WHY THEY CALL IT POLITICS

SIXTH EDITION

WHY THEY CALL IT POLITICS

SIXTH EDITION

ROBERT SHERRILL

Harcourt College Publishers

Fort Worth Philadelphia San Diego New York
Orlando Austin San Antonio
Toronto Montreal London Sydney Tokyo

Publisher	Earl McPeek
Executive Editor	David Tatom
Market Strategist	Steve Drummond
Project Editor	Joyce Fink
Art Director	Vicki Whistler
Production Manager	Serena Barnett

Cover art and drawings by Julio Larraz
ISBN: 0-15-507274-9
Library of Congress Catalog Card Number: 99-65092
Copyright © 2000, 1990, 1984, 1979, 1974, 1972 by Harcourt, Inc.

Requests for permission to make copies of any part of the work should be mailed to:
Permissions Department
Harcourt, Inc.
6277 Sea Harbor Drive
Orlando, FL 32887-6777

Address for Domestic Orders
Harcourt College Publishers
6277 Sea Harbor Drive
Orlando, FL 32887-6777
800-782-4479

Address for International Orders
International Customer Service
Harcourt, Inc.
6277 Sea Harbor Drive
Orlando, FL 32887-6777
407-345-3800
(fax) 407-345-4060
(e-mail) hbintl@harcourtbrace.com

Address for Editorial Correspondence
Harcourt College Publishers
301 Commerce Street
Suite 3700
Fort Worth, TX 76102

Web Site Address
http://www.harcourtcollege.com

Printed in the United States of America

9 0 1 2 3 4 5 6 7 8   016   9 8 7 6 5 4 3 2 1

Harcourt College Publishers

Contents

Foreword   xi

Chapter 1
The President at Home:
Playing All Sides to Stay on Top   *1*
   Electronic Eavesdropping   2
   Ranking the Good and the Not So Hot   3
   Why Do Nice Guys Finish First?   4
   Clinton's Roller Coaster Takes Off   6
   From Bad to Worse   7
   The Comeback Kid Comes Back Again   8
   On Top Again, but Watch Out Below   10
   Historic Infamy   11
   The Buxom Brunette   12
   The Great Embarrassment   14
   "A Sham Trial"   15
   A Scale of Losers   16
   Ronald Reagan: Enter Laughing   17
   Vague Powers, Cries of Alarm   20
   The Abuse of Presidential Powers   22
   Very Human Beings, Indeed   24
   A Very Welcome Come-Down   27
   The Mystique of the Presidency   31
   How to Succeed in Domestic Politics   42
   The President and Congress   66

Chapter 2
The President Abroad:
Bouquets, Brickbats, and Bombs   74
   War-Making Powers   78

Treaty-Making Powers   82
The President and His Advisers   85
Dollar Diplomacy Begins, Big Time   91
The Myth of Omniscience   93
Looking under the CIA Covers   97
The Difficulty of Making Changes   99
Can the President Be Reined In?   102
The Ultimate Restraint   106

Chapter 3
Cold War, National Security, and the Military   *112*
The High Cost of Winning   115
From Isolation to Intervention   119
Reagan: The Super Cold Warrior   120
Fear of Communism   123
From Ally to Enemy   124
The Ideological Frenzy   126
Military Foreign Policy   130
The Military Move In   130
Pentagon Spending on Manpower   133
The Military-Industrial-Political Complex   136
What Do We Care Whether They Perform?   139
Fraud, Waste, and Sloppy Work   144
American Intervention in World Affairs   148
The Foreign Policy of Spies   150
Disastrous "Successes"   152
Our Arms Hucksters   154
Foreign Policy in Transition   155
Getting Too Tricky   158
The Post-Cold War Perils   159
American Guinea Pigs   161
What Did We Learn from the Cold War?   162
We Weren't So Bright   163
Here We Go Again   164
Science Fiction Revived   165
Breaking the Habit   166

Chapter 4
Congress:
The Most Deliberative Body, and a Swamp   *168*
Signs of Deep Trouble   170
Electorate: Blame Yourself   172

Pay and Freebies   175
Kingmakers Behind the Scenes   177
Need Breeds Hatred   179
Pity the Flunkies   181
A Legislator's Work Is Never Done . . .   182
Never Enough Time   184
The View from Inside   187
Overlapping—and Conflicting—Interests   188
Boodle and Pork Barrel   189
The Mechanics of Congress: Committees   192
Business on the Floor   197
The Battle of Words   198
The Leaders of Congress   201
Congeniality Fades   203
Oh, Yes, the Senate   212
The Seniority System   214
Attempts at Reform   217
A Few Ethics Reforms   219
Pork versus Purity   224
Is Congress for Sale?   227
But There's Hope   233

Chapter 5
The Supreme Court:
A Sometime Fortunate Imbalance of Power   236
The American Court System   240
Whims and Delays   245
The Final Say   247
The Conservative Revolution   251
The Mystique of the Supreme Court   255
How the Court Operates   258
The Court's Role   263
An Evolving Court   267
The "Revolutionary" Warren Court   272
Who Enforces the Court's Edicts?   277
The Burger Court: The Tempo Slows   278
The Rehnquist Court   284
What's in the Future?   288

Chapter 6
Bureaucracy:
Our Prolific Drones   290

Those "Hidden" Workers   294
A Hate-Love Relationship   298
Poster Child of Spending   299
The Unappealing Giant   301
Bureaucratic Indifference   304
Kicking the Underdogs   306
Environmental Revolution   314
There Are Good Guys, Too   315
When Bureaucrats Turn Rogue   319
Congress and the Bureaucracy   325
The President and the Bureaucracy   327
Resistance to Reform   329
"Depending upon the Men Who Administer It"   333
The Premier Example of Sleaze   336
Business in Catbird Seat   337
Can the Bureaucracy Be Reformed?   340

Chapter 7

Parties and Pressure Groups:
Democracy's Gang Warfare   344

Organizing through Parties   348
The Decline of Party Influence   351
A Surface Sameness   356
Voter Disillusionment   366
Birth of "People's Lobbies"   371
Organizing through Lobbying   371
Rise of People's Lobbies   378
Big Business Fights Back   384
Vox Populi   391

Chapter 8

The Media and Government:
Politics, Profits, and Propaganda   394

Data, Propaganda, and Power   397
The Handicaps from Within: Money   400
The Self-Censorship of Bias   416
The Reagan Love Affair   419
The Herd Instinct   421
The Press Conference Carnival   423
Pseudopatriotic Self-Censorship   426
How to Keep a Reporter Down   429
Now and Then a Few Victories   447

Chapter 9

The Economy:

Manipulating That Mysterious Spigot   *448*

The Free Economy Isn't Free   450
Some "Revolution"   453
Life in the Middle Class   461
The Social Security "Fix"   463
Taxation   466
Subsidization   470
Special Subsidies to Banks   472
Regulation   475
Import Complexities   477
Trying to Regulate the Big Boys   481
Debt   485
Managing the Money   488
Fiscal Control: Casting Bread upon the Waters   491
Inflation: the Case of the Shrinking Dollar   495
Killing the Economy to Save the Dollar   496
Opportunities for Reform   503

Chapter 10

So You Want to Go into Politics   *506*

Do You Have What It Takes?   506
The Springboards   511
Are You Squeaky Clean?   515
Enslaved by Television   518
The Stupidity of the Selective Process   523
Polls   528
Money, Money, Money   529
Whose Words Will You Speak?   532
The Top Handlers   535
Smears, Lies, and Other Nastiness   537
Negative Impact   545

Index   547

Foreword

The late film star John Wayne, who for many years was everybody's favorite macho American, once told a reporter, "I hate politics. I regard it as a necessary evil, a citizen's responsibility. There's no way, even if you went back to the days of the Inquisition, that you could get me to run for political office. Politics in the old days was fun. But now it's become an awesome monster and is apt to ruin the country. Politicians don't do what's good for the country. They do what helps them get elected. I just can't get enthused about politics any more."

That's probably the way most Americans feel. They are much more interested in making a living, buying cars, pursuing romance, and watching television than they are in the machinery of government. They leave politics to the politicians, whom they pay very well (more than three times the national average income) and rate very low (lower than garbage collectors in some opinion surveys). Rarely does anyone have something good to say about politics or politicians. But pundits and comics and even some politicians are deeply indebted to both for endless material to ridicule, scorn, or laugh at. From former Senator Eugene McCarthy ("Being in politics is like being a football coach: You have to be smart enough to understand the game, and dumb enough to think it's important") to Abbie Hoffman ("I tend to agree with Woody Allen that politicians are a cut above child molesters"), the insults have been flying.

In fact, politics is a noble profession, or can be. Unfortunately, the evidence of its nobility is often buried under the debris of our shattered expectations. "Exaggerated hopes," says Irving Kristol, is "the curse of our age," and he may have a point. Maybe one reason we become easily disillusioned and frustrated with the system is that we expect too much perfection from our politicians. Is that why we drop out? Barely half the electorate can be counted on to vote in a presidential election—such a feeble turnout as to make the word *democracy* a joke.

But exaggerated hopes are only one cause, and not the most important. Nor is laziness. The decline of interest in politics results mainly from well-founded cynicism. Americans aren't stupid. To the growing number who have a sophisticated awareness of what's going on, it is very hard to sell the notion that we operate under a government of, by, and for the people, with liberty and justice for all.

Many Americans have begun to see it as a government of, by, and for high-rollers, with justice too often going to the highest bidder. A Media General/Associated Press poll showed that at least half the respondents believe government to be dishonest, 82 percent were not surprised to learn of recent bribery in the Pentagon, and seven out of ten called the government mismanaged. They had good reason to think so, for obviously we are passing through an Age of Sleaze. It has been a period symbolized by a U.S. attorney general, the nation's highest law-enforcement official, who had to defend himself from a variety of misconduct charges; by the number of high officials who quit government to become influence peddlers and wound up convicted of illegal lobbying (or, worse, *not* convicted); by a president who undermined the moral tone of government by defending these miscreants and hailing one of his outlaw advisers as a "hero"; and by a Speaker of the House—the third-highest official in the federal government—who rode out of town with the sheriff in hot pursuit.

As the old saying goes, "The more things change, the more they remain the same." Most of the sleaze mentioned in the last paragraph took place in the Republican administrations of the 1980s. But the Democratic administration that followed in the 1990s did not lack for mud with the impeachment of the president, one high Justice Department official convicted of fraud, one cabinet member forced out of office and tried for perjury, another forced out of office and tried for taking a bribe, and a third cabinet secretary probably escaping indictment only by being killed in an airplane crash.

As for the exit of the speaker mentioned above, Jim Wright of Texas, that turned out to be a fitting bridge event into the 1990s because Newt Gingrich, the boisterous Republican Congressman from Georgia who orchestrated the downfall of Wright, eventually became the House speaker himself and was disgraced in 1997 when the Ethics Committee fined him $300,000 for illegal campaign spending. The strong stink of questionable campaign spending hung over both parties throughout the last half of the 1990s, and neither party seemed the least bit interested in bringing about campaign spending reform—although both parties loved to preach about it.

This kind of hypocrisy helped create deep public cynicism, which could be measured in such polls as that of Fox News in early 1997, showing that while 36 percent of the American people thought most politicians were "dedicated public servants," a stunning 44 percent looked upon them as "lying windbags."

We are passing through a period in which, thanks to the people who run Washington, the fat cats are getting much fatter and the rest of us skinnier. Executives of the thrift industry (banks, savings and loans), with the collusion of government "regulators," stole many billions of dollars that you and I are being forced to repay; the government's civil rights, environment, and consumer protection laws are flabby from disuse; federal agencies that are supposed to protect us from drug rackets, monopoly pricing, unsafe food, and cruddy work conditions have gone into hibernation. Everywhere we look, it seems that the motivation of government action is greed, particularly in the hallowed chambers of Congress where members seem to have both hands in the pockets of rich special-interest groups.

Indeed, even the most unsophisticated citizens realize that mere votes are rarely enough to win fair play in politics; they know that big money must have had something to do with persuading Congress, for example, to write a tax code that makes the janitor at General Electric pay more taxes than GE itself, or to write laws forcing ordinary citizens to subsidize the destruction of national forests to make multi-million-dollar lumber companies even richer. The influence of people of no income or of moderate income stops at the ballot box; after a candidate is elected, he or she is more inclined to lend an ear to the desires of those who *paid* for the campaign—which of course means people of wealth, corporations, and well-heeled organizations. True democracy can't be bought, but practical democracy can be, and often is.

Complaints, complaints, complaints. And the list could go on for many pages. What do they add up to? Do they mean that Kurt Vonnegut was wrong when he said, "Make no mistake about it: This nation is the most astonishing and admirable experiment in pluralistic democracy"? No, of course not; he is absolutely correct.

And yet Americans are dissatisfied with their government, and they should be. On paper, the goals may be high, and the framework of the government may be as perfect as any ever devised; but the machinery does not live up to its political platform guarantees, and the operation of it is a constant repair job.

But the John Waynes of the world are wrong when they suggest that this situation is something new. Politics never "used to be fun." Very few people of any era have admired politicians or looked upon the government of their time as a friend. They have suspected and feared it. They have seen government as a swap-off between unwelcome forces. They have preferred pests (politicians and bureaucrats) to pestilence (anarchy and chaos). They have accepted protection from government only because they thought its regulators and police would be less dangerous than the unregulated morality of their fellow citizens.

That may be a harsh view, but it is not unhealthy. By preparing for the worst, one cultivates a more delicate taste for the slightest achievement. Connoisseurs of politics have always begun with the assumption that all government is, to some extent, evil—or at least falls far short of the ideal. Even the most humanely framed constitution, the best-intentioned governors, and the most benign administration of laws will inevitably lead to some loss of liberty, some oppression, some injustice, some waste.

At its most efficient, our government could not be described more honestly than as "a process of making things—including itself—less defective." Just less defective. If we approach our subject in this spirit, we will be radical only in the sense that we will be returning to the radical historical roots of our government. A reading of *The Federalist* papers, for example, will show that those wonderful harangues by Hamilton, Madison, and Jay offered the Constitution only as the best guide through some rough governmental terrain. They did not peddle the Constitution as a magical formula for making the roughness disappear.

As a practical, commonsense instrument, the Constitution has met most of our needs, however, and we can boast that we now operate under the oldest written constitution in the world. But we are still a very young nation; just how young can be measured by the fact that when Ronald Reagan was packing up to leave the White House at the end of 1988, which was the two hundredth anniversary of the ratification of the Constitution, his life had spanned over a third of the history of our constitutional government.

However, if our government is young enough to deserve our tolerance, it is old enough to survive our harshest criticisms. As you read this book, maintain a good sense of humor, because politics, being the best show in town, deserves it; but also read it aggressively, with a chip on your shoulder, eager to challenge and criticize the conduct of your leaders. Don't worry about being too tough on them; any good politician can (and must) learn how to dodge brickbats. When George Bush was campaigning for president in 1988, he made the mistake of visiting a Portland, Oregon, shipyard, where the workers drenched him in taunts and insults and curses. "You immoral scum," was among the nicer epithets hurled at him. But he was a veteran of many political wars and knew how to take the confrontation, calling it a "good challenge." Let this book incite you to do your own challenging, though not necessarily with insults. As you read it, ask yourself again and again: Is this how I want my government to act? Is this the best way to run things? What *should* be the role and conduct of these people we are paying so well and heaping honors upon to govern us?

If you don't like what you see, gear up for the day when you can work to change it. After all, government is not a part of nature. It isn't a geological formation, or a school of fish. Government is something we create for ourselves, to serve us. There is nothing sacred about it. When it needs to be changed to serve us better, we should change it. We have done so many times in the past.

When our government was set up, only property owners who were white and male could vote in federal elections. First we dropped the ownership requirement, then the color requirement, then the sex requirement. For most of our government's existence, U.S. senators were elected by state legislatures. When that became too obviously corrupt a system, we changed it to have them elected by the general public. The structure and rules of our government are always evolving. Most departments of the cabinet were not created until the twentieth century; no doubt there will be other additions and subtractions (we can hope) in the future. Not long ago, a president could be reelected endlessly; now he is restricted to two terms; maybe that should be changed back to the old way, or maybe the president should be restricted to one six-year term. We haven't always had nine justices—at first there were six, then seven, then nine, then ten, then eight, then nine again—sitting on the Supreme Court, and maybe the day will come when we decide to pull another number out of our collective hat. (Franklin Roosevelt had a frustrated plan that could have increased the number to fifteen!) There was a time when a presidential nominee would run on a ticket with a vice-presidential nominee from another party. No one is likely to suggest that we return to that clumsy arrangement. But a number of very smart people *have* suggested that we drop the vice-presidential post entirely, as being mostly useless except as a misleading and confusing way to "balance the ticket."

If you ever get in the mood to try to improve the machinery of government, consider these possibilities:

- *Turn 'em out on a regular basis.* We limit our presidents to two four-year terms. Why should members of Congress get an indefinite run for our money? How about setting a limit of, say, five two-year terms in the House and two six-year terms in the Senate? Even that may be too much.
- *De-deify federal judges.* There are good arguments for giving federal judges lifetime appointments, as at present. But there are also good arguments—maybe better ones—for limiting their service. Once in a while we wind up with a president of questionable integrity and judgment. Does it make sense to give him (or for that matter even a president of high integrity and unimpeachable judgment) the power to shape the laws of the land, indirectly, for many years after he leaves government? Under the present system, he can do it through his authority to put "his" judges on the bench for life. Why not change the system so that their service automatically ends four years (or five, or eight, or whatever you think best) after the president who appointed them leaves office?

Well, you get the idea. If you want to shake up the government—and if you can get enough people to agree with your ideas—go ahead and shake it up. Just make sure that your reforms do not reduce our freedoms. Some people, for example, point out that seven of our twenty-six constitutional amendments deal with the right—but none with the obligation—to vote. They would pass a law requiring all adults to vote, in the name of good citizenship. There is some logic, and considerable emotional appeal, to that proposal. But because *not* voting *can* be a way to make a political statement, forcing a person to vote would deprive him or her of free-speech rights guaranteed under the First Amendment. Watch out that your reforms don't step on constitutional toes.

And don't just concentrate on improving the efficiency of government. As soft-hearted Hubert Humphrey once said, "You can read the Declaration of Independence and all of the grievances therein listed and not once did our founding fathers talk about the inefficiency or the efficiency of government. They had grievances about the injustice and the inequities that were imposed upon them." That's what we should be mostly concerned with. In addition to whatever reactions you may have to the structure and rules of government as presented in this book, also continually question your government's *priorities,* its sense of humanity (or lack), its sense of morality (or lack), its sense of urgency (or lack) in meeting social crises.

Looking at recent conduct in Washington, you may want to ask yourself, for instance, is it desirable to continue having a government:

- that pretends it has "punished" a criminal lobbyist (formerly a top White House aide) by fining him $100,000, when that is *one-fifth* what he was paid by TWA and Boeing for making only *two* of his illegal phone calls?
- that uses taxpayer subsidies to enable foreign lumber companies to buy our five hundred-year-old trees for $5 each?
- that permits a State Department employee convicted of gold smuggling to continue receiving his $66,000 federal paycheck while serving his prison sentence?
- that lavishes $70 billion on a fleet of bombers of questionable value but does nothing to treat five million children and teenagers who have mental disorders?
- that, even while acknowledging that tobacco contributes to more than 300,000 deaths in this country each year, uses taxpayers' money to help the tobacco industry recruit new addicts overseas?
- that dawdles for six months before it passes a bill to stop the fraud in the savings and loan industry, even though each day of delay costs taxpayers $20 million?
- that passes environmental laws but refuses to enforce them, thereby leaving three out of five Americans living in urban areas blanketed by dangerously polluted air?
- that does nothing to control gun ownership by nuts, even though guns have proliferated so much that in one year alone Secret Service agents caught seventy-four tourists wandering through the White House with concealed handguns?
- that declares that the cocaine plague—which has made addicts of 6 million Americans and filled our prisons and hospitals—is our number one problem but that nevertheless maintains friendly relations with (and gives economic aid to) the drug-producing countries that grow rich from our misery?

By now, you must realize that this book is, to say the least, critical of politics as it operates today and critical of many politicians and bureaucrats for their style of operating. Criticism can become tedious, however, unless it is made with the background acknowledgment that we are talking not about scientific absolutes, but about the imperfect human shaping of a sometimes too plastic ideal.

Even while thrashing them with well-deserved scorn and damnation, we must bear in mind that the men and women who run the government are—pardon the expression—human beings. And many are very fascinating human beings. We mean such chaps as Richard Nixon, who after holding a press conference at Walt Disney World, approached a man and boy standing outside the auditorium and asked the man if he was the boy's mother or his grandmother. When the man replied that he was neither, Nixon slapped the man's face, said "Of course you're not," and walked off. (No wonder H. R. Haldeman, Nixon's own chief of staff, called Nixon "the weirdest man ever to live in the White House"!) Hey, they have as much right to be nutty as non-politicians have. They are subject to exhaustion, anger, greed, lust, and all the other impulses that make life worth chronicling. When Senators Strom Thurmond and Ralph Yarborough wrestled on the floor outside a committee room, they were expressing more than a difference in ideology. And the same can be said for the encounter when Congressman Henry Gonzalez hit Congressman Ed Foreman for calling him "pinko." And ditto for Senator Kenneth B. McKellar, eighty at the time, when he punched two newsmen in one day for writing about him as "old."

More often, they substitute oral violence for physical. President Lyndon Johnson privately called Senator Barry Goldwater "a mean, vindictive little man. He is nasty and petty." At the same time, Goldwater was telling *his* circle of advisers that "Johnson was a dirty fighter, a liar, a treacherous rascal who would slap you on the back today and stab you in the back tomorrow." President John Kennedy had a reputation as a sophisticated smoothie, but privately he could be as tough as a longshoreman. By the end of his presidential campaign, the kindest thing he was saying of his opponent Richard Nixon was, "He's a filthy, lying son-of-a-bitch, and a very dangerous man."

The human side of politicians has in recent years often turned the public's attention to the bedroom. Titillating accounts of the women in the lives of some presidents have been detailed in the years since. Perhaps the most destructive Don Juaning in history was done by Gary Hart, whose attention to women other than his wife certainly cost him the Democratic presidential nomination and very likely the presidency in 1988. As the late good ol' boy governor of Alabama, Big Jim Folsom, once said, "Women is a occupational hazard to politicians."

Before man had government, he had instincts and glands, and whether we like it or not in this sophisticated age, instincts and glands still have much to do with what is produced in Washington. When Hal Holbrook was preparing for a television series based on the mythical life of a "Senator Hays Stowe," he spent many hours talking with real senators to get a feel for the job. One senator told him privately that he "hated" having to deal with his constituents.

"In come John Doe and Mary Doe and eight little Does expecting to see you," he explained. "They're on vacation and he's in Bermuda shorts and the kids are mad and tired. When they lean back on that sofa to rest and visit and you've got to make a speech that night and you're not prepared and the mail is stacking up, you just can't imagine the feeling that comes over you. It's almost intolerable. But you've got to see them."

On the other hand, it was disgust with his colleagues, not with the public, that inspired South Dakota's Senator James Abourezk, retiring after only one term in Senate, to exclaim with heartfelt emotion, "I'm sure glad to be getting out of this chickenshit place."

Nervousness, exhaustion, psychotic arrogance, irritation with the public—these have their effects on the shaping of the legislation that runs the country. And the appetites and gross pleasures that touch the lives of barbers and clerks touch also the lives of the mighty. F. R. Pettigrew, who spent two terms in the United States Senate at the turn of the century, wrote of President Cleveland:

> My seat was the first seat on the main aisle. Grover Cleveland was brought in by two or three men and placed in a chair right across the aisle from me. He was still stupidly intoxicated, his face was bloated, and he was a sight to behold. He did not seem to know what was occurring, but looked like a great lump of discolored flesh.

Alas, even Demon Rum has lived into modern-day Washington and has had its influence—small influence—on the outcome of things. It was said, for example, that a senator who normally would have voted against the quarter-billion-dollar Lockheed Aircraft loan instead cast the deciding vote in favor of the measure because he was soused. And for much of his last three years as the omnipotent chairman of the House Ways and Means Committee, Wilbur Mills was "hazy" from an overconsumption of alcohol.

If nothing else, the purpose of this book is to encourage candor and discourage cant. A democratic government in the final analysis comes down to a great many very human beings who aren't especially fond of one another, jostling and shoving with the common hope that each will come out on top.

Still, if our political leaders leave something to be desired, let us not forget that it has always been this way and we have somehow survived.

Of the two great parties which at this hour almost share the nation between them, I should say that one has the best cause, and the other contains the best men. The philosopher, the poet, or the religious man will of course wish to cast his vote with the democrat, for free-trade, for wide suffrage, for the abolition of legal cruelties in the penal code, and for facilitating in every manner the access of the young and the poor to the sources of wealth and power. But he can rarely accept the persons whom the so-called popular party propose to him as representatives of these liberalities. They have not at heart the ends which give to the name of democracy what hope and virtue are in it. The spirit of our American radicalism is destructive and aimless. . . .
On the other side, the conservative party, composed of the most moderate, able and cultivated part of the population, is timid, and merely defensive of property. It vindicates no right, it aspires to no real good, it brands nor crime, it proposes no generous policy; it does not build, nor write, no cherish the arts, nor foster religion, nor establish schools, nor encourage science, nor emancipate the slave, nor befriend the poor, or the Indian, or the immigrant. From neither party, when in power, has the world any benefit to expect in science, art, or humanity, at all commensurate with the resources of the nation.

Ralph Waldo Emerson wrote the above quote in his essay *Politics* in 1844. One must take note of his extravagances; the differences between the two parties and their leaders were not so black and white then. Nor are they now. But in general the *deficiencies* were accurately noted, and they have not changed much in the century and a half intervening between Emerson's complaints and the ones heard today—that either the politicians take little thought before they rush in with their passionate reforms, or they have no passions and no reforms to offer. The defects of the government and of the politicians and bureaucrats who run it may be more critical today simply because of the pressure of people and the pressure of time. But if the nation was able to survive the Whig president and the Congress of Emerson's day, there is reason to hope that life will go on in a reasonably acceptable way despite the Congresses and the bureaucracy and the courts and the Johnsons and the Nixons and the Fords and the Carters and the Reagans and the Bushes and the Clintons of our time, although some of what follows in this book may lead the reader to think differently.

Success in politics is generally measured by its end result: It was a good idea if it worked and it was a lousy idea—no matter how nobly expressed—if it didn't get the job done, the problem solved. On a day-to-day basis these definitions are justifiably emphasized. But politics is more than practicalities; it is also made of glowing presumptions and overwhelming historical IOUs and pipe dreams. The extravagant praise that politicians heap on themselves, the inflated measurements they give to their accomplishments, the flowery Fourth of July oratory that is laid like a crown on the brow of the faceless "common man"— these things should not be underrated for the juice they supply the fruit of politics. If it were not for them, it would dry up. Hope and faith and even charity have an important place in the corners of the smoke-filled rooms. "Your taste is judicious in liking better the dreams of the future than the history of the past," John Adams wrote to Jefferson, twitting him for his idealization of politics and his uncritical faith in democracy. But it is the Jeffersonian dream, not the Adamsian cynicism, that keeps us going.

It might also be valuable to remember some advice former Senator Russell Long once received. When his father, Huey Long, the famous "Kingfish" of Louisiana politics, was assassinated, Russell was still a young man who sometimes needed help, and when he did he often turned to his Uncle Earl, an infamous and very popular politician of rough-and-tumble ethics. When young Russell went off to college, he joined the debate team. One year the issue to be debated was the question, "Is there a place for ideals in politics?" He went to Uncle Earl for advice.

Uncle Earl's response was emphatic and profane: "A place for ideals?" he yelled. "Hell, yes, there's a place for ideals in politics! Listen, boy, you want to hit the opposition with ideals or anything else you got!"

This may not be exactly the ideal role for ideals, but it is the American way, and it has its own charm, and it is worth coming back to from time to time as an antidote for the illness of political melancholy.

CHAPTER 1

The President at Home

Playing All Sides to Stay on Top

*Why be an American if you can't criticize the
president?*
WILLIAM JEFFERSON CLINTON 1997

*People think I want power . . . but all I want is
solace and a little love, just a little love.*
LYNDON JOHNSON

WE AMERICANS, HAVING HAD THE LUCK AND GENIUS TO DE-
velop the world's most successful form of government, are fascinated
by our creation. We are so fascinated by it, in fact, that we have turned
it into a kind of secular religion, called politics, and we have populated
it with divinities, prophets, martyrs, true believers, backsliders, and
devils.

If Washington, D.C., is the Mount Olympus of our secular religion,
the president must be considered our chief deity, for his personality
towers over the city. Don't take the words "divinities" and "deity" seriously. That's just playful hyperbole that some historians like to use.
In his book on the presidency, for example, the renowned scholar
Robert Dallek writes that "once in office . . . the president takes his
place among the divinities of our national mythology . . . someone 'almost more than human.'"

But Dallek quickly goes on to say that there is also an equally strong
"national impulse" for "demythologizing" presidents.

That's putting it mildly.

We see our political deities in the same way that the Greeks saw their mythical gods—as subject to some very human weaknesses. In recent decades the press and scholars have become much more aggressive in pointing out these weaknesses, sometimes in prurient details. In 1998, for example, they welcomed evidence (through DNA testing) that Thomas Jefferson, as long rumored, had had children by one of his female slaves. And biographers keep telling us that Franklin D. Roosevelt, who is viewed by many as America's most effective moral leader of the twentieth century, engaged in a long clandestine affair with Lucy Mercer, a former social secretary. Nobody wrote about such things when John Kennedy was in the White House, but since his death there has been a flood of books describing what one author called his "insatiable hunger for debauchery" including an affair with a gangster's moll, another affair with a woman suspected of being an East German spy, and naked frolics in the White House swimming pool with favored nymphs, while Secret Service agents stood guard.

As for Bill Clinton, he was plagued throughout his presidency by lawsuits and exposés relating to his reckless womanizing, both before and after he reached the White House. One of these affairs culminated, as we will discuss later, in his impeachment and trial, after what former Senate Majority Leader George Mitchell called "the most investigated sexual relationship in all of human history."

Electronic Eavesdropping

Making it uniquely easier to peek, with hindsight, into the private thoughts and secret dealings of three recent presidents was the existence of a taping apparatus in the White House. Presidents Kennedy and Johnson used the tapes selectively, but Nixon let it all hang out. From 1971 to 1973, he let the tapes run constantly. If he hadn't, Senate investigators would never have found evidence of the criminal activities that drove Nixon from office.

On these tapes you can hear Nixon talking about wanting to blow up a safe at a Washington think tank, paying off Watergate burglars to keep them quiet, spying on the Kennedys, shaking down corporations and labor unions for millions of dollars, selling ambassadorships, and—over and over—venting his hatred for Jews.

Not surprisingly, ever since Nixon had to flee Washington to avoid impeachment, presidents have decided it would be wise to shut down the taping apparatus. For Americans who like to see behind the presidential curtain, it was an unfortunate development. Since then, in recreating presidential careers, historians have had to fall back on the standard, duller stuff: official documents, press accounts, letters, memoirs, and so forth.

On the other hand, if allowing our presidents to maintain a special aura serves any useful purpose, perhaps it is just as well that the tapes were suspended. And besides, they may distort the facts of presidential lives. It is certainly reasonable to assume that had the tapes been humming in the White House since the founding of the nation, the historical ranking of our presidents might be very different indeed.

Ranking the Good and the Not So Hot

Five years into his presidency, Clinton admitted privately that history would probably not rank him very high. That was a good guess, but he shouldn't feel too bad about it. Achieving greatness is a difficult trick for any president to pull off. It usually requires the help of a crisis, preferably a huge one. That's why, when historians and political scientists rank the presidents, they virtually always put Abraham Lincoln, George Washington, and Franklin Roosevelt at the top.

Obviously, they are seen as great because of the way they handled the most significant military crises in the nation's history. This is particularly true of Lincoln, whose administration spanned the Civil War.

But it is encouraging to realize that—as Washington and Roosevelt showed—greatness can also be achieved by leadership in periods of peace. We owe as much to Washington, the president who launched our new federal government, as we do to his generalship during the Revolutionary War. And we owe as much, indeed probably more, to Roosevelt for pulling the nation through the Great Depression as we do for his service as commander in chief during most of World War II.

Unfortunately, if we can believe what seems to be a consensus among presidential scholars, America has had only middling-to-bad luck with its presidents during the past four decades. Not that they haven't had a chance to prove themselves via crises.

Two recent polls tell the story.

One poll, taken by historian Arthur M. Schlesinger, Jr., at the behest of the *New York Times Magazine*, sought the opinions of thirty-two experts. They concluded that since 1960 only Lyndon Johnson and John Kennedy could be rated even as "average high." Gerald Ford, Jimmy

Carter, Ronald Reagan, George Bush, and Bill Clinton got an "average low" rating, and Richard Nixon was considered a flat-out failure.

The other poll of 719 historians and political scientists was done for the Citadel Press. Of the forty-one presidents being judged (James Garfield and William Harrison were excluded because they didn't serve long enough to make an impression), Lyndon Johnson was ranked 10th, Kennedy was ranked 15th, Carter 19th, Bush 22nd, Clinton 23rd, Reagan 26th, Ford 27th, and Nixon 32nd.* (These polls were taken before Clinton's impeachment.)

In other words, both polls showed that if the last eight presidents received college grades for their work, only two would have gotten as high as B's or B−, five would have gotten C's or C−, and one would have received a D− or F. Not exactly an outstanding class of politicians.

The Citadel Press poll is the most interesting because it gives numerical ratings to the presidents according to five categories: their leadership qualities, their accomplishments and ability to manage crises, their political skills, their ability to pick the right people for government service, and, finally, their character and integrity.

The first thing you would notice in reading this poll is that some of these fellows who reached the White House since 1960 were not exactly Boy Scouts—judging from the way they are rated for "character and integrity." Nixon, the only one in history forced to resign, is ranked right smack at the bottom, 41st; Reagan is 39th, Clinton 38th, Johnson 37th, Kennedy 34th. (If you're wondering who filled the 40th notch, it was Warren G. Harding, whose administration from 1921 until the day he died in 1923—some think he was murdered by his wife—was one big scandal.) The other presidents fall in the mid-range, except for Carter—who continued to teach Sunday school even while he was in the White House. He is ranked number five, which puts him very close to those sterling characters, Lincoln and Washington, in that category.

Why Do Nice Guys Finish First?

Is there a relationship between character and integrity on the one hand and effective leadership on the other? Does history give any guide for an answer to that?

---

*The Associated Press, February 8, 1997. The Citadel Press (Carol Publishing Group) book is *Rating the Presidents* by William J. Ridings, Jr., and Stuart B. McIver.

Those who argue that character and integrity are of little value in creating strong leadership will point to Carter, who had the reputation of being a man of strong character and ample integrity but whose accomplishments were not impressive. And to make their argument from the other direction, they will point to Lyndon Johnson, who was woefully short on integrity but was a ruthless whizbang as a leader and a near-genius as a politician. As for Johnson's accomplishments, he was a disaster in foreign affairs, but in domestic affairs—civil rights, medical care, child care, and so forth—he brought more humanitarian progress to America than any president since Franklin Roosevelt put together the New Deal in the 1930s.

Those are reasonable arguments, but in fact Carter and Johnson were among the exceptions. History's rule seems to be that integrity and character do indeed go together with achievements. Most of the best presidents have had strong moral fiber. At least that's what the scholars in these polls tell us. Seven of the ten presidents rated "great" or "near great" were also rated as having the most character and integrity. Two others came close.

Scholars may care about such things. But does the general public? Do the voters? Let's hope so. Then how do we explain the fact that the only presidents reelected to second terms since 1960 were three of those rated lowest in the integrity department: Nixon, Reagan, and Clinton?

If you wish, you can blame it on the public's ignorance and you can blame its ignorance on the press (which we will return to in a later chapter) for failing to adequately inform the public of the deceptions, blunders, and underhanded actions that occurred during their first terms. Or you can say that the electorate was in fact probably correct in believing that those three presidents—despite their many major character flaws—had shown in their first terms that they were still likely to use presidential powers better than their challengers, most of whom, it must be admitted, did not convey an impression of strength.

The use of power: that's what fascinates the electorate. Voters know that in electing a president they have made him the most powerful politician in the world, so naturally they watch closely—with the help of the press—to see if and how he uses his power. Indeed, watching and measuring the use of power is one of America's favorite spectator sports. Is the president losing his grip? Is he winning or losing support in Congress? Will his failures be fatal? Will his successes make him too uppity? Keeping score on the president is part of what Hedrick Smith, longtime *New York Times* bureau chief in Washington, calls "The Power Game."

It's a game that is great fun to watch, but spectators should hedge their judgments with the modest awareness that reputations change with new evidence and new perspectives, and that using power is never at a constant pitch. It's breathtakingly up and down, a veritable roller coaster. This can be seen in the careers of the last two two-term presidents, Clinton and Reagan.

Clinton's Roller Coaster Takes Off

Many of the reporters who traveled with Bill Clinton in his 1992 presidential campaign referred to him privately as "Slick Willie" because he was such a smooth operator.

But Clinton gave himself a kinder nickname—"The Comeback Kid"—and he deserved it. He seemed the strongest Democratic candidate by far. But halfway through the first primary the press hit him with a couple of devastating rumors—that he had been a draft-dodger in the Vietnam War and that he had been a marathon skirt-chaser as governor of Arkansas. (There was, in fact, supporting evidence for both rumors.)

Almost overnight, the polls showed his popularity plummeting 50 percent and his campaign seemed doomed. But he refused to be sidetracked by the rumors. With the nation in the middle of a modest recession and unemployment at a daunting 7.71 percent, he continued to pound away at his central campaign theme that the national economy needed fixing. His main campaign slogan was, "It's the economy, stupid!" Another of his slogans, "Putting People First," was meant to suggest that he was a great populist and that President Bush was a patsy for the super-rich and for big corporations.

Clinton's eloquence, sloganeering, and stubbornness paid off. The Comeback Kid regained enough strength to take the Democratic nomination and then the White House, although his share of the popular vote was only an anemic 43 percent (the eccentric Texas billionaire Ross Perot won 19 percent of the vote as a third-party candidate, thus making it virtually impossible for either Clinton or Bush to win a majority).

Neither candidate had stirred great enthusiasm, but the outcome of the race clearly indicated there was an unusually strong desire for change running through the electorate. For thirty-two years there had been a steady decline in voter participation, but this time 55 percent of the eligible voters turned out, compared to 50 percent four years earlier.

It seemed an atmosphere custom-made for the new president, who had been selling himself as a magician of change. Clinton took office amid much fanfare emphasizing youth; he was forty-six, Vice President Albert Gore was forty-four. He was hailed as the vanguard of a "new generation" of politicians, as the first president since the end of World War II who had not served in that war, and as the first president elected since the end of the Cold War.

With all polls—and the defeat of a sitting president—showing that the public was fed up with the frequent "gridlock" between the White House and Congress, it seemed a perfect time for Clinton to try to invade Congress—which was still controlled by his own party—and push through some of the major reforms that he had promised. Instead of jumping into the legislative arena, however, Clinton decided he would first do something he could do on his own, by executive order. He decided that one of his first acts as President would be to lift the ban on homosexuals in the military—something he had promised to do for the gay groups who were important organizers and fund-raisers in the Democratic party.

From Bad to Worse

Immediately, he ran into a hornet's nest. To a man, the admirals and generals at the Pentagon seemed ready to rebel. Clinton backed off, agreed to "study" the issue for six months, and then agreed to a compromise that satisfied neither side and seriously weakened him with Congress, which thought he had made a stupid mistake by gambling so many of his political chips so early in his term on such a marginal issue.

He was off to a bad start, and it didn't get better when most of the big progressive programs he had promised to fight for were compromised, put on hold, discarded, or defeated. The one dramatic reform he vigorously tried to pass—legislation to make medical care available to all Americans, including the 40 million who could not afford any insurance—was presented to Congress late, was complex and confusing and not explained in a way that would get public support, and was soundly defeated.

The only major piece of legislation Clinton did manage to move through Congress in his first two years was the North American Free

Trade Agreement (NAFTA), which lifted tariffs and allowed the United States, Mexico, and Canada to trade with each other virtually as though they were one country. But this was a Republican bill, a hangover from the administrations of Reagan and Bush, and many Democrats felt Clinton betrayed them by pushing it. Organized labor, which (correctly) feared many U.S. corporations would move their plants into Mexico's cheap labor market, hated it. Many others (including 300 environmental groups that petitioned Clinton against the bill) feared NAFTA would undermine our environmental laws and make our borders more porous to drug traffickers.

Critics were quick to point out that the populist campaigner had, as president, quickly fallen under the influence of powerful moneyed interests. Now it seemed his primary goal—virtually unmentioned while he was campaigning—was to lower the deficit to please Wall Street's bond market.

As the mid-term (1994) Congressional elections approached, Clinton was so unpopular even with many in his own party that some Democratic candidates didn't want to be seen with him. He was blamed for the results of that election, in which Republicans, picking up fifty-two seats, took control of the House for the first time in forty years and regained control of the Senate.

With different parties controlling the White House and Congress, "gridlock"—the kind of bitter partisanship that had afflicted the Bush administration—crippled Clinton's, too. There were days, during fights over the budget, when the government literally came to a halt and the bureaucrats stayed home. As a campaigner, Clinton had promised to avoid gridlock, but now he was up to his neck in it.

It was during this period that Clinton first hit bottom on the roller coaster that every president, sooner or later, must ride. And it triggered the old ritual that can be called The Pundits' Pessimistic Appraisal of Power. Now the pundits began to measure his political biceps and shake their heads in pity. Would he have the machismo to deal with a Republican Congress? They doubted it. Would he be able to patch up his relationship with his own party in Congress? They doubted it. Most predicted Clinton was doomed to be just another one-term president.

The Comeback Kid Comes Back Again

Looking toward the 1996 presidential election, which was still a long way off, Ed Rollins, one of the Republican party's most brilliant strategists, warned his colleagues not to underrate Clinton: "Though getting better, he's largely been a third-rate president. But make no mistake, he's a world-class campaigner."

He was right, and that's how Clinton rescued his administration: He began campaigning.

What? Start campaigning with the election a year and a half away? Start running campaign ads so early? Incredible! Maybe so, but it worked so well for him that it may become the presidential style of the future: government by a permanent campaign. Actually, using a permanent campaign to govern was not new to Clinton. He had used the technique with great success to hold the governorship of Arkansas for five terms.*

The heart of Clinton's permanent campaign was polling. He never made a move, never offered a bill, never made a speech without first taking an opinion poll to find out what the public would like. The strategy was not to let personal convictions—or a personal sense of direction—interfere with what the constant, daily polling of voters showed would get their support. In terms of leadership, it was blowing with the wind, but it worked. But at a cost to his reputation. David Maraniss, the best biographer of Clinton's early career, says critics felt that Clinton's habit of letting polls shape his thoughts "made him so malleable that his word was unreliable."

Clinton became an expert fence-straddler. To avoid appearing "too liberal" he went along with some of the legislation proposed by Republicans—some tax cuts for the upper class, harsh welfare reform, a much tougher stance on crime, a tougher stance on immigration—but to avoid appearing "too conservative" he used the threat of a veto to force Congress to make some humanitarian changes in those bills before passing them.

Enough voters accepted that centrist wobble that Clinton, who not so long before had been written off as a loser, easily won reelection (granted, economic prosperity and the dullness of his opponent, Bob Dole, helped a lot).

---

*Clinton was not the originator of the strategy; that credit, or blame, belongs to the ubiquitous Dick Morris, a political soldier of fortune who would happily work for either party—if the price was right—and sometimes for both at the same time. Clinton did not particularly like Morris—once in an argument he had socked his adviser on the jaw—but he knew that Morris's strategies had saved his political hide in Arkansas and he hoped for the same miracle again, so he called him back. And he kept him as a consultant until the supermarket tabloids reported Morris's strange attraction for a prostitute's toes, and the bad publicity forced Clinton to dump him.

On Top Again, but Watch Out Below

For the moment, the presidential roller coaster had reached a peak. But the ride was far from over and a breathtaking descent lay just ahead. The first year of his second term included some legislative victories but also some important defeats. Most important (because Clinton himself had made such a big deal of the legislation) was his failure to persuade Congress to give him special powers to make foreign trade agreements—and to Clinton's great embarrassment, the defeat was brought about not by Republican opposition but by the "no" votes of his own party.

From that evidence alone, the pundits began to write Clinton's obituary. William Safire, the *New York Times* columnist, said: "Clinton in the first year of his second term is like Bush in the last year of his only term: an exhausted volcano." A writer for the *New Yorker* magazine said, "It's tempting to say out loud what most Beltway types secretly believe: that the Clinton Administration isn't merely in the doldrums—it's over."

Nothing could have been farther from the truth. The most exciting—if ignoble—part of his time in office was not far away. It would begin with the disclosure that Clinton, true to form, had had a long-term affair in the White House with a twenty-four-year-old intern, and it would end with his being impeached by the House and tried by the Senate for perjury and obstruction of justice.

The most fascinating feature of this mean catfight between Clinton and his Republican antagonists was the attitudes of the public. A year after it all began—a year sodden with press accounts showing that Clinton was a sex nut, a marathon liar, a marital cheat, and a hypocrite—it was hardly surprising that opinion polls showed 71 percent giving a negative rating to Clinton's moral and ethical standards. But the polls also showed that two out of three Americans liked the job Clinton was doing as president and were sick and tired of Washington's fixation on Clinton's private life and wanted the Republicans to shut up and let him finish his term.* As one Los Angeles mother told a pollster, "The guy's a dog" but his punishment should be left to Mrs. Clinton. "Hillary will take care of him." In other words, to the astonishment of many politicians, many preachers, and many edi-

---

*For a full year the public said it was sick and tired of Monica Lewinsky. Yet only two months after the Senate trial ended, Barbara Walters interviewed her on ABC and drew the largest audience in history for a news show. Seventy million watched all or part of the two-hour program. That was second only to the Academy Awards and the Super Bowl. (*New York Times,* March 5, 1999)

torial pundits (twenty-four newspapers had urged Clinton to resign) most people said it was okay for a president to be a cad if he was also a good executive.

Historic Infamy

Since this was only the second time in our history that a president was impeached (indicted) and tried for committing what the Constitution calls "high crimes and misdemeanors," we're obliged to review the steps leading up to the Congressional showdown, and the combatants involved in it.*

Step One: In 1994, Paula Jones sued President Clinton for sexual harassment, claiming that in 1991, when he was governor of Arkansas and she was a clerk employed by the state, he had lured her to a Little Rock hotel room where he made a lewd proposition. In 1997, to the surprise of most legal scholars, the U. S. Supreme Court voted unanimously to let the lawsuit go forward, even though no sitting president had ever before been subjected to a court trial. In casting his vote, Justice John Paul Stevens made one of the dumbest predictions of all time, saying the case "appears to us highly unlikely to occupy any substantial amount" of the president's time. As it turned out, the Paula Jones's lawsuit and its spinoff into the Monica Lewinsky scandal poisoned every hour of Clinton's remaining years in office.†

Step Two: Kenneth Starr, a rich Republican attorney, was appointed in 1994 to run the federal Office of the Independent Counsel to investigate several questionable actions involving Clinton both before and after he became president. Since an independent counsel is supposed to be unbiased and politically neutral in his search for facts, it's important to note Starr's background and the way he was selected.

Mrs. Clinton called Starr "a politically motivated prosecutor" who was part of a "vast right-wing conspiracy" dedicated to destroying Clinton's presidency. She had some grounds for thinking so. Right-wingers in and out of Congress were the principal instigators of the impeachment crusade. Also, a right-wing foundation subsidized the Paula Jones lawsuit, and Richard Scaife, the fanatically right-wing

---

*The first was more than a century ago. Andrew Johnson, who became president when Lincoln was assassinated, was impeached and tried after Congress accused him of using his powers illegally. He was acquitted by one vote on May 26, 1868.

†In April 1998, a federal judge threw her case out of court, but Ms. Jones appealed to a higher court, and to get her to drop the appeal, Clinton paid her $850,000.

heir to the Mellon banking fortune, subsidized books and magazine pieces suggesting the Clintons were guilty of everything from fraud to murder.

She might also have called it, with some exaggeration, a Southern right-wing conspiracy, since the House speaker, the House majority leader, the House whip, and the Senate majority leader were all extremely conservative and all were from the South, as were the four most tenacious House prosecutors of the impeachment. There was one other Southern touch of significance: The conservative three-judge panel that selected Starr to be prosecutor was headed by a North Carolinian who had consulted Senator Jesse Helms and Senator Lauch Faircloth of North Carolina, two of the most reactionary members of the Senate, before deciding on Starr.

Starr, too, was a southerner, born in Vernon, Texas, the son of a fundamentalist preacher. One anecdote often told to illustrate the father's character was about the time when he was out hunting his cow. He came across a woman wearing shorts and milking a cow in the privacy of her own cow barn. This so offended him that the following Sunday he preached a sermon damning women who wear shorts. Kenneth Starr never strayed from his father's strict Calvinist teachings, and he approached his prosecution of Clinton with all the zeal of a Salem witchhunter.

During his first three years in office, Starr spent $40 million trying to pin something on Clinton, but all of his investigations fizzled. Undiscouraged, he kept sniffing around for sin. And lo!, some dirt finally blew his way.

The Buxom Brunette

Step Three: Because her father had been a generous contributor to Clinton's presidential campaign, Monica Lewinsky, a buxom Los Angeles brunette, got a job as a White House intern. She was young but not inexperienced in manipulating the male libido. She set out to capture Clinton's attention, which she did one day when she encountered him in a White House hallway and lifted the back of her dress to let him see her thong underwear. Over the next two years, they had ten sexual encounters around the White House, until Ms. Lewinsky's supervisor began to suspect she was up to no good and had her transferred to a job in the Pentagon.

Step Four: At the Pentagon, Ms. Lewinsky struck up a friendship with Ms. Linda Tripp, an older woman who had once worked in the Clinton White House. In after-work phone conversations with Ms. Tripp, Ms. Lewinsky spoke in great detail of her affair with the president. Ms. Tripp taped twenty hours of these conversations and then betrayed her young friend by telling Kenneth Starr and Paula Jones's lawyers about them. That was in January 1998.

Step Five: Now Starr had a way to get at Clinton, through his sex life. Starr's grand jury investigation would continue for the next nine months—and, though the jury's activities were supposedly secret, what went on behind those closed doors was constantly leaked and became the all-consuming focus of press coverage. In several appearances before the jury, Ms. Lewinsky supplied intimate memories, including the times when, even as they were having sex, Clinton was eating pizza and carrying on phone conversations with congressmen. She told how Clinton had suggested ways to cover up their relationship, and of the gifts he gave her, and of their heavy-breathing late-night phone conversations.

While others were being summoned to testify to Starr's grand jury, Clinton would go on television to assure the public he had had no sexual relations with Ms. Lewinsky, just as privately he assured his family and aides and congressional allies. But lies spoken to a television audience or in private conversations aren't against the law. Lies spoken under oath are perjury. On January 17, 1998, Clinton lied about the Lewinsky affair in a sworn deposition taken by Paula Jones's lawyers (who were intent on showing the pattern of Clinton's womanizing over the years). Finally, it came his turn to testify to the Starr's grand jury on August 17, 1998, and he again lied about the relationship. On that occasion—which was videotaped—Clinton grudgingly admitted that "on certain occasions in early 1996 and once in early 1997, I engaged in conduct that was wrong. These encounters did not consist of sexual intercourse. . . . But they did involve inappropriate intimate contact."* As the four hours of intense grilling continued, Clinton defended himself with what a *New Yorker* writer called "one of the most improbable arguments in the history of human sexuality"—that oral sex isn't really having a sexual relation, and therefore he hadn't lied.

---

*Just how intimate was shown when Starr subpoenaed a blue dress Clinton had given to Lewinsky. There was a stain on the dress. The FBI, using a sample of Clinton's DNA, proved the stain had been made by the president's semen.

The Great Embarrassment

Independent Council Starr sent that videotape to the House Judiciary Committee along with 30,000 pages of grand jury testimony, plus his own 445-page summary—full of steamy details (many Congressmen wondered why the religious prosecutor was so eager to circulate material that many considered downright pornographic)—and recommended impeachment.

The House of Representatives would get around to that in due time, but first Clinton's enemies in the House—ignoring the rule of secrecy that legal ethics demanded of grand jury testimony—drew immediate blood by releasing the video tape to the public. Was any president ever before subjected to such embarrassment?

For the next twenty-four hours, around the clock, all or portions of the tape rolled across the nation's television screens, and viewers heard the president being repeatedly asked about touching and kissing various parts of Ms. Lewinsky's body. *The New York Times* sent reporters into the streets to get the reaction of people watching this incredible inquisition. They found viewers responding with "fatigue, shame, and a distinct dollop of sympathy for a man being painfully humiliated before their eyes. 'Brother, what a screwball, what a sick man,' muttered Albert Navarrate, a jeweler from Queens, more in sadness than in anger. . . . 'I mean he's a good president. He just got screwed up. But children shouldn't be exposed to this,' he said, as the words 'oral sex' were heard on the screen and flashed by again and again on the electric ribbon on the building rising above him."

One year closed and another opened with the prosecution winding its increasingly repetitive, increasingly boring way through the House Judiciary Committee, the full House, and into the Senate, where the nation was finally put out of its misery. During the impeachment and trial, members of Congress kept claiming that they were "voting their conscience," not voting out of partisan biases. Perhaps they were, but if so, it was interesting that their consciences usually voted along party lines. This made the outcome quite predictable.

Impeachment (indictment) requires only a majority vote, and since Republicans held a majority in the House, Clinton was of course impeached. Conviction, on the other hand, requires a two-thirds vote in the Senate, and since the Republicans held only fifty-five of the one hundred seats in that chamber, Clinton was in little danger of being convicted. The Senate fell short of even a majority vote on either of the charges against him. It rejected the charge of perjury, fifty-five to forty-five, with ten Republicans voting against conviction. It then split fifty–fifty on the charge of obstruction of justice, with five Republicans breaking ranks.

"A Sham Trial"

By the final vote, the event was about as exciting as the rerun of an old soap opera. "There was no dramatic search for the truth in Congress's deliberations," *The Wall Street Journal* correctly observed, "for the basic truth of the whole episode was known months before impeachment deliberations began. There weren't even any real moments of drama to capture the public fancy—just a sordid tale repeated over and over again." Senator Arlen Specter of Pennsylvania, one of the Republicans who voted against convicting Clinton on either charge, also sized it up accurately: "In a series of halting half-steps, the Senate stumbled through a pseudo-trial, a sham trial—really no trial at all." Few senators had their hearts in it. The basic reason was that many senators may lack brilliance and some may lack decency, but it can be said of most senators that (1) they are not fanatics and (2) they respect the Constitution.

For all the talk about perjury and obstruction of justice, what the Clinton scandal boiled down to was simply a guy who cheated on his wife and lied about it. That may be a sin, but it is not a sin that is rare in Washington.* And only a fanatic would consider it a crime serious enough to deserve the removal of the president from office, thereby invalidating the votes of the 47,402,357 Americans who backed him in the last election.

Two other harsh critics of Clinton's ethics also were exposed: Representative Dan Burton, Indiana Republican, confessed to fathering a child during an extramarital affair, and Representative Helen Chenoweth, Idaho Republican, admitted she had once had a long sexual fling with a married man.

No doubt influencing many in the Senate was the fact that virtually all legal scholars agree the Constitution's yardstick for measuring impeachable conduct—"treason, bribery or other high crimes and misdemeanors"—is not meant to cover personal misdeed and moral

*While the impeachment was going on in the House, several of the most righteous-sounding members were exposed for their hypocrisy. Judiciary Chairman Henry Hyde, who was leading the impeachment crusade, had to admit that in his younger days he had had a six-year affair with a married woman; and Speaker-elect Robert Livingston, knowing that *Hustler* magazine was about to reveal his several adulterous affairs, made a public confession and resigned from Congress on the spot.

failures; it's meant to cover only the most serious crimes and abuses of official power that subvert the government or the Constitution, neither of which is likely to be endangered by illicit sex in the White House shadows.

A Scale of Losers

Except that the impeachment and trial supplied political cartoonists and late-night comedy shows plenty of material, everyone came out of this long ordeal a loser—Clinton, Starr, Congress, their reputations indelibly smudged. "There were no victors—nobody won," said Herbert Stein, the economist and social commentator. "If anybody is the hero in this, it's probably Clinton. But he's not a real hero either. He just eluded capture." True, but the great irony of this melodrama was that the guilty person, though a loser, came out better than his adversaries. Well, maybe. His hope for a shining "legacy" was trashed, and his personal legal costs reached $6 million.

At the conclusion of it all, polls showed pornographer Larry Flynt, publisher of *Hustler,* had an approval rating higher than either the pious Kenneth Starr or the Republican Congress. Indeed, the public's opinion of the Republican Party was at its lowest in fourteen years. Party leaders had thought the scandal would give them twenty more seats in the House in the 1998 elections. Instead, they lost five seats.

As for Clinton, he deserved an Oscar for acting unfazed by it all. During a year of increasing infamy, with new charges bursting like land mines every day, Clinton went about his business as blithely as though these things weren't happening. He filled his roles without a hitch. As commander in chief, he launched bombers to punish foes in Iraq and Afghanistan; as the nation's chief peacemaker, he tried to end feuds in Bosnia and the Middle East; as our top trade wheeler-dealer, he bopped around China, Korea, Mexico, South America, Britain, smiling all the way.

In domestic affairs, he made important environmental changes by fiat and worked as best he could with a distracted and sullen Congress. His State of the Union address for 1999, made with incredible gall right in the middle of the Senate trial, was delivered with such bravura and laid out such soaring plans for the nation's future, that even Pat Robertson, founder of the rabidly anti-Clinton Christian Coalition and a leader in the effort to oust the president, admitted defeat: "From a public relations standpoint, he's won. They might as well dismiss this impeachment hearing and get on with something else, because it's all over as far as I'm concerned." Apparently the public felt the same way, for in an annual Gallup Poll it named Clinton "the most admired man," far ahead of the Pope.

For the moment, the Comeback Kid was on top again. But he had two more years to go, so there would inevitably be other downers. Like the northern lights, presidential power flares up with awesome brilliance one moment and then diminishes at a frightening rate the next. It happens to just about every president, the scintillating and the dull, the smartest and the ones who aren't so smart. Speaking of which, no recent president had more of a dramatic ebb and flow of power than Ronald Reagan, the fortieth president, the publicly charming but rather dense ex-actor who liked to pretend that he was a cowboy and the world was his horse.

Ronald Reagan: Enter Laughing

At the end of President Reagan's first year in office, early in 1982, newspapers were filled with stories about his overwhelming string of victories in pushing programs through Congress—he had had a phenomenal 82.4 percent success rate—and about the abject surrender of the Democrats. Editorial writers sounded frightened by the tilt of power. Was it tilting too far?

But a year later, after Reagan had suffered several congressional setbacks and lost a few points in the popularity polls, the tone of the commentaries was quite different. Typically, on February 22, 1983, *The New York Times'* Washington correspondent Leslie H. Gelb wrote dolefully, "Advisers to President Reagan . . . frankly concede that there is a presidential power vacuum."

Reagan's roller-coaster ride would continue, with the next high coming on the Fourth of July, 1986. Reagan and his wife, Nancy, stood on a platform near the Statue of Liberty in New York Harbor as fireworks framed the skyline and bounded off the dark waters. Spotlights threw the silhouette of the Reagans, much larger than life, onto the statue, making them seem part of the symbol being celebrated. Then Reagan pushed a button and a laser beam lit the statue's torch, while the crowd burst into "America the Beautiful," joined no doubt by some of the millions who were watching on television.

For Reagan, who always preferred symbolism over substance, it was a euphoric moment, casting him in the role of the Hollywood-to-Washington Myth Maker who had captured the hearts of America. Much of the press played along. "Ronald Reagan," bubbled *Time* magazine, "has found the American sweet spot. The seventy-five-year-old man is hitting home runs."

Public-opinion polls showed a stunning 70 percent approval rating for Reagan, with 75 percent of those polled believing him to be a strong leader.

And yet—for such can be the transience of popularity and its some-time companion, power—the shining mirage was again about to blow away, the magic was about to disappear in a puff. It happened with the revelation of the Iran-contra scandal, one of the most disgraceful pres-idential episodes of this century.

For seven years Reagan had been boasting of what a tough guy he would be with terrorists, particularly with Iranian terrorists. When he ran for president in 1980, he repeatedly shamed President Carter for allowing fifty U.S. embassy workers to be kidnapped and held hostage in Tehran, Iran. Reagan promised voters that *he* would never allow that sort of thing to happen to U.S. citizens overseas, that *he* would never forgive or make concessions to terrorists or do business with what he called the "Loony Tunes" and "squalid criminals" in Iran.

But only four short months after he celebrated the Statue of Liberty's birthday, all of Reagan's flamboyant antiterrorist rhetoric exploded in his face. The world discovered in November 1986 that America's Big Macho was, in fact, a marshmallow who for nearly two years, even while talking his toughest, had been selling an enormous tonnage of arms to Iran's leader, Ayatollah Khomeini, the one man in the whole world that polls showed Americans hated most, the fanatic who was widely believed to be behind most of the kidnappings and killings of Americans in the Middle East.

The scandal became even worse when it was discovered that Reagan had used some of the millions of dollars obtained from the Iran sales to secretly, and illegally, support Nicaraguan rebels in a war that Congress had specifically forbidden money to be spent on. In short, Reagan had broken the law, had violated his oath to uphold the Constitution.

Temporarily, Reagan's public support plummeted. Opinion polls showed that a majority of Americans thought his word was no good. Whatever persuasive power he had once had with Congress dried up; *Congressional Quarterly* found in the following legislative session that his success in lobbying bills to passage had fallen almost forty points, to an abysmal 43.5 percent in 1987, the lowest since ratings were first compiled in 1953.

His loss of face drove Reagan into a psychological funk, drained him physically and psychologically. He became befuddled, listless, unresponsive. All he seemed to want to do was watch television and old movies. For a while he showed little interest in running the country, and some White House advisers were afraid he was losing his grip on the office. His spirits eventually revived, however, but not his influence with Washington officials. The so-called Great Communicator ended his presidency as an ordinary politician, just a likable old man best known for a good grin and an endless supply of jokes.* His reduction in political stature in his last years was cynically summarized by one Republican leader: "Reagan's not just a lame duck. He's a capon."

Aside from the entertainment that such a downfall provides citizens who enjoy watching politics, there are two serious questions that Reagan's experience raises: At the height of his popularity, was he dangerously powerful? And was he, when the shame of the Iran-contra scandal washed away his mystique, too weak to govern properly?

Some variation of those questions has been heard in several administrations during the past fifty years. When a president has overwhelming success with Congress (as Lyndon Johnson also had in his first years in office), editorial writers are apt to comment with dismay on the lack of congressional independence and to raise fears of a runaway presidency. They rush to suggest that such a president could damage the traditional balance of power between the three branches of government.

And when Congress fights back, stalemates a president's efforts at least momentarily, and the president begins losing points in the popularity polls, the journalistic winds change 180 degrees. Now the editorial writers and political pundits begin to worry that the enfeebled president—as Johnson, seriously damaged by the Vietnam War, and Nixon, even more seriously crippled by the Watergate scandal, were in their final years—will be unable to give the guidance needed for the executive branch. Might such a president allow the ship of state to drift onto shoals?

These outbursts of nervous commentary should be taken seriously, but not too seriously. They raise legitimate points (such as loss of

---

*Nevertheless, right to the end, polls showed that most of the public continued to hold an allegiance to Reagan even though it admitted his many serious failings. As Reagan got ready to turn the White House over to George Bush, a Media General–Associated Press survey (December 27, 1988) showed most Americans gave Reagan a negative rating for his handling of every social issue: civil rights, education, housing, welfare, and ethics in government; majorities said Reagan had hurt the poor and helped the rich; and two-thirds said he had done a lousy job handling the economy. And yet—incredibly—six of ten approved of his presidency and seven of ten rated his leadership as excellent or good. Apparently those being surveyed gave extra weight to his handling of foreign policy, which most approved, or the outcome of the survey simply proves the old political axiom that no politician ever failed by overestimating the stupidity of the electorate.

mental equipment, which will be discussed later), but they are a bit melodramatic. That's just the way we are. History shows we have always tended to be melodramatic when measuring our chief executive.

Vague Powers, Cries of Alarm

From the founding of our government, Americans knew they didn't want a king, but they weren't sure just how much less than a king our chief executive should be. We have been debating the point for more than two hundred years. Should the president be the omnipotent guide, or the handyman of Congress, or something middling? The presidency is, a great historian once said, the "dark continent" of our government—explored many times but still terra incognita. No two scholars, no two politicians can agree on its correct boundaries.

The Constitution itself is typically vague on the matter. Originally the framers wanted the powers of government centered in Congress, the lawmaking body, and they specified in some detail how Congress should do its work. The president's powers were outlined in almost cryptic terms, specifying little more than his responsibility for the conduct of foreign relations, his duties as commander in chief of the armed forces, and his vague obligation to see that the laws are "faithfully executed." Of course these powers evolved into something much more expansive and complicated than could have been foreseen.

At the time of its founding, ours was the only government established on the principle of separation of powers, with three distinct branches—the executive, legislative, and judicial—checking and balancing each other from their autonomous centers. That's the way it is in theory; that's what we have been brought up to believe is the arrangement. But, in practice, the operation of the government clearly shows a gross imbalance in this tripodal structure. It also clearly shows that the powers are not in fact very separate.

Article II of the Constitution states that "the executive Power shall be vested in a President." That seems simple enough. But the president's powers do not stop at the executive boundary. His veto power gives him a strong hand in the legislature. His appointive powers can be used to shape the federal judiciary and the executive agencies that have immense quasi-judicial influence over the life of the nation.* Through his constitutional role as commander in chief of the armed services, as head of his political party, and as the only federal politician (except for the vice president, of course) elected by the nation as a whole, the president also has available a multi-levered apparatus for creating pressure and propaganda that is not available to either the legislature or the judiciary.

In short, there is a separation of powers, but the separation is not clean and absolute, and the three branches are not equal in strength. The weight is significantly on the side of the presidency. The Supreme Court has increasingly construed the Constitution to favor the presidency. In thinking up new solutions to the needs of our increasingly complex society, the Congress has granted more and more authority to the chief executive, including, in 1921, the power to prepare the budget.

The expansion of the presidency was, periodically, accompanied by complaints from some citizens who believed that the executive branch was overflowing the mold built by the framers of the Constitution. This complaint was first heard widely in modern times during the administration of President Franklin Roosevelt, who was extraordinarily successful at manipulating Congress (at least during his first term) and who made a blatant effort to stack the Supreme Court with members who agreed with him. A few Americans were genuinely convinced that Roosevelt had dictatorial designs on the office. The next significant cry of alarm over the power of the presidency came in the late 1960s and early 1970s, when some editorial writers and some members of Congress warned that America was in the grip of an "imperial presidency." It was a foolishly extravagant phrase, but forgivably so, for it was born of the frustration and fear created by the Vietnam War and by the Watergate scandal. Those two episodes showed that the president could be dangerously high-handed, could abuse his powers in such a way as to singlehandedly do lasting damage to the government and to the people's psyche.

---

*Occasionally a president will openly state that he is not guided by the Constitution so much as by his own feelings or intuition or conscience—whatever that means. "The Constitution is the supreme law of our land and it governs our actions as citizens," said President Gerald Ford, but he then added, "Only the laws of God, which govern our consciences, are superior to it" (quoted in *Newsweek*, February 5, 1975). But who's to say what the laws of God are? Or the laws of conscience? The reliance on conscience over law is a position that anarchists adhere to, and revolutionists, and seems to give no clear idea what that particular conservative Republican president had in mind as to the constitutional limits of action. Metaphysics seem to afflict every president at some time in his career.

The Abuse of Presidential Powers

About 2:30 A.M. on June 17, 1972, Washington, D.C., police entered the offices of the Democratic National Committee in the Watergate office-apartment complex and caught five men burglarizing the place and attempting to bug the telephones in the DNC chairman's office.

That was the beginning of what Senator Charles Percy, a Republican from Illinois, called, with some restraint, "the darkest scandal in American political history." Over the next two years, newspaper, grand jury, and congressional investigations uncovered the most weird series of political activities ever put together. Many, if not most, of the activities were traced back to sources either in the White House or in what was called the Committee for the Re-Election of the President (CREEP), which had been set up to keep President Richard Nixon in office and was headed by officials recently resigned from the Nixon cabinet and subcabinet.

In addition to the five burglars caught on the spot, two White House staff members were also convicted of being directly involved in the burglary. That was just the beginning. Top officials in the White House or at CREEP were also found to have inspired several other burglaries; the burning of incriminating evidence by the acting director of the FBI; the use of the FBI to gather data on political opponents and "radicals"; the planting of FBI provocateurs in antiwar groups to encourage them to violence and thereby discredit Senator George McGovern, the Democratic presidential nominee and a leading opponent of the Vietnam War; plans to bomb or set fire to the Brookings Institution, a center of academic criticism of some of Nixon's policies; and the compilation of a list of a hundred "White House enemies,"* who might be subjected to special harassment by the Internal Revenue Service and to character assassination (one black congressman was targeted for notoriety because he supposedly "likes white women"). There was also—by what smacked very heavily of extortionist techniques—the solicitation of an enormous campaign slush fund from corporation executives and industrialists who did business with the government and who were fearful of suffering reprisals if they did not kick through.

The men charged with these sometimes criminal and always unethical actions gave excuses that made their behavior seem all the more ominous. They said that they had countenanced burglaries and spying and the suspension of civil liberties because they thought these were necessary for "national security"—the very excuse, some observers re-

---

*The author of this book was honored by being named by the White House as one of its "enemies."

called, that had been used by the Hitler faction in its rise to power in Germany. Others in the inner White House circle excused their actions by saying that they felt President Nixon's reelection was necessary to "save the country"—a singular evaluation of one politician in a democracy. One person who gave this as his excuse was John Mitchell. At the very time he was the U.S. attorney general, the highest officer of the law in the land, Mitchell was associating with—if not encouraging, as some have charged—men whom he knew to be planning felonies. He admitted that he had obstructed justice and lied under oath, both felonies. Moreover, documents obtained by *The New York Times* indicate that in 1970 President Nixon himself approved a domestic espionage plan, parts of which he had been warned were "clearly illegal." The plan included burglary, monitoring private phone conversations, and opening private mail.

Writers began using extravagant words and phrases not often directed toward the White House: "Gestapo" (Mary McGrory), "tide of Nazism" (Carl T. Rowan). Even Barry Goldwater, conservative Republican senator from Arizona, referred to the Watergate events as growing out of "a Gestapo frame of mind."

Many opinion-shapers were, in short, likening Nixon to Hitler. They got encouragement from some politicians. "I am convinced that the United States is closer to one-man rule than at any time in our history," said Senator McGovern, who had just been defeated by the man he was calling a tyrant. And another liberal senator, Alan Cranston of California, added, "The presidency—by nature remote from the people, monolithic in structure and with a huge bureaucracy at its command— is the one branch most in danger of degenerating into dictatorship."* The reality of presidential power, together with its monarchical symbols, began to be spoken of as "the imperial presidency," and to be feared as such. Where would it end? How aloof would the "sovereign"—as Nixon called the occupant of the White House—become from his presumed subjects? Would future presidents feel they could commit crimes with impunity—would they act on the belief, as Nixon

---

*Such black warnings make good headlines, but before taking them too seriously, when they are heard during any administration, one should remember several things. It is extremely difficult for even the toughest of presidents to "command" that giant beast, the bureaucracy. No president can fully overcome the constitutional powers invested in Congress, especially the House of Representatives, to dominate the budgetary process. No president is immune from Congress' power to override his veto by a two-thirds vote. No president can conjure up magical powers to overcome the Senate's right to reject presidential appointments. And if Congress feels that the Constitution gives the president too much power, it can pass by a two-thirds vote a constitutional amendment that whips right past the White House on its way to ratification by the states. Congress need worry much less about a presidential dictatorship than about its own default.

put it, that "when a president does it, that means that it is not illegal"? These were dark concerns that ran through the nation's psyche and prompted the U.S. House of Representatives to crank up the clumsy machinery for impeachment. When the political atmosphere became so cold as to make certain that Nixon would certainly be impeached by the House, tried and convicted by the Senate, and removed from office, he resigned. But the national bitterness did not end there. When Gerald Ford, Nixon's hand-picked successor, pardoned the former president of all crimes, many Americans felt that justice had been thwarted (indeed, many believed—despite Ford's denials—that, as a precondition to his being named vice president, Ford had promised Nixon a pardon). This feeling figured heavily in Ford's defeat in 1976.

Watergate showed the potentially vicious side of the presidency, when the office is filled by someone willing to abuse his power.

The same lesson was given in foreign affairs by the expansion and conduct of the Vietnam War, which, although begun by John Kennedy, was not brought to its full scope until after the election of Lyndon Johnson in 1964. As it always does when recruited to support patriotic adventures and misadventures, the public at first supported the war.

A slow awakening came with the weakening of the domestic budget, as a result of war-born inflation and waste, and with the body count in Southeast Asia. When the longest war in American history officially limped to a semiconclusion in early 1973, the bodies were stacked like statistical cordwood: U.S. combat dead—45,943; U.S. dead from noncombat causes (accidents, illnesses)—10,298; U.S. missing—1,333; U.S. wounded—303,616; South Vietnamese combat deaths during the U.S. period—166,429; South Vietnamese wounded—453,039; North Vietnamese and Vietcong combat dead—937,562; civilians killed—415,000; civilians wounded—935,000.

Overwhelmed by these numbers, accumulated during a war that was often questioned on constitutional as well as moral and strategic grounds, many people of both liberal and conservative persuasion began seriously to reexamine the office of the presidency, where American participation in the war was hatched. The war had been joined and prolonged by three presidents, three very human beings, but the terrible cost was not, to put it mildly, borne by them but by the whole nation, and some wondered if it would ever fully recover.

Very Human Beings, Indeed

Just how human those three presidents were was revealed years after they left office, and those revelations go back to the point we mentioned earlier, that it is not melodramatic to assume that presidents may sometimes be mentally incapacitated to such an extent that they cannot provide the leadership the nation needs.

For example, because of an old war injury, Kennedy had back problems that often subjected him to intense pain. Did he take drugs to alleviate the pain—it would have been reasonable for him to have done so—and if he did take drugs, over what period of time did he take them and in what mental state did they leave him? In 1972 Dr. Max Jacobson, well known for administering the powerful stimulant known as "speed" to famous patients, admitted that he had accompanied President Kennedy to Vienna in 1961 when the president participated in a summit conference with Soviet Premier Nikita Khrushchev. Jacobson acknowledged that he gave Kennedy shots, but he would not say what they were. Thus, eleven years after the fact, the nation learned that some of its war-and-peace diplomacy may have been conducted by a president who was feeling like Superman, thanks to amphetamines.

But whether or not Kennedy took therapeutic but mind-warping drugs really isn't of continuing concern since very few presidents experience such physical pain that they need to take opiates. Much more to the point is the question of whether stress—to which all presidents are subjected, and some in a very intense way—may temporarily affect their minds.

There is considerable evidence that this may have happened to some recent presidents. As mentioned earlier, Reagan's response to the Iran-contra scandal was to sink into such a listless, do-nothing mood that some of his closest aides feared he had become unstable. Four of them met by prearrangement in the West Wing of the White House on the morning of March 2, 1987, "to watch the president closely, to determine whether he appeared mentally fit to serve," and if not, whether to recommend that Vice President Bush invoke the Twenty-fifth Amendment of the Constitution, which would have temporarily removed Reagan from office.* (It would have been a fearsome step to take. Not being

---

*According to *Landslide, The Unmaking of the President, 1984–1988* (pp. x–xi), by Jane Mayer and Doyle McManus, the four aides were: Howard Baker, Reagan's third and last chief of staff; A. B. Culvahouse, the White House counsel; Thomas Griscom, the White House's new director of communications; and James Cannon, Baker's confidant and counselor.

Amendment 25, Section 4, states that whenever the vice president and a majority of the cabinet declare "that the President is unable to discharge the powers and duties of his office, the Vice President shall immediately assume the powers and duties of the office as Acting President." If the president challenges the move, then Congress has the last word; he can be ousted only by a two-thirds vote in both houses.

psychiatrists, they didn't know how to measure his actions, so when he told a couple of jokes they were only too happy to conclude that he had snapped back and was "normal" enough to leave alone.)

Much graver evidence of mental instability was to be found in the conduct of Nixon, under stress from the Watergate scandal, and of Johnson, apparently tormented by the Vietnam War.

Nixon finally reached the point that he walked the halls of the White House talking to the portraits on the walls. His son-in-law, David Eisenhower, fully expected Nixon to "go bananas" (as Eisenhower expressed it) and commit suicide. Other close associates noticed that he was losing control of himself. Senator Barry Goldwater recalls an evening at the White House when Nixon's "mind seemed to wander so aimlessly that I asked myself the unthinkable: is the President coming apart because of Watergate?" Nixon's chief of staff, Alexander Haig, tried to bring Nixon's mind back into focus by taking away the president's tranquilizers and sleeping pills. Secretary of Defense James Schlesinger, believing that Nixon was dangerously impaired, ordered the military to accept no directives from Nixon unless they were cosigned by Schlesinger himself.

With Lyndon Johnson, it was always hard to tell whether he was just engaging in his customary hyperbole, or whether he was going off his rocker. In any event, he frequently said things that frightened those who knew him. For instance, according to the former wife of Congressman Don Edwards, at a dinner party Johnson confided to the Austrian ambassador that every morning around 2 o'clock he was visited by the Holy Ghost, who told him whether to bomb North Vietnam that day. Mrs. Edwards said that the ambassador feared that if the Soviets heard about these alleged visits from God and concluded that "he's completely crazy, they might be forced into doing something," like a preemptive nuclear strike. On another occasion, Johnson talked of how wonderful it would be if he could "become dictator of the whole world, and then I could really make things happen." In his book *Remembering America,* Richard Goodwin, who held a variety of posts in the Kennedy and Johnson White Houses, says that Johnson thought "communists already control the three major networks and the forty major outlets of communication" and were "taking over the country." He said that when Johnson showed "increasingly irrational behavior," both he and Bill Moyers, another White House aide, consulted two psychiatrists and described Johnson's actions. "In all cases," writes Goodwin, "the diagnosis was the same: We were describing a textbook case of paranoid disintegration, the eruption of long-suppressed irrationalities." Johnson had become "a very dangerous man."

They were not alone in viewing Johnson with alarm. Eric Goldman, another high staff member, looked upon Johnson's conduct after two and a half years in office as "downright frightening." And two *Washington Post* reporters who interviewed Johnson in his last year in office found him "battered and stumbling over his words, driven to the point of physical collapse."*

A Very Welcome Come-Down

Although only a few White House insiders were aware of these unnerving mental eccentricities, there was certainly a widespread perception among the general public that Lyndon Johnson and Richard Nixon had wonderously inflated notions of their role, were imperiously high-handed, and were as thin-skinned to criticism as any monarch.

Because of the unpleasantness that accompanied these two presidents, the electorate welcomed with relief the rather plodding presidency of Gerald Rudolph Ford (of whom Johnson one said, "Jerry can't chew gum and cross the street at the same time") and then the presidency of James Earl Carter, Jr., a seemingly self-effacing peanut farmer from Georgia. One of Carter's most appealing traits was that he apparently was determined to maintain his ties with the grass roots and to resist the temptation to become kingly. His effort was not appreciated by everyone. Many—including quite a few in his own party—ridiculed him for it. Tip O'Neill, Speaker of the House during those years, recalled in his memoirs:

> I'm a pretty down-to-earth guy, but it used to irritate me to see the president of the United States carrying his own luggage. One morning, when we were leaving Blair House together a few days before the inauguration, Carter picked up his garment bag and a valise. I grabbed the bag away from him, but he snatched it back.
> "People love to see you carrying your own bags," he said.

---

*Some observers—particularly mind doctors—cite examples such as these to argue that, given the stresses of the presidency, a psychiatrist trained to watch for telltale signs of mental collapse should be on the White House staff. As Dr. Julian Lieb, former director of the Dana Psychiatric Clinic at Yale–New Haven Hospital, wrote in the *Washington Post Weekly* of February 20/26, 1989, "The present system is untenable. Members of the president's staff, who would never presume to prescribe treatment for their own family and friends, have the sole responsibility for the mind that can start an atomic war in seconds."

"Not if you're the president, they don't," I replied. "And what about the bellhops? They vote too, you know."

What Carter failed to understand is that the American people . . . *want* a magisterial air in the White House, which explains why the Kennedys and the Reagans were far more popular than the four first families who came in between. The fact is that most people prefer a little pomp in their presidents.

Perhaps. But at least Carter had the satisfaction of being the most unregal president since Harry Truman. No sooner was he sworn into office at the Capitol inaugural ceremony than he began deflating the imperial style. Instead of riding back to the White House in an armor-plated limousine, Carter and his wife climbed out of the car and walked the length of Pennsylvania Avenue, hand in hand.* Within a few days he began trimming the White House perquisites: He ordered that the two presidential yachts be sold; he reduced the motor pool by 40 percent and ended the practice of giving staff big-shots chauffeur service from their homes to work; he ordered White House aides to use military aircraft as rarely as possible and instead to fly commercially, tourist class; he ordered 300 television sets and about 200 AM-FM radios removed from the White House.

Before Carter's administration, a presidential entrance at a major social event was always accompanied by the marine band playing "Ruffles and Flourishes" and "Hail to the Chief," not to mention several salvos from a column of trumpeteers. Carter temporarily ended most of that. In his first television address to the nation as president, he wore a cardigan sweater. At his first cabinet meeting—a hastily convened emergency session and therefore understandably less formal— he wore no tie. He warned the press that, whether they liked it or not, he would try to lead the life of a normal man: "I'm not going to relinquish my right to go to the zoo with my daughter, to the opera with my wife or pick up arrowheads on my farm without prior notice to the press." He taught Sunday school at a Baptist church in Washington, just as he had in Plains, Georgia. Shortly after taking office, he opened his personal telephone line to the public and, over a two-hour period,

---

*In his memoirs, Carter explained how the idea for the walk blossomed. It had been suggested to him by Senator William Proxmire as a good example for the nation's physical fitness program. Carter dismissed that as "rather silly." But then, after thinking it over, he realized that the symbolism of the act would be invaluable in another way—"I felt a simple walk would be a tangible indication of some reduction in the imperial status of the President and his family" (*Keeping Faith* [New York: Bantam, 1982], pp. 17–18).

took forty-two calls from citizens in twenty-five states. The implied message: The president was an available neighbor.

For taking these steps to reduce pomp, some critics charged that Carter was merely symbol minded, earning popular support by cheap and insignificant actions. This was a woeful misjudgment. Every action a president takes is weighted with significance. Actions that *in themselves* are of no great importance take on considerable importance at a time when the public is looking for signs by which to interpret the president's administration. For this reason, even the seemingly trivial actions of new presidents are subjected to especially intense magnification and scrutiny by the public.

Unfortunately, Carter's admirable efforts to convey an air of democracy were, as the result of bad management and a long spell of bad luck in the second half of his administration, also accompanied by an air of impotency. The same voters who had welcomed him as an antidote to the expansion of power during the Johnson and Nixon years were yearning by 1980 for the return of a decisive president, and he was rejected in his try for reelection.

With Ronald Reagan, America once again got glitz and glamour and $220,000 china sets for the White House and $5,000 dresses for the first lady. But with George Bush—like Carter, determined to make his image drastically different from his predecessor—the symbolism swung back to folksiness, starting with a Carter-like postinaugural walk up Pennsylvania Avenue. And an extra dose of folksiness came with Clinton, who did not think it beneath his dignity to play the saxophone (he had been a champion sax player in high school) at impromptu jazz sessions or to duck into a McDonald's for a quick burger during a jog around Washington.

These swings in style and outer trappings, however, have done little to answer the old questions that puzzle scholars of the presidency: Is too much potential power available to the president? Given congenial circumstances, is it possible for him to become "imperial" in a real sense?

Probably the answer is that the presidency offers far too much power in foreign affairs for occupants of the White House who are thoughtless or arrogant. But in domestic affairs *no* president—especially an imaginative one—has half as much power as he needs to carry out his plans for the country.

The minority of assertive presidents have measured their power—or lack of it—in long periods of frustration and anger, usually triggered by the sight of their programs disappearing in the swamp of geriatrics, obstreperousness, and parochialism on Capitol Hill. "By

God," cried Theodore Roosevelt, on the verge of a tantrum, "I'd like to have 16 or 20 lions to set loose in the Senate." In recent decades an increasingly ponderous and independent bureaucracy has joined Congress in frustrating activist presidents, until the latter have been stung to make crassly bitter summations of their impotence. "They talk about the power of the president," said Harry Truman. "They talk about how I can just push a button to get things done. Why, I spend most of my time kissing somebody's ass." The same feeling was expressed in more decorous terms by President Carter: "There are so many things that I would like to do instantly that take a long time. The most difficult thing [about the presidency] is to recognize the limitations of a president's power."

President Reagan was never known to complain about lack of power, perhaps because, more than any president since Calvin Coolidge (who was the president Reagan admired most among his predecessors), he took little interest in the day-to-day operation of government. He rarely met with congressmen, rarely tried to twist arms on Capitol Hill or put his personal imprint on legislation. He was famous for dozing off in cabinet meetings. He was inattentive to details, ignorant of facts, largely disengaged from management, and totally willing to delegate power to subordinates. On some major policy matters dear to his heart, such as his belief that taxes should never be raised, he went stubbornly his own way and would not listen to advisers, but overall Reagan's White House was the most staff-dominated of modern times. Reagan wasn't exactly a puppet but, as Hedrick Smith says, he was "legendary for bending to the advice of whichever person or group among his trusted advisers was the last to see him." Once, when asked by reporters if he'd be visiting the Vietnam War Memorial on Veterans Day, he replied, "I can't tell until somebody tells me. . . . I never know where I'm going." On another occasion he told reporters, cheerfully and without complaint, "They tell me I'm the most powerful man in the world. I don't believe that. Over there in that White House someplace there's a fellow that puts a piece of paper on my desk every day that tells me what I'm going to be doing every fifteen minutes. He's the most powerful man in the world." Some reporters may have thought he spoke in jest, but those who were aware of how the Reagan White House operated knew it was the truth. Reagan's aides laid out every minute of his day for him. And his advisers usually told him where he was going legislatively, too.

And yet, partly because of his genius for public relations, he was seen by most Americans as an activist president. It was a reputation that stood on three legs.

One leg was his willingness to talk tough in foreign affairs and occasionally take, without congressional approval, surprise (even illegal) actions against insignificant enemies (Grenada, Libya, Nicaragua). Another leg was his willingness to veto congressional actions and to talk tough with Congress, threatening it with John Wayne and Clint Eastwood clichés. He loved to dare Congress, "make my day." (And such is Congress's timidity, his threats sometimes worked.) And the third leg was his incredible ability to wrap himself in the flag and present himself as the preeminent symbol of traditional, American family values. He proved, more than any modern president, the power of symbols. He was no fighter, no activist. Most of the things he promised to do when he arrived in Washington—reduce the size of government, reduce the budget, outlaw abortions, restore prayer in the public-school curriculum—he never tried to achieve. He never really tested his power by fighting for them. But he was a great talker. He never stopped *talking* about those things. And because he talked a good fight, most Americans were deluded into seeing him as an activist president.

But if *real* activist presidents have had honest grounds for complaining about their lack of power, and about their frustrations in seeking to exercise power, where do we get the idea that the president is so powerful? Partly it is from an accurate perception of his real, arbitrary, and far-reaching power in foreign affairs (discussed in the next chapter) and partly it is from the myths, presumptions, and folklore that have grown up around this unique office.

The Mystique of the Presidency

Shortly after his swearing in, following Kennedy's assassination, Johnson approached key members of Kennedy's staff and begged them to stay on and help him, arguing for their transferred loyalty with an irrefutable logic: "I'm the only president you've got." Although the statement was probably supposed to convey no more than the uncharacteristic humility he felt at the moment, in its simplicity it nicely sums up the problem every president confronts throughout the easy days as well as in the crises—that there is only one of him. The president is singular. Aside from the vice president, he is our only national politician. He is the only politician whose decision-making powers are neither duplicated elsewhere nor shared with somebody else as an equal.

The problems he deals with are generally no different from the problems that ricochet around all federal halls, the same problems Congress wrestles with in a more lumbering fashion, but in dealing with these problems only the president can justifiably have on his desk (as Presidents Truman and Carter had) a sign proclaiming with as much resignation as pride: "The buck stops here."

The uniqueness of his potential power deludes the public into thinking that it is also limitless. And this dangerously misleading notion is hyped by the press, which knows what its readers and viewers want. Hedrick Smith, who covered Washington many years for *The New York Times*, puts it this way:

> As a nation, we focus obsessively on the president, out of proportion with other power centers. This happens largely because the president is one person whom it is easy for television to portray and whom the public feels it can come to know. Other power centers are harder to depict: The Supreme Court is an aloof and anonymous body; Congress is a confusing gaggle of 535 people; the bureaucracy is vast and faceless. It is almost as if the president, most politicians, and the press, especially television, have fallen into an unconscious conspiracy to create a cartoon caricature of the real system of power.
>
> There is a strong urge for simplicity in the American psyche, a compulsion to focus on the single dramatic figure at the summit, to reduce the intricacy of a hundred power-plays to the simple equation of whether the president is up or down, winning or losing on any given day or week. Television and the viewing millions seek to make a simple narrative of complex events.

Because of this singularity, we wrap the presidency in a cocoon of pomp and mystique that is no doubt very satisfying to the ego of the person in the job and in fact augments enormously the powers he has by law. But this deference also keeps him from serving the nation with the openness and efficiency that the job deserves, for the most harmful misconception of the president is that his singularity somehow gives him a power that is total and, since he is above the people, a power that to a degree is inherently against them. Although it was partly a desire by right-wingers to deliver an insulting wallop to the memory of Franklin D. Roosevelt, who had had the gall to break tradition by being elected four times, it was also the national monarchophobia that pushed through the Twenty-second Amendment to the Constitution in 1951 to limit the president to no more than two terms. Coincidentally, by making every second-termer automatically a lame duck, the amendment robs the president of a great deal of the influence that he would need to carry out his constitutional role.*

The fear that our top politician will somehow be able to perpetuate himself indefinitely gets no support from experience. The electorate in its caution, or its fickleness, has elected only fifteen presidents (Washington, Jefferson, Madison, Monroe, Jackson, Lincoln, Grant, Cleveland, McKinley, Wilson, FDR, Eisenhower, Nixon, Reagan, and Clinton) out of forty-two to even a second term, much less allowed a permanent grip on the post.

With this safe history behind us, why, then, the persistent concern over whether the president may be too powerful?

The concern is understandable, considering the libertarian nature of the American people. We revere champions, but we dislike the boss. We are passionately orthodox, but we rebel against those who impose orthodoxy. As a people we have regrettably indulged ourselves in romantic admiration for the wheelers and dealers of politics at the neighborhood and state levels—the Mayor Daleys and the Boss Crumps and the Mayor Curleys and the Huey Longs—but at the same time we suspect and fear and even hate the respectable attributes that smack of national monarchy. To the colonists, one-man rule meant monarchy, which was, in turn, synonymous with tyranny; many Americans still use the two words interchangeably. With the degrading rule of George III so fresh in their memories, it is understandable that the leaders of the new nation were too quick to see clues of a return to monarchy in some aspects of the new government. The Constitution frightened Patrick Henry. "It squints toward monarchy," he warned. "Your president may easily become king."

A reading of *The Federalist* papers—written in 1787 and 1788 to soothe the myriad fears of the populace in respect to governmental bugaboos—reveals that no other problem was so vexing as that of the presidency. It was this office and what Alexander Hamilton called the constant "aversion of the people to monarchy" that the opponents of the new Constitution found most useful in promoting unrest. Hamilton accurately pointed out—using an argument any schoolchild

---

*The longer a president is in office—that is, the closer he comes to the probable termination of his service—the less power he has to swap with the power brokers in Congress. Even before the second term was made automatically lame duck, presidents had their problems maintaining the muscle of their office. After the passage of the Social Security Act in 1935, FDR carried little weight with Congress except in military matters, although he served ten more years.

could develop today—that opponents were dealing heavily in fiction when they likened the presidency to the British Crown of that day, since the presidency was a four-year term, whereas the Crown was hereditary; the president's veto of legislation could be overridden by two-thirds votes of both houses, whereas the king's negation of parliamentary acts was final; and the president could be removed by congressional impeachment and trial, whereas the king could only be removed by assassination or banishment.*

The most obvious miscalculation on Hamilton's part was in hooting at those who raised the specter of a president with "imperial purple flowing in his train . . . [or] seated on a throne surrounded with minions and mistresses, giving audience to the envoys of foreign potentates in all the supercilious pomp and majesty."

The splendor that Hamilton thought so ridiculous to imagine has in fact arrived. Acknowledging that as things go in the world of potentates, the presidency isn't a bad place to serve, Nixon said, with a smile of candor, "We're roughing it pretty nicely." It's getting nicer all the time.

---

*Adding the procedure for impeachment to the Constitution was favored by Benjamin Franklin for the very reason that otherwise assassination would be the only way left to get rid of a chief executive who was judged to be wrecking the country. Yet Americans have cheated on the Constitution and have treated their presidents to the decencies of democratic unhappiness only twice, when efforts were made to impeach and convict Andrew Johnson and Bill Clinton. For the most part, Americans have dealt with their presidents as though they were monarchs, removing four of them from power by assassination and attempting to remove five others in that fashion.

Regrettably, the result has been to force the president further from the people. He fears them. The Secret Service force that protects him from the people has been more than doubled since 1963. Its budget is up tenfold. The president rides among the people in a car built like a tank. Even when he goes to his "informal" quarters at Camp David, he goes with great caution. Referring to the double steel fence around Camp David's two hundred acres, plus the guard of forty-eight Marines who patrol the area night and day, plus the cleared "no-man's land" along the perimeter, a White House aide understandably assessed the presidential retreat as "the nearest thing we have to a medieval castle with a moat and foot guards." Indeed, Charles the Bald was not so protected. The White House is bathed in protective floodlights at night. There are bulletproof guardhouses at the gates. And traffic is no longer allowed in front of the White House.

Such defenses are a recent phenomenon. Even until the 1930s, the White House was almost unguarded. Security was so easygoing in President Hoover's time that sightseers sometimes wandered into Hoover's private rooms by error. Until the turn of this century, thousands of Americans felt that there was no way to usher in the New Year quite like dropping by the White House to shake the president's hand—sometimes the line stretched for blocks. How distantly innocent that all seems today. Now there is distrust on both sides. Fearing the people, the president becomes more physically remote and seemingly more mentally aloof.

There were always elements of pomp around the president; but stark plainness was, for a long time, also present. If Washington loved to move grandly among the citizenry in a regal coach pulled by six horses or on a white stallion with leopard-skin trappings, the populace cannot be said to have encouraged this kind of ego, nor did many of Washington's successors seek to present themselves so regally as he. When Thomas Jefferson took the oath of office on March 4, 1801, he "dressed plainly and without ostentation" for the occasion, walked from his boardinghouse to the Capitol (accompanied only by two men who would be in his cabinet), and delivered his inaugural address only to members of Congress. Then he walked back to his boardinghouse for supper, only to find that all the chairs were taken and that no one offered to surrender his place at the table to the new president. From that egalitarian era the United States has moved to inaugurals that cost $50 million, at which wealthy friends of the first family have the privilege of paying $1,000 to watch the new president dance or hear seventy-year-old Hollywood stars crack political jokes.

Whether or not it has been in the right direction is perhaps debatable, but U.S. presidents have come a long way since 1853, when Franklin Pierce moved into a White House so ill-equipped that he could find only a single candle to light his way to bed, which on that first night was a mattress on the floor. Calvin Coolidge thought it not at all beneath his dignity to retire from the White House to a $36-a-month rented duplex. When Harry and Bess Truman left the White House for the last time, they went to the railroad station and paid their own fares back to Independence, Missouri; not until Truman had been out of office for six years did Congress decide that all presidents and their widows deserved to be paid a pension. It was a far cry from the way Lyndon Johnson, only sixteen years later, was moved into luxurious retirement—flown back to Texas in the presidential plane and given $450,000 to draw on for "transitional expenses." Subsequent presidents have retired to similar treatment.

The president is paid $400,000 a year plus expenses; no matter how wealthy in their own right the occupants of the White House may be—Kennedy, Johnson, Nixon, Carter, Reagan, and Bush were millionaires before they reached the highest office—only two this century have shown, by returning their entire salaries to the U.S. Treasury, that they considered the privilege of serving their country to be reward enough (the two were John Kennedy and, three decades earlier, Herbert

Hoover). Presidents have become increasingly lavish in their style of living.* A hundred years ago the annual cost of operating the 132-room White House was $13,800. Today the cost is estimated at about $150 million (it's hard to be sure just what the White House does spend, for the details are widely scattered throughout the budget). Sixty years ago, President Hoover got by with a staff of 42. When Clinton took over, there were about 500 persons (including 75 butlers) working in the White House itself and another 1,500 working for the Executive Office of the president in the Old Executive Office Building, next door to the White House, and in the newer Executive Office Building across the street. Flunkies are available for every purpose, though their assignments vary from administration to administration. One man in Nixon's White House was assigned the task of walking beside the president and telling him in advance whether to turn left or right at a corner or how many steps were in a stairway, so Nixon wouldn't stumble. Every recent presidential candidate has promised to reduce the White House staff; but when they get in office, they change their minds.

Any president would like for you to think he is working his heart out for you every waking moment. John Ehrlichman tells us in *Witness to Power* that his boss, Nixon, ordered aides to put out the message to the press that "the president has slept only four hours a night. He goes to bed at eleven or twelve, then awakens at two and works from two to three. That's when he does his clearest thinking. Then he sleeps until seven-thirty." All hokum. In fact, Nixon usually had a good eight or nine hours of uninterrupted sleep. So do most presidents. Nor do they labor throughout the day. The White House complex is outfitted with tennis courts, a movie theater, and a swimming pool—and occupants of the White House use them often.

---

*We give our ex-presidents generous treatment, too. In 1955, when the first legislation regarding support and perquisites for ex-presidents was passed, the cost to the taxpayers was $64,000. Of course, there were only two living former presidents in those days: Herbert Hoover and Harry S Truman. Today we have Ford, Carter, Bush, and Reagan, as well as a presidential widow, Lady Bird Johnson. To take care of them all, taxpayers are now shelling out close to $30 million. Each ex-president gets a $300,000-a-year office allowance, and round-the-clock Secret Service protection. The Secret Service assigns twenty-four agents—eight per shift—to guard each former president; some of the agents are used as porters and flunkies. Phone bills run around $95,000, and so on. Some members of Congress are beginning to wonder if the perks might not be a bit excessive, particularly in light of the fact that recent ex-presidents (with the notable exception of Carter) have made millions by peddling their title—sitting on corporate boards of directors, demanding exorbitant fees for speaking engagements, and writing books for fortunes. Reagan, for example, got $2 million for speaking in Japan and $5 million for his memoirs, which of course he didn't even write.

Reagan's day, for example, started at 9 A.M., but after the 9:30 National Security Council meeting he was pretty much on his own, except for ceremonial duties. Aides who met with him after lunch found he would often go to sleep while they were talking. His "work" day was over at 4 P.M. During the day, he usually found time for an hour of lifting weights (he liked to have visitors feel his biceps). Reagan spent hours answering fan mail and watching old movies, the latter being what occupied most evenings for him and wife Nancy. A member of Reagan's cabinet says that whenever he visited the president after 6 P.M. he was always in his pajamas. He usually toddled off to bed by 11.

When the president grows restless amidst the grandeur of the White House, he can escape to the 180-acre playpen, Camp David, in the Maryland mountains near Washington. There he can romp and play at a heated, free-form swimming pool, a bowling alley, archery and skeet ranges, tennis courts, a pitch-and-putt golf green, a movie theater, or on the miles of nature trails. Carter's chief of staff writes in his memoirs that Carter had been president only one month when he made his first visit to Camp David and after that it was hard to keep him in Washington. "In fact," writes Hamilton Jordan, "over the course of his administration, his family spent the equivalent of nearly an entire year, using the retreat more than any other first family. I was always a little worried that someone in the media might make the same calculation and criticize us for it."

All presidents take vacations, of course, and Reagan took slightly fewer than John F. Kennedy, who had one day of vacation for every three and a half days in office. Not only did Reagan smash Carter's record for playtime at Camp David, he also spent well over a year vacationing at his California ranch and at Palm Springs, at no small cost to the taxpayers. The *Los Angeles Times*, which tried to keep a tab on the Reagans' expenses, figured that they spent considerably more than $8 million of public money on their California vacations. One twenty-five-day vacation in 1987 cost $600,298.

When the president travels, he can call on one of a half-dozen jets in the presidential fleet. *Air Force One* is followed by both a back-up plane of the same size and the National Emergency Airborne Command Post, or the "doomsday plane" (a modified Boeing 747), which is a kind of mobile Pentagon.

Every presidential plane is a flying palace, and the new ones built for Bush were even more so: two 747 jetliners equipped at a cost of a mere $250,000,000. And what did taxpayers get for their president at that price tag? They got 4,000 square feet of interior space (compared to the "cramped" 1,300 square feet on the 707's used by Reagan and previous presidents). On board the new *Air Force Ones* you would find 100 telephones, 16 televisions, 11 videocassette recorders, 7 bathrooms, and enough food and water to feed 70 passengers and a 23-member crew for a week without resupply. The only beds on board are for the president and first lady. Bunks are available for the flight crew, and thirty-one "executive sleeper seats" await White House staff members and guests. The fourteen seats reserved for journalists are first-class width but non-sleepers. Everyone has headphones that offer six channels of stereo music. To serve the president (not guests), the plane has a laundry and an office for his doctor. The president's suite has twin beds, a two-sink lavatory with a shower, and a vanity desk. Next to the bedroom is his executive office with couches that can seat five people and a full-size desk that doubles as a table designed to let the president dine with one other person. The plane has two kitchens and a large dining/conference room. Naturally, the plane is outfitted with a shredder capable of destroying fifty pounds of "top secret paper" an hour.

Are such elaborate planes necessary? The United States is the only nation in the world where, when the head of state moves, the office of the head of state moves with him. Are we better off for that? Perhaps an argument can be made for it when the president goes abroad. But what about lesser jaunts? A cross-country trip costs taxpayers $100,000.

The shooting of Kennedy, the attempted assassination of Ford, and the wounding of Reagan are reason enough to guard the president against crazies. But sometimes security precautions reach such totality that an onlooker might be forgiven for thinking that the Secret Service regards the president's body as sacred. In December 1982 President Reagan visited Costa Rica—an extraordinarily peaceful country, a democracy without an army, where the police are unarmed and the president of Costa Rica walks around unescorted by guards because his only danger is in being kissed by admiring women. Costa Rica is the most pro-United States country in Latin America. And yet here came Reagan armed and guarded like a Roman emperor visiting Carthage: His presidential plane was accompanied by a C-5 cargo plane carrying three bulletproof Lincoln Continentals; his entourage included 300 Secret Service agents. It was just a normal visit by a U.S. president.

Some presidents might like that kind of protective coddling, but Clinton found it highly irritating—at least at first. When he arrived at the White House, he found, to his amazement, that Secret Service agents were even stationed inside his living quarters: He promptly made them move outside. And he couldn't understand why an agent needed to accompany him in the elevator when he was only going between two floors. He was appalled to find his office guarded by one agent on the walkway outside, two in the hallway, and a third in the hall outside the Roosevelt Room, where Clinton held meetings. And when Vice President Gore traveled the few steps from his own office to Clinton's, accompanied all the way by two Secret Service agents, that made *four* agents left outside to guard the hall.

Reminiscent of medieval kings who took their retinue and scepter and movable throne and other regal gewgaws with them as they moved about their kingdoms, some presidents carry along the glitter of state on their travels. When Lyndon Johnson traveled abroad, he often took along White House china and crystal for entertaining chiefs of state. Nixon topped that on his trip to Rumania by airlifting not only State Department china, White House crystal, and vermeil flower bowls for the luncheon he gave dignitaries of that country, but also the White House maitre d', five butlers, and twenty-six stewards.

The presidential addiction to the motor car was grandly displayed when Bush attended the economics conference in Paris in 1989; not only was he the only one of the seven national leaders to have brought along *two* limousines, but that was just the top horsepower; all told, he traveled around the city in a twenty-car motorcade.

When President Clinton visited China in 1998, he took along only ten armored limousines for the official delegation, but since there were 1,000 people in his retinue (more than three times as many as Nixon took when he visited China in 1972), Clinton's party rented 350 cars in Shanghai. Among the luxuries the Clintons took along was enough bottled water so that the president and first lady wouldn't have to open a tap to bathe in the luxurious Chinese guest houses and five-star hotels where they stayed on their nine-day trip. But at least Clinton didn't make such regal demands in China as he had made the year before in Brazil, where he asked the government to suspend daylight saving time during his visit to allow him another hour to prepare for his evening schedule. (He was refused.)

The pharaohs of Egypt, the caesars of Rome, and the fathers of the Catholic Church built pyramids and temples of various kinds to celebrate their immortality by enshrining their sacred writings, relics, and bones.

In the same spirit, American presidents, on leaving office, carry away tons of their sacred papers, around which they build self-aggrandizing monuments called libraries. Valuable depositories they may be, but they are also ego trips. These libraries (11, at present) are built with private funds but cost taxpayers about $30 million a year to operate. They contain hundreds of millions of pages of written material, more than 5 million still pictures, millions of feet of film, and more than 200,000 artifacts. To give you a way to visualize some of that, consider just one of the libraries, the Jimmy Carter Library in Atlanta. If you stacked all the written material into a single pile, it would reach 2.5 miles—which is the paper equivalent of twenty-eight Great Pyramids of Egypt balanced base to point. Think how high it would be if he had been reelected.

So sacred is every presidential word presumed to be by his coterie (a presumption often shared by the president, no doubt) that nothing is considered so trivial as to be cast aside. Thus on Nixon's visit to China, the White House press officials dutifully recorded for posterity, and photocopied for the press corps, such momentous pronouncements as these: on viewing the Great Wall of China: "I think that you would have to conclude that this is a great wall"; on viewing the mountains overshadowing the city of Hangchow, immortalized by Marco Polo: "It looks like a postcard."

The best reporters know they are participating in a foolish extravaganza. When Martin Tolchin was covering the White House for *The New York Times,* he admitted, "I have had stories on page one just because the president burped. I don't think they belonged there at all."

When a president leaves his home, he will always be accompanied by a planeload of reporters—ordinarily between two hundred and one thousand. There is little reason for most of them to be there. Coverage of the president's activities while traveling is done by a "pool"—a small group, usually about four reporters and a television camera crew—who actually travel with the president. Members of the pool are expected to share what they learn with the other reporters tagging along in the other plane. It's flackery at best, sycophancy at worst.

Flattery, Strokes

Some believe that there is a monarchical quality to the president's life because he surrounds himself with courtiers and jesters, advisers more adept at flattering and stroking the president's ego than in giving him their hard opinions. George Reedy, President Johnson's press aide, likened life in the White House to "the life of a court" because the president "is treated with all of the reverence due a monarch. No one interrupts a presidential contemplation for anything less than a major catastrophe somewhere on the globe. No one speaks to him unless spoken to first. No one invites him to 'go soak your head' when his demands become petulant and unreasonable."

He exaggerates somewhat. Some advisers are not reluctant to challenge a president's opinion and challenge it quite sharply, and some presidents will accept such opposition without harboring thoughts of beheading the critics. But it does take some courage to go up against a president's wishes, perhaps because, as many have said, the aura of the Oval Office sets up nerve-wracking vibrations for those who come there to oppose the president on policy matters.

When Army Chief of Staff Douglas MacArthur went to see President Roosevelt about radical cuts Roosevelt had proposed in the size of the Army, they got in a bitter argument. MacArthur shouted, "When we lose the next war, and an American boy, lying in the mud with an enemy bayonet through his belly and an enemy foot on his dying throat, spits out his last curse, I want the name not to be MacArthur but Roosevelt." Roosevelt shouted back, "You must not talk that way to the president!" Eventually they calmed down, and in fact Roosevelt admitted that MacArthur was correct. But, as MacArthur related in his memoirs, because he had lost his self-control in front of the president of the United States, he "felt like vomiting on the White House steps."

After President Johnson finished giving seventy members of the House of Representatives a briefing on the Vietnam War at the White House, Congressman Frank Thompson of New Jersey stood up and said, "Now, is someone going to tell us the truth?" Johnson strode over and grabbed him by the arm, said, "I want you out of my house right now," and led him down the corridor to the exit. Thompson recalled, "I'm an inch taller than he is. But he seemed so big, I felt overwhelmed. God, he was a frightening man."

Perhaps it is because confrontations like those are so unpleasant that presidents—like any political bosses, let alone monarchs—surround themselves with aides and advisers with whom they will feel comfortable, which means a group of which the majority are yes men. James Baker III, a top official in both the Reagan and Bush administrations, humorously concedes this. "The president wants no 'yes men' around," Baker said. "When he says 'no,' we all say 'no.'" For Kennedy the claque was the so-called Irish Mafia from Massachusetts. Johnson kept many of Kennedy's staff but he added his inside layer of Texans. Nixon's closest aides and advisers were young, bloodless executives from his home state, California, or old pals from his congressional days. Gerald Ford's innermost circle was old friends from his hometown, Grand Rapids, Michigan, or longtime cronies from his House career. Carter picked Georgians overwhelmingly. And Reagan, of course, surrounded himself mostly with Californians, particularly those who had served him when he was governor of that state. Not surprisingly, Bush picked for his cabinet and top White House posts mostly people he had worked with during his fourteen years of federal service, or who had helped him in his campaigns, and who, as *The New York Times* put it, "are prepared to defer to his judgments." At the center of his circle was a group known as "The Untouchables" because of their unquestionable personal loyalty to Bush. (Bush, an avid tennis player, was also careful to pick mostly people who played tennis.)

And Clinton at first surrounded himself with people he had worked with or known for years when he was governor of Arkansas or who had helped him in his 1992 campaign. Clinton had known his first chief of staff, Thomas F. McLarty III, since they were classmates in kindergarten—but that, as Clinton soon discovered, did not mean his former playmate was suitable for the job, and he was soon replaced. Indeed, by the beginning of his second term, most of the people Clinton had started with were gone, some of them departing because they were fed up with his lifelong habit of blaming his staff for blunders that in fact were his fault.

How to Succeed in Domestic Politics

If an observer looks only at the outward trappings, luxuries, and presumptuous "ego trips," it is possible to construct a persuasive argument about the imperial quality of the presidency. But if one begins to assess the awesome labors, demeaning compromises, endless negotiations, and inevitable frustrations that any president is confronted with when attempting to move his programs through Congress and have them administered enthusiastically by the bureaucracy—then one is apt to get a different impression.

There is no formula for presidential success in domestic affairs, but, looking back over some of the characteristics of our more successful presidents, one might justifiably conclude that the person who sits in the top political chair in this country has the best chance for achievement if certain ingredients, discussed next, are present.

Luck

"In the queer mess of human destiny," historian William Woodward reminds us, "the determining factor is Luck." Recent history gives a perfect example.

The basic reason for the relative failure of Jimmy Carter's administration and the relative success of Ronald Reagan's (measured by the public's response to the two presidents) comes to this: the price of oil.

And this was something that neither president had any control over.

Carter's heaviest burden, and probably the burden that crushed him in his effort to remain in office, was inflation. The main cause of this inflation? The price of oil, the world's most important commodity because its price affects that of all other commodities (even food, because of the petroleum needed for tractors, irrigation pumps, the manufacture of fertilizer, and so on). During Carter's term, oil prices— driven up by foreign suppliers over whom he had no control—more than doubled.

As a result of absolutely nothing Reagan did, but simply as a result of world market forces and squabbling among foreign producers, oil prices dropped 85 percent during his administration. Just luck.

Reagan also had what historian Stephan E. Ambrose calls the "very good luck" of coming to power after a string of failed presidents— Kennedy assassinated, Johnson driven from office by the Vietnam War, Nixon driven from office by the Watergate scandal, Ford only a caretaker president, Carter a luckless bungler. "If he just stayed out of war and avoided a major depression, almost *anybody* would have" been as popular as Reagan, argued Ambrose.

Economic luck also shaped the careers of Bush and Clinton. More than anything else, the recession of 1992 spelled Bush's downfall. And apparently it was the continuing prosperity that lulled Americans into ignoring the sex and campaign finance scandals surrounding Clinton's presidency. With inflation under control and unemployment dropping—though these were conditions that Clinton could rightfully claim little credit for bringing about—polls showed Americans wanted him to remain in office, and that undoubtedly influenced a number of votes at his Senate trial.

Enthusiasm

Considering the way our forty chief executives have performed in the job, the debate on the power of the presidency does not on the surface make much sense. Few historians would rate more than ten presidents as "strong" and usually for no better reason than their eagerness to call out the Army and draw blood, either in military adventures or as strikebreakers. No more than three or four at the most could be rated as strong if the criterion were the pushing of domestic reforms. Two-thirds of our past presidents, viewing themselves primarily as ribbon-cutters, were thoroughly intimidated by what they considered much more powerful congressional prerogatives; far from desiring to swell the office, they were uncomfortable at the thought of exercising power.

During the depression of 1873, President Grant surrendered his authority without firing a shot: "It is the duty of Congress to devise the method of correcting the evils which are acknowledged to exist, and not mine." And that bleak philosophy was perpetuated by succeeding presidents down to 1933 and the advent of Franklin D. Roosevelt. In the interim, other spiritless pronouncements were issued from the White House.

With unemployment at 12 percent in 1921—the highest in this century, except for the unemployment rate of the 1930s—President Warren G. Harding looked the situation over thoughtfully and, with the kind of fatalism that has marked most presidential decision making, decided that assisting the jobless unfortunates in any way, including the manipulation of the economy in their behalf, was not a federal responsibility. Eight years later, with steam gushing out of Wall Street's safety valve and the seams beginning to give, President Herbert Hoover modestly excused himself from action, saying he had "no authority to stop booms." For men like these, the question of the power available to the presidency was beside the point.

The White House's dismal record for getting things done on the home front is due partly to the obstinacy of Congress and the torpor of the bureaucracy. But there has also been a general failure of presidential energy in domestic affairs; the derring-do that marks presidents in foreign affairs is usually absent when they confront Congress.

The most magnificent exception to that rule was a nine-month period in 1965, Lyndon Johnson's first year as an elected president. For the only time in this century (except for four years in the late 1930s) the president's party had a two-to-one majority in both houses of Congress. Johnson didn't let members forget that many had ridden into office on his coattails. The economy was strong and growing. The national mood was upbeat, and most Americans believed with Johnson that it was the government's duty, and within its power, to end poverty and racial injustice. Johnson launched a campaign of eighteen- and twenty-hour days, browbeating Congress and whooping up public support. The result at the end of the nine months was what he called, with little exaggeration, "the greatest outpouring of creative legislation in the history of the nation."*

But even Johnson's enthusiasm for domestic politics didn't last. After operating for two years as a daemonic power broker, LBJ began to retrench and fudge on his domestic promises in the second half of his term so that he could try to find an answer to the question he posed one day to reporters in the White House Rose Garden, "How the f—— do I get out of Vietnam?"

Kennedy's attitude was often one of gentlemanly passiveness; if he ran into stiff opposition from Congress, he was likely to pass it off with a wry, "Well, it looks like this one will be a twelve-month baby."

If a president doesn't want to do much, if he doesn't want to take hold of the mildewed elements of the government and drag them into the sunlight, if he is more interested in shooting quail with rich friends in Georgia (Eisenhower) or in watching Western movies (Reagan) than he is in wrestling with Congress and the bureaucracy, then he won't suffer many disappointments. Calvin Coolidge, whose typical twenty-four hours in the White House included a long nap in the afternoon and eleven hours of sleep at night, seemed quite content with the country's slowly decaying status quo. Eisenhower never expressed keen disappointment in the unfulfilled ambitions he had for the country, perhaps because his ambitions were so modest and his interest in the presidential job so slight. Even with the clarity of hindsight, it is impossible to reconstruct anything resembling an "Eisenhower domestic program" and nearly as difficult to fit together the pieces of his foreign policy. He was, as James David Barber has written, a noble void.

> Should he engage in personal summitry on the international front? "This idea of the president of the United States going personally abroad to negotiate—it's just damn stupid." With the new Cabinet, wouldn't it make sense to oversee them rather carefully? To George Humphrey [Treasury Secretary], the president said, "I guess you know

*These are some of the milestones that became law in 1965: Medicare, providing health insurance for the elderly, financed by payroll taxes; Medicaid, which pays for health care for the poor; the first general federal aid to public schools; the first broad-based federal scholarships and loans for college students; the Voting Rights Act, which has enabled large numbers of blacks to register and vote, and therefore hold more elective offices; the National Foundations for the Arts and Humanities, which have brought cultural activities to communities across the country; rent supplements for poor people; highway beautification; grants, loans, and training programs for doctors and other health professionals; and special development assistance to Appalachia.

about as much about the job as I do." And his friend Arthur Larson writes that the president found patronage "nauseating" and "partisan political effect was not only at the bottom of the list—indeed, it did not exist as a motive at all." In 1958 the president said, "Frankly, I don't care too much about the congressional elections." . . . His heart attack in September 1955 was triggered, Eisenhower said, when he was repeatedly interrupted on the golf links by unnecessary phone calls from the State Department.

Into a vacuum so tempting, strong congressional leaders—if such there be at that moment—will inevitably move. Thus Eisenhower's lethargy was a godsend for Senator Lyndon Johnson, Democratic majority leader, for it gave him, rather than the president, the opportunity to seem the initiator of a domestic program. From that national exposure Johnson moved on to the vice presidency and then the White House. Johnson gave Ike a great deal of cooperation, but he was motivated to a great extent by his own ambitions. If a president does not lean heavily on Congress, that mulish animal will normally not move for him voluntarily. Congress watches for every weakness in the presidency with the intent of taking advantage of it. One of Congress's principal preoccupations is to strut its power and, if possible, humble the chief executive. Presidents come, presidents go, but the congressional wheelhorses go on, seemingly, forever.

Most presidents, confronted with that kind of obstinacy on Capitol Hill, give up easily, especially if they have no driving enthusiasm for domestic affairs. "I've always thought this country could run itself domestically, without a president," Nixon told Theodore H. White in 1968. "All you need is a competent Cabinet to run the country at home. You need a president for foreign policy; no Secretary of State is really important; the president makes foreign policy." Actually, he was not nearly as indifferent to domestic affairs as the remark to White suggested; indeed, Nixon was personally involved in making decisions on such crucial issues as abortion, school integration, aid to parochial schools, labor legislation, crime, welfare, and taxes. But even when he had a domestic bill worth fighting for and that he personally believed in, Nixon's mind wandered and his energies flagged when he ran into opposition. On August 11, 1969, he proposed for the first time in American history legislation to establish a floor under the income of every family with children. It was called the Family Assistance Plan, and Nixon himself thought it was "the most important piece of social legislation in our nation's history." It easily passed the House, but it got bogged down in the Senate Finance Committee, where liberals said it offered too little and conservatives said it offered too much. Nixon, fascinated by Vietnam and China and Russia and their more exotic challenges, quickly lost interest in the fight. By 1973 he announced that although he recognized the fact that the country's welfare system was a "crazy quilt of injustice and contradiction," he was junking his plan because he did not think Congress was in a mood to make "overall structural reform."

Thereafter Nixon sought to exert presidential power in domestic affairs not by leading Congress but by obstructing it—by slowing things down or dismembering them, by vetoing legislation, and by refusing to spend money that Congress had appropriated for domestic programs. As one member of the White House staff put the matter: "The president has never said this to me in so many words, but I think he simply gave up on Congress fairly early in the game, when he saw he simply didn't have the horses to create and bring into being a major domestic agenda that he could call his own." So Nixon retreated into foreign affairs.

President Carter did not melt so easily as Nixon under the fire of Congress, but he, too, lacked the driving willpower (and the popularity) needed to win passage for his domestic programs. As a presidential candidate, he had promised to institute sweeping welfare and tax reforms, to reduce the bureaucracy, and to establish a national health insurance program. But once he reached the White House, his enthusiasm for these reforms seemed to evaporate. He proposed them to Congress in a lackadaisical fashion, and when they were butchered or killed outright, he blamed lobbyists and corrupt congressmen—or, in his melodramatic words, "a pack of powerful and ravenous wolves." Carter also blamed the public for his failures. We the people were too dumb, he wrote in his memoirs, to understand the "extremely complicated and difficult" issues and therefore didn't give him the support he deserved. These weren't very good excuses, for all presidents must contend with lobbyists, corrupt members of Congress, and an ignorant public.

Reagan, in contrast, swept into office with the enthusiasm of a cheerleader. So why wasn't he more successful at pushing legislation through Congress? He had been elected with a majority of the votes everywhere but in Georgia (Carter's home state) and the District of Columbia; he also had a Republican-controlled Senate for the first time in thirty years. He could have exploited the situation to push a host of practical programs, but in fact he wanted only two: a huge tax cut (that would make his rich pals richer) and more money for the Pentagon. He got both without any trouble. He won even in the House of Representatives, which was nominally controlled by Democrats. But after the first year, Reagan would never again be as persuasive with Congress. Nor would he try to be.

When Reagan continued with flaming enthusiasm to speak of the need for Congress to pass support for such things as prayer in the schools and to oppose such things as abortions, he did not expect Congress to comply with his desires (or at least there was no evidence he did, since he never really pushed that kind of "family values" legislation). He was preaching. He was exhorting the public with symbols. Congress paid no attention, but the public did. The unique popularity generated by Reagan's enthusiasm was the popularity of the great evangelist (before evangelists fell into such disfavor) or the charming con man, more than it was the popularity of a president. *The New York Times* said Reagan "has come across as something like Professor Harold Hill, master salesman of Meredith Wilson's brilliant 1957 musical, 'The Music Man.'" Historian Arthur M. Schlesinger, Jr., gave this appraisal: "He's like a nice, old uncle, who comes in, and all the kids are glad to see him. He sits around telling stories, and they're all fond of him, but they don't take him seriously."

But they did take him seriously, in a way. Generally, the public was fond of Reagan, particularly after they got used to his quirks (he believed in ghosts and consulted a soothsayer) and his amiable blunders and his fantasies. But apparently they also saw something more in him. Even during the harsh recession years of 1982 and 1983, when opinion polls showed the public had little faith in his handling of government and little belief in his economic nostrums, the polls also showed the people liked him—and took him seriously—as a *symbolic* leader.

In his soothing, reassuring, positive address to the Republican convention in 1988, Reagan said, "It is our gift to have visions, and I want to share that of a young boy who wrote to me shortly after I took office. In his letter he said, 'I love America because you can join Cub Scouts if you want to. You have a right to worship as you please. If you have the ability, you can try to be anything you want to be. I also like America because we have about 200 flavors of ice cream.'"

That was the strength and weakness of the Reagan presidency: If it wasn't Cub Scouts and ice-cream cones, it was communists with horns, or welfare mothers in Cadillacs. The public rated him high for symbolism, but for little else. The president couldn't be defeated, but his legislative program sure could be.

By the end of Reagan's first year in office, Congress realized that the public loved his Hollywoodish vision of America, circa 1938 (the nice guy always winning the girl; the pioneers always defeating the savages; the underdog always clobbering the evil bully), but not the reactionary policies he wanted to impose on real life. The public loved to hear him describe Americans as self-reliant boot-strappers, but they didn't want him to take away their social welfare programs.

So Congress, while praising the man, started voting against him. Toward the end of Reagan's administration, Richard Darman, one of his most trusted aides, admitted that virtually all of Reagan's basic right-wing proposals were dead before they ever reached Capitol Hill. In other words, enthusiasm can generate a potent image and popularity, but it isn't enough to enact a political agenda.

Intelligent, Well-Behaved Advisers

Every president should memorize this observation of the famous sixteenth-century political guru, Niccolo Machiavelli: "The first opinion that is formed of a ruler's intelligence is based on the quality of the men he has around him."

True enough. A president is judged by his appointees. If he picks stupid and immoral people for his White House staff and for other top positions in his administration, the public invariably concludes that the president must be at least a little stupid and immoral himself; and this conclusion is strengthened if, out of misplaced loyalty, he fails to get rid of appointees once their defects have been revealed.

President Clinton felt obliged to fire some of his closest aides— including old friends from Arkansas—after they were accused of illegal, or at least improper, actions. Housing Secretary Henry Cisneros, one of the ablest cabinet members, was forced out after he was charged with lying to the FBI about how much money he had given a former mistress. Agriculture Secretary Mike Espy, a former Congressman from Mississippi and one of the few blacks to reach cabinet level, resigned after he was accused of taking several thousand dollars in favors from the giant Arkansas poultry firm, Tyson's, at a time when regulations affecting poultry firms were under consideration at Espy's department. (Later, a federal jury found Espy innocent.) David Watkins, who had been a business partner of Hillary Clinton and was now the president's assistant for management and administration, was forced to resign after he was caught using a government helicopter to "check out" a nearby Maryland golf course and playing a round there. Webb Hubbell, who had been one of Hillary's law partners in Little Rock before becoming assistant attorney general, resigned and later confessed to stealing money from the law firm where he had worked before he moved to Washington; his resignation was a special blow to Clinton because Hubbell was one of his favorite golfing partners. There were others who departed under a cloud.

It is a cliché that power breeds corruption, so it is hardly surprising that virtually every president is victimized by a few rotten apples in his barrel. Truman and Eisenhower had White House aides who took kickbacks and were guilty of conflict of interest (although, it must be admitted, their sins were insignificant by today's standards), and the wheeling and dealing of Bobby Baker put a real tarnish on the Johnson White House.

But the Reagan administration gave new meaning to sleaze. More than 100 top officials were indicted or actually went to jail for a variety of crimes (more on this later), and those who wound up behind bars included some who had been his closest aides in the White House. Reagan defended even those who were guilty beyond question—leaving the public to wonder at his own sense of ethics.

Early on, Bush had to face the question of how much tolerance should be shown to aides and cronies of questionable ethics. Trying to get rid of the stench left over from the Reagan years, he announced during his campaign that in his administration there would be an absolute ban on outside earned income for services rendered while in office and that he would not permit even the appearance of impropriety. But shortly after he took office, it was revealed that Boyden Gray, who had served full time as Vice President Bush's counsel and was now President Bush's *adviser on ethics,* had been earning hundreds of thousands of dollars from private companies without reporting the income to the Office of Government Ethics and that he continued to serve as chairman of his family-owned $500 million communications company although it was subject to numerous government regulations—thereby violating a White House ethics policy dating back at least twenty years. It was also revealed that James A. Baker III, Bush's closest political ally and his recently appointed secretary of state, held $3 million worth of stock in a bank that had greatly benefitted as the result of a ruling he made when he was secretary of the treasury under Reagan.

Embarrassed by these revelations, Bush had Gray quit his corporation and Baker sell his bank stock and other officials take similar actions. But there were so many cries of pain from the millionaire bu-reaucrats that Bush apologized, saying "I hope I haven't created some-thing that just carries things too far."

Next came a wave of congressional and press investigations that showed how some high-ranking Republicans, and their relatives, had made many millions of dollars during the Reagan–Bush administra-tion by wheedling highly questionable contracts from the Department of Housing and Urban Development. What should have been even more embarrassing to Bush was that some of the influence peddlers, having helped run his election campaign, were now holding top jobs in his own administration.

In his speech accepting the GOP nomination, Bush had said, "Every time I hear that someone has breached the public trust, it breaks my heart," but he seemed more casual than heart-broken about the pervasive smell of corruption at HUD. Even after it became clear that the mess could cost taxpayers as much as $6 billion, he said he was "not prepared to pass judgment at this point" and that "I don't think you gain much" by assessing "who's to blame, who's not to blame."

Kennedy surrounded himself with advisers who diluted idealism with wardheel politics and who pandered to Kennedy's more frivo-lous instincts. Under the influence of these men, Kennedy made many pretty speeches, but he seldom gambled his political chips on a good but risky cause.* Kennedy had one other fatal flaw in the standard by which he picked his closest advisers. Harris Wofford, who was Kennedy's special adviser for civil rights, put it this way: "The president was open to any view, any analysis, any person, no matter how iconoclastic, with one limitation: Kennedy did not want to be bored. . . . In the Kennedy White House there was hesitation about saying anything unless it was amusing." Those who knew how to wrap their suggestions with wit and sophistication and toughness (Kennedy was macho) could get him to consider their ideas, no matter how foolish they were, says Wofford, but advisers who were dull, no matter how wise, got little attention. Chester Bowles tried to persuade Kennedy not to launch the disastrous Bay of Pigs invasion, but Kennedy considered Bowles a stuffed shirt and wouldn't listen.

---

*As Johnson did in 1964, when he informed his Senate leaders that he was prepared to lose all other legislation if necessary to wear down and break the filibuster against his civil rights bill.

Carter's justified reputation for decorum and probity was hurt in 1978 by the allegedly harum-scarum conduct of his top aide, Hamilton Jordan, who was accused of spitting on a woman in a Georgetown bar and of remarking "I always wanted to see the pyramids" while peering down the bodice of the Egyptian ambassador's wife at a private dinner party. In his memoirs, *Crisis,* Jordan denies the accuracy of these reports but acknowledges that they gravely reduced his usefulness: "In less that a year, I had become a caricature. . . . I was seen as an arrogant, impolite rube." Later he was accused of taking cocaine at a New York night spot. Although he was ultimately exonerated, the charge plagued him for the rest of his time in Washington, and damaged the reputation of the entire administration.

Carter's key staff members often rubbed Congress the wrong way. Jordan lost no time alienating House Speaker "Tip" O'Neill by refusing the simple courtesy of finding a couple of extra tickets to the inaugural ball. After that, O'Neill regularly referred to Carter's aide as Hannibal Jerkin. Jordan also offended other top congressmen. When Congressman John Moss, the powerful California Democrat, wrote the White House asking for information about its concern for human rights practices in the Middle East, Jordan added a memo to the Moss letter saying "Moss is an asshole." When word of this got back to Moss, he said he wasn't surprised because Jordan regularly snubbed or insulted congressmen and had helped create the worst President–Congress relationships he had seen in a quarter century.

If Moss had stuck around Washington for another dozen years, he would have encountered a White House chief of staff, John Sununu, who was so rude and crude in his treatment of some congressmen as to make Jordan seem downright diplomatic by comparison. As governor of New Hampshire, Sununu had helped rescue Bush just when it seemed that Bush's candidacy was doomed in 1988, and in gratitude Bush made him chief of staff. Ed Rollins, the Republican political strategist, said Sununu "mostly surrounded himself with weaklings and sycophants" and "was particularly inept in his dealings with Congress. He never understood that Capitol Hill is a place where some of the world's greatest buffoons still have one vote, and a few are even committee chairmen who can destroy you or your president's agenda in a heartbeat." Brian Kelly, a *Washington Post* editor, remembers Sununu as "simply a pathological bully. For reasons only his analyst knew for sure, he lived in order to be nasty to someone. He treated Congressional leaders . . . as though they were countermen at McDonald's waiting to take his order."

Some Staffs' Foul Atmosphere

Special attention should be paid to Reagan's administration because it offers such a dramatic lesson in the ways staffs can affect a president's reputation.

Reagan thought he was a good manager; in fact, he was a terrible one. He gave little guidance and demanded no accounting from his staff or cabinet. They were on their own.* Although in setting the broad policies of his administration he was stubborn almost to a fault, in the day-to-day operation of his office he was passive. He signed whatever his aides stuck in front of him. Whatever speeches they wrote for him, he delivered, usually without having changed a word. They gave him cue cards instructing him on what to say in conversation, where to go, where to turn, where to sit, what jokes to tell, what to do every hour of every day; he followed their instructions faithfully—like a good actor taking direction.

So long as he had a sensible, pragmatic staff, its domination worked out reasonably well. In his first term, Reagan was lucky enough to surround himself with aides who were veterans of his political wars; most of them had known him or worked for him since the 1960s when he was governor of California, and most were intensely loyal to him. They knew where he was vulnerable and they knew his strengths; they knew how to protect him from his ideological excesses.

But in his second term, the key members of this first staff drifted away to other jobs in the administration or to rich lobbying positions, and they were replaced by a much different sort: men who apparently were ambitious not for the president but for themselves, who were unfamiliar with the political process or were contemptuous of it, and who were uninterested in Reagan's strengths and only too eager to take advantage of his weaknesses.

The new chief of staff, Donald Regan, who had been a big power on Wall Street but knew little about government before he reached Washington, seized more and more of Reagan's responsibilities and

---

*Isolating himself from knowledge of what went on in his own government left Reagan free to claim innocence when things went sour. It was hypocritical and a betrayal of his promises, to say the least. When he campaigned for president in 1980, he repeated this theme in many speeches: "Billions of dollars of waste, extravagance, fraud and abuse in federal agencies simply are being ignored . . . by the Carter administration." He pledged to "put the corruption fighters back in charge" in every nook and cranny of the executive branch. But when it was discovered that his own officials had looted millions of dollars from HUD, he pleaded ignorance and shrugged his shoulders: "I didn't have the slightest idea of what was going on" (*The New York Times,* June 26, 1989).

narrowed the access of others to the president.* According to Max Friedersdorf, the White House congressional affairs director, Regan "built up a staff that was completely loyal to himself. . . . The president was just an appendage." Knowing Reagan's dislike for grubby details, Regan and his tight circle of loyalists increasingly acted on their own, leaving Reagan out, making decisions on important issues without "bothering" him.

You might ask why Reagan allowed this second-term crowd, plus the gang in the National Security Council and the CIA who helped him create the Iran-contra scandal, to achieve so much influence and to use it so damagingly. One reason was that he didn't like to be bothered with personnel decisions and hated to bawl people out or fire them. Once he had the family lawyer come in to settle a dispute with a troublesome maid. Reagan didn't even know, or apparently care, that Regan would become his new chief of staff until another aide informed him, "I've got a new playmate for you, closer to your age." Mrs. Reagan was more interested in running the White House than was her husband. She loathed Chief of Staff Regan and most of his aides, and eventually was successful in driving him out of his job. In some ways, she was de facto chief of staff; she even decided which of the ten thousand photos taken of Reagan every month by the White House photographer would be released to the press and how many people could shake hands with the president at a party.

But probably the main reason the Reagans found the second-term staff infiltrated with irresponsible and even lawless people was that they themselves set a poor moral example and demanded no high ethics from those around them. In 1982, stung by criticism of her practice of accepting expensive designer dresses as "loans" or gifts, Mrs. Reagan had promised that she would never accept them again. In 1988

---

*In Donald Regan's defense, one must realize that the temptation to move into a power vacuum at that level is probably difficult to resist. And, after all, somebody has to make the decisions if the president won't. When a president is passive, his chief of staff can become one of the most powerful men in government. In his memoirs of White House days, *For The Record,* Regan writes: "It was a rare meeting in which the president made a decision or issued orders. . . . Nearly everyone was a stranger to this shy president." It was the same appraisal made by Reagan's former aide, Martin Anderson, in *Revolution:* "He made no demands and gave almost no instruction." Anderson likened Reagan to a "Turkish pasha, passively letting his subjects serve him." No president has had so many ex-aides write so many tattletale memoirs. Is this disloyalty? One former staff member told *Time* magazine, "People are not loyal to the Reagans, because they are not loyal" ("Why He's a Target," *Time* magazine essay, May 23, 1988).

it was discovered that she had lied fulsomely, and that in all the intervening years she had gone right on "borrowing" a $1.4 million wardrobe. Two biographers note, "It was as if the Reagans felt the rules were never meant to apply strictly to them or to the people who worked for their administration." Reagan joked about breaking his oath to uphold the Constitution; at a meeting of those planning to sell arms to Iran, one of the plotters said that if they were caught somebody might go to jail, which prompted Reagan only to grin and say, "But visiting hours are Thursday."

When the Iran-contra illegalities surfaced, Reagan tried to cover them up, just as he tried to brush off the seriousness of the conduct of dozens of officials in his administration who either resigned or were forced out of office under allegations of wrongdoing—conflict of interest, taking bribes, working with organized crime, cheating on taxes, and so on. In short, Reagan brought his staff troubles on himself.

But of course the supreme example in our political history of how the conduct of presidential advisers can almost destroy a president came as the Nixon administration ended its first term. "The Watergate affair"—the generic name for an almost endless catalog of political corruption, dirty work, and downright criminal conduct—began in 1971. When national polls showed that Nixon might have a difficult time being reelected, a coterie of fanatical aides to Nixon launched an operation aimed at winning his reelection at any cost in money or morality. Their basic objective was nothing less than to rig the election of 1972, and they continued their scheme even after polls showed Nixon would be a sure winner.

By the spring of 1974, Nixon's closest White House aides, H. R. Haldeman and John Ehrlichman, along with the White House counsel, John Dean III, and Nixon's former law partner and attorney general, John Mitchell, were among those indicted for a variety of crimes.

Not since president Harding's corrupt pals broke his heart had a president been so poorly treated by those in whom he had invested most of his management powers. What had made the poison of the Nixon administration so deadly was that it had been concentrated in a small circle nearest the head of state. The public was left with an unpleasant choice: Either Nixon had known about and perhaps even had participated in the corruption, and must be unethical, or he had not known about it and must be an inefficient manager of his own household. The result was a president who, for the first time in history, was forced to resign.

Perhaps the worst service Nixon's aides did for him was to cut him off from continual, refreshing contact with the outside world. Even news reports were passed on to him in "digest" form.* His aides wrapped him—with his consent, to be sure—in a thick cocoon of unreality. "Cocoonizing" a president is a sure way to cripple him, for the smaller the circle of his advisers, the less chance a president has to act wisely.

Staffs that know how to serve a president efficiently will make sure there is a constant flow of up-to-date information into and out of the White House, to and from Congress, to and from the cabinet offices, to and from all major nerve-centers of the bureaucracy. Staffs that fail to carry out this function will put the president in many an embarrassing position by making it appear that he either is ignorant of what others in government are doing, or doesn't care. He cannot personally take all phone calls from congressional and bureaucratic leaders; he cannot personally fill them in on administration strategy—these tasks must generally be done by his staff, who, in a very literal sense, serve as his mouth and ears. When they fail, feelings are hurt, efficiency plummets, the president's reputation is damaged, and his influence dwindles.

If a president surrounds himself with intelligent people, he mustn't waste them; he mustn't treat their talents frivolously. Of all recent presidents, Reagan was guiltiest of disregarding the counsel of aides who wanted only to prevent his appearing stupid and calloused. Hundreds of man-hours went into trying to prepare him for every nationally televised press conference. Five days before each conference, most of the cabinet departments sent him thick books of questions and answers on subjects that would likely be raised by reporters. But Reagan disregarded these completely. *Washington Post* reporter Lou Cannon, who knows Reagan very well, recalls the results: "Most of the time, president Reagan was intuitively keen but intellectually lazy. . . . Because of Reagan's knowledge gaps, his presidential news conferences became adventures into the uncharted regions of his mind. His advisers prepared the president as carefully as they could and crossed their fingers in hopes that the questioning would coincide with the preparation."

---

*And since he never read the newspapers, Nixon didn't know when his staff was leaving him in the dark. For example, in 1971 Nixon vetoed a childcare bill, denouncing it as "the most radical piece of legislation" of the year. His staff apparently had forgotten to tell him that his wife was the honorary chairwoman of a group that had fought for two years to get the bill through Congress.

Their hopes were often dashed. At one press conference in February 1982, for example, Reagan gave wrong employment figures, misstated a U.S. Supreme Court position on civil rights, misquoted Pope John Paul II, wrongly remembered details of the California abortion law, and inaccurately described a program for the elderly in Arizona. His mistakes, both in news conferences and in speeches on the road, became so commonplace that embarrassed White House aides informed the press that they would no longer attempt to correct them.

A Crisis, Either Real or Contrived

A democracy the size of ours operates in a very sluggish fashion except in times of crisis. This is a fortunate or unfortunate characteristic of giant democracy, depending on your point of view, but it is a fact. Inertia—political and social status quo—is our ordinary condition. To get us off dead center, to start us slowly moving, takes a psychic explosion.

Presidents who manage to take a strong hand in government either have been supplied with a natural crisis or have concocted one by clever propaganda. War is the greatest natural crisis. Give a president a war and he can do just about anything he wants to do, at home or abroad—freeze prices, allocate jobs, censure the press, even suspend habeas corpus (as Lincoln did during the Civil War). Although there will be some cries of outrage from civil libertarians and some grumbling from Congress, the president will get by with any of these actions in the name of national security.

Civil crises, such as widespread urban riots and economic depressions, are much rarer and, when they occur, much less generous in the power they instill in the presidency.

The most massive economic crisis in the nation's life, the Great Depression of the 1930s, allowed president Franklin Roosevelt to assume powers almost equal to those available to a president during wartime. What he asked from Congress, he got, immediately. But these unusual peacetime powers were available to him only during the first year of his first term, a potentially explosive time when Congress was willing to take whatever drastic curative actions Roosevelt might dream up. Once the panic was past, however, Roosevelt's momentum was blocked. The depression persisted, but there was no longer a feeling of crisis to exploit; by his second year in office he was complaining to his adviser, Thomas G. Corcoran, "You know, in this business, you remember Ty Cobb. If you bat .400, you're a champion."

After the assassination of President Kennedy on November 22, 1963, the nation was seized by a crisis of conscience; for some reason having little to do with logic, there seemed to be a national feeling of guilt because of Kennedy's death, and an accompanying urge to make amends to Kennedy (who had not, in fact, been very popular with Congress before his death). Lyndon Johnson, elevated to the presidency by the assassination, recognized the leverage he had with Congress because of the national hangover of emotionalism and cleverly pushed several key pieces of his legislative agenda as "Kennedy programs." For two years they passed with little trouble.

Except politically, Reagan could hardly count the attempt on his life on March 30, 1981, to have been "lucky." But he turned it magnificently to his own advantage. He spent two hours in the operating room while doctors removed the bullet and put him together again. He nearly died. But he showed enormous pluck and his usual sense of humor, telling his wife, "Honey, I forgot to duck," and his doctors, "Please tell me you're Republicans." Until he could talk, he scribbled the one-liners on a notepad, and to reassure the nation, his staff passed them along to the press. In any major crisis, but particularly in a personal assault, the nation rallies around its president. Reagan's gutsy response to his very close call created enormous public sympathy. He was looked upon as a hero.

Before the assassination attempt, polls showed his popularity beginning to slip. Now it went soaring again, quite enough to start his highly controversial economic legislation moving through Congress. Richard Darman, a top official in both the Reagan and Bush administrations, gives this appraisal of the political effect of the shooting:

> That [whole episode] was crucially important. I think we would have been way out of the normal presidential honeymoon at the time of the crucial votes on the budget and tax cuts if there hadn't been a "second life." The shooting and Reagan's recovery was not only a second life for Reagan but a second life for Reagan's honeymoon. Sheer chance— and extraordinarily important. In fact, I think we would have had to compromise on the tax bill without it.

Any crisis, real or contrived, demands dramatic presidential action. The public expects it. The public, indeed, relishes decisiveness. On the day Franklin Roosevelt closed the banks to end the panic of 1933, humorist Will Rogers probably spoke for most Americans: "This is the happiest day in three years. We have no jobs, we have no money, we have no banks; and if Roosevelt had burned down the Capitol, we would have said, 'Thank God, he started a fire under something.'" An unexploited crisis, a crisis that gets only a limp response from the president, a crisis that just lies there and festers, will poison an administration and the whole nation.

This was shown convincingly by Carter's pitiful inability to cope with the Iranian problem. On November 4, 1979, a mob of fanatical Iranians seized the U.S. Embassy in Tehran. For more than a year—until the very day that Carter left Washington for good—fifty U.S. citizens were held hostage by the Iranians. The effort to free the hostages consumed Carter's interest for the remainder of his term, and everything he tried—diplomacy, economic sanctions, an armed rescue mission—failed miserably. Carter's bungling of the hostage crisis contributed more than anything else to his defeat in 1980 because it deprived him of the one thing that voters demand of their president, namely:

The Ability to Inspire Confidence

The people seemingly want, almost desperately, to believe in the president. Members of Congress are often as softhearted on this point as the general populace. Perhaps it occurs because in such a disparate, splintered, sprawling, geographically inchoate nation it is comforting to have one peg at the top to hang one's political hopes on. In any event, the president who can inspire confidence and moral leadership is equipped with a special armament in his political wars with Congress. Naturally, such confidence can be obtained only if the president's aims are fairly obvious. His values must be, accurately or not, out in the open. For if the president doesn't seem to believe wholeheartedly in certain goals and values, how can he inspire the public?

Eisenhower's hands-off paternalism, although somewhat shapeless, conveyed a strong sense of laissez-faire values. The Great Society programs of the Johnson years conveyed an extraordinarily robust hands-on paternalism. Nixon had more trouble signaling his values. In his 1968 campaign he ran on what was basically a conservative platform, and promptly repudiated most of it once he was in office. At the time of Nixon's second inaugural, Robert Semple, White House correspondent for *The New York Times*, wrote that "what he wants the country to be and what he is prepared to fight for—remains as ambiguous as ever."

The ambiguity of Jimmy Carter was a great handicap to his administration, too. Carter, a political outsider to Washington, had boasted of this during his campaign. He asked the electorate to vote for him as someone with a "fresh" view of the federal apparatus. But no sooner had he arrived at the White House than he began to sound and act like just another politician. As a presidential candidate, he had issued many a populistic tirade against the fat-cat corporations; but as president he offered one appeasement after another to the big-business community and did everything in his power to avoid offending them. As a presidential candidate he had described the tax system as "a disgrace to the human race" and promised to launch a reform of the tax system as soon as he became president; but once in office, he announced an indefinite postponement to that reform effort.

George Bush's inability to convey a consistent philosophy or describe his goals got him in trouble from the very beginning. In his inaugural speech, he had promised to control the drug crisis in America ("Take my word. This scourge will stop."). But his budget contained even less money for drug control than Congress had asked for. In his inaugural speech, Bush had promised to help create "a kinder, gentler nation," but a few weeks later he refused to back efforts to ban the sale or ownership of the kind of semi-automatic assault rifles that drug pushers and madmen were using to make urban life harsher and crueler.*

After Bush had been in office a couple of months, David Gergen, editor-at-large of *U.S. News & World Report* and once director of communications for the Reagan White House, warned that the world was beginning to see Bush as a skittish lightweight, "dashing madly from one event to the next—even the Secret Service has nicknamed him 'The Mexican Jumping Bean'—improvising a theme a week," instead of settling down and acting presidential, by which Gergen meant "focusing the nation on long-term goals, driving it steadily toward them. . . . And he must do it all with an occasional touch of majesty."

On into his presidency's maiden summer, Bush's proposals for domestic improvements continued to be lightweight or contradictory. As a candidate he had promised to put criminals behind bars, but the money he suggested spending on prison construction would leave the federal system still short by 15,000 cells. In a July press conference, he declared, "I am strongly committed to equal opportunity for all Americans" but waved aside as a mere "technicality" the recent Supreme Court decisions limiting the ability of minorities and women to sue in discrimination cases, and said he had no legislation

---

*Bush did ban the import of assault weapons, but the manufacture and sale of U.S.-made assault weapons continued unabated—and according to the Bureau of Alcohol, Tobacco and Firearms, about 2,000 domestic assault weapons figure in violent crimes every year (*Los Angeles Times*, July 9, 1989).

in mind to restrengthen civil rights. He had promised to be the "education president," but then outraged Hispanics with cutbacks in bilingual education. He promised to "put America on the path toward markedly cleaner air," but the weak plan he proposed in 1989 would make America wait well into the next century for clean air, even though the technologies for achieving it were available right then. Why wait?

As we have mentioned earlier, Clinton was just as guilty as Bush was in making promises that he made only half-hearted efforts to carry out, or discarded altogether.

Admittedly, it is impossible, given the arena of issues within which the modern president must operate, not to appear ambiguous and wobbly and even deceitful from time to time. The president is expected to keep too many ill-balanced bills in the air. He is, for example, expected to administer complicated environmental laws while promoting industrial growth, to control hospital costs while improving health care, to ensure product and industrial safety without raising the ire of business, and so on and on and on. Congress has passed such a multiplicity of conflicting laws for the president to execute that it is difficult for him to avoid accusations of hypocrisy and treachery as he proceeds.

A Clear and Potent Image

The president's image of himself and the public's image of him combine as his most important tool. Politicians, especially in this television era, are often accused of valuing style over substance; presidents are always being damned for this. It may be a sin to value style so highly, but it is not so great a sin as some critics suppose. Indeed, a president's style is crucial to his success. He cannot pull off the substance *without* an effective style. It is what people *think* he is that counts: Do the mass of Americans and their representatives in Congress see the president as strong or weak, as clearheaded or confused, as reasonably flexible or stubborn? Franklin Roosevelt and John Kennedy were not nearly so liberal and idealistic as most Americans perceived them to be; Richard Nixon was not nearly so conservative and Gerald Ford was not nearly so clumsy (intellectually as well as physically) as they were nearly always painted. But it was the public's perception (or misperception), not the true character of these men, that counted. It was what got them elected or defeated, and it was one of the things that made their dealings with Congress difficult or easy.

If a president is to have any significant influence with Congress, he must have the strength of public popularity.* Mere public approval is not enough. Nixon won an overwhelming reelection in 1972 because the public approved of the way he was then running the country and because it especially approved of his foreign policy, which already had reopened relations with Communist China and improved relations with Russia. Nixon did not win the election on his popularity—because he was not a popular man, not an appealing person, as he was wise enough to know. "I'm an introvert in an extrovert profession," he said. When CBS reporter Dan Rather asked him why many people thought he "failed to inspire confidence and faith and lacked personal warmth and compassion," Nixon responded in such a way as to equate those characteristics with trivial political fluff. "My strong point," he replied, "is not rhetoric; it isn't showmanship; it isn't big promises—those things that create the glamour and excitement that people call charisma and warmth."

Charisma, secondary virtue though it may be, offers an extra quantum of power. When a president is very popular, members of Congress (except those from safe districts, who don't worry about such matters) may reason that giving support to his programs will make them popular too. Of course, simply because a president gets top ratings with the public does not necessarily mean that his tax program is equally popular or that he can make it popular by "going to the people." But politicians can never be sure about that, and in the House, where members must confront the public so frequently, the barometer of the president's popularity is watched with especially keen regard.

The most popular presidents have been those who—believing that the medium is part of the message—paid close attention to the details of imagery. Franklin D. Roosevelt was limited to radio, but he used it to its fullest in his frequent "fireside chats." Before Roosevelt went on the air, a Navy pharmacist's mate would "carefully clean out his sinus passages to make his lovely tenor voice resonant." Michael Deaver writes that, to prepare Reagan for a television debate, he would let the

---

*Often he begins his term at a disadvantage caused by the democratic process. In sixteen presidential elections—including Truman's in 1948, Kennedy's in 1960, Nixon's in 1968, and Clinton's both in 1992 and 1996—the nation wound up being led by a man whom less than a majority of the voters had endorsed. This does not escape the notice of Congress, which prefers to view its opponent at the other end of Pennsylvania Avenue as something less than the embodiment of the people.

president have "one glass of wine" to instill "a little color for his cheeks."*

Nixon's first lesson in the importance of such details came in 1960, when a serious attack of staphylococcus and an inhumanly rigorous schedule left him looking haggard and mean in the early television debates that were the focal point of his presidential contest with John Kennedy. This was reinforced by the black imbedded stubble of his beard—wretchedly disguised by his makeup crew and contrasted in such a way with the fresh, boyish Kennedy that this alone is thought by some to have cost him that close election.

After that, Nixon always appeared on television well prepared with expert grooming; a cosmetician-hairdresser applied what he called "just a little beard cover and dusting powder." Nixon even wore this facial covering in public if the television crews were around; Americans, accustomed to such theatrical tricks from their politicians, think nothing about it, but when Nixon visited China the residents would ask, "Why is he orange?" Nixon also used a rinse to keep down the gray at his temples. White House correspondent John Osborne observed on one occasion that the rain falling on Nixon's head resulted in brown-colored water dripping down the chief executive's neck. Johnson was even more vain about his looks; he used hair dye lavishly and sometimes had his hairdresser give him a subtle marcel. He also occasionally padded his hairline with "wings" on either side of his head. Once, as he stepped out of a helicopter, a gust of air from the whirring blades blew his hair-padding away. Secret Service agents went into a panic, thinking something violent had happened to Johnson's head.

To Eisenhower, an appearance on television was painful because he had a normal person's perspective of himself. "I keep telling you fellows," he once complained to his staff, "I don't like to do this sort of thing. I can think of nothing more boring, for the American public, than to have to sit in their living rooms for a whole half-hour looking at my face on their television screens." To Nixon, the pain came from the tedious but necessary cosmetic preparations and from knowing that the hot television lights gave his face a sweaty, "guilty" look.

President Carter's first adviser for television was a young Texan named Barry Jagoda, who operated on the principle that Carter's strength came from his low-keyed, natural style—a minimum of

---

*Deaver would have been wise to limit himself too to one glass. When he was later convicted of perjury as a lobbyist, he blamed his troubles on alcoholism contracted during his White House service.

pancake makeup, the natural hemming and hawing of conversation, the offhanded, unrehearsed style. Jagoda saw to it, for example, that the president's podium at press conferences was a small one. He did not want it to appear to be a wall, or a bunker, between the president (a small man physically) and the reporters; he wanted the "open" look, the easy-access look, the I've-got-nothing-to-hide look.

The Jagoda approach was successful in building the informal image, but as Carter's popularity plummeted in 1978, the president decided he needed another image creator, so he brought in Gerald Rafshoon, who had been his media adviser during the campaign. Rafshoon was ensconced in the White House as a senior assistant in charge of reshaping Carter's image—that is, he was to inflate Carter's political sex appeal and make him seem more "presidential." A new official photograph of Carter was issued, obviously more presidential than the first one because the famous grin was less pronounced—the new photo showed only seven teeth compared to the ten displayed in the first. Always generous with press conferences (Carter was averaging one conference every two weeks), the president decided to call more conferences during prime television time and to hold additional televised call-in shows in which he would take questions from the public. Carter's press aide, Jody Powell, announced that for his part he would start courting Washington columnists, notoriously available for a quick presidential romance, in order to "get our story out." All this was being done to get a firmer grip on the most powerful of tools, imagery, and to use this tool to manipulate Congress via the public.

But Carter was an amateur compared to his successor, Ronald Reagan, whom the press dubbed "The Great Communicator." Strangely, Reagan's powers of communication were potent only in public. To the world at large he was hail-fellow, bubbly, and sentimentally friendly. Privately, he was stiff, remote, and aloof, unwilling to confide in anyone but his wife. *The Washington Post* called him "one of the most isolated chief executives since World War I." Privately he built an insurmountable wall around himself, but publicly he drew upon his Hollywood training and his natural Irish theatricalness to become perhaps the most effective manipulator of imagery since Franklin Roosevelt. His slant grin and his ready one-liners and his whimsically wrinkled brow and his gee-whiz, all-American boyishness (quite a trick for a man in his seventies) came across so appealingly that he got away with gaffes and strange opinions that if expressed by other politicians would have ruined their careers. In short, he may not have been a great thinker but he was, for a politician, a great actor. He was so masterful at presenting himself as just an innocent bystander when things went wrong that he was dubbed "The Teflon President," because things didn't stick to him. It was a talent that prompted humor columnist Art Buchwald to observe, "If Reagan drove through a car wash in a convertible with the top down, only Jimmy Carter would get wet."

At a fund-raising dinner for Nicaraguan refugees, Reagan went into one of his damp-eyed speeches and hugged an eight-year-old girl who was presented as having fled her war-torn homeland. Later it was discovered that in fact the girl was the U.S.-born daughter of a banker. Was Reagan embarrassed? Not at all. It was just part of show biz.

Everything he did was staged by his strategists to appeal to the television audience. His life as president was scripted as carefully as the movies he had starred in, such as *Bedtime for Bonzo*. For example, when he went to the demilitarized zone in Korea in 1984, his strategists wanted him to convey to the folks back home the image of a daring soldier. To accomplish this, they planned to have him photographed standing up in the most exposed American bunker at the front. But they didn't want to get him shot by North Korean sharpshooters, so they had the Army string 30,000 yards of camouflage netting from telephone poles to shield Reagan from the enemy's eyes—but to do it in such a way that the netting wouldn't be seen in the photographs. And while his strategists wanted Reagan to look daring, they didn't want him to look foolhardy—so they let the sandbags be piled up to exactly four inches above his bellybutton. Above that line, Reagan's heroic form, swaddled in Army parka and flak jacket, could be photographed as he lifted his binoculars and peered toward the unseen enemy. William Henkel, chief White House advance man and a specialist in concocting "photo opportunities," boasted of the Korean achievement: "This was it, the commander in chief on the front line against Communists. It was a Ronald Reagan statement on American strength and resolve." Henkel admitted that he was just selling a product, like soap. "Many of our little playlets, or presidential events, have a relationship to the advertising business."

Clinton, who as governor of Arkansas was used to a laid-back style, had a hard time adjusting to the image-makers of Washington. When he first arrived in the nation's capitol, writes Elizabeth Drew, those concerned with his image were horrified because: "In television scenes of him at various events, or being shown some object, or listening to an explanation, his mouth often hung open, which didn't look presidential. The sight of his chunky body in his jogging shorts wasn't wonderful to behold; he resisted his staff's efforts to get him to wear a track suit, just as he resisted their efforts to get him to stop making policy pronouncements as he finished his jog, sweaty, sometimes out of breath, and with a baseball cap shading his face. In his daily life, he had taken to wearing suits with big jackets and reverse-pleat trousers . . . that were fashionable in certain circles but on him looked baggy and emphasized his bulk."

In time, they got him to shape up—somewhat.

The President and Congress

There are several devices a president can use in his effort to push his domestic programs through Congress, although even in victory it is difficult for a president to come out of an encounter with Congress looking like a statesman. This is because the weapons at his disposal are rather base ones for the most part: deals, favors, threats, vetoes, and propaganda. The most important tool, however, is perfectly aboveboard and positive: the personal touch, one-on-one.

The Personal Touch

Most presidents, especially those who have spent time in Congress, enjoy dealing with its members. Bush liked to shmooze with them, so did Ford, and most emphatically so did Johnson, Kennedy, and Truman. Nixon, though an alumnus of Congress, was too shy to enjoy it. And Eisenhower, perhaps because he was used to giving orders, didn't like the kind of negotiations such dealings called for. Carter, having practiced only on Georgia legislators, was stiff and clumsy even though he tried his best to be otherwise. Reagan was comfortable with congressional visitors as long as the conversation stayed at the joke-swapping level, but when it moved on to the technicalities of legislation, he would open the discussion, then quickly step aside and let his aides continue it. Most presidents have their pet hates among members of Congress, but they are willing to swallow their personal feelings—they know they *have* to—in order to negotiate successfully. Not Reagan; he had a hard time dealing with the Democratic leadership because he could not overcome his dislikes. He strenuously avoided meetings with Senator Robert Byrd of West Virginia, the Senate Democratic leader, because he considered Byrd "sanctimonious and overly verbose" (which in fact he was). As for House Speaker Tip O'Neill, Reagan even ridiculed his massive body, saying "I sometimes try to stay in shape by jogging three times around Tip." Naturally, these powerful members reciprocated by making things much tougher for Reagan.

No president, at least no president of modern times, had more delight in trying to persuade and manipulate members of Congress—or anyone else—than Lyndon Johnson. His powers of persuasion, one-on-one, were legendary. If standing, he would grab a politician's arm and lean into his face, preferably taking advantage of his height to tower over him, while Johnson stroked his ego or titillated him with Texas stories and unpresidential remarks. Or he might engulf the politician in a bear hug. If they were seated, Johnson would pull his chair up close and grip the politician's knee while they talked. Johnson did most of the talking. These conversations were like an athletic event to him, very physical. He would do anything to intimidate.

One of his favorite techniques of intimidation was to summon somebody to talk to him while he was sitting on the toilet, or to talk to him while he was naked. Senator Barry Goldwater recalls "the 'skinny-dip Johnson,' who invited you to the White House pool and insisted you swim in the raw with him. Some fellows got embarrassed when Johnson began leading them around the basement without a towel. A few would agree to almost anything to keep their shorts on. Not me. I've been swimming in the nude since I was a kid."

CBS reporter Robert Pierpoint recalls an occasion when he was summoned to Johnson's bedroom and watched as the president "took off one piece of clothing after another and handed each one to the valet, until finally there stood the most powerful man in the world, as he would have put it, 'bare-assed nekkid,' while I tried to discuss serious issues and he tried to avoid them." Was this just exhibitionism or was there purpose in such odd behavior? Johnson's aide, Richard Goodwin, insists that it was the latter: "His display of intimacy was not gross insensitivity, or an act of self-humiliation, but an attempt to uncover, heighten, the vulnerability of other men—the better to know them, to subject them to his will."

The "Lyndon Johnson touch" resurfaced, to a lesser degree, with the Clinton presidency. Clinton did not enjoy the challenge of the one-on-one manipulation of opponents, but when he did take them on in privacy, he bowled them over. From the minute Ward Connerly stepped into the Oval Office and heard President Clinton say, "I like your tie," Connerly said he knew he was in the presence of a master. Connerly was an outspoken critic of Clinton and a powerful foe of racial preferences (affirmative action was one of Clinton's favorite causes), but when he emerged from his ninety-minute session with the president, he gushed with praise for his host's understanding of racial issues (Connerly is black) and confessed that he came away with a "warm and fuzzy" feeling about Clinton.

Phil Gramm, the far right-wing Republican senator from Texas, came out of budget negotiations with Clinton saying that in terms of salesmanship, "We have . . . probably the most talented president of my lifetime." Another top Republican senator, John McCain, came away from his session at the White House saying he believed Clinton was "clearly one of the most charming men I've ever met. He has the unique ability to communicate. He does a lot of it physically. He'll not only shake your hand, but he'll grab your arm. He looks right into your eyes." McCain said on one occasion that Clinton said to him, "'John McCain, you're the most amazing man I've met in my life.' He looked into my eyes, and I'm sure that he meant every word." But, McCain added, "I'm not sure for how long" Clinton meant it. Others who fell under Clinton's spell also expressed doubts about the president's steadfastness of opinion.

Deals

Many liberals have the notion that their heroes are above making dirty deals and that they grudgingly consent to deals of any sort. This is a quaint pipe dream.

On September 26, 1961, President Kennedy nominated Thurgood Marshall, counsel for the NAACP, to become a judge of the second Court of Appeals as a stopover on his way to the Supreme Court. For fifty weeks his nomination remained bottled in the Judiciary Committee, ruled by Senator James O. Eastland, a Democrat from Sunflower County, Mississippi. Then one day Attorney General Robert Kennedy met Eastland in a Senate corridor, and Eastland remarked, "Tell your brother that if he will give me Harold Cox I will give him the nigger" (meaning Marshall). Marshall was thereupon cleared, and Cox, who had roomed with Eastland in college and was the senator's protégé, was appointed a federal judge in the circuit that handles most of the Deep South's civil rights cases. He subsequently made something of a name for himself on that bench by such tricks as calling black defendants "chimpanzees." Many would say that Kennedy had made a disastrous bargain.

Senator Everett McKinley Dirksen of Illinois, one of the Republican bulls of his era, helped President Johnson pass the Civil Rights Act of 1964 and was endlessly praised in the press for his supposedly "rising above partisanship" to help. What the public didn't know was that to get Dirksen's cooperation, Johnson had had to okay a massive Corps of Engineers project for Illinois.

In 1978 Carter needed to win the support of Senator James A. McClure, a Republican of Idaho, to get his natural gas pricing bill out of conference committee, where it had been in a deadlock for nine months. McClure, from a state with substantial atomic power research facilities, wanted Carter to make a strong commitment to the support of the atomic breeder reactor program (a "breeder" reactor is one that produces more radioactive fuel than it consumes), when in fact Carter opposed the breeder reactor program altogether because he thought it was dangerous. To get McClure's vote, Carter reversed himself and agreed to support the spending of an extra $1.5 billion on the breeders.

Threats

Threats are probably the president's least effective way of dealing with Congress, but at the same time few presidents would be quite so reluctant to use them as Calvin Coolidge, who said, "I have never felt that it is my duty to attempt to coerce senators or representatives or to take reprisals."

The trouble with threats is they can blow up on the president and leave him with a sooty face. When Nixon got fed up with Senator Charles Percy's opposition to legislation to build an anti-ballistic-missile (ABM) system, he had his aide John Ehrlichman invite Percy to the White House for lunch. In "very blunt" terms, Ehrlichman let Percy know that if he didn't shut up about the ABM, he would get no help from the president for his bill to establish a governmental housing corporation. Percy, who probably wasn't all that interested in the housing legislation anyway, not only refused to bow to Ehrlichman's intimidation but used it to burnish his own image; he called a press conference and told the story of Nixon's pressure in such a way as to make himself seem a very courageous fellow.

The president can go far beyond a mere threat in his battle to influence Congress if he is willing to use the power of criminal investigation to disturb political campaigns. Nixon aide Charles Colson was reported to have helped develop a *Life* magazine article (from confidential government records) showing that Senator Joseph Tydings of Maryland had helped a company in which he held stock to get a profitable contract with a division of the State Department. This alleged conflict of interest became a major issue in his reelection campaign in 1970. After Tydings' defeat by a Republican, the State Department disclosed that its investigation of him had turned up nothing to suggest that he had done anything illegal. More important, however, is the fact that reporters learned that the administration had come to this conclusion *before* the election but had withheld the clearance for obvious reasons.

Vetoes and Other Negative Actions

The presidential veto is a perfectly legal and useful device to make Congress pause and think twice about whether it really wants a particular piece of legislation. If a president says no to a bill, Congress must drown him out with a two-thirds vote. Given the ideological and sectional schisms among the 535 members, that overriding vote is seldom easy to muster.

The liberal historian Arthur M. Schlesinger, Jr., once wrote: "Where a parliamentary Prime Minister can be reasonably sure that anything he suggests will become law in short order, the president of the United States cannot even be sure that *his* proposals will get to the floor of Congress for debate and vote. And no executive in any other democratic state has so little control over national economic policy as the American president." He was thinking, no doubt, of the great presidents who had attempted to control the economy, and the budget, for *positive* programs—what critics call "social welfare." But in fact presidents have considerable power over economic matters, at least negatively.

President Ford proved the intrinsic power of negativism. Even though he was an "accidental" president (he had never run on a national ticket, had never even been nominated as a candidate for either vice president or president, and had been chosen by Nixon and Congress—not the electorate), and even though he had no national constituency and was a weak president, he still was upheld in most of his vetoes of supposedly popular programs—farm subsidies, middle-income housing, day-care funds, and so on.

For a president whose policy is to dismantle and obstruct, or for one who is simply thrifty, the veto is a most convenient weapon, especially when it is fired like a blunderbuss, with a half dozen or so pellets hitting Congress at once. One day in 1972 Nixon vetoed nine social bills. From 1970 to 1973 he was averaging about ten vetoes a year, including seven education, nine health, four economic development, three veteran, and four aid for the elderly bills. It is difficult for Congress to do more than stay on its feet, much less move forward, in the face of such gusty opposition from the chief executive.

Propaganda

Of necessity, the president is in the strictest sense a rabble-rouser. And to arouse the rabble to support him and give him the strength he must have to deal effectively with Congress, a president will use every propaganda device, even turning the bureaucracy into a propaganda machine. In 1973 the Nixon administration issued propaganda kits called "The Battle of the Budget, 1973" to top officials in the bureaucracy and ordered them to start making speeches denouncing the "wasteful" Democratic-controlled Congress. Specifically, the officials were told to denounce fifteen programs that were up for legislative approval. The kits supplied "sample epithets to call Congress," explained how "Horror Stories Might Be Used" in the speeches, and gave sample editorials to plant with newspapers and television stations (such as "Each day the Congress persists in its efforts to foist on the American public a gaggle of runaway spending schemes"). A 1926 statute makes it illegal to use taxpayers' money to lobby for or against legislation, and the General Accounting Office ruled that the White House probably broke the law in its campaign against the fifteen bills. Nevertheless, Nixon's crowd was not doing anything that Kennedy had not done to push his antipoverty programs or that Johnson had not done to build public support for the Vietnam War.

The White House's chief propaganda advantage is that all spotlights are on it; it has the magic of glamor, and what would be considered trivia in other surroundings takes on a sheen of importance there.

One of the corniest but least dangerous propaganda devices is simple hyperbole. Of his trip to China, Nixon said, "This was the week we changed the world." When he signed a revenue-sharing bill, he hailed it as the beginning of "a new American revolution." He called the astronauts' moon-landing the greatest event since the birth of Christ. At the conclusion of the Smithsonian Agreement in December 1971 that devalued the U.S. dollar, Nixon said it was the "greatest monetary agreement" that had ever been made—an evaluation that sounded a bit hollow only fourteen months later when the "greatest monetary agreement" fell apart, and the dollar was devalued again. But, of course, as an ol' politico like Nixon knew, and as he admitted in an interview with *Time* magazine, "Where you need a lot of rhetoric, a lot of jazz, a lot of flamboyance, is when you don't have much to sell."

When Reagan took office, he had an economic program to sell that most economists looked upon as a fairy tale (his own vice president had once described it as "voodoo economics") and that most members of Congress were extremely suspicious of. So he hyped it by declaring that the nation was falling apart—"the worst economic mess since the days of Franklin Roosevelt," he said grimly, adding that only his program would bring America back from the "brink of disaster." His hyperbole worked, even though his program didn't.

As shown also in Chapter 8, the press is easily manipulated by presidents who know the entertainment value of the presidency. Moreover, the press knows it is being manipulated, but it accepts the White House's self-serving leaks, puffery, background pep talks, and staged performances because that is one way, albeit a sometimes grubby way, to get news. The swap-off is part of a complex partnership. In return for carrying water for the elephants and shoveling out the donkey stalls, reporters and editors get to watch part—a rather small part—of the inner circus and sometimes even get to speak to the ringmaster. This gives them a pleasant glow of importance, and in return they put together stories that make the circus seem much more glamorous and important than it really is. Through their promotion and participation, it becomes *their* circus, too. They feel that they have a vested interest in it; they feel, too, that the more they inflate the importance of what happens at the White House, the more this importance reflects back on them.

Knowing this, every president and every president's staff quickly learn how to apply pressures on the press to "cooperate." However, they do not even bother with the regular press corps, who are brushed aside, but instead deal almost exclusively with the top of the media pyramid: reporters representing the "national" press, the biggest newspapers, the newsmagazines, the networks. The White House likes particularly to deal with those network people who, buried deep in the mud of status quo, are so accurately called anchorpersons, and with those columnists who have gained fame by peddling the same portentous clichés for decades. These are the journalists who can reward the White House with the greatest exposure, and besides, White House officials feel comfortable with them, for they have refined the art of barter to its ultimate.

For example, consider Time Inc. President Nixon did not like Hugh Sidey, a Washington correspondent and columnist for Time Inc., and for five and a half years Nixon avoided him. Then, because Nixon was going to make a trip to Europe and felt that he needed a little extra hoopla to launch him in style, he offered a deal to Time's executives: he would give Sidey an interview—if *Time* magazine would put Nixon on its cover. The editors agreed to this.

Presidents negotiate trade-offs of one kind or another all the time. Lyndon Johnson was the most blatant trader in recent years; after he left the White House, he spoke candidly about the technique. "There's only one sure way of getting favorable stories from the reporters and that is to keep their daily bread—the information, the stories, the plans, and the details they need for their work—in your own hands, so that you can give it out when and to whom you want. Even then nothing's guaranteed, but at least you've got the chance to bargain."

In ticking off the devices and stratagems that are available to and often used by the president, one is apt to leave the melodramatic impression that he is living in a hostile world as a kind of political Daniel Boone, grimly coping with savages (the press) and wild animals (Congress) and chancy weather (public opinion), hacking out a few new trails, and pushing back the frontier a trifling amount. Well, of course, the chief executive's existence is not quite that dramatic. He is merely called upon to match wits with generally friendly adversaries and to manipulate fellow patriots for what he conceives to be the common good.

Usually the political game of wits-matching is played at white heat, with enormous financial interests and group pride at stake; to that extent, the president does work in a hypertense atmosphere and is often called upon to exert unusual efforts to win even partial victories. How far short of monarchy—indeed, how far short of true "executive" power—he falls in domestic affairs is evidenced by the fact that if the president had a hundred times as many devices and stratagems to call upon, victory for him would still be a random thing (or at best a seasonal thing) and as rare as a program actually aimed at the public welfare.

CHAPTER 2

The President Abroad

Bouquets, Brickbats, and Bombs

> *Now there are many, many who can recommend and*
> *advise and sometimes a few of them consent. But*
> *there is only* one *that has been chosen by the*
> *American people to decide.*
>
> Lyndon Johnson
> *speaking in Omaha, Nebraska, 1967*

WHEN JIMMY CARTER WENT OFF FOR HIS FIRST LONG VACA-
tion, a raft trip down the Salmon River in Idaho, he was asked how
he would deal with world crises from such an out-of-touch spot. He
replied, "I've issued a directive that there be no world crisis."

Jokes aside, it is quite true that of a president's substantive powers,
only one—more through tradition and the accidental attrition of congressional power than through law—approaches the absolutism of
one-man rule. This is his power that comes through the creation of foreign policy.

No one in the world has more power than the president to influence, if not to decide, the ultimate question: war or peace? The awe-
someness of that power is underscored by the fact that when Truman
dropped atomic bombs on Japan, "the president became forever the
man with his finger on the button, the one American who could destroy an enemy, perhaps the world, with a single order."

But let's not get too dramatic about the president's clout. In some of
his important foreign policy decisions, a president can be held in check
by Congress. For one thing, treaties the president makes with other
countries do not become binding until they are approved by the

Senate. And since Congress holds the government's purse strings, presidential military adventures overseas can be cut short (though they rarely are) and his economic dealings with other countries can be frustrated.

However, a clever president can sometimes sidestep monetary restrictions, as Clinton did in 1995. Mexico was on the verge of bankruptcy and needed a quick loan. Congress refused to come up with the money, so Clinton dipped into an emergency fund that he controlled and on his own authority lent Mexico $12 billion.

In many ways, a president can, strictly by his own actions, encourage or inhibit social and commercial ties with other countries. Carter, for example, refused to let U.S. athletes participate in the 1980 Olympic games in Moscow; that was supposed to punish the Soviet Union for its invasion of Afghanistan. Ronald Reagan banned travel by U.S. citizens directly from this country to Cuba; they could travel to distant Communist countries—the Soviet Union or China, for instance—but not to the little Communist neighbor next door. Carter decided to limit the amount of wheat that U.S. farmers could sell to the Soviets; Reagan decided to rescind Carter's wheat edict and replace it with a ban on the sale of pipeline equipment to Russia. In foreign affairs, presidents are rarely required to explain the logic of their actions, and this holds true not only for their relatively insignificant decisions in social and commercial matters but for their decisions relating to war and peace.

Professor Edward S. Corwin states the accepted wisdom: "There is no more securely established principle of constitutional practice than the exclusive right of the president to be the nation's intermediary in its dealing with other nations."

But having the "exclusive right" to serve as an "intermediary" is a long way from having the right to absolute power in foreign affairs. The Constitution approves the former; it does not approve the latter. Some presidents forget the distinction, or they insist on interpreting the Constitution differently. They are impatient with the idea of sharing power with Congress. In 1983, when the House Select Committee on Intelligence voted to withhold funds to pay for covert military action in Nicaragua, President Reagan denounced this as an irresponsible, dangerous precedent that would leave the executive branch unable "to carry out its constitutional responsibilities." He proved he meant it by defying Congress and setting up an illegal, secret method for raising money from arms sales to an enemy nation (Iran) and funneling it to the ragtag Nicaraguan rebels, the contras.

When Reagan spoke of his "constitutional responsibilities," he was speaking from the perspective of modern presidents, who enjoy powers distorted via evolution, not from the perspective of the writers of the Constitution. *They* intended that Congress should be at least co-equal, and perhaps superior, to the president in foreign affairs. And the reason they took precautions to establish this power-sharing was, as James Madison pointed out (anticipating by two hundred years the conduct of modern presidents), "The management of foreign relations appears to be the most susceptible to abuse of all the trusts committed to a government."

To ease their fears in that regard, the framers of the Constitution gave Congress unqualified power "to regulate commerce with foreign nations." Congress was given the power "to raise and maintain" armed forces, to control immigration, to set tariffs. While the president was given the power to negotiate treaties and to *direct* the military forces once the nation was engaged in war, the writers of the Constitution required that treaties be approved by two-thirds of the Senate before going into effect and gave to Congress, not the president, the right "to declare war" (Article I, Section 8).

Having lived so recently under kings who would sweep up a generation of men and march them off to war simply to fulfill some monarchical ambition or grudge, the writers of the Constitution were determined that the new nation would have a better, saner system. They intended to establish such safeguards that no one person would have the total say in war and peace.

Alexander Hamilton assured readers of *The Federalist* papers that

> the president is to be commander in chief of the army and navy of the United States. In this respect his authority would be nominally the same with that of the king of Great Britain, but in substance much inferior to it. It would amount to nothing more than the supreme command and direction of the military and naval forces, as first general and admiral . . . while that of the British king extends to the *declaring* of war and to the raising and *regulating* of fleets and armies— all which, by the Constitution under consideration, would appertain to the legislature.

That assurance lost its validity long ago.

One of the key reasons that the president's role in determining our national security policy in foreign affairs has changed so radically is that armies are so much larger, weapons so much deadlier, transportation so much swifter, and the world is so much smaller and so much more vulnerable. Decisions must sometimes be made with great urgency and acted upon without delay.

Or at least that is the argument of those who believe that the old, constitutional balance of power between Congress and president is dangerous to follow in the modern world. Dean Rusk, who was to become Kennedy's and Johnson's militant secretary of state, said in 1960: "As commander in chief the president can deploy the Armed Forces and order them into active operation. In an age of missiles and hydrogen warheads, his powers are as large as the situation requires." The next year, with the Vietnam War on the distant horizon, Senator William Fulbright, chairman of the Senate Foreign Relations Committee, argued that "for the existing requirements of American foreign policy we have hobbled the president by too niggardly a grant of power." He conceded that it was "distasteful and dangerous to vest the executive with powers unchecked and unbalanced," but he felt that there was no choice: "The price of democratic survival in a world of aggressive totalitarianism is to give up some of the democratic luxuries of the past."

Unworthy excuses for unconstitutional actions? In hindsight, many critics would say so. It seems that excuses can always be found to meddle in another nation's affairs when one is big enough to get by with it; excuses can always be dredged up from "necessities" when a president has large military forces at his disposal.

War-Making Powers

In the first year of our nation's life, there were fewer than a thousand soldiers in the Army and no Navy at all, so if the president had wanted to make war he would first have had to persuade Congress of the need to recruit fighters. But when the chief executive (and commander in chief) has a sizable standing Army and Navy at his disposal, he manages to get around the need for formally declaring war. Invariably a president who uses troops without consulting Congress will excuse himself with one or several of the following arguments: He will say there was precedent for the action—that for more than one hundred years other presidents had done the same thing. (He will conveniently forget to mention, though, that military actions taken by unilateral executive decision in the nineteenth century usually did not involve conflicts with foreign states.) He will say that he is operating under the nineteenth-century "neutrality theory" for the protection of United States citizens or property caught in foreign tumult. He will say there was a "sudden attack." Or he will say that he is acting under a "collective security" treaty with another nation.

That last excuse was the one Clinton used in 1999, when he joined other members of the North Atlantic Treaty Organization (NATO) in going to war against Yugoslavia. Of course, being as sly as most presidents, he didn't use the term "war." But if it wasn't war, what were all those missile-launching U.S. warships doing in the Adriatic Sea and what were those hundreds of U.S. bombers and fighter planes doing in the sky over Yugoslavia?

In the twentieth century, only two conflicts—World War I and World War II—were congressionally declared wars. But there was a sufficient number of undeclared wars to kill well over 100,000 American soldiers and sailors.

Without asking for the approval of Congress, presidents have sent troops into Southeast Asia, Korea, Lebanon, and into a dozen South American and Caribbean island dominions in this hemisphere. Between 1798 and 1800 John Adams fought an undeclared, limited war against France. Jefferson sent our ragtag Navy after the Barbary pirates in 1801. Wilson, with no congressional authority, sent troops into Mexico in 1914. From 1900 to the outbreak of the Second World War, United States military forces were used in a dozen "expeditions" and "interventions."

Somewhat cynically, Major General Smedley D. Butler of the Marine Corps recalled this glorious period of our history in a letter to the editor of *Common Sense* on November 19, 1933: "I helped make Mexico, and especially Tampico, safe for American oil interests, I helped make Haiti and Cuba a decent place for the National City Bank boys to collect revenue in. I helped Nicaragua for the international banking house of Brown Brothers. I brought light to the Dominican Republic for American sugar interests. I helped make Honduras 'right' for American fruit companies."

When Truman took us into the Korean War in 1950, he did so without congressional approval. Kennedy, without consulting Congress, used the Navy to blockade Cuba during the missile crisis of 1962 and eased us into the South Vietnam war by a progressively larger commitment of "advisory" troops. Johnson made a major, and subsequently much criticized, invasion of the Dominican Republic with 23,000 troops, without the consent of Congress. President Nixon, without notifying Congress, much less asking its approval, sent troops into Cambodia in 1970 and into Laos in 1971 to establish these areas as active battlefield extensions of the Vietnam War. In March 1969, just two months after taking office, he had launched a top-secret, fourteen-month bombing campaign in Cambodia that involved 3,650 B-52 raids. Congress didn't find out about that little presidential adventure until 1973.

In 1980 Carter invaded Iran with eight helicopters loaded with a special military strike force, backed up by three C-180 cargo planes. To be sure, this was not aggression in the usual sense; it was a rescue mission, aimed at freeing fifty hostages held in the U.S. Embassy in Tehran. Even so, it was an armed invasion and could have provoked a war. Did he get approval from Congress for the venture? No. He didn't even tell Congress—much less ask for permission. In his diary entry dated April 24–25, 1980, written just after the mission had failed, Carter stated, "I had planned on calling in a few members of the House and Senate early Friday morning, before the rescue team began its move into Tehran. . . . But I never got around to that." Presidents seldom do get around to taking Congress into partnership in such decisions.

In the fall of 1982, President Reagan sent a contingent of 1,200 Marines to Lebanon. In 1983, he sent the Army, Navy, and Marines to crush the leftist government on the stamp-size island of Grenada. At about the same time, a presidentially dispatched battalion of the 82nd Airborne Division was in the Sinai as part of a peacekeeping force. However benevolent the motivation for such assignments, they were radical steps to take. For thirty years, it had been a cardinal tenet of American foreign policy that there would be no American military presence in that troubled area. For the first time, U.S. troops were involved in Mideast politics—and it was strictly a one-man decision.

Since the beginning of the republic, the president has interpreted his constitutional role as commander in chief in such a way as to involve the United States in more than two hundred foreign military adventures, only five of which were declared wars. Apparently this is something in which our presidents take pride: Hanging from standards behind the president's desk are more than 200 streamers commemorating these military campaigns. Indulging a presidential whim to hunt pirates is one thing, but that sort of itch in the nuclear age can get a nation in trouble, and it raises an extremely relevant question: Is such power constitutional?

Saul K. Padover replies:

> The answer is that it is not patently unconstitutional. There is nothing in the Constitution that says that the president may not wage war abroad at his discretion. The Constitution merely states that only Congress can "declare" war. But it does not say that a war has to be "declared" before it can be waged.

Many others, however, are not so tolerant of presidential arrogance as Padover and believe the makers of the Constitution meant to allow the chief executive to mount military interventions in foreign nations without prior consultation with Congress *only* when attacks on the United States required immediate reaction.

But most presidents have no interest in such scholarly debates, and when they are questioned sharply by Congress about their excursions, they talk back just as sharply. Claiming that two United States destroyers had been attacked by enemy seacraft in the Tonkin Gulf, off Indonesia, on August 4, 1964, President Johnson sought and obtained open-end authority from Congress to pursue the war in South Vietnam in any manner he thought proper. Later, when it was discovered that Johnson had distorted this highly questionable "encounter" with the enemy for no apparent reason but to obtain war powers from Congress, the Senate Foreign Relations Committee, feeling duped, summoned Undersecretary of State Nicholas Katzenbach to give an explanation of the executive department's attitude. Katzenbach, rather crisply and without the slightest sign of humility, informed the committee that the constitutional provision reserving to Congress the right to declare war had become "outmoded in the international arena."*

Knowing President Johnson's habit of looking over the shoulder of anyone who testified for the executive department, the committee members realized that they were hearing the saucy rebuttal of Johnson himself.

But—as we will argue more fully later on—to blame only the president for the various methods by which we have become heavily entangled overseas is going a bit too far. Congress has been only too proud of the mutual-security pacts that proliferated around the world, under the presidential hand, since the Second World War. Even the seemingly extravagant extension of presidential powers through the war in South Vietnam was no more than the American people and their federal representatives had long been tacitly encouraging the chief executive to do.

When learned people in and out of Congress have played along with the president in the old ad hoc game of armed interference in foreign governments, the "strength" of the presidency can hardly be held wholly to blame for things when they go to pot. This is a truth that has

---

*On July 28, 1970, Katzenbach, out of office, appeared again before the committee, this time to urge repeal of the Tonkin Gulf Resolution, which gave the president full support for any action he thought necessary in the Vietnam War. In this way he hoped to take away what he now called the president's only legal excuse for being in Southeast Asia, thus repudiating his former argument. Which goes to show, perhaps, that the undersecretary of state is used not for his brain but as a messenger boy. His brain is called back into service after he returns to private life.

even begun to trickle through the consciousness of the politicians themselves. Writing with the newfound wisdom that comes to defeated presidential candidates, Senator George McGovern allowed as how it was all very well to talk about Congress's regaining its power in foreign affairs, but that

> if we are willing to concede the president dictatorial authority where we happen to agree with him, as liberals have tended to do over the years, we will have little chance of tying his hands when we do not. Examine the broad grants of power we pushed through with a Roosevelt, a Truman, a Kennedy, or a Johnson in the White House, and you will see why many of us in the Congress understand how Dr. Frankenstein must have felt when *his* creation ran amok.

Treaty-Making Powers

Another assurance on which Alexander Hamilton missed the mark has to do with the president's treaty-making powers. The eighteenth-century king of Great Britain was "the sole and absolute representative of the nation in all foreign transactions," and as such "can of his own accord make treaties of peace, commerce, alliance, and of every other description." Hamilton promised that the presidential powers had been nipped far short of that by the constitutional provision that the president could make treaties *only with the advice and consent of the Senate,* providing that two-thirds of the senators present concurred.

It hasn't worked out that way. In the first place, the formal writing of treaties has become almost an insignificant element in foreign policy. By the time an aggressive president gets through announcing policies (Monroe Doctrine, Truman Doctrine, Johnson's and Nixon's Asian doctrines) and making handshake commitments and agreements with foreign potentates and recognizing or refusing to recognize new regimes (which he has the power to do), the making of formal treaties is reduced to almost an antiquated function. An old-fashioned—and in some ways comforting—atmosphere surrounded Senate ratification of a treaty with Panama in 1978 (giving that country control of the Panama Canal by the year 2000). Unused to practicing its treaty-ratification power, the Senate seemed to enjoy itself so much that the debate over the agreement dragged on for thirty-eight days.

How are nation-to-nation agreements solidified if treaties are not entered into? There are several devices. One, which involves Congress, is the joint resolution. Whereas a treaty requires two-thirds of the Senate to approve it, a joint resolution needs only a simple majority of both houses—which is often easier to obtain. When the Senate rejected a treaty to annex Hawaii in 1898, for example, Congress as a whole annexed it by joint resolution. When the Senate rejected the Versailles Treaty that would have ended the First World War, Congress as a whole brought the war to an official end through joint resolution.

But an even more popular substitute (popular with presidents, that is) for the treaty is the executive agreement.* Historians aren't sure just exactly how the executive agreement was born. Apparently, like many other governmental creatures, it is the offspring of convenience. Whether or not the Constitution is also its parent is debatable. In any event, as one historian has put it, presidents, beginning last century, "found this form of compact a practical convenience in making once-and-for-all international arrangements, at first of minor consequence. The Senate accepted the device if only to spare itself the tedium of having to give formal consideration to a multitude of technical transactions."

As always happens when Congress allows the chief executive to invent a substitute power, the power will be exploited and aggrandized. By the end of the nineteenth century, executive agreements were being used for some of the most important international activities. McKinley used one to work out the preliminary terms for ending the Spanish-American War. And Theodore Roosevelt established the Open Door policy in the Far East through executive agreement.

The potency of executive agreements has continued into modern times; with such important foreign alignments and deals as the Atlantic Charter in 1941, the Yalta agreement in 1944, and the Potsdam agreement in 1945 being made by presidents without consulting the Senate. The restoration of normal diplomatic relations with mainland China, one of the most significant developments of the 1970s, was started under Nixon and completed under Carter without consulting with, or gaining the approval of, Congress; it was a supreme example of presidents winging it on their own. Carter's part in these executive agreements was also a supreme example of how to lose friends in Congress. The Senate had passed a nonbinding resolution asking Carter to consult with Congress in secret while the negotiations in Peking were going on. He totally ignored this request and did not even tell members of the

---

*An executive agreement is just what it sounds like: an agreement between the United States and a foreign government made by the executive branch of the U.S. government alone without approval by the Senate.

Senate that the U.S.–China agreement had been completed until one hour before the announcement was made publicly.

The presidential broken-field running around treaties is especially dramatic when one considers that in some recent years presidents concluded twenty times more executive agreements than treaties.

Perhaps just as impressive as the president's treaty-making power is his power to ignore treaties that have been made.

As French President Charles de Gaulle once said, "Treaties are like roses and young girls. They last while they last." How long a nation keeps its treaty promises depends entirely on what it considers its national interests to be at any given moment. One treaty the United States signed and swore to uphold is the Charter of the Organization of American States, which says unambiguously: "No state . . . has the right to intervene, directly or indirectly, for any reason whatsoever, in the internal or external affairs of any other state." And yet President Bush sent 24,000 troops into Panama, in an action he dubbed "Operation Just Cause," to seize the country's military dictator, Manual Noriega. The reason for the invasion was never really clear, although Bush said it was to restore democracy in Panama and to protect the thousands of U.S. civilian and military citizens stationed there. He cited the recent murder of one U.S. soldier in Panama as proof that things were unsafe down there.

But U.S. soldiers stationed overseas are always getting killed off-base, and we don't invade the countries where it happened. In any event, one might wonder if the invasion made much sense; to punish Panama for one death, the United States launched an invasion in which 26 Americans were killed and 300 wounded, not to mention hundreds of Panamanians, virtually all of whom were innocent victims. As Retired Admiral Eugene J. Carroll, deputy director of the Center for Defense Information, pointed out, Bush's revenge was oddly inspired by a "level of pre-invasion violence . . . lower than exists in Washington, D.C., every day."

And sometimes a president makes headlines because of treaties he refuses to sign. This was true in 1997 when Clinton rejected a treaty, which 100 other nations had signed, to outlaw antipersonnel land mines—the first international agreement in eighty years to ban a widely used weapon system. It is estimated that every year nearly 30,000 people—mostly civilians—are killed or crippled from the 100 million land mines left over from old wars around the world. An American, Jody Williams, won a Nobel Peace Prize for her work on the treaty, and when Clinton was slow to congratulate her, she got her revenge in the press by referring to him as "a weenie," and asked sarcastically, "He has time to call the winners of the Super Bowl, but the winner of the Nobel Peace Prize he can't call?"

The President and His Advisers

After a meeting with Soviet premier Khrushchev in Vienna in 1961, Kennedy felt that he had come out looking weak. He told James Reston of *The New York Times* that "Khrushchev had decided that 'anybody stupid enough to get involved in that situation [the Bay of Pigs] was immature, and anybody who didn't see it through was timid, and therefore, could be bullied.'" Not because he was especially interested in Vietnam but only to show that "he couldn't be bullied," Reston says (and others close to Kennedy have said the same), Kennedy sent 15,000 American men to Vietnam—and we were on our way to a commitment of half a million troops.

Lyndon Johnson told his biographer, Doris Kearns, that he extended "that bitch of a war on the other side of the world" out of personal pride, fearing that if he pulled out "I would be seen as a coward . . . an unmanly man."

Reagan bombed Libya to save face. Ever since he reached the White House he had been spouting some tuh-rrific rhetoric about what he was going to do to terrorists. When they blew up the U.S. embassy in Beirut, he vowed revenge on "the cowardly, skulking barbarians"; when they blew up the U.S. Marine barracks with great loss of lives, he swore "swift and effective justice." But there were more bombings, more kidnappings, more murders of U.S. citizens by terrorists overseas, and still he did nothing. Seven highly publicized U.S. hostages were being held in Lebanon by Muslim extremists. Critics asked if he was just abandoning them. Finally Reagan agreed with his image-makers: Some flashy showmanship was called for.

But what was the proper stage? Government intelligence experts were convinced that the real promoters of terrorism were Syria and Iran. But an attack on either of them would have meant real war. Neither Reagan nor his advisers wanted that; they simply wanted a resounding public-relations gesture. So the White House commissioned two public opinion polls to find a good substitute target. Would the public approve the bombing of Libya's cockeyed leader, Colonel Qadaffi? The polls showed they would. So Reagan sent the planes flying. It was a botched attack that did little damage, but it was an immensely successful P.R. stunt, what one reporter characterized as "the counterterrorism equivalent of invading Grenada—popular, relatively safe, and theatrically satisfying."

The moral of these little stories is that presidential planning of foreign policy is not always done at a very high intellectual level. Often it has as much to do with ego as with brains, more to do with self-promotion than with national interests. Just because the president sits on top of the heap does not mean he exercises his power with cool detachment. He does not withdraw like a Tibetan guru and make foreign policy decisions based on profound contemplation and personal philosophy—although some of that, too, may be involved. Nor, when he goes outside himself for advice, does he limit his circle only to his national security adviser and his secretary of state and their lieutenants, important though those certainly are. In charting the road the United States will take in dealing with other nations, the president listens not only to his own conscience and biases and to experts within the diplomatic establishment but also to representatives of the military-industrial complex, to multinational corporate executives, to international bankers, to ethnic power brokers with ties abroad, to lobbyists for foreign nations, to cronies, to the first lady, to party bosses, to campaign contributors, to congressional leaders.

Presidents rely on some unlikely advisers, even in crisis situations. Abe Fortas was a good lawyer but he knew absolutely nothing about foreign affairs; nevertheless, even after he went on to the U.S. Supreme Court he continued to slip back secretly to advise President Johnson on how to conduct the war in Vietnam.* President Kennedy made Richard N. Goodwin his adviser on Latin American affairs although Goodwin was nothing but a bright young speechwriter who, as Goodwin admits, "had never set foot south of the border, aside from one orgiastic night just beyond the Texas border during the campaign." President Carter's chief of the White House staff, Hamilton Jordan, was perhaps Carter's key negotiator in trying to free the American hostages held in Iran. What experience had Jordan had in foreign relations? None at all. Nor had Jody Powell, Carter's press aide, nor Gerald Rafshoon, Carter's ad man, nor Patrick Caddell, Carter's pollster. These young men were professionals when it came to running political campaigns and manipulating public opinion, but when it came to dealing with the leaders of foreign countries and weighing the subtleties of interna-

---

*Doubtless the reason Johnson continued to welcome Fortas' advice was that he had "become a yes-man on Vietnam," unfailingly agreeing with all of Johnson's bad judgments (Bruce Allen Murphy, *Fortas: The Rise and Ruin of a Supreme Court Justice* [New York: William Morrow and Co., 1988], pp. 240–241).

tional relations, they were rank amateurs. And yet during the Iranian crisis, the most important crisis that Carter faced during his administration, he relied heavily on them for advice. There are no rules that govern where a president gets his advice.

The most obvious sources of advice are the secretary of state, the secretary of defense, the director of the Central Intelligence Agency, and, within the White House itself, the national security adviser. The influence of these experts has varied from era to era.

Since Franklin Roosevelt, most chief executives have viewed the Department of State as antiquated, cumbersome, and strangled by red tape. It is said that instructions from the State Department in Washington to an ambassador overseas may require as many as twenty-seven signatures before they can be dispatched and that processing the message in a week's time is considered speedy. Efficiency is a code word that few of the State Department's 25,600 employees have deciphered. Such a sluggish morass of inefficiency may be—as some argue—a safeguard against reckless action: that is, if the policies that emerge from the State Department are not especially brilliant, at least most Machiavellian juices have been squeezed from them after going through the bureaucratic wringer.

That comforting theory has not carried much weight with most recent presidents; they have treated their secretaries of state in various ways, but mostly they have treated them with indifference. Since the Second World War, only Dwight Eisenhower—who wanted to delegate as much of his work as possible so that he would have more time to play golf—had a powerful secretary of state, John Foster Dulles. He, not Eisenhower, set the course of foreign affairs for this country during most of the 1950s. But under Eisenhower's successor, Kennedy, the State Department fell into disuse; under Johnson its vitality continued to decline. Dean Rusk, the secretary of state for both Kennedy and Johnson, was a lightweight, a mouthpiece, and an apologist—no more. All important foreign policy decisions were made by the president and his staff advisers, with the Pentagon brought in because of its specialized data.

Under Nixon, the State Department became virtually a haunted house. The creation of foreign policy was strictly a White House operation—Nixon surrounded by his tight little circle of national security advisers under the direction of Henry Kissinger, the master conniver, the global strategist who had virtual carte blanche in matters of foreign affairs for Nixon and for Nixon's successor, Gerald Ford. The secretary of defense could often claim a place in that circle but the secretary of state hardly ever.

If any occasion signified the new centralization, it was when President Nixon, in February 1969, signed the document that laid down America's foreign policy for the 1970s. At that White House ceremony, Henry Kissinger was present. But not Secretary of State William P. Rogers. Like a good scout, he was off in Ghana handling a routine chore. When Nixon visited China, he took both Kissinger and Rogers, but while Kissinger and some of his aides sat in with Nixon at the principal meetings with Mao Tse-tung and Chou En-lai, Rogers was shunted away in tea-drinking ceremonies with second-level Chinese dignitaries.

In the fall of 1973 Rogers stepped down, and Kissinger was named secretary of state. Most observers interpreted this not as an upgrading of the status of the State Department but as a further upgrading of the status of Kissinger, and as a crystallization of what had become known as the "Nixinger" foreign policy, filled with bold efforts to reach friendlier relations with Russia and China but marred by such misadventures as the unconstitutional air warfare in Cambodia.

President Carter, as was his fashion, struck an ambiguous middle ground in his use of the State Department. His national security adviser, Zbigniew Brzezinski, was not nearly so influential as Kissinger, but because he sat in the White House he had quicker access to Carter's ear than did Secretary of State Cyrus Vance. There was a bitter rivalry between Brzezinski, a hard-liner, and Vance, a soft-liner. Carter himself vacillated back and forth between the two poles, with the result that outsiders could never be sure which adviser was in the ascendancy at any given moment. In fact, they were not coequal. Brzezinski had by far the greater influence. Sometimes this was evident in ways that grossly insulted Vance, who was left out of so many important decisions that he quit in disgust.

With the Reagan administration, the feuding between the State Department and the White House started up again. Reagan's first secretary of state, Alexander M. Haig, a former Army general who had run Nixon's White House during the final days of the Watergate scandal, was hired on Nixon's recommendation ("He's one of the most ruthless, toughest, ambitious s.o.b.'s I know. He'd make a great secretary of state."). But he wasn't tough enough to overcome the rivalry of Reagan's White House advisers. Frustrated beyond endurance, Haig quit in a huff in 1982 and was replaced by George Shultz, another retread from the Nixon cabinet who was known as a "team player"—meaning that he would do the formal diplomatic chores and shut his eyes to some of the more nefarious schemes cooked up by others on Reagan's foreign affairs team. Chief among these others were CIA

Director William Casey and two national security advisers—first Robert McFarlane and then Admiral John Poindexter. They, along with an adviser to the National Security Council (NSC), Lt. Col. Oliver North, joined forces in what some journalists who covered the White House have described as a "junta"—an unauthorized government within the government.

They were a strange and motley crew. McFarlane was a Marine colonel with a problem. He finally left his White House post after breaking into tears so many times that it was presumed he was having a nervous breakdown; later he tried to kill himself. Admiral Poindexter was obsessively secretive and looked upon Congress as "outside interference." Although he was reputed to have a photographic memory, when called to testify before Congress he was seized with spasms of forgetfulness. CIA Director Casey was a hard-drinking, hard-cussing old man (Bob Woodward says he changed his clothes only when friends told him he was beginning to stink) who had been a whizbang campaign manager for Reagan in 1980 and had become wealthy as a Wall Street lawyer, but hadn't been near a spy agency since the Second World War. Like Poindexter, Casey hated Congress, described it as filled with "assholes," and was notorious for lying to congressional committees. Secretary of State Shultz loathed Casey and felt he had sabotaged most of the State Department's best programs, but President Reagan preferred Casey's company because he fed the president lots of spy gossip (Anwar Sadat of Egypt, he said, "smoked dope and had anxiety attacks"; Muammar Qaddafi, the wild colonel who ran Libya, sometimes "wore makeup and high-heel shoes" and liked toy teddy bears). Casey was woefully old-fashioned about intelligence gathering. All U.S. spy agencies have incredibly advanced technology, such as satellite cameras that from several miles in the sky cannot only count Soviet tanks but can even determine which of them are in working order, and radar systems that can take photos through clouds; but Casey favored the old trenchcoat and false-mustache kind of spying that he had learned forty-five years ago. Consequently, much of his information was dead wrong.

As for their notorious underling at the National Security Council, Lt. Col. North, he was a complex and somewhat tragic figure who had done heroic service in Vietnam but then cracked up and spent time in a military mental clinic. With that background, he should never have been let near the NSC and all its temptations. But since he did get into the NSC apparatus, he needed close supervision. He didn't get it. McFarlane, because he had become psychologically worn out himself, and Poindexter, because he was a dim bulb, were happy to let North take over and run things—and he ran away with them. He worked with such fanatical intensity and for such long hours that he became exhausted and began having hallucinations about kidnapping Iranian officials and holding them in cages all over Europe. In directing the Iran-contra scam, North relied heavily on the guidance and advice of an Iranian triple-agent who, in taking a CIA lie-detector test of fifteen questions, had failed all but two—his name and his nationality.

These weirdos, chiefly North, persuaded Reagan to go along with their scheme to sell arms to Iran (they convinced him, wrongly, that it would result in freeing all U.S. hostages held in the Middle East) and then use the money to support Nicaraguan rebels—all in violation of congressional mandates. Vice President Bush, being a member of the National Security Council, knew about the illegal sales but apparently made no effort to argue Reagan out of them; nor did Secretary of State Shultz. So Reagan wound up with bad advice from one side and no advice from the other.

But couldn't Reagan see for himself, without advice from Bush or Schultz or anybody else, that the NSC gang were outlaws—and not even efficient outlaws, at that? Typically, at one point the plotters made a mistake in numbers and sent millions of their loot to the wrong bank account in Switzerland. North exclaimed to Poindexter as their scheme unraveled, "So help me, I have never seen anything so screwed up in my life." This was indeed the gang that couldn't shoot straight.

So why was Reagan such an easy pushover for them? Why in the world did he allow himself to be so easily led into mischief? One reason is that, like most presidents, Reagan didn't consider it very mischievous to violate congressional mandates. He believed himself to be above such laws. But, more important, he was only too willing to leave the detailed operation of the presidency to his aides and to accept their advice without question; this was particularly true in foreign affairs. He gave his approval so readily they stopped asking for it. Unlike all other modern presidents, he was bored by the National Security Council meetings. When terrorism or some other jazzy subject came up, he seemed alert. But when his advisers moved on to more intricate international subjects, "his mind appeared to wander" and his eyes glazed over. "Foreign policy wasn't terribly important to the president," McFarlane said later. "He was defensive about foreign policy, didn't know a lot about it himself." Everyone seems to agree on that point. They also agree that he made little effort to educate himself. Before the economic summit at Williamsburg in 1983, his aides gave him briefing books to study, but he didn't crack them; instead he watched *The Sound of Music* on television. His first secretary of state,

Haig, urged Reagan to set aside just one hour a week to study foreign issues. He got no response. Only after much prodding did Reagan give Secretary of State Shultz an hour a week—which was one-seventh the time Reagan spent lifting weights and much less than he spent answering fan mail. Sometimes while Shultz was talking to him, he would doze off (just as he once did at a meeting with Mikhail Gorbachev and again at a meeting with Pope John Paul II).*

Dollar Diplomacy Begins, Big Time

President Bush, who had come to the Oval Office with the reputation of a passive flunky willing to do even some of the illegal errands assigned by Reagan, moved quickly to establish himself as the champion of a foreign policy apparatus dominated by the old Eastern Establishment/multinational corporations cadre. There was nothing surprising about this, nor of his relationship with it. During the eight years he had just spent on the National Security Council and during his one year as director of the CIA on the way up, those were the people he had become comfortable dealing with. He signaled his intention to make the State Department more active, but very much under his thumb, when he appointed his old Houston Country Club pal James Baker III to head the department; it was assumed Baker would be Bush's vigorous alter ego.

Bush appointed Lawrence S. Eagleburger to be Baker's deputy and Brent Scowcroft to head the NSC. Here was the tip-off as to what lay ahead. Eagleburger and Scowcroft were notorious examples of the revolving door. In previous administrations, both had held the same jobs they were taking under Bush, but in the meanwhile they had been partners with ubiquitous Henry Kissinger in a firm offering advice on foreign affairs to thirty leading global companies, including ITT, American Express, Anheuser-Busch, Coca-Cola, H. J. Heinz, Fiat, Volvo, I. M. Ericsson, Daewoo, and Midland Bank. They promised—for the sake of anyone who still believed in the tooth fairy—that they would not let their corporate relations influence

*Apparently Shultz finally caught on that sleep was more important to Reagan than international events. Speaker of the House Tip O'Neill (*Man of the House* [New York: Random House, 1987], p. 366) relates that when a Russian fighter plane shot down a Korean airliner carrying a full load, including a number of Americans—the sort of incident that could trigger a militant response—Shultz called the leaders of Congress in the early hours of the morning. When O'Neill asked Shultz what Reagan's reaction had been, Shultz said, "I haven't told him yet. I'll tell him when he wakes up."

their conduct of U.S. foreign policy. With Eagleburger and Scowcroft on the inside again, and their ex-partner Kissinger on the outside among the multinationals but often serving at the most secret levels of government as a consultant, too, it was getting hard to figure out where the line was to be drawn (if at all) between national interests and corporate interests. As for Secretary Baker, he promised not to let his family's large holdings in major oil companies such as Exxon, Mobil, Standard Oil of California, and Standard of Indiana, plus a rich assortment of stock in other major international corporations, color his judgment. The weirdos were out (maybe); big business had returned in full force.

Bush was doing what came naturally to a capitalist government entering the free-wheeling post–Cold War era, which began in the first year of his presidency. With the fall of the Soviet Union (more on that in the next chapter), U.S. foreign policy quickly shifted from an emphasis on ideology—that is, democracy versus communism—to an emphasis on commerce. The new foreign policy was: Make profits, not war. And President Clinton continued that policy with even greater enthusiasm than Bush had. To be sure, Clinton's secretaries of state, first Warren Christopher and then Madeleine K. Albright, were kept busy running around the globe trying to put out brush fires and ease tensions in the usual State Department fashion, but at the same time some of the other cabinet members and Clinton and Vice President Gore were working even harder at helping U.S. corporations beat competitors in the global marketplace. When the crash of a U.S. military plane in Croatia in 1996 killed Commerce Secretary Ron Brown, it was symbolic of the new foreign policy that two dozen American corporate executives were with him—he was opening important doors for them as they globe-trotted in search of business contracts. He had previously escorted other groups on the same mission.

Money made our foreign policy quite malleable. For instance, because the United States believed Iran supported terrorist organizations such as the one that blew up a U.S. military barracks in Saudi Arabia, the Clinton administration threatened to punish any foreign company that invested in Iran. But in the fall of 1997, Russia's premier private company, Gazprom, announced that it was going to pump natural gas off the Iranian coast. Our government couldn't stop the pumping, but it could have put a crimp in Gazprom's plan to raise $1 billion in the world financial market. So why didn't it carry out its threat? Possibly because queering the deal would have hurt the Wall Street firm of Goldman, Sachs and Company, which was underwriting the Gazprom bond offering. Goldman, Sachs, aside from being one of the largest financial supporters of Clinton's 1996 campaign, was also the firm which Treasury Secretary Robert E. Rubin had been co-chairman of before moving into Clinton's cabinet.

The Myth of Omniscience

If Reagan was fed tons of bad information and half-baked advice, he wasn't the first president to be served that way and he will not be the last.

Although in fact the president's decision-making apparatus is often very ordinary, the public assumes quite the opposite. One reason the president has so much power in foreign affairs is that he is surrounded by the myth that he must know what he is doing and should not be challenged because he has access to intelligence and military reports that are not available to the rest of us. Supposedly he draws upon the collective wisdom of a global network of spies who are right on top of what's happening everywhere in the world. Newspaper feature stories and spy novels and James Bond–type movies have created the illusion that the world's leaders are constantly being fed "the inside stuff" via their spies and undercover operatives and crafty embassy officials around the world. Nobody is supposed to be more generously supplied with this than the president of the United States, who can rely not only on the Central Intelligence Agency but on the even larger intelligence systems operated by the Army and Navy. The very mention of a "top secret cable" landing on the president's desk from these spies is enough to make Congress, and the general public, bow their heads with respect.

However, some officials who have served close enough to presidential desks to know exactly what goes on have suggested that such blind faith is misplaced. Historian Arthur M. Schlesinger, Jr., a close adviser to President Kennedy, tells us that

> as one who has had the opportunity to read such cables at various times in my life, I can testify that 95 percent of the information essential for intelligent judgment is available to any careful reader of *The New York Times*. Indeed, the American government would have had a much wiser Vietnam policy had it relied more on the *Times;* the estimate of the situation supplied by newspapermen was consistently more accurate than that supplied by the succession of ambassadors and generals in their coded dispatches.

Rarely is the public treated to such refreshing candor as exhibited by President Bush during the political upheavals in China in early 1989. The situation was so volatile that accurate news was skimpy; at a press conference, journalists asked Bush if he knew more than they did. Cheerfully he acknowledged that he didn't, and that Chinese officials had repulsed all his efforts to get more information. "They won't answer the phone," said Bush. A White House aide later told journalists, "We may be sitting at the center of things, but sometimes we just have to turn on the Cable News Network to find out what's going on."

George Reedy, President Johnson's first press secretary, once told the Senate Foreign Relations Committee that the executive department's legendary information-gathering machinery is "basically a multiplier and it multiplies misinformation as well as information." Even a person who works closely with the president, he said, can never be sure "whether he is acting on information, misinformation, verified data, questionable data, or just a plain hunch."

In 1965, when public criticism of Johnson's policies was mounting, he told his speechwriter Goodwin that the "real problem" was not his Vietnam adventure but "that everybody in America think they know everything about everything, like Vietnam. They don't realize that the leaders are the ones who've got the secrets, and that's something they should respect."

And what "secrets" did the "leaders" have that made them so specially wise? Why, they had secrets that showed North Vietnam could be bombed into submission. So in 1965 they began bombing North Vietnam in what would be the largest sustained campaign of aerial attack in the history of warfare—the total tonnage dropped on North Vietnam, an area the size of Texas, was three times the Allied tonnage dropped on Europe, Africa, and Asia during the Second World War. It was called "Operation Rolling Thunder." Defense Secretary Robert McNamara at the beginning was its most enthusiastic supporter. But two years later, this "expert" told a congressional committee that it had been a total failure and that no amount of bombing "that I could contemplate in the future would significantly reduce the flow of men and material to the South."

But it took thirty years for McNamara to work up the moral courage to admit publicly that he and Johnson's other pro-war advisers—including the secretary of state, the national security adviser, and Johnson's closest military advisers—had been giving their advice out of almost total ignorance. In his 1995 memoirs, McNamara wrote,

"When it came to Vietnam, we found ourselves setting policy for a region that was terra incognita." And what made it worse was that "our government lacked experts for us to consult to compensate for our ignorance" because all of the State Department's East Asian and China experts had been purged during the 1950s by Senator Joseph McCarthy and other hysterical congressional hard-liners who suspected them of being Communist sympathizers.

If Johnson (and the nation) paid a bitter price for putting too much faith in his advisers, so did his predecessor. Within weeks after John Kennedy took office in 1961, Allan Dulles, director of the Central Intelligence Agency, began encouraging him to move swiftly on a rough plan, left over by President Eisenhower, to invade Cuba (at the Bay of Pigs) and overthrow Castro. The CIA's plotters made it sound like a sure thing—even though the 1,200 invaders, a ragtag army of Cuban immigrants, would be going up against Castro's army of 200,000. Also, the spot at which the invaders landed was surrounded by swamp, and they had no radio equipment and were short of ammunition because those things were aboard an old freighter that had been blown up. It was, as one of Kennedy's aides later admitted, "a preposterous, doomed fiasco" and Kennedy was a fool to believe the CIA. Later, with the invaders crushed, Kennedy admitted it: "How did I ever let it happen? I know better than to listen to experts. They always have their own agenda. All my life I've known it, and yet I still barreled ahead."

But the CIA was not alone in giving bad advice. Before making his final decision, Kennedy had summoned his twenty top advisers in military and foreign affairs and asked for their guidance. With only one exception, all voted to invade. Obviously, they were voting from ignorance. And once again in his 1995 memoirs Defense Secretary McNamara confessed his part in the group ignorance: "I had entered the Pentagon with a limited grasp of military affairs and even less grasp of covert operations. The truth is I did not understand the plan very well and did not know the facts."

"You always assume," Kennedy later lamented, "that the military and intelligence people have some secret skill not available to ordinary mortals." He wasn't the only president to make that foolish assumption.

Fortunately for the United States—and for the world—Kennedy learned his lesson and, at the most critical crisis of the Cold War, ignored some of the bad advice he was getting and showed real leadership. This was in 1962, when our government discovered that the

Soviet Union had placed intercontinental missiles in Cuba. That was too close for comfort. What should Kennedy do about it? For thirteen horrendously tense days he and his advisers debated the solution. At various times during those meetings Kennedy was urged by the highest generals at the Pentagon and by the chairmen of congressional armed services committees to launch an atomic attack on the Soviet Union and (as one of these experts put it) "try to get it over with as quickly as possible." If Kennedy had done that, the resulting exchange of nuclear explosives would doubtless have destroyed both nations. Instead, Kennedy stayed cool and worked it out diplomatically.

The vulnerability of the president to the bad advice of so-called experts has never been better illustrated than in 1978, when Iranians began to complain about the Shah's oppression. The Shah was considered one of the United States' most trusted allies; he was also the supplier of a significant amount of the oil consumed by our allies. Strategically, it was highly important that the Shah stay in power. When rumblings of discontent began to shake Iran in 1978, President Carter asked the CIA to appraise the situation. The CIA reported in August that Iran "is not in a revolutionary or even in a prerevolutionary situation." The CIA's report went on to say that the Shah was in total command of the military and that forces opposing his regime did not have the popularity to be more than a minor nuisance. Five months after that report was handed to Carter by what was supposedly his top spy agency, the Shah had fled for his life, the military had deserted him and the supposedly weak opposition, led by a seventy-five-year-old religious fanatic whom the CIA had taken scant notice of, was firmly in control.

Before the year was out, Carter was once again the victim of "expert" advice. The Shah wanted to take refuge in this country. Carter feared that if he gave asylum to the Shah, Iranian fanatics would seize our embassy and take its workers hostage. But all his top advisers urged him to let the Shah come into the country to receive medical treatment (treatment he could just as easily have received elsewhere). Finally, Carter went against his own instincts and caved in to their advice. What he feared would happen, immediately did happen. And for the next 444 days—despite threats, despite seizure of $13 billion in Iranian assets, despite a bungled attempt to rescue them by force—the fifty embassy workers were held prisoner, critically damaging Carter's image, making him appear helpless and the United States weak, and probably costing him the election in 1980.

Looking under the CIA Covers

Since the Central Intelligence Agency has obviously been a key adviser to the president in matters of foreign affairs, a closer look at that agency is deserved.

Until the end of World War II, spying on other countries was something that our government scarcely considered to be proper or necessary. But we came out of that war feeling very nervous and paranoid about the Soviet Union and its communist allies. What mischief were they up to? Were they plotting against us? For that matter, what were our allies up to?

Our goal was to maintain our position as the world's most powerful nation, even if it meant stooping to conduct that polite society would frown on. So in 1947, Congress passed the National Security Act, which set up the Central Intelligence Agency. Other spy agencies were also established, but the CIA outranked them and to some degree supervised them. It was expected that its agents' most useful work would be in collecting information from abroad. The CIA also created what came to be known as the "dirty tricks department," which carried out foreign sabotage, espionage, propaganda, political bribery, and almost anything else the spies could think up to lessen the influence of unfriendly governments.

We'll save an appraisal of the CIA's "dirty tricks" for the next chapter. Right now we'll deal with this question: How reliable have its spies and analysts been in the information they fed the president and others in shaping foreign policy? Probably some of the information was highly useful, but because the CIA has made every effort to keep its work super-secret, there can be no complete answer to that question.

Of its failures, however, much is known. Senator Patrick Moynihan, a former member of the Senate Intelligence Committee, was being conservative when he said, "For a quarter century the CIA has been repeatedly wrong about the major political and economic questions entrusted to its analysts." CIA historian David Wise saw its failures over a longer time span: "Its analysts misjudged almost every major development in the post–World War II world, including the most spectacular misjudgment of all—the flat-out failure to predict the collapse of the Soviet Union."

As already mentioned, the CIA supplied disastrously inaccurate information about Cuba and Iran. Its intelligence was just as nonexistent or faulty when the United States faced crises in Indonesia, Korea, Iraq, and a dozen other countries.

The CIA failed to foresee the Soviet invasion of Afghanistan in 1979. It supplied no useful advice for the U.S. invasion of Panama in 1989. It totally misinterpreted the political situation in Central America; in 1990, the CIA predicted the Sandinistas would lose the election in Nicaragua by 15 percent; they won by 15 percent. In an unusual burst of honesty, the CIA recently acknowledged that only 10 percent of its informants in Guatamala were "deemed reliable."

But the CIA's most harmful failures were in its handling of information about the Soviet Union. From the end of World War II until the early 1990s, the CIA gave the White House and Congress wildly exaggerated estimates of the Soviets' strength. Its economy was reported to be growing 50 percent faster than the U.S. economy; its military industry was said to be the equal, if not the superior, of our own. The fallacy of these reports, which frightened U.S. leaders into wasting billions of dollars in a senseless arms race, was exposed when the Soviet Union collapsed in 1991 and the world could finally see, as William Greider has written, that the Soviet "economy was a crude joke . . . not second strongest in the world or third, probably not even fourth or fifth. Americans, in other words, were propagandized by their own government for forty years. Were citizens deliberately deceived or were the CIA spies so befogged by their own ideological biases that they missed the reality themselves?"

Some of both, probably. In 1995, the CIA's director stunned Washington by confessing that even though the agency knew that some of the reports it received from Russia over the previous decade were being sent not by our spies but by Russia's own double agents, the CIA had turned these reports over to the president and the Pentagon without one word of warning that they were fatally flawed. Pentagon officials said the false information caused them to spend billions on weapons they didn't need.

Sometimes the CIA's mistakes have been so stupid that they would be funny if they weren't so tragic. During the 1999 war with Yugoslavia, the United States and its allies depended heavily on the CIA for information as to what targets should be hit by their bombers. In one instance, the CIA identified a building in the middle of Belgrade as headquarters of a Yugoslav arms agency. So bombs were dropped, the building was destroyed, three people were killed and twenty injured. Oops! it turned out that the arms agency was really 200 yards to the south. The building bombed was the Chinese embassy. How could the CIA have made such a dreadful mistake? After all, the embassy had been there for three years. Its identity was hardly a secret; the Belgrade phone book and tourist maps identified the embassy at that address. The blunder momentarily shattered diplomatic relations between the United States and China, but at least it was fuel for Jay Leno, who explained to his television audience that "CIA stands for Can't Identify Anything."

The Difficulty of Making Changes

The posture of this nation toward other nations does not change much from administration to administration, not even when one party replaces the other. The main reason for this is that those who seek and win the presidency tend to share similar philosophies. Why not? Most people schooled in this country receive more or less the same lessons in history and political science. Most Americans are bombarded day after day throughout their lives with the same news reports, the same editorials, the same preachments. They reach adulthood having more or less the same view of the world and believe in the same truisms: The United States is "God's country" and free-enterprise capitalism made us great; countries that follow the communist doctrine are a malicious, evil influence in the world (this was a particularly strong belief until 1991, when the Soviet Union expired); our allies in Western Europe, Mexico, Japan, and what once made up the British empire can be trusted completely, but allies elsewhere must be watched closely; most Middle Eastern, Asian, and African nations—the so-called Third World nations—are dangerously in flux; Central America and South America "belong" to our sphere of influence and must be protected from radical incursions at almost any cost.

Though oversimplified, that is the world as seen by most Americans—and it is the world as seen by most presidents. So it is hardly surprising that a new president will not veer wildly from decisions made by previous presidents. And the cumulative effect of a foreign policy carried through several administrations can be strong indeed, and very resistant to change, even if a president should desire to change it. Though each administration is theoretically free to do its will, each administration is bound to some extent by tradition, customs, precedents, and commitments made by its predecessors.

"The essence of good foreign policy," David Halberstam once wrote, "is constant reexamination." True enough. But for the reasons given above, reexamination is sometimes very difficult to carry into reform. And there is another reason: Presidents often inherit massive foreign policy problems. Truman inherited the Second World War from Roosevelt. Eisenhower inherited the Korean war from Truman. Johnson inherited from Kennedy a South Vietnam policy that had sent 16,000 American military "advisers" to that country; Nixon inherited from Johnson a full-scale war with 500,000 Americans in Vietnam; Ford inherited from Nixon a war that, by that time, had fallen apart; Clinton inherited from Bush a chronic, armed confrontation with Iraq.

Only a president who comes into office with no U.S. troops involved in belligerencies anywhere in the world can have the luxury of time for cautious and careful reappraisal of foreign policy. Carter was the first president in fifteen years to be blessed with that luxury, and he made use of it. He was not so stridently anticommunist as were the presidents who had to maintain a rationale for their military actions. He put less emphasis on our hectic relationship with the Soviets and more emphasis on developing ties with Third World countries and strengthening our friendships with old allies in Europe. Carter was a religious person and he looked upon foreign relations as a missionary operation.

Boiled down, Carter's foreign policy was—in addition to the traditional anticommunism—based on human rights. Countries that showed respect for human rights would receive our friendship and help. Countries that suppressed civil rights, that imprisoned and tortured political prisoners, and in other ways violated basic freedoms, would not receive our friendship and help. That was the ideal. In practice, not surprisingly, Carter fell far short of attaining that goal. He discovered he could not enforce fixed standards when dealing with 150 other nations. There had to be some flexibility, chiefly to meet our national security requirements. For example, the South Korean government was notorious for torturing and killing political dissidents, but Carter overlooked that and continued giving South Korea aid because he felt that the country's support was vital to our global defense plan. And he continued to maintain a close friendship with the government of the Shah of Iran, even though the jails of Iran were crowded with political prisoners. Looking back on the administration's successes and failures, Brzenzinski had to admit that the human rights program had greater influence "with weak and isolated countries than with those with whom we shared vital security interests." In short, Carter imposed his human rights policy on nations that needed our help more than we needed theirs; with other nations, he sometimes held his nose and forgot the ideal.

Nevertheless, despite its frequent failures, the human rights policy did force some nations—particularly in Africa and Latin America—to be a little more humane. Under pressure from Carter, thousands of political prisoners were released from jails. Similarly, the Soviet Union for the first time allowed thousands of Jews to escape its suppression and emigrate to Israel.

At the same time, Carter's approach also proved that only foreign policies based on war can be certain to overlap from one administration to another. As soon as Reagan became president, he deemphasized human rights almost to the point that it became a dead issue. He, like Carter, came into office with U.S. troops uninvolved in wars anywhere in the world and had the opportunity to take his foreign policy in new directions. Instead, he decided to go back to the standards that had guided most of our foreign policy since the Second World War: For another country to be considered our ally, worthy of our financial assistance, it needed only to be fervently anticommunist. For example, the government of El Salvador murdered 13,353 civilians in 1981 (according to a survey conducted by the Archdiocese of San Salvador), and the slaughter continued through 1982. But because that government was anticommunist, Reagan considered it a force for "stability" in Central America and asked Congress to send it millions of dollars in military aid to fight left-wing guerrilla insurgents. When congressional critics in 1982 complained that the Salvadoran government was too brutal to deserve our support, the Reagan administration argued that things were improving there—in the previous six months only 3,000 civilians had been executed by the government's death squads.

Nevertheless, congressional pressure finally moved Reagan to act. In December 1983, he sent Vice President Bush to El Salvador with a message for its government: Curb the death squads or lose military aid. Since that would have meant the loss of more than $1 million a day in subsidies, the warning worked. For several years there was a sharp reduction in murders, but then El Salvador slid back into wholesale human rights violations, and this time the Reagan administration was silent. By the time Bush became president, U.S. aid to El Salvador had soared to $533 million a year—half that country's budget—even though there was little evidence that violent repression had abated.

Like Carter, President Clinton talked a lot about making human rights a centerpiece of his foreign policy, but he did even less than Carter to bring this about—especially when dealing with countries that were big enough to be important to our economy. Saudi Arabia, for example, is notoriously repressive to its women and it allows nothing like free speech or free press to anyone. Its idea of criminal justice is something out of the Middle Ages. Similar, or worse, conditions prevail in China, which kills or imprisons its political dissidents. But where is the president who would propose that until those countries reform along American standards, we should not buy Saudi oil or trade with China, whose population of 1.3 billion makes it the largest market in the world? Such a president may surface eventually, but none has appeared so far.

When Clinton ran in 1992, he scolded President Bush for "pampering dictators" in Beijing. But when he became president himself, pampering was pivotal to his China policy, which emphasized trade. He said his objective was "cooperation, not confrontation," as he welcomed China's repressive chief of state, Jiang Zemin, to the United States in 1997 with a state dinner at the White House, to which he invited scores of corporate executives but only one human rights activist.

A president's hospitality—whom he invites to drop by the White House for a visit—can convey an eloquent message to the rest of the world. The first African leader that the Bush administration honored with an invitation was Mobutu Sese Seko of Zaire, who came to power with the assistance of the CIA in 1965 and began busily looting his own country. His people were wretchedly impoverished, but he was reportedly worth $5 billion. When the president gets chummy with a fellow like that, what does it say to other African leaders? That they have our blessing to steal?

Can the President Be Reined In?

Let us restate our opening premise: Over the years, various presidents, often acting on faulty or false information, have launched the United States into dangerous and degrading military adventures overseas. They have done this on their own, by whim, without consulting Congress, though the Constitution says that only Congress can declare war. And they have sometimes prolonged these military outings through secrecy and lies.

The problem, obviously, is so serious that it demands the creation of some legal apparatus that could keep a president under control. What should be done? What *has* been done? One might suppose that Congress, from injured pride if for no other reason, would have taken steps long ago to rein in the president. One would certainly think that the experience of presidential power run amok during the Vietnam War would have prompted significant congressional reform. Unfortunately, such is not the case.

By 1973 even many of the hawks in Congress were so irritated by the Johnson–Nixon military escapades and all their seemingly endless variations that they decided that something should be done to check future presidents. Something, but not much, *was* done. Culminating three years of ponderous deliberations, Congress passed a War Powers Resolution. This is what it said: If the president sends U.S. troops overseas to fight without the consent of Congress, he must within sixty days go to Congress and gain its approval for his actions, or bring the troops home. However, there was a loophole in the law: It said that the president could keep his emergency troops overseas for another thirty days if he felt that this was "necessary to protect U.S. forces." So the law gave the president power to send troops overseas for emergency action and keep them there for a total of ninety days without permission from Congress. At the end of the ninety days, if Congress hadn't declared war or given its blessing to the expeditionary force, the president would have to bring the troops home. In addition, if at some point during those ninety days Congress concluded that the president's actions were just too outrageous to be allowed to continue another minute, it could pass a concurrent resolution—not subject to the president's veto—bringing the boys home immediately.* It was a wobbly law, and perhaps even a dangerous one. Some critics believe that instead of limiting the president, Congress actually wrote into law powers that he previously had not had under the Constitution. In any event, every president has ignored the law—and gotten away with it.

Before expecting much relief from Congress, one should remember that only once in modern times has it reduced the budget for an armed action in which U.S. troops were involved, although members of Congress were well aware that closing the purse would be the quickest and surest way to reduce the scope of the foreign adventure.

The one exception occurred when Congress cut off funds to U.S. troops in Somalia and thereby forced their withdrawal in 1994. This action—all the more amazing because it was done to a Democratic president by a Democratic Congress—was literally forced on Congress by the public's outrage when two U.S. helicopters were shot down in Somalia, eighteen U.S. servicemen were killed, and television showed Somalians dragging an American soldier's body though the streets of Mogadishu.

But that was a very minor military engagement, the type of foreign involvement that recent presidents prefer to call "peacekeeping." Much more typical was Congress's compliance during the Vietnam War.

---

*These restrictions on the president's emergency war powers won the approval of none other than McGeorge Bundy, national security adviser to President Kennedy and President Johnson. There's no reformer like a reformed sinner.

Not until Nixon had withdrawn all U.S. ground troops from Southeast Asia did the House of Representatives timidly cut off funds for the administration's bombing action in Cambodia. This was one decade after the first U.S. bomb was dropped in Southeast Asia. All the horses having been brought home, the alert members of the House were then ready to shut the barn door. Understandably unintimidated by this action, Nixon's spokesmen said they would carry on the bombing raids with or without approval from Congress—and with or without specifically authorized money. On the Senate side, Mike Mansfield, Montana Democrat, mumbled something about this attitude raising a "constitutional crisis," but neither he nor any other senator seemed willing to engage the White House in a showdown fight over the matter. Consequently, the White House bluffed its way into getting congressional approval for a "final" one hundred-day bombing orgy.

In 1976 Congress passed the Arms Control Export Act, giving itself a method by which to block White House weapons export plans.* In 1978 Congress passed the Nuclear Nonproliferation Act, giving itself the right to pass on presidential decisions concerning the export of nuclear fuel and sensitive technology. And in 1985 Congress passed a law saying that any nation breaking the worldwide Nuclear Nonproliferation Treaty (which forbade spreading material for making nuclear weapons to nations that did not already possess them) would be forbidden to buy U.S. nuclear products and technology. Such laws sound good, but they are meaningless, of course, unless enforced. In 1992, after selling nuclear-war material to Iran, Iraq, and Algeria, China signed the nonproliferation treaty; but then it broke its word by selling nuclear materiel to Pakistan. Nevertheless, with giant corporations like General Electric and Westinghouse vigorously lobbying for a chance to sell an estimated $15 billion in nuclear reactors to China over the next ten years, President Clinton ignored evidence that China was a treaty violator and declared that it was eligible to buy our nuclear products. Congress went along with that judgment. Big money often prevails in such matters.

President Carter's sale of planes and other weapons to a variety of Middle Eastern nations ran into a series of delays and hurdles in congressional foreign relations committees, while members debated and fought over details—the friends of Israel arguing one way, the friends

---

*Thus Congress won a negative voice in foreign affairs. The Arms Control Export Act stipulates that the president does not need overt congressional approval of weapons sales but that, on the other hand, if a majority of both houses vote *disapproval* within thirty days after the president announces a sale, then the sale cannot go through.

of Saudi Arabia arguing another, and so on. Even so, Carter generally got his way, for Congress rarely likes to stand in the way of military sales.

Even during what passes for peacetime, Congress quickly falls in line with presidential desires when troops are sent to a potential trouble spot. In 1982 Reagan dispatched marines to help "keep the peace" in Lebanon. To be sure, they were there not to engage in war but to serve as a police force; it was, however, an extremely sensitive situation and the Marines were soon being killed by, and killing, snipers. By the middle of 1983 the situation had become so hot that some members of Congress moved that the War Powers Resolution be invoked, forcing Reagan to bring home the Marines within ninety days. Instead, a bipartisan majority of Congress decided to let Reagan have a free hand in Lebanon for another year and a half. A few weeks after Reagan got that go-ahead, Arabs drove a truck loaded with dynamite into the Marines' barracks in Beirut and killed 230 of the servicemen—the biggest military death toll on one occasion since the Vietnam War; but not even that embarrassing episode moved Congress to limit Reagan's adventure in Lebanon.

Three days after the Marines were blown up in Beirut, Reagan launched another adventure—without consulting members of Congress, much less seeking their approval—on the West Indies island of Grenada, population 109,000. Some close observers felt that the invasion was a charade, swiftly concocted by Reagan to divert public attention from the death of U.S. servicemen in Lebanon. Even Reagan's own press secretary, Larry Speakes, later referred to the invasion as a "public relations" action. Reagan claimed he invaded the island because the unstable, left-leaning government of Grenada posed a threat to the U.S. students in medical school there, but there was never any evidence that the students were in the slightest danger. Reagan was in such a rush that he forgot to inform British Prime Minister Margaret Thatcher of his plans, although Grenada is part of the British commonwealth. The smallest independent nation in the Western Hemisphere, Grenada is about twice the size of Washington, D.C., has only one industry (the manufacture of rum), and virtually no armed forces. Against this mighty kingdom, Reagan sent in 500 Marines and 5,500 paratroopers, backed up by eleven U.S. Navy warships, to evacuate the Americans, and, while at it, to crush the existing government and set up a new government more sympathetic to U.S. policies. Naturally, the Grenadians, even with the help of about 100 armed Cubans who were building an airstrip on the island, didn't stand a chance—Speakes said the encounter was "the equivalent of the

Washington Redskins scheduling my old high school team, the Merigold Wildcats." But the invasion was so stupidly mismanaged that 18 U.S. servicemen were killed and 116 were wounded. It was also a failure as foreign relations (the United Nations condemned U.S. actions by a vote of 108 to 9). But because Congress and most of the public are totally uncritical of gunboat diplomacy, Reagan's action went over big in the opinion polls.*

To be sure, later—much later—House Speaker Tip O'Neill denounced the invasion as a cover-up, saying, "As far as I can see, it was all because the White House wanted the country to forget the tragedy in Beirut." But at the time of the invasion, O'Neill came out solidly behind the president, adding this to the jingoistic remarks of the day: "It is no time for the press of America or we [sic] in public life to be critical of our government when the U.S. Marines and Rangers are down there." Every president knows that the most successful Pied Pipering is done with a military bugle.

The Ultimate Restraint

Is there any way to guarantee that a president will not assume a fire-breathing generalissimo role and run wild? Is there any way to check him effectively if he does? As already mentioned, we must rely on Congress (and, in a distant, vague, philosophical way, the Supreme Court) to check him—and we will often be disappointed in the reluctance of Congress to do so. The ultimate weapon at its disposal is the power of impeachment. It is a power that has been available to Congress since the Constitution was written. It could be used on the very next president who performs his duties in reckless contradiction to what Congress conceives as the national interest. The machinery of impeachment should not be looked upon as an antiquated device to be used only in the most extreme instance of presidential anarchy. It should be seen as a perpetually modern device that can in the most effective way serve as what Hamilton called in *The Federalist* papers "a bridle in the hands of the legislative body upon the executive."

Many will receive this as a crude suggestion, but there is really no reason why a job that the voters hand out on a regular schedule should

---

*The Army was so pleased with its conduct in this toy war that it handed out 8,612 decorations, including 170 for valor. There were more medals awarded than troops on the island (Geoffrey Perret, *A Country Made by War: From the Revolution to Vietnam—the Story of America's Rise to Power* [New York: Random House, 1989], p. 552).

not be taken back on an irregular ad hoc schedule when they dislike the results. No portion of the Constitution is fairer or more democratic than Article II, Section 4, which gives the ultimate power to change the government to the people through their federal representatives. It provides that "The President, Vice President and all civil Officers of the United States, shall be removed from Office on Impeachment for, and conviction of, Treason, Bribery, or other high Crimes and Misdemeanors." That last phrase keeps the situation loose, since it can be made to mean just about anything you want it to mean. In the impeachment of President Andrew Johnson in 1867 for high crimes and misdemeanors, the House of Representatives was instructed to consider as a crime "anything highly prejudicial to the public interest," or "the abuse of discretionary powers from improper motives or for an improper purpose."

In 1985, Congress approved what was called the Boland Amendment, which specifically prohibited the CIA, the Department of Defense, or any intelligence agency—including the White House's National Security Council—from spending any money that "would have the effect of supporting, directly or indirectly, military or paramilitary operations in Nicaragua." Reagan went out of his way to violate that law by selling arms to Iran (some of them through Israel, in violation of the Arms Export Control Act) and using the proceeds secretly to support the war in Nicaragua; and then he repeatedly lied to Congress to cover up his actions. Was this an "abuse of discretionary powers"? Members of Reagan's closest circle, including Attorney General Edwin Meese III, thought so and were sorely afraid that Congress would punish Reagan accordingly.

In 1970, Kenneth O'Donnell, one of the intimates of the White House in President Kennedy's tenure, disclosed in a *Life* magazine article that Kennedy had concluded by 1963 that our participation in the Vietnam War was wrong. O'Donnell claims that Kennedy intended to pull our troops out completely but meant to delay this action until 1965 because he was afraid that to do so sooner would hurt his chances for reelection.

O'Donnell's version of Kennedy's Vietnam intentions has been confirmed by another member of the Kennedy clique.* Had Kennedy lived and had his reasoning been discovered, should he have been impeached and tried? Risking the lives of thousands of American soldiers only for political gain—could this be fairly indicted as "the abuse

---

*See Arthur M. Schlesinger, Jr., *Robert Kennedy and His Times* (Boston: Houghton Mifflin, 1978), p. 660.

of discretionary powers from improper motives or for an improper purpose"?

Or consider the infamous Tonkin Gulf incident, the alleged attack by North Vietnamese naval vessels on U.S. destroyers in the Gulf of Tonkin. Was the attack real or contrived? Was it used to mislead Congress into giving Johnson war powers? The answers began to come out when Daniel J. Ellsberg, who had done a highly secret study of the development of the Vietnam War—the so-called "Pentagon Papers"—leaked the study to *The New York Times*. According to the *Times'* interpretation of the Pentagon Papers, "for six months before the Tonkin Gulf incident in August, 1964, the United States had been mounting clandestine military attacks against North Vietnam while planning to obtain a Congressional resolution that the Administration regarded as the equivalent of a declaration of war."

But an emotional incident was needed. It was created when the U.S. destroyer *Maddox*, on an intelligence patrol in the Gulf of Tonkin, fired on North Vietnamese PT boats and received return fire (one bullet hit but did not damage the *Maddox*; it was hardly enough to escalate a war). This seemed to be a suitably sensitive area, so two days later the *Maddox* was sent back in, this time accompanied by the destroyer *Turner Joy*.

On the night of August 4, some members of the destroyers' crews thought—or said they thought—they were being attacked by enemy craft. No one actually identified enemy vessels on that pitch-black night. A great deal of shooting took place, but so far as can be proved, *all* of it came from our own ships. There is considerable reason to believe that the only serious encounter was with hysteria. Details transmitted to Washington by the destroyers' officers made it clear that they really didn't know what had happened, but suspected the "enemy" was imaginary.

Here are the recollections of James B. Stockdale, who was the senior Navy aviator flying over the ships on the night in question (he would later be shot down over North Vietnam, spend eight years in a North Vietnamese prison, and ultimately rise to the rank of vice admiral):

> I situated myself just where I could scan all horizons best. . . .
> And throughout the hour and 15 minutes of the "sea battle" that the McNamara Pentagon later reported to have "raged," with burning ships and all the rest, there was not one break in the total darkness within the six or eight miles from our destroyers that I could keep under visual surveillance . . . not one American out there ever saw a PT boat. There was absolutely no gunfire except our own, no PT boat

wakes, not a candle light, let alone a burning ship. None could have been there and not have been seen on such a black night.

Yet the White House—backed by the Pentagon and the State Department—inflated the encounter into a critical international situation. They were assisted by such willing suckers as the *Time* reporter who wrote (using data conveniently put in his hands by the Pentagon):

> The night glowed eerily with the nightmarish glare of air-dropped flares and boats' searchlights. For 3½ hours the small boats [of the North Vietnamese] attacked in pass after pass. Ten enemy torpedoes sizzled through the water. Each time the skippers, tracking the fish by radar, maneuvered to evade them. Gunfire and gun smells and shouts stung the air. Two of the enemy boats went down. Then, at 1:30 A.M., the remaining PTs ended the fight, roared off through the night to the north.

Most of that is pure hogwash. The White House conveyed similarly inaccurate information to Congress, and on the basis of that information Congress, by a vote of 502 to 2, passed the Tonkin Gulf Resolution that gave President Johnson carte blanche "to take all necessary steps, including the use of armed force"—and the main act of the tragedy of Vietnam was under way. Later, reporters discovered that Johnson had been carrying in his pocket for weeks a draft of the total power resolution, just waiting for the right opening. The people, the press, the Congress were all tricked.

Does that sound like an impeachable situation?

The question is academic, of course, because not until Johnson had been out of office more than a year did the Senate even work up enough energy to vote its repudiation of the Tonkin Gulf Resolution. Yet weak as the voice of dissent was in Congress, it was stronger than the public voice of dissent. Symbolically, voters turned out of office the two senators (Gruening and Morse) who voted against the Tonkin Gulf Resolution. It was the weak insistence from within Congress, not the public's even weaker complaint, that persuaded the Johnson administration periodically to try a bombing pause. As late as the spring of 1968 the electorate was still urging Congress—by 52 percent to 30 percent, according to a Harris poll—to pursue the Vietnam conflict, even if it meant ignoring domestic ills. The reason doubtless had something to do with the chilly observation of Dr. Arthur Burns, chairman of the Federal Reserve Board: "The military-industrial complex has acquired a constituency including factory workers, clerks, secretaries, even grocers and barbers." Adds Jack Raymond, the former *New York Times* Pentagon reporter: "The military budget provides $6,000 for flowers for American battle monuments. Flower growers, too, can be part of the military-industrial complex."

In short, so long as the economy was booming (and there was an unparalleled run of prosperity during the Johnson administration), it would have taken a foreign policy disaster of unimaginable proportions to turn the public—or its more shining image, Congress—to thoughts of impeachment on account of a war concocted by a president.

The electorate didn't resoundingly declare that it wanted the government to get out of Vietnam until the nation's economy had fallen into a sharp recession under President Nixon, partly as a result of the war. The enormous costs of keeping personnel in Vietnam had drained money away from the Pentagon's "normal" research and development contracts, away from the "normal" military industries (planes, tanks, naval craft—none of which had been manufactured for Vietnam's mostly jungle and rice-paddy warfare in the quantities that a traditional war would have demanded), and away from other federally subsidized industries. The boom of the early war years faded. In 1969 the hard-hat construction workers were beating up young people who dared to parade on behalf of peace. By 1971 the hard hats, many of them unemployed, were joining anti-war demonstrations. Not until they had the leisure of waiting in line for their unemployment checks did many people feel the shame of the My Lai massacre* and pause to question the morality of spreading the war (into Cambodia and Laos) with the excuse of wanting to shorten it.

Likewise, from the Second World War almost to the present, a majority of Americans approved whatever military budgets were requested by their presidents, since these requests were always made in the cause of anticommunism. Not until the unemployment rolls in 1982 reached proportions not seen since the Great Depression of the 1930s did a sizable percentage of the electorate decide, as shown in opinion polls, that perhaps it would be wise to spend a little less fighting Reds overseas in order that we have more money to fight hunger in this country.

Since is hardly improves politics to denounce a president for doing something a majority of his constituents for so long considered to be

---

*On March 16, 1968, a squad of U.S. soldiers massacred 122 unarmed men, women, and children in the South Vietnam village of My Lai; some of the younger women were raped before they were murdered. Only one member of the squad, an officer, was ever tried; though convicted, he spent no time in prison.

patriotic, perhaps we must come back finally to some vague, far-off dream that—by education or voodoo or some other as yet untried method—the American people, the ultimate source of presidential power, will become less supportive of the worst impulses of our generals and hard-line diplomats. Henry Steele Commager was right on target when he said:

> Abuse of power by presidents is a reflection, and perhaps a consequence, of abuse of power by the American people and nation. . . . As we have greater power than any other nation, so we should display greater moderation in using it and greater humility in justifying it. . . . In the long run, then, the abuse of the executive power cannot be separated from the abuse of national power.

But the changing of the national character by lecturing to the people and praying for them to lay aside their ugly impulses is, to say the least, a long-range, almost metaphysical goal. Meanwhile, it will do no harm to inquire further into the question of how we as a nation developed such a militant frame of mind.

CHAPTER 3

Cold War, National Security, and the Military

Our government has kept us in a perpetual state of fear—kept us in a continuous stampede of patriotic fervor—with the cry of a grave national emergency. . . . Yet, in retrospect, these disasters seem never to have happened, seem never to have been real.

GENERAL DOUGLAS MACARTHUR
mid-1957, quoted in The Military-Industrial Complex
by Sidney Lens

IT WAS QUITE A CHRISTMAS GIFT FOR THE NON-COMMUNIST world.

Early in the evening of December 25, 1991, Mikhail Gorbachev took a seat in a room across the hall from his Kremlin office and stared into a television camera. In a twenty-minute, remarkably unemotional address to the Soviet nation, he informed his television audience that he was stepping down as president of the Union of Soviet Socialist Republics.

Although he did not say it in so many words, what he meant was that the USSR had passed into history. It was dead. Kaput. Finished. The union was thereby splintered into fifteen republics, the largest of which, Russia, would now inherit whatever faded power and glory remained of the USSR.

A few minutes later, the Soviet flag above the Kremlin was lowered and the Russian tricolor of white, blue, and red horizontal stripes was

raised in its stead. It was an eerie moment. The end of the Soviet empire—created three generations earlier by the Communist revolution—was one of the most dramatic moments of the twentieth century, and yet the empire seemed to disappear almost casually.

And its disappearance was one of history's most stunning surprises. It seemed that few outsiders—or at least nobody in a position of power in this country—fully understood all the reasons for the Soviet debacle. Jack F. Matlock, Jr., the last U.S. ambassador to the Soviet Union, who had spent his life studying that country, admitted he didn't know what the decisive events were that brought it about.

Although for the past few years there had been tremors of rebellion in the outlying republics of the USSR, none of our spy agencies had foreseen the collapse. They had failed to fully comprehend what in hindsight was one of the most obvious clues—the Soviet economy was falling apart. The grotesquely bloated military machine, the inefficient government-owned industries, the obese bureaucracy, the all-encompassing welfare programs had simply bled the nation dry. The USSR was broke.

Russia's transition from the one-party tyranny of communism to a rickety democracy (and an equally rickety free-market economy) has been marred by many failures, and there is still no certainty that it will succeed. But at least for the moment it seems unlikely that anything as menacing as the old, once-powerful USSR will reappear in that part of the globe.

Russia is in such sorry condition that the United States—fearful that if things get too desperate in that country it might turn to another militaristic dictator for salvation—has even given its old enemy economic assistance. Corruption is rampant in Russia's business world and in its government, which has been penetrated by the Russian Mafia. Agricultural production is at a thirty-year low. Scores of factories have closed, and those that remain open commonly pay less than $100 a month in wages. Unemployment, hunger, and despair have turned many to drugs—there are more than two million addicts in Russia.

Life for the common Russian soldier is worse than for his civilian counterpart. The standard conscript's pay in 1997 was $3 a month and army privates received 5,000 rubles (about 70 cents) a day for food—50 percent less than the food allotment for prisoners. Fifteen naval cadets starved to death in 1997. It is commonplace to see soldiers begging in the streets of Moscow. Only 10 percent of Russian servicemen are issued boots or topcoats (in Moscow, the average high temperature in January is twenty-one degrees and the average low is nine degrees) or full uniforms. The average pay for officers is $300 a month, but 100,000 families of officers are homeless. It's no surprise that each year more than 500 soldiers kill themselves.

Russia's armed forces are so skimpily equipped that analysts say they could fully supply only one of its seventy-eight divisions for battle. In every port, its naval vessels lie rotting in their berths. Once the Soviet boasted the largest military machine in the world. Today that machine has virtually disappeared and is not likely to be reappear soon, for Russia is spending less than $20 billion a year on defense— about 8 percent of what the United States spends.

The High Cost of Winning

In other words, we have lost our most feared adversary and the Cold War is over. What an incredible relief! For nearly half a century, or more than twice as long as most readers of this book have been alive, there was the constant threat that the Cold War might turn hot. With the lifting of that threat, the outlook of the entire industrial world and of many developing nations began to change. But profound questions remain, and historian Ronald Steel asks some of the most difficult:

> What happened to our enemy? For decades our leaders warned that this evil, yet somehow seductive, force was poised to take over the world. . . . Yet in the end there was no colossus: only an inept, strife-ridden, and impoverished regime—a gigantic Potemkin village.
>
> What were we so afraid of? Indeed, were our leaders really afraid of the power of the Soviets to seduce and intimidate the entire world? Or did they find it to be a useful enemy that allowed them to build up the military and economic power that created what has been justly called the American Century?

What the Cold War cost the United States and the Soviet Union in lives lost (in such places as Vietnam, Korea, and Afghanistan) and in an existence filled with fear and hate is beyond measure. As for the enormous economic damage done by the Cold War to the Soviet Union, by goading it into military preparedness it did not need and could not afford, that is now easy to see. But what about the damage to us? Professor Steel gets to the heart of that question: "Yes, the other side lost. But did we win? And if so, was it because of our superior strength and values? Or did we merely have deeper pockets than our foe? And what does it mean to win?"

It means we are the only super power left in the world, but that sometimes seems to carry as many burdens as blessings. Apparently our political leaders think that even though we have no major enemy in the offing, we must continue to spend as much on military affairs as all other nations in the world combined. It also means that—largely because of our gigantic military budget over the last half century and particularly during the 1980s—we now have a national debt of nearly $6 trillion (yes, trillion), on which the U.S. taxpayer pays $250 billion each year in interest alone. For that $250 billion, the taxpayer receives nothing at all in return; it's just down the drain.

Some experts believe that our total defense spending for the Cold War years (with 1990 the make-believe cutoff point) was roughly $10 trillion—or enough to buy everything produced in the United States in the last two years—every factory, every skyscraper, every house, every plane, every auto, every stick of furniture, every piece of clothing, all the meat and vegetables and fruit, all the lumber and cotton, all the liquor, all the books and newspapers, all the art, all the movies and television shows, all the sporting events, just everything—plus pay for all the labor that went into them.*

To imagine the *moral* enormity of the defense budget, consider the statement of President Dwight Eisenhower in 1953, at the bitterest moment of the Cold War, as he saw the direction the world was turning:

> Every gun that is made, every warship launched, every rocket fired signifies, in the final sense, a theft from those who hunger and are not fed, those who are cold and not clothed. This world in arms is not spending money alone. It is spending the sweat of its laborers, the genius of its scientists, the hopes of its children. . . . This is not a way of life at all in any true sense. Under the cloud of threatening war, it is humanity hanging from a cross of iron.

If the Cold War robbed us of the chance to build a finer material life for all Americans, it also robbed us of some integrity. In the name of national security, we distorted our traditional concepts of honesty and allowed large segments of our industrial world to profit from sham. Aided and abetted by high officers of the armed forces who wanted to hold more power, the defense industry grew fat (as we will show more fully later in this chapter) by building many weapons systems that

---

*There is much talk these days about caring for the homeless. Our Cold War defense spending could have built *one hundred million* $100,000 homes. Among those who made the $10 trillion estimate was Carl Sagan, who fairly arrived at that figure by using not only Pentagon costs but appropriate fractions of outlays for "international security" at the State Department, the Energy Department, NASA, and the Veterans Administration.

were not needed and that were so poorly made that they gave us little defense. But the corruption was the fault not only of generals and admirals and industrialists, it was also the fault of Congress, which made no real effort to reform the system, and of the thousands of citizens who were willing to close their eyes to corruption as long as they got jobs from it. And because the military budget always included generous grants to university scientists, campus leaders were very timid about criticizing the corruption.

Dr. George Wald, in a famous speech at the Massachusetts Institute of Technology, argued that the military budget "is buying up everything in sight: industries, banks, investors, universities, and lately it seems also to have bought up the labor unions."

Wald was overdramatizing to make a point. Not everyone touched by defense money is "bought." But heavy reliance on defense money for livelihood does tend to warp an individual's or an institution's view of the defense budget and does tend to generate tolerance for the spending (and wasting) of vast sums on guns that might more usefully be spent on housing or roads or medical care. One does not usually think of universities as part of the military–industrial complex, but in any list of the 100 companies receiving the largest dollar volume of Pentagon prime contracts, one is likely to find institutions such as MIT, where Dr. Wald voiced his criticism, ranking right up there with the likes of Tenneco and IBM as suppliers of what it takes to run the military machine.

Today, the arms manufacturers and the military constitute an elite, and they have taken advantage of their new status by intruding into every important element of civilian life.

More than 8 million Americans are involved in the defense business, one way or another, and "these 8 million Americans have a vested interest in keeping the Cold War going," says retired Admiral Gene LaRocque, former head of the Center for Defense Information, a privately supported think tank.

The military–industrial complex has become a little kingdom of its own. The $260 billion defense budget includes $50 billion for buying new weapons and almost $40 billion for research and development each year (69 percent of all federal research money goes into defense). The capitol of this kingdom lies just across the Potomac River from Washington, D.C. The world's largest office building, with twenty miles of corridors and 10,000 filing cabinets and a veritable army—23,000—of military bureaucrats, this capitol is politely known as the Pentagon, but those who know it best sometimes refer to it as Fort Fumble or Camp Chaos.

To rationalize the ever-increasing military budget of the Cold War and win the support of taxpayers, our leaders frightened us by concocting "perils" that really didn't exist. The most effective peril was the claim that we were falling behind the Soviets in military power. The "bomber gap" bogey of the Eisenhower years was followed by the phony "missile gap" of the Kennedy years, which was followed by the "megatonnage gap" of the Goldwater campaign, which cropped up again in Reagan's first campaign. Nixon had a "security gap" campaign in 1968. Four years later his secretary of defense cranked up a new gap—the "free world security gap"—which was nicely vague enough to mean just about anything. And when they can't think up a good gap, politicians and Pentagon officials wanting to inflate the budget could always fall back on the claim that we were losing "momentum" to the Soviet Union in the arms race.*

They also whipped up our belligerency by claiming that we were in great danger from tiny outposts of communism, some as far away as Southeast Asia, some as close as the Caribbean, and this was their excuse to meddle in the affairs of other nations, even to invade them. Such actions have often been illogical, even downright farcical. Why, for instance, does our government allow U.S. tourists to travel to, and U.S. industrialists to trade with, potentially our most powerful ideological enemy, communist China, while forbidding U.S. tourists to travel to, and U.S. businessmen to trade with, our weak and struggling communist neighbor, Cuba, just ninety miles away? A great deal that happened in the Cold War, and still happens, doesn't make much sense.

Are these troubles inevitable? If we had been guided by more common sense and cool headedness, could we have escaped them? Can we escape them still—since many are continuing troubles? Probably.

---

*If it is any comfort, the leaders of the supposedly "enemy" nations went through the same absurd ritual. When Eisenhower was president, he was host to Communist party boss Nikita Khrushchev. One afternoon they took a stroll, and a conversation took place that Khrushchev recounted in his memoirs.

Eisenhower opened by asking, "Tell me, Mr. Khrushchev, how do you decide the question of funds for military expenses? Perhaps first I should tell you how it is with us. It's like this: My military leaders say, `Mr. President, we need such and such a sum for such and such a program.' I say, `Sorry, we don't have the funds.' They say, `We have reliable information that the Soviet Union has already allocated funds for their own such program.' So I give in. That's how they wring the money out of me. Now tell me, how is it with you?"

"It's just the same," said crusty old Khrushchev. "They say, `Comrade Khrushchev, look at this! The Americans are developing such and such a system.' I tell them there's no money. So we discuss it some more, and I end up giving them the money they asked for" (quoted by Clayton Fritchey, syndicated column, June 16, 1973).

But to some extent our hardships and mistakes have been the natural result of being new at our present role; they add up to the price we have had to pay for becoming a global nation. To anyone born in the last five decades, such a statement may seem rather strange. To such a person, being "global" will seem the normal condition for this nation. But historically, it is a relatively new role, a relatively new perspective for us.

From Isolation to Intervention

During the Revolutionary War, the French were our allies and fought by our side against the British. But we canceled that treaty of alliance and went to war on the seas against the French (a sort of informal war) in 1796, when the French treated our commerce in what we considered an arrogant fashion. From that year until 1941, when we were pulled into the Second World War, "the United States never entered into close political association with any European power." In his Farewell Address, President Washington had warned against "entangling alliances." For most of our history, America's leaders looked upon that advice as the highest wisdom.

Until the First World War (1914–1918), no general war induced our participation; and when we went late into that war (not entering until 1917), we mingled our soldiers with our allies without at the same time mingling our political destinies. President Wilson's efforts to bring the United States into the League of Nations were repulsed by the U.S. Senate in 1919, and the electorate turned down the "League" candidate in the presidential election of 1920.

We were a people who wholeheartedly believed in, and had had an almost unbroken tradition of, isolationism for the first 170 years of our national existence.

That all changed with the Japanese attack on Pearl Harbor on December 7, 1941, and our entry into the Second World War. On this point Ronald Steel expounds:

> The change from the old isolationism to the new interventionism flowed almost inevitably from the Second World War. The unavoidable war against fascism revealed the bankruptcy of isolationism and destroyed the illusion that America could barricade herself from the immoralities of a corrupt world. . . . As a result of her participation in the war, America became not only a great world power but *the* world power. Her fleets roamed all the seas, her military bases extended

around the earth's periphery, her soldiers stood guard from Berlin to Okinawa, and her alliances spanned the earth.

Some historians might dispute Steel's insistence on the unavoidability of the Second World War, but there is no question that the war moved us irretrievably out of the backwater of isolationism and swept us helter-skelter into the broad and turbulent stream of interventionism. The war left the United States as the only major power capable of meeting the threat of "global communism" (as it was seen then) posed by the Soviet Union and China. As a result, for most of the past half century three things dominated American foreign policy: (1) fear of communism, (2) militarism and nuclear weapons, and (3) concern with the affairs of other nations, including actual interference in them.

Oversimplified, all of those interrelated influences were offshoots of one thing: rivalry with the Soviet Union. They can be stated in a different way as goals: to weaken the communist alliance, to avoid an atomic war, and to draw the uncommitted nations of the world into the United States' orbit of influence.

The goals of the Soviet Union were precisely the same, but from its own perspective, of course: to weaken the Western alliance, to avoid an atomic war, and to draw the uncommitted nations into its orbit. One can always say, of course, that the Soviet Union pursued its goals unethically, fiendishly, callously, or whatever, but that does not change the fact that Soviet goals were really no different from our own. And Soviet suspicions of us were exactly the same as our suspicions of them—the worst.

To be sure, the United States called the Soviet Union an ally in the Second World War, but that did not mean we liked or admired them; we didn't. It only meant that, for a very few years, we found them useful. But the last shot of the war had scarcely been fired before we squared off against the Soviets: capitalism versus communism. The Cold War had begun.

Reagan: The Super Cold Warrior

If we focus on the 1980s, a decade shaped by Ronald Reagan's presidency, we can see how recently the full fervor of the Cold War was with us.

When Reagan became president, he announced plans to spend $1.7 trillion over the next five years on arms and warriors to defend this country against the Soviet Union, which he judged to be "an evil empire," "the focus of evil in the modern world." He called on Americans to join him in his crusade against the Soviets with a religious fervor because "we are enjoined by Scripture and the Lord Jesus Christ to oppose . . . with all our might" the "sin and evil in the world."

One trillion seven hundred billion dollars is as much as it cost to operate the *entire* government—not just the military arm of it—for the first sixty-five years of this century. In short, Reagan proposed lavishing upon his military program in just five years what eleven other presidents spent to see the country through the First and Second World Wars, the Korean War, the start of the Vietnam War, and fifty-eight peacetime years scattered in between.

The enormous increase in the defense budget was justified, Reagan argued, because the Soviet Union was spending 12 to 14 percent of its gross national product on arms every year while we were spending only about 5 to 6 percent. (What he didn't tell the public was that the United States' gross national product was more than double that of the Soviet Union.)

The Reagan five-year plan for a military buildup prompted 575 opinion-shapers, including twenty-five former cabinet members (among them, two former secretaries of defense), plus dozens of the nation's top bankers, corporate chairmen, lawyers, and university presidents, Republican as well as Democratic, to write an open letter to Reagan. The letter, published in a two-page advertisement in *The New York Times* to arouse public opinion for their effort, pleaded with him to reduce defense spending immediately and to plan for a "more gradual and affordable multiyear buildup in [the nation's] defense capability."

It was hard to understand what had prompted this impressive display of concern from these Establishment people. Did they think Reagan had flipped? Was he going in a direction so different from his predecessors? Was he a uniquely fierce militarist?

Unique in degree, perhaps, but certainly not unique in kind. Shoveling megabucks to the Pentagon was nothing new. Doing it in the name of capitalistic piety while denouncing communistic sin was old hat. And supporting defense budget requests with misleading data was a time-honored technique used by every administration at least since the Second World War.

If Reagan was following tradition in the way he stoked the Pentagon furnace, he was also following tradition in the way he loved to play the nuclear game and to mix into the affairs of smaller countries. In 1982 the U.S. military had five hundred thousand times the nuclear destructive power in its arsenal that it had had in 1945. But that wasn't enough for Reagan, and by fiscal 1984 he was spending twice as much for nuclear arms as had been spent just four years earlier. He was doing it with the hoary argument that if we didn't equip ourselves with more and still more nuclear warheads we would be vulnerable to a Soviet "first strike"—meaning that they could clobber us with so many atomic bombs that they would have little to fear from a "second strike" retaliation. And by the end of his first three years, Reagan had invaded Grenada, "policed" Lebanon, and dragged the United States into the civil wars of Central America as patron, adviser, and covert participator. In each instance he said he acted to checkmate "communist influence." He moved into Central America with an argument that was as questionable as it was threadbare: If we didn't stop the communists in the wretchedly poor villages of that region, he argued, they might ultimately be a force to be reckoned with north of the Rio Grande. "If guerrilla violence succeeds" in El Salvador, Reagan said, that country (whose population is less than half of Florida's) "will join Cuba and Nicaragua as a base for spreading fresh violence to Guatemala, Honduras, even Costa Rica. The killing will increase, and so will the threat to Panama, the Canal and ultimately Mexico." So, he said, what's "at stake in the Caribbean and Central America . . . is the United States' national security."

It is known as the "domino theory" or the "rotten apple" theory: If one country falls—or one goes bad—pretty soon, by an inevitable progression, our own domino will fall; our own apple will turn rotten. Far-fetched? Many thought so. Many considered it to be a childishly simple explanation of the threat from communist aggression. But presidents used it without shame.

Speaking for President Truman in 1947, Secretary of State Dean Acheson warned that "like apples in a barrel infected by one rotten one, the corruption of Greece [by communism] would infect" Asia, Europe, and Africa. If "we and we alone" did not step forward with military aid that would stop the communists in Greece, he suggested, we might fight them on the shores of Maryland. President Johnson once said that if Vietnam fell to the communists, the United States might have to start defending San Francisco against them.

Indeed, the most remarkable thing about the conduct of foreign policy is that there were so few significant changes in style and viewpoint in the forty years from Truman to Bush. They were frozen by fear of the "Red Menace."

Fear of Communism

Communist doctrine advocates public ownership of everything. Theoretically, it outlaws economic competition and economic inequality, and it would create a classless society in which each citizen contributed according to his or her abilities and received according to his or her needs—no more, and no less.

On paper, such social formulas have the soothing appeal of utopia. But true communism, as a government in which the people have total power, has never been practiced anywhere in the world. Instead, the most important communist experiments, in the Soviet Union and China, have been dictatorships functioning like all other ideological dictatorships, and Americans have been wise to their defects. The vast majority of Americans have never shown any interest whatsoever in adopting communism. To the citizens of this country—which William Howard Taft judged to be "really the most conservative country in the world"—communism is probably the least appealing of any major political ideology alive in the world today.

Of the dozens of thousands of men and women elected to Congress, only one—Vito Marcantonio—ever publicly acknowledged sympathy for the Communist party USA. Communists won only 100,000 out of 40 million ballots cast in the presidential election of 1932—a time of economic disaster, and by the mid-1950s the party in this country was as extinct as the dinosaur. Most Americans have never laid eyes on a real communist except in the newsreels, and they would have a hard time even defining the meaning of communism. And yet, strangely enough, nothing arouses Americans to such panic as the suggestion that they are in danger of being brainwashed or "taken over" by communists. There were two periods in this century when the nation was seized by a mindless frenzy of anticommunism. The first was the Great Red Scare of 1919–1920, when Attorney General A. Mitchell Palmer sent federal agents on illegal raids (they had no warrants) sweeping through "suspicious" bowling alleys, pool halls, cafes, club rooms, and even homes to seize anyone who looked like a "communist." Hundreds of "suspicious" aliens were, without hearing or trial, hauled aboard an Army cargo ship and shipped to Finland, for their final train ride to the Soviet Union.

The second period of hysteria came in the late 1940s and early 1950s. This time the intensity and craziness of the anti-Red fervor was symbolized by Indiana's requirement that professional wrestlers sign an oath of loyalty to the United States. Tennessee ordered the death penalty for those seeking to overthrow the *state* government. The Mississippi legislature passed myriad laws hemming in the Communist party—and its one member in that state. In New Rochelle, New York, the city commission ordered all communists to register; only one citizen showed up at police headquarters to comply—he thought the new ordinance applied to *commuters*.

These periods of hysteria were largely created, and always exploited, by some portions of America's Establishment—its more reactionary politicians, businessmen, and publishers—who acted as though they honestly feared communism was imminently threatening to seize the electorate's mind and heart. This fear, whether real or contrived, was useful to them, for it gave them an excuse to denounce any liberal reformer, labor agitator, or civil rights leader as "communistic." Most reform movements that would upset the status quo had to run this gauntlet.

The supposed threat of communism also gave our political leaders an easy excuse for supporting some of the world's most repressive right-wing rulers, even some who were major drug dealers: They were "anticommunist" so they were "our friends." It was also used as an excuse for supporting a gargantuan military establishment that bled domestic programs of money.

From Ally to Enemy

During the Second World War, political leaders had to soft-pedal the anticommunist line because the Soviet Union was our ally in the war against the German–Italian–Japanese axis. On April 25, 1945, American and Soviet troops met on the banks of the River Elbe and embraced. The two great powers of the world, allies then, had come together, severing forever the Third Reich. But within two years the governments of the United States and the Soviet Union were totally wary, viewing each other as the primary enemy. U.S. leaders did not try to hide their feelings that communists posed a much graver threat to our future than had the German Nazis or the Italian Fascists or the Japanese war party.

When Chiang Kai-shek, China's nationalist leader, was driven off the mainland and China fell to the communists in 1949, this was offered as proof positive that the red tentacles were moving swiftly to embrace the world. The rise of the "iron curtain" across Europe, behind which the Soviet Union solidified its domination over most East European countries, was seen as further proof, as was the postwar strength of communists in French and Italian labor unions, the communist coup in Czechoslovakia, the revolution triggered by communists in Greece, and countless provocations on every continent.

These were indeed troubling developments that our leaders could not take lightly. Nor could they be faulted for feeling threatened by the devious maneuvers and belligerent talk of Soviet Premier Joseph Stalin. In February 1946, less than a year after the meeting at the Elbe, he spoke of the impossibility of peace in the face of "the present capitalist development of the world economy." Understandably, many of our leaders thought this sounded very much like the preamble to a declaration of war against the United States. President Truman was convinced that "force is the only thing the Russians understand. . . . The Russians [are] planning world conquest." From their point of view, the Soviets interpreted our actions in the same way. On January 29, 1949, the Soviet Foreign Ministry stated flatly, "The Soviet Union is compelled to reckon with the fact that the ruling circles of the U.S.A. and Great Britain have adopted an openly aggressive political course, the final aim of which is to establish by force Anglo-American domination over the world."

For the first dozen years after the Second World War—and especially during such periods as the Soviet blockade of Berlin in 1948—the possibility of open combat between the two countries was constant. So grim was the atmosphere that any proposal for dealing with the Soviets short of nuclear war was hailed as moderate. This was the response to the anonymous article in the now-famous July 1947 issue of *Foreign Affairs* (subsequently it came out that the author was George F. Kennan, chargé d' affaires at the American Embassy in Moscow), in which it was predicted that "the Soviet pressure against the free institutions of the Western world is something that can be contained by the adroit and vigilant application of counter-force at a series of constantly shifting geographical and political points . . . but which cannot be charmed or talked out of existence." This proposal of mere "containment" rather than a policy of annihilation of the Soviets was hailed as the talk of a peacemaker.

There was much that was rotten in the containment policy: It rationalized our support of any government, even the most inhuman right-wing dictatorship, so long as it was anticommunist; and it accustomed American leaders to sticking their "dirty, bloody, dollar-crooked fingers" (in General David Shoup's phrase) into the affairs of other countries. But for all that, containment was not a hot war. Although it was a policy that strengthened Europe by a threatening presence—the militarily well-equipped and well-manned North

Atlantic Treaty Organization—containment was mainly operative through economic assistance. The United States, through its financial aid to countries impoverished by the war (the Marshall Plan pumped $12 billion into the Western European economy in three years), achieved a kind of sullen stalemate with the Soviet Union. Those in the Pentagon who urged that the United States launch a "preventive" nuclear attack on the Soviet Union—urgings that were still heard even after it was learned in September 1949 that the Soviets had discovered how to build the atomic bomb—were no longer able to get as many followers.*

The "containment" policy—although it was itself aggressive, tremendously expensive, and risky—was built around the hope that if we managed to stall long enough without actually going to war with the Soviet Union, somehow the passage of time would soften the Soviet heart and open the Iron Curtain, permitting the two powers to coexist in peace if not in friendship.

The Ideological Frenzy

The fault of our political leaders at this time lay not in establishing a defense against possible Soviet attacks, but in stirring up the general public far beyond the level necessary to guarantee support for their actions. For example, in 1947 Turkey and especially Greece were torn by communist provocations. President Truman wanted to send economic and military aid to the established governments in those two countries to counteract the Soviet aid to the communist insurgents. Senator Arthur Vandenberg, chairman of the Foreign Relations Committee, and Undersecretary of State Dean Acheson persuaded Truman that he should present his request to Congress not simply as aid for two na-

---

*In his book *Neither Liberty Nor Safety: A Hard Look at U.S. Military Policy and Strategy* (New York: Holt, 1966), General Nathan F. Twining, who had served as chairman of the Joint Chiefs of Staff from 1957 to 1960, recounts how the National Security Council set up a national security policy, approved by Truman in April 1950, in which the concept of "containment" was reaffirmed. But this concept had some stiff competition, writes Twining, from those who advocated the "pre-emptive action" of clobbering the Soviet Union with atomic bombs, the theory being that "the world would become much too dangerous to live in if the Soviet Union were allowed time to develop a nuclear arsenal. While preventative war may be considered immoral, a much greater immorality would result if we were to allow our enemies to destroy our values and inherit the world." At that NSC meeting in 1950, says Twining, the hit-them-first argument "was presented and defended by some very dedicated Americans. However, the Administration ruled out this course of action."

tions but as the first blow to be struck in the cosmic conflict with communism. Truman bought the argument, and on March 12 he went to Congress with what was to be known as the Truman Doctrine—promising a global commitment "to support free peoples who are resisting attempted subjugation by armed minorities or by outside pressures," not only in Greece and Turkey but everywhere.

It was a hollow, grandstanding promise that could not possibly be fulfilled. It raised false hopes (and subsequent disillusionment) in many oppressed nations, and perhaps worst of all, as former Ambassador Charles Yost has explained, it "helped create an enduring and militant climate of opinion in the United States . . . which, two decades later, was to lure three other American presidents into the morass of Vietnam."

Exaggerating the threat of communism became a vice in both major political parties. It was a technique used to whip up a lather of enthusiasm in Congress for steadily escalating defense budgets, and to whip up hysteria among voters to win power. Democratic and Republican politicians entered into a frenzied competition to appear the most "patriotic," the most "anticommunist"—which was supposed to equate with pro-American. It was during the late 1940s and the first half of the 1950s that Republican politicians such as then-Senator Richard Nixon and Senator Joseph McCarthy, an alcoholic, pathological liar, won national attention as anticommunist demagogues.

In 1952, when Nixon was Dwight Eisenhower's vice-presidential running mate in what was probably the bitterest campaign of this century, he also gladly served as the party's hatchetman, boasting of his role: "If the record itself smears, let it smear. If the dry rot of corruption and communism, which has eaten deep into our body politic during the past seven years, can only be chopped out with a hatchet—then let's call for a hatchet." Nixon said that Eisenhower's opponent, Adlai Stevenson, the former governor of Illinois and a highly moral and patriotic fellow, "holds a Ph.D. degree from Acheson's College of Cowardly Communist Containment." (Dean Acheson had been President Truman's secretary of state.) Even Eisenhower, a war hero, who was so popular with the electorate that he could easily have stood above the Nixon level, allowed himself to be dragged into the mud and failed to speak up in defense of his great Army colleague, George Marshall, when right-wingers called Marshall a traitor. The right wing accused the Democrats of harboring traitors, of selling out China to the communists, and of being too soft with the Soviets. To prove that they were just as "patriotic" as Nixon and McCarthy, Democrats such as Senator Hubert Humphrey proposed outlawing the Communist party and setting up concentration camps in which to imprison "unpatriotic" Americans during crises.

This senseless competition in demagogy to win the support of the electorate had a devastating effect on America's foreign policy. It left no room for moderation, for flexibility. Only the most rigid, hard-line belligerence could be offered by politicians, unless they wanted to be smeared as "communist dupes." Only because he was a military hero could General Douglas MacArthur say in 1952, without damage to his reputation:

> Indeed, it is part of the general pattern of misguided policy that our country is now geared to an arms economy which was bred in an artificially induced psychosis of war hysteria and nurtured upon an incessant propaganda of fear. While such an economy may produce a sense of seeming prosperity for the moment, it rests on an illusionary foundation of complete unreliability and renders among our political leaders almost a greater fear of peace than is their fear of war.

The "incessant propaganda of fear" continued to be the basis of American foreign policy down to the present. It was difficult for our leaders to change, for they were captives of their own success as propagandists. Having sold the electorate on the evils of communism, they found it difficult—even politically dangerous—to try to unsell them.

Escape from such a dilemma sometimes is accomplished only in the most ironic fashion. For example, Richard Nixon built a career by denouncing Democrats for being soft on the communist Chinese and the Soviets. As a result of such charges, the Democrats feared acting too friendly with either nation. They especially avoided suggesting that we should reopen diplomatic channels to communist China or even support its membership in the United Nations. But when Nixon became president, *he* reopened friendly channels with China and established detente with the Soviet Union—and he got by with it. After all, nobody could possibly accuse the great communist witch-hunter of being a communist dupe.

And yet this turn of events also shows the tragedy that resulted from a generation of anticommunist demagogy. So spooked were the Democrats by it all that when President Carter, a Democrat, succeeded Nixon and Ford, he felt no urgency to continue the mellower atmosphere established by Nixon. Although formal diplomatic relations were restored with China, detente with the Soviet Union was played down. Instead, foreign policy continued to be built around the fear of communist expansion. The arms race picked up again and defense spending continued to rise.

As a candidate Carter had warned against "an inordinate fear of communism," but as president he began to talk about "ominous" Soviet aggression. And he apparently felt obliged to sound like a tough guy, as when he told a cheering crowd of Texans, "We're not going to let the Soviet Union push us around."

With the election of Ronald Reagan, much of the shrill anticommunist vocabulary of the 1950s was returned to high fashion, at least in presidential politics. Throughout his 1980 campaign, he tried to arouse the electorate (with considerable success) with warnings that Carter had let our defenses down, when in fact Carter was spending much more for arms than Nixon or Ford had. "We're in greater danger today than we were the day after Pearl Harbor," Reagan told *The New York Times.* "Our military is absolutely incapable of defending this country." He said then, as he had been saying for years and kept saying after his election, that we were second in military strength to the Soviet Union, although Reagan's own officials at the Pentagon and the State Department admitted the two nations' forces were equal in strength. Shades of the 1950s, he even accused persons supporting the nuclear freeze movement of being dupes of communist "foreign agents."

To be sure, seven years into his presidency Reagan took the amazing step (in the same way Nixon's China overture had been amazing) of signing with the Soviet Union the first superpower agreement actually abolishing some nuclear weapons. Had the great hater of what he called the "evil empire" suddenly grown soft on communism? Not at all. He had been forced into his new position by two outside pressures. First, because of his involvement in the Iran-contra scandal, Reagan had reached his lowest point of public support. The surest way of regaining some of that support, as all public opinion polls had shown, was to lessen tensions with the Soviet Union. Second, Reagan was pushed to the treaty table by the new Soviet premier, Mikhail Gorbachev, who had come into power in 1985 with the clear intent of reducing global tensions as a way to cut back on the Soviet Union's military budget and thereby, perhaps, save that nation from an economic debacle. Gorbachev was so insistently willing to reduce nuclear capabilities that Reagan could not say *nyet.*

But the political and economic use of anticommunism was not yet quite dead. In his victorious campaign for the presidency in 1988, George Bush fell back on some of the old smear–scare tactics. He accused his opponent of being "soft on defense" and of being a "card-carrying member of the ACLU," resonant of the "soft on communism" and "card-carrying communist" epithets of the McCarthy era.

Military Foreign Policy

Throughout the Cold War, our military policy was based on what Winston Churchill, one of its creators, called a "balance of terror." The theory was that both the Soviet Union and the American government knew that no matter which side launched the atomic attack, the answering attack from the other side would be just as devastating, and at least one hundred million would die in each nation. Therefore, realizing that "victory" was impossible and that only mutual suicide would result, neither side would want to strike the first blow. Paradoxically, many saw the balance of terror as a benign influence, and, in a perverse way, it was.

But there was another level at which our policy makers could still think of war: the old-fashioned way. And so they also responded to real and imagined threats by circling the wagons, so to speak, with conventional weapons. "Conventional weapons" had such a comforting sound to them that they bought enough in the 1960s to bolster Secretary of Defense Robert McNamara's two and a half war contingency plan: that is, enough weapons to *simultaneously* fight Russia and China, while carrying on a dust-up (a "half" war) in some smaller country. Although the world has changed completely since McNamara's era and the United States hasn't even one major enemy in sight, the Pentagon still demands enough arms to fight two wars at once.

The Military Move In

The evolution of a multiwar mentality among those who have shaped our foreign policy for the past generation can be partly accounted for by the fact that the supposedly civilian part of the government is not so civilian. It has become a civimilitary hybrid: Dozens of generals and admirals have infiltrated policy-making jobs originally designed for civilians in the Office of the Secretary of Defense, which is supposed to be the impregnable citadel of civilian control over the military.

To traditionalists, this trend undermines the spirit of the Constitution. The constitutional provision for civilian control of military matters—beginning at the very top, with the president serving as commander in chief—is based on the rationale that wars are too important to be left solely to the generals and admirals. Of course, despite the troubling invasion of brass into previously civilian policy-making jobs, the defense machinery is still ostensibly under civilian control. But this control is weak. Ironically, its weakness is the result of what was supposed to be its strength. In creating the Department of Defense, the National Security Act of 1947 explicitly stated that the purpose of bringing the Army, Navy, Marine Corps, and Air Force under one departmental roof was to ensure "unified and civilian control" over the military services. The Joint Chiefs of Staff, representing the four services, outwardly are subject to the secretary of defense. In fact, the National Security Act (in the opinion of General David C. Jones, U.S. Air Force, retired, who was chairman of the Joint Chiefs from 1978 to 1982) produces "a loose confederation of large, rigid service bureaucracies . . . with the secretary of defense powerless against them." The secretary has only an oblique control over the Joint Chiefs, and the Joint Chiefs have only a pro forma control over their military bureaucracies. As General Jones pointed out, "The bureaucratic resistance to change is enormous and is reinforced by many allies of the services—in Congress and elsewhere—who are bent on keeping the past enthroned."

Generals and admirals do not always take orders happily from civilians, not even when the civilian is the president. There is a constant feeling of tension between top civilian officials and top brass. And, on the part of the latter, there is occasionally a showing of impudence, if not rebellion. For example, when President Nixon set out to reopen relations with communist China, he did so in utmost secrecy. Not even his secretary of state knew what he was up to. Nixon had a good reason for this secrecy: He knew that most military men saw China as forever the enemy. Military leaders who felt this way might have tried to subvert his effort. So he worked only with his foreign affairs adviser, Henry Kissinger. Sensing that they were being left out of high-level policy making, the Joint Chiefs placed a spy in their White House liaison office, who stole carbon copies of "eyes only" documents, including private reports from Kissinger to President Nixon.

In other crucial ways too the military sometimes operated at odds with Nixon. In his *Memoirs*, Nixon tells of ordering the Pentagon to resume intelligence flights over North Korea:

> It was nearly three weeks before my order was implemented. Even worse, we discovered that without informing the White House, the

Pentagon had also cancelled reconnaissance flights in the Mediterranean. Thus from April 14 to May 8, the United States had not conducted its scheduled aerial reconnaissance in the Mediterranean and the North Pacific—two of the most sensitive areas of the globe. I was surprised and angered by this situation. . . . Thanks to this incident I learned early in my administration that a president must keep a constant check not just on the way his orders are being followed, but on whether they are being followed at all.

Is it possible that the military establishment might, in addition to occasionally frustrating the president's wishes, actually try to take over the government? This plot made an excellent book and movie (*Seven Days in May*), but is it too far-fetched to be considered a real-life possibility? President Kennedy was asked that very question. His answer: "It's possible. It could happen in this country, but the conditions would have to be just right." According to historian Arthur M. Schlesinger, Jr., Kennedy encouraged the filming of *Seven Days in May* "as a warning to the Republic."

But to frustrate and ultimately control their civilian masters, our military leaders do not have to take over the government. They can establish our defense policies simply by withholding information, or giving false information, or frightening the president and Congress into accepting bad guesses.

These tactics are especially effective because there is such a rapid turnover among the senior civilian officials. In the five decades since the Department of Defense was established, there have been twenty-two secretaries of defense. When it comes to buying complex weapons systems, the inexperience of civilian officials makes them particularly vulnerable to misguidance. The top brass spend a lifetime learning about weapons; their civilian counterparts at the Pentagon are relatively transient. Most of them are at their posts less than three years, and it takes them at least a year simply to master the basic Defense Department routines. Thus the top civilian officials at the Pentagon, realizing they don't have the information needed to run the procurement program independently of the military, go along with the brass rather than appear foolish. They fall easy victims to exaggerated claims of a "missile gap" or a "bomber gap" or a "submarine gap."

The growth of the Pentagon in size and in influence cannot be blamed altogether on ambition or misplaced efficiency. To some extent this growth was in response to a vacuum made by the shrinking of the State Department's influence.

Few government leaders have been able to admit that the military sets foreign policy.* To save face in a nation operating on the theory that the civilian element in government is preeminent, these leaders go on pretending that the State Department runs the show, strongly counseled by the Senate Foreign Relations Committee. But occasionally the rumble of caissons and the scream of jets and the firing of arms become so noisy that even members of Congress are jarred into candor.

Stung by the invasion of Cambodia by United States troops—an invasion that was accomplished apparently without the foreknowledge of the State Department and certainly without the foreknowledge of Congress—Senator William Fulbright said on "Face the Nation" (November 29, 1970) that it was obvious the secretary of defense had far more power in the formulation of United States foreign policy than did the secretary of state.

A reporter then asked if Fulbright thought that perhaps the difference in the strength of Defense and State might not be traced to a matter of style. Said Fulbright sourly, and with the best of logic: "I don't think $80 billion a year [the defense budget at that time] is a matter of style. In our kind of economy this is muscle, this is influence, this is power. It controls everything that goes [on] in our government to a great extent. It's the primary control."

If the federal budget can be used as a measure of clout, then the Pentagon does indeed overwhelm the State Department. The latter's annual budget in the 1990s was around $5 billion, while the Department of Defense was luxuriating in a budget more than fifty times larger.

Pentagon Spending on Manpower

The Pentagon employs nearly 80 percent of the civilian and military individuals who work for the federal government. More than half of the Pentagon's budget goes for personnel support. As of 1997, the Department of Defense was handing out paychecks to 1.5 million

---

*The most dramatic example of how the military can determine foreign policy came with the discovery in late 1972 that General John D. Lavelle had, between November 1971 and April 1972, been ordering air strikes over North Vietnam in violation of the president's orders. To cover what he was doing, Lavelle falsely reported the circumstances of the strikes. Was he punished? Hardly. Although demoted to the rank of major general, he was allowed to retire on a full general's pension.

active-duty military personnel; 1 million civilian employees; 881,000 military reservists and national guardsmen (at a cost of more than $2 billion, although many experts believe that the reservists and guardsmen are not qualified for meeting an emergency); and 1,200,000 military retirees.* This last group eats up about one-twelfth of the defense budget.

The Department of Defense is, in short, the nation's biggest employer. As such, it has an enormous number of citizen boosters. Aside from the people who draw their checks directly from the Pentagon are the many thousands whose livelihood depends on defense contracts with the federal government—the Lockheed–Grumman–Boeing kind of conduit for military spending.

All these workers constitute such an enormous pressure group that whittling down the cost of military spending has become an extremely difficult task, even in times of relative peace. Although military enlistments and defense employment, in and out of the Pentagon, have dropped 25 percent since the end of the Cold War, defense planners say that isn't nearly enough to compensate for the sharply escalating cost of weapons and other military equipment.

Of special concern to the budget makers is the military pension burden. The decision, made shortly after the Second World War, to break with the American tradition and maintain a large standing army in peacetime has created a crisis: Military pensions that cost $14 billion annually in 1981 are expected soon to cost several times that much. Members of the armed forces can retire as early as age thirty-seven (after twenty years of service) at half their basic pay. A military officer who retires after thirty years, at age fifty-three, could be expected to earn an average lifetime pension, enlarged by an allowance for inflation, of $590,000. (In private industry, a person who retires at sixty-two receives, on the average, a pension whose lifetime value is $135,000.)

Americans born since the Second World War probably think that a large standing military force is traditional. About 1.5 million of their fellow citizens are serving at one of the hundreds of military installations in this country or at U.S. military bases in twenty-five countries around the world. There are more admirals and generals at large today

---

*Concern over the quality of Army National Guardsmen is prompted by such situations as in South Carolina, where 40 percent of the 15,400 enlistees were found to read at the ninth-grade level or below, although 25 percent of these semiliterate guardsmen work with high-tech weapons that have manuals written for tenth graders (*Tallahassee Democrat*, March 14, 1989).

than there were at the height of the Second World War. Is that a normal situation?

It depends on what one calls normal. It is certainly not a "traditional" situation, in the historic sense. At the end of the Revolutionary War, George Washington dissolved the Army and sent the soldiers home. Later he thought the United States should have a small standing army, but Congress disagreed and wouldn't give him any money for it. In 1784 Congress passed a resolution stating that "standing armies in time of peace are inconsistent with the principles of republican governments, dangerous to the liberties of a free people, and generally converted into destructive engines for establishing despotism."

For the greater part of our history, this nation has maintained very small forces in relation to its population and its sprawling domain. When we entered the War of 1812, we were a nation of about 7 million, but we had only 12,000 in the Army. By the time we went to war with Mexico in 1846, the number had actually declined to 7,640 servicemen. Although the United States did enlist 3.5 million men and women for the First World War, the return of peace quickly shriveled the armed forces to fewer than 150,000 enlistees.

At the end of the Second World War, the draft would have died, as it did after the First World War, except that our political and military leaders managed to contrive such a frightening scenario—based on false information—that the draft was revived in 1948 and extended down to 1973.* The nation's bitter disillusionment with the

---

*The manner in which the peacetime draft was foisted off on Americans is instructive in the way anticommunism was used as a policy-making tool. Here's how the draft was cooked up: First came an intelligence report from the Army that, as the *Chicago Tribune* related, "pictured the Soviet Army as on the move when actually the Soviets were redistributing their troops to spring training stations." Whether this report actually frightened Truman or whether he only pretended it did, on March 17, 1948, he went before a joint emergency session of Congress to demand action on the Marshall Plan and Universal Military Training and Selective Service. Although members of Congress were later privately told that the Russian buildup was a phony, the frightened impression left with the general public was never corrected, and the fires were stoked in April and again in June 1948 by General Omar Bradley, Army Chief of Staff, who said on both occasions that war with the Soviet Union was quite possible. General Lucius D. Clay, American commander in Berlin, warned that war could break out with "dramatic suddenness."

The Army did all it could to make it appear that its fighting strength had slipped to a dangerous low and that voluntary enlistments could not be depended on to supply the men it needed. Thus on June 24, 1948, a bill to extend the draft for two years became law. (This and much other information relating to the early Cold War in this chapter depends heavily on John M. Swomley, Jr., *The Military Establishment* [Boston: Beacon Press, 1964].)

Vietnam War, just then limping to an indecisive conclusion, finally forced the politicians to surrender their automatic hold on the nation's youth.

The end of the draft was accompanied by an increase in personnel costs that threatened to sink the military budget. In an effort to lure enough volunteers into uniform, base pay went up radically (it was $900 per month in 1997).

Despite the higher pay, middle-class whites generally look upon defense as somebody else's job—namely the white population's least educated and lowest-income segments, and minorities, who apparently feel that a job in uniform is better than no job in civvies.

Ironically, it is partly because of this that the Department of Defense can argue that its massive budget is benign. Out of uniform, wouldn't most of these young men and women be also out of work? The Pentagon can cast itself in a father image, pointing out that a wide range of federal benefits and services are available to the 25.5 million veterans and their families.

The military can claim that a hitch in the service has given more people a college education or on-the-job training than all the civilian school-aid programs ever invented (8,420,000 Second World War vets, 2,391,000 Korean vets, and 3,500,000 post-Korean vets). It can be pointed out that the military alumni system has built the largest hospital chain in the world, which treats one million veterans each year in its beds and accounts for 21.5 million outpatient visits. The military can also justify its system by saying that without a hitch in the armed services, the more than 12 million veterans who have bought homes since the Second World War on GI loans would have had to borrow money at higher interest rates elsewhere and might not have qualified. Such benevolent spinoffs of military activities enable the Pentagon to polish its image far beyond its merits and counterbalance a long record of weapons failures, cost overruns, waste, and corruption.

The Military–Industrial–Political Complex

The same fear that has produced and cultivated our foreign policy also has produced and cultivated much of our civilian economy. The corrupt exploitation of the economy for defense purposes has left most Americans unable to judge whether their foreign "enemies" were truly their enemies or were only necessary symbols for the perpetuation of a way of life, a way of defense, that they did not know how to get rid of.

With the end of the Second World War, the defense industries were faced with a crisis of influence, for never in American history had a war been settled without an accompanying diminution of the arms industry and of the military establishment. To counteract this anticipated slump, steps were taken to integrate the military with big business. When the end of the war was in sight in January 1944, Charles E. Wilson, then president of General Electric, told the Army Ordnance Association that the national goal must be "a permanent war economy," which could be best begun if every key defense industry named a special liaison official, with the commission of a reserve colonel, to serve with the armed forces. In the same year, Navy Secretary James Forrestal helped organize the National Security Industrial Association to assure a clublike approach to industry's dealings with the military. Every arm of the military now has its own special civilian alumni organization—the Association of the United States Army, the Navy League, the Marine Corps League, and the Marine Corps Association—which serve as powerful lobbies and as links between the defense industry and Congress.

The political and economic—not defense—nature of so-called defense work was heavily underscored in 1973 when Richard Nixon announced that he was closing 40 bases and cutting back 219 other military facilities, eliminating 16,600 military and 26,200 civilian jobs over the following year. The move seemed to make good sense. But there was one strange fact about these cutbacks: Two-thirds would have to be absorbed by Massachusetts, the only state to vote for Democratic presidential candidate George McGovern in the 1972 election, and Rhode Island, which had a solidly Democratic slate in Congress and which had given Nixon one of his narrowest margins of victory in 1972.

If all the obsolete military bases in the country were closed, taxpayers could save an estimated $2 billion annually. But Congress has usually resisted this kind of thrift. A fort in Utah that had been established 125 years ago to protect stagecoaches against Indians and that had become so useless it was scheduled to be closed in 1964 was saved by Utah's congressmen until they were finally defeated in 1989.

Since then, Congress has permitted three other rounds of base closings, but none since 1995, and from all indications it will permit no more until well into the next century—even ones that are antiquated and of little use. Closing them would save money that could strengthen the military in other ways. So why does Congress resist? It does so to protect the home folks whose civilian jobs are tied to the bases. It's not hard to sympathize with them. Insignificant adjustments in the defense budget—just a scratch through some line in a military appropriations bill—can bring depression to small towns. For example, when the Army closed its ammunition depot near Edgemont, South Dakota, the town lost one-third of its population—those who moved away had to sell their homes for as little as $3,000—and the town has been so desperate to revive its economy that it has tried to lure a string of potentially hazardous industries, such as toxic waste and municipal garbage dumpers.

T. Coleman Andrews, former Commissioner of the Internal Revenue Service, told a group of businessmen in 1960, "If the Soviets should present a sincere and reliable proposal for peace, it would throw us into an industrial tailspin the like of which we have never dreamed." Andrews was assuming that the defense budget would be cut back accordingly. He foresaw the kind of recession that happened in 1969–1971, as the war in Southeast Asia wound down. At a midway point in the recession, Sanford Rose reported:

> The layoffs have hit with shattering force—in West Coast aircraft factories, in ammunition plants across the South, in electronics firms outside Boston. From the beginning of 1969 to mid-1970 about 500,000 defense-related jobs disappeared. From June 1970 to June 1971, another half million are scheduled to vanish. Dozens of communities are realizing to their dismay how deeply they are involved in the mammoth business of defense. The occupational dependency is also far greater than one would expect. For example, close to 40 percent of all physicists and one-fifth of all engineers in the country depend on defense work.

Today, with the United States at peace with Russia, why haven't we gone into a similar, or worse, economic tailspin, as Andrews predicted? There are several reasons, one being that today the industry is cushioned by a much fatter budget—six times larger than it was when Andrews issued his warning. Another reason is that the government has become much more adept at using the military budget as a public works project, a gigantic industrial welfare program. The philosophy behind that program was perfectly expressed in the following congressional encounter.

When Congress closed out the summer of 1971 brawling over whether or not to guarantee a $250 million loan to keep the Lockheed aircraft company afloat, the proponents of the loan did not pretend it should be approved for security reasons. Indeed, Deputy Defense Secretary David Packard admitted in testimony before congressional committees that the company wasn't needed for that purpose. The only issue was jobs.

In an exchange with Senator William Proxmire, Treasury Secretary John Connally made the point with candor:

> Proxmire: Lockheed's bailout is not a subsidy; it is different from a subsidy; it is the beginning of a welfare program for large corporations. I would remind you that in a subsidy program there is a *quid pro quo.* You make a payment to an airline and they provide a certain amount of services for it. In welfare you make a payment and there is no return. In this case the government gives a guarantee and there is no requirement on the part of Lockheed to perform under that guarantee. A guarantee of $250 million and no benefit, no *quid* for the *quo.*
> Connally: What do you mean no benefit?
> Proxmire: Well, they don't have to perform.
> Connally: What do we care whether they perform? We are guaranteeing them basically a $250 million loan. What for? Basically so they can hopefully minimize their losses, so they can provide employment for 31,000 people throughout the country at a time when we desperately need that type of employment. That is basically the rationale and justification.

What Do We Care Whether They Perform?

Connally's attitude has been the commonly accepted attitude in government, of course, but not many officials have been brazen enough to come right out with it. Politicians usually pretend that all defense spending is for defense and that its usefulness in priming the economic pump is just an accidental, though much appreciated, spinoff.

The big selling point in Congress for the construction of the controversial MX missile was the claim that it would generate an average of 32,132 jobs a year, with twenty-eight states getting a piece of the action. Of course, Representative Charles E. Bennett of Florida was correct when he said, "That's not a way to choose a multi-billion-dollar weapons system. To think a member of Congress would be so parochial as to spend money on a faulted weapon because it might produce jobs in his district is awful. Ye gods, that's no way to do it." But that's the way it is done and so long as the Pentagon's billions are distributed with the rationale of welfare checks, even those members of Congress who oppose certain weapons systems will line up for their cut of the pie.

Representative Thomas J. Downey was a liberal Democrat who represented a district on Long Island where the defense industry is the biggest employer. Because he thought many of the Pentagon's programs were foolish, he voted against them. Weapons manufacturers hit him so hard in his very first reelection, which he barely survived, that Downey immediately learned his lesson. He began voting the straight Pentagon ticket (or at least the straight ticket as it relates to Long Island). He said that it violated his idealism—"This is not what I envisioned my career being, hustling people for weapons"—but that he was just doing what everyone else in Congress was doing. "The Texas guys will make sure they rally around LTV, the St. Louis guys around General Dynamics and the Seattle guys around Boeing. The issue is straight jobs."

When some members of Congress opposed developing the B-1 bomber (the fleet of 100 ultimately cost $28 billion, or $280 million per plane) with the argument that it would be outdated before completed, they were reminded that parts and subsystems for these bombers were manufactured in forty-eight states. Sure enough, long before the last of the B-1s had rolled off the assembly line, its replacement—the B-2, or "Stealth" bomber, a revolutionary plane designed to evade radar—was in the works. This raised two questions. If the B-2 was needed, did this mean the B-1 hadn't been needed? If the B-1 was a good plane, was the Stealth just wasted money?

The answer is that both planes were costly flops. The congressmen were right to warn that the B-1 would be outdated before it ever flew. The whole purpose of building it was to have a long-range aircraft that could hit the Soviet Union with nuclear bombs. But by the time it finally went into service in 1998—twenty-eight years and five presidents after Nixon approved its development in 1970—its "target," the Soviet Union, was ancient history. During those twenty-eight years of endless tinkering, the B-1 was plagued with design problems (three crashes, one caused by a bird), mechanical problems (it couldn't fly in the snow because of a lousy deicing system), and engine problems.

As for the B-1's successor, the B-2 Stealth bomber, it has been one of the all-time biggest busts in Pentagon history. The Air Force planned originally to build 132 of the planes for $22 billion. But after eight years that sum had been spent and the Air Force had only a single plane to show for it. After the "experimental" stage was supposedly over, Northrop Grumman Corporation settled down to building twenty-one more Stealths at a cost of $44.7 billion. At $2 billion per plane, it was the world's most expensive aircraft. But it had two fatal defects. First of all, the plane's radar system was so cockeyed that it couldn't tell a rain cloud from a mountainside—or any other obstacle. Secondly, the plane's thermoplastic skin—which was supposed to give it "stealth" qualities—was so fragile that it deteriorated in rain, heat, or humidity. In other words, unless a war was fought in ideal weather, the Stealth bomber would have to stay home in a climate-controlled hanger. And since no climate-controlled shelters are available overseas, it can't leave this country except for short periods. This is why the Stealth bombers used in the war against Yugoslavia in 1999 were not stationed at European bases. Instead, they were flown from their base in Missouri—a thirty-hour roundtrip requiring two mid-air refuelings each way.

Rarely does the Pentagon cancel a weapon system once it's in production, no matter how faulty it may be. But embarrassment forced it to cancel the Army's Divad antiaircraft gun (after wasting $1.8 billion on it) when in one test the radar-guided, computer-operated instruments aimed the gun at a rotating latrine fan in a nearby building, having identified it as the closest threatening target.

To keep the military–industrial world in the chips, the Pentagon accumulates mountains of some commodities that it obviously does not need. It certainly didn't need the 40 million yards of textile goods—enough cloth to cover the earth's equator with a band three feet wide—that investigators found stashed away in a Memphis military warehouse. And since it already had enough depleted uranium (to make armor and armor-piercing shells) to wage a one hundred-year war, why did it spend millions of dollars to buy more? Because the stuff was coming from a South Carolina company and the chairman of the Senate Armed Services Committee was from South Carolina, that's why.

Savvy critics know that while many of the irrational military purchases can be blamed on the admirals and generals, a great many can also be blamed on Congress, which often forces the Pentagon to take things it does not want. For instance, the Pentagon asked for just enough money to build one C-130J transport plane. But Congress appropriated money to build nine. Why the unwanted generosity? Because the planes would be built at the Lockheed Martin plant just one block outside House Speaker Newt Gingrich's district in Georgia, that's why.*

Since pump-priming of the economy, not defense needs, is the objective of much of the spending, it is hardly surprising that so much money is spent on poorly made things. One of the costliest planes is the C-5A transport, which the Pentagon said would cost only $28 million per plane but which wound up costing nearly $60 million. And, as Senator Proxmire pointed out, "as cost went up, the performance of the C-5A declined. Landing gears collapsed. Motors fell off. Wings cracked." *The Wall Street Journal* reported, "Despite the C-5A's ignominious past, Air Force officials insist the plane isn't a flying turkey. 'The C-5A does everything it is supposed to do except fly a long time,' asserts Lt. Gen. Alton Slay. Adds Maj. Gen. Charles F. Kuyk, Jr.: 'We like the airplane.' But he concedes, 'having the wings fall off at 8,000 hours is a problem.'"

The production of inefficient weaponry can have embarrassing, even tragic, results.

- In 1980, President Carter authorized the Pentagon to train a special rescue squad to try to free the fifty Americans held hostage in our embassy in Tehran, Iran. Eight helicopters were launched from an aircraft carrier in the Persian Gulf. Three of the helicopters suffered mechanical failures en route to Tehran, ruining the mission, since at least six of the aircraft were needed for the airlift.
- In 1985, Arab terrorists hijacked the Italian cruise ship, the *Achille Lauro,* and murdered one passenger, a sixty-nine-year-old American, and threw him overboard in his wheelchair. Reagan ordered the ship seized and the terrorists captured and brought to this country for trial. On their way to carry out the plan, a Navy squad of experts in antiterrorism arrived at Shaw Air Force Base in Charleston, South Carolina, and

---

*Military construction can be just as wasteful as arms. In the 1960s, the Pentagon started building a "defense" highway on the main island of Hawaii. The highway, which cost $1.3 billion, finally opened in 1997—twenty-five years late and eighteen times more expensive than the original estimate. Some critics called it "The Road to Nowhere." Others called it "Danny's Highway," because Senator Daniel Inouye kept the federal funds flowing for three decades, to the benefit of ten general contractors, forty-five subcontractors, and forty-one design consultants. (Associated Press, December 6, 1997).

climbed into an Air Force airplane for the flight to the Mediterranean. The plane had mechanical problems and couldn't get off the ground. After a long delay, they climbed into a second plane. It also had mechanical problems. They boarded a third plane; it also was too broken down to use. Hours after their planned departure, they found a fourth plane that could make the trip; but by the time they reached the Mediterranean, the *Achille Lauro* had reached an Egyptian port and couldn't be touched.

- In 1986, Reagan decided to kill Muammar Qaddafi, ruler of Libya. The plan was for nine F-111 bombers, each carrying four two thousand pound laser-guided bombs, to attack Qaddafi's residence. Thirty-two bombs were supposed to hit it. But only two bombs landed in the compound. It was such a high-tech failure that even Pentagon intelligence agents weren't given details of the botched raid. Qaddafi wasn't injured.

- In 1988, the U.S.S. *Vincennes* shot down an Iranian civilian airliner and killed 290 people.* How did the terrible mistake occur? It happened because crewmen operating the *Vincennes'* radar system thought that the blip of the civilian Airbus (which was 177 feet long, with a wingspan of 147 feet) was in fact a hostile Iranian F-14 fighter plane (only sixty-two feet long, with a wingspan of sixty-four feet). It was another terrible electronics failure, this time, to the Navy's embarrassment, involving the $500-million Aegis system of three-dimensional radars, computers, and batteries of video displays—which the Navy boasts is the most sophisticated missile-system ever made. The failure offered a choice of only two explanations: (1) The Aegis system is grossly overrated and is in fact a half-billion-dollar lemon, or (2) it is so complicated that it is beyond the capacity of ordinary sailors to operate.

- The Navy blames defective gearboxes on Navy F-18 fighter planes for seventy-one emergency landings and several in-flight fires, as well as the loss of an F-18 during the Gulf War. (They came to that conclusion after inspecting 150 gearboxes and finding all—100 percent—were defective.) The outfit that made

---

*In December 1988 a bomb aboard Pan Am flight 103, leaving London, blew up the plane and killed 270 people, mostly Americans. Investigators believed the bomb had been placed by terrorists in retaliation for the destruction of the Iranian airliner. If this assumption is correct, it means that, directly or indirectly, the *Vincennes'* error cost the lives of 560 people.

the lousy gearboxes, Lucas Industries, pleaded guilty in 1996 to falsifying quality records and was penalized $106 million (a piddling fine, considering that Lucas has estimated yearly revenues of $6.7 billion).

"What do we care whether they perform?" Those five episodes suggest that our military leaders and our defense industry don't care. They have been much more interested in throwing money around and feathering each other's nests than they have been in supplying the nation with efficient equipment.

Fraud, Waste, and Sloppy Work

If the true objective of the military establishment was to provide the best weapons possible at a price fair to the taxpayers, the Pentagon's procurement system would not be hidden behind such an enormous cloud of dishonesty.

We are talking now about what President Eisenhower called the "permanent armaments industry of vast proportions." Vast indeed: There are 20,000 prime contractors and 150,000 subcontractors pushing and shoving for a piece of the annual $50 billion procurement budget. In the struggle for booty, morality often gets mangled. Sometimes the results are scandals of a sort that the public can easily understand, as in the mid-1980s when defense contractors were caught charging (and the Pentagon was caught paying) for $7,000 coffee pots, $16,000 refrigerators, $600 toilet seats, $180 flashlights, and $748 pliers.

At any given time, more than half of the Pentagon's top 100 weapons suppliers are under investigation for procurement fraud. Additionally, in any given year, thousands of smaller contractors and subcontractors and military procurement officers are indicted or convicted of fraud. The number of contractors barred from doing business with the Pentagon because of illegal activities has risen 1,000 percent in the past decade. Needless to say, many Pentagon officials are totally honest and are offended by fraud. They attempt to stamp it out, or at least to reduce its scope, and to this end the number of investigators specifically assigned to track down fraud has tripled in the last decade. But it seems to be a losing battle.

The problem is an old one. Since the Second World War, six different panels of business leaders have suggested remedies. Each study has criticized these characteristics of the procurement system:

- *"The revolving door,"* through which Pentagon officials and military officers leave the government and go to work, directly or indirectly, for the contractors they had been overseeing. The best way for a Navy procurement officer, for example, to make sure that he can leave the service and step into a high-paying job with, say, General Electric, is for him to slip GE secrets that will help the company submit a contract-winning bid. In one recent year, more than 13,000 former civilian and military employees at the Pentagon parlayed their training into higher salaries with the defense industry.
- *The fantasy—the fiction—that the defense industry operates as part of the free-enterprise system.* Nothing could be further from the truth. The great majority of defense contracts are awarded on a non-competitive basis, and those that are awarded "competitively" are really no more competitive than agreements made within a family.

The fiction of free enterprise exists for both big and small contractors. One study by the General Accounting Office (GAO) of 256 randomly selected "consultant" contracts awarded by the Defense Department showed that the fix was in: Three-fourths of the contracts, valued at $2.6 billion, had gone to former Pentagon employees, 80 percent of the contracts had been awarded without competition, and all but one of the contracts showed signs of significant waste or fraud.

Many of the major defense companies are creations of the Pentagon; they live only through the largesse of the Pentagon. The notion that they could survive according to the rules of free enterprise—of competition—is ridiculous. They are propped up entirely by Pentagon contracts. The Pentagon feels it can't afford to let them die, because their specialty production might be needed in a time of crisis.

In theory, the Pentagon could open all its purchases to competitive bids and could give its business to the one company in each line that makes the lowest bid. But this might put the other companies out of business. So even the losers are awarded some part of each new project, enough to keep their production lines open. And if they pad their bills, if they claim some fraudulent expenses, the Pentagon closes its eyes and pays up in the name of national security.

The friction of free enterprise became increasingly—some would say alarmingly—apparent under President Clinton. His administration encouraged defense companies to merge, thereby further radically reducing competition. In the first four years of his administration, the number of major players in the aerospace and defense field shrank by more than half. Before the orgy of mergers and acquisitions ends, many analysts believe there will be no more than half a dozen eight hundred pound gorillas dominating the defense industry. There will, of course, be many smaller companies acting as "suppliers."

Consider two of the largest gorillas: Boeing Company, which commands two-thirds of the world market for large commercial jetliners, bought the aircraft builder McDonnell-Douglas, which gets three-fourths of its income from defense work; Boeing-McDonnell thereby became the nation's second largest weapons contractor, annually drawing about $10 billion from the Pentagon. It was just behind Lockheed and Martin Marietta, two aircraft corporations that had combined two years earlier and together get $11.5 billion in defense contracts annually.

The Pentagon does not expect any genuine "competition" from these monsters. For example, in 1996 the Pentagon didn't ask Boeing and Lockheed to compete in the bidding for contracts to develop a new generation of fighter planes; no, it gave contracts to both companies for that work. As the number of defense companies shrink through corporate mergers and acquisitions, the Pentagon will require less and less competitive bidding. For the taxpayer, this would be a very unfortunate development.

The "low" bid is often very phony indeed and deserves no more credence than the high bid. This is particularly true if the project is extremely complex. Let's say the low bidder is awarded a contract for a new fighter plane. The contract will run to literally millions of pages, a mountain of details leading into areas of design never tried or tested before. Between the signing of the contract and the actual production of the plane, countless changes will be made in the design. By the time the plane rolls off the assembly line, it may easily cost twice what the "low" bidder said it would cost.*

Since the low bid was meaningless, what usefulness did it serve? It served simply to get the contract for the company that was the most successful at pretending. David Packard, former Deputy Secretary of

---

*Another GAO study showed that 147 major defense projects had increased in cost by 82 percent (from $233 billion to $424 billion) over original estimates and that some of the increases were well over 1,000 percent (John D. Hanrahan, *Government by Contract* [New York: W. W. Norton, 1983] p. 106).

Defense, says "one could do as good a job in awarding the major contracts by putting the names of qualified bidders on the wall and throwing darts."

Richard Halloran, who once covered the Pentagon for *The New York Times*, appraised the system this way:

> Competition in procurement is at base artificial. Because many big companies have monopolies on certain kinds of weapons or other military equipment, and the Defense Department is a single buyer, arms makers need not respond to the marketplace. Overpricing, late delivery, poor design, bad engineering, shoddy workmanship, substituting inferior materials, and inadequate testing only begin the list of practices tolerated in a self-enclosed system, in which many of the actors pass through a revolving door taking turns at playing the roles of buyer and seller.

Or as Representative Denny Smith, Oregon Republican, who was a member of the Congressional Military Reform Caucus, summed it up:

> The problem is not that there is fraud in defense procurement. The problem is that defense procurement has itself become a fraud. It has little or nothing to do with defense of the nation and armed forces that can win in combat. The victims of the fraud are three-fold: the people in our armed forces, who are given ineffective weapons; the taxpayers; and the nation, which needs a real defense, not just contractor, career or congressional welfare disguised as defense.

The auxiliary harm that comes from wasting so much money in the major weapons systems is that there isn't enough money left over to give members of the armed forces the pay they deserve or the training they need. Reportedly, 12,000 military families are on food stamps. The backlog of maintenance at military depots is at an all-time high. For lack of money, some of the tank crews sent to the Persian Gulf War had been poorly trained, to say the least; in fact, they had "had to park their tanks and conduct their platoon training dismounted, with soldiers walking the ranges and pretending to be tanks." And some tank platoons had never been through a live-fire exercise. As one Army colonel appraised the situation, "It was a recipe for disaster, a disaster averted only because the Iraqis chose not to fight."

American Intervention in World Affairs

During and after the Second World War, we entered into a veritable maze of treaties with other nations. Most of these treaties were based on the idea of collective security—that is, readiness for general international action against an aggressor nation. The most important of our military treaties, signed in 1949, is the North Atlantic Pact (usually known as the North Atlantic Treaty Organization, or NATO), to which a dozen European and Mediterranean nations also belong. A similar collective security pact was signed with nine nations for Southeast Asia (SEATO). Nonmilitary and military alliances formed in the Western hemisphere include the Alliance for Progress, the Rio Pact, and the Organization of American States. Since the Second World War, we have poured hundreds of billions of dollars into military and nonmilitary foreign aid in order to strengthen noncommunist countries (and to profit our own businessmen, for most of the aid money was then spent on U.S. goods and services).

The most dramatic demonstration of the United States' departure from an isolationist mentality after the Second World War came with the creation of the United Nations in 1945. Less than three decades after Congress had rejected the similarly conceived League of Nations, the United States became the foremost advocate of an international organization. The United States offered land, and most of the money, for constructing the UN's headquarters in New York City; and the United States has been the most generous financial supporter of the UN—until recently.

Idealists once saw the UN becoming a supreme global court, enforcing world law for world peace, but they have long since given up that dream. To be sure, the UN has on rare occasions served as a kind of front for "law enforcement"—as when United States servicemen, ostensibly fighting under the UN flag, went to the defense of South Korea in 1950. But, generally, the UN has served as a forum in which nations could vent their tempers. The primary responsibility within the UN for maintaining international peace rests with the small Security Council, which for all practical purposes is run by the five major countries—the United States, Russia, the United Kingdom, France, and China. From the end of World War II until the fall of the Soviet empire, the Security Council was made virtually useless by internal ideological feuding. Since the end of the Cold War, its members have shown considerable cooperation in approving a number of military "peacekeeping" operations, but with only spotty success. During the decades of Security Council paralysis, the UN's main operations were in the 185-member General Assembly, where most of the time was taken up by clusters of small emerging nations voting to condemn various actions of the large nations.* Useful as this exercise in global democracy may be, it has become a spectacle that does not inspire much admiration among Americans. Fed up with the UN's sloppy management, Congress refused to pay our dues to that organization (we were $1 billion in arrears as of 1997) until the UN cleaned up its bloated, corrupt bureaucracy.

Despite its numerous defects and disappointments, the United Nations serves an extremely useful purpose as a symbol of the possibility of world government. It is *not* world government—it is indeed many light years from being so—but it is still the nearest thing to a world parliament that mankind has seen. If it thus far functions at a level not much higher than a debating society, critics must bear in mind that letting off steam by debate, by an exchange of verbal abuse, by insults hurled back and forth within a parliamentary pit, may very easily have offered sufficient release to pent-up feelings that war has been averted on several occasions. When Soviet Premier Khrushchev took off his shoe and used it to pound on a desk during a debate in the United Nations Assembly, it may have seemed like a childish thing for him to do—a temper tantrum—but who knows what dangerous tensions were thereby released in the Soviet psyche? Temper tantrums, if kept within a peaceful context, can be very healthy in foreign relations.

---

*The UN operates at two levels. At the bottom is the General Assembly, in which all nation members of the UN have an equal vote—the vote of Chad equals the vote of the United States. At the top level is the Security Council, where at first only the five great powers—the United States, the Soviet Union (now Russia), the United Kingdom, France, and China—had votes. When the UN was created at the end of the war, these five nations, so recently allies, were expected to work closely together to enforce agreements and to dampen conflicts that threatened world peace. However, in response to the spirit of nationalism, each of the five was given a veto power. Thus, any one of the five that felt a proposal threatened its national interest had the power to kill the proposal. Almost immediately intense rivalries between the Soviet Union and the Western nations surfaced, and the resulting veto duels fought between communists and noncommunists in the Security Council effectively prevented the United Nations from becoming a unified voice for peace. The Security Council now has fifteen voting members, but the Big Five are the only permanent ones (the others are elected to two-year terms), and affirmative votes from all five are required for any important action.

As for the UN's "police actions," some of those have been criticized as merely smoke screens behind which our presidents could go to war without asking Congress for a formal declaration, as the Constitution requires. Truman did it in the Korean War and Bush did it in the Persian Gulf War. Both presidents claimed we were not going to war alone but were participating in "multilateral" action with other UN forces. In reality, the "multi" boiled down mostly to multi-troops from the United States—with this nation supplying 95 percent of the UN troops in Korea and 70 percent in the Gulf War; furthermore, American pilots flew 85 percent of the combat missions over Iraq.

The Foreign Policy of Spies

The results of our interventionist attitude have sometimes been malignant, as in the creation of bullying spy agencies. A passage of the National Security Act of 1947 brought into being those cloudy agencies—the Central Intelligence Agency, the National Security Council, the National Security Agency—that bridged both military and diplomatic services and created a force entirely new to the American experience. Thus the military was wedded permanently to civilian diplomacy and, in fact, made preeminent. Too often thereafter the government gave its heart to the spooks, the spies, the underhanded wheelers and dealers in foreign affairs, especially to the CIA—an agency that David Wise and Thomas Ross called the Invisible Government and described in a book by that name.

"An informed citizen might come to suspect," they pointed out, "that the foreign policy of the United States often works publicly in one direction and secretly through the Invisible Government in just the opposite direction." And one reason for the efficiency of the secret maneuvering is, in the words of former CIA director Allen W. Dulles, that "the National Security Act of 1947 has given Intelligence a more influential position in our government than Intelligence enjoys in any other government in the world."

In his book *Veil*, the biography of then-CIA Director Bill Casey, *Washington Post* reporter Bob Woodward tells of a conversation in which Casey asked the staff director of the Senate Intelligence Committee why he thought people joined the CIA. The staff director replied, "For the excitement and for patriotic reasons."

"No, no, no!" yelled Casey, who then explained that the real reason was: "We have a chance to establish our own foreign policy."

Did he mean a CIA foreign policy separate from the government's legitimate foreign policy? Judging from the way the CIA has operated, that's exactly what he meant. In pursuing its own foreign policy, the CIA has sometimes been what the late Senator Frank Church called "a rogue elephant"—meaning, a vicious elephant that roams alone. Caught up in the anticommunist frenzy of the post-war years, every administration granted the CIA extraordinary freedom and secrecy. Too often, presidents and members of Congress preferred not to know—or pretended not to know—what the CIA was doing because there was plenty of evidence to show that in fact many of its actions and alliances violated U.S. law, international law, and the United Nations charter.

CIA activities overseas have included armed intervention, disruption of labor unions, propaganda attacks, kidnapping, sabotage, spying, planned invasions, support for one regime, opposition to another—in British Guiana, France, Italy, Brazil, the Dominican Republic, Bolivia, the Congo (Zaire), Nigeria, and on and on. All over the globe. But to what extent, and by whose order, and to what end—who can be sure? Not even the president is always aware of what the CIA is up to.

The CIA has worked arm-in-arm with some of the world's worst thugs. In the aftermath of World War II, its payroll included numerous Nazi war criminals, including men like Otto von Bolschwing, who helped Adolph Eichmann plan the extermination of Europe's Jews and who himself was responsible for fomenting a riot in which Jews were killed and hung on meat hooks. (The CIA appreciated him so much they sneaked him into the United States illegally and helped him become a citizen.)

Another CIA employee was Panama's former dictator, Manuel Noriega, now in U.S. prison, who, even while he was helping Colombian drug lords get their cocaine into the United States, was being paid $200,000 a year by the CIA as an informer.

And then there was Mobutu Seso Seko. In 1965 the CIA helped him seize control of Zaire (now called Congo), the third largest country in Africa. Over the next thirty-two years the United States supported his "anticommunism" with $1.5 billion in military aid while he was looting Zaire and hanging anyone who complained. When he fled to Europe in 1997, he left a nation that was largely deprived of roads, health care, electricity, telephones, or schools.

In Central America, throughout the 1980s the CIA hired as inform-ers hundreds of military officers who were expert at kidnapping, tor-turing, and killing persons suspected of being enemies of their right-wing governments. Investigations that brought out these details in the mid-1990s also discovered that during the Reagan administra-tion's clandestine war in Central America, the CIA taught police and military personnel in at least five countries how to extract information from people in a "sophisticated" fashion—not by pulling out their fin-gernails but through psychological torture.

The list of scoundrels supported and protected by the CIA could run many pages, but let's turn instead to its four most publicized "successes."

Disastrous "Successes"

Three of those "successes" resulted in the overthrow of governments. Were these things done to "push back the tide of communism," as the CIA claimed, or were they done primarily to help U.S. capitalists? Robert Reich has noted that it was not "mere coincidence that the Central Intelligence Agency discovered communist plots where America's corporations possessed, or wished to possess, substantial holdings of natural resources."

- In 1953, Kermit Roosevelt, head of the CIA's Middle East division, led a riot that overthrew Dr. Mohammed Mossadegh, Iran's elected prime minister, and restored the Shah to total power. Mossadegh had nationalized Iran's oil fields. The Shah reopened them to foreign companies and the United States' largest oil firms were given generous access for the first time. Fittingly, Roosevelt later became a vice president of Gulf Oil Company.

   Long-range results: Enough Iranians hated the Shah that he was overthrown in 1979, and religious fanatics replaced him with Ayatollahs, who look upon the United States as "the Great Satan" and have made our position in the Middle East precarious ever since.

- The United Fruit Company virtually owned Guatamala—many thousands of acres of its land. In 1952 Jacobo Arbenz was elected president and promptly seized much of the land and turned it over to the peasants. So the CIA rigged a revolution in 1954, threw Arbenz out of the country, returned the right-wing military government to power, and United Fruit got its bananas back.

Long-range results: Peasant outrage triggered the longest guerrilla conflict ever fought in the Western Hemisphere. It didn't end until 1997. More than 100,000 people were killed, most of them massacred by military "death squads" (some of whose officers were trained in this country).

- In 1970 the CIA tried, but failed, to prevent Salvador Allende, an unabashed Marxist, from winning election as Chile's president. The U.S. business community became very unhappy with him when he nationalized property owned by the local subsidiaries of such U.S. corporations as International Telephone and Telegraph and the giant mining companies, Anaconda and Kennecott. A revolt in 1973, to which the CIA gave strong support, ended with the murder of Allende and his replacement with a military government.

  Long-range results: The military has dominated Chile's government directly or indirectly ever since.

- The CIA's only major success not tied to corporate profits but done for purely ideological reasons was in Afghanistan. But once again there was a negative spin-off, this time of frightening proportions. When the Soviet Union invaded Afghanistan in 1979, the CIA began pouring billions of dollars into training guerrilla fighters—Muslim "holy warriors"—and supplying them with rifles, explosives, and Stinger missiles. They fought well. On February 15, 1989, when the last Russian soldier crossed Afghanistan's northern border in retreat, jubilant officials at CIA headquarters exchanged champagne toasts. And well they might, for the defeat damaged Soviet morale and finances enough that it helped bring down that already crumbling government.

  Then came the horrendous spin-off: Thousands of the radical Islamic fighters who had been in the CIA program now took their expertise to other nations and became terrorists in what they considered a holy war. Two bombings in Saudi Arabia that killed twenty-four American soldiers and wounded 250 were blamed on terrorists who received explosives training in Afghanistan. And an Afghan veteran was convicted of being the mastermind behind the explosion at the World Trade

Center in New York City on February 26, 1993. It killed six people, injured one thousand, and caused half a billion dollars in damage.

American taxpayers have spent many, many billions of dollars to support the CIA. Was it well spent? David Wise, probably the most astute historian of the spy agencies, has written: "The CIA itself did not make much difference in the ultimate outcome of the Cold War. From the Bay of Pigs to Iran-contra, its covert warriors hatched one disaster after another."

Sometimes the CIA's incompetence has been mind-boggling. During the 1999 war with Yugoslavia, the United States and its allies depended heavily on the CIA for information as to which targets should be hit by their bombers. In one instance, the CIA identified a building in the middle of Belgrade as headquarters of a Yugoslav arms agency. So bombs were dropped, the building was demolished, three people were killed and twenty injured. Oops! It turned out that the arms agency was really 200 yards to the south. The building our bombers hit, using a CIA map, was the Chinese embassy. How could the CIA have made such a mistake? After all, the embassy had been there for three years; the Belgrade phone book and tourist maps identified it at that address. The CIA explained that their maps hadn't been updated.

Our Arms Hucksters

There is another area of our foreign affairs, a netherworld that takes on some of the features of everything we have mentioned—spying and diplomacy and militarism—but has a life of its own. That is our international commerce in armaments.

Because of our interventionist attitude, and because our leaders have come to look upon armaments as just another commodity, America has become the world's largest arms salesman. Under President Clinton—despite his campaign promise to reduce the arms trade—the United States has exported tens of billions of dollars worth of weapons annually and now holds a 70 percent share of the world market. U.S. weapons were being used in most of the thirty-five to forty regional conflicts underway around the globe.

Most arms exports are handled through the Pentagon, government to government. But there is also a thriving trade in private sales, with our defense contractors getting permits from the State Department to sell directly to foreign military and police forces, a practice that invites bribery. Walter Mondale appraised the situation accurately: "America is no longer an arsenal of democracy; it is quite simply an arsenal." The most depressing part is that our arms sometimes go to both sides in a war, or to nations that have been at war with each other and may soon be again—to both Israel and the Arabian countries, to India and Pakistan—and to nations that can least afford the luxury of belligerencies. They buy tanks and guns and planes from us when they should be buying tractors—and our arms merchants and our officials encourage them in this folly.

Until the economic crisis hit governments in that part of the world in 1997, Asia, particularly Southeast Asia, was a big market for fighter planes, missiles, tanks, and other armaments. Then those countries, on the verge of bankruptcy, began backing out of arms contracts—and U.S. taxpayers sometimes got stuck with the bill. For example, our government contracted for $392 million worth of fighter jets from Boeing Company, and then sold them to Thailand. But when Thailand backed out on the deal, our government was left holding the bag.

Foreign Policy in Transition

Since entering its interventionist era, the United States has had a spotty record. On the one hand, it has done much good. The generosity of the Marshall Plan rebuilt a shattered Europe after the Second World War. U.S. food assistance programs—though also helping American farmers get rid of surplus commodities—helped several nations escape wholesale starvation. NATO, though often mismanaged and wasteful, is one military alliance that probably accomplished what it was aimed at: discouraging the Soviets from taking some foolishly aggressive steps.

But as interventionists we have also bungled so many times, and sometimes with such costly results, as to revive among many Americans in recent years a noticeable yearning for a return to isolationism—or at least a kind of semi-isolationism whereby we would not withdraw from the world but would mind our own business much more vigorously than in the recent past.

The principal cause of this new feeling of temperance was our bad showing in Asia. The first frustration was in Korea. After the

Second World War, Korea was divided into two nations, the north being run by the communists, the south by a right-wing regime. In June 1950, the communists invaded South Korea. President Truman, under the rather feeble pretense that we were supporting a United Nations "police action," sent U.S. troops to help the South Koreans. It was a savage war in which more than 54,000 Americans died and which ended in an unsatisfactory armed truce. It was a war that did not improve conditions in Asia, did not improve our reputation around the world, inspired no enthusiasm among our troops or Americans at home, and is seldom mentioned by historians or politicians or just plain citizens (who seem almost to have forgotten it). It was a futile war that left such outstanding military leaders as Douglas MacArthur (who led the U.S. forces through most of the Korean War), Matthew B. Ridgway, and James Gavin convinced that we should "never again" send an expeditionary force to the Asian continent.

Yet within ten years of the Korean fiasco, American troops were again in Asia—this time in South Vietnam—where they stayed for the longest war in our history. We suffered more than 211,000 casualties, spent $150 billion, and lost the war—the first time in history that our military machine was not simply kept from achieving victory (as in Korea) but was actually defeated. The worst aspect of the war was that we spent so much of our spirit and blood and money on such a shoddy cause. Our troops were fighting in South Vietnam to keep in office a government that was corrupt, tyrannical, and vastly unpopular with the South Vietnamese people.

The war had a devastating effect on this nation's psyche. Before we had withdrawn from Southeast Asia, Americans were bitterly divided over what course to follow—"turn tail" or drop atomic bombs or stay on and on, wasting more lives and money as we sank deeper and deeper into the Southeast Asian quagmire. Hundreds of thousands of Americans staged peace marches in Washington and other large cities. A few marches in favor of the war were also staged. Tempers of both hawks and doves, as the antagonists called each other, were high and difficult to control. There was so much hatred for President Lyndon Johnson, who had escalated our involvement to 500,000 troops in South Vietnam, that he was afraid to go out among the general public; in the final months of his administration he made most of his appearances at military bases, under tight security. Public abhorrence of his military policies finally forced him to decide not to run for reelection.

As a result of our unhappy Asian experiences, polls have shown that the American people have become much more cautious about wanting their leaders to get involved in the affairs of other nations, especially the smaller developing nations whose destiny, in the early stages of development, seem likeliest to provoke armed conflict. How long this quasi-isolationist mood will hold is anyone's guess.

Nor is it clear that America's leaders have learned much from the Asian experience. It should have taught them two things: (1) Perhaps some emerging nations do not want to be "saved" by the well-meaning Americans. Perhaps they want to work out their own destiny, even if that means—to our dismay—going down the communist or socialist road. Just because capitalism and democracy work well for us does not necessarily mean they are the right formula for all nations. The fanatical resistance, and sluggish support, we encountered in Korea and Vietnam should have told us that much. (2) Superior military might will not necessarily win wars. The United States has the greatest air force in the world, and its bombers dropped more bombs on North Vietnam than we dropped on all enemy nations in all of the Second World War; North Vietnam had no air force at all. Our warships could freely shell North Vietnam's shoreline, for there were no comparable warships to resist such assaults. The North Vietnamese had no tanks to meet our tanks. Their military supplies were conveyed less often on trucks than on the backs of men and women.

The military odds were heavily against the North Vietnamese. So how did they defeat us—as they had earlier defeated their colonial "masters," the French? Apparently it is fair to conclude that they won because they believed in their cause—a united Vietnam free of foreign rulers—and would not quit. It was a lesson that our political and military leaders could have learned without wasting so many lives. They might have known what to expect if they had remembered the history of the American Revolution and the often "hopeless" condition of the colonial troops, without shoes and with little food, who nevertheless kept fighting.

Other recent experiences have proved that the great nations that once dominated the Age of Intervention must change their foreign policy formulas to acknowledge not only shifting strengths within their own ranks but also the wishes and ambitions of nations they once held in contempt—and even of governments they still hold in contempt. Trying to run over them doesn't always work, as recent presidents have learned. President Reagan made no greater effort in foreign policy, both by legal and illegal means, than he made to overthrow the Sandinista government of Nicaragua. But when he left office, the same people were running that country as when he came in eight years earlier.

An even better example of how small nations have learned to humble large ones is in the Middle East. Our oil companies, with the blessing of our State Department, exploited those oil-producing nations unmercifully until the 1960s. Finally fed up with being pushed around, the Middle East nations took back their oil fields, made the great oil companies mere renters, and forced the world to pay homage at the gasoline pump.

Getting too Tricky

If further proof is needed that smaller countries no longer quake at our military might, that proof can be found in Iraq. Also, our relationship with Iraq shows how dangerous it sometimes is to try to manipulate smaller nations with behind-the-scenes schemes. In this case, our leaders got much too tricky for their own good—and for ours.

The two most explosive regimes in the Middle East in the 1980s and 1990s were Iran and Iraq. Both governments supported terrorists who prowled the world doing their deadly mischief. Iran was ruled by religious fanatics who wanted to dominate the Middle East by spreading militant Islamic fundamentalism. Iraq was ruled by an extremely dangerous crackpot named Saddam Hussein who wanted to dominate the Middle East simply because he desired more wealth (oil) and more power. Hussein was totally unpredictable. He was also ruthless, as he had shown by using poison gas to kill thousands of Iranians (in the six-year Iraq–Iran war) and rebellious Kurds in his own country. And he wasn't kidding when he threatened to "burn half of Israel" with his chemical weapons.

Why side with either of those obnoxious governments? Middle Eastern politics are extremely complex and mysterious, and President Bush would have been wise not to have butted into the Iraq–Iran equation. Instead, he decided to build up Iraq as a counterweight to Iran; so he secretly cleared the way for Hussein to receive $1.5 billion worth of American technology and $5 billion in loans. Ostensibly the money was for "food" but in fact—as Bush should have guessed would happen—Hussein spent it on his army and on his chemical, biological, and nuclear warfare programs.

Bush's manipulations backfired. In 1990 the army he had subsidized invaded Kuwait. Fearing Hussein might next attack Saudi Arabia and cut off one of our major sources of oil, Bush sent 500,000 American warriors to crush the invaders.

Hussein's army was easily defeated. But Hussein himself was not. In 1999, as this book was being revised, he was still ruling Iraq, cocky as ever, daring the United States to come after him again.

When Hussein refused in 1998 to permit United Nations' scientists to continue going through his armaments to see if he was building atomic bombs and missiles filled with poison gas and germs, President Clinton launched a three-day air attack on Iraq. But if the eighty-eight thousand tons of bombs dropped by Bush hadn't brought Hussein to his knees, a few more tons were also bound to fail. So there we were, confronted with our first major post–Cold War military challenge, and not knowing how to end it.

Iraq was just one of a rash of "little" conflicts that confounded Clinton, the first president whose administration was totally in the post–Cold War era. He sent U.S. troops to Haiti to "establish democracy," but that failed. He sent troops on a "peacekeeping" mission to Bosnia, promising that they would be home within a year, but as the century ended, it looked like they might be in Bosnia for decades. In 1999, the United States sent bombers and missile launchers to punish Serbia's dictator, and that seemed destined to be another quagmire. Our missile attack on Afghanistan, an effort to assassinate a terrorist who had blown up a U.S. embassy, was a failure.

In short, our leaders were learning once again that having overwhelming military superiority does not guarantee victory. So much for the honor of being the world's only superpower.

Though he didn't always act on his own advice, President Kennedy had the right idea: "We must face the fact that the United States is neither omnipotent nor omniscient, that we are only 6 percent of mankind, that we cannot right every wrong or reverse each adversity and that therefore there cannot be an American solution to every world problem."

The Post–Cold War Perils

It's been half a century since the first atomic bomb was dropped in anger. A U.S. Air Force bomber dropped it August 6, 1945, and the explosion completely devastated four square miles in the heart of Hiroshima, Japan, killing an estimated 66,000 persons (including an estimated 3,000 American prisoners of war), and injuring an estimated 69,000. Three days later, American airmen dropped another atomic bomb, this time wiping out 40 percent of Nagasaki, Japan, killing an estimated 40,000 persons and injuring 25,000. Two bombs, two cities. Five days later Japan surrendered.

Never again was an atomic bomb used in war. But the threat of its use, either by us or by the Soviet Union, was the darkest cloud hanging over the Cold War. Making it all the darker was the development, in the mid-1950s, of the hydrogen bomb, which, having the explosive power of seven million tons of TNT, was capable of devastating 150 square miles by blast and 800 square miles by searing heat.

After the 1962 Cuban missile crisis, mentioned in the last chapter, when the world came close to war, the use of nuclear weapons was never again considered a serious option to the major nations. Instead, the United States and the Soviets adopted the doctrine of "Mutually Assured Destruction," better known as MAD, whereby both sides maintained so many atomic weapons that each knew if they made a first strike it would trigger a reprisal that would ensure their own destruction. It was logical madness, yes—and it worked.

It worked because only two nations, the United States and the Soviets, were involved. Grudgingly, over the years the two sides cooperated in lowering, bit by bit, the nuclear threat. From the pinnacle of the Cold War, when each side had more than thirty thousand atomic warheads, the stockpile had been reduced 50 percent by the mid-1990s, and, if things go as planned, by the year 2003 the United States and Russia will cut the total number of nuclear warheads to thirty-five hundred—which is progress of a sort, but still leaves them equipped to blow up most of the world. And slimming down the arsenal does not mean our military scientists and engineers aren't still working to "update" our nuclear weapons.

But what the United States and Russia do with their nuclear programs has become almost irrelevant. The genie is out of the bottle and has gone global. The technology and know-how for building atomic bombs are now in the hot little hands of at least a dozen countries, and Pentagon experts predict that by the turn of the century a dozen more will join the nuclear club. Some are brimming over with grudges toward other nations. What's to keep them from using their new power? In the good old, bad old days, America and the Soviets could maintain a balance of terror. But when so many nations are involved, how can a balance be struck?

America, as the oldest member of the nuclear club, can preach to the newcomers about the virtues of restraint, and with some justification. But if we were restrained in the use of the bomb, we were not restrained in its development.

Tragically, even if an atomic weapon is never used against this country by a foreign enemy, we will have greatly suffered as a result of this silent war. Because of incredibly sloppy and callous management, over the years the Atomic Energy Commission and the Energy Department allowed millions of pounds of radioactive waste, produced in our weapons plants and deposited in military dumps across the nation, to seep into the air and water supplies of dozens of communities from Washington state to South Carolina.

For all this, you can blame the government, which in the name of "national security," allowed the nuclear arms plants to operate as closed societies. They were a law unto themselves and they permitted no outsiders to inspect their facilities for safety flaws. Mismanagement and sloppy work habits led to accidents, but the accidents were covered up. Even when they became commonplace, radioactive leaks into the air, water, and soil were kept secret from the outside world. Today the Energy Department estimates it may cost us $110 billion to clean up forty-five years' worth of radioactive contamination. And what price can be put on what has happened to the thousands of people who lived near these plants, many of whom today believe they developed cancer, blood disorders, and unexplained illnesses because of the contamination?

Those responsible show little remorse for the cover-up that endangered whole communities. Dr. Glenn T. Seaborg, who was chairman of the Atomic Energy Commission from 1961 to 1971, now says:

> Rightly or wrongly, there was a feeling that national security was the most important factor to consider in managing information. You had to live through that era to understand the situation then. We were in a very serious race with the Soviet Union. In some sense they were ahead of us. Our very survival depended upon staying abreast of them. Secrecy led to things that we are horrified about today.

American Guinea Pigs

Even more unconscionable were the hundreds of atmospheric atomic bomb tests from 1944 to 1974—in the South Pacific and in Nevada—

which exposed many thousands of persons, military and civilian, to nuclear fallout. They were not warned of the danger. Also, between 2,000 and 3,000 servicemen were subjected, without their knowledge, to secret biomedical experiments connected to the nuclear weapons research.

Many of the 300,000 U.S. servicemen who had been exposed to above-ground nuclear tests at close range and the thousands of civilians who were living downwind from the blasts began complaining in the late 1970s about unusually high rates of cancer and about birth defects among their children.

The government scoffed at their complaints and the AEC referred to the complainers as "the Crazies." But in 1993 a wonderful thing happened. Secretary of Energy Hazel O'Leary, who had been in office only a year, decided "that if just 10 percent of what the so-called Crazies were saying was true, I was working for an evil agency." So she declassified all the secret documents relating to the charges. Among other things, these documents showed that the AEC had funded and covered up radiation experiments on many human guinea pigs—pregnant women, prison inmates, hospital patients, and even orphans (who were fed radiated oatmeal).

What Did We Learn from the Cold War?

The United States and the Soviet Union have to be given a lot of credit for one thing—they didn't take the fatal step, and never before in history had such a bitter rivalry lasted so long (fifty years) without the antagonists going to war. Indeed, it went on so long that many assumed it would last forever, and some—unbalanced ideologues and greedy defense industrialists and a few hardline military brass—probably hoped it would.

But of course it couldn't because the Cold War was not just a deadly struggle between ideologies; it was also a competition in economic bankruptcy. We won only because we were richer, and because Soviet leaders were totally irrational in the way they robbed—ruined—their economy in their mad effort to attain supreme military power.

The United States came out of the Second World War unscathed. Not one bomb fell on its territory. Its manufacturing capacity was intact and booming. The United States could splurge on its military budget—for a while—and not be hurt. But the Soviet Union had been devastated by the war: In the German-occupied part of that country, 137,000 tractors had been destroyed, 49,000 grain combines, 15,800 locomotives, 65,000 kilometers of railway track, half of all its railway bridges, half of all its urban living space. Towns lay in ruins. At the end of the war, many Soviet citizens were living in holes in the ground.

But instead of following the only sensible postwar path of pouring all resources into rebuilding its civilian economy, the Soviet Union wasted huge amounts on military equipment and personnel. Five years after the war had ended, the Soviet Union was spending more billions of dollars on its armed forces than was the United States, and three times more than Britain, France, and Italy combined. The Soviet Union succeeded in its frenzied effort to become a military superpower, but only by siphoning off vast stocks of trained manpower, scientists, machinery, and capital investment, which were desperately needed to rebuild the civilian economy. Consequently, the Soviet Union never came even close to becoming a first-rank economic power. Throughout the 1970s and 1980s, its economy did not grow at all—except in the production of alcohol.

We Weren't So Bright

But as many sections of this chapter have illustrated, U.S. leaders during the Cold War were also sometimes guilty of irrationally wasteful military expenditures. However, the only time they came close to showing real mental derangement was during the administration of President Reagan. Over the eight years he was in the White House, the military budget was raised a total of $1 trillion—that's $1,000,000,000,000—over the average spent in the previous eight years. That $1 trillion was added to the national debt. Let's say we pay 5 percent interest on the debt. That means U.S. taxpayers will be paying $50 billion a year—forever, or close to it—in interest on the defense madness of the Reagan years.

And don't forget the trillion dollars Reagan flushed down the sewer was spent to protect us from what he called "the evil empire," the Soviet Union, at the very moment that it was falling apart.

As Clinton's first secretary of defense, Les Aspin, acknowledged, "In the short run the national security of the United States is protected by a strong military force; in the long run, the national security of the United States is protected by a strong economy." That makes sense. And as one way to get a stronger economy, our leaders might consider bringing home more of our troops; that is, they could stop letting our trade competitors freeload off our military budget. Doesn't it seem odd that the United States still stations troops in Europe to defend nations that are rich enough to pay for their own defense?

You might also wonder why we continue to drain our economy of billions of dollars to keep 37,000 troops in South Korea, when that nation has grown into the eleventh largest economy (admittedly, a bit shaky at times) in the world.

Japan has had an even better deal. As a part of its surrender in the Second World War, Japan was forced by the United States to agree not to build a large armed force. Lucky Japan. Today the average Japanese citizen pays only $98 for defense, compared with the average American's $1,023. Protected by U.S. armed forces, Japan is thus free to spend its money on technological research and manufacture, devoting itself to the pursuit of sustained economic growth, especially in export markets. Sixty-nine percent of U.S. federal funds for research and development are devoted to defense; the corresponding figure for Japan is only 4.5 percent. In other words, our military budget has helped Japan develop its manufacturing base to such a degree that the nation we conquered with arms has begun to conquer us with trade. Every auto, every television set, and every VCR that we import from Japan has indirectly been subsidized by the U.S. taxpayer.

Here We Go Again

What are we doing with a Cold War–sized defense budget when it seems safe to say—despite the several dozen small conflicts always flaring up somewhere in the world—that a new breeze is blowing? With most nations clearly more interested in making money than in making war, and with trade barriers falling everywhere, the hottest battles these days are being fought at the cash register. For some time we have been on reasonably good terms with our old enemy, Russia. (The perfect symbol for the new age was the appearance of Mikhail Gorbachev, former head of the Soviet Union, in a Moscow television advertisement for Pizza Hut in 1997. He is shown offering a piece of pizza to customers, who cry out: "Long live Gorbachev, who brought us Pizza Hut!" That's a long way from Karl Marx.) In America, "anticommunism," once the Cold War era's most powerful political theme, is quite out of style and no longer stirs even the slightest whiff of hysteria.

Some in our government, especially those who favor a bulging defense budget, find it hard to adapt to the post–Cold War age. They get very nervous when the United States has no major foe, active or potential. But at the moment the only one they can scare up is China. Indeed, some in Washington consider China the next great security threat and would agree with Representative Jim Bunning, a Kentucky Republican, who complained that "the Chinese government is engaged in a massive expansion of its own military machine, taking up where the Soviet Union left off, using the profits from trade with us to pay for it."

Well, we needn't get too panicky about that massive buildup for a while. According to the International Institute for Strategic Studies, as of 1997 this is how we compare with China: The United States has 178 long-range strategic bombers; China has none. The United States has 17 ballistic missile submarines; China has one. The United States has 11 aircraft carriers; China has none. The United States has 4,450 tactical aircraft; China has 697. And so on, all through the armory.

But long-range missiles—what about those? So far as was known as we approached the new century, China had none that would come even close to reaching the United States, and certainly none that would reach this country with accuracy. So there was little to fear on that score either. But in a surprise move in 1998, communist North Korea launched a primitive missile over Japan and into the Pacific, and in 1999 the FBI named a Chinese–American working at the Los Alamos National Laboratory was under investigation as a possible spy for China. He was suspected of having stolen the data for one of America's most advanced nuclear warheads.

Science Fiction Revived

Those two events were enough for the hawks in Congress to revive "Star Wars"—one of the costliest lemons ever squeezed by the Pentagon. In the early 1970s, the Pentagon spent $5.7 billion—and back then a billion was really a billion—to build the country's first anti-ballistic-missile (ABM) system. But it was almost immediately declared obsolete against the Soviets' new multiple-warhead missiles, and shut down. In the weapons industry, however, it is very hard to kill a bad idea. So, although many weapons experts argued it would be impossible to build a truly efficient ABM system, the Reagan and Bush administrations spent tens of billions of dollars pursuing the pipedream of constructing an impregnable space shield that could repel thousands of warheads.

When Clinton came in, he junked the program—temporarily. Then in 1999, he reversed himself, as he so often did, and backed the expenditure of $10.5 billion over the next six years to develop a missile defense system even though, as *The Wall Street Journal* pointed out, "Serious questions remain whether the technology will work, and if it does, whether it will make the world a safer, or a more dangerous place. The Russians are already threatening to block further nuclear reductions if the United States breaks out of the 1972 ABM treaty that bars a national missile-defense system."

Many believed that the program was not being revived because of real fear of rogue missiles but simply in response to what a Carnegie Endowment official called "the politics of defense procurement." Already lined up for big contracts were those perennial feeders at the defense trough, Boeing Company and Raytheon Company.

Breaking the Habit

That's a bit of bad luck, but there's still reason to hope that the future will belong to those in Washington and around the country who want America to shed what Max Frankel, an editor for *The New York Times*, calls "the heavy armor that shaped and sustained American diplomacy for half a century." Some of the old architects of the Cold War, like George Ball, a former secretary of state, have changed their view and now condemn those members of the foreign policy community who "have fallen into the habits of the past and don't know how to extricate themselves."

That, of course, is the great obstacle: old habits. The defense bureaucracy—the Pentagon, the spy agencies, and some portions of the state department—is notoriously rigid, and even more rigid are their allies in the military industry. To them, the challenges of peace must be traumatic.

Which is what Georgi Arbatov, director of Moscow's Institute for the Study of the U.S.A. and Canada, meant in that slyly humorous remark he made shortly before the Soviet Union collapsed: "We are going to do something terrible to you—we are going to deprive you of an enemy."

CHAPTER 4

Congress

The Most Deliberative Body, and a Swamp

The Congress is the mirror of the people, and it reflects the aggregate strengths and weaknesses of the electorate. Its membership might include just about the same percentage of saints and sinners, fools and geniuses, rogues and heroes as does the general populace. Congress is a highly concentrated essence of the virtues and faults of the nation as a whole.

JIM WRIGHT
Reflections of a Public Man

WHEN THE FIRST CONGRESS WAS CALLED TOGETHER IN 1789, the new nation's life depended on it alone. There was not yet any federal court system; Congress would have to set one up. There was not yet a president or a vice president; Congress would have to count the ballots of the first electoral college to see who had won, and then make arrangements for inaugurating the first president.

With such crucial responsibilities on its collective shoulders, did Congress step smartly about doing its business? Not at all. At the first meeting of the House of Representatives, only thirteen members had straggled in—less than one-fourth the membership. (The eleven states that ratified the Constitution had elected fifty-nine men to the House.) In the Senate, the turnout was even worse—only eight out of twenty-six senators were there, so few that they did not constitute a quorum

and the Senate had to adjourn. It took more than three weeks for the Senate to round up a quorum so that it could hold its first meeting.

If this was not exactly an auspicious beginning, at least it gave fair warning of what lay ahead. Congress has almost always been slow to action, clumsy in movement, and insensitive even to most crises. Former Senator Joseph Clark was right when he claimed that "since the foundation of the Republic, Congress has rarely initiated anything, rarely faced up to current problems, even more rarely resolved them." Major initiatives, major solutions have almost always originated in forces outside Congress, either in the executive branch or in citizen reform groups that pushed their demands on the federal legislature. When Jimmy Carter was campaigning for the presidency, he asserted that "Congress is inherently incapable of leadership. In the absence of strong presidential leadership, there is no leadership." That was one bit of campaign rhetoric few would refute.

Stewart Alsop once remarked that the periods of congressional dominance in federal life, "as after the Civil War, or in the nineteen-twenties, or in the early McCarthy period, have not been proud chapters in American political history." He left out at least one important period in this shabby series—the era, following Andrew Jackson, when Congress moved into the vacuum resulting from the loss of a strong president and permitted its proslavery element to take control and ride the nation into the Civil War.

Signs of Deep Trouble

There are exceptions. One should not forget the moment of congressional domination in *domestic* affairs—in Nixon's first term—when the United States saw its greatest outburst of environmental and consumer protection laws. Among Congress's many enthusiastic environmentalists was Senator Gaylord Nelson of Wisconsin. The first Earth Day, April 20, 1970, was his brainchild. It became a media event, with millions participating in demonstrations, cleanups, and rallies across the country. Caught up in the spirit, Congress launched a new era of environmental law. In 1970 it created the Occupational Safety and Health Administration (OSHA) and passed the Clean Air Act. In 1972 came the first pesticide regulations, the Noise Control Act, and a series of laws protecting marine mammals and coastal beaches. The next year, Congress authorized the Endangered Species Act, regulated toxic chemicals, and passed new green laws governing the use of public lands. The 1970s, the environmental decade, fittingly culminated in passage of the Alaska National Interest Lands Act in 1980, which protected about 110 million acres of wilderness, an area larger than the state of California.

Congressional domination had another impressive outburst in 1987–1988, when the Reagan presidency was so weakened by the Iran-contra scandal that it could give no direction, Congress (though the House was itself handicapped by deep scandal surrounding the speakership) improved two major civil-rights laws, gave the first complete overhaul to the federal welfare system since its inception in the 1930s, passed an $18 billion Clean Water Act over the president's veto, expanded federal programs for the homeless and drug addicts and AIDS victims, passed a catastrophic health insurance plan for millions of elderly or disabled people (a badly written law, but Congress meant well), ratified the first U.S.–Soviet arms reduction treaty, and churned out a host of other laws—thereby bringing to a close the one hundreth Congress (a "Congress" lasts two years, so this was the two hundreth anniversary of its founding) with a record that its leaders boasted was the most productive in two decades. The doyen of political columnists, David Broder, ordinarily no admirer of Democrat-controlled Congresses, admitted that "it probably ranks among the handful of Congresses in the last four decades which clearly left an enduring mark in many fields."

But the very fact that the one hundredth was such an exception simply underscores that Congress is in trouble. How could a Congress be called "the best in twenty years" or "one of the best in forty years" when in fact it failed to come to grips with some of the most important problems facing the nation—the budget deficit, the out-of-control entitlement programs (pensions, etc.), the corruption of the Pentagon, the crisis condition of the savings and loan industry, the long-delayed cleanup of toxic and nuclear waste, and many et ceteras.

The fear that as it is presently organized Congress may be nearly incompetent to cope with the problems and needs of more than 250 million people has penetrated even the mind of Congress itself. Former Representative Richard Bolling, an outstanding moderate from Missouri whose thirty-four years in the House left him limp with cynicism, described the House as "ineffective in its role as a coordinate branch of the federal government, negative in its approach to national tasks, generally unresponsive to any but parochial economic interests"—well, at least most of the time.

When Senator Howard H. Baker, Jr., Tennessee Republican and Senate majority leader, announced that he was not going to seek reelection, he said it was impossible to stay in touch with the electorate—to learn what they are thinking, to get a true sampling of their sentiments—as long as Congress stayed in session year-round. He stated in an interview:

> I still go home almost every weekend for a hurried grazing pass at the people of my state, masquerading in the guise of a man trying to find out what is going on. Who in the world can find out what is going on in the people's minds on a Saturday or Sunday when people would rather not be talking to politicians to begin with?
>
> I get home and find out that things I worried about daily in Washington, people at home couldn't care less about. And people down there mention things repeatedly that barely surface up here as issues.

One hears despair everywhere from those who try to do their job. "There's a sense that the whole system is breaking down," said Senator Daniel Evans, who quit in frustration in 1989 after only one term. One day in the midst of a tax debate, Senator Daniel Patrick Moynihan yelled at his colleagues, "What on earth are we doing? This system is collapsing." Another time he likened senators to white mice who "run around wanting different things and end up within hours lying on their backs with their feet in the air." As Senator Tom Eagleton prepared to flee the Senate after three terms, he said that body was in the grip of "unbridled chaos."

And Senator David Pryor of Arkansas, a member of a tougher group determined to stay and try to change the rules so that the machine will start working again, said, "I think we're spending a lot of time basically doing nothing. Being in the Senate is like getting stuck in an airport and having all your flights cancelled." Later he likened the Senate to a "huge, giant lumber mill, with all the high technology . . . and the biggest saws in the world, which is making toothpicks."

In the midst of one nerve-wracking dysfunctioning period, Senate Chaplain Richard C. Halverson opened a session with the prayer, asking God to "spare the senators . . . from becoming like a powerful engine frozen because of the friction of its parts. . . . Preserve it, gracious God, from becoming a muscle-bound giant, victim of its own rules, procedures and precedents."

Electorate: Blame Yourself

Disenchantment with professional politics, and especially with Washington's variety, can no longer be considered merely the grumpiness of the sophisticates. In just one brief period has the public stated its confidence in the conduct of Congress, 1964 to 1966, the most productive years since Franklin D. Roosevelt's first term. Before and since that unique 1964–1966 blossoming, only about one-third of the public has consistently said it thinks Congress is doing a good job (and in gloomy periods support sinks to half that).

Admittedly, a lot of the public's attitude stems from the fact that it simply doesn't pay much attention to the everyday workings of Congress. That august body may seem like the center of the universe to people living inside the Washington, D.C., beltway, but, as journalist Howard Kurtz has wisely observed:

> To most of America, Congress is just a faraway collection of overpaid and over-pampered hacks who mouth off on Sunday TV shows that no one watches and who now and then stay up all night working themselves into a lather over wild-eyed flagburners. In one recent poll, fewer than 30 percent of those interviewed could name their congressman, and fewer than half could name one of their senators. The degree of political disinterest out here in the regions, which campaign reporters rediscover every four years, is hard to exaggerate.

Does Congress deserve such unrelenting disdain? Yes and no. It does deserve disdain because although in general the public allows Congress wide latitude in writing of laws, Congress insists on pursuing the most cautious and most expedient course of action in just about any situation. In short, Congress deserves disdain because, in a country that was founded on revolution and whose Fourth of July tenets are lofty and idealistic, Congress shoots only for the safest and lowest common denominator of action—if it shoots at all.

On the other hand, no, Congress does not deserve the public's disdain because Congress is the creation of the people. Congress is the only part of the federal government that is elected directly by the people. The president is one extra step removed from the electorate; the popular vote decides who is to be in the electoral college every four years, and the electoral college elects the president. As for the federal judges, they, of course, are appointed. So only the 535 members of Congress—435 in the House, 100 in the Senate—feel the moist touch of the voter on their shoulder, directly, without any intermediate cushioning.*

---

*Originally only the House was elected by the popular vote. It was the part of Congress that was supposed to represent the rabble. The Senate was elected by members of the state legislatures. Since the Senate was not directly responsible to the populace, it was seen as a "balancing" influence on the House. Actually, it was seen—and so acknowledged by anyone of candor—as the voice of the moneyed interests. And indeed it was. Since most of the state legislatures were notoriously in the palm of special business interests, they naturally selected senators who would be lackeys for those interests. And they were seldom disappointed in their selections. But since 1913 the Senate, too, has been elected by the general populace.

When Congressman Lloyd Meeds of Washington state was getting ready to retire from Congress in 1979, after fourteen years in the Capitol, he was asked, "What is wrong with Congress?" He replied:

> There's nothing wrong with Congress that isn't wrong with this country. Congress, particularly the House of Representatives, is a mirror of what's happening and of the views that are being expressed in the households all across this country today. And to expect Congress, particularly the House, with its short tenure of two years, to be better or worse than the country as a whole is to expect something that our Founding Fathers never intended, and something that is never going to happen.
>
> It is necessary to differentiate between fact and perception. Meeds's "First Law of Politics" is that there is no fact, only perception. The public's perception of the institution of Congress is that it is terrible, that it has fallen on bad days and bad ways, and that it is a lousy institution. But let me tell you I think that Congress is a much better institution today than it was in 1965 when I first came here. We have made it a better institution by adopting reforms in the committee system. These reforms have taken place in the last fifteen years. . . . When I first came here freshmen and sophomore members were to be seen and not heard. Today they are an effective, integral part of Congress.

But Representative Henry S. Reuss, who retired in 1983 after twenty-eight years in the House, including six years as chairman of the Banking Committee, had a somewhat different appraisal. "The quality of the average member today," he said, "is the finest in history, in terms of general education and outlook on public life. But the institution has moved backward, and is less effective today than twenty-eight years ago." The reasons, he said, are the "evolution of the electronic Congressman" who lives by the television set and computer; the accompanying decline of the parties, "especially mine" (Democratic); and "unbridled" campaign expenditures that put a "psychological mortgage" on members. "Congress is less collegial," he said, "because there's more egotism and less team spirit."

There is some truth in what both Meeds and Reuss say, even though they sometimes seem to be at odds. The typical member is better schooled today than twenty years ago; members are also more independent, because with enough money and a good television package, they can sell themselves directly to the voters without the aid of their parties. This has created "less team spirit," as Reuss noted. Dictatorial control has been taken away from the old mossbacks in

Congress, and the freshmen and sophomore members are, as Meeds claims, carrying their full weight. But with the decline of respect for elder members, and the lessening power of seniority, institutional authority has fallen on hard times. Members are more honest and accurate in telling the public where they got their campaign money; Meeds is right about that, and it is an improvement. But on the other hand, there are now many ways of hiding the true sources of campaign funds, through the creation of political action committees (PACs). These PACs representing special-interest groups have become so uncontrollably generous in giving to campaigns that Congress has become the best that money can buy—which, as Reuss was implying, is not exactly a compliment.

So reforms have been offset by new defects, and the public is accurate in its perception of Congress as, at least in part, "lousy" (to use Meeds' word). That perception cannot be offset by saying that Congress is only a reflection of, and no better or no worse than, the public. In many ways its membership is far better off than the general public.

Pay and Freebies

Congress is much better paid, much more pampered, much more insulated from hardships—it is much more haughty and aloof and conceited and self-centered—than any cross-section of the public at large. And the public, which pays for Congress's privileges, properly resents this attitude—especially when it is not accompanied by efficient performance.

Members of Congress are paid $140,673, which is nearly four times the national average income. It is also more than most members were earning before they were elected. And do not for a moment think that their congressional salary is all that many members have to live on. At least thirty of the senators are millionaires and more than fifty members of the House are believed to be that well heeled, or nearly so. Probably the richest is Senator John Kerry of Massachusetts, who married the widow of another senator, John Heinz of Pennsylvania (the ketchup-and-pickle heir), who left an estate estimated at more than $700 million. Many members augment their congressional salaries with pensions from having served as governors or members of state legislatures before reaching Washington, or from military service; many have income from investments. On the other hand, some members are in hock up to their knees. And while $140,673 is a very nice salary, for members who have only that much to keep up two homes and a family, it may seem pretty skimpy. Which is why there are a handful of members who, to avoid maintaining a second home, sleep in their offices.

Members receive full pensions at age sixty after only ten years of service, compared to twenty years for civil service employees and considerably more years than that for people in nonfederal employment. According to a Labor Department study, a worker in the private sector earning $50,000 or more is usually eligible for pension benefits averaging $17,062. That wouldn't be considered even peanuts to congressmen. Several long-term members retiring in 1999 will receive $98,694 a year—three-fourths their salary—with automatic increases thereafter.

Americans love to argue over whether congressmen are overpaid or underpaid. A recent pay raise drew this wry observation from a *Chicago Tribune* columnist: "Actually, I don't have any strong feelings against congressmen getting pay raises. I've known some congressmen who weren't worth $8.95 a year. Others would be a bargain at $895,000 a year. So maybe it balances out." And anyway, "The fact is, the average congressman is not the average American. He is better educated, smarter, reads more, watches fewer game shows and soap operas on TV, knows more about law, foreign affairs, national problems, and assumes greater responsibilities. So why shouldn't a congressman be paid as much as a weak-hitting utility infielder?"

A nice argument, repeated by many supporters of the raise in less colorful language, but it had one basic flaw: Utility infielders are paid with private money, not public. And as his performance declines, so does his pay. Though the congressional pay raise would have been an infinitesimal part of the budget, it was the principle of the thing that galled people. Thus this argument from David Keating, executive vice president of the National Taxpayers Union:

> Decisions on trillion-dollar budgets? Give me someone in Washington to make those decisions whose pocketbook is being squeezed, not someone making nearly $150,000 annually. Decisions on war and peace? Those with the most to lose are generally the ones most ready to fight to protect it. Let us have representatives in Washington for reasons of principle, not property, and we will be more likely to have peace. If pay for members of Congress is 'low,' why are so few quitting? Only 15 of 535 members of Congress voluntarily quit politics this election cycle, and few, if any, of those fifteen cited pay as a major cause of their decision to retire."

Shed no tears for our federal lawmakers. They will not starve, nor will they go unhonored with physical comforts. Aside from their salary, they get a pension that is five times higher than the average citizen's pension and that, because of automatic increases members voted themselves in 1963, often pays more in retirement than members earned in salary. Former House Speaker Carl Albert, for example, had a salary of $65,600 when he retired from Congress in 1977; today he collects a pension of just under $100,000 a year. He is one of several ex-members who have earned more than $1 million each since leaving Congress. Members also have given themselves free medical care, cut-rate insurance, cut-rate hospitalization, free flowers, free picture framing, cut-rate meals in fine private dining rooms, free trips to foreign tourist spots, and all sorts of luxurious office allowances, free trips home, phone allowances between 9 A.M. and 5 P.M. and free phone service at all other times, free mailing, and numerous other freebies that contribute to the joys of being a member of the congressional club. (Which is, by the way, still overwhelmingly a white male domain: In 1998 there were fifty-three women in the House, nine in the Senate; thirty-nine blacks in the House, one in the Senate (Carol Moseley-Braun of Illinois, but she was defeated in 1998 after only one term); twenty-one Hispanics, all in the House; five Asian-Pacifics in the House; two in the Senate.

Kingmakers Behind the Scenes

It costs taxpayers nearly $2.5 billion a year to let members live and work in the style to which they have become accustomed. And the cost is rising steadily. A big part of the expense comes from providing them with enough space to accommodate their princely ambitions. The latest addition to the Roman grandeur of Capitol Hill is the marble and glass Hart Building, the Senate's third office building, completed in 1982. It cost $137.7 million—a mere $90 million more than officials predicted when the building was first planned in the early 1970s. It was the costliest federal building up to that time. Why so much money? Exterior windows that are twenty-feet high and five-feet wide, $1.5 million in wood paneling, sixteen-foot-high office ceilings, two private bathrooms for each senator, elevator doors made of bronze, $3 million worth of marble, a three-story underground garage, a rooftop tennis court. In short, the works.

In the past forty years, two new Senate office buildings have been built, although during that time the number of senators increased by only four. The Capitol architect predicts that the Senate will have to start constructing another office building soon. Over on the House side, expansion has been almost as impressive.

What's going on? Why the explosion of construction? Two things are happening. The first and most obvious is that Congress is simply indulging in an orgy of extravagance, an irresponsible spending on itself. That accounts for the luxurious paneling and marble and gymnasiums and splendid restaurants and the like. The second reason is that Congress is becoming buried under its own self-breeding bureaucracy. You must look upon the Capitol Hill community as a little kingdom unto itself, and it is a sizeable one. There are more than 37,000 Congressional workers—from majority leader to venetian blind technician. About half are people who work within the members' offices or in committee offices, and their number has grown 300 percent in the past thirty years. Clerks, secretaries, publicists, legislative aides, case workers, administrative assistants—the hired hands swarm over the Capitol, filling space as soon as it is built.

Some staff members are highly prized professionals and very powerful in their own right. The public rarely knows of their existence. Such a one was Richard Conlon, who for twenty years preceding his death in 1989 was executive director of the Democratic Study Group in the House of Representatives. It was said that virtually no major legislation could pass without his personal support. On one occasion, he organized 110 House members to sue the president to comply with a legislative resolution.

The top staff members are well paid. A few are paid nearly as much as their bosses. When former Speaker Jim Wright's thirty-six-year-old legislative aide stepped down in 1989 as a result of publicity about a savage beating (hammer and knife) he had given a young woman sixteen years earlier—a beating for which he had served time—it was revealed that he was earning $89,500—the same level as a congressman at that time. Some who receive that kind of salary are worth it, considering that they do more of the actual running of the office and the dealing with lobbyists and the writing of legislation and the dickering with other members' offices than do their bosses. When Senator Howard Baker, Jr., was Senate majority leader, reporters who called him about his position on a bill would often be told that he didn't know because "I haven't talked to Tommy yet"—meaning Tommy Griscom, his young press aide. When Tip O'Neill was Speaker of the House, he relied on Stephen Airel Weiss, an aide in his early thirties, to put together major legislation and devise the strategy for passing it. O'Neill excused Weiss's enormous influence by saying, "He thinks exactly as I think."

Perhaps. But there is great danger in this sort of thing. The aides, not having to face the electorate for their jobs, cannot possibly feel the same responsibilities. Furthermore, there is always the possibility that the aides, with an eye to yet-higher-paying jobs in business, may get too thick with the lobbyists who represent those businesses. And it is the aides and the lobbyists who do most of the actual writing of legislation, working together on it. Busy members surrender the chore to them, rationalizing that they can't do otherwise in a day that overflows with committee meetings, meetings with constituents, meetings with donors, meetings with lobbyists, meetings with staff, debates on the floor, and so on.

Before Democratic whip Tony Coelho of California resigned from the House, he was candid enough to admit that "I've lost control. . . . What I've done now is put things in the hands of lobbyists and staff. I'm going to go home tonight with two or three [large manila] envelopes of memos to read, and I'm going to say yes or no. Who wrote the memos? My staff. I'm going to respond to their interpretation of the issues."

Need Breeds Hatred

Another danger from the growth of staffs is that these bright manipulators are ambitious and like to expand the power of their little dukedoms. The best way to do this is to think up more legislation for their boss to push—to get more publicity, more newspaper space and television time—and the legislative pipeline thereby becomes further clogged.

Ninety percent of Congress's work is done at the committee and subcommittee levels, and it is here that staff experts carry the most influence. The elite group of specialists who make up the staffs of the congressional committees put their imprint on almost every bill passed by Congress. One report sees their influence in this way:

> Most casual visitors to the Capitol probably overlook altogether the role of committee employees in the work of Congress. In committee hearings and floor debate, senators and representatives wholly monopolize the limelight.
>
> But a close look at Congress in action reveals the importance of staff workers. At hearings, they sometimes can be glimpsed whispering in the ear of a senator or representative, planting a question for a witness or appraising a witness's answer.

When a committee "marks up" a bill, the aides labor at their bosses' elbows on the wording of proposed amendments—amendments to be affixed to a measure that most likely was itself drafted by the staff.

Likewise, when a committee chairman takes a bill to the floor for action by the full House or Senate membership, committee aides troop right along with him. They do not engage in debate; the rules forbid that. But they sit beside elected officials, sometimes passing notes to them as questions arise.

This hidden government of advisers is largely faceless, but occasionally in crucial moments we get to see who is really running the country. Such a moment occurred in 1986, when the Senate was wrestling with the monumental tax-reform bill and Senator Bob Packwood of Oregon, chairman of the Senate Finance Committee, called a press conference to explain the bill. Only he didn't try. He turned the conference over to David Brockway, silently admitting that he didn't know nearly as much about what was going on as Brockway, chief of staff of the Joint Committee on Taxation.

Leon G. Billings, Norvill Jones, Michael R. Lemov, Richard J. Sullivan, Donald M. Baker, Kenneth A. McLean, Bernard M. Shapiro—these are not exactly household names, but these men have probably done as much as, and very likely more than, any seven senators to shape pollution laws, foreign affairs, pork barrel authorizations, job safety laws, tax laws, and banking laws in the committees where they hold top staff jobs and their advice is considered golden. Their success is usually voiced in a grudging acknowledgment, as when the late Senator James B. Allen complained: "Senators supposedly make the decisions and tell the staff to write the reports. But, unfortunately, to a large extent, staffs orchestrate and call the tune for Senate committee members. We're being taken over by nonelected, mushrooming staffs."

Many members, frustrated and shamed by their growing dependence on staffs, have come almost to hate the very people they employ. Said Senator Ernest Hollings of South Carolina:

A senator the other day told me another senator hadn't been in his office for three years. It is just staff. Everybody is working for the staff, staff, staff, driving you nutty. It has gotten to the point where the senators never actually sit down and exchange ideas and learn from the experience of others and listen. Now it is how many nutty whiz kids you get on the staff, and to get you magazine articles and get you headlines and get all of these other things done.

Pity the Flunkies

But of course most of the people who work for members of Congress are far from being powerbrokers; their jobs, hardly engulfed with glamour, differ little from office work done in Spokane, San Antonio, or Schenectady. And much of what passes for "glamour" is nothing but acting as a servant to a cranky and demanding boss. One of Senator Robert Byrd's press aides quit when he discovered that his duties included mowing the senator's lawn. Representative Gerry Sikorski, Democrat of Minnesota, may have set a record for variety of demands, if some of his aides were correct in saying he had required them to shovel snow from the sidewalk in front of his home, pick his daughter up from school, wash dishes, get his dry cleaning, and help his wife care for their dogs. Some assortment of that kind of service is par for many congressional offices. And it is not uncommon to hear female employees complain that their bosses try to pressure them into performing sexual favors as well.

Which brings us to one of the notorious characteristics of Congress: It operates by the rule that the rule-maker should not have to obey the rules. It has carefully exempted itself from the kind of reform laws it has imposed on the rest of society. "It is the rankest form of hypocrisy," said retired Senator John Glenn of Ohio. "Laws that are good enough for everybody else ought to be good enough for us." Illinois Congressman Henry Hyde added with disgust, "Congress would exempt itself from the laws of gravity if it could."

Probably so, for it has exempted itself from every minimum-wage law since the first one it passed in 1938.

Until recently, both chambers exempted themselves from fair employment laws. They could, if they wanted, keep minorities and women at the bottom of the scale, or not hire them at all. In 1988, the House took a step toward fair play: It extended the same protection against job discrimination to its own employees that most American workers had received twenty-four years earlier, but it still left itself a couple of big loopholes for arbitrary action. Although the House refused to put itself under the Civil Rights Act of 1964, like other portions of society, it did amend its rules to prohibit hiring and promotion discrimination on the basis of race, color, national origin, religion, sex, physical handicap, or age. However, the new rule allows House members to refuse to hire someone whose way of life they disagree with. Workers who feel they have been discriminated against can't take their case to court, as the Civil Rights Act permits other workers to do. They must instead complain to a House panel, and the panel's decision is final. It's a slender reform—although more than the Senate has done—and the status quo it goes up against is quite awesome.

Some offices hire no blacks. Because Congress has exempted itself from keeping such records, there is no way to know how many are employed by members.

A Legislator's Work Is Never Done . . .

A principal reason for the growing staff is that in the last forty years Congress has been overwhelmed by a flood of new issues. Suddenly it finds itself required to be expert on environmental problems, energy problems, job safety, equal rights, medical needs, and a laundry list of social programs. A generation ago Americans lived in a different social and political world: Medical aid programs for the needy had not been passed; the great civil rights laws had not been passed; the women's equal rights movement had hardly been heard of; the middle-class drug problem was nonexistent; illegal aliens were only trickling, not flooding, into the country; the Third World countries of Africa and Asia were still somnambulant; the spread of toxic chemicals in the environment had not yet reached such proportions as to arouse many fears; the atomic energy industry had hardly started; auto exhaust poisons were considered a nuisance in a few cities but not seen as a national problem; the intolerable decay of the inner cities and the flight to the suburbs had not yet reached a frightening pace.

As these problems began to accelerate, the public began to demand assistance from Washington. Gradually, often grudgingly, and often with insufficient information and half-cocked notions, Congress passed legislation to meet the problems. Considering how varied and complex they were—and are—it is something of a miracle that Congress grappled with them as well as it did, occasionally achieving an authentic victory: Some of the safety, environmental, and racial fair-play laws have given Americans a fighting chance to pursue happiness.

But some of the new laws were written so hastily and so carelessly that they created as many problems as they solved. Sometimes they were almost bad jokes. For example, when the drafters of the Coal Mine Health and Safety Act were told that an "Auer breather" (a West German device) was available to provide coal miners with a closed-circuit oxygen rescue apparatus in case of fire, they thought their informant was saying "hour breather." So they wrote into the law that the United States Bureau of Mines must provide miners with a portable sixty-minute breather. Unfortunately, no device in the world would provide more than twenty-five minutes of life-supporting oxygen for the miners. Bureaucrats being bureaucrats, officials at the Bureau of Mines spent the next ten years trying to perfect a sixty-minute breather—rather than go back to Congress and tell the law's drafters that no such device was available.

Such loose, sloppy drafting of legislation is not uncommon. After working for eighteen months to put together a natural gas bill, members of Congress came up with an incomprehensible mass that ran to 171 pages. They accompanied it with a report of 130 pages, intended to explain what was meant by the 171-page bill. A typical section of the bill read: "This special rule limits the operation of indefinite price escalator clauses in existing intrastate contracts for which the contract price on December 31, 1984, is higher than $1.00 per MMBtu's so that the contract prices may not exceed the new gas ceiling price as of January 1, 1985, adjusted by the monthly equivalent of the annual inflation adjustment factor, plus 3.0 percentage points."

If you can't understand that, don't be ashamed. Neither could experts at the Department of Energy. In fact, the person in charge of the department's Office of Enforcement sent out a confidential memo stating that the bill "is so complex, ambiguous and contradictory that it would be virtually impossible for this commission to enforce it in a conscientious and equitable manner."

Sometimes there is nefarious method in the madness of legislative gobbledygook. A so-called tax reform bill contained hundreds of passages with language so impenetrable that the public could not realize it was giving billions of dollars in tax breaks to corporations and wealthy individuals. For example, this passage:

> In the case of a partnership with a taxable year beginning May 1, 1986, if such partnership realized net capital gain during the period beginning on the first day of such taxable year and ending on May 29, 1986, pursuant to an indemnity agreement dated May 6, 1986, then such partnership may elect to treat each asset to which such net capital gain relates as having been distributed in proportion to their distributive share of the capital gain or loss realized by the partnership with respect to each asset.

That may sound like garbage to you, but it was pure gold—$8 million in tax exemptions—to the partners of one unnamed Wall Street brokerage firm.

In his valedictory session, Senator Barry Goldwater complained:

> Senators often don't know what they're voting on. That's a lousy way to run a lemonade stand, much less our national legislative process. My bill to reorganize the Department of Defense ran 645 pages. I myself had a helluva time understanding everything in it. Multiply that several thousand times and you begin to have some idea of the confusion in which Congress operates.
>
> Worse yet, members often haven't the foggiest notion of the long-range implications of a law they have passed. Members of the federal bureaucracy wind up interpreting and finalizing the law. No one elected them. They are responsible to nobody. So off they go into the wild blue yonder!
>
> The final weeks of almost every session of the Congress now look and sound like a bargain-basement sale. Bills are passed so wildly that they often contain unprinted amendments. That means Congress is passing legislation it has never read!

Indeed it does. And occasionally some of this unread law floats to the surface to everyone's surprise—including Congress's. In 1988, it was discovered that Congress had appropriated $8 million to build day schools in France for Jewish immigrants from North Africa. Now, the U.S. Congress passes a great deal of humanitarian laws, but wasn't that taking its generosity down strange roads? Where in the world had the legislation come from? Well, it turned out that Senator Daniel K. Inouye of Hawaii had tucked it into the massive appropriations bill, unread by anyone else apparently, as a favor to a Jewish foundation based in New York. When the benevolence was uncovered (and later rescinded by an embarrassed Congress), the head of the foundation explained why they had asked Senator Inouye for help: "When we found out that the Congress of the U.S. was giving out money to cats and dogs and who knows what, we thought we could get a piece of it." Not so illogical, at that.

Never Enough Time

Much of Congress's shoddy workmanship can be traced to the foolish way it allots its time. The first several months of a typical year will be dawdled away; then in the last two weeks of the year, members will frantically process eighty or a hundred major bills, whisking them through with such haste that the contents of only a few can be painstakingly analyzed by all members. Real legislative issues will sometimes drag on to intolerable lengths while the days pass in limp salutes to protocol, tradition, and ancient egos, until, in a whirlwind of despair, Congress will pass laws the contents it knows not of.

Typical of the kind of mess Congress gets itself into by dawdling was the crunch of 1998, when members faced the next fiscal year, only four weeks away, and had not yet passed even one of the thirteen major spending bills that had to be passed to prevent another shutdown of the government (as occurred in 1995). While President Clinton threatened to veto seven of the bills if they were passed without changes he demanded, Republicans quarreled among themselves over a tax cut and foreign affairs spending; there were interparty clashes over campaign spending reforms, managed health care, trade policies, and such esoteric questions as abortion rights. There was no way in the world all these issues could be handled sensibly in such a short time.

Time—there is never enough of it for Congress. To be sure, they squander it, waste it, but much of their time is legitimately consumed by demands that they can't keep up with: constituent demands for help, national demands for answers, staff demands for space to work in or for more machines to process more paper. And always, perpetually, overwhelmingly, maddeningly, there is demand of the brain for time in which to pause and contemplate, to think, to study.*

Senator James B. Pearson of Kansas, nearing the end of his second decade in Washington, complained:

> In my more cynical moments, I say that if this government ever falls, it won't be from any external pressure. It will be because those people assigned to make judgments never had any time to read or contemplate or think. The days of the great Senate specialists are passing, and senators, by and large, are being forced to become generalists. Congress really doesn't have the capacity to deal with highly scientific technical issues like energy and weapons systems. This problem is not going to pass away. If anything, issues will get more technical.

---

*The House Commission on Administrative Review found in 1977, probably the last study of the problem, that an average member of the House puts in an eleven-hour workday but has only eleven minutes daily to devote to reading and twelve minutes to spend in his or her office on legislation and speech-writing. The study noted, "Rarely do members have sufficient blocks of time when they are free from the frenetic pace of the Washington 'treadmill' to think about the implications of various public policies."

So great are the demands on their time that members, as already mentioned, have increasingly turned over more and more duties to their staffs and have themselves become more and more remote from the public. This is especially true in the Senate, where a member's constituency can be well into the millions. Senate members receive more than 50 million pieces of mail in a typical year. Senators from a large state may receive 20,000 letters a week. In return, Congress spews out 12,000 letters for every one it receives; at latest count, that came to an annual total of 759 million pieces of mail.

Not only are telephone calls and mail from constituents flooding over the Capitol, so are constituents themselves. With budget air fares, a voter who gets up and reads something in the morning paper that offends him about his government can be in Washington that afternoon knocking on the door of a congressperson to do something about it. This is no small concern. There isn't enough time in a congressperson's day to meet half the people who want to see him or her. The staff becomes a buffer—glad-handing the visitors, giving them passes to the congressional galleries, loading them up with brochures about what to see while they are in Washington, but keeping them away from the member.

Federal politicians protect themselves not only by hiding behind five thicknesses of staff but also by hiring a heavy cordon of police. Congress is protected by 1,255 police officers, which is a larger force than protects Nashville, a city of more than half a million. Is life really that dangerous on Capitol Hill? Well, it's true that in 1998 a madman from Illinois shot and killed two Capitol police officers and wounded a tourist. But these were the first shots heard in the Capitol in forty-four years, a peaceful interlude interrupted only by two rather minor explosions, one in a Capitol restroom. So it is hard to believe that the horde of police are there to ward off criminals. A better assumption is that they are there for the same reason many of the halls within the Capitol complex most trafficked by Congress's lawmakers are off-limits—to ward off the public, to keep it at a distance from the politicians, who prefer to preserve most of their time for attending committee meetings, discussing work with their staffs, going to the floor to vote (and occasionally to debate or to listen to others debate), huddling with big-money campaign contributors, taking long lunches, visiting one of the several congressional gymnasiums for a workout or a massage.

That may sound heartlessly undemocratic, but it is probably necessary if they are to get anything done, even if what is done turns out to have been a waste of time.

The View from Inside

One of the smarter and more industrious members of the Senate was, until he retired in 1992, Senator Warren B. Rudman, sixty-five, a New Hampshire Republican. He says that when he was in the Senate he felt like he was seventy-five years old, and departing the Senate made him feel like thirty-five. Was it really such a depressing job? Here is one of his typical days, as he recreated it for *The New York Times* in 1995:

6 A.M. You head to Capitol Hill for breakfast with constituents. You find they have been shocked by an editorial that morning in the largest paper in your state. It accuses you of driving the children of America into the arms of atheism. Why? Because your view of the Constitution obliged you to vote against a bill to require prayer in the public schools.

8 A.M. You discuss the day's agenda with the staff. An aide brings in hundreds of letters that arrived yesterday, and you read as many as time permits.

9 A.M. You have three committee hearings going on simultaneously, and you attend parts of all three, knowing you are spread too thin. Your press secretary slips you a note: Twenty reporters have called about your criticism of the president last night. You return some of the calls between hearings.

Noon. Your state party chairman calls to say that a handsome golf pro who recently married a very rich woman has decided he wants to be a senator. You think you can defeat him, but will have to raise $10 million in the next two years, instead of $5 million for a normal race.

Noon. You take prominent businessmen from your state to lunch in the Senate dining room. They agree on the urgency of a balanced budget—of course, only if it does not mean higher taxes or reduced benefits for them. You pick up the tab.

1 P.M. to 6 P.M. Bells start calling you to votes on the Senate floor. They ring all afternoon. Many are on amendments relating to abortion, flag-burning, pornography, and school prayer. None will pass, but their sponsors are eager to make statements for the papers back home. New senators, the ones obsessed with protecting the flag, don't seem equally concerned about protecting the economy. The number of votes, in committee and on the floor, has nearly doubled since 1980, when I entered the Senate.

You go to your party's campaign office (on the Hill) and get a list of people to ask for money. You have to call from there: It's illegal to call from your office. You hate asking strangers for money, but you have the golf pro to worry about.

6 P.M. You attend fund-raisers for two colleagues. . . . You choke down peanuts and two small sausages for dinner.

8 P.M. You are back on the Senate floor for debate on major budget amendments. The mood is angry, people are bitter, ideologues on both sides reject compromise. Some people won't speak to each other.

1 A.M. The majority leader gives up and adjourns. Late nights have become the rule. You wonder if you'll be able to leave the next afternoon to spend the weekend in your home state. It will be filled with meetings with constituents, fund-raising, town meetings, and press conferences.

1:30 A.M. You're home. The family is sleeping. You ask yourself, "Who needs this?"

Overlapping—and Conflicting—Interests

Since 1978, members of the House of Representatives have had to make public disclosure of their personal incomes from sources other than their congressional paychecks. The resulting data show that a significant percentage of members earn outside income from the very industries that are controlled to some extent by the committees on which they serve. Some members of the Agriculture Committee, for example, own farms or ranches. Some members of the Banking Committee have bank stock.

The conflict-of-interest questions raised by situations such as these could be asked, one way or another, of the many members who hold investments in defense companies, oil and gas companies, insurance companies, banks, and other major corporations. It seems reasonable to assume that their outside income sometimes seriously dilutes the public spiritedness of their work in Congress.* Voters have a right to ask the obvious question: How much do outside activities affect the legislators' votes?

Another possible conflict of interest is that between narrow constituent interests and broad national interests. Some committee assignments in Congress are prized because they offer an inside track to

---

*An "outside" income worth special notice is the military pension, which isn't exactly outside, since it also comes from the federal treasury, but does threaten to lessen the objectivity of members. Nobody knows for sure how many, but several dozen members of Congress receive either veterans' pensions or veterans' disability payments, and dozens of others will receive veterans' pensions at the end of their "reserve" service. This may be one reason—although it isn't necessarily the main reason—why Congress has made virtually no effort to control the amazing growth of military retirement benefits.

getting more subsidies for the folks back home and for special interests that reward members at campaign time. Committees that handle oil legislation, coal legislation, Western water resources, federal grazing rights, and farm bills dealing with cotton and wheat production are packed with members whose home areas stand to benefit. Under a republican form of government, it is inevitable that each member will vote in the interests of the people who elected him or her. But there is always the danger that in some committees the sum of these narrow, parochial interests will outweigh the broad, national interests. Ideally, every committee would be made up of a healthy mixture of ideological and geographical interests, balancing each other and keeping each other in line. On some of the more important committees, this is not done.

Because overlapping interests, if not outright conflicts of interests, are so common in Congress, it is probably to be expected that members see nothing wrong in taking favors from their moneyed allies. To suggest that the relationship might be otherwise often brings an incredulous response from our politicians. When Edward Garmatz of Baltimore was chairman of the House Merchant Marine Committee, he had a singularly cozy relationship with the big shipping lines. Asked why he received most of his election money from the maritime industry, he snorted: "Who in the hell did you expect me to get it from—the post office people, the bankers? You get it from the people you work with, who you helped in some way or another. It's only natural."

Boodle and Pork Barrel

Congress is distracted by its political venality, by the fact that it is usually motivated by mundane rewards. The more candid members of Congress admit, as Representative Richard Bolling once did, that "the mortar that binds the system consists largely of what has been called inelegantly but properly 'boodle.'"

> Boodle includes the location of a military installation, with a construction payroll followed by a steady payroll of civilian and military employees who live and spend and pay taxes in a member's district. It also includes a wide variety of public works—dams, rivers, and harbor projects, federal post office and office buildings, conservation and reclamation projects. The boodle in itself is legitimate and productive. The hitch is in the way it is distributed. Generally, the stay-in-line orthodox members will come away with the fuller plate.

A perfect example of boodle could be found in the budget for the Army Corps of Engineers passed in 1997. Thirty million dollars was set aside for "South Central Pennsylvania Environmental Improvement." It required the government to pick up 75 percent of the tab for water and sewer system improvements in twenty-one Pennsylvania counties. Wow! Such generosity! Most local governments never get that kind of aid. Why this exception?

The answer was obvious: These counties are in the congressional districts of Republican Joe McDade, chairman of the subcommittee that wrote the bill; Democrat John Murtha, a senior Appropriations Committee member; and Republican Bud Shuster, chairman of the House public works panel.

The other phrase for this is, of course, pork barrel, and Bolling is incorrect when he suggests that it is always legitimate and productive. Sometimes it is; often it is not. But for the majority of members of Congress, the paramount issue is not legitimacy and productivity but whether the barrel supplies enough pork to go around in the right places—namely, the business community and the middle class, which provide campaign contributions and votes.

Representative Jamie L. Whitten of Mississippi, when asking for speedy approval of a $3 billion public works (dams, post offices, and so on) appropriations bill, asserted, "Since the works provided reach into every nook and corner of the country, the report has had the attention of practically all the membership of the House." There was, in short, plenty of pork to go around, and it was the kind of pork that fed contractors, labor unions, building-material manufacturers, builders—just the sort of people who keep politicians in office.

Do not suppose, however, that members of Congress are always moved to act by evidence that legislation touches many lives in every area; that has never been a consistently effective way to evoke congressional support. For example, medical care for the aged was proposed in every session of Congress for a generation before it was finally, reluctantly, passed; yet there were certainly people in every district who needed this protection. Every year industrial hazards kill more than 14,000, injure 260,000, and lay up 390,000 workers with occupational illnesses. But it took thirty years for legislation shoring up occupational health and safety standards to be passed. Stiff controls on the sale of guns have been advocated for years by the FBI, the associations of police chiefs, and most scholars of crime (in addition to the public, which polls regularly find to be in favor of controls). After the assassination of John Kennedy, fresh efforts were made in Congress to pass a gun control act; after the assassinations of Martin Luther King, Jr., and Robert Kennedy and the assassination attempts on Gerald Ford and Ronald Reagan, the campaigns were renewed. And they were renewed again in the late 1990s, after teenagers at several schools across the nation shot and killed a total of 26 students and teachers, and wounded dozens of others—most shockingly at Littleton, Colorado, where the death toll was 15 students and one teacher. Yet with the exception of a clamp-down on mail-order sales, restrictions on importing and manufacturing some types of military-style assault weapons, and some requirements for checking the background of buyers, Congress has done little to curtail the booming gun trade that has put an estimated 250 million weapons in the hands of U.S. residents.

It isn't that Congress cannot work swiftly if it chooses to. As Senator Howard M. Metzenbaum, Ohio Democrat, once observed sarcastically, "We don't have time to do anything that is important, but we have plenty of time to take up every special interest bill that any high-priced lobbyist pushes before the Congress of the United States."

Not that all special-interest legislation needs "plenty of time" to get action. Indeed, some speeds right through, such as the $5 billion highway "improvement" bill that had only one day's hearing and came to the floor with most members not even able to guess at the goodies it contained, or the $4.6 million "emergency" jobs bill for which there were no public hearings, no public drafting sessions, no public notice of where the money would go. The public knew nothing about this until a draft bill was presented to the full Appropriations Committee for action. It had all been done smoothly and swiftly and secretly. Representative William Lehman, Florida Democrat and chairman of the subcommittee, met privately ahead of time with other members of the panel, told them how much money would be allocated in the bill, and, as one member recalls, asked his colleagues, "If you've got a project, let me know." Zip: That's all it took to get action.

And sometimes the swiftest pork can be delivered simply by a decision not to act at all. In 1997, somebody on the technical staff of the House Ways and Means Committee "mistakenly" inserted a provision into the tax bill (things are easy to hide in the huge and complicated tax legislation) that would greatly benefit the few hundred people who die each year and leave estates worth more than $17 million. Because of the "mistake," each of those estates will be saved more than $200,000 in taxes and the government will lose $880 million in revenue over the next decade.

Mistakes of that significance are usually corrected the next year. Not this time. Bill Archer, chairman of the Ways and Means Committee, is a Republican who represents a district in Houston, Texas, that is one of the richest in the country and one of the likeliest to have residents who die with $17 million estates. He persuaded his colleagues to leave the tax break in the law.

The pattern is clear. When the action benefits friends in the party or indulges special interests to whom the lawmakers are indebted (or hope to become indebted) or helps somebody make money on a grand scale, speed is not out of the question.

The Mechanics of Congress: Committees

One reason for Congress's sluggishness in enacting legislation is the mechanics of the place. President Kennedy, in a television interview in 1962, summarized the various booby traps:

> The Constitution and the development of the Constitution give all advantage of delay. It is very easy to defeat a bill in the Congress. It is much more difficult to pass one. To go through a committee, say the Ways and Means Committee of the House—to go through one of its subcommittees and get a majority vote; and then the full committee and get a majority vote; then go to the Rules Committee and get a rule; then go to the floor of the House and get a majority; then start over again in the Senate—subcommittee and full committee—and then go to the Senate floor, where there is unlimited debate (so you can never bring a matter to a vote if there is enough determination on the part of the opponents, even if they are a minority); and then unanimously get a conference between the House and Senate to adjust the bill, or, if one member objects, to have it go back through the Rules Committee, back through the Congress, and have this done on a controversial piece of legislation where powerful groups are opposing it—that is an extremely difficult task. So that the struggle of a president who has a program to move through the Congress, particularly when the seniority system may place particular individuals in key positions who may be wholly unsympathetic to your program and may be, even though they are members of your own party, in political opposition to the president, this is a struggle which every president who has tried to get a program through has had to deal with. After all, Franklin Roosevelt was elected by the largest majority in history in 1936, and he got his worst defeat a few months afterward in the Supreme Court bill.

You will notice that Kennedy laid the greatest emphasis on the hurdles a bill must pass over, or under or around, at the committee and subcommittee level. This is the realistic view of Congress. The romantic, and inaccurate, view is that the most important work of Congress is done in the main chambers of the House and Senate. Crucial as the final votes may be, and dramatic as the debates preceding the votes may sometimes be, they are merely the final flourish to the real work of Congress—which goes on in the more than 50 House and Senate committees and in the 300 or so subcommittees (the exact number shifts from year to year in the ebb and flow of power struggles). That's where the wording of legislation is largely completed; that's where most of the tough compromises are agreed on; that's where endless testimony from outside experts is taken, pointing out the weak and strong points of the bills under consideration.

Committees have three functions: They are the primary factories in which legislation is put together. They are the laboratories in which programs established by Congress are analyzed to see how well they are being carried out by the bureaucracy (this is called the congressional oversight function). And they conduct investigations; they can investigate anything they want to investigate. Sometimes investigations are aimed at exposing criminal conduct, sometimes they are meant to embarrass and harrass enemies of the Establishment (a favorite objective of the infamous House Un-American Activities Subcommittee), and sometimes the investigations are simply to probe some aspect of our lives to see whether corrective legislation is needed. In recent years various committees have investigated auto repair costs, broadcast ratings, the Mafia, foreign agent lobbyists, the munitions lobby, nuclear waste disposal, radioactive fallout, television crime and violence, and Wall Street crime.

Not all, but most, investigations done to help ordinary people and control corporate bullies have come when Democrats were in the majority. Impressive reforms were accomplished by such men as: Senator Frank Church, Idaho Democrat, whose Foreign Relations Subcommittee probed unfair oil industry prices; Warren Magnuson, the great populist from Washington State, whose Senate Commerce Committee spotlighted an array of anticonsumer abuses; and William Proxmire, Wisconsin Democrat, who used both the Senate Banking Committee to investigate the bilking of consumers by banks and the Joint Economic Committee to uncover defense contract cheating. When Democrats controlled the House, progressives like Henry Waxman and Fortney Stark uncovered conflicts of interest in the medical–industrial–pharmaceutical complex; and George Brown, Don

Edwards, and John Moss, all of California, used their positions to investigate assaults on civil liberty and privacy.

Most committee investigations done when Republicans control Congress tend to be aimed at relaxing what they consider to be excessive government safety and health regulations and reducing government restraints on corporations that don't mind abusing the public for profit.

Scattered Jurisdiction

Because committees and subcommittees have proliferated so extravagantly—the number of subcommittees has increased 200 percent in the last two decades—their jurisdiction is often unclear and it becomes difficult to focus clearly on problems. The more the substructure of Congress spreads out in a mishmash of competing fiefdoms, the harder it is to pull legislation together and pass it. Twelve different House committees have jurisdiction over drug policy After the stock market crash of 1987, no fewer than ten committees and subcommittees held hearings about securities laws; jurisdiction was so scattered that the nation is still waiting for Congress to come up with some good ideas on how to prevent the next crash A dozen committees have subcommittees attending to international economics. The secretary of the Department of Health and Human Resources may have to fight his way through as many as forty committees and subcommittees before bringing his whole program together.

In 1989, Congress began investigating the Department of Housing and Urban Development, where housing programs for poor people had been destroyed through waste and fraud. Why was Congress so late in taking action? Six congressional panels—subcommittees on appropriations, banking, and government operations in both the Senate and House—have the authority to oversee HUD activities. And from the very beginning of the Reagan administration in 1981, HUD's inspector general had sent messages to these subcommittees describing thousands of cases of fraud and waste in the department. "There was plenty of evidence for those of us who had the responsibility to get involved," said William Proxmire, who had chaired one of the HUD subcommittees in the Senate during that period, "and we just didn't do it." Because of the lazy and indifferent oversight, taxpayers lost several billion dollars.

Seeking the Spotlight

Only the permanent standing committees can approve legislation, but they share the adventure of investigations with the "select" committees (a panel of members Congress appoints specifically to study one problem). Although select committees cannot author legislation, they can, through adroit use of hearings, reports, and public relations techniques, sometimes throw a spotlight on problems that have been ignored by the more established and more rigid power structures in Congress. In any event, investigations, whether handled by permanent or select committees, are the most fruitful source of publicity available to members because they concentrate on the dark side of life—waste, corruption, greed, stupidity, conspiracy—which most appeals to the news media and their audiences.

Which is why, when the president of the other party gets in trouble, the committees of Congress go after him like chickens after a grasshopper—as Nixon and Clinton discovered. In 1998, seven Senate committees and half the House committees were conducting thirty-one separate investigations of reported wrongdoing by Clinton, his administration, or the Democratic party.

A member's committee assignments will largely determine the degree of power, prestige, and publicity received during his or her career. Especially prized as rich sources of those commodities are seats on the House and Senate money committees (Finance, Appropriations, Ways and Means, Banking) and on the armed service committees. Some committee assignments are also sought because they give members a chance to please special interests and win constituent votes. And some assignments, especially on the foreign relations and armed service committees, lend themselves easily to being exploited by junketeering members. (A "junket" is a trip abroad, usually made with the excuse of wanting to "study" military cemeteries or air bases or corn production or some other serious matter; but the trip usually includes many stopovers at nightclubs and tourist spots. One of the favorite junkets is to the annual Paris Air Show, which some members concede is nothing more than a big cocktail party.)

What determines a member's committee assignment? There are many influences. His seniority is important, though less so than it used to be in the House. His willingness to be a "team player," to cooperate with the congressional leadership, is also important; mavericks usually don't get the best committee assignments. The influence of powerful interest groups is also crucial. Representative Henry A. Waxman, a California Democrat who is one of the most adroit string-pullers in Washington, pointed out, "There are enormous policy implications in the committee selection process. A number of issues on the Energy and Commerce Committee, for instance, were decided by one or two votes. Millions, if not billions, of dollars are at stake for major industries in this country when committee assignments are being made." Which is why major industries work zealously behind the scenes, cashing any chip they can get their hands on to guarantee that friendly members are assigned to the key committees.

Faulty Guidance

The primary reason for the committee system is that about 8,500 pieces of legislation are introduced in each Congress. Hundreds of these are duplicates, and hundreds more are so trivial or so parochial as to not warrant the attention of the full Congress.* Still there remain several thousand bills that are of such substance that Congress could well consider their passage. It is inconceivable that a member could give even a hundred bills, much less a few thousand, the consideration they deserve. In fact, only about 200 are enacted into law.

So the committee system is supposed to give the members at least a fighting chance. The bills are parceled out according to broad fields of specialization—banking, military affairs, appropriations, taxation, public works, education, and so on.

But the committee system, logical as it seems, falls woefully short of a solution to the workload of Congress. A senator from a major state may find himself assigned to three or four committees and half a dozen subcommittees; he may face a morning in which six of these groups are holding hearings. He cannot possibly give personal attention to all that is going on. He may spend half an hour in each of the hearings, flitting from one to the other to make a *pro forma* appearance, and leave the actual studying of the bills to his aides.

Because most House members hold membership on only one important committee, they have more time to at least read the legislation that comes to their committee and to make their own legislative compromises. That isn't saying much. The day that a bill comes to the floor in either house is usually the first time that the members have seen it, much less studied it. That may seem, as former Representative Richard L. Ottinger once declared, "absolutely incredible," but that's the way Congress has been operating for years.

Thus, the fate of legislation within the committee is of vital importance to its reception on the floor. If a bill receives a committee's unanimous approval, it is virtually guaranteed approval by that chamber of Congress. The meaning is simply that the rest of the chamber looks to

---

*When we say some bills are trivial, we mean trivial—bills, that is, commemorating National Sewing Month, Snow White Week, National Fishing Week, National Asparagus Month, and the like.

the committee for guidance. The committee vote is a weather vane that members not familiar with the legislation can use for a quick reading of a bill's value.

The major defect in this follow-the-committee system is that, as we have already seen, many of the most important committees do not reflect a cross-sectional viewpoint. Often they represent a very narrow viewpoint, ideologically or commercially or geographically. Membership on the money committees is largely conservative, and the cues these committees give are based more often on ledger balances than on human needs; the military committees are loaded with hawks; the farm committees are crowded with neofarmers; and so forth. The guidance given the full house by committees of this sort is biased in the extreme, heavily weighted against reform and in favor of the status quo.

And the follow-the-committee system can also be demolished by powerful lobbies. This happened in 1998 in a dramatic way. The Senate Commerce Committee voted nineteen to one to approve tough legislation that would have made the tobacco industry pay many billions of dollars in compensation for the deaths its products had caused, and for the enormous drain tobacco-related illnesses had inflicted on government health budgets. Passage in the Senate seemed almost certain. But then the tobacco lobby responded with a $40-million television ad campaign discrediting the legislation with half-truths and lies. Result: The Senate refused to follow the Commerce Committee's lead.

Business on the Floor

If the committees do the real work of Congress, what goes on in the House and Senate chambers? Very little. Members stay away from the floor as much as possible.

The Senate, which historically has been the chamber of the great debates, needs fifty-one senators to transact business, but if no member challenges the lack of a quorum, bills can be passed with an almost empty chamber, and that's what the chamber often almost is. One day a reporter asked Senator Warren B. Rudman, Republican of New Hampshire, if there were enough senators left to establish a quorum, and he answered only half jokingly, "We not only don't have a quorum, we don't have enough for a good poker game." Often the floor is occupied only by the majority and minority leaders and a couple of other senators. Even the most important legislation seldom stirs an honest-to-goodness debate. When the Senate was debating the

Panama Canal Treaty, a treaty heralded as a major step in better hemispheric relations, there was seldom more than half a dozen senators on the floor at any one time. When the Senate is in a real hurry to get out of town for the weekend, it may even vote on a measure *before* debating it. Senate debate—once a garden of lush oratorical flowers in the heydays of Everett Dirksen and Hubert Humphrey—is a dying art. And in the House, where time restrictions seldom encourage long speeches or rhetorical artistry, it never thrived.

You would never guess this arid condition from reading the *Congressional Record*, which is supposed to be a record of congressional debate. But the *Record* is not a verbatim account. In fact, it often comes closer to fiction than fact. Members have five days in which they may "correct" the record of the day's proceedings. This gives them a chance to insert long speeches that they never gave, sometimes even to reconstruct bogus "debates." Often they were hundreds of miles from Washington when the actual debate took place. It also gives them time to delete thoughtless and inaccurate remarks and to knock out insults.

Some typical cleaning up occurred after Representative B. H. Solomon of New York got so angry with Representative Patrick J. Kennedy of Rhode Island that he threatened to throttle him. If you read the *Congressional Record* of that day's debate, you will detect no sign of anger, much less a physical threat.

An extreme example of *Congressional Record* "ghosting" was a day when it ran to 112 pages. Yet the Senate had met for only eight seconds; the House not at all. The *Record* was done by remote control—by adding, by revising, by expanding from the comfort of the members' offices—and often was done not by the members themselves but by their staffs.

The Battle of Words

With 435 members in the House, time for debate is precious. It must be parceled out stingily. Whenever an important issue comes up for discussion, the House leadership sets the total debate time to be expended on it. Rarely does any one member get more than five minutes to speak. The Senate, with only one hundred members, can be more expansive. Traditionally, any member can speak for as long as he chooses, subject only to the imposition of gag rules when his colleagues get tired of listening and want to press on to other matters. But this is rarely done.

However, even senators must show some restraint on their windiness or they won't get all their work done. Every senator has his pet bills that he is eager to push through, and time must be found for the push. This situation lends itself to a form of blackmail called the filibuster, an attempt to talk a bill to death. When a group of senators oppose a piece of legislation but know that they cannot muster enough votes to defeat it outright, they can filibuster and bring the work of the Senate to a halt with their nonstop debate. Their hope is to fritter away so much time on that one bill that the majority of the Senate—preferring to get on to other legislation rather than win that one fight—will give up.

Opponents call the filibuster a harmful, undemocratic, obstructionist device to get around rule by the majority. Proponents of the filibuster argue that sometimes the majority is wrong, and, in any event, the filibuster is the only sure weapon the minority has to escape tyranny by the majority.

For many years liberals hated the filibuster because it was used so frequently, and so effectively, by Southerners fighting civil-rights legislation. Senator Strom Thurmond, Republican of South Carolina, holds the record for the longest speech in the history of the Senate. Filibustering against the Civil Rights Act of 1957, he spoke for twenty-four hours and eighteen minutes in a round-the-clock session. Liberals—as well as conservatives—have found the filibuster a useful weapon in fighting economic bills. The late Senator Wayne Morse, a liberal Democrat of Oregon, spoke for twenty-two hours and twenty-six minutes against the tidelands offshore oil bill. In 1978 two other liberals, Senator Howard Metzenbaum of Ohio and Senator James Abourezk of South Dakota, filibustered in an effort to kill a bill to decontrol the price of natural gas.

In 1982, Senator Jesse Helms, a rock-ribbed conservative from North Carolina, filibustered against a gasoline tax. In 1983 he was back with a filibuster against creating a national holiday to honor Martin Luther King, Jr. But that was just a ruse. What he really wanted was passage of a bill favoring the tobacco industry, and when the Senate gave it to him, he dropped the anti-King filibuster.

It used to be that filibusters sometimes ran through the night. Senators would drag out cots and turn their cloakroom into a bedroom, grabbing a few minutes' sleep when they could, then arising to don a bathrobe and bedroom slippers to continue the debate. Many claimed to hate the discomfort of filibusters, but many secretly admitted they loved the battle. As Senator Alan Cranston of California exclaimed after a filibuster in 1982, "Oh, God, was it exciting!"

But the frequency of filibusters increased so much that many senators' nerves began to fray, so they changed the rules. These days the filibuster has become so ritualized that it is carried out without the dramatic all-night endurance tests. Now the Senate allows the chamber to go on to other business even while a filibuster is technically under way. Every few days the Senate then attempts to vote on the issue to see if the body can muster the sixty-vote super-majority needed to stop the filibuster. If it can't, the Senate meanders off to other legislation once again.

Or at least it tries to. During late 1997 and throughout 1998, so many filibusters were going on at the same time that it was hard to remember who was objecting to what. Many outside critics think the process has gone wildly awry and that the filibuster is used so often and so indiscriminately that the principle of majority rule is dying; it's getting to the point that essentially a bill needs sixty votes to be guaranteed passage.

But the filibuster is still treasured as a leverage by most senators, who argue that the founding fathers intended for the Senate to be the place that tempered the passion of populist majorities. Legend has it that George Washington once told Thomas Jefferson, "We pour legislation into the senatorial saucer to cool it."

There are other ways to pour legislation into the saucer. Even after cloture has been voted on a filibuster, the process can be slowed to a crawl by offering dozens and dozens of amendments to the legislation at issue. In the battles over oil and gas legislation, Senator Howard Metzenbaum of Ohio and Senator James Abourezk of South Dakota introduced 508 amendments to a bill. Each amendment requires a vote by all members and can take up to half an hour to dispose of.

Yet another way to stop action in its tracks is with the "hold." This is a time-honored prerogative by which members can—anonymously, if they so choose—call for a "hold" on specific bills and nominations. They thereby serve notice on Senate leaders that, if the bill or nomination is brought to the floor, they are willing to wage a filibuster to defeat it. The identity of the members calling for the hold and the reason for their objections are often unknown to the public and other senators. Sometimes one senator will put a hold on another's project just to retaliate for a hold against a pet idea of his own. The hold is valued as a way to extract concessions from federal agencies, the White House, and from other senators.

The beneficial quality of legislation cannot save it from being smothered, at least for a while. From October 1995 to February 1996, various Republican senators used the hold to block consideration of a widely popular bill to make health insurance more readily available to Americans who lose or change jobs. When the holds were finally released, the legislation was approved by votes of 98 to 0 in the Senate and 421 to 2 in the House.

Every president has to put up with dozens of holds on his nominees. Congress took particularly keen delight in frustrating Clinton in this way. Scores of his nominees to federal judgeships were put on hold—sometimes for as much as two and a half years. At one point, with three dozen judicial nominees held in limbo, Chief Justice William Rehnquist complained that the Senate was creating a critical logjam in the courts.

The Leaders of Congress

Contrary to a rather common romantic assumption, the firm hand of authority is not fatal to democracy. Nowhere is the need for a sensible degree of firm direction more evident than in Congress. As the late Senator Hubert H. Humphrey once put it, "You can't run this Congress on the basis of mutual admiration, affection and being nice guys. We have 535 prima donnas up here and unless somebody takes charge, we're just going to wander around and get in trouble."

Party Influence

The "somebodies" who take charge are determined along party lines. Although members—largely because of new methods of financing their campaigns—are becoming more independent of parties, partisanship is still the dominant power in Congress. It provides discipline, organization, guidance, fellowship, and cohesion. Members of the same party usually hang out together; they socialize together. The veteran members "look after" the younger; they give tips on how to cut corners, how to save time, and how to save face. It should not be supposed, however, that party membership plays a constant, conclusive role in determining how members vote. Party leaders, though they doubtless wish they could, aren't able to call signals like a football quarterback and expect members to vote accordingly. Too many other influences—ideologies, lobbying pressures, personalities—are competing with partisanship. As a result, the two parties do not operate strictly as opposites but, in fact, sometimes cooperate in the shaping and passage of legislation.

The willingness to ignore party lines on votes is much more common among Democrats than among Republicans. The reason is simple: Although the Democratic party is programmatically liberal, many Democratic members are conservatives; the Republican party is programmatically conservative, and very few Republican members swerve from that philosophy.

Sometimes the indifference to party lines has been so extreme as to seem outright disloyalty. A striking example of this came in the years when Ronald Reagan was in the White House. Republicans took control of the Senate during those eight years, and the Democratic majority in the House dwindled in number. Many southern Democrats, whom loyalist Democrats scornfully referred to as "boll weevils," deserted their party leadership in droves and gave the Republicans the margin of votes they needed to seriously cripple some of the social programs that had been established in Democratic administrations.

Their party disloyalty was not surprising. Indeed, for many years the core of Democratic conservatism has been among southern members. Most were ideologically so far to the right that they logically should have been in the Republican party, even its most conservative wing. They gave little allegiance to the national Democratic party, except during the Great Depression of the 1930s, when the South got more financial aid from the federal government than any other region, and during the war years of the 1940s, when hundreds of military camps and defense plants brought bountiful payrolls to the region. In other words, they were simply Dollar Democrats.

Why did they run for office as Democrats? The answer is historical: Their native region for generations had been guided politically by the bitter memories of the Civil War and the Reconstruction—both of which the South blamed on Lincoln and the Republican presidents who followed him. As many a bumper sticker in Dixie proclaimed: "Hell, No, We Ain't Forgettin'!" Obviously, as a practical matter, in that atmosphere anyone who expected to be elected ran as a Democrat.

But all that began to change radically in the 1960s when the national Democratic party enthusiastically pushed for racial integration and enforced the right of southern blacks to vote. With the newly enfranchised blacks moving heavily into the Democratic party, southern Democratic politicians began moving out—transferring their allegiance to the Republican party, which, once dead, was born again and flourished. As a result, the often arrogant drawl of the old-style southern Democrat has virtually disappeared from the halls of Congress. In its place is the often vitriolic and sometimes downright wacky drawl of some southern Republicans, such as Senator Jesse Helms of North Carolina, who, as chairman of the Senate Foreign Relations Committee, seems primarily interested in trying to destroy the United Nations.

Congeniality Fades

One of the regrettable shifts in the 1990s was toward more animosity between Democrats and Republicans in both houses. Bipartisanship, which once had been a staple, was at a very low ebb. There was much more rudeness, more crude one-upmanship. Partly the mood was the fault of President Clinton, who obviously did not like to deal with Congress, not even with members of his own party; being in the minority in Congress and unwelcome at the White House, congressional Democrats were left to feel almost leaderless and adrift, which put them in a sullen mood.

The House's harsher attitude was obviously a slop-over from Newt Gingrich's take-no-prisoners crusade leading to the Republican victory in 1994 (which we will discuss later). At least two dozen of the young members elected in that year were such extremists that they even suspected Gingrich of being too moderate, and in 1997 plotted to unseat him as Speaker (he squelched their rebellion, but he remained in danger). Most of these rebels felt free to defy the Republican leadership because they didn't expect to be in Washington very long. They were not just bomb-throwers like Gingrich, the man they followed to Washington and then temporarily turned against. They were suicide bombers, true believers who behaved as if they had nothing to lose. "Washington doesn't have anything we want," said Representative Tom Coburn, a doctor who delivers babies on weekends. "That's what makes us so dangerous."

To pacify right-wing Republicans, Gingrich continued to use insulting rhetoric about Democrats and moderate Republicans, and so did his chief lieutenants, Majority Leader Richard Armey and Majority Whip Tom Delay, and some of the other GOP leaders. Sensitive issues such as gay rights and abortion rights caused snarling fights between the parties, and within the party. On several occasions, Democratic members denounced Republicans as "Nazis" and "fascists." Armey referred to Representative Barney Frank, a Massachusetts Democrat, as "Barney fag," obviously a slur on Frank's homosexuality. Armey claimed it was a "slip of the tongue."

On the outside looking back, some retired Republican leaders were appalled at the contrast between the Congressional atmosphere of the nineties and what they remember it to have been in their day. They warned their successors they were behaving absurdly. Former Senator Alan Simpson likened the new Republicans running the House to "a slave ship where they've escaped from the hold and come up and murdered everyone on deck, leaving nobody who knows how to get back into the harbor."

Most of the old courtly combatants in the Senate who knew compromise as an essential part of the game have retired. Thad Cochran, who started in the House in 1973 and left the Senate in 1997, recalled, "I had just as many close, personal friends on the Democratic side as on the Republican side. Now you are viewed with suspicion for having friendships on the other side. Certainly that is true if you join with the other side in offering legislation and amendments."

To understand the "new" atmosphere, one must understand that the conflicts have almost a religious fervor. The New Deal programs set up by Franklin Roosevelt and the Great Society programs set up by Lyndon Johnson and extended even by Richard Nixon—programs protecting the elderly and the poor, protecting the environment, ensuring the safety of workers, regulating the stock market and banks—have all been around so long that they are (as polls show) accepted by most of the public as almost a kind of established political religion. Virtually all Democrats in Congress consider it their sacred duty to protect these programs. Some Republicans are their allies, up to a point, and especially on environmental issues. "I think there are divergent forces in the Republican Party, and it is going to take some time to sort out where we are going," says Representative James H. Saxton, a moderate from New Jersey. "The younger members, especially from the West, are less than sensitive to the environmental issues as we know them in the East, and they comprise a sizable number, or chunk, of Republicans in the House."

Members in this "chunk" have a different political religion. Ronald Reagan is still their Martin Luther, and their scripture is: Get government out of our lives, cut back federal regulations, make private charities take a bigger role in the care of the old and helpless, open more of the federal lands and forests to industrial development.

Religious wars are always the messiest.

But we run the danger of exaggerating. Bipartisanship may be weaker, but it is not dead. For example, in 1998 when the fights were over liberalizing food stamps for immigrants and protecting managed-care patients and reforming the campaign reform law, between fifty-one and ninety-eight House Republicans broke with Gingrich and joined Democrats to make a majority in favor of the bills.

And there have lately been impressive examples of individual bipartisan teamwork. Republican Christopher Shays of Connecticut and Democrat Martin T. Meehan of Massachusetts coauthored the House's finance reform bill. In the Senate the fight for campaign finance reform brought together a team of dramatically different fellows: On the one hand John McCain—Arizona Republican, sixty-one, very conservative, Episcopalian, son and grandson of four-star admirals, former fighter pilot, Vietnam War hero; on the other hand, Russell D. Feingold—Wisconsin Democrat, forty-four, a Jew, very liberal, no military experience, bookish, a former Rhodes scholar.

Also, there were signs that the institutional power of Congress and the changing mood of the electorate were wearing down the hardliners. Of the seventy-three firebrands who roared into the House as part of Newt Gingrich's 1994 revolution, vowing to blow the place up, twenty-three had packed their bags by 1999. This was a striking attrition rate for a chamber that routinely returns 95 percent of its incumbents. Most of the departed were turned down for reelection or in races for higher office. Voters, apparently, had tired of their cynicism. Some who remained in Congress were beginning to sound much tamer (or "squishy," as the hardliners called the defectors). Representative Joe Scarborough, a thirty-five-year-old Floridan who was one of the hardest chargers in '94, said in '99, "I'm a chastened revolutionary. The revolution that got us here is over. Now it's time for us to decide whether we want to govern effectively or move into the minority, and I choose to govern."

Top of the Heap

The Speaker is the most powerful member of Congress and stands third in line to become president, if the president and vice president die or are incapacitated.

At the beginning of a new session, each party in the House of Representatives offers a nominee for Speaker, and the full House chooses between the two. This is merely a technical concession to the spirit of interparty democracy; actually the majority party always wins. The losing nominee then serves as the floor leader for the minority party.

In addition to electing a Speaker, the majority party in the House elects a floor leader. Each party also elects an assistant floor leader, called a "whip," who is assisted by a dozen regional whips. The Senate goes through a similar routine of selecting its leaders except for the office of Speaker—which does not exist in the Senate.

The floor leaders keep members informed about when certain bills are coming up for debate and what the bills are all about; they try to build support or opposition to bills; and they try to get members of their parties to be on hand for votes. Equally important, they try to determine how much support their side will have, for it is very embarrassing for the leadership to predict incorrectly the outcome of a vote.

Negative powers are widely dispersed through both the House and Senate. Chairmen can stall; committees and subcommittees can mangle legislation and sit on it for months on end; senators can filibuster; members of both houses can crush legislation under a load of extraneous and frivolous amendments. As Nelson W. Polsby has pointed out, "the power and the responsibility to get things done—especially big things—is predominantly in the hands of party leaders."

This does not mean the leaders always work in harmony. In Congress, the greatest power struggles have been in the House, between those who felt that committee chairmen should hold dominant power and those who believed that the House Speaker should hold the nucleus of power. This is an old, old war. There has never been, and will never be, a final victor; the tide of battle swings back and forth, with first one side and then the other winning a temporary advantage.

Although the Speaker is chosen from and by the majority party, he is supposed to show a high degree of fairness in the way he presides over the House—he is expected to let minority party members have a fair share of the time to present their views. Nevertheless, he is a creature of his party and naturally favors his party's legislative programs. There's nothing unfair about that; that is simply party politics.

The Speakership of the House is a constitutional office. But the Constitution is silent about what the Speaker's powers and duties are to be, other than that he presides over the House. This silence has allowed such leeway that the Speakership is probably the second most powerful political job this nation has to offer, and during some periods of our history the Speaker has been considered as powerful as the president. Throughout the nineteenth century and briefly into the twentieth century, the Speaker had the exclusive power to name members to the standing committees and to pick the chairmen of the committees. With all members dependent on him in this regard, the Speaker could build a great reservoir of loyalty in return for favors rendered in committee assignments. Early Speakers also had one other important power: From 1850 to 1910 the Speaker was automatically chairman of the House Rules Committee, which regulates the legislative traffic and sets the rules for debate.

With such awesome powers at their disposal, naturally some Speakers abused them. The pinnacle of abuse was reached during the Speakership of Joseph (Uncle Joe) Cannon, a Republican. He ruled the House from 1903 to 1911, and in retrospect can accurately be seen as the most powerful person ever to sit in Congress. Foul-mouthed, flinty, reactionary but likable, Cannon exploited the House rules like a tyrant, bottling up virtually every progressive piece of legislation. During his seven-year tenure, all fresh ideas were smothered quickly. Gleefully he explained his do-nothing attitude: "Everything is all right out West and around Danville [his district]. The country don't need any legislation." It may have been funny for a while, but finally Cannonism was seen as a national peril and enough members of Cannon's own Republican party joined the Democrats to strip him of his power.

What occurred was not merely the defeat of one Speaker but of *the* Speaker. Never again would the person holding that position wield so much power.

The tyrannical power that had rested with the Speaker now shifted to the committee chairmen, who came to be selected on the basis of seniority. Each ran his own little kingdom, independent of the Speaker. Over the next sixty or so years, the few Speakers who were relatively strong—Speakers like Sam Rayburn of Texas, who filled the job for sixteen years, longer than anyone else—achieved their success not by coercing members but by their ability to affect masterful compromises, to placate and coddle and coax the powerful chairmen to play along with them. Rayburn did his best work at striking deals in what was called "the Board of Education room," using bourbon and branch water, and telling Texas stories.

In recent years the pendulum of power in the House has swung again toward the Speaker as a result of some internal changes. First of all, seniority no longer provides an ironclad guarantee that chairmen will not be deposed by a vote of the members. And the Speaker has re-won the authority to appoint the members of the Rules Committee.

This does not mean they function as rubber stamps, but it does mean he has exceptional influence over which bills will reach the floor for a vote.

Power through Personality

To herd along a majority of the House, the Speaker must still rely to a great degree on his talents (if he has them) for evoking a feeling of loyalty and good fellowship based on his personality and on the favors he does.

Tip O'Neill, the tank-sized, white-maned, bulbous-nosed old pol from Massachusetts whose ten-year tenure as Speaker ended in 1987, could have had much more power if he had not been so easy-going. He was popular with members of both parties, and he enjoyed that popularity so much he often didn't want to crack down and get things done right.

On at least one occasion, as he later confessed, his nice-guy attitude had disastrous results. It was when the Republicans came up with their economics package of 1981. "As Speaker, I could have refused to play ball with the Reagan administration by holding up the president's legislation in the Rules Committee," says O'Neill. But "despite my strong opposition to the president's program, I decided to give it a chance to be voted on." He also says he was "unprepared" for the results. The administration put all its proposals in one huge, complicated package—an eight hundred-page bill—that passed the House so fast most members didn't know what was in it or what they had voted for or against. It turned out that the bill cut various social, health, child care, and education programs. To maintain his role as Mr. Congeniality, O'Neill had unwittingly betrayed his own party.

O'Neill's successor, Jim Wright of Texas—a man with enormous ambition and the grin of a Cheshire cat—had problems for opposite reasons. Instead of working too easily with members of both parties, he was often a loner, sometimes too hot-tempered. Some members thought he was open; some thought he was an enigma. "He's like an onion," said one senior Democrat. "There's layer after layer after layer, and you never get to the core." Some Democrats were ticked off because he didn't ask them for advice. But they all had to admit he was much more aggressive in pushing the Democratic party's agenda and in resisting the president's agenda than O'Neill had been. Republicans complained that he carried his partisanship too far, ruling the House in such an arbitrary fashion that they were left out of the process completely. So there was general rejoicing in their ranks (and some silent satisfaction among a minority of Democrats, too) when the Republican gadfly, Representative Newt Gingrich of Georgia, brought charges of misconduct against Wright, subjecting him to more than a year of excruciating analysis, and finally indictment by the House's ethics committee.* Wright discovered that he had not developed enough strong friendships in the House to withstand the flak that followed, and he was forced out of office. His successor, Tom Foley of Washington, was his opposite: easy-going, cautious.

And then came Newton Leroy Gingrich.

Newt, the Revolutionary

When Republicans took control of the House of Representatives in 1995, it was a truly astounding development. Democrats had been running the House for the previous forty years. In fact, except for a four-year interruption in the early 1950s, they had been running the House for sixty years. Although in the Senate the Republicans, after being down for twenty-five years, had temporarily ridden back to power on the coattails of President Reagan in 1980, in the House they seemed doomed to be the minority party forever.

In short, what happened in the 1994 election was truly a revolution. And the leader of the revolutionaries was Newt Gingrich, a pudgy Georgian, who in many public opinion polls has been rated as one of the most unappealing politicians in America. But among politicians he was seen—and sometimes admired—as one of the most ruthlessly successful leaders of recent decades.

After two unsuccessful campaigns for a House seat from Georgia, he won in 1978. Something happened in that campaign that signaled Gingrich's new approach to politics.

As a student at Tulane University in the 1960s, he had been a radical left-wing activist, and that philosophy continued to show when he became an assistant professor of environmental studies at West Georgia College in Carrollton.

---

*One of Gingrich's most damning charges was that Wright had strong-armed people into buying a book he had "written," and privately printed, and from which he received an incredibly large royalty (55 percent of the sales price). (A quotation from Wright's book opens this chapter.) Two years after Gingrich had sicked the hounds on Wright, it was discovered that he, Gingrich, had also written a book that was promoted in a most unusual fashion, by getting twenty-one investors to cough up $5,000 apiece. The book was aptly titled *Window of Opportunity*.

The billion-dollar corporation that dominated life in that town was Southwire Company, the largest manufacturer of copper wire and cable in the United States. Over the years, it paid hundreds of thousands of dollars in fines for polluting with industrial waste and for violating worker safety and labor laws.

As a professor of environmental studies, Gingrich had denounced Southwire's criminal acts. And in his first two congressional campaigns, in which he was helped by the Sierra Club, he had continued to denounce the company for these violations. But in his 1978 campaign, the bank owned by Southwire's owners generously assisted Gingrich—as they continued to do, ultimately paying over $100,000 to his various political and personal enterprises—and never again was he heard to say anything bad about that company or other corporate violators, or anything good about the federal agencies that punished them. From that time on, he was a rabid conservative—with plenty of campaign money.

When Gingrich arrived in Washington, he found the Republican apparatus in the House being run by men he considered lethargic and defeatist—content to be in the minority party as long as they kept being reelected. Gingrich showed little interest in passing legislation; by the end of his first term, his consuming interest was in seizing power for himself and his party. As Larry J. Sabato and Glenn R. Simpson observe in their book *Dirty Little Secrets: The Persistence of Corruption in American Politics,* "Perhaps the most brilliant political tactician of his generation, Gingrich determined before anyone else that the Republicans' only hope of taking the House of Representatives was to wreck it, as he himself once famously remarked." Democrats had been in power so long, most people thought that party and the House were almost synonymous. Therefore, Gingrich concluded, "Only if Congress were to be destroyed in the eyes of the public would the Democrats also be destroyed, allowing the Republicans the freedom to remake America."

He thereupon launched the most concentrated vilification campaign seen in modern politics. He filed numerous ethics charges against Democrats and, as mentioned previously, one of his charges brought down Speaker Wright. At every opportunity, Gingrich portrayed the opposition party in negative terms. Democrats were "thugs" and "crooks," the Democratic party was totally irresponsible and corrupt, Congress was corrupt, and Washington was a sink-hole of sin that needed to be cleansed by a new generation of politicians (meaning Republican). He got his message out in myriad ways, but primarily through C-SPAN, the federally funded television show that carries all House (and Senate) speeches into millions of homes across the nation.

Exactly how much Gingrich contributed to the development of the nation's ugly mood is, of course, impossible to measure, but by the time the 1994 election rolled around, polls showed the public was fed up with politicians and ready to vote-'em-out, which it did to Democrats in sufficient numbers to put the House under the control of Republicans. Gingrich, of course, became Speaker.

In his first race, in 1974, he had told the *Atlanta Constitution*, "My ambition is to be an old-time political boss in twenty years." He made it right on schedule. Indeed, Gingrich had thought about running the House ever since he was in high school, and he had studied whatever he could find about the tyrannical Speaker Joe Cannon (mentioned earlier). From the day he took over, Gingrich tried to run the House with a Cannon-like authority, and though he failed in that, there were moments when he came close to his ideal. Unlike the Democratic speakers who had preceded him, Gingrich appointed all committee chairmen and determined committee memberships. When chairmen got out of line and failed to show loyalty to his program, he would threaten to take away their power.

But those who seek total power must be ready to take total blame when things go wrong. For Gingrich, they went wrong in 1998, when Republicans expected to gain between twenty and thirty more seats in the House, but wound up losing five, thereby dropping their majority to a dangerously meager six seats. In the last week of the election campaign, the Republican party apparatus, goaded on by Gingrich, had launched a $10 million television advertising blitz that used the Clinton sex scandal as a theme, both directly and with winking innuendo. But the public was tired of the scandal, and the blitz backfired. The results were a disaster both for the party and for Gingrich. He was blamed by enough angry House Republicans that he knew he could not be reelected Speaker, so he stepped down. He went out decrying the "cannibals" in his party who drove him from power. Ironically, he was echoing the Speaker he had helped drive out, Jim Wright, who also departed bemoaning the "mindless cannibalism" of his opponents.

Gingrich was replaced—or almost—by Representative Bob Livingston, Republican of Louisiana, who was elected Speaker but, before he had time to find the chair, resigned in his own minor sex scandal. He was replaced by the very conservative Illinois Republican J. Dennis

Hastert, a high school teacher before he became a politician. Compared to the brilliant but rambunctious Gingrich, he seemed downright backward—except in soliciting big donations from corporations. Even though he had a nonrace for reelection in 1998, he pocketed more than a million dollars. Naturally, he has opposed all campaign finance reforms.

With the overpowering presence of Gingrich no longer dominating the Capitol Hill drama, the Senate leadership finally had a chance to take center stage.

Oh, Yes, the Senate

It may seem that we have slighted the Senate in this discussion. We haven't slighted it, but the Constitution did. The Constitution gave the Senate no officer comparable to the Speaker. The vice president presides over the Senate, and that's about the only relationship he has with the Senate. (Since this is usually a pretty boring role to play, he often turns over the presiding job to whatever senator is handy.) The leadership roles in the Senate are handled by the majority leader and the majority whip, both elected by the majority party from the Senate membership; there is also a minority leader and a minority whip elected by the minority party. The majority leader sets the calendar by which legislation is brought to the floor for debate and vote; a party's whip has the duty to make sure all members are present to vote on crucial issues and to make sure, if possible, that they vote the way the party wants them to.

Whatever strength the majority leader has is squeezed from the job by dint of personality and character, nothing more. When Lyndon Johnson was majority leader in the 1950s, he was reputed to have massive influence because he was an artful persuader, overwhelming other senators by his physical presence—hugging them, talking right into their face, squeezing their arm—and by his melodramatic pleas, sometimes tearful, sometimes homespun and witty, sometimes threatening. Since the departure of Johnson, the men who held the post—three Democrats and three Republicans—have been colorless. Of each it could be said that his success stemmed from the fact that he was a self-effacing servant of other senators, buttering them up, making sure that their pet bills got on the calendar and that they had ample time to be heard in debate, scheduling debate in such a way as not to interfere with campaigning. Compared to a strong Speaker, even a majority leader like Johnson has little power, and certainly this has been true of his successors; they are merely comparable to expert maître d's, who are always able to find a table for an important customer and to keep the food coming fast and hot from the kitchen, and who know how to turn away drunks without offending them.

Alas, senators also measure their majority leaders by their ability to perform on television, because they often have to rebut presidential speeches. This is one reason Senate Democrats were happy when Senator Robert Byrd of West Virginia, who had been their leader since 1976, stepped down from that post at the end of 1988. Although he was an efficient legislative traffic cop, he was a mixture of country corn and bureaucratic stuffiness. On the last day of every session he would come to the floor wearing a garish red vest, dance a jig, and sing a First World War song, "Pack Up Your Troubles in Your Old Kit Bag." But when he had to appear on television, his stiff, pompous side emerged. "On TV, Byrd goes beyond fuddy-duddy," said one Democratic senator. "He's one of the most untelegenic people on earth."

His successor, Senator George Mitchell of Maine, couldn't dance a jig, but he had the smooth television demeanor of a "You're in the Friendly Hands of Allstate" pitchman. And significantly, he boasted of it. "It is an attribute of leadership in our time," he said. "People cannot ridicule or demean it. Two centuries ago the ability to ride a horse and wield a sword were attributes of leadership." Apparently what he was saying was that while leaders no longer depend on horses, they do still depend on their product.

When the Republicans again took over the Senate in 1994, they chose as their majority leader Trent Lott of Mississippi, who was cut from the same cloth as his Democratic predecessor. He had the clean-cut look and soothing voice of a small-town banker, and he was inoffensive on television.

Middling leaders like Lott remind us that in the Senate the committee chairmen, if they choose to use all the power at their disposal, are still top dog. Senator Jesse Helms of North Carolina relishes his power as chairman of the Senate Foreign Relations Committee. He's seventy-five years old but as cantankerous as a young mule. He once held up forty-three ambassadorial nominees in order to protest various State Department policies he disliked. He again dug in his heels when Clinton nominated liberal Republican William F. Weld, a former Massachusetts governor, to become ambassador to Mexico. When Weld appeared before Helms' committee for a hearing, the only person heard was Helms. The old chairman pounded his gavel again and again and wouldn't allow anyone but himself to speak—and what he said boiled down to "no way."

The Seniority System

Usually the leadership of Congress has been determined not on the basis of talent or wisdom or imagination (although these have not been considered demerits) but on the basis of political longevity. Seniority has been the key to power, the key to chairmanships and all that goes with them—the traditional ticket to the top. Once assigned to committees, members are rarely removed unless they want to be. Instead, if they are members of the majority party, they climb the long seniority ladder to the chair (unless, of course, they have aroused a tremendous amount of opposition on the way up).

There are two kinds of seniority: One kind is a member's seniority in the chamber in which he serves, and the other kind is his seniority on his committee. The broader seniority is sometimes ignored in the assignment of members *to* committees. But a member's seniority *on* a committee is almost sacred.

Congressmen who defend the seniority system usually do so with the argument that it is only fair to give the most power to members who have been around the longest; they invoke the spirit of fair play as their argument. This is a ruse. The real reason the congressional establishment likes the seniority system is that it usually passes power into the hands of those who have learned to "get along," who have reached an age when they are staid and conservative (if they were ever anything else in their younger days) and reluctant to rock the boat.

This is certainly not *always* the outcome of seniority; sometimes it has exactly the opposite results. When the voters of Rhode Island finally became so disgusted with Fernand St. Germain for being in bed with bankers, they voted him out of office in 1988. That opened up the chairmanship of the House Banking Committee to the next senior member, Representative Henry Gonzalez of Texas. Gonzalez was anything but staid and conservative. In fact, he was just this side of being a left-wing radical; he was a maverick in all things, including his clothing, which ran to electric blue suits and white silk ties; he socked two men for calling him a communist; he tried to impeach President Reagan in 1987 with the same result that he had when he tried to impeach Federal Reserve chairman Paul A. Volcker in 1981; he was rumored to carry both a knife and a pistol; and he frequently quoted Shakespeare in congressional debates. Gonzalez would never have made it to the chair had seniority not hoisted him into it.

For most political observers, seniority is a dirty word. It is a concept that connotes much of the worst aspects of the popular stereotype of a member of Congress—the white-haired, string-tied, long-winded hack who keeps getting reelected only because he is a master of pork barrel legislation; he is the Senator Foghorn of the deceased comic strip *Li'l Abner*. Seniority is a word that conveys—unjustly perhaps—a system dominated by men who have outlived their usefulness.

To some extent, of course, this impression is justified. Congress does contain hacks who are powerful only because they have managed to hang on. No better example can be found than Senator Strom Thurmond of South Carolina, who has been in the Senate for nearly half a century. As he approached the age of one hundred, he had, some said, "long ago left this planet." Nevertheless, as of 1998, he was still chairman of the Armed Services Committee, where he presided with the help of aides who coached him with big-script cards.

But there is nothing inherently wonderful about youth and nothing inherently awful about old age. If the ancient fools of Congress were weeded out, there is no assurance that they would be replaced by young whizbangs, nor any assurance that some of the wise old men wouldn't be replaced by young asses. The Senate was hardly improved in quality in 1970 when Tennessee replaced Albert Gore (then sixty-three) with William Brock III (then forty), who ran a poorly disguised campaign against Gore as a "nigger-lover." And the Senate was critically shortchanged when Illinois replaced the great Paul Douglas (then seventy-four) with the genteel, mediocre Charles Percy (then forty-seven). There is no inevitable conclusion that can be reached, based on age alone, about the mentality of the congressional leadership. Before his death in 1989, Representative Claude Pepper, approaching his ninetieth birthday and wearing a hearing aid in each ear, chaired the powerful House Rules Committee with a mind as sharp as those of most forty-year-olds in that chamber.

However, historically two extremely detrimental results *can* be charged to the seniority system. First of all, for many years the seniority system created an imbalance of regional power in Congress. Members who come from the safest states and districts—safest in the sense that they would rarely, if ever, receive any opposition from the other party in their election contests—naturally have the best chances to rise to the top, and for a long time the safest seats were in the South. As late as the ninety third Congress (1973–1974), half of the standing committees (and all of the important ones) were chaired by southerners—an overwhelmingly lopsided regional influence over the nation's laws.

Moreover, almost none of the southerners chairing important committees in either house was born, reared, or lived in a major urban area. The great majority of them had rural or small-town backgrounds; they were tuned to the agricultural and small merchant way of life. The problems of sidewalk crime, crowded slums, overloaded sewage systems, and all the other complex ailments of big-city life were things with which they had no personal experience. They were nineteenth-century people leading a twentieth-century legislature.

All these southern chairmen were nominally Democrats. But only a couple of them cast their votes more than 50 percent of the time with the national Democratic party platform, and some cast their votes as much as 80 percent of the time with the conservative Republican opposition. Northern liberals and moderates regularly denounced and frequently cursed them for blocking Democratic social programs; but the seniority system made the chairmen impervious to sticks and stones, or curses.

But as we have mentioned elsewhere, things have changed radically in that region. It still offers safe seats—but now most of them are reserved for Republicans. Anyway, members of Congress from other states are being returned by the voters just as regularly as southerners. Nowadays, most districts and most states are "safe" in that respect; nationally, virtually all incumbents who run are reelected. So northerners and westerners are going up the seniority ladder just as surely as southerners, and they have been doing it for some time.

Revolt of the 1970s

Little could be done about the seniority system in the Senate, where seniority is more sacred and only five times in the last 130 years have senior members of a committee been refused chairs. But the 1970s saw the House flooded with the largest wave of newcomers in two decades, and the freshmen demanded change—they especially wanted the kind of change that would permit them to have an immediate, strong voice in the operation of government. They were rebelling against the other, very harmful effect of the seniority system when it is carried to extremes: It destroys the ambition and enthusiasm of the young members of Congress. At that time, according to studies done via computers, an entering freshman would have to wait thirty or forty years for a chance at a chairmanship. Well, the freshmen of the early 1970s—especially those that came in with the class of 1974—weren't going to stand for that kind of future. They were unintimidated by the seniority system. Working through the House Democratic caucus (where organizational votes are taken), the reform members led a revolt that dumped three southern chairmen from their posts. Representative Reuss, who led the insurrection that allowed him to replace old Banking Committee Chairman Wright Patman, explained his motivation: "I had been in Congress two decades already, and I could see that if I waited for nature to run its course, I would be growing watermelon seeds between my ears before I was chairman."

Since then, the most senior members have not been automatically elevated to the chairmanships but have been subjected to a vote of the caucus and the approval of the Speaker. Additionally, House reformers pushed through a rule that no member could chair more than one subcommittee; this opened up many subcommittee chairs to junior members. Previously, an ancient member might hold not only the chairmanship of a full committee but also four or five subcommittee chairmanships; in this way, about forty senior members controlled the show.

With the stripping of power from many oldsters, and the multiplying of committees and subcommittees, "Mr. Chairman" became a commonplace title. However, the spread of authority diluted responsibility—perhaps too much.

Attempts at Reform

Congress is not devoid of self-criticism. Sometimes, with enormous grunting, it even achieves reforms. The changes in the conduct of committees are a fine example.

Consider the House Ways and Means Committee, which is often called the most important committee in Congress because of its grip on the level of taxation (the constitutional power to "levy and collect taxes" rests primarily with the House, and there, with the Ways and Means Committee). Moreover, Ways and Means controls the Social Security, welfare, Medicare, and unemployment-insurance programs, through which each year the government lays out several hundred billion dollars.

For most of the nation's life, the House has been very proud of this committee and has indulged its often capricious, undemocratic, secretive, and even overbearing way of doing business. Although the committee took testimony on proposed bills in public session, until the 1970s most of its deliberations were done behind closed doors; the public was excluded, and so were most members of Congress who were not members of the committee. After the committee had packaged its legislation, it was sent to the floor under a "closed rule" that permitted no floor amendments except those offered by the committee itself.

Until 1975, the Ways and Means Committee had been presided over for many years by Representative Wilbur Mills of Arkansas. He was no rube. A graduate of Harvard Law School, he had spent years learning the Internal Revenue Service's tax code backwards and forwards; he had, in fact, memorized large sections of it. His power over the committee was virtually absolute, partly because of the respect other members had for his profound grasp of tax law, partly because he was an economic conservative and thereby represented the prevailing philosophy of the committee, and partly because he had a canny way of feeling out the mood of the House and of the public at large and knowing how far he could go. A superb politician, he made all members of the committee feel they shared his power when in fact he shared his power with no one. For sixteen years he even refused to allow the existence of subcommittees, lest their chairmen challenge his power. All legislation began and ended with the full committee, with Mills analyzing every word of it. Mills' power was legendary. When he ran for president in 1972, a colleague asked him, not altogether facetiously, "Why do you want to become president and give up your grip on the country?"

Then tragedy struck. Mills became an alcoholic. For months at a time he was in a daze. He lost his hold on legislation. He lost the respect of the committee. And then a series of escapades with an exotic dancer made ugly headlines that began to enshroud his career. He was stripped of his chairmanship; soon he quit Congress.

If it was the end of Mills' career, it was also the end of the old Ways and Means. The membership of the committee was enlarged from twenty-five to thirty-seven members, and many of the newcomers were moderate or even liberal in their economic viewpoints. Some of the new members were freshmen, with no great regard for House traditions. As part of the reform movement of the early 1970s, the committee was forced to set up subcommittees. Also, the committee was forced to hold most of its deliberations in public meetings and to hold recorded votes. All these things were done to reduce the power of the chairman and to instill more democracy in Ways and Means (and in other committees, too, for the reforms were applied to all). The changes did succeed in bringing some democracy.

Was it all for the best? One of the new members, Representative Fortney Stark, a Democrat from California, thought so: "This committee operated in secret for so long and played it so safe, it became a joke. We've opened up the place to some meaningful dialogue. This is the only way we are going to regain respect."

But Joe Waggoner of Louisiana, a conservative member of the committee, quit Congress out of disgust with the reform changes. He gave this parting criticism: "The rules call for open committee meetings, more sunshine. Actually, this has worked to the detriment of Congress, because the average member doesn't have the fortitude to do in public what he might do if he could sit down and work out a problem behind closed doors. Courage has diminished. If Congress had a total of 435 pounds of guts when I came here, I'd say that number now is down to about 35 pounds."

Both, in a way, are correct. The new rules have brought to all committees much more "meaningful dialogue," as Stark says, and with that has probably come more respect for Congress. But it is also true that under the old rules the work of Congress went more smoothly and more predictably and that compromises were easier to achieve away from the glare of the public eye. That is not to say that the product was better; often it wasn't. In any event, the results of these reforms were not surprising, for an increase in democracy always means an increase in conflict. That was the swap-off: more democracy and less efficiency.

A Few Ethics Reforms

Sensitive to appearances, conscious of its roguish members and the bad press they generate, Congress tries periodically, but at very long intervals, to achieve a higher standard of morality.

Former Congressman Brooks Hays of Arkansas may have been correct when he said of the official morality of members of Congress: "Their standards are about what you would find among 535 bank presidents, or 535 presidents of Rotary Clubs, or 535 stewards in the Methodist Church, or 535 deacons of the Baptist Church." (This is something like what the Pirate King said in *The Pirates of Penzance:* "I don't think much of our profession, but, contrasted with respectability, it is comparatively honest.")

Hays's analogy, if not examined too closely, may give some comfort. And, judging strictly by how many members of Congress have been convicted of serious crimes—fewer than five dozen in this century—it would certainly seem that they are at least as honorable as their constituents. Nevertheless, in recent years there *has* been an unusual rash of criminal indictments, near-indictments, and reports of questionable income and favors involving members of Congress—so much so that congressional morality is once again the cause of public ridicule. Charges have included tax evasion, bribery, perjury, mail fraud, the acceptance of illegal gratuities, and sexual misconduct.

Hoping to improve their reputation, both House and Senate established ethics committees, the Senate in 1966 and the House in 1968.* The ethics committees were supposedly going to ensure that errant members would be swiftly punished. To that end, codes of conduct were written. The Senate's is rather bland, forbidding members to dip into campaign expenditures for personal uses and prohibiting the acceptance of illegal campaign funds. It left most conflict-of-interest questions hanging. The House's code is stricter, not only including the prohibitions of the Senate code but also prohibiting members from accepting gifts of "substantial value" from anyone having a direct interest in legislation before Congress. The House code also laid down the strong general admonition that a member "shall conduct himself at all times in a manner which shall reflect creditably on the House of Representatives."

What happens to members who violate these codes? The Constitution gives Congress the power to punish its members and it leaves open the question of what punishment best suits the crime. The worst that Congress has ever inflicted—and this is done with extreme rarity—is kick the member out. Usually an offensive member is merely censured or reprimanded (even a lighter slap than censuring). Censuring or reprimanding a member is nothing but an embarrassment; the member is officially informed that his or her colleagues think he or she has done wrong. That's all. It involves no loss of pay, no loss of perquisites, and usually no loss of standing. As a result of the censuring, a member may become so unpopular as to be voted off a choice committee or out of a chairmanship, but this seldom happens. In fact, censuring itself seldom happens. The reason is simple: Members of Congress, who are not notably religious in other respects, wholeheartedly believe in the Biblical admonition, "Judge not that ye be not judged." No matter how sneaky or unsavory another member's conduct may be, they would much prefer to leave his or her fate to the voters, lest they establish a pattern of judgment by which their own conduct might be called into question at some future time.

---

*The House was prompted to establish its ethics committee because it had been having trouble punishing a mischievous member, Adam Clayton Powell, Jr., a black from Harlem. Displeased with his conduct, members voted not to allow him to take his seat in 1967. Two years later the U.S. Supreme Court ruled that the House had acted improperly.

In the first decade after establishing its ethics committee, the Senate censured only one member for misconduct although dozens of senators were known to have been involved in questionable campaign financing and other money deals.

Enforcement of the House ethics code has been just as lackluster. When dairy lobbyists and oil companies admitted giving illegal contributions to at least two dozen members, the House Ethics Committee took no action. In the first eight years after the House passed its ethics code, eight members were convicted in civil courts of crimes ranging from perjury to soliciting prostitutes. The House Ethics Committee ignored their cases. Finally, in 1976, a strange thing happened: The committee actually got around to reprimanding a member, Representative Robert L. F. Sikes, Democrat of Florida, for conflict of interest (he had helped pass legislation that benefited a business deal he was involved in). It had been fifty-five years since a member had even been reprimanded.

In 1977 came "Koreagate," as it was called in dark tribute to the infamous Watergate scandal. South Korean agents were discovered to have spent nearly a million dollars trying to bribe House members to influence the outcome of foreign-aid legislation. Naturally, the South Koreans denied they were trying to bribe anyone, but one of the agents admitted distributing $850,000 to thirty members of the House, thirteen of whom were still serving in 1978. After two years of sluggish investigations, Koreagate sank slowly in the west and the House Ethics Committee concluded that only four members were guilty of violating House rules by accepting the money, but that none had done anything worthy of being removed from office. Had they accepted bribes? Oh no, no. They had simply shown poor judgment. Leon Jaworski, the attorney who was hired especially to conduct the committee's probe, observed as he packed up and headed home that "public skepticism and cynicism" about the results of the investigation could not be faulted. He admitted, "There should be—and I think there is—a better method of conducting inquiries into alleged wrongful conduct of high officials in our three branches of government than to resort to self-investigation."

In 1978, Representative Charles Diggs, the senior black member in Congress, was convicted of masterminding a payroll kickback scheme and was sentenced to three years in jail. But the House overwhelmingly refused to expel him from office, and while his conviction was on appeal he continued to serve. Members did not even vote to censure him until nine months after his conviction. Probably the House considered that to be a severe punishment; this was the first time it had censured a member since 1921—and on that occasion it had been another black member who received the jolt.

In 1979, the House censured Representative Charles Wilson, California Democrat, for financial misconduct. Although not as active, the Senate did vote in 1979 to "denounce"—a much kinder rebuke than censure—Senator Herman Talmadge of Georgia, one of its highest-ranking and most powerful members, for submitting bogus expense accounts totaling many thousands of dollars and diverting campaign funds to personal use through a secret bank account. In 1980, the Justice Department decided not to prosecute Talmadge, a decision that surprised few political observers, seeing as how another Georgian was sitting in the White House.

After the most protracted FBI investigation of political misconduct in history, six members of the House and one senator were caught in "Abscam" (Arab scam), in which a phony Arab sheik in the FBI's hire showed that these congressmen were willing to sell their offices for money. Some of them went to jail. (Even in jail, though, those who had served long enough in Congress received their pensions.) But the most surprising result was that one of those convicted, Representative Michael J. Myers, Pennsylvania Democrat, was actually expelled from the House on October 2, 1980—the first time this punishment had been meted out since the Civil War and the first ever for corruption.

In July 1983, the House had an unusual flurry of morality when it censured two members for having sexual relations with congressional pages: Representative Gerry E. Stubbs, Massachusetts Democrat, with a male page, and Representative Daniel B. Crane, Illinois Republican, with a female page. At first the House had merely reprimanded them, but a groundswell of public outrage at such mildness prompted members to upgrade the punishment. "The idea of reprimand was not strong enough for the American people," said Representative Bill Alexander, Democrat of Arkansas. "After all, these guys molested minors. I was out in my district over the weekend and I was overwhelmed. The reaction was brutal."*

---

*Two years later, Congressman Alexander's piety fell under a shadow when it was learned that he and his party of seven—daughter, aides, and friends (no other Congressman went along)—had merrily flown off to Brazil in a C-9 military transport, with a six-member flight crew, a military doctor, and four Pentagon people serving as official escorts. Ordinarily the C-9 carries up to forty-two passengers. Taxpayers paid $50,820 for the flight costs alone, and on top of that were the salaries of the military personnel and the allotment of at least $75 a day to each member of Alexander's party for food and lodging. Alleged purpose of the junket: to inspect alcohol fuel production in Brazil. Uh huh. (*The New York Times,* August 18, 1985)

This was unusual. Apparently the public's harsh response occurred because, as Alexander pointed out, youngsters were part of the sexual escapades. As a rule, the public has not seemed very upset either by members caught rolling in the hay or by those with their hands in the till. Most of the errant members mentioned above were reelected, some even after they were convicted of felonies. A congressman's constituents are much less interested in his morality than in his ability to bring home the pork barrel. That at least has been true in the past.

In 1986, the traditional tolerance of the House Ethics Committee toward powerful members was again fulsomely demonstrated when Representative Dan Daniel, a senior member of the Armed Services Committee, was accused of violating House ethics rules that forbid members to take anything worth more than $100 from sources with a direct interest in legislation. The charges arose from the fact that he had copped at least sixty-eight free trips (and perhaps as many as two hundred) from Beech Aircraft Corporation, whose C-12 transport plane had been touted by Daniel as the very thing the Pentagon needed. Not only were the flights worth more than $100; they were worth, to be exact, $7,663. Also, Daniel billed the government $1,343 for auto mileage on nineteen of the air trips he was making for free. Wasn't that fraud and embezzlement? You may think so, but the House Ethics Committee didn't. It concluded that Daniel—who, after all, had only been in Congress eighteen years—just didn't understand the federal laws and House rules against taking certain gifts and embezzling government funds.

Five senators collected more than $1 million in campaign funds from a savings and loan executive. In turn, they helped keep federal regulators at bay while his S&L looted the government of $2 billion. The executive ultimately went to prison. But the Senate Ethics Committee, which investigated the matter in 1989, did nothing to the members, except mildly reprimand one, Senator Alan Cranston of California. Cranston protested that "my actions were not fundamentally different from the actions of many other senators." Regrettably, he was right.

In the early 1990s, the House Ethics Committee investigated 269 current and 56 former members who had routinely been allowed to overdraw their accounts at the House bank without paying a penny of interest or penalties. Some members had written bad or overdrafted checks totaling more than half a million dollars—and didn't repay the bank for two years or more. Two former members went to prison, but none of the current ones were even scolded. (Newt Gingrich, the great moralist, had written twenty-two bad checks with a face value totaling $26,891. We will return to Gingrich's ethical lapses a little later.)

Also in the early 1990s, it was discovered that some House members had worked up a nice little scheme for stealing from the U.S. Treasury. To send mail within the United States, members use their "frank," which is their signature on envelopes. Each member has an annual allocation for franked mail, and Congress reimburses the U.S. Postal Service for the cost. But to send mail overseas, or to send special-delivery mail, members have to use standard postage stamps. For this, the government also gives them an allotment. Some members figured out a way to cheat. They would charge several hundred dollars worth of stamps to their allotment, and then, a few days later, come back to the House Post Office, turn in the stamps for money, and pocket the money. It was a common practice, but the FBI's investigation caught only one big fish: Dan Rostenkowski, the powerful chairman of the House Ways and Means Committee, who had converted $23,100 in stamps and pocketed the cash. Even he might have gotten off if he hadn't also been accused of authorizing $500,000 in salaries for fourteen "ghost" employees who did little or no work. He pleaded guilty and was sentenced to eighteen months in prison.

One of the hot-potato complaints that the House Ethics Committee received—and quickly tossed aside—focused on Representative Tom Delay of Texas, the Republican whip. It seems that Delay's brother, Randy, had had a remarkable change of fortune. In 1992, having suffered several business reversals, he filed for bankruptcy. But after 1995, when Tom Delay was elected House speaker, suddenly a number of big companies and trade associations hired brother Randy as their lobbyist, though he had zilch experience, and *The Houston Press* reported that between 1995 and mid-1997 he earned $740,000 in fees and expenses. Representative Delay was accused of providing legislative favors for his brother's lobbying clients; he was also accused of pressuring lobbyists to increase their contributions to the Republican party as the price for access in the GOP-led Congress. Apparently the Ethics Committee felt those things were just routine sleaze, so the complaint was dismissed without even being investigated.

Pork versus Purity

The philosophy that guides Congress in ethical matters, though it may be baffling to the outside world, is quite simple to the freebooters of

Capitol Hill. It was once explained in this way by John Swanner, staff director of the House Ethics Committee:

> Everybody tries to relate the House of Representatives to organizations that have a disciplinary structure, where the worker can be disciplined by the supervisor and the supervisor disciplined by the plant manager and the plant manager by the third vice president, et cetera. But there is no boss in the House of Representatives. A fellow can come up here and pick his nose, and so long as his constituents like nose-picking they can send him back, and there's not much anybody else can do about it so long as he doesn't bugger up everything else.

That's generally true. So long as a congressman has been good at shoveling federal money to the home folks, they haven't seemed to mind a little nose-picking; and if they are willing to put up with it, his colleagues have been, too.

Two University of Nebraska political scientists in a decade-long study found that three-fourths of House members who faced ethics charges in Washington were easily reelected. Members with publicized ties to the Mafia have even been reelected in recent years.

The unpredictable operation of the Ethics Committee can be seen in The Case of the Three Speakers. In 1978, *The New York Times,* following up on disclosures made by Boston investigators, found that House Speaker Tip O'Neill had been involved in a series of highly questionable business ventures, and that he had given false information to the House on the eve of his election to the Speakership in 1976. When the *Times* asked O'Neill for clarification, he refused to comment, saying, "I will not answer any questions about my personal or my public life." Meanwhile, investigators for the House Ethics Committee discovered that a South Korean agent had spent $6,500 for parties and gifts for O'Neill.

Did this cloud descend on the Speaker's career and affect it in any way? Not in a detectable way. The House Ethics Committee cleared him of any impropriety.

Now come down ten years. In the meanwhile the nation has seen Gary Hart ruined as a presidential candidate by disclosures of his womanizing; several of Reagan's closest friends and advisers have moved from civil service to felony raps; the Senate has rejected John Tower as Bush's nominee to the Defense secretaryship partly because of his drinking and womanizing record; Congress has passed a new ethics law to prevent its ex-members and employees from lobbying their first year on the town. Ethics are in the air. All of a sudden Washington is full of blue noses.

Caught in this riptide of reform, Speaker Jim Wright gets hauled up in front of the House Ethics Committee on charges of abusing his powers to help a hard-up savings and loan company, of letting his wife take money for work she didn't do, of profiting mightily from an oil well deal that stunk, and of "selling" a book he wrote—or rather, that an aide ghosted for him while being paid by the taxpayers—in such a way as to avoid the House's rule limiting outside income.

Wright didn't get off like O'Neill had, though he may not have been any more of a rascal. The temper of Washington had changed radically, if temporarily, in the meanwhile. This time the Ethics Committee, a bipartisan tribunal, indicted the Speaker for sixty-nine rules violations and turned him over to the House for punishment. (But just as the people of Boston had shrugged off O'Neill's improprieties, the people of Fort Worth, Wright's hometown, indicated they were standing solidly behind him. After all, he, like O'Neill, had been a heavyweight champion pork-barreler.) Before Wright got what he deserved, he resigned.*

But then, by the time Speaker Gingrich came along, the Ethics Committee had changed once more from steel to marshmallow. Many ethical charges were filed against Gingrich in his first years as speaker. The Ethics Committee was very slow to handle them, perhaps, critics said, because the committee's chairman, Congresswoman Nancy "Stonewall" Johnson, had been handpicked by Gingrich—which was understandable, since she admired the Speaker so much she called him "the most visionary thinker in politics today."

One of the charges against Gingrich had to do with the $4.5 million book contract he was offered by HarperCollins. Why in the world would anyone pay him that much for a book that would probably be no more than repackaged old speeches? After all, Gingrich's last book had netted only $15,000. It looked rather suspicious, considering that HarperCollins was owned by the international media mogul Rupert Murdoch, and he had many interests before Congress—especially legislation dealing with his television empire. Could it be that he was trying to buy Gingrich's support? That would be bribery. The Ethics Committee eventually cleared Gingrich, but it did say he had created an "especially troubling" perception of "exploiting one's office for personal gain." (Eventually, and grudgingly, Gingrich admitted "I made a public-relations mistake," and he took only $1 for his book.

---

*And then this rules violator got what many believe he did not at all deserve: a pension of about $83,000, which will be automatically increased every couple of years; a retirement office in his congressional district; and about $100,000 a year for staff salaries and $67,000 for office expenses. Those things come from taxpayers; from the gullible commercial world, he can expect to receive from $10,000 to $50,000 for a single speech.

The Ethics Committee also investigated accusations of tax law violations involving the finances of GOPAC, Gingrich's political action committee. The investigators asked him for certain details—and the information he gave was false. Was this a cover-up? Whatever it was, the committee decided merely to reprimand him—a mere slap on the wrist—for failing to conduct himself "in a manner reflecting creditably on the House of Representatives." And it charged him $300,000 for the cost of the investigation. But for Gingrich there was a very broad silver lining to that cloud. The IRS says lawmakers investigated for ethics violations may deduct their legal fees from their income taxes. That ruling would allow Gingrich, who earned $171,500 a year as Speaker, to avoid taxes for two years.

Is Congress for Sale?

Twenty years ago, Richard Harris wrote in *The New Yorker*, "Probably the most distinctive characteristic of the successful politician is selective cowardice." Since then, the cowardice of our successful politicians has become so accepted, and has become so indiscriminate, that we seldom feel prompted even to comment on it. Anyway, cowardice is now strongly challenged by another of their characteristics—greed—for the title of most distinctive.

"When we think of corruption in Washington, Abscam swims into focus: Televised images of politicians pocketing bribe money, embarrassed only by the lack of depth of their pockets," writes Professor Amitai Etzioni. "Worrying about bribes to politicians is like being concerned about burglars breaking in through a back window—when one leaves the front door wide open."

The front door in this instance was carved out and hinged by the Federal Election Act of 1974. Like so many of the reforms cooked up by Congress, this one went sour almost immediately. The aim was to put a limit on contributions by wealthy individuals (one insurance executive had given a cool million dollars to the Nixon election) and under-the-table contributions by labor unions and corporations. The new law said that no person could give more than $1,000 to any one candidate in a primary or general election, and no more than $25,000 to a political party. As for corporations, unions, and trade organizations, they were not allowed to give money at all unless they formed a political action committee (PAC) and registered with the Federal Election Commission. The rules governing these interest group PACs were firm: No person could give more than $5,000 to a PAC and no PAC could contribute directly to a single candidate more than $10,000. The law also established a system by which the public could finance the bulk of *presidential* elections through tax dollars.

The results were these: First, money that had been going into presidential races was now rechanneled into congressional races. Indeed, the amount spent by special-interest groups on congressional campaigns doubled in the very first election after the law was passed. Second, since no one PAC could give more than $10,000, the number of PACs proliferated like rabbits. They had been around before, but had been few in number. In 1973 there were just over 100 PACs in existence. In 1989 there were 4,828; in the 1988 election, PACs gave $172 million to candidates running for federal office. By 1996 this had increased to $214 million.

While the law allows a PAC to give only $10,000 to each candidate, the Supreme Court ruled that a person, a PAC, or any group can spend an unlimited amount "independently"—for instance, through radio and television commercials touting the candidate's virtues—as long as the givers pretend to be acting on their own and do not communicate with the candidates' campaign organization. This, of course, is a farcical loophole that makes the law's restrictions meaningless.

Money contributed like this is called "soft" money. Being totally unregulated, it is turning the election process into a giant Las Vegas, where only the biggest gamblers win. In 1996, the fifty largest donors—corporations, unions, and trade associations, all prohibited from giving money directly to candidates except under the PAC limits—had used the legal "soft" money bypass to spend more than $800,000 apiece to support the candidates of their choice. Hedging their bets, most big donors gave to both parties. Critics use terms like "legalized bribery" to describe the system.

Professor Etzioni claims that the legalized bribery is done quite openly: "How, then, does the corruption work? The law forbids only explicit deals. A lobbyist may visit a member of Congress shortly before a vote. He'll express the position the lobby favors, will make a campaign contribution some time before the vote, and—if the vote is satisfactory—another after it is cast. So long as no direct link is forged between the contribution and vote, giver and receiver are home free."

Former President Gerald Ford, who served more than two decades in the House, said it is accepted by all members that businessmen give only "so when they walk in with a problem they can say, 'Well, we or my company or my PAC contributed to your campaign.' I mean, it's that pragmatic."

Former Senator Wyche Fowler, a Democrat from Georgia, looking back on his years in Washington, recalled the wretched routine: Make "a list of about thirty lobbyists and start calling them, asking them to be on my [campaign] committee and raise me $5,000 or $10,000 by a specified date. And then they would call and say, 'Wyche, I'd like to talk to you about the agriculture bill or banking bill coming up next week.'" It was the old *quid pro quo* squeeze play. Every member has to play it.

Quid pro quo. Money for a vote. If that's the way things work, it eliminates most people from the political process. Bob Dole, the Kansas Republican who took millions of dollars from giant corporations, explained the obvious: "Poor people don't have a PAC." Most middle-class people don't either, for most middle-class people aren't organized. Does this mean that the special-interest groups have seized the political process by buying it?

Some certainly seem to be trying. Senator Al D'Amato, Republican of New York, raised more than $17 million for his reelection campaign in 1998, one of the biggest campaign slush funds in history. Much of it came from the banking industry. D'Amato is chairman of the Senate Banking Committee. MBNA, the giant issuer of bank credit cards, contributed more than half a million dollars. MBNA wanted him to help wipe out a consumer protection law and, sure enough, an anticonsumer amendment zipped through his committee.

A corporate contributor to a campaign slush fund of Senator Trent Lott told *The Wall Street Journal,* "I give because I have an interest in how he votes. . . . It's self-interest." *Quid pro quo.*

When it comes to campaign financing ethics, Congress's specialty is irony and black humor. What better proof than Representative Dan Burton of Indiana, chairman of the Government Reform Committee, investigating campaign finance abuses of the White House. Is this the same Dan Burton who raised hundreds of thousands of dollars from foreign lobbyists for his 1996 campaign? That's the guy. It's the Dan Burton who was investigated by a federal grand jury after he was accused of trying to cut off access on Capitol Hill to a Pakistan lobbyist, unless he gave Burton $5,000.*

---

*Aside from his questionable qualifications as an ethics investigator, Burton has some odd legislative ideas. Right-wing journalist David Brock says "many colleagues in his own party think he's nuts." Obsessed with the dangers of AIDS, Burton has introduced a bill that would require every person in America to get mandatory testing for AIDS every year (Molly Ivins, *Fort Worth Star-Telegram,* June 3, 1998).

One Man's Bribe . . .

John T. Noonan, Jr., the nation's preeminent expert on bribery, says in his book *Bribes* that ordinary campaign contributions aren't bribes because they aren't big enough to put politicians under pressure. "Size," he writes, "is thus a relevant characteristic. A large contribution can create an overriding obligation; its proper name becomes bribe."

Keep that definition in mind as you let watchdog organizations like Common Cause sift through any federal budget and show you how the influence of ordinary citizens, even when organized into groups, usually adds up to very little compared to the success of big-money lobbies. The 1998 budget is full of examples:

- The highway construction lobby during the previous six years gave $3.4 million to the two major political parties. In return, Congress took $7 billion that was to have gone to paying down the national debt and put it in the highway fund.
- Oil and chemical companies gave $24 million to the political parties over the previous six years; they were rewarded with a $1.7 billion tax break.
- Broadcasters gave $5 million to the parties; they were rewarded with digital spectrum rights worth billions of dollars.

Big contributions are seldom mistaken for anything but a bribe. Everyone in the business admits it. When Russell Long was in the Senate, nobody had his hand out farther and nobody was less hypocritical about it. "The distinction between a large contribution and a bribe," quoth Long, "is almost a hairline's difference."

In truth, the only difference is what an era, or a prosecuting attorney and a judge, decide to make of it. For example, in 1967, Senator Daniel Brewster of Maryland received $14,500 as "campaign contributions" from Spiegel Inc., a mail-order catalog company. He got some money before he promised to try to kill a postal rate increase, and he received some of it after he tried to kill it. He was indicted for bribery and pleaded guilty to accepting money for the performance of an official act. Spiegel Inc. was convicted of bribery and so was the company's lobbyist.

Now let us jump forward sixteen years. In 1983, the Dravo Corporation of Pittsburgh got in trouble with the Navy over its contract to build a steam plant. Dravo went to Senator Arlen Specter of Pennsylvania, to whom the corporation had already given $4,000 in "campaign funds," and asked for help. "Without telling the Navy what he was doing," writes Phil Stern in his aptly named *The Best Congress Money Can Buy*, Specter inserted a brief provision into a ninety-page bill that got Dravo off the hook. Thereupon, Dravo gave Specter another $2,500.

The similarities between the two cases are striking. Similar experiences—intermingling pleas for help with "campaign contributions"—happen every day on Capitol Hill. But Specter was not indicted, nor are other members of Congress these days. Brewster's indictment a generation ago was a historical fluke, his conviction a rarity on a par with being struck by lightning. Indeed, antibribery efforts (not laws, but efforts to use the laws) at the federal level have been almost nonexistent throughout our history. Although bribery is one of only two crimes specifically mentioned in the Constitution (treason being the other) as grounds for impeachment, in practice bribery has been one of the most ignored crimes, particularly in Congress.

The difficulty of proving bribery is that the contribution must clearly be the result, or in anticipation, of a particular vote. Suspicious observers may have no trouble making the connection in their own minds, but that's not good enough for a court. When Senator Lloyd Bentsen of Texas became chairman of the Finance Committee, he wasted no time inviting lobbyists to a series of breakfasts. Price per seat: a $10,000 campaign contribution. Of course, it is always possible that some people in Texas consider $10,000 a normal price for breakfast, and there was no way to prove that the lobbyists were buying anything but his companionship. Still, when the public found out about the breakfasts, there was so many hoots and jeers that Bentsen called them off. Most members are not quite so gauche.

A Vicious Circle

The atmosphere of lawlessness created by PAC money is not, however, the worst of it. What is really destructive is the effect that PAC money has on democracy. Indeed, as Barry Goldwater said, "PAC money is destroying the electoral process." It has practically wiped out the idea of competition between candidates.

Lobbyists like to bet on sure winners, and since 98 percent of House members and 85 percent of senators who try for reelection win, lobbyists give nearly 90 percent of their money to incumbents, not overlooking those with no opponents. It's a vicious circle: Winners get the money, and money keeps making them winners—over and over, as long as they wish.

What makes it even more impossible for challengers is the incredible rise in the cost of campaigns. Since the mid-1970s, the cost of an average House campaign has risen 500 percent; the average Senate campaign 600 percent. If you can't write a check for half a million dollars, don't even think about running for the House, and anything less than $3 million won't get you close to the Senate—even in a small state.

If you want to challenge an incumbent, don't look to PACs for help. In a typical election for the House, incumbents get eight to twelve times more (depending on their party affiliation) than challengers. "Congress," as one political consultant accurately sized up the problem, "has become an incumbent protection society."

For forty years the resulting rigidity of the system was particularly harmful in the House, where, simply because of the PAC system, the Democratic majority seemed almost guaranteed to continue forever. Surely the Founding Fathers, who saw the House as the part of the federal government closest to the people, did not envision *that* chamber being locked up so tightly by special-interest money.

Anyone who agrees with that may almost be grateful to Newt Gingrich—however much they disagree with his right-wing politics—for breaking the Democrats' hold on the lower chamber in 1994. And there was poetic justice in the way he achieved his goal. Yes, partly it was done, as we have already pointed out, by a masterfully mean propaganda attack via C-SPAN television speeches and in other ways, heaping so much vituperation on the Democratic party—throwing so much mud at it—that the public became disgusted with Congress as a whole and wished wholeheartedly for a change in leadership. That was part of his attack.

But the other part was with money. Gingrich agreed with his enemy, President Clinton: "The party with the most money wins." To win the House, Gingrich had to outfox the incumbent Democrats in manipulating the PAC system. He did it sometimes in violation of the spirit of the federal election laws, and sometimes illegally in every respect, but he had learned those techniques by watching the Democrats.

His plan was simple. He had a political action committee called GOPAC. He would solicit tens of thousands of dollars through GOPAC—sometimes by threatening corporate executives with serious retribution if they didn't kick in—and pour those funds into supporting virtually every Republican challenging potentially vulnerable Democrats. The process was tainted. Federal law requires political action committees to name their contributors and the amounts they gave. Gingrich's GOPAC ignored that regulation, for an obvious reason: One wealthy industrialist's PAC gave five times the federal limit; another gave forty-seven times the limit; another, thirty-nine times the federal limit, and so forth.

Gingrich and his followers claimed that theirs was an ideological revolution aimed at cleansing the House of corruption. That's rather hard to believe, since they won by adopting the Democrats' illegitimate fund-raising tactics. And having gained dominance, not many Republicans seem eager to reform campaign laws. At a much-ballyhooed photo op, Speaker Gingrich shook hands with President Clinton in 1995 and promised to give campaign finance reform a high priority on his legislative agenda. He must have been joking. True, the Republican House passed a campaign reform bill in the closing days of the 1998 summer session—but that was just something they could brag about when they went home and started campaigning. They knew the bill would be killed in the Senate, for Senate Majority Leader Lott had promised that it would be. And, sure enough, it was. As Congressman Barney Frank observed sarcastically, "This is a bill that everybody wants to vote for, and nobody wants to become law."

But There's Hope

It would be grossly misleading to end this chapter with the implication that Congress represents only electoral indifference and institutional deterioration. Nor should it be presumed that members of Congress never rise above their lowest common denominator. The fact is that, although they are too rare to exert a prevailing influence on Congress, there are at any given time in history some members whose courage and integrity and brilliance could rival the models of any age.

When the U.S. Supreme Court sensibly ruled in 1989 that burning the U.S. flag as an act of political expression was constitutionally protected free speech, members of Congress became hysterical in their efforts to prove their patriotism by denouncing the ruling. In one session lasting through the night, not one House member rose to defend the Court. But in the Senate, three members—Howard Metzenbaum, Edward Kennedy, and Gordon Humphrey—had the guts (Humphrey needed less of them, since he wasn't running again) to vote against a resolution condemning the decision. On most controversial flag-waving and dollar-waving issues, the gutsy members can usually be counted on two hands. But at least there are always some to be counted.

The two earliest and most consistent critics of our involvement in the Vietnam War, Senators Wayne Morse of Oregon and Ernest

Gruening of Alaska, pursued that course without wavering, although it was evident that by doing so they would risk defeat in the next election; and they were defeated. Senators Ralph Yarborough of Texas and Albert Gore of Tennessee supported antisegregation laws, advocated a moderate course in the Southeast Asian war, voted against the two southern nominees to the Supreme Court (Clement Haynsworth and Harrold Carswell), and opposed favoritism for oil companies and other powerful interests that carried considerable weight in their home states. They took positions that went strictly counter to the general feelings in the South, and they knew it was risky to do so; and they were turned out by the voters.

In July 1983, Senator David Pryor, Arkansas Democrat, rose on the floor of the Senate and suggested that his colleagues delete $180 million from the Pentagon's budget that was to be used to build nerve-gas weapons. He argued that it would be morally and practically wrong to build the weapons, and he warned that they could "mark the beginning of a new kind of arms race." He was so eloquent that he forced the Senate into a 49–49 tie, and the vice president had to cast the deciding vote. It went against Senator Pryor. What made his legislative fight so unusual, so courageous, was that the $180 million was going to be spent at nerve-gas manufacturing facilities in his home state. Rejecting military pork? It was almost unheard of. Chambers of commerce back home were furious with Pryor for opposing this influx of federal money. Some Arkansas newspapers editorialized against him. The other senator from Arkansas, Dale Bumpers, voted against him. But in this case there was a happy ending: Pryor survived the next election.

The late Senator Sam Ervin, Jr., of North Carolina was one of the most obstinate foes of civil-rights laws, but at the same time he proved to be the Senate's most adamant defender of civil liberties. He stood virtually alone among southerners in opposing the Pentagon's program of sending military agents to spy on left-wing politicians and left-wing professors and students. When the Senate was considering whether to expand the witch-hunting powers of the Subversive Activities Control Board, old Ervin, once a small-town judge in the foothills of North Carolina, stood up and with his eyebrows jumping and his judicial jowls shaking for emphasis, told the Senate why he could not vote yes.

> I hate the thoughts of the Black Panthers. I hate the thoughts of the Weathermen's faction of the Students for a Democratic Society. I hate

the thoughts of fascists. I hate the thoughts of totalitarians. I hate the thoughts of people who adopt violence as a policy. But those people have the same right to freedom of speech, subject to a very slight qualification, that I have. I love the Constitution so much that I am willing to stand on the floor of the Senate and fight for their right to think the thoughts and speak the words that I hate. If we ever reach the condition in this country that we attempt to have free speech for everybody except those whose ideas we hate, not only free speech but freedom itself are out in our society.

His side lost that day, as the right side usually does in Congress; but as long as that body can produce such moments as when a southern conservative makes an impassioned plea for society to quit harassing its pariahs, Congress isn't yet hopeless.

CHAPTER 5

The Supreme Court

A Sometime Fortunate
Imbalance of Power

*Do not try to save the world by loving thy neighbor;
it will only make him nervous. Save the world by
respecting thy neighbor's rights under law and
insisting that he respect yours (under the same law).*

E. B. WHITE

*It is my understanding that the Constitution of the
United States allows everybody their free choice
between cheesecake and strudel.*

SKY MASTERSON
Guys and Dolls

LAW IS THE UNDERSTANDING BY WHICH SOCIETY AGREES TO
reconcile its differences. As long as everyone is in agreement on an issue, law can be ignored. Mutually satisfied citizens never take each
other to court or lobby for new legislation. That happens only when
parties fall out, when neighbors disagree over rights of way, when corporations insist on using similar trademarks, when athletes want to
break contracts and move to another team, when sheepmen feel that
cattlemen have too much of the federal range, when people living
downstream decide they are being abused by an upstream utility company's pollution. In short, the law is appealed to for help and relief
only when one element of society feels that others have conspired to
deny it a fair chance at the bonanza of life and liberty.

Where do laws come from? They have varied parentage. Some are born of custom and tradition, the hardy ancestry of common law. Some come from legislation; some from executive fiat. There is a rare breed of law that comes from the deliberation of conventions, as the U.S. Constitution did. Some law originates in, and all law is obliquely shaped by, the whim of judges—both brilliant judges of the highest integrity and judges of the sort once described by California Governor Edmund G. ("Pat") Brown: "superannuated and senile and mentally ill and alcoholics."

People respect law only when it works. And the prime requirement for the successful application of law is impartiality. Over the doorway to the United States Supreme Court are carved the words "Equal Justice Under Law." They really didn't need to say "equal" because there is no justice if the law is unequally applied. Justice means the protection of life and property through even-handed law enforcement. Justice is the settlement of disputes, either between individuals or between individuals and government, in a speedy and fair manner. Justice means that the rights of the individual are fairly balanced with the rights of society, that the rights of a minority are fairly balanced with the rights of the majority, and that neither individual, minority, majority, nor society is allowed to tyrannize any of the others. Justice means maintaining order by the equitable punishment of those who have unfairly deprived others of life, property, privileges of citizenship, privacy, or any other constitutionally protected ingredients of being an American.

How much justice do we have in America?

- Morton Halperin, a former White House aide, sued former President Richard M. Nixon and Nixon's top assistant, H. R. Haldeman, for violating his civil rights by wiretapping his telephone. The court agreed with Halperin, but awarded him only $5.
- A few months after a federal court let Richard Helms, former director of the CIA, get off with a $2,000 fine for lying to a congressional committee about CIA activities, another federal court ordered that Frank Snepp, also a former CIA official, be forced to give up $60,000 in royalties from a book in which he told the truth about CIA activities.
- Thousands of workers and families of dead workers have sued dozens of corporations for sicknesses and deaths caused from working around asbestos. The Rand Corporation, after digging through this legal quagmire, concluded that only 37 percent of

the more than $600 million that defendants and insurers had spent in connection with asbestos damage suits had gone to compensate the plaintiffs. The other 63 percent had been consumed by lawyers and other court costs.

- In 1972 the U.S. Supreme Court threw out the death penalty statutes then in effect, saying they were being applied unfairly. In 1976, in *Gregg* v. *Georgia,* the deeply divided Court allowed capital punishment to begin again, with certain restrictions. Has arbitrariness ended under the new laws? Judge for yourself. A nationwide survey found that in Maryland the killer of a white is eight times more likely to receive the death penalty than the killer of a black, in Arkansas the likelihood is six times greater, and in Texas five times greater.

- For murdering a Mexican-American prisoner, by beating and then drowning him in a bayou, a Houston policeman received a one-year sentence. For murdering a twelve-year-old Mexican-American prisoner—he handcuffed the boy's hands behind his back and then shot him in the head—a Dallas policeman received a five-year sentence.

- Criminals sentenced for drug offenses account for about half the growth in the prison population over the last fifteen years, and African-Americans represent 75 percent of those in prison for drug possession—despite the fact that both races use illegal drugs at about the same rate.

- Theoretically, jail terms are set according to the seriousness of the crime. But despite the fact that in recent years some states have spent more to build prisons than to build schools, jails are getting so crowded that sentences sometimes depend on whether there's room for the convicts. The North Carolina legislature, for example, recently adopted sentencing guidelines for judges based on a computer model showing how much bed space was available in the state's prisons, much like a hotel reservation.

- Some laws seem touched with insanity. For example, in 1973 Michael Rene Pardue, then seventeen years old, was beaten so cruelly by a detective (known for beating confessions from suspects) that he confessed to three shotgun murders, which in fact he had not committed. He was sentenced to life in an Alabama prison. Twenty-five years later the Alabama Supreme Court ruled that all evidence indicated Pardue was innocent of the murders and had been wrongly imprisoned. But would the state release him? No. Three times during his imprisonment he was convicted of trying to escape, and in Alabama three-time losers are kept in jail for life—even though, in Pardue's case, he had merely tried to escape from a prison where he shouldn't have been in the first place.

The American Court System

Stories like the above could be multiplied by the thousands, and that number would only begin to scratch the surface of the overall legal system in America, which Derek C. Bok, once president of Harvard University, called "among the most expensive and least efficient systems in the world." It often seems that the system of justice is about to break down, either because the machinery is overburdened, or because it costs more than most people can afford, or because so many of the officials involved—judges, prosecutors, defense attorneys—are overworked or incompetent.

The most prized myth of the English-speaking world is that the law applies alike to rich and poor, to powerful and humble. Ideally, of course, the law does *not* play favorites; ideally, justice *is* blind—blind, that is, to social status and bank accounts. Unfortunately, justice is not blind and never has been. The law shows favoritism in what it allows and in what it doesn't allow. The wealthy and powerful always get a better shake than the poor and the weak.

As many a low-income felon has discovered, stealing a $200 television set or a $10,000 car is enough to land them in prison for several years. But when Victor Posner—one of the highest-paid American executives with a salary estimated at $8.5 million, who controlled forty companies and had a personal fortune of about $180 million—was caught stealing $1.2 million from the government by not paying the proper amount of taxes, the judge let him off without having to serve a single day.

Ivan Boesky, the infamous stock manipulator who stole upwards of $200 million, pleaded guilty and was sentenced to three years in a minimum security prison in southern California where inmates play tennis and grow flowers. Nobody expected him to serve more than a year.

In the same week Boesky went off to raise roses, a small-time drug dealer passed through the same New York courthouse and received a sentence of forty-five years, without parole, to be served in a *real* prison.

There are lots of ordinary folks serving time whose crime was no worse than growing pot in a backyard garden. They must envy Oliver

L. North, the infamous White House aide who was convicted in 1989 of accepting a $13,800 illegal gift, of destroying extremely valuable national security documents, and of lying to Congress. His trial cost the government millions of dollars. He could have been sentenced to ten years in prison, but he didn't spend even an hour behind bars. He had friends in very high places.

Or consider the blissful immunity of corporations. According to the Bureau of National Affairs, the dollar cost of corporate crime in America every year is over ten times greater than the combined larcenies, robberies, burglaries, and auto thefts committed by individuals. But no matter how foul their crimes, corporations are usually let off with no more than a fine, and in most cases the amount is little more than pocket change to the big company. A study for the United States Sentencing Commission covering the years 1984 through 1987 found that nearly half of the convicted corporations were fined $5,000 or less, and about 80 percent were fined $25,000 or less. Only one out of five of the criminal corporations was even put on probation.

Crooked bankers and other insiders are looting billions of dollars from America's thrift institutions, yet "the chances of getting caught and going to jail are minimal," the House Government Operations Committee reported. Even when fraud is uncovered and prosecuted, sentences tend to be light. The House committee's report cites the American Heritage Savings & Loan in Chicago, where executives made $15 million in fraudulent loans. The firm collapsed and taxpayers had to shell out $45 million to clean up the mess. The longest sentence handed out: one year and a day, plus community service.

Complained Anthony Valukas, a U.S. attorney in Chicago, "If someone had walked in the door of the bank with a note saying this is a robbery and walked out with $1,500, I dare say he would have received five to ten years in prison."

All of which proves the accuracy of C. Wright Mills' formula: "It is better to take one dime from each of ten million people at the point of a corporation than $100,000 from each of ten banks at the point of a gun. It is also safer."*

*Perhaps one reason the rich and the mighty get off with such light (if any) punishment is that their crimes are so often financial ones that land them in federal courts, where the well-heeled judges are likely to feel sympathy for those out to make a few million extra bucks. A survey by the Associated Press in 1989 found that a majority of federal judges, in addition to their salaries ranging from $89,500 to $115,000, had "six-figure investment portfolios and many make more money off the bench than on it." As many as one out of five federal judges may be millionaires. Judge Gerhard A. Gesell, who handled Oliver North's trial, is one of the millionaires. The great majority of federal judges were attorneys for corporations before they went on the bench.

Most people would probably agree that the scales of justice are weighted unfairly. If the typical American were given the opportunity, he or she would probably end the imbalance between the punishment of crimes in the street and the punishment (if any) of crimes in the executive suite. A Louis Harris poll showed that a manufacturer of unsafe automobiles was regarded by the public as worse than a mugger (68 percent to 22 percent), and a business executive who illegally fixed prices was considered worse than a burglar (54 percent to 28 percent). But never in the history of this country has anyone served time for making unsafe autos, and only once has someone served time for fixing prices. That kind of barren justice has a dangerously debilitating effect on the public's attitude toward law and government.

S-l-o-w Help for the Poor

The Bill of Rights, as we call the first ten amendments of the Constitution, are what Americans hear most frequently referred to in Fourth of July speeches—particularly the First Amendment's guarantee of freedom of speech, freedom of the press, and freedom of religion.

But equally important—as anyone who has run afoul of the law will tell you—are the procedural rights guaranteed by the Fifth, Sixth, Seventh, and Eighth Amendments—rules for the conduct of the government itself before, during, and after a trial. These amendments guarantee, among other things, that a person accused of a crime has the right to keep silent, the right to a jury trial, the right to a lawyer, the right to fair bail, and the right to equitable punishment.

Sounds swell. But the Bill of Rights was adopted in 1791, and for the first seventy-seven years of our nation's life, it was generally assumed that the Bill of Rights applied only to federal courts. But most criminal cases wind up in state courts, and the right to a lawyer didn't apply to state courts—until the Fourteenth Amendment was passed in 1868.

And even then the right didn't mean a thing if you didn't have money to hire a lawyer. That's always meant big bucks (today a cheap lawyer costs $125 an hour; the lawyers hired by Monica Lewinsky for her White House sex case cost $450 an hour).

Gradually, from the mid-1930s to the 1970s, the U.S. Supreme Court took actions to provide lawyers for penniless defendants, whether in state or federal courts.

The job was almost finished in 1963, when the court ruled that Florida had not given one of its inmates a full share of constitutional protection. Clarence Gideon, fifty-one, an experienced felon, had been sentenced to five years in prison for burglarizing a pool room and stealing several bottles of booze. Penniless, Gideon had asked the Florida judge to provide him with a lawyer and had been refused. When the case got to the U.S. Supreme Court (*Gideon* v. *Wainright*), Justice Black wrote the majority's decision in terms just as simple as had been written into the Sixth Amendment nearly two centuries earlier: "[I]n our adversary system of criminal justice, any person hailed into court, who is too poor to hire a lawyer, cannot be assured a fair trial unless counsel is provided for him. . . . The right of one charged with crime to counsel may not be deemed fundamental in some countries, but it is in ours."

That took care of defendants in all felony cases. And in *Argesinger* v. *Hamlin,* in 1972, the U.S. Supreme Court extended the right to counsel down through all criminal cases, even misdemeanors, in which conviction could lead to jail.

It had taken a mere one hundred and seventy-nine years for the Sixth Amendment to reach full flower. The wheels of justice do indeed move slowly.

Poor Get Poor Help

These were giant steps forward, theoretically. But in fact indigent defendants often still have no lawyers. For lack of money, lack of lawyers, or lack of sympathetic judges, "there are still many jurisdictions that don't meet the standard," according to Howard B. Eisenberg, executive director of the National Legal Aid and Defender Association. "I think it is clearly a crisis."

In a typical year, federal, state, and local governments spend more than three times as much per capita on prosecution as they do on public defense (and this doesn't count the help the prosecutor gets from police investigations, medical examiners, crime labs, and ballistics labs).

In many jurisdictions, the public defender's office—which is supposed to supply lawyers for the poor—is broke. In many other jurisdictions, the office operates on a shoestring. Alabama, for example, spends only 45 cents per capita on defense for poor people, compared to $4 in California. Alabama, in fact, will not spend more than $1,000 to defend a person for any crime, including murder. Obviously, in places like Alabama, indigent defendants must rely on volunteer, unpaid legal assistance. And good lawyers, because their time is worth big bucks, don't like to volunteer. There are exceptions—some of the most expensive law firms do a considerable amount of *pro bono* (charity) work—but as a rule the best lawyers avoid it. In Texas, a study by the State Bar found that only seven out of every one hundred lawyers do *pro bono* work.

The result is that people who have no money, even those who are charged with murder and whose lives depend on getting good lawyers, sometimes wind up with court-appointed lawyers who are senile, or who are intoxicated or under the influence of drugs while trying their cases; lawyers who handle cases without any investigative or expert assistance; lawyers who sleep during trial* or are absent during crucial parts of the trial; and lawyers who use racial slurs to refer to their clients.

Defendants whose luck isn't that bad still may get help that is pitifully bad, often winding up with young lawyers with no trial experience or old lawyers whose talents have faded.

John Paul Penry got one of the latter. Penry, a thirty-two year old with the intelligence of a six year old, had been convicted for rape–murder in Texas and sentenced to die. When his case got to the U.S. Supreme Court, he was represented by a good-hearted but over-the-hill lawyer whose performance is described by the renowned Harvard law professor, Alan Dershowitz:

> To say the least, his presentation was a disaster. The attorney spoke haltingly and his words were difficult to understand. He seemed not to understand some of the justices' questions. When he did, he frequently gave the wrong answers. He couldn't find needed references. He became so bogged down in technical detail that Justice Sandra Day O'Connor had to remind him, with only three minutes left in his argument time, that he had not addressed the main issue—whether it was constitutional to execute a mentally retarded prisoner.

Obviously the scales of justice, said Dershowitz, are out of whack. "While lawyers help the rich get richer through leveraged buyouts and other fancy financial footwork, those most in need of excellent legal representation—the mentally retarded, the poor, the homeless, the stateless—have to rely on well-motivated volunteers, retired lawyers and underpaid public defenders. There is something drastically wrong with this system."

---

*A judge in Harris County, Texas, responding to a murder defendant's complaint that his lawyer slept during the trial at which the death sentence was imposed, stated, "The Constitution doesn't say the lawyer has to be awake." (pp. 800–801, "Judges and the Politics of Death" by Stephten B. Bright and Patrick J. Keenan, *Boston University Law Review*, Vol. 75, No. 3, May 1995).

Whims and Delays

There is an appalling amount of inconsistency found in our courts. Depending on whether they are swamped with work, prosecutors may try diligently to send a defendant to prison—or refuse to handle the complaint. (In one study, it was found that U.S. attorneys, the prosecuting arm of the Justice Department, refused to prosecute 62 percent of the criminal complaints over a period of six years because they said they didn't have the time.) It is commonplace for prosecutors to "cut a deal" with a defendant—offer to let him off on a lesser charge if he will plead guilty to it, thereby avoiding the time and expense of a trial. But the "deal" varies from prosecutor to prosecutor, depending on how rushed they are and what mood they're in.

Judges are also very inconsistent in their sentences. A study by the Federal Judicial Center showed that whether a bank robber received one year or ten years in prison could depend on which of two courtrooms he was processed through. Fifty judges were surveyed; in 16 of 20 cases they were sharply divided over whether even to impose a prison term. Tom Goldstein, who wrote on legal affairs for *The New York Times*, describes the multifaceted arbitrariness of the courts: "Differences in sentencing reflect differences in the defendants' race, wealth, age and sex, differences in the geographical location of courts, differences in plea bargains, and probably most importantly, differences in the personality and ideology of the judges doing the sentencing."

The breakdown of justice is not only seen when serious crimes and serious disputes are at issue, but also when citizens need the assistance of a court for a moderate problem—a dispute over a product's performance, say, or a dispute over whether the neighbor's hedge should be allowed to block the view, or a fuss over a roofing job that wasn't done well. Talbot D'Alemberte, former president of the American Bar Association says, "Many aggrieved parties, regardless of socioeconomic status, effectively have *no* access to any forum for the resolution of disputes because the time, money and trouble involved are simply worth far more than the loss involved."

In other words, they feel that life is much too precious to be wasted in the stalled traffic-jam of justice, a legal process that former Chief Justice Warren E. Burger called "one of the slowest in the world." They've heard the horror stories about people who waited years to get their day in court, and then more years to get a final ruling. Ten years ago, the median time from filing suit to the commencement of trial in a federal district court was less than a year; today it exceeds a year and a half. But that's just the beginning. Some cases commonly take more than five years from commencement to final disposition; and complex litigation, such as antitrust claims, can linger more than a decade. In 1987, IBM settled an action that had been churning around the courts for eighteen years.

Why this interminable backlog of cases in most urban courts? For one thing, there is a shortage of courtrooms, a shortage of judges, a shortage of prosecutors; taxpayers are reluctant to build and hire enough to handle the soaring crime rate and the populace's growing love of civil litigation. But another reason for the slowdown, according to Burger, is that many lawyers are unfit to practice law; they simply don't know how to prepare for trial, or they make clumsy mistakes that result in mistrials. He estimated that about 50 percent of all lawyers are incompetent.

But what did Burger mean by "competent"? Is it knowing all the tricks that the law allows? As one veteran court observer has written:

> Opposing lawyers work more to win victory for their side than to seek truth. Witnesses are primed for testimony by one side and misled on cross-examination by the other. Pertinent evidence is purposely suppressed. Lying by witnesses is commonplace and tolerated. At the same time, each side and the judge must observe every appropriate technicality; a mistake leads to a lost case, and there often is no opportunity to correct even an inadvertent oversight. . . . Constant back-and-forth and jigsaw-puzzle presentation of the evidence often leaves jurors baffled at the end of a trial, only to have their minds further scrambled by overly emotional, completely one-sided, and often distorted summary arguments by each lawyer.

This is called the "adversary system" of justice, and our legal profession is proudly trained in it; textbooks used in law schools often read like military strategy textbooks. The result in the courtroom does indeed often leave the poor jury (not always of the highest mentality) floundering and drowning in technicalities. After an assault trial in Washington, D.C., which ended with the defendant sentenced to a three-year prison term, nine of the twelve jurors went to the judge and asked him to give the man another trial because they *thought* they had been voting for *acquittal,* not conviction. (The judge refused.) Such is the competence of some juries. Researchers for the National Science Foundation, surveying a random sample of prospective jurors, found that they understood only 54 percent of the crucial elements of each of the standard instructions given jurors. Only one, a Ph.D. holder, grasped the entire meaning of "proximate cause." Four people came away with a total blank.

Some judges make such a grotesquely distorted effort to seat an "unbiased" jury that they deliberately exclude jurors of normal mentality and normal experience. For example, in the trial of Lt. Col. Oliver North in Washington, D.C., Federal Judge Gerhard Gesell refused to allow anyone to sit on the jury who had ever even *heard* of the Iran-contra scandal, which North was accused of masterminding. This was the most notorious political scandal of the 1980s. For months newspapers across the nation had bannered it and the television networks crammed it nightly into their reports from Washington. Only people living in caves could have avoided hearing about it. But judges don't have to make sense in order to be obeyed, and Gesell got the know-nothing jury he wanted.

For the above and other reasons, the ordinary citizen has come to look upon the much-vaunted "day in court" as overpriced, overwrought, and overrated, and would wholeheartedly agree with Judge Learned Hand that "as a litigant, I should dread a lawsuit beyond almost anything else short of sickness and death."

The giant corporation with its army of attorneys can afford the slow-motion waltz of justice; however costly and tedious it may be, the courtroom ordeal can be written off simply as another business expense. To the professional criminal, the legal process is taken as just another risk of his chosen career. But to the ordinary citizen—who comes to court expecting simplicity of procedure, expert judgment, and speedy disposition of his or her case—the interminable delays, the legal expense, the sometimes poorly trained judges and attorneys are extremely disillusioning.

The Final Say

The ultimate voice in the legal system belongs to the judge. Government at every level imposes a great blanket of rules, regulations, edicts, and laws on the citizenry in an effort to keep the machinery of civilization running smoothly. Every part of the bureaucracy—from the city tax assessor to the Federal Trade Commission—issues a constant flood of regulations. City councils, county commissions, state legislatures, and the U.S. Congress pass thousands of new laws every year. But human beings cannot be regimented with total precision. Their lives and businesses are too complex, and the regulations and laws are almost always too loosely written to cover the complexities. As Justice Felix Frankfurter noted:

> Anything that is written may present a problem of meaning. . . . The problem derives from the very nature of words. They are symbols of meaning. But unlike mathematical symbols, the phrasing of a document, especially a complicated enactment, seldom attains more than approximate precision. . . . The imagination which can draw an income tax statute to cover the myriad transactions of a society like ours, capable of producing the necessary revenue without producing a flood of litigation, has not yet revealed itself.

Words that seem simple—*tax evasion, abortion, trespass, bankruptcy, theft, smuggling, price-fixing, pollution, false advertising, child support*—words and phrases that everyone feels completely familiar with and probably feels quite capable of defining in theory and recognizing in practice, become terribly elusive and multidimensional when society tries to apply them in individual cases. They are sources of endless dispute.

Which is why there are judges. Somebody has to be the final arbitrator. Somebody has to be the final interpreter. Whether they are right or wrong, judges do the necessary job of bringing disputes to a conclusion so that society can stop wrangling and get about its work. Not that judges themselves always agree. They are often in fierce disagreement over the meaning of a law. That's why there are arbitrators even for the bench—judges of judges—in the courts of appeal, both on the state and federal levels. At the very top is the United States Supreme Court, the final appellate court to which all state and federal courts at the lower levels must look for guidance.

In recent years, some of our society's hottest arguments have centered on the Second Amendment to the U.S. Constitution, which reads, "A well regulated Militia, being necessary to the security of a free State, the right of the people to keep and bear Arms, shall not be infringed." To the National Rifle Association (NRA), one of the most powerful lobbies in Washington, this means that citizens have a constitutional right to own guns, without government interference. Polls show a majority of the public agrees with that, but a significant minority is just as heated in disagreement. As for the lower federal courts, they have almost universally rejected the NRA version, and say instead that the right is guaranteed only to state militias, not to individuals. But the lower courts are not enough. Until the U.S. Supreme Court speaks the final word, the argument will go on and on.

Behind the Bench—Politics

All judges are political creatures. At the municipal and county levels, practically all judges are elected. Some state judges are elected and some are appointed. All federal judges are appointed by the president for life.* Once a federal judge makes it to the bench, he can be removed only by impeachment by Congress, which almost never occurs. No Supreme Court justice has ever been impeached, and only two judges at the federal appellate level have been impeached in the last half century.†

There are several good reasons for the life appointment. For one thing, it removes judges from a great deal of political pressure—though some political pressure continues to be felt, as do political loyalties and political gratitude. For another thing, life appointment gives a judge the courage of his convictions. He can do just about anything he wants to do and get by with it. For example, Federal District Judge William Wayne Justice, who presided in Tyler, Texas, until he retired in 1998, had by 1982 managed to get most state officials and millions of ordinary Texans wanting his scalp. He had struck down a state law that denied free public education to illegal aliens (his action was upheld by the U.S. Supreme Court); had ruled that the entire 30,000-inmate Texas prison system was so badly crowded that it was unconstitutionally "cruel and unusual punishment" and ordered sweeping prison reforms; and had even found time to reach down and straighten out some local trivia, such as ordering Tyler Junior College to admit long-haired males.

Aside from irritating Texans who felt that the federal courts had no business messing with their local biases and social apparatus, Justice's rulings promised to cost the state many millions of dollars. He may have made himself the most unpopular man in Texas; he received

---

*Federal judges have two other outstanding characteristics: Most are male and most are white. Not until 1981 was a woman appointed to the Supreme Court—Justice Sandra Day O'Connor. Her rise to the highest court was an extremely tardy victory for women, but her start on that climb was a classic tale of what women have had to put up with in the legal "fraternity." Although she graduated third in her class at Stanford Law School, she was refused a position in every major law firm in southern California except one, which offered her a job as a secretary.

†The importance of impeachment to get rid of bad apples is clearly seen in the case of U.S. District Judge Walter Nixon of Mississippi. He was convicted of perjury and given a five-year prison sentence. But even in prison he received his $89,500 annual salary and was eligible to return to the federal bench when he completed his sentence. Only his impeachment could put an end to the travesty of justice, so in 1989, Congressman Don Edwards, chairman of the House Judiciary Subcommittee, began the impeachment process (Associated Press, March 23, 1989). But impeachment does not always mean banishment from public life. Alcee L. Hastings, Florida's first black federal district judge, was impeached for bribery. But in 1992 he was elected to Congress by south Florida's heavily black 230th district. (*The New York Times,* April 6, 1998.)

much hate mail and many obscene phone calls. But Judge Justice was smilingly unperturbed. "The plain fact of the matter is that the majority is sometimes wrong," he said. "Getting a lot of flak because of your decisions just kind of goes with the territory. That's why they appoint you for life."

Since presidents are profoundly political animals, it is natural that they are partisan in the people they select for the federal bench, particularly for the Supreme Court. If their political advisers say a certain lawyer is right for the job, there's a good chance they'll take the recommendation even if they personally know very little about the nominee. For example, transcripts of White House tapes of a conversation between Richard Nixon and his aide John Ehrlichman on July 24, 1971, show that Nixon wasn't even sure of the name of the man he was about to name to the Supreme Court:

> President: You remember the meeting we had when I told that group of clowns we had around there. Renchburg and that group. What's his name?
>> Ehrlichman: Renchquist [sic].
>> President: Yeah, Rehnquist.

Three months later Nixon would nominate William H. Rehnquist to the Supreme Court as "one of the finest legal minds in this whole country today." Nonsense. "What's his name" had had no judicial experience, and except for a few years in a routine law practice in Phoenix, his career was mainly that of a political operative. He had come to Washington to work as the Republican administration's point man on Capitol Hill in all legal matters, a job that required more political craftiness than legal profundity.

Griffin Bell, who was a federal judge before he became President Carter's attorney general, describes the heavy influence of politics that took him—and all federal appointees—to the bench: "For me, becoming a federal judge wasn't very difficult. I managed John F. Kennedy's presidential campaign in Georgia. Two of my oldest and closest friends were the two senators from Georgia. And I was campaign manager and special, unpaid counsel for the governor [Carter]." He winked. "It doesn't hurt to be a good lawyer either."

Another highly regarded federal judge asserted flatly: "You can't get on the federal bench in this country without a political claim. I had a political claim, and so did every one of my colleagues."

The Conservative Revolution

Partisanship in the process of appointing federal judges has intensified in the past several decades. Presidents appoint them, but their appointments must be confirmed by the Senate (those are the Constitutional rules of the game). And when one party controls the White House and the other party controls the Senate, things can get pretty rough, as was demonstrated in 1999. Senator Orrin G. Hatch, a Utah Republican, was chairman of the Senate Judiciary Committee, through which all judicial appointments must pass. He wanted President Clinton to name one of Hatch's political pals from Utah to a federal bench. Clinton didn't want to. So Hatch simply slammed the door on all judicial confirmation hearings—forty two were pending at that time—until Clinton was ready to compromise. It was the first time in forty years that a senator had shut down the confirmation process in a feud with the White House.

The political struggle to control the Supreme Court has also become more intense. Prior to 1968, there had been only one rejection of a nominee to the Supreme Court in the previous eighty years. Since 1968 the Senate has rejected three nominees, two others have withdrawn their names from consideration because they feared they would be turned down, and one confirmation fight turned into a fierce brawl that was decided by a mere two votes. Getting on the Supreme Court can be a tough gauntlet to run, and the reason is ideological rivalry.

Ever since the activist years of the Warren Court in the 1950s and 1960s (which we'll come back to a little later), the power that the Supreme Court can exert in shaping the nation's "social agenda" —civil rights, civil liberties, and so forth—has been evident. Democrats (particularly liberals) loved what the Warren Court did; conservative Republicans hated it.

Republican presidents have tried to bring about what was called "the conservative revolution" by appointing justices who would undo the Warren Court's reformation. From Warren Burger in 1969 to Clarence Thomas in 1991, all ten appointments to the Supreme Court were made by Republican presidents. (Ruth Bader Ginsburg in 1993 was the first appointment by a Democratic president in twenty-six years.) Through all those years, Democratic influence came only by trying to muster enough Senate votes to block what they considered to be the worst appointments. They usually lost, but when a nominee was exceedingly conservative, the Democrats did put up a strong fight.

Their assault on Clarence Thomas was one of their strongest. President Bush had appointed Thomas to take the seat being vacated by Thurgood Marshall. The only similarity between the two men was that they were both black. Before being appointed to the Supreme Court in 1967, Marshall was probably the foremost civil rights lawyer in the United States. As head of the NAACP Legal Defense and Education Fund, he argued such historic cases as *Brown* v. *Board of Education.* After serving four years on a federal circuit court of appeals and two years as solicitor general, President Johnson selected Marshall to be the Supreme Court's first black justice.

Totally opposite to Marshall in ideology, Clarence Thomas was not merely a conservative but an unabashed reactionary. Unlike most blacks, he did not believe in affirmative action and was often at odds with the NAACP over civil rights matters. He had had only a mediocre legal career when President Bush appointed him to a federal circuit court of appeals, and Thomas had hardly got his seat warm on that court bench before Bush nominated him to the U.S. Supreme Court. But before the Senate could vote on his confirmation, Thomas was accused by a black woman of repeatedly subjecting her to sexual harassment when she worked for him at the Equal Employment Opportunities Commission (of which he, oddly, had been chairman at one time).

After a nationally televised Senate Judiciary Committee hearing at which lurid charges were made and passionately denied (Thomas likened the hearings to a lynching), liberals thought they had the ammunition to bring Thomas down. But they failed, barely. After what became the bitterest confirmation battle of this century, the Senate gave his nomination its approval—fifty-two to forty-eight—the narrowest margin in the history of Supreme Court confirmations.

A Lasting Legacy

"Presidents come and go," said President Nixon, on announcing his last two appointments to the Supreme Court, "but the Supreme Court goes on forever." Indeed, one of the most powerful and lasting imprints a president can make on government is through his Supreme Court appointments. If he appoints judges who closely reflect his own ideology, then he continues to have, by proxy, a strong influence long after he leaves politics. Perhaps long after he is dead. In the early 1980s, for example, four members of the Supreme Court had been appointed by presidents who by that time had died. Four members had been appointed by a president, Richard Nixon, who had left office under threat of impeachment. And the final member had been appointed by a president, Gerald Ford, who had himself been nominated by Nixon as his successor. So five members of the Court were put there, directly or indirectly, by the only president in history who quit in disgrace. Some observers felt that this was a miscarriage of political justice and an unfair extension of Nixon's powers. Congresswoman Elizabeth Holtzman would comment three years after Nixon's departure, "Although Mr. Nixon is gone, his ghost glares down at us balefully from the Supreme Court."*

Ironically, one of the most ethical of recent presidents, Jimmy Carter, was the only president in our history who, because no vacancies occurred during his term, was unable to appoint a single justice to the Court.

Ronald Reagan, departing Washington at the age of seventy-nine, left behind on the Court three appointees who would doubtless be putting flowers on his grave for many years: Anthony M. Kennedy, fifty-two; Sandra Day O'Connor, fifty-eight; and Antonin Scalia, fifty-two.

What Reagan did to inject a more conservative philosophy at the lower-court level was perhaps even more important, because federal trial judges handle some 300,000 cases annually and federal appellate tribunals decide 18,000; of these, the Supreme Court only reviews fewer than 100. So what the lower courts decide usually sticks. By the end of his tenure Ronald Reagan had appointed more than four hundred federal judges, more than half the country's federal judiciary. (Fewer than 2 percent of Reagan's judicial appointees were black, fewer than 5 percent Hispanic, and fewer than 9 percent female.) Thirty-four percent of Reagan's second-term appointments were under forty-five years old. Reagan often chortled, "They will be there for a long time . . . making rulings after I'm dead." Under President Bush, the "Reaganizing" of the judiciary continued.

In other words, presidents have an eye to the future as well as to the present, and they try to clone their ideologies into the future by appointing justices whose attitudes toward governmental matters resemble their own. Generally they get what they aim for—but not

---

*In his memoirs, the former president wrote that aside from Justice William Rehnquist's extremely conservative philosophy, his "most attractive attribute was his age: He was only forty-seven and could probably serve on the Court for twenty-five years" (*RN: The Memoirs of Richard Nixon* [New York: Grosset & Dunlap, 1978]). Obviously, Nixon saw his own influence extending through Rehnquist (and his other appointees) for at least a quarter-century.

always. Justice Byron R. White, though appointed by Kennedy, a liberal, quickly evolved into a loyal member of the Court's conservative bloc. Eisenhower, a conservative, appointed Justice William J. Brennan, mistakenly thinking Brennan was also a conservative; as it turned out, Brennan, over his thirty-four distinguished years on the Court, became the leader of the liberal bloc in pushing individual rights for blacks, women, and homosexuals; defending freedom of the press; and opposing capital punishment.

When presidents are disappointed in their Supreme Court appointments, they can become quite angry. On discovering how liberal Earl Warren was, Eisenhower said that the appointment was the "biggest damfool mistake I ever made."

President Reagan must have been disappointed in his appointee, Justice Anthony Kennedy, who started off his service in 1988 as a wobbly conservative, but by the mid-nineties had become a centrist with occasional libertarian impulses. In fact, on the four most controversial social issues of our day—abortion, school prayer, flag burning, and gay rights—Kennedy stunned and disappointed his conservative supporters by casting crucial votes to extend "liberal" protections.

And President Bush must have suffered the same disappointment in Justice David Souter, a low-keyed judge from New Hampshire who was considered the "stealth justice" because his judicial philosophy was so little known at the time he was appointed. It turned out he wasn't as conservative as Bush thought. He became the center's intellectual force and conscience; a conservative, yes, but a moderate one.

These two justices and Reagan appointee Justice Sandra Day O'Conner (a thorough-going conservative) shocked—to put it mildly—America's political right-wing in 1992 when (in the case labeled *Planned Parenthood* v. *Casey*) they joined Justices Blackmun and John Paul Stevens to form a majority that, at least for the moment, kept alive the abortion rights of *Roe* v. *Wade*. Writing for the majority, Souter, sounding much like Earl Warren, explained that they felt they could not overturn a ruling that women had depended on for two decades, knowing that abortions would be available "in the event that contraception should fail. The ability of women to participate equally in the economic and social life of the nation has been facilitated by their ability to control their reproductive lives."

Presidents have learned that, except for hard-liners like Antonin Scalia and Clarence Thomas (who almost always vote together on the right), most justices are never completely predictable.

The Mystique of the Supreme Court

To the ordinary citizen, the Supreme Court often seems to sit high above the grubbiness of the police court and the divorce court, at an Olympian distance from the politically smudged county and state courts. So it *seems,* and in that seeming is one of its greatest services. To the ordinary citizen, the United States Supreme Court is the embodiment of the majesty of the law, which makes all of us somewhat more willing to accept its edicts in good faith.

The public's opinion has helped implant in the "brethren" (as the justices call each other) a false sense of their own superiority—what one critic of the Court, Judge Jerome N. Frank, once described as "the cult of the robe," meaning that human beings who don the judicial robe think that they thereby become automatically instilled with a sagacity that is beyond other people in government; that they float with purity above the fray, as oracles of constitutional truth, looking down with mild contempt on the gadflies of the press and on the ordinary mortals in Congress who grapple messily with day-to-day problems. They forget, as the late Justice Robert Jackson once remarked, that Supreme Court justices are infallible because they are final, not final because they are infallible.

In fact, we are dealing here with very human beings. Justices have been known to shout at each other and exchange catty, even vicious remarks about each other's talents and character. Justice Jackson denounced Justice Hugo Black as a "stealthy assassin" of judicial proprieties. Justice Felix Frankfurter despised Justice William O. Douglas and called him "the most systematic exploiter of flattery I have ever encountered in my life." Justices sometimes display their tempers in public. Chief Justice Earl Warren may not have been exaggerating when he said that he would "strangle with my own hands" anyone who showed pornography to his daughter. Chief Justice Warren Burger personally chased television reporters out of a hall where he was about to deliver a speech.

Some justices are witty, some are solemn; some are creative, some much less so. Justice Thurgood Marshall was known as a habitual jokester.* Justice Harry A. Blackmun liked to quote "Casey at the Bat."

*His humor was sometimes rather gruff. At a luncheon for the Court's clerks, Marshall was asked a particularly silly question about what he would do, if all-powerful, to solve the problem of racism in America. After a perfect pause and in perfect deadpan, he gave his response: "Kill all the white people." (Edward Lazarus, *Closed Chambers: The First Eyewitness Account of the Epic Struggles Inside the Supreme Court* [New York: Times Books, 1998] p. 278)

Chief Justice Burger was a talented painter; Justice Abe Fortas, an excellent violinist. Justice Scalia plays the piano. Justice White, a former professional football player, liked to unwind with a fast game of basketball. A former Supreme Court clerk recalls coming upon White in the gym, dribbling the ball. White, lost in thought and mumbling, suddenly shouted, "What if . . . ," asking a question relating to a case then before the Court. "And that question presented the key that unlocked the case," according to the clerk, "and after that he played a hell of a game."

While members of the Court have quite normal passions and quite normal political biases, they keep them reasonably in check compared to the president and to members of Congress, who are constantly under pressure and responding to a volatile public opinion that often seems to operate in accordance with the physical principle of a Duncan yo-yo. In some ways the most comforting characteristic of the Supreme Court is that in the midst of political fluidity, it is relatively stable. Its membership is slow to change. Presidents and members of Congress seem almost transient by comparison. There have been forty-two presidents and thousands of members of Congress, but as of 1999 there have been only one hundred and eight members of the Supreme Court. On the average, a justice will serve fifteen years, but Justice Black served thirty-four years before retiring in 1971 and Justice Douglas thirty-six years and six months (a record) before retiring in 1975. As we said earlier, justices can be forced off the bench only by being impeached and convicted by Congress of misbehavior; this has never happened. So, in effect, members of the Supreme Court, whether of good, mediocre, or poor quality, stay on for as long as they want. Some stay much longer than they should. Determined to set a record for service, Douglas stuck around until his eyesight was so haywire he couldn't read briefs, his mind sometimes wandered, he sometimes could not remember even the names of the other justices, and he often fell asleep during their conferences. When a friend asked Douglas how he could do this job when he couldn't read, he snapped, "I'll listen and see how the Chief [Burger] votes and vote the other way."

Knowing that the mystique of the Court is the source of much of their influence, members have done all they could possibly do to maintain an aura of majestic aloofness, of remoteness and secrecy. They may even believe it to be their patriotic duty to create this atmosphere as a way to help implement their decisions, for it is certainly true, as law professor Telford Taylor once put it, that "the Court is in large part what people think it is. . . . It is an 'image.'"

The Shades Are Down

Photographers rarely can catch justices shorn of their black robes. Until the 1980s, the justices virtually never gave interviews. That changed, though only slightly, beginning in 1982 when Justice Blackmun stunned the world by allowing a television crew to come right into his court chambers for an interview; a few months later, Chief Justice Burger granted his first interview in twelve years. The trend toward greater openness quickened with the national observance of the bicentennial of the Constitution; suddenly, to the surprise of nearly all outsiders, every member of the highest court agreed to be interviewed on television to talk about the Constitution and their role in interpreting and protecting it.

But these rare ventures into the open did not signal a basic change in the Court's secrecy; they did not mean the Court had gone so far as to apply to itself Justice Louis D. Brandeis' observation that "sunlight is said to be the best of disinfectants." Cameras and recording equipment are still banned from the Court's public sessions. The Court still refuses to disclose who was on which side when a case ends in a tie vote.* The justices never explain their judgments. They adamantly resist all attempts by reporters, lawyers, or any other "outsiders" to find out what they said in conference, what went into their private debates, how they arrived at their decisions.† Their contact with the outside world is officially through a "public relations officer," a government employee whose principal duty is to tell the public as little as possible. When columnist Ellen Goodman asked this official to explain the functioning of the Court, for example, he replied, "The justices in a very judicial manner sit in thoughtful judgment."

While some of this posturing and pretense is good theater, some of it is also poor democracy. Like the executive and legislative branches, the

---

*Ties occur when there is a vacancy on the Court, or when members disqualify themselves from a case, for reasons that they don't have to explain and rarely do. For example, a justice might step aside rather than risk the appearance of a conflict of interest. Justice Powell, who once held a great deal of oil stock, used to disqualify himself every time a case involving an oil company came up.

†One of the rare occasions when that curtain was penetrated was with the publication of *The Brethren: Inside the Supreme Court* by Bob Woodward and Scott Armstrong ([New York: Simon & Schuster, 1979], p. 359). Depending largely on court clerks who served the justices, Woodward and Armstrong portrayed a court whose members often arrived at their decisions at least partly as a result of spite, envy, and ego. Typical of the very human behind-the-scenes glimpses that this book provides is of Justice Brennan ticking off on his fingers how his various colleagues had voted, saving for the last his middle finger, which he "raised in an obscene gesture" to count Chief Justice Burger's vote.

judicial branch does the *public's* business and, as is the custom (however grudging) in the other two branches, as much of its work should be done openly as is possible. The Court's mania for secrecy sometimes does a great disservice to lawyers and to lower-court judges who must take directions from the high court. When the Supreme Court says of the ruling of a lower court only that "the judgment is affirmed," without explanation, nobody knows for sure what it means. Does it mean that the Supreme Court literally adopts all the principles incorporated into the lower court's decision? Or does it mean the high court is too busy to be bothered with thinking the problem through? Or does it mean the high court is willing to go along with the lower court's decision for a while but will probably overturn it later on? Trying to interpret skimpy decisions, says Charles Alan Wright of the University of Texas School of Law, is somewhat "like a lottery."

How the Court Operates

The Supreme Court decides which cases it will accept and which it will reject. It can't handle the 3,500 or so cases that are filed with it each year, so it selects about 70 or 80 cases that it considers somehow the most important. Traditionally, it takes the votes of four justices to accept a case, but they never tell the public why they accept a case or turn one down. Specialists on the outside of the Court are often puzzled by the choices. So are some members of the Court. In 1989 Justice White publicly scolded his colleagues: "Many cases that deserve review are being denied." Citing 14 cases the Court had recently turned down and 12 that it had granted review, he said that any difference between the two groups "is elusive, to say the least." One thing is certain: Every burning legal question that the Court bypasses, every conflict among the lower courts that it leaves unresolved, is an issue left to fester somewhere else.

Even 70 or 80 cases sometimes strain the Court's facilities and abilities. In a single term, the justices can be called on to wrestle with profound complexities arising from quarrels about such problems as taxation, freedom of the press, obscenity, abortion, separation of powers, and antitrust legislation. They must show, or at least pretend, some expertise in economics, psychology, political science, engineering, history, semantics, and ethics. Issues that would never have come to the Court in an earlier era—such as pollution and consumer quarrels—are commonplace. To grapple with this intellectual octopus, the justices have the assistance of a meager research staff and an equally lean clerk staff.

A special note should be made of the clerks because they are very important—some believe *too* important—in the operation of the Court. There are three dozen or so young men and young women presently clerking for the justices. Most of them were law students only two years ago, and they were distinguished students or they would never have been selected for the clerkships. But now they have more to say about which cases the world's most powerful tribunal will hear and how its opinions will be worded than anyone but the justices themselves.

Edward Lazarus, now a federal prosecutor in Los Angeles, was clerk to Justice Harry Blackmun. He paints a rather scary picture. Often, he says, even the best-intentioned clerks are too caught up in their own ambitions and ideologies to give sound advice to their bosses, and some clerks are downright malicious, "seeking to influence votes by telling their bosses exaggerated stories about how other justices demeaned them behind their backs." He recalls "the very significant power that clerks wielded at the Court" and the "very abusive manner in which" some clerks "wielded that power for partisan ends."

Although the justices don't reveal how they select the cases to be judged, this much is known: The justices don't read the actual petitions for review; instead they read the memorandums, written by the clerks, that summarize the petitions. This means that these clerks, most in their twenties, have a good chance to persuade the justices which petitions to accept and which to reject.

Also, the clerks are usually the only people with whom the justices privately discuss and debate the cases in any detail, for they have little time for out-of-Court consultation with one another.

And finally, the clerks have considerable influence in the wording of the Court's opinions. Bear in mind, these opinions are pored over and studied in the minutest detail by lawyers and lower courts seeking to discover the Court's faintest nuances. Little do they realize (or perhaps, to their irritation, they do realize) that some of the justices tell their clerks in a general way what points they want to make in the opinion and then leave the actual drafting—including the rhetorical flourishes and the footnotes—to them. It is well to remember, when reading a Supreme Court opinion, that what you think is the distilled wisdom of an eighty-year-old jurist may be simply a twenty-seven-year-old's well-schooled flight of idealism.

But let us not be unappreciative of the help of the clerks. Indeed, the justices need all the help they can get. The truth is the judges of the highest court, like their brethren below, make many judgments in the dark. Sometimes, recognizing the limits of their expertise, they simply sidestep complex cases.

Myriad Influences

The popular belief is that the Court takes guidance solely from a great body of law, of which the Constitution is the heart. Actually, when the justices shape their decisions (or "opinions"), they are influenced not only by the written law but by logic, history, and custom, as well as by utility, accepted standards of conduct, patterns of social welfare, and their own instincts, beliefs, and political leanings. But above all they are influenced by legislative intent and by previous opinions handed down by the Court. Since stability and consistency are the two great strengths of the Court, it at least likes to pretend devotion to the principle of *stare decisis* (which means literally "to stand by what has gone before") and decide cases according to precedents. But when the Court is seized with tumultuous ideological change, as at present, precedents often get mangled. Major opinions not two decades old are being overturned these days.

When precedents are unavailable or do not fit, judges must then be intellectual pioneers and fashion new law. But judge-made law is secondary to law made by legislatures (statutory law), and statutory law is subordinate to constitutional law.

In other words, when the meaning of a statute is clear, judges are obliged to shape their rulings to agree with it. When the wording of a statute is unclear, then the Court is duty bound to return to the legislative record at the time the statute was passed and try to deduce what the legislators probably *meant* for the statute to do. The Court must try to go along with the wording of the law or the intent of the legislature *unless*—and this is the crucial exception—unless the Court feels the statute is unconstitutional. The unconstitutionality of a statute is the Court's only justification for invalidating it. Likewise, the Court of one era will not overturn Court decisions of previous eras except with the excuse of a reinterpretation of the Constitution.

When a case is accepted for review, the justices receive written briefs in which each side presents its arguments. Then a day is scheduled on which lawyers for opposing sides present oral arguments in court. The oral argument is one of the few operations of the Supreme Court open to public view. It is the only time that the lawyers and the justices meet face to face. The questioning from the justices can be stiff, even harsh. The pressure on the lawyers is intense. Some have been known to faint; at least one attorney had a heart attack.

For these oral arguments, the Court ordinarily allows either an hour or half an hour to each side of the case. The time limit is strictly enforced. Five minutes before a lawyer's time is up, a white light flashes on; a red light means he or she must stop instantly—one lawyer was stopped on the word "if."

All in all—counting the time used in reading the lower courts' opinions and the briefs and the time to hear the oral arguments—a case that will intimately affect the lives of 260 million Americans may not get more than half a dozen hours of each justice's attention before he or she must render a decision.

A few days after the oral arguments have been heard, the justices meet to discuss the case briefly and to make their tentative decision. The chief justice opens the discussion by stating the facts of the case, summarizing points of law and suggesting ways to dispose of the case. He then asks each justice for views and conclusions. A majority vote decides the case. If the vote is a tie, the decision of the lower court stands.

If the chief justice sides with the majority, he assigns the writing of the Court's opinion; if not, the senior justice among the majority assigns the writing.

The "Court's opinion" is what a majority of the nine justices decide. On that point, at least, there is a democratic quality about the Court. Before the justice who is assigned to write the majority opinion is done with it, it has passed through the hands of all concurring brethren, who criticize it, edit it, quibble with it, and often force it through several rewritings.

A well-written majority opinion will be, above all else, instructive and easy to understand. The first duty of the justice who writes the opinion is to explain, in unmistakable terms, the rationale by which the majority reached its decision. Clarity and completeness are prized because the reasoning behind the decision guides the judges of lower courts and the legal fraternity in general. The power of the Court stems, in large measure, from its success in impressing courts and the bar with the clarity and precision of its thinking.

Value of Unanimity

Psychologically, the larger the majority supporting the Court's opinion, the better. Sometimes justices will swallow their true feelings in order to bolster the *seeming* solidarity of the Court. Justice Lewis F.

Powell, Jr., conceded that this was the motivation behind at least one of his votes: "In order to avoid the appearance of fragmentation of the Court on the basic principles involved, I join the opinion of the Court."

The impact of a unanimous opinion is intense because the public is naturally impressed when none of the nine strong-willed and independent justices can find an excuse to go his or her separate way. To gain this kind of impact, Chief Justice Warren filibustered, wheedled, and coaxed his fellow justices into line in the landmark segregation case, *Brown* v. *Board of Education*. In May 1954, when the vote stood at eight to one, Warren told Justice Stanley F. Reed, "Stan, you're all by yourself in this now," and argued persuasively that a unanimous decision would be in the national interest.

One of the worst things the Court can do is to make a ruling that is not clear, that is ambiguous. The effect of failure of that sort was dramatically illustrated in the famous case, *Regents of the University of California* v. *Bakke* (1978).

In 1974, Allan P. Bakke, who is white, applied for admission to the University of California School of Medicine at Davis but was rejected. It wasn't that he failed the entrance exam; he did well on it. In fact, he was better qualified for admission than the sixteen Hispanic, black, and Native American applicants who were admitted to the school under a special admission plan aimed at helping minorities catch up. Bakke sued, charging discrimination. In 1978, the Burger Court handed down a confusing ruling that gave no guidance at all. It ruled that Bakke had indeed been discriminated against and should be admitted, but it also ruled that a policy allowing for the admission of lower-scoring minority applicants is constitutional: "Government may take race into account when it acts, not to demean or insult any racial group, but to remedy disadvantages cast on minorities by past racial prejudice." In other words: yes, and no—Bakke was the victim of reverse discrimination and that's bad, but reverse discrimination is okay if it corrects a situation resulting from direct discrimination.

The ruling resulted in total confusion, and it was made all the more confusing by the fact that there was not one Court opinion but *six* opinions. *Each* justice on the majority side wrote his own opinion! Bedlam. Consequently, the *Bakke* opinion has had a very indefinite effect on the recruiting of minority students for medical and law schools.

Twenty years after the Bakke ruling, some universities trying to increase minority enrollments by using "affirmative action" programs were still having to defend their action in court battles—sometimes winning, sometimes losing.

The Court's Role

The Constitution is a simple document. It is a short document; it can be read in an hour. Its wording is highly generalized. Yet it remains, in our extremely complex age, as useful and alive as it was when written; it was as potent in dealing with the millions of specific problems of the second half of the twentieth century as it was in dealing with the broad problems arising with the founding of the nation. The explanation for this is quite obvious. "We are under a Constitution," said Charles Evans Hughes in 1907, "but the Constitution is what the judges say it is," and the Supreme Court says various things about it depending upon the era. Each new generation becomes a different prism for catching the light by which the Court must read the Constitution. Try as it may, the Court would find it impossible to maintain a historical consistency. "Throughout its entire history . . . the Supreme Court has been in search of the Constitution," writes Carl Brent Swisher, "as the judges sitting were able to see and define the Constitution, and throughout its entire history the Court has been seeking to determine the character and dimensions of its own role in the government."

The search is perpetual because the Constitution is elusive. It seems to be only words, but it is much more than words; words alone are never enough, and they are never certain. The Fifth Amendment guarantees that the government cannot take life, liberty, or property "without due process of law." That language could not be vaguer; in fact, its imprecision has driven some justices—Frankfurter and Brandeis, for example—to suggest that it be repealed. It has meant something different to every new line-up on the Supreme Court. The same is true for such guarantees as the Sixth Amendment's right to a "speedy and public" trial. The First Amendment says, "Congress shall make no law respecting an establishment of religion." Does that mean Congress cannot permit prayers in the schools? The national debate on that issue, begun in the 1950s and continuing today, shows there is no simple answer. The First Amendment goes on to guarantee "no law . . . abridging the freedom . . . of the press." Does this clear the way for the press to advocate an overthrow of the government? The Fourth Amendment prohibits "unreasonable" searches. It is rather unlikely that the framers of the Constitution had in mind the seizing of evidence through electronic eavesdropping, yet the amendment must somehow be made to apply to this modern instrument.

And so it goes throughout the Constitution. It is a marvelous piece of elastic reasoning that must be stretched into new shapes with every generation. The best people who have sat on the Supreme Court are quick to acknowledge that this is true.

In 1968, Richard Nixon promised that if elected to the presidency he would appoint to the Supreme Court only "strict constructionists," meaning those who would interpret the laws of the land in the light of the exact meaning of the words of the Constitution, without stretching the words in any direction or "modernizing" the intent of the Constitution in any way.* If the Constitution were an extremely detailed document, touching every conceivable action that might take place in commerce and in the lower courts and in the schools and in religion and in the press and in Congress, then there might be some justification for hoping that a strict construction of the Constitution would actually meet the needs of life in twenty-first-century America. But the Constitution is not that kind of instrument, and to suggest that a strict construction of it will do the job is, at best, gross deception.

When they speak of being "strict constructionists," conservative judges usually do not just mean that they want to do only what the Constitution says they can do and no more; they mean also that they do not want to do anything that can be done by Congress or the president. They believe the Court should keep its hands off social problems, as long as there are still channels for change open elsewhere. For the most part this attitude leaves reform and progress up to the legislative branch, to the political process; in other words, this attitude involves wholehearted belief in the principle of majority rule. This is a pretty principle, but it simply does not take care of all our problems.

It was this attitude that permitted segregation to hang on so long without federal interference. Conservatives reasoned that if the blacks living in the South did not like the Jim Crow laws, they could always elect state legislators who would change them, couldn't they? Well, theoretically. And if they were blocked from making change in that way because state laws prevented them from voting in the state elections, the blacks could always send people to Congress who would institute safeguards, couldn't they? Yes, *if* they could get the white folks to let them vote in a federal election.

The "strict constructionists" belong to a simpler age. And so do those many people who feel that the Supreme Court's main job is

---

*And yet the late liberal Justices Douglas and Black were a great team of strict constructionists of the First Amendment. When the Constitution says, "Congress shall make no laws . . . abridging the freedom of speech, or of the press," they judged it to mean just that—*no law*, and that includes no laws against pornography, for example. Is this what Nixon meant, too?

judicial review—testing the constitutionality of the work of Congress, holding up each new law to the supposedly "fixed" criteria of the Constitution. If this were the case, the Supreme Court could be considered the most inactive and most tolerant arm of government, for in its first sixty years of existence the Court nullified only two acts of Congress; in its first one hundred years, the Court nullified only twenty acts. Even in the period of the sharpest clashes between the Supreme Court and the Congress—when President Franklin Roosevelt was pushing his reform programs through Congress at a record clip between 1933 and 1935—the Supreme Court nullified only seven acts of Congress. The truth is, the Court allows Congress enormous leeway in the writing of laws.

The most valued service of the Supreme Court has not been to hold back Congress and the chief executive, operating as a kind of brake or "negative balance," but to throw its weight wherever needed to create a fortunate imbalance, to revive old concepts of justice and fair play, and to encourage Congress—to the extent that that body can be encouraged—to take progressive action. Whether or not history will prove it to have always taken the wise course of action, the most important function of the Supreme Court has been to try to act as the federal conscience when Congress seemed incapable of serving in that way—best seen in the 1950s and 1960s.

Above all else, the Court is supposed to be a uniquely strict guardian of our basic constitutional rights—particularly in those moments when public and Congress have drunk too heavily from bootleg patriotism and 150-proof piety. Just imagine for a moment that we had direct democracy in this country; say that we did not use elected representatives to pass our laws but that—through some sort of electronic gadgetry hooked up to our homes—we could vote directly on all laws. We would probably make some disastrous decisions on bread-and-butter issues, but the republic would survive those fumbles; bureaucracy would somehow keep the planes flying, the butter warehoused. The *big* worry is whether the electorate, given its head, would maintain anything resembling our traditional constitutional democracy for longer than forty-eight hours. For the truth is that a dangerously large slice of the American public is willing to settle for totalitarian solutions. "It is in protecting our civil liberties," said Representative Don Edwards, "that Congressmen run into the most serious opposition from their constituents. We have had poll after poll that shows the people would not reenact the First Amendment to the Constitution [freedom of religion, speech, press, and assembly] if the question were put to them today."

There is an abundance of lip service to the principles of the Constitution. But in practice, other emotions grip the electorate. High-flying generalizations of fair play and constitutional law easily win popular support in the abstract, but their application at the practical level often runs into strong opposition. Just about everyone believes racial segregation is bad, but many don't want integration in their neighborhood. Just about everyone believes in free speech, but many would like to silence Ku Kluxers. Most people believe in freedom of religion, but many would be offended were an admitted atheist to run for high office. Pollsters encounter these conflicting attitudes all the time. In one survey, to the statement, "No matter what a person's political beliefs are, he is entitled to the same legal rights and protections as anyone else," 94 percent of the sampled "general electorate" agreed, yet three-quarters of these same people turned around and agreed with the statement, "Any person who hides behind the laws when he is questioned about his activities doesn't deserve much consideration." While 81 percent of the sample agreed with the broad concept of freedom of the press ("Nobody has a right to tell another person what he should and should not read"), more than half of these same people changed their minds when the principle was given a particular application ("A book that contains wrong political views cannot be a good book and does not deserve to be published").

It is not difficult to imagine the sort of clobbering the electorate would deliver to the Bill of Rights if the voting button was pushed according to their transient sentiments.

Many in Congress, of course, would like to oblige the electorate in such matters. Lawrence Speiser, former head of the Washington office of the American Civil Liberties Union, says that "hundreds of bills" are introduced every session of Congress to undo the civil libertarian decisions of the Supreme Court. (Fortunately, most of these bills contract a fatal dose of congressional torpor.) Against such impulses the United States Supreme Court stands as a bulwark, if it wants to—and as an antidote to national disinterest and lassitude in the face of pressing social needs.*

---

*But lest the Supreme Court seem too much to fill the hero's role, let it be hurriedly added that the efficacy of the Court as a restraint and antidote varies with its composition and with the public's willingness to heed the Court. The recent changes in the Court's makeup suggest that it may be less of a bulwark against public passions in the future. Many Court-watchers were chilled to read that the majority's opinion in 1989 giving approval to the execution of sixteen year olds was in response to (as Justice Scalia wrote) a "national consensus." No one assumes the Court can fully escape the pressures of public opinion, but rarely has the Court so openly admitted capitulation to it. The ruling was as puzzling as it was troubling. Linda Greenhouse of *The New York Times* asked, "What is 'consensus' and how is the Court to decide whether society has arrived at one?" (*The New York Times*, July 2, 1989).

And yet, this could be a tricky and even dangerous situation, for the question finally comes down to this: If the democratic process—voting and petitioning—leaves some ills untouched, should the courts step in and do what the legislatures, state or federal, refuse to do? If the answer is yes, then the next question is: When courts step out of their traditional role of interpreting law, and *create* laws, thereby becoming legislators of a sort (and usurping the duties of the real legislature), do they do more harm or more good thereby? If the answer is that they do more good, then the question is: Is the immediate good outweighed by a long-term harm? Helping a part of society that seemed to be helpless is good, but interfering with and disrupting the constitutionally prescribed three-way balance between executive, legislative, and judicial branches *could* set a dangerous precedent. How can the Court be sure that it is not setting such a precedent? It doesn't know. Each new Court simply does its work as it sees fit, and especially in the 1950s and 1960s, the Court saw fit to make an impressive number of what it considered to be "socially desirable" laws that had been long neglected by the legislative branch.

An Evolving Court

To understand and appreciate the modern Supreme Court, we must take a hasty run through the Court's history. The most important thing to bear in mind is that for almost all its life, the Supreme Court has been primarily interested in property rights, rather than in human rights. In this, it simply reflected the spirit of the men (very few women were involved) who ran the country—the industrialists, the businessmen, the financiers, the speculators, the bankers. In hindsight, and by modern-day standards, this may seem a callous attitude, but it was an attitude that carried its own logic. The courts were eager, as were politicians generally, to promote the industrial revolution and give protection to the growing infant industries. Thus, beginning in the early part of the nineteenth century, for example, it was the prevailing opinion of the courts that a worker was free to pursue the occupation of his or her choice and that freedom also entitled the worker to all the risks of that occupation. If a coal miner was killed when rotten beams collapsed, or if a mill worker lost a hand in machinery that was not property guarded—those things, said the courts well into the twentieth century, were simply unfortunate adjuncts to being employed, and the employers should not be held financially responsible.

The probusiness attitude of the courts expanded in the second half of the nineteenth century as the philosophy of laissez faire capitalism took over. Laws passed by Congress with the intent of assisting individual citizens were manipulated by the courts to assist corporations instead. This was especially evident in the way the Supreme Court twisted the Fourteenth Amendment to the corporations' advantage.

The Fourteenth Amendment, which became law on July 28, 1868, had been added to the Constitution with the specific intent of helping the newly freed slaves gain full citizenship. The states as well as the federal government were to see that no person be deprived of life, liberty, or property without due process of law. But instead of using this amendment to protect blacks, the Supreme Court used it to protect the corporations. They managed to do this by ruling that a corporation is also a "person" (*Santa Clara County* v. *Southern Pacific Railroad*, 1886). The Supreme Court thereby shifted the emphasis of the Fourteenth Amendment from human rights to property rights, from the protection of individual freedom from government interference to the protection of corporate laissez faire from government interference.

In effect, this ruling freed business and industry from significant government regulation down to the 1930s. Some state legislatures and Congress occasionally passed laws prohibiting child labor, guaranteeing minimum wages, regulating hours of labor, protecting women workers from excessive chores, and clearing the way for union organizers. But during the first quarter of the twentieth century, the courts, using the due process clause of the Fourteenth Amendment like an axe, invariably struck down these legislative efforts, ruling that a corporation must be as free to buy a worker's labor as a worker is free to sell it (as if a hungry person is "free" to negotiate on equal terms with a corporation), and that the legislatures could not intrude into that relationship.

The courts, and especially the Supreme Court, became in this negative way a superlegislature. In 1913, Theodore Roosevelt condemned judges for their "well-meaning" intrusions into the legislative process, declaring them to be ignorant bunglers with "no special fitness to decide nonjudicial questions of social and economic reform. . . . They ought not to be entrusted with the power to determine, instead of the people, what the people have the right to do in furthering social justice under the Constitution." (Later, this same damnation, but from the other side of the political spectrum, was leveled at the Warren Court.)

The Court's rigid, mechanical interpretation of the Constitution and the probusiness bias of courts at every level continued long after

Theodore Roosevelt's denunciation. Henry Steele Commager accurately wrote that the record of the pre-1937 Supreme Court

> discloses not a single case, in a century and a half, where the Supreme Court has protected freedom of speech, press . . . against congressional attack. It reveals no instance . . . where the Court has intervened on behalf of the underprivileged—the Negro, the alien, women, children, workers, tenant farmers. It reveals, on the contrary, that the Court has effectively intervened, again and again, to defeat congressional attempts to free the slave, to guarantee civil rights to Negroes, to protect workingmen, to outlaw child labor, to assist hard-pressed farmers, and to democratize the tax system.

Commager picked 1937 for his backward look because that was a watershed year. When Franklin Roosevelt became president in 1933, the nation was in the midst of such a terrible economic depression that some observers feared there might be a revolution. Business and industry were barely operating; the stock market was in a shambles; hundreds of banks had shut their doors permanently; bread lines were commonplace. The situation was desperate, and Roosevelt, with the assistance of Congress, provided laws needed to start the economy moving again. Their rescue effort was to be based on a new alliance—government would provide the money to get the bankrupt economy on its feet, and, in return, business and industry would accept radically new rules and regulations as to how they conducted themselves. These laws went directly against the Supreme Court's established philosophy of protecting business from government interference—and so the Court struck down the laws. Laws to help the farmers, laws to help the banks, laws to regulate prices, laws to help organized labor—all were killed by the Court.

Furious, Roosevelt asked Congress in 1937 to enlarge the Court so that he could appoint enough new justices to achieve a majority and thereby save his "New Deal" program, as it was called. In his message accompanying the "court-packing" bill, Roosevelt argued:

> Modern complexities call for a constant infusion of new blood in the courts, just as it is needed in executive functions of the government and in private business. A lowered mental or physical vigor leads men to avoid an examination of complicated and changed conditions. Little by little, new facts become blurred through old glasses fitted, as it were, for the needs of another generation; older men, assuming that the scene is the same as it was in the past, cease to explore or inquire into the present or the future.

What he said was absolutely true. There were nine old men on the Court, and their viewpoints, like their arteries, had hardened. They still believed in a narrow interpretation of the Constitution, one that protected the business status quo. They did not seem to realize that their rulings could no longer protect the business status quo, since it had been destroyed by the depression.

Roosevelt's proposal was shocking to Congress and to much of the public. Already imbued with enormous emergency powers, he now seemed to be reaching for still greater powers. If he gained control of the Court in this way, would he become a dictator? The question was asked by many members of Congress, and Roosevelt's court-packing plan was smothered.

Abruptly, however, the attitude of the Court (or of a majority of the Court) changed. Apparently fearful of the outcome of the fight, the Court speedily endorsed a number of major New Deal laws while Roosevelt's court-packing legislation was still under consideration in Congress. Fate threw a bonus to Roosevelt in the death of one of the most conservative members of the Court, allowing him to name Hugo Black (one of the most liberal justices of all time) as a replacement. By the end of 1937, the old die-hard reactionaryism of the Court was gone forever. By the end of 1940, Roosevelt had appointed five members, all of whom could be classified as "moderates" or "liberals" and who either tolerated or enthusiastically approved government's dominant partnership with business. Several rulings in the late 1930s and through the 1940s also made faint but certain advances for civil rights.

Caught in War Frenzy

Nevertheless, the "improved" Court was guilty of one of history's most shameful and embarrassing examples of how, in periods of patriotic passion, the Court—normally a small island of relative stability—sometimes gets swept away by outside pressures. Bowing to the hysteria that rolled across the nation after the Japanese attack on military installations at Pearl Harbor, Hawaii, on December 7, 1941, President Roosevelt authorized the military commanders to round up and intern some 70,000 native-born U.S. citizens of Japanese ancestry. We were also at war with Germany and Italy at the time, but no citizens of German or Italian descent were put in detention camps. It was done only to the luckless Japanese-Americans because they "looked different," not because they were a threat—no act of espionage or sabotage was ever proved against a Japanese-American.

Here was a situation, if there was ever one, that called for relief via the cool, restraining character that the Supreme Court is supposed to possess and with which it is supposed to temper popular actions in moments of crisis. But the Court ducked its responsibility. Twice it received appeals from Japanese-Americans who had been interned, and twice it refused to rule on the constitutionality of relocating and interning citizens for no reason except that they were unwelcome neighbors to a majority of hysterical people. "Among nine judges who were as a group more alert to claims of individual rights than any Court in our history until then," writes Robert G. McCloskey, "only three dissented against ratifying the most extreme invasion of rights in our history." Ironically, the three who stood fast for freedom did *not* include either Justice Black or Justice Douglas, who later gained reputations as libertarians in cases that took much less courage to rule on.

After Roosevelt's death in 1945, the Court began to change for the worse. President Harry Truman's four appointments ranged from mediocre to poor. Limited in their abilities as constitutional scholars, they took their cues from the mood of the times, which was shaped by an anticommunist hysteria. Loyalty oaths became quite the fad. Liberals were suspected of being socialists, and socialists were suspected of being communists, and communists were looked upon by many Americans—including some of its highest officials and politicians—as unfit to receive the same constitutional protections given other citizens. Congress and state legislatures passed a number of very repressive laws during this period, and the Supreme Court, presided over by Frederick Vinson, an old Truman crony, generally came out on the side of government strictures and against individual freedoms.

After Chief Justice Vinson died in 1953, the Supreme Court moved into its most dramatic era. President Eisenhower, faced with his first Supreme Court appointment, offered the Chief Justice post to California Governor Earl Warren. Eisenhower's decision had more to do with politics (the appointment would be popular with California Senator William F. Knowland, who had recently become Senate majority leader) than with admiration of Warren's legal knowledge. In fact, his potential as a judge was something that could only be guessed at. Within a year that mystery had been cleared up, and by the time Warren stepped down in 1969, the Warren era had been firmly established in Court annals as probably the most revolutionary of all time.

The "Revolutionary" Warren Court

Never before in its history had the Court served as the nation's conscience more forcefully than it did under Chief Justice Warren. The Court's responsiveness brought from Justice Brennan the happy comment that "law is again coming alive as a living process responsive to changing human needs. The shift is to justice and away from finespun technicalities and abstract rules."

By the mid-1950s, the Court had begun to free citizens from the need to shout their undying loyalty to fatherland. In 1956, the Court threw out state laws punishing "sedition" against the federal government (*Pennsylvania* v. *Nelson*). The same year it made it a little less easy for the witch-hunters to have their way by ruling that only federal employees in "sensitive" jobs could be fired as security risks (*Cole* v. *Young*). The infamous Smith Act of 1940 had made it a crime to "advocate," either orally or in writing, even the "desirability" of overthrowing the government. In 1957 the Court somewhat eased the threat to free speech and free press by ruling that simple advocacy as an abstract doctrine was not enough to sustain guilt; to be guilty, a person had to actually get out and recruit and incite others to take *action* to overthrow the government (*Yates* v. *United States*).

These refreshing actions were taken at a time when the House Un-American Activities Committee, the Senate Internal Security Subcommittee, the Subversive Activities Control Board, a number of loud if not always powerful individual members of the House and Senate (Joseph McCarthy, Richard Nixon, Karl Mundt, William Jenner, to name but a few), the State Department, the Department of Justice, the FBI, and a great portion of the daily press were thumping the anti-communist drum in ragtime.

The Warren era saw the Court most dramatically influential in three areas: the equalizing of political representation, the equalizing of the machinery of justice for the poor as well as the wealthy, and the equalizing of civil-rights protection.

Political Representation

For many years the outlines of political districts had remained the same, despite the fact that the population had shifted radically, especially from rural to urban areas. The result was that politicians representing rural areas had relatively few constituents—it was sometimes said that these politicians represented more trees than people—while politicians from urban areas had to carry the burdens of a great many more citizens, proportionately. Never mind feeling sympathy for the urban politicians. That wasn't the trouble. The trouble was that if 400,000 citizens are represented by one person in the state legislature or in Congress and another group of 100,000 citizens is also represented by one person, it means that it takes four voters in the first district to equal one voter in the second. It also means each member of the smaller group is obviously going to have a better chance of having his or her voice heard and thereby enjoy more protection of political interests.

Until 1962 the courts had regularly ruled that setting the boundaries of political districts was a state's right, not to be interfered with by the federal powers. With reform left up to the state legislatures, the situation seemed pretty hopeless because many state legislatures were dominated by politicians from districts with the smaller populations; they would hardly want to lessen their per capita power. But in 1962, in the Tennessee case *Baker* v. *Carr*, the Warren Court ruled that political boundaries were the business of the federal courts because it was an issue that fell under the equal protection clause of the Constitution. Not content with merely giving the lower federal courts the go-ahead for handling political boundary disputes, the Warren Court in 1964 laid down specific guidelines—an "equal population" principle for legislative apportionment. It was the "one-man, one-vote" principle. The result was a dramatic shift away from the rural and toward the urban and suburban flavor in most state legislatures. The ruling forced reform in some states where the legislative district lines had not been redrawn for forty to sixty years. Instead of having some lawmakers represent three or seven or even ten times as many voters as other lawmakers, all districts were made more or less equal through reapportionment. Warren said he believed this to be the most important ruling of his years on the bench.

Machinery of Justice

The Bill of Rights (the first ten amendments) was added to the Constitution at the insistence of those founders who felt that the Constitution would not otherwise offer sufficient protections for the individual citizen against the misuse of government power. The Bill of Rights lists specific guarantees—freedom of speech, freedom of the press, freedom of religion; prohibition against unreasonable searches and seizure of private property; guarantees of felony indictments only by grand jury; safeguards against being forced to testify against oneself; the right to a speedy trial; the right to an impartial jury; the right to have an attorney;

prohibition against excessive bail, excessive fines, or unusually cruel punishment. These were to be bulwarks between the individual citizen and a potentially bullying government.

But what government? Central? State? Both? Until ratification of the Fourteenth Amendment in 1868, it was generally agreed that the Bill of Rights was aimed at the central government. But the Fourteenth Amendment was clearly aimed at the states, and it included this language: "No State shall make or enforce any law which shall abridge the privileges or immunities of citizens of the United States; nor shall any State deprive any person of life, liberty, or property, without due process of law; nor deny to any person within its jurisdiction the equal protection of the laws."

To many students of the Constitution, this language unmistakably extended the guarantees of the Bill of Rights to state government as well. But those who held that opinion remained in the minority until the Warren Court came to their rescue. Utilizing the "due process" clause of the Fourteenth Amendment (an extremely vague and flexible clause) in the freest fashion, the Warren Court ultimately succeeded in extending so many pieces of the Bill of Rights to the states that today, practically speaking, it all applies to states as well as to the central government.

One of the most dramatic steps in this direction came with the *Gideon* v. *Wainwright* decision in 1963, which we mentioned earlier but is worth mentioning again. Clarence Earl Gideon was an inmate of the Florida penitentiary; Louis Wainwright was the warden. Gideon wrote a letter to the Supreme Court pointing out that he had asked the state to supply him with an attorney for his trial because he could not afford to hire one for himself, but the state had refused. He argued that without an attorney he had not been able to defend himself adequately, that justice therefore had not been done, and that Mr. Wainwright should be forced to release him.

Gideon's plight was not an unusual one. Most states did not provide indigents with attorneys in felony trials. Were defendants under these conditions being denied the constitutional protection of due process of the law? Were they being improperly denied the Bill of Rights' guarantee of a lawyer? Should these rights be dependent on whether or not the defendant could afford an attorney? In earlier eras, the Supreme Court had ruled against the indigent defendants.

Now that philosophy was to be overturned. The Court's majority said paupers must have lawyers even if the public has to foot the bill.

Two companion rulings extended defendants'—or even suspects'—rights even further. The first was *Escobedo* v. *Illinois*, handed down in the spring of 1965. Five years earlier a twenty-two-year-old Chicago man named Danny Escobedo was arrested as a suspect in the shooting death of his brother-in-law. He was interrogated by the police for hours. He asked to have his lawyer present, but the police refused. At no time during the interrogation was Escobedo told of his constitutional right to remain silent (the guarantee against self-incrimination). In a five-to-four decision, the Warren Court ruled that because many confessions are obtained in the period between arrest and indictment, this is a critical period when "legal aid and advice are surely needed."

Many police and prosecutors were outraged at this interference with their traditional style of treating suspects. They were even more outraged when *Miranda* v. *Arizona* was handed down in 1966. Again the Court was sharply divided, five to four, but the majority held firm for the rights of the accused. The decision spelled out in detail what police and prosecutors must do to comply with the Court's interpretation of the Constitution: Before beginning their interrogation, officers must inform the suspect of his or her right to remain silent and they must emphasize that anything the suspect says thereafter can be used against him or her. Also, the suspect must be told at the very beginning of the process that he or she has a right "to the presence of an attorney, either retained or appointed."

Civil Rights

The Warren Court will be longest remembered for the reforms it made in the area of civil rights, and particularly for its ruling in *Brown* v. *Board of Education* (1954). This was the Warren Court's first major decision, and its most controversial, for it overturned an old decision that had upheld an entrenched social practice—racial segregation. The first act of this drama began long ago with a famous train ride.

Homer Plessy was one-eighth black. He bought a train ticket in New Orleans and sat down in a car reserved for whites. The conductor said he had to move to the blacks-only car. Plessy sued, arguing that the Louisiana law that allowed segregated cars violated his right to equal protection, as guaranteed by the Fourteenth Amendment. The case went all the way to the Supreme Court, which ruled in *Plessy* v. *Ferguson* that it was ridiculous to assume "that the enforced separation of the two races stamps the colored race with a badge of inferiority." The Court decreed that segregation alone was not unconstitutional; only inequality of treatment was unconstitutional.

That ruling came in 1896. And—despite a few Supreme Court rulings during the 1930s and 1940s that chipped away at the corners of discrimination—"separate but equal" remained the law of the land until the Warren Court came along.

Actually, for more than half a century after *Plessy,* blacks languished in separation that was far from being equal. Stuck away in their own ghettos, in their own schools, their own restaurants, their own theaters, at their own end of the trolley, blacks proved the old cliché, "out of sight, out of mind." Most white officials did put the blacks out of their minds so far as they were able.

The new era was opened on May 17, 1954, with the Court's ruling in *Brown* v. *Board of Education.* This ruling came from a suit filed in Topeka, Kansas. The complainant was a black girl, Linda Brown, who attended a segregated school.

The unanimous opinion of the Court: Segregation violates the equal-protection guarantee of the Fourteenth Amendment. The opinion was written by Warren himself. It was sophisticated reasoning that avoided getting tangled up in the quarrel over equal facilities. Even if black schools were as new and as well equipped as white schools, education in segregated schools could not possibly be equal because separation affects the minds of the students. Warren wrote:

> In approaching this problem, we cannot turn the clock back to 1868 when the Amendment was adopted, or even to 1896 when *Plessy* v. *Ferguson* was written. We must consider public education in the light of its full development and its present place in American life throughout the nation. Only in this way can it be determined if segregation in public schools deprives these plaintiffs of the equal protection of the laws. . . .
>
> We come then to the question presented: Does segregation of children in public schools solely on the basis of race, even though the physical facilities and other "tangible" factors may be equal, deprive the children of the minority group of equal educational opportunities? We believe that it does. . . .
>
> Segregation of white and colored children in public schools has a detrimental effect upon the colored children. The impact is greater when it has the sanction of law; for the policy of separating the races is usually interpreted as denoting the inferiority of the Negro group. A sense of inferiority affects the motivation of a child to learn. . . . In the field of public education the doctrine of "separate but equal" has no place. Separate educational facilities are inherently unequal.

Although the *Brown* opinion theoretically applied only to the handful of school systems named in the case, it was written in such a way as to have the broadest application in public education. Also, by using the Fourteenth Amendment to severely limit state sovereignty (which is to say, to extend the equal protection of the Bill of Rights to the states), the ruling led directly and naturally into the reapportionment and criminal-process decisions mentioned earlier.

Who Enforces the Court's Edicts?

The Warren Court made some revolutionary decisions, but it is well to consider how effectively they were carried out and enforced. No matter how much politics and public opinion actually shape, or fail to shape, the Court's edicts, they certainly determine the effectiveness of the edicts. When public opinion and politicians fail to respond to a Court's decision, it makes the whole concept of justice look sick. Justice Felix Frankfurter, fearing, with good cause, that the public was not ready for a desegregation ruling from the Supreme Court, warned in 1952, "Nothing could be worse from my point of view than for this Court to make an abstract declaration that segregation is bad and then have it evaded by tricks."

If conditions are contrary to the enforcement of its judgments, the Court can be the most helpless branch. It is a natural helplessness: The Court can decree, but Congress and the president have to back it up or the decree is so much air. President Andrew Jackson, infuriated when the Supreme Court invalidated a Georgia law that in effect permitted the state to steal land from the Indians, said, "[Chief Justice] John Marshall has made his decision, now let him enforce it."

It was a petty but effective remark, and southern foes of the Supreme Court have enjoyed repeating it or paraphrasing it on appropriate occasions. In 1956, when Governor Allan Shivers of Texas refused to send state police to protect black students trying to integrate the high school in Mansfield, Texas, he also said, "The Supreme Court passed the law, so let the Supreme Court enforce it." The same philosophy was applied to congressional action after passage of the Civil Rights Act of 1964, when Alabama Governor George Wallace announced, with his usual rococo embellishments: "The liberal left-wingers have passed it. Now let them employ some pinknik social engineers in Washington to figure out what to do with it."

In some parts of the South, organized prayer—at school athletic events, assemblies, and commencement exercises—has remained a common activity despite decades of federal court rulings against the practice. In Decatur, Georgia, recently, school officials allowed the pastor of a Baptist church to conduct a service at the high school during school hours. The county's public safety commissioner, a member of that church, told the students, "We are here in defiance of the Supreme Court, calling on the name of Jesus Christ." Defiance of that sort is often politically popular, and quite safe.

The efficiency of law in a democracy, as Justice Frankfurter once pointed out, depends almost entirely on "the habit of popular respect for law." Laws and court decrees have no intrinsic power. If the people don't obey, then some method must be contrived to make them obey. And if the executive branch makes only a halfhearted effort, or no effort at all, to enforce the Court's rulings, and if public disobedience is widespread enough, it is likely that the people's recalcitrance will prevail.

Total success could not be claimed for any of the three reform areas marked out by the Warren Court, but there was far more success than failure in these three reforms, no matter how unpopular they were. More citizens of the United States live in urban areas than in rural ones, and their representatives rushed to the support of the reapportionment edict. Although there was continued resistance to the desegregation edicts, by and large the nation accepted the idea that the desegregation laws were here to stay and that there would have to be at least a modest adjustment toward obedience. And although there was widespread criticism of the Court for "coddling criminals" by extending constitutional protection to all criminal suspects, no matter what their income, there was even more general support for the new rules of fair play in criminal justice.

That's what made the Warren Court outstanding—it got some support from the public and from Congress. Not an overwhelming amount, but some. Congress, buoyed along by public opinion, passed the strong Civil Rights Act of 1964, opening public accommodations to blacks, and the Voting Rights Act of 1965, which at last made it possible for blacks in the South to overcome the manipulations of local elections boards to keep them off the voting rolls and out of the voting booths. With these statements from Congress, and at least lukewarm attention to the matter of civil rights on the part of the Department of Justice, the racial walls at last began to crack, if not crumble, a decade after the Supreme Court had spoken in the *Brown* case.

The Burger Court: The Tempo Slows

When the Court moves too far ahead of the crowd, it inspires widespread suspicions and even hatred. Many see it as a subversive body, "foreign" to the temper of the general populace. In the twilight of the Warren Court era, Robert H. Bork of the Yale Law School charged that the Court had created an atmosphere in which "political retaliation [aimed at the Court] is increasingly regarded as proper. This raises the question of the degree to which the Warren Court has provoked the attacks."* Conceding that the Warren Court operated with the best of will, Bork still felt that "in its eagerness to reform wide areas of national life, it has made its own job impossibly difficult. It has assumed an omnicompetence in problems of political philosophy, economics, race relations, and criminology, to name but some of its areas of activity, that no small group of men, particularly no group with very limited investigatory facilities, could conceivably possess."

Perhaps the Warren Court deserved that criticism. But if so, the same criticism could apply to any other generation on the Supreme Court. But so what? That's just the way our government operates. The fact is, the Supreme Court is obliged to be available to rule on all areas under the umbrella of the Constitution, which, in these regulatory times, covers an enormous ground indeed. This duty, always pressed on the Court, was not accepted with great enthusiasm until the Warren era.

The Court's enthusiasm for reforms, however, made it a convenient political target. The latter half of the 1960s and the early 1970s found the nation faced with considerable social unrest. There were, on college campuses and in the streets, constant demonstrations against the Vietnam War. There were race riots and confrontations. There was a sexual revolution. Many young people were experimenting with drugs. Nudity in public entertainment was almost commonplace. Traditional values were being challenged as never before. More and more people, young and old, were paying less and less respect to social codes and customs.

A significantly large minority of the American people welcomed the new breeze. They felt liberated by it. But a majority of Americans were frightened by the change. And many blamed the Warren Court's progressive decisions for shaking the social structure. Sensing the widespread mood of fear and disenchantment, Nixon in 1968 made a

---

*Before reading Bork's opinions further, one should bear in mind that he is a very conservative gentleman who does not believe in rocking the Establishment boat. When Attorney General Elliot Richardson and Deputy Attorney General William Ruckleshaus resigned rather than carry out President Nixon's command to fire the special prosecutor in the Watergate investigation, Nixon measured Bork as the kind of chap who would go along with his orders, and he made Bork acting attorney general. In 1987, President Reagan nominated Bork for appointment to the Supreme Court, but the Democratic-controlled Senate refused to confirm his appointment.

campaign promise to appoint such men to the Court that the Warrenesque influences could be reversed.

With an opportunity that rarely comes to a president, Nixon was able to appoint four justices during his first term. He had selected them so accurately for their conservatism that by the time he was up for reelection he could claim to have made a beginning toward fulfilling his 1968 promise.

In the months before the voters went to the polls in 1972, the Committee for the Re-Election of the President—which was, ironically, the organization later revealed to have financed the Watergate burglary and other political espionage that year—sent out campaign brochures boasting: "The courts are once more concerned about the rights of law-abiding citizens as well as accused lawbreakers. President Nixon has appointed four members to the Supreme Court—Chief Justice Warren Burger, Justice Harry Blackmun, Justice Lewis Powell, Jr., and Justice William Rehnquist—who can be expected to give a strict interpretation of the Constitution and protect the interests of the average law-abiding American."

The Burger Court did shift directions. Although the old Warren Court was not reversed in a wholesale fashion, the bold thrust of the Warren days had been stopped. There was a tempering, a shading, a caution about the Burger Court's actions that pointed to a new generation of justice.

The Burger Court reversed the evolutionary liberalism of the Warren Court on "obscenity," which is routinely the stickiest and most difficult question that confronts every new Supreme Court. The difficulty, of course, comes from definition. What *is* obscene? Every generation has a new definition, and every judge does too. Justice Potter Stewart measured the problem properly when he said that he didn't really know how to describe hard-core pornography, but "I know it when I see it."

In 1973, the Burger Court (split five to four) gave broad new powers to local authorities to crack down on what the Chief Justice called "the crass commercial exploitation of sex" by defining obscenity as that which offends local, not national, tastes. Replacing the Warren Court allowance that obscenity was material "utterly without redeeming social value" was the Burger majority's stricter definition of it as material that, taken as a whole, "does not have serious literary, artistic, political or scientific value."

As expected, the Burger Court began to take a sterner law-and-order posture. New powers of intrusion and prosecution were given to governments when the Court ruled that even if a defendant were brought to trial in a state court under a law that is probably unconstitutional, the federal courts should not interfere except in the most flagrant cases of abuse (a critical retreat from the Warren years), and that police and the FBI do not need a warrant to let informers carry electronic bugs on their persons to record conversations.

One rather frightening development was the Burger Court's attitude toward the Fourth Amendment's guarantee that "the right of the people to be secure in their persons, houses, papers, and effects, against unreasonable searches and seizures, shall not be violated." This guarantee was clearly aimed at preventing government officials from using whimsical pretexts for rummaging through innocent persons' homes or offices or other property, simply because they think they "may find something." Burger Court decisions made it extremely difficult to appeal a case on the grounds that evidence used against a defendant was unconstitutionally seized.

The Burger Court also ruled that a grand jury might require reporters to disclose their confidential sources to grand juries; that a shopping center could be closed to peaceful pamphleteers; that a member of the U.S. Congress was not immune from a grand jury summons to tell how he had acquired classified documents (in reference to Senator Mike Gravel's publishing of the Pentagon Papers); that the attorney general had the proper power to prohibit a Marxist journalist from coming to this country to participate in academic conferences and discussions; and that civilians who are targets of surveillance by military spies cannot take the Army to court unless they can show that the spying suppressed their activities.

Progovernment Tilt

Among this lush tangle of decisions, some thought they could see the sproutings of a suppression of dissent. The Warren Court had tilted in favor of the individual and against the arbitrary powers of government. The Burger Court tilted back in favor of government and against individual rights.

It also developed a friendlier attitude toward big business. The Court made it much more difficult to launch antitrust suits. It significantly restricted the rights of investors to sue a corporation. It ruled that a state cannot prevent business executives from spending corporate funds to propagate personal and political views unrelated to their companies' business purposes.

No Revolution

But the most significant feature of the Burger Court was not that it sometimes chipped away at rulings beloved by liberals; the significant feature was that it did so little of this. Once again the justices were proving that presidents cannot predict how their appointees will act once they got on the Court.

By the end of 1981, three conservative presidents—Nixon, Ford, and Reagan—had appointed six members of the Court. But this heavy majority did not function in a heavy-handed conservative fashion, or at least it rarely did so. Just as the Warren Court, notwithstanding right-wing claims to the contrary, had not operated in a radically liberal fashion, neither did the Burger Court operate in a radically conservative way. Like any modern Supreme Court, it had much too sophisticated and complex a membership to be predictable. Nixon certainly did not get everything he desired. Considering his constant problems with campus demonstrators, he would hardly have wanted "his" appointees to rule, as they did, that the radical Students for a Democratic Society could not be prohibited from organizing on campus even if they advocated violence—as long as they behaved themselves while on campus. And the Court killed a ninety-year-old law banning all unauthorized demonstrations on the grounds of the U.S. Capitol—a law often used in the past to justify arresting antiwar and other protestors who had brought their messages to Congress. So the Burger Court was not as insensitive to First Amendment guarantees as some of its critics feared; it was just moderately sensitive.

The Burger Court widened the separation between church and state by denying the constitutionality of a state act requiring every school room to post an enlargement of the Ten Commandments. It sharply restricted the use of capital punishment and reversed the death sentences of hundreds of convicted murderers by finding that the death penalty, although not unconstitutional itself, was applied in an unconstitutionally arbitrary fashion. And if the Burger Court seemed eager to put new tools in the hands of the prosecution and police, it was also willing to help the accused. In a historic extension of the Sixth Amendment, the Court ruled for the first time that a defendant must have a lawyer even in a misdemeanor trial, if conviction could carry a jail term of any length.

The Burger Court ruled unanimously that people could not be jailed simply because they are too poor to pay fines—a ruling that, as Fred Graham of *The New York Times* noted, "outdid the Warren Court's best egalitarian efforts by creating a right that exists only for the poor. An affluent person can be put in jail forthwith for failing to pay his fine, but some other method of collecting fines from the poor (installment payments, perhaps) must be tried first."

Not content with that magnanimity, the Court went on to rule that people who want to obtain divorces but are too poor to pay filing fees and court costs must be given cost-free divorces by the states.

Abortion Landmark

One of the most controversial decisions of the Burger Court was *Roe v. Wade*. Widely praised and widely hated, it became more of a political issue than any decision of the twentieth century other than *Brown v. Board of Education*. "Roe" was the court name of Norma McCorvey, a twenty-five-year-old, divorced, carnival worker. She had a love affair and became pregnant, but she didn't want to keep the child. Abortions were illegal in Texas, except to save the life of the mother. Desperate, she made up a story that one night, walking back to her motel from the carnival, she was knocked down and raped repeatedly by three men. If she thought that sad story (which she didn't admit was a lie until fifteen years later) would soften the hearts of Texas officials, she was wrong. She didn't have enough money to travel to California, where she could have had the operation legally, so the situation seemed hopeless. Then she met Linda Coffee and Sarah Weddington, two of only five women to graduate from the University of Texas Law School in 1967 (women lawyers were still looked upon as freakish in Texas). They wanted to challenge the state's abortion law. Did Ms. McCorvey want to be their test case? Bitter and fighting mad, she was only too willing.

Eventually the case reached the U.S. Supreme Court (long after Ms. McCorvey had had her baby). On January 22, 1973, by a vote of seven to two, the Court handed down one of the most remarkably nonstrict interpretations of the Burger era—and one that flew in the face of President Nixon's expressed political position. The Court overruled all state laws that prohibit abortions during the first three months of pregnancy and liberalized abortion laws during the remainder of the pregnancy period except for the last ten weeks, during which time a state may prohibit the killing of the fetus. Not only was the rejection of the president's position supported by three of the justices he had appointed—Burger, Powell, and Blackmun—but the majority opinion was written by Blackmun.

Moreover, the decision was written with all the flights of introspection and sociological guesswork that might have accompanied even the most imaginative rulings of the Warren Court. Almost apologizing for the fact that justices cannot escape their humanness, Blackmun wrote, "One's philosophy, one's experiences, one's exposure to the raw edges of human existence, one's religious training, one's attitude toward life and family . . . are all likely to influence and to color one's thinking and conclusions about abortion." And, for that matter, about almost any other topic that would come before the Court.

Ten years later the Burger Court reaffirmed the proabortion ruling and strengthened it by striking down an array of local legislative restrictions that prevented access to abortions.

Further buttressing the rights of women, the Burger Court in 1983 barred pension plans that force women to work longer than men before they become eligible to receive payments, or that pay women less than men for the same length of service.

Analysts, struggling for words to describe the Burger Court, have seized upon such adjectives as *centrist, fragmented, shifting, floating,* and *unpredictable.* In the preface to a book of scholarly essays, *The Burger Court: The Counter-Revolution That Wasn't,* Columbia University law professor Vincent Blasi concluded that "the Burger Court's work does not lend itself to any concise, comprehensive characterization. In certain areas, the Court consolidated the landmark advances of the Warren years. In other areas, a mild retrenchment took place."

The Rehnquist Court

With the coming of the Reagan and Bush administrations, the ultra-conservatives at last had a chance to control the Court. When Chief Justice Burger stepped down in 1986, Reagan promoted the most conservative member of the Court at the time, Justice William Rehnquist, to succeed him. And then Reagan named as the new ninth member Antonin Scalia, who was even more conservative than Rehnquist. When two holdover centrists retired, Potter Stewart in 1981 and Lewis Powell in 1988, Reagan replaced them with two solidly conservative justices, Sandra Day O'Connor and Anthony Kennedy.

Those four—Rehnquist, Kennedy, Scalia, O'Connor—plus Justice Byron White held the majority and began moving the Court sharply to the right. Such a decided shift in the Court's orientation had not been witnessed in a generation.

Not that liberals were left with nothing to cheer about. Indeed, it seemed like an echo of the good old days when the Court struck down a Louisiana law requiring schools to "balance" the teaching of evolution with the teaching of creationism; ruled that the states may require employers to grant special job protection (including leaves of absence) for employees who are physically unable to work because of pregnancy; endorsed the constitutionality of rent control; and made it easier for defendants in criminal cases to plead entrapment.

Particularly heartwarming for liberals was the Rehnquist Court's attitude toward First Amendment cases. It reaffirmed the "freedom of speech" protection to those who criticize public figures, even if the criticism is outrageous and offensive. In one case, a jury had awarded the Reverend Jerry Falwell $200,000 in compensation for "emotional distress" because *Hustler* magazine had implied, in an "ad parody," that Falwell had had a drunken incestuous rendezvous with his mother in an outdoor toilet. The Court overturned the jury's award, ruling that public figures can't be libeled unless they can prove that the defendant knowingly, or with malicious recklessness, made a false statement of fact. *Hustler*'s parody was malicious all right, but it didn't even pretend to be a statement of fact. The remarkable thing about the decision was that it was written by Chief Justice Rehnquist, who in twenty previous libel cases had rejected First Amendment defenses every time.

The Court also upheld the First Amendment right of adults to receive "dial-a-porn" phone calls so long as the messages are merely naughty but not obscene. The Court also ruled that the First Amendment bars police from seizing the inventory of adult bookstores before any of the publications have been found at trial to be obscene.

But the First Amendment ruling that caused an earthquake of outrage among conservatives (and probably seemed too liberal even to some liberals) came in a case involving the burning of the U.S. flag. During the 1984 Republican convention in Dallas, Gregory Lee Johnson set fire to an American flag in a nonviolent demonstration against the Reagan administration. Sentenced under Texas law to a year in jail and fined $2,000, he appealed to the Supreme Court, claiming that the flag burning was symbolic speech covered by the First Amendment. In a five-to-four decision (Rehnquist was among the angry dissenters), the Court agreed with Johnson and thereby invalidated the flag-desecration laws of forty-eight states and the federal government. Writing for the majority, Justice Brennan said, "If there is a bedrock principle underlying the First Amendment, it is that the government may not prohibit the expression of an idea simply because society finds the idea itself offensive or disagreeable."

More in keeping with the Court's new temper, however, were several rulings that narrowed the kinds of expression the Court would allow on government property. Federal officials, for example, were allowed to limit the type of messages that could be displayed on sidewalks outside post offices. And public television stations were allowed to pick and choose among the political candidates they would allow on the air, even though this could mean barring candidates who, lacking funds for commercial television, had nowhere else to go.

In religion cases, the Court lowered the barrier between church and state by allowing the federal government to give grants to religious groups for sex counseling (score one for the conservatives); at the same time, it raised the barrier by ruling that a Nativity scene sponsored by a government body, if the scene is unadorned by any secular symbols of the season, amounts to an unconstitutional endorsement of the Christian religion (score one for ultraliberals).

On the other hand, the Court was extremely conservative in all capital punishment cases. It upheld the death penalty for black murderers even though statistics show that racial bias often determines who is executed and who isn't; ruled that the Constitution permits states to execute murderers who are mentally retarded as well as those who were as young as sixteen years of age when they committed their crimes; and ruled that indigent convicts on death row do not have a constitutional right to a lawyer to assist them in a second round of state appeals.

Civil Rights Retreat

But the most dramatic action of the Rehnquist Court came in those landmark areas that had made the Supreme Court—particularly in the Warren era but also into the Burger era—a beacon light guiding the federal government toward the expansion of minority and women's rights. Here, the conservative majority said not merely, "Stop, enough," but "Stop, too much, turn around and go back."

One of the significant achievements of the civil-rights movement was the establishment of government affirmative-action programs that set aside a portion of public-works contracting for companies owned by minorities. The Rehnquist majority ruled that that kind of an arrangement was "discrimination in reverse" and violated the constitutional right of white contractors to equal protection of the law. Similarly, the Court ruled that affirmative action hiring agreements could be legally challenged by white workers (this ruling permitted white firefighters in Birmingham, Alabama, to challenge an eight-year-old, court-approved settlement intended to increase the number of blacks hired and promoted in the department). Another severe blow to the civil-rights movement was the ruling that in class-action suits alleging discrimination, the burden of proof was on the plaintiffs; this overturned a 1971 opinion in which the Court had placed the legal burden on employers for justifying policies that seemed, statistically at least, to screen out women and members of minorities.

The reaction among black leaders was heavy pessimism. "Night has fallen on the Court as far as civil rights are concerned," said Benjamin L. Hooks, then executive director of the National Association for the Advancement of Colored People. "We are seeing the unraveling of gains we thought were secure."

On the other hand, the Rehnquist Court can be credited with virtually creating the law banning sexual harassment in the workplace. Title VII of the Civil Rights Act of 1964 outlawed "discrimination because of sex." Note, the law said discrimination, not harassment. Not until various rulings of the Rehnquist court in 1986 and 1993 was the meaning of discrimination expanded and retranslated to mean harassment as well. At that point, the law only protected women from harassment by men.

The next giant step took place when a male oil-rig worker filed a federal suit claiming that several coworkers and supervisors had singled him out for crude sex play, unwanted touching, and threats of rape, making his job intolerable. In 1998, the Supreme Court ruled that federal law protects employees from being sexually harassed in the workplace by people of the same sex, too. (The ruling did not open the door for homosexual discrimination cases, as such; it simply addressed discrimination whatever the sex.)

Abortion Retreat

The most miraculous happening under the Rehnquist Court was that *Roe* v. *Wade*—although truncated and a bit mangled—was still alive as the century approached its conclusion. *Roe,* you will remember, was the 1973 ruling of the Court that prohibited states from blocking abortions until the third trimester of pregnancy; or, to put it another way, *Roe* declared that women have a right to abortions in the first trimester and a limited right in the second trimester.

In the years following *Roe,* no other issue so dominated the political landscape or was fought over with more virulent passion. Pro-abortionists (who call themselves "pro-choice") believed with all their heart that women should have control over their own bodies and government should not try to regulate their child-bearing decisions. Antiabortionists (who call themselves "pro-life") just as passionately felt that abortion was murder. They sought a constitutional amendment that would grant full rights to fetuses from the moment of conception. They also persuaded Congress not to fund abortions for poor people. Many antiabortionists picketed abortion clinics, and the more wildly fanatical among them occasionally bombed the clinics and shot the doctors who performed the abortions.

The antiabortion crusade was joined by most conservative politicians. And since conservatives controlled the White House from 1969 through 1992 (except for Carter's four years; but he had no influence on the Court because no vacancies occurred during his presidency), it was logical for antiabortionists to think that "their" presidents would get to appoint enough conservative justices that *Roe* would be overturned.

It didn't happen. Yes, *Roe* was changed. In 1989 (*Webster* v. *Reproductive Heath Services*) and in 1992 (*Planned Parenthood* v. *Casey*), the states were allowed to impose new restrictions on abortion. But the heart of *Roe* remained intact.

Its survival in *Planned Parenthood* v. *Casey* points to a truth that has been stated several times in this chapter: The justices are not always predictable. Each may usually vote "conservative" or "liberal" (though those categories are sometimes meaningless in law), but now and then they will confront a decision that will affect the nation so profoundly that they set aside all personal (and political) preferences and, if need be, switch sides. As Justice Anthony Kennedy once put it, "The hard fact is that sometimes we must make decisions we do not like."

Kennedy's vote was one of the crucial—and unexpected—votes that saved the right to abortion. He had first intended to vote the other way. He hates abortion. But when it came time to cast his vote, Kennedy says—and even today when discussing this, his eyes fill with tears—he felt it wasn't right for him to impose his personal views on the nation.

What's in the Future?

When people talk about the "Warren Court"—and they usually talk about it either with great admiration or anger—they conjure up the image of a Court that was bold, creative. When they talk about the "Burger Court," they usually mean a Court that was not very creative but was valuable for maintaining a steady course in a turbulent era. It is too early to guess how history will judge the "Rehnquist Court." Its image is still too fractured to be seen clearly. It seemed to favor state governments over the federal government, and to favor any government over the individual. But as it closed out its session in 1999—the thirteenth year Rehnquist had presided over the Court—its preference for states' rights over fedreal laws went far beyond the "seeming" stage. In decisions that stunned much of the legal world, the Court ruled five to four that states could ignore provisions in labor, patent, and unfair-competition laws enacted by Congress.

The conservative majority held, for example, that without the consent of the states, 4.7 million state employees cannot sue when they are underpaid in violation of federal minimum wage or overtime requirements. The rulings were based on what the Court called the "sovereign immunity" of the states—ironically, these words are not found in the Constitution.

Four of the five conservative justices were appointed by President Reagan. The other was appointed by President Bush. It underscored the accuracy of Justice Blackmun's forecast in 1988, as the nation prepared to decide whether it wanted to elect Vice President Bush, a conservative Republican, or Michael Dukakis, a liberal Democrat. "For better or for worse," said Justice Blackmun, "this election will be a very significant one. If Vice President Bush wins, the Court could become very conservative well into the twenty-first century." His prediction seems right on target. Four years later, Clinton replaced Bush in the White House and named two justices (Ruth Bader Ginsburg, a mostly moderate, and Stephen Breyer, a liberal by the Rehnquist Court's standards), but the twelve years of a Reagan–Bush White House still dominated life in the Supreme Court even into the end of Clinton's second term: Simply proving the obvious once again, not even justice can escape the political past.

CHAPTER 6

Bureaucracy

Our Prolific Drones

Every once in a while one gets the view down here in Washington that the respective departments are members of the United Nations, and that each has a separate sovereignty.

SENATOR HUBERT HUMPHREY
quoted in Emmet John Hughes,
The Living Presidency

BEGINNING IN THE 1930S, MOST LIBERALS BECAME CONVINCED that our best chance for progress lay with the federal government. They believed that since the federal government had an almost unlimited source of funds and the best apparatus for creating national unity and for enforcing its will on the people, it could also be utilized most easily for doing good—far more than could the disparate state governments with their varied incomes (some very poor) and their great range of consciences (some apparently almost nonexistent). The building of highways, dams, utility plants, post offices, and docks; the subsidizing of farms, airlines, banks, railroads, school programs, and publishing houses; the protection of bank deposits and labor unions; the policing of the stock market; the regulation of transportation fees and schedules; the underwriting of housing loans—activities of this sort, multiplied endlessly, were seen as the natural benevolence of big federal government.

Many of the programs were successful; most of them received wide and permanent popular support. After they had been well established, even conservative politicians supported them, or at least were silent in

their opposition; in some cases conservatives even pushed to expand such programs as Social Security, which once were held to be anathema by the conservative Establishment.

But with these benefits came a sharp decline in direct electoral control of the government. Each of the beneficent programs created its own bureaucracy. Congress could not administer the burgeoning programs. Neither could the president and his executive department, nor did Congress desire that the president have enough supervisory power to do the job. So the bureaucracy of the welfare state swelled both in size and independence, until, as archconservative Barry Goldwater correctly appraised it:

> It is so massive that it literally feeds on itself. It is so large that no one in or out of government can accurately define its power or scope. It is so intricate that it lends itself to a large range of abuses, some criminal and deliberate, others unwitting and inept. The government is so large that institutions doing business with it or attempting to do business with it are forced to hire trained experts just to show them around through the labyrinthine maze made up of hundreds of departments, bureaus, commissions, offices and agencies. . . . It would be downright laughable if it were not so serious to consider how many of our people actually believe that a national administration firmly controls the Federal Government. It is true that broad overall policy is determined at the White House level or at the cabinet level in the government bureaucracy. But its implementation is too often left to the tender mercies of a long-entrenched bureaucracy.

Presidents come and presidents go, and so do members of Congress, but the faceless bureaucrats live forever, and so (seemingly) do their often outdated and irrelevant policies.*

These days many liberals, no longer so certain that the federal foundation can support a utopian superstructure, are tempted to join con-

---

*Before going further we had better give a working definition of bureaucracy. By that we mean the fourteen cabinet departments and the commissions, agencies, and boards that have been erected as governmental needs have arisen. The earliest administrations had War, Navy, State, and Treasury departments. A young country needs only the basics: Some way to protect itself, deal with other countries, and handle its finances. There was also an attorney general, but the Department of Justice that is now thought of as his domain came almost a century later, in 1870. Interior was added in 1849. The Commissioner of Agriculture, added in 1862, was promoted to cabinet rank in 1899. The Office of Postmaster General, created in 1789, was made a cabinet department in 1872 (and in 1971 was made an independent agency). Commerce and Labor came into existence in 1913, Defense (unifying in a clumsy way the various military services) in 1947, Health, Education and Welfare (now called Health and Human Services) in 1953, Housing and Urban

servatives in agreeing with former Senator Goldwater's tone as well as with his theme. Two recent presidents, Jimmy Carter and Ronald Reagan, rode to the White House primarily by playing on the public's disenchantment with the government and by promising to reduce and reform the bureaucracy. (It is instructive that they were among our most unproductive modern presidents, perhaps for the very reason that they held the government in such contempt.) In the 1976 presidential campaign, Carter spoke of "that mess in Washington" and promised to do something about the "complicated, confusing, overlapping and wasteful government bureaucracy"—that most despised of all parts of the government—to streamline it, get rid of the fat, make it shape up and serve the people. He considered his antibureaucracy pitch one of his most important: "There has been no theme that I have emphasized more often than a need to reorganize the federal government. The American people overwhelmingly support this idea and that's one reason I was elected president."

But whatever "mess" Carter found in the bureaucracy when he took office was still there four years later. And his promise to trim the bureaucracy turned out to be a pipe dream. In fact, Carter *added* two cabinet departments, the Department of Energy and the Department of Education, which by consensus of most Washington observers are two of the most inefficient units of government.

Development in 1965, Transportation in 1966, Energy in 1977, Education in 1979, and the Department of Veterans Affairs in 1988.

As business and industry began to abuse their powers under the laissez faire philosophy that dominated our nation's life in the second half of the nineteenth century, Congress began creating regulatory and administrative commissions. Because the railroads mistreated the farmers in the way of rates and service, the Interstate Commerce Commission was established in 1887. In an effort to end the boom-and-bust cycles by stabilizing the dollar (and by regulating the banks), the Federal Reserve Board was established in 1913. Unfair trade practices and monopolistic activities of the period gave birth to the Federal Trade Commission in 1914. The utility robber barons and the buccaneers of the natural gas fields helped create the Federal Power Commission in 1920. The chaos of the airwaves industry resulted in the Federal Communications Commission in 1934. The disastrous stock market crash brought about the creation of the Securities and Exchange Commission in 1934, and the brutal labor–management wars of the early 1930s were responsible for the establishment of the National Labor Relations Board in 1935. The Civil Aeronautics Board (1940), the Atomic Energy Commission (1946), and the National Aeronautics and Space Administration (1958) were responses to the need for controls and policy guidance in the new industries of aviation, atomic energy, and space—all of which are just as subject to exploitation in these sophisticated times as railroads, banks, and stock markets were subject to exploiters in those more rugged eras. In 1977, the Federal Power Commission and Atomic Energy Commission were made a part of the Department of Energy. When the airlines were deregulated in the 1980s, the Civil Aeronautics Board ceased operations.

So in 1980 Ronald Reagan came with the same promise: He, too, would clean up the mess; he, too, would trim the bureaucracy. Particularly he promised to get rid of the Energy and Education departments. "In this present crisis," he said in his inaugural address, "government is not the solution to our problem, government is the problem"—and he promised to reduce its size radically. What came of his promise? When he left office in 1989, the bureaucracy was more chaotic, more inefficient, more poorly administered, more hostile to the public's needs than at any time in recent history—and it was larger by 142,284 employees than when he took office, and costing twice as much as during Carter's term. Not only were the Energy Department and the Education Department still in place, but in the last year of his term Reagan created a new and very wobbly leg for the bureaucratic centipede—the Department of Veterans Affairs.

Those "Hidden" Workers

We'll skip President Bush, who, except that he was lighter-weight and less colorful, was a carbon copy of Reagan. President Clinton sounded like his Republican predecessors, declaring "the era of big government is over," and he also promised cuts to the executive department. To everyone's amazement, he did cut it—by 300,000 workers, down to 1.87 million in the executive force (which doesn't count the 1.9 million military personnel and the 850,000 postal workers). But, aha, there are other ways to count the size of the federal government. Paul Light, a scholar at Brookings Institute, reasonably argues that to get the true picture, one must count not only the groups mentioned above, but one must also count what he calls the "shadow" workers, hired through contracts and grants. This group, by his figuring, adds 12.7 million workers to the federal payroll for a grand total of 17 million employees.

Actually, no one knows exactly how many government contract workers—call them consultants, if you like—are on the federal payroll, how much they cost, what they do, or how well they do it. John D. Hanrahan, who wrote *Government by Contract*, guesses a lower total figure than Paul Light does. But Hanrahan states flatly that "in some agencies or units within agencies, the major parts of their budgets were spent on contractors. The Department of Energy, for example, had spent between 80 percent and 94 percent of its budgets on contracts" with outsiders to do the work that the regular bureaucrats were supposed to be doing.

How do the "contract bureaucrats" benefit the regular bureaucracy? Three ways: (1) They let agencies dodge personnel ceilings. If Congress or the president tries to cut the cost of government by freezing the number of permanent employees, the bureaucracy simply uses its budget to hire consultants instead. (2) Consultants allow the bureau to operate in secrecy. The regular bureaucracy is bound to divulge most of its information under the Freedom of Information Act (well, at least it is supposed to). But the courts have ruled that private consulting firms working for the government are not covered by the act. (3) Contractors also get by with bullying employees in ways the Civil Service wouldn't allow. Workers who complained about safety and environmental problems at four military nuclear plants run for the government by private contractors (Rockwell International, NL Industries, and General Electric) say they were harassed by their superiors and ordered to see psychiatrists for their "mental problems." A contractor at the government's nuclear weapons plant in Hanford, Washington, fired employees for complaining too loudly about the massive pollution from radioactive leakage.

If those contract workers had been in the Civil Service, their fate would have been different. In fact the Civil Service is so extraordinarily sympathetic that complainers line up by the thousands to gripe. Minorities make up about 29 percent of the federal workforce, but many minorities still complain the government isn't doing enough to provide equal opportunities. The Government Accounting Office (GAO) disagrees. Its latest five-year study concluded that while women are underpaid for their job description, minority workers are more than twice as likely to be overpaid; the GAO thought this might be because supervisors feared bias charges. Civil rights' complaints in government rose 70 percent between 1990 and 1997. One-fourth were filed by whites, alleging reverse discrimination.

A survey of the bureaucracy by the U.S. Merit Systems Protection Board found that more than two women in five (42 percent) claimed they had been sexually harassed at work and 14 percent of men made the same complaint. For the most part, the harassment didn't go beyond touching, pressure for "sexual favors," suggestive gestures, or "unwanted sexual teasing, jokes, remarks, or questions," but apparently it was enough to make the office atmosphere unpleasant. The Merit Systems Board found that the hanky-panky cost the taxpayer $267 million over a two-year period in paying sick leave to distressed employees who missed work, in replacing employees who quit in disgust, and in reduced productivity.

No Heavy Lifting

But in general federal workers have a much cushier life than workers in the real world. Dr. Sharon Smith, an economist with the Federal Reserve Bank in New York, after spending several years studying the comparison, concluded that the same kind of work is paid between 13 percent and 20 percent more in the federal government than in the private sector. And that doesn't take into consideration benefits such as higher pensions that sweeten a civil servant's life.

A typical federal employee retires on a pension more than twice as high as the average Social Security pension that other taxpayers can look forward to. And while a Social Security beneficiary can't retire until sixty-five and receive full benefits, the bureaucrat can retire at age fifty-five, if he or she has put in thirty years on the job. Most private pensions are not indexed to inflation; in fact, most retirees have no private pension. But those lucky enough to retire from the federal government get generous increases every time the cost-of-living index rises. Quite a few federal employees retire, take their pensions, and then get another job with the government—they're known as "double dippers."

How hard do bureaucrats work? Maybe most earn their pay, but it isn't hard to find the other kind.

Karen Elliott House, a reporter for *The Wall Street Journal,* visited the Department of Agriculture to check the work pace. A typical bureaucrat, she reported, was an assistant to an assistant administrator for management in the Foreign Agricultural Service. His desk top, when she dropped by to chat, held a candy bar, a pack of cigarettes—and his feet. He was tilted back in his chair reading real estate ads in *The Washington Post.* Asked what he did for the public, he chuckled and replied that he assessed the adequacy of the department's fats and oils publications.

Marjorie Boyd, a contributing editor of the *Washington Monthly,* also noted the absence of a crushing workload: "Anyone who spends much time visiting government offices in Washington cannot help but be struck by the fact that there are many workers who seem to be literally doing nothing except reading newspapers or magazines and drinking coffee. Many others seem to be engaged in dubious make-work projects." And yet, wrote Boyd, "with all this inactivity and questionable activity, there is total job security. The figures show beyond doubt the reluctance of government employees to fire one another." Year in and year out, about one-seventh of 1 percent of the workforce is fired for inefficiency. To put that in perspective: If a small business employing ten people fired employees for cause at the same rate as the federal government, it would discharge one worker every seventy years.

There are other ways to measure the production of the federal bureaucracy. For instance, you will notice that many statistics used in this book are four, five, or six years old. The reason is that the bureaucracy takes that long to grind out its findings. Many bureaucratic reports are ancient history by the time they are made public. Though we live in the Computer Age, you can easily get the impression that federal workers are still using the abacus and stylus.

One of the most dramatic examples of bureaucratic slowness surfaced in 1997 when the National Cancer Institute released portions—just portions, it wasn't yet through—from a long, long-awaited study begun fourteen years earlier. It was information vitally needed about how much cancer-causing radiation had been spread across the country by atomic bomb tests in the 1950s.

Incredibly, an initial draft of the study was completed in 1989, but it couldn't be released then because the word-processing software that researchers used had become obsolete. So more time was wasted while a new draft was typed on a computer that didn't have enough storage capacity. So they tried another computer, but this time nobody but the programmer could understand the database. While the National Cancer Institute fumbles along, Americans all across the country are left to wait and wonder who among them was dangerously exposed to drifting radiation.

Things like that should remind us that many times we trust our very lives to bureaucrats, who sometimes fail us. The federal nuclear weapons plant in Hanford, Washington, has the nation's largest concentration of radioactive waste. For almost fifty years, managers of the plant steadfastly claimed that leaks were insignificant because the radioactive stuff would be trapped by the surrounding soil. But in 1998, they admitted they were wrong. The Energy Department had said for decades that no waste from the tanks would reach the ground water for ten thousand years at least. But it is already there. About 54 million gallons of radioactive waste are stored at Hanford in 177 underground tanks. Already, 68 tanks have leaked nearly a million gallons into the soil, and all the oldest tanks are expected to eventually leak. The Energy Department has known about the leaks for at least a decade, but it kept quiet. And now, as the poison moves toward the nearby Columbia River, it admits it doesn't know how to correct the horrendous blunder.

A Hate–Love Relationship

The public gets emotional about the bureaucracy because that is the part of the federal government that citizens know best. It is tangible; we encounter it daily. Bureaucracy's job is to administer all the tasks assigned it by Congress and the president, in every particular. The civilian employees keep the enormous, clanking, steaming machine lumbering along. Without the bureaucracy, we would have no mail, no Social Security checks, no food stamps, no passports, no protection from untested drugs or spoiled meat or unfair prices, no college loans, no subsidies for business, no legal aid. Bureaucrats make a thousand judgments that affect the day-to-day lives of all Americans. Without the bureaucracy, our servicemen and servicewomen would not be housed, fed, armed, and maneuvered into position. Relations with other nations would be difficult to maintain; international trade would become unpredictable and even more avaricious than it is.

Critics of the bureaucracy are ambivalent. This is understandable, for in many respects it is a magnificent achievement, a stalwart and surprisingly efficient operation that has somehow managed to survive two centuries of tinkering by members of Congress and often-hyperactive presidents. In other ways, it is a Rube Goldberg contraption that takes a thousand movements to turn one screw. The contradiction was expressed by Senator Patrick J. Leahy of Vermont:

> Most federal workers are intelligent, dedicated people who do a day's work for a day's pay. Unfortunately, when you put these same people into the crazy-quilt of departments, agencies, commissions and bureaus that comprise the federal government, too often you get a radically different result: an intractable bureaucracy which in size and power is one of the most difficult-to-control creations man has ever yet devised.

Along with doing its useful duties, the bureaucracy often performs in ways that seem wasteful, unnecessarily intrusive, and silly. Although many of its unwelcome practices are traceable directly to orders from the White House or Congress, the bureaucracy gets the blame—and the headlines. Consequently, the bureaucracy has come to stand for government in its most derogatory sense. It has become the symbol of governmental indifference to citizen needs, the symbol of government waste.

So very much money—$1.7 trillion dollars a year—is tossed around by the federal government that it is hardly surprising that some of it is spent foolishly. To most citizens, a trillion dollars—even though it comes out of their pockets—is an unreal sum. Some of the things the money is spent on also seem comically unreal: There was the $375,000 that the Navy spent to test the flight characteristics of frisbees; there were the twelve films produced by the Defense Department, all on the same subject, "How to Brush Your Teeth"; there were the 371,875 letters sent out to postal employees warning them not to stick pencils in their ears or to let their toenails grow to excessive lengths; there was the safety pamphlet (costing $500,000 to produce) sent to farmers, warning them that if they stepped in wet manure, "you can have a bad fall."

The National Science Foundation (NSF), an independent government agency, is especially, well, "imaginative" in the way it hands out our cash. The NSF spent $46,100 to study how the sight of scantily clad women affects men's driving in Chicago and $84,000 to find out why people fall in love; $107,000 to a University of Illinois professor to study the reaction of people to jokes concerning flatulence and nonreproductive sex acts (this will complete a study he began in 1989 with a $122,851 grant from the National Institute of Mental Health). All told, the National Science Foundation dispenses more than $3 billion a year in grants for about 20,000 research and education projects, most of which, we may hope, are not quite as far-out as the above.

When any large group of people have so many billions of dollars to give away, it's natural to expect them to show some dim-wittedness and make some quaint slip-ups. But, in fact, these are more than quaint slip-ups; they are symptoms of a deeper problem that has to do with ethics and priorities. The deeper problem is the gigantic waste that results from what seems to be simply a pathological love of spending. The bureaucrats throw money around so recklessly and so callously that one gets the feeling they do not consider themselves part of the same public that must foot the bill.

Poster Child of Spending

How else, except for this attitude, does one explain the Pentagon's spending $50 million to supply its retirees Viagra? Or the Department of Interior's spending $100 million in the early 1970s to transform Washington,

D.C.'s Union Station from a railroad depot to a tourist center, and then ten years later spending $80 million to make it a train station once again? Or the U.S. Army Corps of Engineers spending $29 million to straighten the Kissimmee River (Florida) in the 1960s, and then spending $80 million in the 1980s to put the bends back in the river?

Indeed, the Army Corps of Engineers could be used as the poster child of pathological spending. It never met a river it didn't want to dredge, and dam, and dam again. It has a passion for gouging out new channels that don't work. It has one of the greatest talents in the bureaucracy for making money disappear without a trace, doing its fanciest disappearing acts at rivers and beaches. For example, one spring the Corps added 405,000 tons of sand along 12,000 feet of Lake Michigan shore, at a cost of $1.5 million. By summer's end, the sand had all washed away. An Ocean City, New Jersey, beach rebuilt in 1982 at a cost of $5 million disappeared in a storm about ten weeks later. The Army Corps was back at Ocean City in 1997 to do a $10 million shore-building job, only to have it disappear in a storm one year later.

Almost every year a new scandal surfaces in the General Services Administration, the housekeeping agency of the government. It is notorious for doing such things as buying a "bargain" building for $22 million that government workers couldn't move into for ten years because it was so filled with noxious fumes. Another of its brilliant moves was to lease an eight-story building for $14 million a year to house the Federal Communications Commission (FCC). But it sat empty while the government continued to pay $1.2 million a month to keep the FCC in its old offices.

It might have been a bit late to get around to it, but in 1994 Congress decided it would be a good idea to look at the government's financial books, so it ordered a comprehensive audit of the entire federal government—the first in two centuries. Five years later, the General Accounting Office (GAO) published its results, and, as you might expect, it had found that most of the Cabinet departments' accounting systems were a mess. Assets and liabilities were all mixed up. Billions of dollars in transactions and property couldn't be accounted for. The Housing department had lost records for many of its older loans. The Medicare program, auditors found, overpaid claims by billions of dollars in 1996. The Pentagon was the worst; it admitted it had lost many things you wouldn't think would be hard to find—like a $1 million missile launcher and a $460,000 floating crane. All in all, the GAO gave passing grades to only seven of twenty-four government agencies. But, what the heck; it's just your money.

The Unappealing Giant

Above all, the bureaucracy stands for what many citizens have come to fear and loathe the most: bigness. It started small, even for a new country. When the federal government moved from Philadelphia to Washington in 1800, the bureaucracy consisted of about 130 clerks. By the end of the Civil War, the ranks had swollen to 7,000. As we moved into the twentieth century, the federal government employed 26,000 bureaucrats. The New Deal jumped the payroll to 166,000 by 1940, on the eve of the Second World War. That was the point of no return. By war's end, the civilian employment had pushed well past two million. The queen bee may be in Washington, but the drones in this hive are everywhere; only one in ten of the federal employees work in the nation's capital.

Today the dimensions of the bureaucracy, whether measured by bodies or concrete, are stunning. The federal government owns 400,000 buildings. Everyone knows there are fourteen cabinet departments. But below that level, things get fuzzy. How many independent and regulatory agencies are there? Between forty-four and seventy-five; the answer depends on who does the counting. How many offices, bureaus, and agencies are there in the fourteen cabinet departments? President Carter tried to find out, but after three months of searching, a White House official told him, "We were unable to obtain any single document containing a complete and current listing of government units which are part of the federal government." *The United States Government Organization Manual,* which runs to more than 800 pages, scarcely begins to convey the size and complexity of the United States government.*

Some parts of the bureaucracy hang in there long after they have lost their usefulness. The Rural Electrification Administration was set up in 1935 to help bring electricity to rural America. Ninety-nine percent of the homes in rural America now have electricity, but the REA budget and staff continue to grow.

The Interstate Commerce Commission, established in 1887 to control the railroad robber barons, was once one of the most powerful parts of the federal government, regulating trains, buses, trucks, and

---

*The labyrinth of government being what it is, one can hardly be surprised that workers in one part don't know what is going on in other parts. And so we have situations, as reported by the Library of Congress, in which "the federal government spends nearly $4 billion annually on research and development in its own laboratories, but it does not know exactly how many laboratories it has, where they are, what kinds of people work in them, or what they are doing."

just about anything else that crossed state lines in commerce. But by the 1960s, it had become so corrupted by the industries it was supposed to be regulating that its usefulness had dropped almost to zero. Every president in the 1970s and 1980s, Democrat and Republican, tried to kill the commission, but it somehow survived by bureaucratic guile. One Republican congressman called it "the dinosaur that wouldn't die." But after a quarter century of uselessness, it was finally killed on December 28, 1996, when President Clinton signed its death warrant.

Federal giantism is best seen in the Department of Defense, the biggest bureaucracy in the world. The department spends so much money, and spends it so inefficiently, that it actually doesn't know whether the cash is coming or going. Not long ago lobbyists for the Pentagon were all over Capitol Hill demanding more money and pleading poverty, although at that moment $92 billion appropriated for defense was lying unspent in the U.S. Treasury—which the Pentagon had forgotten about. In 1996, the Pentagon got Congress to give it an extra $37.5 million to build 2,000 housing units for military families on a waiting list. It promised they would be built within one year. Instead, it spent every penny on consultants without breaking ground on a single new housing unit. Easy come, easy go. A special presidential task force appraised the Defense Department as "an impossible organization." The chairman of the group, Gilbert W. Fitzhugh, who was also chairman of the Metropolitan Life Insurance Company, said they had found that "everybody is somewhat responsible for everything, and nobody is completely responsible for anything. They spend their time coordinating with each other and shuffling paper back and forth, and that's what causes all the red tape and big staffs in the department. Nobody can do anything without checking with seven other people."

Actually, that isn't a bad description for most portions of the Civil Service.

Next in size and chaos is the Department of Health and Human Services (which, before education was spun off into its own department, was known as Health, Education and Welfare). Like a frantic hen that has hatched too many squabbling chicks, it broods over forty rivaling agencies that deal with problems ranging from abortion to smoking. Some cabinet secretaries have found the department completely unmanageable; one HEW secretary of the Nixon era, Robert Finch, had a physical breakdown trying to run the place.

Another typically chaotic piece of the bureaucracy is the Department of Agriculture (USDA) with 102,000 full-time employees (one for every fifty farms), it fills five huge buildings in Washington and overflows into 16,000 other buildings across the nation. It does everything from write standards for watermelons to run self-awareness programs for farm women. It has built more dams (about two million so far) and loaned more money to Americans (about $10 billion a year) than any other part of the government. It is one of the three biggest publishers in government; for instance, it prints up about 28,000 forms that are circulated internally and filled out by employees in an effort to let their bosses, and ultimately the secretary of agriculture, know what they are doing. It's mostly in vain. Thomas Foley, who used to be chairman of the House Agriculture Committee, told *The Wall Street Journal:* "No Secretary of Agriculture runs the department. It's just too big."

Hurting the Little Farmer

So who does run it? All sorts of big agricultural business groups and other heavyweight special interests in the food industry. No, they don't run it directly, but they have powerful influence on USDA programs and policy. The one group that has the least influence on the USDA is ordinary, small farmers.

Small farmers get an especially harsh shafting from the USDA if they are black. In 1920, 14 percent of the nation's farms were owned by blacks, mostly in the South. Today, there are fewer than 1 percent. Most lost their farms because they were discriminated against by white USDA county agents who made it virtually impossible for them to get farm loans, crop subsidies, and other federal benefits. The blacks were being shafted long before President Reagan came along, but he made it even worse by abolishing the USDA's office of civil rights in 1983. President Clinton restored the office, but by that time the remaining 18,000 black farmers were in desperate condition.

They filed a class-action lawsuit against the USDA for $3 billion in 1998 and began holding large protests in Washington, at one point tying a mule to the White House fence. In 1999, the USDA finally acknowledged that the blacks had been grossly mistreated over the years and offered a settlement of $50,000 tax free to every complainant. Many farmers said that was too little, too late, particularly for those who lost their farms in foreclosures.

Typically, the settlement did not punish the USDA county agents for their lawless discrimination.

As has already been made clear, inefficiency seems to follow growth. Take the Secret Service, for example. A generation ago the Secret Service was a rather humdrum and out-of-the-way agency that mostly hunted counterfeiters. It assigned a few of its idle agents, but not many, to accompany the president as bodyguards. Then came the assassination of President John F. Kennedy in 1963. Using that tragedy as an excuse for growth, the Secret Service became a veritable army. In 1963, it had 450 agents. Today, it has more than 2,300, and its budget has jumped twentyfold. With typical bureaucratic ambition (and the support of the agency's congressional allies), it pushed its authority into new areas. It began serving as the bodyguard not only of presidents, vice presidents, and past presidents and their families, but of major presidential candidates; and, having plenty of agents to spare, it even began bodyguarding cabinet members. It spent millions of dollars on new technology, including a computer in which it stored the names of 50,000 troublemakers. And for all that expenditure, how successful has the Secret Service been? Though presidential candidate George C. Wallace was accompanied by Secret Service agents in 1972, he was shot by a gunman not three feet away. In 1975 it was only by great good luck that President Ford escaped assassination in Sacramento, where the Secret Service failed to apprehend a demented young woman armed with a pistol until she got within two feet of Ford. And then in 1982, because the Secret Service violated its own security procedures, an assassin got close enough to put a bullet in President Reagan.

Bureaucratic Indifference

Many Americans believe the bureaucracy is indifferent or else downright hostile to the idea of helping or protecting the general public.

They have good reason for thinking so. Those who have worked for the government and are candid about the experience will admit that it is not unusual for secretaries to ask callers, "Are you from a law firm or are you a member of the public?" In that context, being from a "law firm" equates with "lobbyist." The bureaucracy is very chummy with lobbyists, but stray citizens are often viewed as nuisances. Occasionally this attitude is displayed with special starkness, as when the broadcast bureau at the Federal Communications Commission sent a memo to all secretaries: "Please eliminate the use of the closing paragraph, 'If I can be of further assistance, please let me know,' from all letters for the chairman's signature."

When this attitude exists at the top, it seeps all the way down to the clerks. After dozens of phone calls to a variety of bureaucratic offices where the underlings treated him rudely, former Representative John Rousselot, a California Republican, declared furiously that if a congressman was so treated—moreover, a congressman who sat on the committee overseeing the Civil Service Commission—"God help the average citizen trying to get help!"

While corporations have a relatively easy time dealing with the government in money matters, ordinary citizens often get roughed up. The Internal Revenue Service (IRS) admits that many of the ten million taxpayers who telephone for assistance in filling out their tax forms receive wrong answers, but when these victims try to get the errors straightened out, they are often treated as though they were trying to cheat. No wonder taxpayers are confused—and no wonder the IRS gives some wrong answers and is cranky; both taxpayers and agency have had to deal with 6,493 tax law changes since 1986. Still, that's no excuse for being mean.

IRS officials are occasionally brought before Congress and lambasted for their treatment of ordinary taxpayers. This is an old morality play, repeated decade after decade—and little changes. The Senate Finance Committee heard hundreds of horror stories, and IRS confessions, at its extraordinary three-day hearings in 1998. Agents told about being trained to lie and bully moderate-income people but to go easy on "corporate America or the wealthy people, because those people can bring an accountant or a tax attorney and fight the system." Other IRS bureaucrats admitted it was commonplace for agency employees to snoop through supposedly confidential tax files of celebrities, neighbors, local public officials, and anyone who publicly criticized the agency.

One woman testified that her husband, a forty-seven-year-old lawyer, killed himself after learning that the IRS had prompted a bank to foreclose on their home. Then the IRS put liens on the life insurance benefits from her husband's death.

In another case, the IRS made a bookkeeping error about a $3,500 tax payment, and because of that mistake a southern California homemaker's life was ruined for the next nine years.

Another California woman told the Senate of going through a seventeen-year nightmare with the agency that was caused by a mix-up over her husband's identity.

Congress responded by passing the IRS Reform Act of 1998, which mandates that agency employees must be fired if they commit any of ten abusive acts. Top IRS officials promised that their 98,000 employees would treat taxpayers much gentler in the future.*

People who deal with the Social Security Administration (SSA) may have an equally painful experience. Because of staff reductions at the SSA dating back to the Reagan administration, would-be retirees have an awful time trying to get advice on how to apply for pensions or for Medicare.

And the information they receive is often wrong, costing them thousands of dollars in deserved benefits. At last count, 300,000 pensioners were appealing SSA rulings, and 50,000 of these had actually gone to court for help.

Kicking the Underdogs

The lower you are on the social and economic totem pole, the less courteous your treatment is likely to be. No group is lower on that totem pole than the Native Americans, who for more than a century have been cheated and abused by the bureaucracy (primarily by agencies within the Department of Interior), and continue to be. Although the government spends $3 billion a year on Native American programs, much of this is wasted. The Bureau of Indian Affairs has done little to reduce the alcoholism, child abuse, and unemployment on the reservations; and bureaucrats either did nothing to stop, or actually participated in, the theft of oil and gas from Native American lands. After his special committee had investigated the corruption for seventeen months, Senator Dennis DeConcini, the Arizona Democrat, said, "I cannot think of any area where the federal government has so completely abdicated its responsibility as it has in Indian affairs."

More evidence of that surfaced in 1999 in a lawsuit. For more than a century, Native Americans had asked the federal government for a simple accounting of money and land held in trust for them since the days of the treaty signing, in the 1880s, when the government broke up

---

*Ironically, while the new law may have made the IRS "kinder," it also frightened workers so much that they seemed to lose interest in doing their job to collect unpaid taxes. Statistics released in 1999 showed that IRS seizures were down 98 percent and tax liens were down two-thirds—costing the government at least $15 billion in unpaid taxes. (*The New York Times*, May 18, 1999)

the tribal land ownership system and awarded individual allotments of 80 to 160 acres per Native American. These units—belonging to as many as 500,000 Native Americans—were "managed" by the government, usually leased out to gas, oil, and timber companies. The income was supposed to be passed on to the descendants of the original owners.

Instead, the Native Americans were royally cheated, perhaps by as much as $10 billion. The government had simply made no real effort to carry out its responsibilities. So the Native Americans sued Interior Secretary Bruce Babbitt and Secretary of Treasury Robert Rubin, demanding a full and proper accounting. When the federal judge handling the case ordered the cabinet officers to turn over their records, they said most of them had been lost. They admitted that the trusts were earning about $300 million a year, but they had no idea how many properties, leases, contracts, and investments were in the trusts. In other words, for several generations the government had held back the wealth that belonged to thousands of Native Americans, many of whom lived in poverty. Typical of the victims was the Native American woman who had six gas wells on her property but was receiving only $5 a month from the government.

Indifference to Health and Safety

It's bad enough when the bureaucracy is indifferent, but there is always the danger that indifference to the public's needs will turn to callousness.

The operation of the Occupational Safety and Health Administration (OSHA) is a good example of this danger. In 1980, OSHA said it would limit the amount of dust that could pile up in grain elevators (grain dust can be as explosive as TNT), but not for another nine years—with fifteen workers being killed and seventy-four others seriously injured in the meanwhile—did it get around to setting standards for grain dust.

OSHA has slightly over 1,000 inspectors to cover nearly six million workplaces—an impossible task for such a small force, and made all the more impossible by the fact that the Reagan–Bush administration cut the number from 1,328. Most of the fines imposed on outlaw industries are not for unsafe working conditions but simply for record-keeping violations. And often OSHA doesn't even levy fines for that. It didn't fine Iowa Beef Processors for more than 1,000 unreported injuries and illnesses.

Each year about 10,000 fires start with upholstered furniture, causing more than 500 deaths, 1,100 injuries, and $150 million in property damage. Federal regulators have known for nearly three decades that the foam in most sofa cusions is highly flammable. But to please furniture makers, they delay new safety regulations.

What happens when a 5,000-pound sport utility vehicle hits a midsize family sedan of, say, 3,300-pounds? Plenty, and it's all bad, and most of it happens to the sedan. Sport utility vehicles account for only one-third of the vehicles on the road, but they kill more people in cars than other cars do.

Officially administered tests by the National Highway Traffic Safety Administration (NHTSA) are usually the first step toward the government's requiring vehicle design changes that reduce injuries and deaths. So why was it that the NHTSA waited until 1998 to run the tests—seven years after the introduction of the Ford Explorer set off a surge in sales of sport utility vehicles?

Could it be because of the old bureaucracy-industry "revolving door" that Ralph Nader justifiably complains about? Here are just some of the dozen top officials who had passed through the revolving door as of 1998: Barry Felrice, for twelve years head of the critical rule-making branch of NHTSA, is now director of regulatory affairs at the American Automobile Manufacturers Association; Andreas Card, former secretary of the Department of Transportation, under which NHTSA operates, is now president of the Automobile Manufacturers Association; and Diane Steed, who headed NHTSA for six years in the anything-goes Reagan years, now heads a consulting firm for auto industry front groups.

They have a lot of clout with the buddies they left behind in the bureaucracy.

Trucks and Atoms

Okay, let's move on to the really humongous trucks with single trailers (60 feet long), double, and triple trailers—the latter, up to 120 feet long, as long as a ten-story building, and weighing, with cargo, up to 80,000 pounds. Accidents involving heavy trucks killed 4,903 and injured 116,000 in one recent year. "That's an average of thirteen Americans every day in truck crashes, with twelve of the thirteen being occupants of passenger cars," says John Claybrook, chairman of Citizens for Reliable and Safe Highways (CRASH), a grassroots safety organization. "That death toll is equivalent to having more than thirty fully loaded 737 jetliners crashing. If this were the airline industry, it would be grounded."

Given the amount of influence the trucking industry has in Congress, the government will never force a reduction in truck size.

But there are other safety factors. Many truckers complain that their employers force them to meet schedules that allow them very little sleep. Most truckers admit dozing off at the wheel occasionally. The National Transportation Safety Board estimates that truck drivers who fall asleep at the wheel are a factor in 750 to 1,500 road deaths every year. So what does the agency mean to do about it? In 1997, it said that new regulations updating the 1937 federal rest rules for commercial truck drivers were on the agency's list of "most wanted" safety improvements. Note that date: 1937! They hadn't updated the rules in sixty years, not since the biggest trucks on the highway were a mere 35 feet long—half the length of today's single-trailer trucks, and highway traffic was one-sixth as much as it is today. Nothing is more sluggish than a sluggish bureaucracy.

The Atomic Energy Commission (AEC) is another prime example of bureaucratic callousness. When it began testing nuclear weapons in the Nevada desert in 1951, it presumed—on no scientific evidence whatsoever—that nearby ranchers would not be harmed by radioactive fallout from the explosions. But tests soon showed that the fallout was enormously dangerous and led to an increase in certain kinds of cancer. So what did the AEC do? Warn the ranchers? Buy their property and move them out? Did it take any precautions at all? No. Instead, the AEC, and later the Energy Department, became even more secretive and issued reassuring press releases about how safe the bomb testing was. When concerned scientists tried to warn the public by publishing studies showing the fallout dangers, the atomic bureaucracy tried to shut them up by threatening to cancel their grants or, if they worked for the government, to fire them. More than a thousand people died or became seriously ill from what they or their families believed was the fallout, but the government successfully fought all efforts to pay damages to the victims. "When mistakes were made," writes Nick Kotz, a Pulitzer Prize–winning journalist, "crushingly powerful bureaucracies plowed ahead, intransigently refusing to admit error and forgetting government's guiding purpose—to serve the people."

More Callousness

The Federal Aviation Administration (FAA) is the watchdog that is supposed to make sure those thousands of planes flying over America every day don't fall. It has 3,000 inspectors, but only 600 of them are assigned to inspect the 2,500 shops that work on commercial airplanes—that is, they are supposed to make sure the repair stations really do the repairs and maintenance they are supposed to do.

But according to the General Accounting Office, Congress's investigative arm, the FAA routinely fails to make a return visit to see if the violations that its inspectors uncover at these repair stations are ever corrected. Does such sloth matter? If they could talk, the 110 people who died in the May 1996 crash of a Valuejet DC-9 in the Florida Everglades would have some comments to make about that question. The crash was caused by a fire from oxygen generators improperly shipped by a repair station. The FAA seems strangely casual about the problem. It began a process to update the regulation of repair stations in 1989, but still hasn't finished. The FAA was also supposed to update the requirements for maintenance personnel, but it suspended that effort in 1994.

The National Transportation Safety Board, which investigates plane crashes and advises the FAA on proper ways to prevent their happening again, got fed up in 1998 and said a commuter plane crash near Detroit that killed all 29 people aboard could have been prevented if the FAA had put into effect the lessons learned from a similar crash two years earlier. James E. Hall, chairman of the safety board, said, "The bottom line in responsibility for safety in our country is a government regulator. The government regulator is the one we pay our taxes to." And the public is not getting its money's worth, Hall said, because the system is breaking down.

Not Enough Workers

If it is breaking down, it's probably because the bureaucracy's workforce is not allocated sensibly, or perhaps it has been cut too much. Some parts do have a surplus of employees. But some very important parts have so few workers that they cannot possibly do the job Congress assigned them to do. They may at times seem incompetent, but if you look more closely at the complexity and immensity of their duties, you will soften your judgment, for they are faced with almost impossible tasks.

This is particularly true of departments and agencies assigned to protect us from harmful foods and drugs, or to prevent illegal aliens and illegal merchandise from getting into the country, or to protect workers and the environment from being unfairly exploited. These tasks are so enormous they cannot be done right without employing more enforcement officers than the federal government has ever had. For instance:

- It's estimated that workers would get an extra $19 billion a year if they were paid the overtime they are legally entitled to and are being cheated out of. The U.S. Labor Department receives about 20,000 overtime complaints a year, and that is probably a small fraction of the actual overtime illegalities that occur. The Labor Department makes no real effort to discover the true scope of the crime. Why not? Because the department has only 800 investigators—and they also have to handle minimum-wage, child-labor, and other enforcement covering hundreds of thousands of workplaces across the nation.

In 1997, a sample compliance survey limited to New York City's garment factories found 63 percent in violation of wage and hour laws. Imagine how many thousands of lawbreakers would be uncovered if the survey was done nationally! But also think how many inspectors it would take.

- The U.S. Customs Service must enforce 600 different laws from sixty different agencies. Mostly, it tries to stop the flow of drugs into this country, but it also tries to block all sorts of other illegal goods. How is it possible to inspect more than the tiniest fraction of the goods entering the country? In 1997, a typical year, ships docking at U.S. ports unloaded 4.5 million cargo containers—a favorite hiding place for smuggled contraband; 6 million trucks entered the United States either from Mexico or Canada and 118 million cars traveled across the same borders; 68 million air passengers arrived in the United States from overseas, and more than 8 million arrived via ships.

But wait a minute. Customs agents are also expected to stop the outflow of cars, motorcycles, computers, hi-fi gear, software, guns, appliances—things that are stolen here and smuggled to eager buyers around the world. Insurance investigators believe more than 200,000 stolen cars are shipped out of the United States annually, for an estimated loss of $1 billion or more.

Give the Customs Service ten times more inspectors and they probably still wouldn't have enough.

That would also be true of the Immigration and Naturalization Service (INS). Immigration is like a tidal wave, and the INS is barely staying afloat.

The Immigration Flood

We have the most generous immigration policy in the world. The number of legal immigrants living in the United States has almost tripled since 1970, rising from 9.6 million to 26.3 million today. The foreign born now account for nearly one in ten residents. People who favor immigration believe the newcomers help bring dying inner cities to life; many businesses look to immigrants either as cheap labor or as an expanding market. And indeed they do expand the market, for immigration and births to immigrant women are said to account for 70 percent of the increase in the U.S. population since 1970 and *all* of our projected population growth in the twenty-first century.

Those statistics frighten many people. A poll conducted by *The Wall Street Journal*/NBC News found that 70 percent of Americans favor tighter restrictions on immigration because they believe first-generation immigrants tend to be poorer (the newcomers account for one out of seven persons living in poverty), less educated, and more likely to be on welfare.

Half of all immigrants are Spanish speaking—27 percent come from Mexico. Nearly half the estimated 5 million illegals in the United States are thought to be living in California. Not surprisingly, many California taxpayers do not feel hospitable, since every year they pay an estimated $2 billion to educate the children of illegals and about $400 million to imprison criminal illegals.

States like California, New York, Texas, and Illinois, which attract the bulk of the immigrants and feel the greatest financial burden, put heavy pressure on Congress to stop the illegal flow, and Congress puts heavy pressure on the INS. But although the agency has several thousand border agents, its task of keeping out illegal aliens is virtually hopeless. Our borders are too easy to slip across. Many come in by plane or ship, using a visa, and then disappear in the masses.

For every illegal the INS catches and turns back, at least three or four get through. In short, the agency works in a highly frustrated atmosphere. Just how frustrated can be seen in the fact that in one recent year, 3,000 illegals caught in southern Texas were turned loose because the INS didn't have enough space to detain them.

The frustration can result in unprofessional conduct. In 1996, faced with a mountainous backlog of 1.4 million applications for citizenship from legal immigrants, the INS cheated. It gave citizenship to 180,000 without first checking their backgrounds to see if any were major criminals.

Frustration can also lead to harshness. Sometimes illegals marry legal immigrants, have children, get jobs, and settle down to establish a home. Then the IRS finds the illegal spouse and deports him or her, thereby breaking up the family. Is that humane? Is it fair? The INS would probably answer that it doesn't have the time, the manpower, or the legal flexibility to always ask itself those questions.

More Headaches from Abroad

Aside from illegal aliens, drugs, and other contraband, federal inspectors must try to keep out foreign foods that contain dangerous diseases. Again, we're talking about a task so immense, and a policing and inspection force so ridiculously small, that any success we have in keeping out polluted food can be mainly credited to just plain luck.

With the growing "global economy" and an explosion of trade going in both directions, the problems have multiplied astronomically. Some countries from which we import food have no sanitary code at all in the production of fruits, vegetables, and meats. As one Food and Drug Administration official put it, "Look, in a lot of countries, the field workers often get paid by the number of bushels they pick. They often don't have any place to go to the bathroom, so they just do it in the field, right on top of the food sometimes. And they don't wash their hands. Then if the produce is washed in polluted water and shipped in a truck that hauled garbage that morning . . ." He didn't finish the sentence, but the conclusion was clear: Food handled like that is bound to be highly contaminated.

The Department of Agriculture (USDA) has the duty of monitoring all domestic and imported meat and poultry. The Food and Drug Administration (FDA) is charged with safeguarding Americans from contamination in all other food, including fruit, vegetables, grains, and seafood. Neither the USDA nor the FDA have enough inspectors to do the job right. The FDA, for example, has 235 inspectors. But with 2.2 million shipments of foreign food—30 billion tons—arriving every year, those inspectors can only give a swift sniff and a poke to less than 1 percent of the foreign food that winds up on grocery shelves.

It's not surprising that in recent years there have been outbreaks of disease, such as the 2,000 Americans who were made ill for weeks from parasites never before seen in this country. The bugs arrived on Guatamalan raspberries. And 200 children in Michigan got hepatitis A after eating strawberries from Mexico. There are thousands of contaminated shipments the FDA can't catch.

President Clinton, saying, "We have millions of people getting sick every year," asked Congress in 1997 for an extra $24 million to hire 100 inspectors. They would go abroad and check foreign food–safety systems, banning fruits and vegetables from countries that didn't regulate strictly enough. But many in the food industry, preferring profits over safety, urged Congress to go slow because we export twice as much food as we import, and they feared other countries might retaliate.

Environmental Revolution

The United States entered the "environmental era" in the late 1960s and early 1970s. Ironically, leading the parade was Richard Nixon, who may have been a weird president in many ways, but he was a master politician and he recognized that the most popular issue of the moment was environmentalism—protecting America's air, water, and land. Nixon was personally lukewarm on the subject, but the force of Congressional and public opinion was too powerful to resist. So in 1970 he joined Congress in establishing the Environmental Protection Agency (EPA). The EPA took over most of the government's widely scattered environmental oversight and was given greater regulatory power. In the same period several other landmark environmental laws were passed.

They have resulted in great benefits. For example, despite stiff opposition from auto manufacturers and the smokestack industries, which complained about clean-up costs, the Clean Air Act has indeed resulted in a sweeter atmosphere. In 1988, Los Angeles suffered through 239 days that did not meet acceptable air quality. In 1995, the unacceptable days had dropped to 103. In the same time span, Chicago's days of unacceptably dirty air dropped from twenty-three to four, New York City's from forty-six to eight.

Some of the rivers that in the 1960s were so heavily polluted with chemicals that they sometimes literally caught on fire are once again clean enough to support fish. Many of the pesticides that were killing birds and fish, and sickening human beings, have been outlawed.

Which isn't to say that all our environmental problems are under control. According to the EPA, the water in more than a third of our rivers and lakes is still substandard. And every year, we—meaning, our vehicles and industries—are releasing more than 2 *trillion* pounds of toxic chemicals into the air, water, and soil.

And there are still 1,254 hazardous-waste sites waiting to be cleaned up—which is only a few hundred less than polluted the land eighteen years ago, when the Federal Superfund Program was enacted. Corporations that did the polluting were supposed to clean them up, but, faced with a probable cost of $40 billion or more, they are in no rush. It's cheaper for them to hire million-dollar lawyers to get delays by tying up the EPA's meager legal staff in court.

But perhaps the major handicap faced by the EPA is the same as with other regulatory agencies: It doesn't have enough inspectors for the task assigned. The states are responsible for the day-to-day enforcement of federal laws like the Clean Air Act and the Clean Water Act, with federal agents giving supervision. But the inspector general of the Environmental Protection Agency in a two-year nationwide examination that began in 1997, found that this system simply isn't working in many western states. Hundreds of factories and waste water treatment plants had not been inspected for ten years and were operating without a valid permit, and polluters were almost never punished.

There Are Good Guys, Too

Considerable evidence supports former Senator William Proxmire's claim that "there is little room in the government service for men of character, independence and guts. The government doesn't want the free spirits—the highly intelligent, strong-minded, truthful men—working for it. What it wants instead are time-servers, conformists and 'yes' men."*

On the whole, that's probably true. But there are quite a few notable exceptions. Indeed, as a percentage, there are probably as many exceptional people in the bureaucracy as there are in the general population, which may or may not be saying much. People such as Ernest Fitzgerald, a weapons-buying expert at the Pentagon, went before a Senate committee and revealed that the C-5A transport plane was going to cost $2 billion more than Air Force officials had previously claimed. For being honest, he was fired. After a ten-year battle that put Fitzgerald heavily into debt, he was rehired, but banished to a job with virtually no responsibilities. Anthony Morris, a virologist at the Food and Drug Administration, warned that the government should not embark upon a swine flu vaccination program. Morris was fired. As it turned out, he had been very right. There was no swine flue epidemic; the needless program cost millions of dollars; 97 persons died from their injections; many others were crippled; and the government was left facing billions in claims. But Morris received neither an apology nor his old job back.

---

*Yeah, but on the other hand, the government does include some gutsy, truthful people; it doesn't do much good, however, unless Congress listens to them. For several years, the inspectors general at the Department of Housing and Urban Development sent reports to Congress warning of the fraud going on there. If anybody paid attention, it should have been Senator Proxmire, who was chairman of the HUD subcommittee of the Senate Appropriations Committee. "There was plenty of evidence," he admits, "for those of us who had the responsibility to get involved, and we just didn't do it." Uh huh, just a little $2 billion goof-up (*New York Times,* July 3, 1989).

Another hero at the Food and Drug Administration, but fortunately one who was listened to, is Dr. Frances Kelsey. As background to her legendary victory, you should understand that pharmaceutical companies are always screaming at the FDA to hurry up and approve their new drugs so they can put them on the market and start making zillions of dollars. And it is the FDA's duty to pay no attention, but to take all the time that is necessary for a full testing of new drugs, to make absolutely sure they are safe. It takes lots of time—sometimes eight or ten years—because the laboratories are overloaded with work. Under pressure from the drug companies, Congress in 1992 and 1997 ordered that the approval process be speeded up. Result? Several drugs had to be yanked off the market because they had been approved too early and were killing people. The same results, but worse, would have happened in 1960 if Dr. Kelsey (who still works at the FDA) had not flatly refused to be rushed into approving the drug thalidomide, which was being sold in Europe and elsewhere as a popular sedative for pregnant women. Result: Around the world, 10,000 babies were born with severe defects—missing arms, hips, and so forth—but the United States escaped with only seventeen deformed babies, all born to mothers who had bought the drug overseas.

In other words, don't get the idea that all bureaucrats are shiftless hacks just interested in serving their time with as little work as possible and then drifting off into the sunset of posh retirement. Not true. In every department, in every agency, there are workers who are as irritated and frustrated as the general public is by the bureaucracy's overall spirit of lethargy and indifference. They want to cut through the red tape, cut out waste, and implement programs smoothly to help the public. They are delighted when the press or congressional investigators turn up bureaucratic corruption because that makes their jobs easier to do right. Some of these reform-minded bureaucrats are "whistle-blowers"—passing information to press and Congress about their crooked coworkers and bosses. To keep the proper perspective about government, one has to constantly remind oneself that these honest, hardworking bureaucrats—though in a significant minority—do exist.

Now and then, the nation is treated to a high-level bureaucrat who has the guts to expose himself to hostile fire from both ideological sides, "that rarest of Washington officials—a rugged individualist who follows his own agenda, not a predictable ideologue who espouses the party line." Surgeon General C. Everett Koop was that kind of fellow. Because he opposed abortions, Senate liberals fought his confirmation for nine months (they called him "Dr. Kook"). But once he became surgeon general, he took such a sympathetic position towards AIDS victims and ignorant young lovers, and became such a belligerent foe of the tobacco industry that liberals came to love him and conservatives to hate him. As *The Washington Post* reporter Sandra G. Boodman noted, conservatives "accused Koop of promoting immorality because he advocated sex education beginning 'at the lowest grade possible' and recommended condoms in addition to abstinence." They were convinced he was a devil when he modified his antiabortion position to say that a pregnant woman infected with the AIDS virus must be given the option of abortion.

The very conservative Dr. Koop took the loss of his old allies without flinching. "I think," he said,

> sometimes when my right-wing critics talk about family values, they don't realize how few families there are. I'm thinking about the eighteen-year-old girl in the South Bronx who's fat and unattractive and black and she had a pregnancy two years ago and had an abortion and she never knew her father, and her mother is trying to take care of a bunch of children and grandchildren. She has no education that will help her get a job and she has very few choices in life. I'm not willing to let those kids go down the drain by preaching the unrealistic message of abstinence rather than giving them practical advice about condoms.

Good ol' GAO

And if one really wants to get a rosy glow of faith in the civil service, then one only has to remember that the General Accounting Office is on the job.

The GAO is full of real experts—far better than investigative newspaper reporters—at detecting the corruption, waste, boondoggling, and stupidities of the government. It employs several thousand accountants, lawyers, engineers, sociologists, and management specialists, who produce about 1,000 reports a year, and hardly a day passes that one of the reports doesn't make a news story. It may be something as comparatively slight as the revelation that too many government agencies regulate the content of pizza, or a medium-level (but symbolic) revelation that the Pentagon allowed another defense contractor to charge Super Bowl tickets to the B-1 bomber budget, or major disclosures, such as the fact that NASA never has analyzed 90 percent of the information it spent billions of dollars to collect from space, or that the U.S. Forest Service doesn't charge enough rent from resorts operating on federal lands and is losing 75 cents of every $1 it spends to market lumber, for a total loss of billions of dollars.

The GAO was the first to discover and publicize that the Federal Savings and Loan Insurance Corporation, supposedly the Savings and Loan "insurance company," was insolvent to the tune of $6 billion. The GAO found that the State Department allowed its employees to cheat the taxpayers out of at least $20 million by charging off luxury trips to bogus accounts with fictitious names and Social Security numbers. (It was bad enough that one crooked foreign service employee signed his expense account Ludwig Van Beethoven, with a Social Security number of 123-45-6789, but he doubly deserved to be fired for misspelling the composer's name.)

It was the GAO that discovered the Army had spent half a billion dollars for new heavy-construction machines to replace machines that were still usable. Machines that were replaced at a cost from $74,000 to $148,000 each could have been repaired, said the GAO, for $300 to $13,000 per machine.

With no exaggeration, the GAO can boast of saving the taxpayers $20 billion in a typical year by providing solutions to administrative inefficiencies. On the other hand, it recently complained that the government had ignored 1,298 problems the GAO had pinpointed.

Also of great value are the 1,800 criminal investigators of the government's Offices of Inspectors General. These are the junkyard dogs of federal law enforcement—low-status sleuths prowling the backrooms of their agencies sniffing out corruption, fraud, and abuse. About two dozen executive branch agencies maintain these in-house investigators, who have cracked many big criminal cases. Agents at the Department of Transportation uncovered a nationwide bid-rigging conspiracy among highway contractors that ended with seven hundred criminal convictions and $66 million in fines. At the Department of Agriculture, agents slapped forty-eight criminal indictments on sugar brokers for illegally dumping about 400 million pounds of foreign sugar on the domestic market. And it was agents of the Small Business Administration inspector general who led the investigation of Wedtech, Incorporated, the Bronx military contractor that got more than a quarter-billion dollars' worth of government contracts through bribery and fraud. So vigorous is the law enforcement of these agents that they are beginning to fear for their lives, and have asked for the right to carry guns.

When Bureaucrats Turn Rogue

The worst thing that can happen in the bureaucracy is for an agency to lose touch with the rest of government, to create its own isolated world of unreal priorities and secret agendas—to become a rogue organization.

Two agencies have, historically, achieved rogue strength to a particularly dangerous degree. One (discussed more fully in our third chapter) is the Central Intelligence Agency, the CIA, our primary, or at least our most notorious, international spy agency. The other is the Federal Bureau of Investigation, the nearest thing we have to a national police force. The FBI is also an intelligence-gathering (domestic spy) agency.

Since the Second World War, both agencies have operated without much supervision from either Congress or the presidency, except for occasional encouragement for their dirty work. They have broken countless laws. Using patriotic propaganda in a masterful fashion, they welded public support in such a way as to make themselves invulnerable to criticism by civil libertarians. Their top officials felt so powerful—and for good reason—that they saw no need to obey even the president, although the directors of both the FBI and the CIA could be fired by him if they stepped out of line. In his memoirs, former President Nixon tells of trying to get some documents from the CIA. First he sent the order through a White House aide and when that didn't get the documents he wanted, he personally gave the order. He still didn't get them. "The CIA was closed like a safe," he writes, "and we could find no one who would give us the combination to open it."

Being information-gathering agencies, both the FBI and the CIA have their ultimate power in the way they release or withhold key information. By withholding vitally needed information from which to make a judgment, the CIA in 1961 persuaded President Kennedy to go ahead with the disastrous Bay of Pigs invasion in Cuba. According to the findings of Senate Intelligence Committee investigators, senior officials of both the CIA and the FBI covered up crucial information in the course of investigating President Kennedy's assassination.

Rarely does the public get to catch a glimpse of the activities behind the CIA's curtain. One of those rare occasions was in the mid-1970s, when it was discovered that the CIA had, for many years, conducted burglaries, wiretaps, mail interceptions, and other disruptive tactics aimed at people *in this country* whose politics it disapproved of. It had done these things despite the fact that the statute under which it operates strictly forbids all domestic activities. When CIA horror stories, including its assassination contracts with the Mafia, began coming to light, James R. Schlesinger, former director of the CIA, responded with the kind of shrugging attitude that makes real bureaucratic reform very difficult to achieve. He said tolerantly, "All bureaucracies have a tendency to stray across the line."

As the century came to a close, the CIA's reputation reached an all-time low. The end of the Cold War had left it in limbo. No longer could it pose as a great warrior against Communism, and many of its most experienced spies retired because of old age or boredom. The left-over spies and the recently embraced electronic spy equipment were making major mistakes. So in an effort to regain public respect, the agency tried what for it was a unique ploy: honesty. For the first time in its history it began admitting that for many years it had been covering up or lying to Congress and the public about some of its dirty and/or dumb activities. For one thing, it admitted it had lied when it told Congress it didn't know its pals in the Honduran military (supported by millions of covert dollars from the United States) had carried out hundreds of human rights violations, including murder, torture, and kidnappings.

An even more dramatic outburst of honesty occurred in 1998 when it opened a vault that had been locked for thirty-six years and released a report written by the CIA's own inspector general. It acknowledged that the agency was totally to blame for the disastrous invasion of Cuba in 1961 and had failed to warn Kennedy that the CIA's top officials knew long before the invasion was launched that it was doomed.

And for the first time in fifty years, the CIA voluntarily disclosed its annual budget for spying—$28 billion, which is one-tenth the entire defense budget. And yet, for all the money the agency was tossing around, it failed to foresee India's nuclear tests. The chairman of the Senate Intelligence Committee called it "the intelligence failure of the decade." The House Intelligence Committee concluded that the CIA and its sister spy services (thirteen in all) lack "the analytic depth, breadth and expertise to monitor political, military and economic developments worldwide." Despite such harsh criticisms, the CIA would doubtless, as in the past, be allowed to continue merrily on its bungling way without much Congressional supervision.

The Nutty Top Cop

However obnoxious the CIA's activities have been, they have not been so harmful to the rights of our citizens as have the FBI's high-handedness, illegalities, and kingly goofs, especially during the half-century reign (1924–1972) of Director J. Edgar Hoover. One does not, perhaps, expect a high degree of morality from the CIA, for from its very beginnings one side of its operations was officially established as a dirty-works factory. But the FBI is supposed to be different. For three generations, the movies and the comic strips assured us that FBI agents were trim, brave, unflappable gangbusters, the United States' first line of defense against the "underworld rats." That image was the result of the most successful public-relations campaign in bureaucratic history, and it was largely the doing of the bull-dog-jawed Hoover.

But then—some of it toward the end of Hoover's career and a flood of it after he died—came the unsettling details of what had really been going on behind the FBI's wall of autonomy. Hoover had become eccentric to the point of nuttiness, in his personal life as well as in his management of the bureau. He would summon agents to his office and talk for hours, neither stopping nor allowing them to interrupt, on every topic under the sun, often making little sense. Agents who feared they were being summoned to be bawled out would take Hoover a little present—a coconut cake (his favorite), perhaps, or a "cocktail-hour wristwatch." He was like a little boy with these trinkets and sweets.*

For decades before Hoover left the bureau and for a while thereafter, the FBI was something of a fraud, in both the quality and the kind of work it did. In 1982, congressional researchers concluded almost half of the criminal history records that the FBI sent to the police, state agencies, banks, and other institutions were incomplete or inaccurate and unjustly tainted the reputation of millions of Americans.

While the Mafia and other sophisticated crime syndicates went about their business relatively undisturbed, Hoover kept his agency spying on "radical" organizations that he hated—mostly antiwar and civil-rights groups that were no threat to either the public peace or the

---

*Although Attorney General Robert Kennedy told several friends that he considered J. Edgar Hoover "dangerous . . . rather a psycho . . . senile . . . frightening," he said that he and his brother, President John Kennedy, felt that it was better to keep Hoover on as head of the FBI because "he was a symbol" and retaining that symbol in the administration might help get Kennedy reelected in 1964 (Arthur M. Schlesinger, Jr., *Robert Kennedy and His Times* [Boston: Houghton Mifflin, 1978]).

public's well-being. At one point, the New York office had over 400 agents working on communism, four on organized crime. The FBI operated mainly to harass those Americans whose left-wing ideology offended Mr. Hoover. He hated homegrown socialists, and he didn't like liberals much better. Hoover especially detested Martin Luther King, Jr., the civil-rights leader. He tapped King's telephone and bugged his hotel rooms, and then passed these tapes out to selected journalists in an effort to show that King was immoral. In the FBI's hysterical war on the left-wing, Hoover's agents committed hundreds of illegal burglaries and wiretaps, paid informants who later lied under oath, furnished funds and arms to paramilitary right-wing groups that burned and bombed offices of left-wing groups and carried out assassination plots against left-wing leaders, incited police violence, and blackmailed and slandered critics.

Hoover's hang-up over what he called "leftwing dupes" sent FBI agents scurrying down some strange trails. They put together a dossier on a seventeen-year-old girl in Newark, New Jersey, who wrote a high school essay on the Socialist Labor Party. In Washington, D.C., they tried to get a socialist kindergarten teacher fired lest she lead her tots into Marxism. Hoover's hatred for draft dodgers was so intense that he would sometimes assign a hundred agents to run down one draft evader. Records from FBI files indicate that the agency under Hoover spent at least 40 percent of its time in political surveillance and in trying to disrupt political organizations with techniques that post-Hoover Attorney General William B. Saxbe called "abhorrent in a free society."

Fear of Blackmail

But no attorney general, though nominally Hoover's boss, ever dared talk that way about Hoover's work while he was alive. One reason was that he had put together files that many politicians feared could be used for blackmail: files full of data about the private lives of important people, such as presidents and members of Congress, including their sexual and drinking habits. This was one reason that the FBI budget always sailed through Congress without challenge.

Sometimes presidents asked the FBI to perform political dirty tricks, but most of its illegal activities were done on the FBI's own initiative and often without the knowledge of either the attorney general or the president.

How does a fellow like J. Edgar Hoover turn his part of the bureaucracy into a private kingdom? Several factors go into the formula:

longevity, propaganda, fear, cronyism, control of information. But perhaps the most important factor was secrecy. Hoover operated behind a wall of secrecy: Presidents did not know what he and his agents were up to; the outer ring of the FBI often did not know what the inner ring was doing.

Hoover left the FBI in such disarray and in such disrepute that the four directors since then have had their work cut out trying to get rid of the stink. They haven't fully succeeded. Two directors, William H. Webster and William S. Sessions, were embroiled in race scandals. The bias against minority races that existed under Hoover is still very much present. A black FBI agent was tormented by other agents (an ape's head was taped over his son's face in a family photograph on his desk; a photo of a black man who had been beaten was placed in his mail slot; he received obscene phone calls and anonymous threats). His supervisor considered these incidents "pranks" and said they were "healthy" and a sign of "esprit de corps" in the office. There were 11,548 agents at the FBI in 1999. Of the total, 84 percent were white, 7.1 percent were Hispanic, 5.7 percent were black, and 2.5 percent were Asian. There were 1,871 female agents who comprise 16.2 percent of the total.

Shades of the Hoover era, the FBI under Director Webster was also caught spying on U.S. citizens for no reason except that they opposed the Reagan–Bush administration's Central American policy. Hundreds of citizens were secretly followed and photographed, their license plates recorded, their trash searched for incriminating evidence. And then the FBI was caught in what the press sarcastically dubbed "The War on Spies in the Stacks," referring to the FBI agents who went around to libraries asking what books and periodicals people were reading, and if they had patrons "with Russian-sounding names."

On the other hand, it must be acknowledged that since the departure of Hoover, the FBI has been much more faithful at tending to its proper business. Among other things, it exposed widespread corruption in the Chicago court system that led to the conviction of a dozen judges, thirty-five attorneys, and fifteen law-enforcement officers. It broke up a gigantic Mafia heroin conspiracy popularly known as the Pizza Connection, uncovered bribery involving billions of dollars in Pentagon military contracts, caught on videotape a handful of crooked congressmen in the famous Abscam sting, and in a sting operation that swept from Long Island to the Canadian border, the FBI caught dozens of local officials taking bribes and kickbacks.

When President Clinton appointed Louis Freeh to be director, there were hopes the agency would avoid the major pitfalls of the past. But some remained. The FBI continued to show little interest in investigating civil rights crimes and cases of police brutality. And it seemed particularly reluctant to go after corporate criminals. David McGee, a highly regarded federal prosecutor, said, "This resistance to paper cases [corporate and white-collar crime] is a big deal, because if you don't do paper you leave out a broad spectrum of criminal matters, often the most important crimes. All that too many agents want to do these days is kick down doors." A veteran FBI agent agreed: "Many younger agents have become obsessed with breaking down doors, with going after the bad guys like they do on television."

This preference for violent conclusions resulted in two of the most misguided episodes in FBI history. The first was a shoot-out (the FBI gave a "shoot-to-kill" order) at a white supremacist's cabin in Ruby Ridge, Idaho. The man's wife and fourteen-year old son were killed, as was a U.S. marshall. An even more disastrous use of violence came in 1993, when the FBI ordered an assault on the building near Waco, Texas, where more than seventy members (many of them children) of a weird religious cult were living. The building went up in flames and all inside were burned to a crisp.

After that, "Ruby Ridge" and "Waco" became battle cries among many wacko, right-wing, gun-toting groups around the country who cited those incidents as proof that the federal government was tyrannical. Timothy McVeigh indicated it was partly in revenge for Ruby Ridge and Waco that he bombed the federal building in Oklahoma City in 1995, killing 168 people.

Hoover, who loved to snoop, would be jealous of the increased powers given to the FBI in recent years for break-ins, wire-tapping, bugging, and especially for accumulating a database of constantly updated personal information about not only criminals but millions of ordinary citizens.

An agency with those powers should have close oversight, but in fact the FBI operates with considerable autonomy. Since it is a wing of the Justice Department, most people assume that the attorney general supervises it. Not so. With the passage of a law in 1976 giving the FBI director a ten-year term of office, he remains, as Hoover was, very much his own master. Director Freeh himself understands that a more vigorous oversight would help. As he told the House Judiciary Subcommittee on Crime in 1997, "We are potentially the most dangerous agency in the country."

Congress and the Bureaucracy

How can the bureaucracy operate in such a freewheeling, chaotic fashion? Why are steps not taken to control it? Doesn't Congress have the power to do it? Doesn't the president?

Yes, indeed. Powerful and influential as the bureaucracy may be, it is not impregnable. It does not function in a walled and armored city, repelling all intruders. It does not manufacture its own money and determine its own life—except by congressional and presidential license, mandate, or default. For members of Congress or the president to say that the bureaucracy is an omnipotent force in itself is nonsense. Any time it wants to, Congress, with the president's approval, can tear the bureaucracy apart and put it back together just about any way it chooses. But although Congress mildly despises the bureaucracy as a kind of poor relation that is willing to act as toady to Congress whenever necessary to get a handout, the crucial point is that Congress *does* look upon it as a relative, an offspring (perhaps a clone). The jobs the bureaucracy carries out are jobs that Congress created. Many of the bureaucracy's policies are written into law by Congress. And Congress and the bureaucracy have close working ties with pressure groups.

And those close working ties can have results very harmful to the public. For a good example, let's look at the western states, where three of the most powerful lobbies are the cattle, timber, and mining interests. They have cheated the public for many years. They got away with it by putting plenty of campaign money into the pockets of congressmen on the committees controlling the Interior Department, which hands out the grazing and mining permits, and the Agriculture Department, whose Forestry Service handles logging permits.

The big cattle ranchers lease federal land for a fraction of what private leases would cost and leave much of it so overgrazed it looks like a desert. The Forestry Service exists mainly to help the big timber companies make a profit by destroying our national forests. Whatever the companies spend to build roads through our national forests to get at the trees is deducted from what they pay for the timber. Often, this means they get the timber for nothing. Not only does the taxpayer lose tens of millions of dollars a year, but the land is left scalped and rutted with roads—totaling 380,000 miles nationwide today—enough to circle the globe nearly fifteen times.

The mining rip-off supervised by the Interior Department is incredible. The Mining Law of 1872 was passed to stimulate small-scale economic activity on the frontier. It allowed people to prospect on federal land, and, if they found promising deposits, to buy it for $2.50 to $5 an acre. Believe it or not, that's still the price. Big corporations long ago displaced small prospectors and "an area the size of Connecticut has been sold for practically nothing. Some 3.2 million acres of federal land, containing $240 billion worth of minerals" is now in corporate hands and "between $2 billion and $4 billion worth of royalty-free minerals are extracted each year" from them. While the corporations take away our minerals, they leave us with polluted groundwater, 12,000 miles of ruined streams, and abandoned mines that may cost as much as $60 billion to reclaim.

The Iron Triangle

Which brings us to the arrangement sometimes called the "iron triangle" or the "unholy trinity": (1) a particular government bureau chief teamed up with (2) a lobbyist, who represents the industry or business most affected by the actions of the bureau, and (3) the senior members of Congress who sit on the committees with jurisdiction over the bureau. For example, members of the agriculture committees of Congress, officials in the Department of Agriculture, and representatives of the giant agribusiness industries whose welfare is uppermost in the USDA's bureaucratic heart, are mostly cut from the same mold. They are old friends. They have worked on legislation together for many years. They play golf and poker together. They send one another Christmas presents. The same can be said of the people on the military committees, Pentagon officials, and the military-industrialists; of the people on the interior committees, those at the Interior Department, and the big landholders and timber barons of the West; and so forth.

They are *comfortable* with each other. The leaders of Congress are very reluctant to rearrange the bureaucracy in any way that might disrupt those pleasant old relationships that are so profitable to all involved, if not so profitable or constructive for the public in general.

Furthermore, Congress, being somewhat lazy, has come to rely on the bureaucracy so heavily that the bureaucracy exploits the need— as crafty servants have a way of dominating lazy masters. It is the bureaucracy's store of information that gives it the upper hand over Congress. The bureaucracy gathers data about everything from weather trends to how to grow onions; data about the inner workings of the latest ballistics missile and how much the tax-exempt foundations didn't give away last year and how much marijuana is sold at what prices in Abilene, Kansas. There is no aspect of life in America that the bureaucracy does not know something about or does not have ways of investigating.

The bureaucracy's power comes from the kind of basic data around which an industrial nation revolves. That data can be cashed in for big bureaucratic budgets and for the kind of legislation that can be enormously profitable for the bureaucracy's allies in the corporate business world. With its data, the bureaucracy can shade and weight legislation to suit itself and its friends, manipulating the information to show why a particular piece of legislation should or should not be passed. And it can withhold information that would help "the other side," sometimes by simply refusing to supply it but usually by delaying tactics or by pretending it does not know what Congress really wants.

Two-thirds of the bills passed by Congress were not written by Congress nor were they written by those portions of the executive branch specifically responsive to the president; they were written, usually with the assistance of private pressure groups, by agencies within the bureaucracy.

It's good when Congress can get the information it needs out of the agencies, but it's bad when that is the only place Congress can get the information. The executive assistant of one Midwest senator summarized Capitol Hill's complaints:

> We're in their hands. We rely too much on the executive's bureaucracy downtown. . . . We make hundreds of calls a day to the agencies. All these bills are so complex we can't understand them without help from the bureaucrats. At the conference-committee hearing on an education bill, say, somebody is constantly running out in the hall to ask one of the HHS flunkies hanging around the door to call down and find out what a particular formula means. Sometimes I get to feeling there is only one branch of the government—the executive and its bureaucracy.

The President and the Bureaucracy

Although presidents always complain that they have precious little control over the bureaucracy, in some ways they have quite a bit. For one thing, the president appoints all cabinet secretaries and more than 3,000 other top officials. He appoints all members of the independent and regulatory agencies. In short, he hires and can fire at will everyone with an auspicious title like Cabinet Secretary, Assistant Secretary, Deputy Secretary, Deputy Assistant Secretary, *ad infinitum*—everyone entitled to a chauffeur or a silver water pitcher or a private bathroom.

The president has great power to make changes within his own personal fiefdom, that special portion of the bureaucracy known as the Executive Office of the President. Special attention must be paid to the Executive Office, because it came into existence in the one great reorganization achieved by a president. When Franklin D. Roosevelt became president in 1933, he launched his New Deal, which was an assortment of hundreds of new programs that had never been tried before and did not fit easily into the established bureaucracy. Since most of the federal workers were holdovers from the archconservative Republican administrations that had preceded him, Roosevelt feared that if his programs were left to the discretion of the established bureaucracy, they would be mangled. So he set up, within the bureaucracy, new units that were committed to his liberal Democratic administration.

But creating this "new" bureaucracy within the "old" bureaucracy resulted in a Frankenstein's monster—a bureaucracy grown so enormous and so complex that Roosevelt had a hard time finding out all he needed to know about its activities in order to operate the White House intelligently. The answer, he felt, was to expand his supervisory staff, and he asked the Congress to let him do this. Congress, though suspicious of his ambitions, gave him permission to create a little kingdom of advisers and lieutenants.

On September 8, 1939, Roosevelt issued Executive Order 8248, which has been described as a "nearly unnoticed but nonetheless epoch-making event in the history of American institutions." The order created the modern "presidency"—as seen apart from the president. To be exact, it created the Executive Office. Under that general title are grouped the president's White House staff and, in addition, such command lines as the Domestic Policy Staff, the Council of Economic Advisers, the National Security Council, which sometimes has more immediate influence with the president than the Defense Department and the State Department put together, and the Office of Management and Budget (OMB).

The OMB is the nerve center of the president's organized effort to control the bureaucracy and to influence (and sometimes threaten) Congress. The OMB puts together the president's budget, which is another way of saying that it establishes, in a dollars-and-cents way, the president's and the nation's priorities.

Aside from the potent brain trust centered in the Executive Office, the president has significant—though not total—organizational powers. Under authority granted him by Congress (through the periodic extension of the Reorganization Act of 1949), the president can shift duties from one department to another, can shift duties from one bureau to another within the same department, and can create new bureaus, new agencies, new cabinet departments. He doesn't have to get congressional approval; he simply has to avoid evoking congressional disapproval. If both houses of Congress have not passed a resolution vetoing the restructuring within sixty days after the president has ordered it, the restructuring automatically takes place.

A president can establish by edict (so long as Congress likes the idea) even whole new cabinet divisions. In 1977 Carter established the Department of Energy and ordered that it swallow two independent agencies, the Federal Power Commission and the Atomic Energy Commission, as well as a host of other scattered energy-related chips of the bureaucracy. In 1979, with congressional approval, Carter divided the Department of Health, Education and Welfare into two departments: the Department of Education and the Department of Health and Human Services. And in 1988, Congress grudgingly ("I can't begin to tell you how many colleagues have told me they wish they had the guts to vote against it," said Representative Steve Bartlett of Texas) allowed Reagan to create the Department of Veterans Affairs.

A president has a good chance to make his imprint through the so-called independent regulatory agencies. The terms of members are staggered to prevent any one president from making appointments in wholesale numbers at the beginning of his term, but it doesn't take long—thanks to deaths and pressured resignations—before he can claim a majority of appointees on every agency.

Resistance to Reform

Still, since the passing of the spoils system,* few presidents have been able to lay their ideological or methodological imprint very deeply on

---

*Operating on the maxim "to the victor belong the spoils," this political patronage system rewarded campaign workers and contributors with public office, with little attempt to match job and appointee. The spoils system flourished unchallanged during most of the nineteenth century; reforms finally took hold after the assassination of President Garfield by a disgruntled office seeker, and in 1883 the Civil Service was created.

the bureaucracy. Naturally, from president to president there will be changes in bureaucratic moods and ideals; the quality of federal work will fluctuate according to the morality and public-spiritedness of the president and the people he brings into government with him. If, on top of the normal inefficiency of government, one president success-fully encourages an additional quantum of inefficiency, that does not mean another president down the pike cannot swing the pendulum of efficiency back to at least the historical status quo and, with prayer and luck, perhaps even a bit further. But only a bit. No president can hope to herd along like sheep the several million people on the federal payroll.

Perhaps the best-known quote to illustrate a president's lack of con-trol as "chief administrator" came from President Franklin D. Roosevelt. Roosevelt reportedly had this exchange with one of his aides:

> When I woke up this morning, the first thing I saw was a headline in *The New York Times* to the effect that our Navy was going to spend two billion dollars on a shipbuilding program. Here I am, the Commander in Chief of the Navy having to read about that for the first time in the press. Do you know what I said to that?
> No, Mr. President.
> I said: "Jesus Chr-rist!"

Divine expletives have been invoked by many frustrated presidents. Another old story around Washington is about the White House visi-tor who suggested a management innovation to President Kennedy. "That's a first-rate idea," Kennedy replied. "Now let's see if we can get the government to accept it."

After leaving the Kennedy administration, Arthur Schlesinger wrote, "Getting the bureaucracy to accept new ideas is like carrying a double mattress up a very narrow and winding stairway. It is a terri-ble job, and you exhaust yourself when you try it. But once you get the mattress up it is awfully hard for anyone else to get it down."

Another celebrated outburst of frustration was President Nixon's to his White House aides:

> We have no discipline in this bureaucracy. We never fire anybody. We never reprimand anybody. We never demote anybody. We always promote the sons-of-bitches that kick us in the ass. . . . We are going to quit being a bunch of goddamn soft-headed managers. . . . When a bureaucrat deliberately thumbs his nose, we're going to get him. . . . The little boys over in State particularly, that are against us, we'll do it: Defense, HEW—those three areas particularly. . . . There are many

unpleasant places where civil service people can be sent. . . . When they don't produce in this administration, somebody's ass is kicked out. . . . Now, goddamnit, those are the bad guys—the guys down in the woodwork.

Presidents, like the public, have learned that there can be times when cursing is one of the few comforts available to those who attempt to deal with a wayward and obstinate bureaucracy. The sad story is echoed by their henchmen. Frank Carlucci, who has served in top jobs everywhere from the White House to the Pentagon, says that it takes "from six to eight months for a presidential directive to be translated into agency guidelines and reach the action level," and in some extreme cases, he says, the decision-to-action translation takes two or three years.

Carter came into office vowing to make a sweeping overhaul of the ninety-five-year-old Civil Service system. But the reform law passed in Carter's second year did not accomplish a great deal. During his campaign for the presidency, Carter had promised that he would reduce the 1,900 federal agencies to 200, but after he took office he quietly jettisoned that idea and no hint of it is found in the new law. The timid spirit behind the much-ballyhooed reform was illustrated in talks Carter made to Civil Service employees to win their support for the legislation; he promised them, "No one will be demoted, have their salaries decreased, or be fired as a result of reorganization. You need not fear that." So much for the great crusade.

Why the caution? Why the tentativeness?

There are several reasons why even the most reform-minded president moves slowly, if he moves at all, in overhauling the bureaucracy.

Stubborn Voting Bloc

First of all, he is not confronted with bricks but with people. And since he is not a dictator, he must depend to a large degree on persuasion. The attitudes of the bureaucracy run deep through many layers and become locked in by time. A president, whether he wants to or not, inherits all these old attitudes of the bureaucracy.

Charles Frankel, who served as assistant secretary of state long enough to know why things fall apart, explains: "A new policy dispossesses people; it takes their property away. The point of what they know how to do, of what they have always done, is lost. The old outfit, the old group, loses its rationale, its importance, its internal pecking order." Resistance, therefore, is massive.

The resistance can be broken successfully only by convincing the key members of the bureaucracy, which usually means the bureau chiefs, that the proposed changes are worth making on behalf of the country and that they will not hurt the individual bureaucrats. That kind of persuasion takes time.

Selfishly, and practically, a president also is aware that people who work in Civil Service, especially those who belong to government labor unions, are vigorously active in politics—when they think their livelihoods are threatened. The government employee unions give generously to political campaigns. The civilian federal labor force—plus wives or husbands and children over age eighteen—make up a voting bloc of well over six million that would frighten just about any president away from radical reformation of the Civil Service. Where is the politician who would risk losing the next election merely for the sake of a better government?

Prisoner of Rich

But the most important reason presidents never seem to get very far with reform of the bureaucracy is that they are also subject to the same intense business–industry pressures that shaped and welded together the previously mentioned "iron triangle." By the time a politician reaches the White House, he has become a prisoner of big money. Try as he will (though few seem to give it much of a try), he cannot escape its influence. He has become indebted to people who contributed to his campaigns, gave him introductions to people who could help him rise, gave him inside tips on stock investments so he wouldn't be dependent on his political salary, voted him into the best clubs and made him feel important. They asked him to speak to their trade organizations (and paid him handsomely for sharing his clichés with them).

And all they ask—demand—in return is that the tone and thrust and mechanism of the government be maintained primarily to benefit big money. If there are any significant changes in the mechanism, they expect the president to let them help chart the change.

When a president picks his departmental secretaries, undersecretaries, and other top-level officials, he usually selects them from the economic interest groups with a stake in their duties. This is as true of liberal presidents as of conservative ones. You should be able to guess the results of these appointments, but if you can't, then take guidance from what William Proxmire said when he was chairman of the Senate Banking Committee:

It is a truism, supported by hundreds of examples, that the great departments of the government routinely act on behalf of the major economic interests under their jurisdiction rather than in the public interest. The Treasury represents banks. The Defense Department promotes the military–industrial complex. The Agriculture Department puts the interests of big farmers ahead of the public interest. These great agencies of government, designed to protect and promote the interests of all citizens of the country, end up promoting the interests of the few and promoting them against the public interest when the two conflict.

This is particularly true when the occupant of the White House not only permits, but wholeheartedly encourages, the special interests to take over the bureaucracy—as we shall now see, by examining the Reagan administration.

"Depending Upon the Men Who Administer It"

Presidents do have two potent ways of influencing the bureaucracy: By writing budgets that drastically curb (or generously expand) the bureaucracy's ability to carry out its congressionally mandated programs, and by his imposition of a moral or immoral tone—an atmosphere of wanting to do, or ignore, what is right—through the people he appoints to high positions. (Congress, of course, can frustrate a president by changing his budget and rejecting presidential appointees, but this entails more skirmishes and battles than Congress usually is willing to handle on a broad basis).

Reagan, who truly hated some portions of the bureaucracy, did more than any other modern president to tear it down in these two ways. Agencies handling such propeople regulations as environmental protection laws, industrial safety laws, and antitrust laws received much less money than they needed to carry out proper enforcement, though Congress prevented Reagan from starving them to death.

Every agency, big or small, with the responsibility to police business conduct was reduced to a skeleton staff of investigators, and many remain in skeleton condition today.

If there is one thing that taxpayers need for their protection, it is more and better federal auditors. They are in incredibly short supply. The scarcity of good auditors allowed the savings-and-loan industry to run wild (more on this in Chapter 9) in an orgy of thievery and bad loans, leaving taxpayers to pick up the $150 billion bill. In addition to guaranteeing the S&L loans, the government has $745 billion outstanding in other subsidized loans and loan guarantees (home, farm, college, veterans' loans, and so on), and the bureaucracy has kept such a loose watch that *no*body has even a good guess as to how much these programs have lost to bad management. The Federal Housing Administration, which insures $275 billion worth of American mortgages, didn't have its first full audit until 1989, the year after Reagan left office—at which time it was discovered that it was almost broke.

In short, Reagan left the bureaucracy with too few investigators and law enforcers to operate properly, even if they wanted to.

Quality, too, declined radically. Of Reagan's top- and middle-level appointees, scores were convicted of crimes or resigned under a cloud or, even worse, were allowed to stay in their jobs even after being caught in disgraceful actions. Some were corrupt because they refused to carry out either the spirit or the letter of the laws they were being paid to enforce. Others were just downright crooks. And some of those who participated in the unethical activities continued to hold high office in the Bush administration.

When President Franklin Roosevelt signed the Securities and Exchange Act in the mid-1930s, a group of his closest advisers was at the ceremony standing in the semicircle behind him. One was Ferdinand Pecora. As Roosevelt scrawled his signature, he asked, "Ferd, now that I have signed this bill and it has become law, what kind of a law will it be?"

"It will be a good or a bad bill, Mr. President," Pecora replied, "depending upon the men who administer it."

Reagan Most Corrupt?

There, more than the budget, is the key to the success or failure of a bureaucracy. Good laws can be ruined by bad administrators. Bad laws can be rescued at least in part by good administrators. To a very significant degree, a president is responsible for the reputation of his administration because of the men and women he appoints. By that measure, Ronald Reagan will probably go down in history as one of the most corrupt presidents, not because he was personally so but because of the multitude of administrators who came into his administration and went sour.

The character of the federal government under the Reagan administration is easy to read from these comparative statistics, compiled by the U.S. Justice Department in a Report to Congress on the Activities and Operations of the Public Integrity Sector for 1986:

Federal Officials	1975	1985
Indicted	53	563
Convicted	43	470
Awaiting trial	5	90

Lying ahead in the remaining two years of the administration were some of the most notorious cases, such as that of Michael Deaver, once one of Reagan's closest advisers, convicted of perjury, and that of Lynn Nofziger, convicted of illegal lobbying—a conviction that was later overturned by an appellate court dominated by Reagan appointees. And then there was Edwin Meese III. After spending four years on Reagan's White House staff, Meese wound up his government career with three years at the Department of Justice—three years marked by crisis and scandal.

In fact, so many scandals and rumors of illegal conduct swirled around Meese that he came to personally represent the "sleaze factor" in the administration, and his usefulness as attorney general was seriously reduced; he had to excuse himself from participating in many key cases. For instance, because he had obtained Teamsters Union support for Reagan, he was unable to participate in the Justice Department's decision in 1988 to file suit against the crime-ridden union.* Early in 1988, Meese's chief deputy, Arnold I. Burns, and the head of the department's criminal divisions, William F. Weld, quit, saying that Meese had lost touch with reality and that he had turned the department into a nut house—"a world of illusion and allusion: a world in which up was down and down was up, in was out and out was in." Furthermore, said Weld, he believed Meese should have been prosecuted on charges of accepting bribes from his longtime friend, E. Robert Wallach, who was later convicted of racketeering.

After a fourteen-month investigation of Meese's misuse of his office, a special federal prosecutor concluded that he had probably violated federal tax and conflict-of-interest laws.

---

*In his memoirs, Allen Friedman, who was at one time vice president of the Teamsters Union, says that in 1980 he delivered a suitcase filled with money to Meese in a Washington hotel room, to be passed on to Ronald Reagan. Friedman, who describes the money as a "bribe," says it persuaded Reagan to appoint Jackie Presser to be one of his economic advisers. Presser, then president of the Teamsters, had very close ties with the Mafia (*Power and Greed: Inside the Teamsters Empire of Corruption* [New York: Franklin Watts, 1989]).

The Premier Example of Sleaze

What happens when the bureaucracy is run by people of questionable ethics who receive no supervision from the White House or from Congress? The most chilling answer to that question can be found in the conduct of the Department of Housing and Urban Development during the Reagan years.

HUD was established in 1965 primarily to provide housing for low-income people. The Reagan administration, which had no interest in helping the poor, cut HUD's budget by 75 percent; this still left many millions for Reaganites to plunder, and plunder it they did. When this scandal started coming to light in 1989, Reagan offered his usual excuse: "I didn't have the slightest indication of what was going on." What went on was this:

Samuel Pierce, who was HUD secretary throughout the Reagan years, had time to help friends and political cronies get fat contracts, but otherwise had little interest in the department and turned over much of the department's operation to aides such as his executive assistant, Deborah Gore Dean, whose training in "housing" was as a bartender in a hotel restaurant her family owned. She may not have been academically sharp (it took her eight years to get through college), but she sure knew how to exploit bureaucratic power for political friends. A Republican consultant said of HUD in those days that it was "known in the street" as "sort of the last place where you can legally steal money in the government."

A lot of illegal stealing went on, too. Private escrow agents, hired by HUD to handle sales of foreclosed properties, stole at least $20 million and maybe as much as $100 million. (An agent who stole $5.5 million became known as Robin HUD.) An estimated $1 billion was lost through private mortgage insurers who snookered HUD officials into bad deals. Because Pierce is black, one might suppose that he would have zealously protected programs that were meant to supply housing for poor blacks. He didn't. In one instance, $1 million set aside for low-cost housing was spent instead to build a swimming pool for Republican Senator Alfonse D'Amato's neighbors.

Perhaps the most outrageous scandal had to do with the many top Republicans who creamed off millions of dollars as "consultants." They got rich for doing nothing but making a couple of phone calls. Among the better-known members of the gang were James Watt, Reagan's notorious Interior Secretary (we'll have more to say about this charming chap later on), who received $420,000 for what he cheerfully admitted could be described as "influence peddling"; and that old crooked retread, John N. Mitchell, Nixon's attorney general who went to jail for his part in the Watergate scandal. He dropped around to pick up $75,000 for "consulting."*

Business in Catbird Seat

Outright illegalities were not so omnipresent as were conflicts of interest and Reagan's tendency to turn the government over to special interests, particularly big business.

Some of Reagan's most notorious appointments were at the Department of Interior, which is supposed to serve as trustee for the American people of invaluable wilderness areas, vast tracts of timber, millions of acres of grazing lands, and some of our most promising deposits of minerals, including oil and gas.

Eleven of the top sixteen officials appointed to the Interior Department by Reagan had previously been employed by or served clients in the five major industries regulated by the department: Six had past affiliations with the oil and gas and mining industries, three with the timber industry, two with the livestock industry, and three with the utilities industry. Talk about conflict of interests: Reagan's first interior secretary, James Watt, was president of the Mountain States Legal Foundation, which used money from oil, gas, mining, utility, and timber companies to fight conservationists and environmentalists. Robert Burford, director of the Interior Department's Bureau of Land Management, was part-owner of a ranch that leased 32,000 acres of federal land, and was on record as advocating the transfer of public land to private ownership. The department stopped filing criminal charges against violators of the strip-mining law and stopped trying to collect millions of dollars in civil penalties. The Bureau of Land Management dropped more than 805,000 acres from wilderness protection in ten

*One of the most discouraging spinoffs of having rot develop in a part of the bureaucracy is that even when reformers come along, it seems to take forever to clean up the place. Ten years after the Reagan gang had departed, much of the rot was still at HUD, and President Clinton, after two false starts, appointed Andrew Cuomo to take it over and get tough. Accepting the job, Cuomo asked and answered: "What is HUD? It is scandal. It is inefficient. It is wasteful. It is the destroyer of neighborhoods. It is the place where good taxpayers have their dollars ripped off. I'm going to change everything you believe about HUD. But first of all, I'm going to acknowledge all of this. Acknowledge it, then resolve it." Lots o' luck. (*The New York Times,* January 4, 1998.)

Western states (thus enabling commercial exploiters to get their hands on it).

Awful OSHA

Ethics at the Occupational Safety and Health Administration could be measured in the career of Thorne Auchter, Reagan's first head of OSHA, who resigned in 1984 after it was alleged that he approved the dismissal of $12,080 in penalties and a dozen safety citations against a Kansas company owned by a firm of which he was president. He also refused to establish a formaldehyde standard that DuPont opposed; coincidentally, perhaps, Auchter owned almost $22,000 in DuPont stock. Auchter was replaced by Robert A. Rowland, who resigned in 1985 after being accused of taking part in the decision not to impose tougher rules for the use of chemicals manufactured by companies in which he held more than $1 million in stock. Another of the sterling chaps at OSHA was Leonard Vance, director of the Health Standards Programs. When a congressional subcommittee, investigating rumors that Vance had blocked efforts to curtail the use of a cancer-causing chemical after meeting privately with the chemical's manufacturer, ordered Vance to turn over office log books showing whom he had met with and when, he said he couldn't because the log books were thrown away after his dogs got sick and vomited on them.

EPA the Worst

But the pinnacle of conflict of interest and servitude to big business during the Reagan administration was reached in the Environmental Protection Agency (EPA).

Referring to Reagan's EPA appointees, *The New York Times* was stung to observe, "Seldom since the Emperor Caligula appointed his horse a consul has there been so wide a gulf between authority and competence. Mr. Reagan's EPA appointees brought almost no relevant experience to their jobs. His administrator, Anne Gorsuch Burford, was a telephone attorney and two-term state legislator who learned about environmental issues fighting Clean Air Act provisions in Colorado." She finally resigned after many members of Congress accused her of withholding documents and of delaying a toxic-waste cleanup grant to California so as not to help the Democratic Senate campaign of then-Governor Jerry Brown.

The top officials surrounding Mrs. Burford were of a similar character. Rita M. Lavelle, assistant administrator for hazardous waste, was a former public-relations officer for Aerojet-General, which was in trouble with the EPA before she arrived in Washington. In 1984 Lavelle was convicted, and served part of a six-month term, for lying to Congress about Aerojet-General waste dumping and for obstructing a congressional inquiry. Robert Perry, general counsel for the EPA, was formerly an Exxon lawyer; he was investigated for possible perjury for telling Congress, despite evidence to the contrary, that he had not participated in a settlement to clean up a toxic waste dump used by an Exxon subsidiary. Mrs. Burford's chief of staff, John E. Daniel, was a former lobbyist for the Johns-Manville Corporation, the largest manufacturer of asbestos, a leading cause of fatal lung diseases.

In short, the EPA, one of the most important and complex regulatory agencies in the government, was being run by industry lobbyists and industry lawyers who couldn't seem to forget their old alliances.

The Beat Goes On, and On

Reagan may have been unusually bad in his misuse of the bureaucracy, but other abuses in other administrations are all too easy to find. If it's because powerful economic interests run the show, we shouldn't be surprised. It's what to expect from the "physics of politics," or at least one law of that physics, namely, that more pressure can be exerted through a narrow opening than through a broad opening. The narrow opening is at the top of the economic power structure. As Adolf Berle pointed out:

> Eight hundred corporations probably account for between 70 percent and 75 percent of all American business activity; 250 corporations account for perhaps two-thirds of it. . . . Far and away the major part of the American supply-and-exchange system is constituted of a few hundred (at most) clusters of corporate enterprises, each of whose major decisions are determined by a central giant.

Needless to say, it is much easier for a dozen of those central giants to agree on ways to promote their policies than it is for millions of random citizens to make countermoves. The advantage in pressure politics, therefore, is always at the top. And since these special-interest groups maintain an unrelenting pressure on the bureaucracy and especially on the regulatory agencies, it is to be expected that these elements of government eventually give in, to varying degrees, and become subjects rather than masters of industry.

Can the Bureaucracy Be Reformed?

Because so many portions of the bureaucracy are no longer responsive to the needs of the general public, and because they do their narrowly selfish work without fear of reprisal from the public, it may seem useless to talk of reform. But it isn't useless to talk of reform; it is only naive to expect much.

How do we go about trying to change the bureaucracy for the better? There is no magic formula. But whatever formula we use, there will be one essential ingredient: outrage. Nothing that is deeply entrenched in government can be changed without the public's raising hell. This is true in electoral politics; it is doubly true in dealing with the bureaucracy. It was the concentrated anger of miners that forced the government to start making more than a perfunctory enforcement of mine safety laws. It was the organized anger of Nader's followers that forced the government to set and enforce auto emission standards. It was the organized outrage of Common Cause and its allies that brought about the passage of the Freedom of Information Act and pried open the bureaucrats' secret files. Only if the public maintains its anger at being cheated by the people it supports so royally can the reform continue. But reform won't come by marching around this Jericho until its walls suddenly come tumbling down; it will be a matter of picking the wall apart, one stone at a time, one problem at a time, one issue at a time, one agency at a time. And it will be done by a dozen methods—by lawsuits, by editorial campaigns, and especially by making the defects of bureaucracy such a hot topic that politicians eagerly seek office to get a chance to carry out proposed changes that the public is demanding.

Here are a couple of guidelines worth keeping in mind:

Shun "Good Business" Reformers

It can't be repeated too often: Reform of the bureaucracy should never, never be turned over to any person or group that proposes to do it in the name of "good business."

For proof of the wisdom of that advice, one need only recall that it was "good business" reforms in 1970 that changed the Post Office Department, then a part of the cabinet, into the United States Postal Service (USPS)—one of those strange, semi-independent government operations. The USPS was the brainchild of a commission headed by Frederick R. Kappel, former chairman of the board of American Telephone & Telegraph. Potent lobbying for the "reform" was carried out by a so-called Citizens Committee for Postal Reform, which included such "citizens" as E. I. du Pont de Nemours, Standard Oil of New Jersey, Bank of America, and Pan American World Airways. These citizens persuaded Congress that some "good business" management was needed to keep the Post Office from running at a deficit. So Congress went along with the argument, without pausing to ask why big business didn't mind if the Defense Department and Agriculture Department and other departments ran at a deficit, but insisted that the Post Office Department—the one department that aided even the lowliest citizen's daily life—should be forced to try to pay its own way.

Big business's reformed post office was something less than a howling success. The business-bureaucrats said that the service needed to be mechanized, so billions of dollars were spent on mail-processing machinery—and today mail service is no more reliable than it was in the last year of the old Post Office. In the good old days when the government ran the show, one could depend on overnight service between, say, Washington and New York. Today, with the business-bureaucrats running the show, the only sure way (well, *almost* sure way) of getting overnight service between Washington and New York is to pay the special express mail rate of $11.75. Regular postal rates increased 100 percent during the first decade, an added expense that drove some magazines and newspapers out of business. (That was an ironic turn of history, considering that, from the beginning of our nation, Congress viewed cheap postal rates as the best way of promoting the press and thereby uniting the nation and maintaining a free government.)

While the Postal Service is considered an independent agency, it is legally subject to the will of Congress, just like all the other independent agencies—or at least it is supposed to be. But something is haywire, because Congress voted 393 to 12 not to raise the first class stamp to 33 cents (from 32 cents) in 1998, but the Postal Service Board of Governors ignored Congress and approved the increase anyway—and got away with it. That 1 cent increase is no small matter. It translates into another $1 billion in annual revenue. And why did the Postal Service need it? After all, it had been making billion dollar profits for several years at the old postal rate.

Perhaps they wanted more money to play with. When Postmaster General Marvin Runyon stepped down in 1998, he got a retirement party costing $124,000, paid for by us postal customers. And 900 postal executives received year-end bonuses that averaged $10,400. Every time you buy a stamp, you help pay for those bonuses, whether you want to or not. That's government run like a business.

Perhaps "reformers" who come to the government from a corporate background are at a disadvantage. Perhaps they are accustomed to thinking of government as something to be exploited rather than as an opportunity to provide better service. Alfred Bloomingdale, the Diner's Club president who helped his old friend Ronald Reagan select his top bureaucrats, was quite candid about their criteria. "We're surrounding Ronnie with the best people—the ones we'd hire for our own business," he said, explaining that he looked upon the federal government as "twice General Motors or three times General Motors, but it's General Motors."

He couldn't have been farther off base. Government isn't General Motors. It isn't AT&T or Exxon, either. And as the bureaucratic debacle of the Reagan years ultimately proved only too clearly, the first rule of reforming the bureaucracy should be to keep the reformation out of the hands of those who think it is just another big business.

Increase the Accountability of Bureaucrats

Make it easier to get rid of the officials who get too chummy with the special interests they are supposed to be regulating. Job security is nice, but the security of the consumer and our national interests should have a higher priority. It wouldn't do to return to the spoils system, but perhaps President Jackson was right: The bureaucracy needs shaking up from time to time.

But even bureaucrats of good conscience must be given guidelines, whether they work in a regulatory agency or elsewhere in government. Reshuffling the bureaucracy is not enough. Each unit in government must be told not only what it is in existence for, but in which direction it must move. Its marching orders should be specific. It is not enough, for example, to tell an agency to figure out a way to conserve energy resources. The agency must be given a specific target to shoot for. It must be made to come up with a plan by a certain date. If the plan is a sloppy one or does not fit with the nation's priorities, the officials who wrote it must be made to realize that they will be either fired or banished to a pencil-sharpening post in Kansas.

Even while mulling over these possible remedies, one should bear in mind that, to paraphrase John Donne, no bureaucrat is an island. The bureaucracy is not an island either. It draws its guidance and power from Congress and the president. When and if other elements of the government become more honest, industrious, and public spirited, the bureaucracy will probably follow suit. Good political habits are just as capable as bad habits of inspiring imitation.

CHAPTER 7

Parties and Pressure Groups

Democracy's Gang Warfare

*One of the greatest disabilities of citizens in this
country is that they don't know their own power.*

RALPH NADER

ONE BALMY APRIL MORNING IN 1989 AN ESTIMATED 600,000
people, mostly women, poured like a slow-moving flood from the
Washington Monument grounds down Pennsylvania Avenue and
Constitution Avenue, converging on the Capitol and on the U.S.
Supreme Court building. Many were wearing clothes of white, purple,
and gold—the colors of the women's suffrage movement. Everywhere
were signs and T-shirts and buttons and banners proclaiming such
things as "My body, my baby, my business" and "Keep your laws off
my body." Some, like actress Jane Fonda, came with their children.
One woman pushed a baby carriage emblazoned, "Motherhood by
Choice." A fourteen-member delegation from one cluster of families
carried a sign, "Four Generations for Choice and Equality." But the
most prevalent signs bore the messages "Never Again" and "Keep
Abortion Legal." A few women waved coathangers, a hateful symbol
of the days when women who were desperate for abortions had to
submit to quack doctors operating with strange instruments and under conditions of questionable sanitation.

But the proabortion demonstrators were not without opposition. A
few hundred antiabortion protesters lined the parade routes, standing

344

back on the sidewalks and holding up signs such as "Abortion Is Murder" and "What If You Were Aborted" and, sarcastically, "Save the Seals and Whales but Kill the Children." Several in this group were dressed as babies, in bonnets and bloomers, shouting repeatedly, "What about the babies?" At one point, the two sides faced off angrily, one side shouting, "Life! Life! Life!" and the other side screaming back, "Shame! Shame! Shame!"

The month before, there had been 67,000 antiabortionists in Washington and at that time they had won President Bush's support for their cause.

This time, for the pro-abortionists, the White House was silent. But the pro-abortionists weren't in Washington to lobby the president. Or Congress. Their mission was a strange one: to intimidate the U.S. Supreme Court and to persuade it that public opinion would not stand for the clock to be turned back to the days prior to *Roe* v. *Wade,* which allowed pregnant women to choose abortion—a blazingly controversial decision that the Court was scheduled to review within two weeks.

Never before had any massive group of demonstrators tried to influence the Supreme Court's opinion. The Court was supposed to be sacrosanct. But these women weren't impressed by that reputation. Said Molly Yard, president of the National Organization of Women and one of the parade's leaders, "The Justices are all political creatures, and they do understand political opinion. And I have to believe the Supreme Court doesn't really want to tear apart the social fabric of the country."

The presence of these pro and con hordes of women on the streets of Washington may have posed the possibility of violence. Their demonstrations may have been an inconvenience to Washington police, who had to bring out their mounted patrols and work overtime. And perhaps the Court's members may have been embarrassed to hear speakers refer to them so rudely. But were the demonstrations undemocratic? Were they unconstitutional? Were they "un-American"?

And the same could be asked of demonstrators who act more aggressively—like the hundreds who sat down in the middle of a Washington avenue, inviting arrest (and they were arrested), to protest the lack of government concern for the homeless; and like the hundreds of farmers, protesting falling farm prices, who drove their huge tractors through downtown Washington, intentionally tying up traffic and creating a public nuisance. Were *they* doing something unconstitutional, undemocratic, un-American?

No way. These demonstrators were all exercising their rights under the most revered part of the Bill of Rights, the First Amendment, which guarantees "the right of the people peaceably to assemble, and to petition the government for a redress of grievances." To enjoy that right, Americans (and some foreigners), in every imaginable configuration and every degree of political clout, sometimes somberly and sometimes cheerfully, never tire of thronging to Washington. Farmers, Native Americans, women's liberationists, antiwomen's liberationists, coal miners, Iranian students, marijuana advocates, save-the-whalers, ban-the-bombers, homosexuals, senior citizens, truck drivers, traveling salespeople—organizations representing an endless list of groups are always marching on the government.

Sometimes they are accused of acting selfishly. But that's a foolish complaint, for selfishness is part of the foundation of politics. President Kennedy's most famous admonition was "Ask not what your country can do for you; ask what you can do for your country." That may be a nice ideal to shoot for, and even to practice in one's nobler moments. But the practical citizen is more often motivated by the thought, "What's in it for me?" So long as it is balanced by a reasonable amount of compassion, there is nothing wrong with that. There is a great deal right with it, in fact.

Power of Togetherness

People can't be motivated to pay taxes and go to the polls simply to be "good citizens." They pay taxes and vote for the best available politicians because they hope their money and ballots will result in jobs, homes, recreation, old-age security, and all of the other standard life supports, not only for themselves but for their neighbors. (The decent citizen doesn't want the good life *only* for himself or herself. To that extent, politics is something more than selfishness.)

So the basic question confronting the citizen is: How does one translate desire into fulfillment? How does the individual citizen make the politicians take notice, and make them respond properly?

The answer, unfortunately, is that the average individual citizen won't get very far acting alone. Success in politics depends on cooperation, on working with others, on *organizing*.* The most pleasant myth shared by Americans is that the individual ballot is pivotal in a democracy. The myth—although, like all good myths, there is an element of truth in it—is

---

*No one knew that better than the early leaders of the labor movement, whose first objective was to receive the protection of the political establishment. As the legendary labor leader Joe Hill told one of his allies shortly before he was executed by a Utah firing squad (on a hoked-up charge): "Goodbye Bill. I die like a true blue rebel. Don't waste any time mourning. *Organize!*" (M. B. Schnapper, *American Labor* [Washington, D.C.: Public Affairs Press, 1972], p. 377).

perpetuated by such pep talks as this, from John Gardner, former Secretary of Health, Education and Welfare:

> What difference does one vote make? It can make a lot. In most
> elections, those who fail to vote could have changed the result had
> they gone to the polls. For every vote in Richard Nixon's plurality over
> Hubert Humphrey in 1968, 150 people did not vote. The 1960
> presidential election was decided by less than one vote per precinct.
> In 1962, the governorship of Minnesota was decided by ninety-one
> votes out of more than one million cast. The outcome of the 1968 U.S.
> Senate election in Oregon turned on four-tenths of one percent of the
> 814,000 votes cast. Local races—for mayor, for city council, for school
> board—have sometimes been decided by a single vote.

One might also point out that Lyndon Johnson would probably never have gotten on the road to the White House if he had not won his first senatorial race in Texas by a mere 87 votes; and that Jimmy Carter would not have been elected president in 1976 if 8,000 votes in Ohio and Hawaii had gone instead for President Ford—a mere 8,000 out of 79,633,000 cast. Such slender victories do lend an aura of power to the individual ballot, supplying the kind of drama that the rather dry electoral process sorely needs. But it is quite misleading. There is a cumulative potency to individual ballots only because there is an *organized framework* that holds them together. This organized framework is the political party.

Organizing through Parties

We might be able to function politically without parties, but that's doubtful. Even in their most impotent condition, parties serve necessary functions.* First, they supply the machinery by which candidates

---

*Sometimes major parties get so sick they seem ready to die; but they always bounce back. In August 1977, a Gallup poll found that only one American voter in five wanted to be identified as a Republican. This 20 percent slice of the electorate was, Gallup said, "the lowest point [for the Republicans] recorded in Gallup surveys conducted over the last four decades." Robert Teeter, whose Opinion Research Company takes surveys for the Republican National Committee, said, "The thing has bounced around between our 18 percent and 23 percent for a long, long time." The Gallup poll mentioned above found 49 percent of the persons interviewed identifying themselves as members of the Democratic Party—a healthy six percentage points higher than five years earlier. To reverse the trend, Republican leaders contemplated radical changes. Ronald Reagan even suggested that a change in party name might be in order. But four years later Reagan was in the White House, and Republicans—who were outnumbered sixty-two to thirty-eight in the Senate in 1968—were now comfortably in the majority, at least temporarily.

are weeded out and nominated. Second, they are a convenient rallying agency—collecting campaign money for politicians at most levels and recruiting campaign workers at all levels. Third, parties offer a kind of shorthand way for a voter, with luck, to figure out what the candidates stand for. That is, parties offer labels, and labels simplify choices, identify alliances, and almost always communicate something about orientations. In politics with far-flung mass electorates, party labels and party identification have served as the principal links between candidates and voters.

Third-party labels have usually been especially eloquent. The States' Rights Party, the Prohibition Party, the Greenback Party, the Socialist Labor Party—all these parties laid their beliefs on the line. The voters may not have known much about the candidates, but the party labels gave them a good clue as to why that political organization had sprung into being and what changes it offered.

Third parties generally appeal to persons powerfully motivated by ideology. The ultraliberals or the ultraconservatives or the ultrasomethings are most likely to be found supporting third-party candidates. It is fair to say that these citizens would probably rather make a strong statement in defeat than a bland statement in victory. As a rule, third parties are electoral protest movements; their followers, fed up with the Establishmentarian arrogance and seeming indifference of the major parties, do not really expect to win but do hope to throw a monkey wrench into the normal two-party procedure.

For example, Ross Perot and his Independent Party followers, about whom we'll have more to say later on, threw several monkey wrenches into the presidential election of 1992 and drew off enough wild and disenchanted conservative voters to ensure the defeat of President Bush. And lately the Green Party—with a heavy emphasis on environmental matters, as its name implies—has achieved some influence, largely at the state and local levels, in some western states.

The Greens' power is mostly negative, siphoning strength from the Democratic Party, which is the party most of its members would probably otherwise support. In a 1998 special congressional election in New Mexico, the Green candidate won 15 percent of the vote and thereby ensured the election of the Republican candidate. Sometimes third-party voters have to ask themselves: Is making our "message" in this way worthwhile if it results in electing politicians we really don't like?

One or the other of the two major parties nearly always wins. There is no written guarantee to that effect, of course, but the odds are so heavily stacked in favor of the two-party system that even the strongest third party can only hope, on a long chance, to deprive either of the major parties of a victory in the electoral college and thereby throw the election into the House of Representatives.* If this should ever happen, the third party's leaders might carry enough influence in the House to swing the election—at least, that is the perpetual pipe dream.

The weakness of third parties is easily seen in the fact that only five times since the Civil War have third parties polled more than 10 percent of the vote in presidential elections: in 1892, the Populists, whose candidate was James Baird Weaver; in 1912, the National Progressives and Theodore Roosevelt; in 1924, the National Progressives and Robert M. LaFollette; in 1968, George Wallace leading the American Independent Party; and in 1992, Ross Perot and his Independent Party. The only successful third party was the fledgling Republican Party, which in 1860 elected Abraham Lincoln.

The two major parties, being in control of the state and federal legislatures, have passed electoral laws that make it extremely difficult for third-party challengers to get on the ballot and to obtain adequate campaign funds. Democrats and Republicans have written the rules so that only they can win; not since Zachary Taylor was elected as a Whig in 1848 has anyone taken up residence in the White House as anything but a Democrat or a Republican. Not since Theodore Roosevelt won eighty-eight electoral college votes in 1912 (behind the Democratic winner, Woodrow Wilson, who got 435 electoral votes, but far ahead of Republican William Howard Taft, who won only eight electoral votes)

---

*The only federal elective officials not chosen directly by the people are the president and the vice president. They are elected by the electoral college, as it is quaintly called, an ancient institution that has been with us since the nation's founding and whose usefulness is much debated. This is how it works: When we vote for a presidential candidate, our votes are translated into votes for a slate of electors representing that candidate's party. Each state has as many electors as it has senators and representatives. The District of Columbia, though it has no senators or representatives, has three electors. So there are 538 members of the electoral college. It takes 270 to elect the president and vice president. The electors meet on a specified day in December and cast their votes, virtually always (though there has been a maverick or two over the years) for their party's nominee. If no candidate gets 270 votes, the presidential election moves into the House of Representatives, with each state's delegation of members combining to cast one vote (thus, for example, Nevada's one representative would have as much clout as New York's thirty-nine representatives). That last-ditch routine has not been utilized in modern times.

Another bizarre possibility of the electoral college system is that a candidate could win the presidency and yet fall heavily short in the popular vote. It could have happened in 1988. *U.S. News & World Report* estimated that although Dukakis lost by 7 million votes, a shift of 700,000 votes in close states like California, Illinois, Missouri, and Pennsylvania would have given him an electoral college majority (Kevin Phillips column in *Christian Science Monitor,* December 1, 1988). *The New York Times* estimated that Dukakis could have won the presidency in the electoral college by a shift of only 590,000 votes in 11 states (November 20, 1988).

has a third-party candidate won more votes than a presidential nominee of a major party.

But in recent years, the two major parties, despite their continued dominance of national politics and despite their acknowledged usefulness, have begun to lose influence and status. Several things have brought about the parties' decline, especially in presidential elections.

The Decline of Party Influence

It used to be that most delegates to national conventions were chosen in party caucuses, and candidates were picked in the legendary "smoke-filled rooms." It was a clubbish sort of thing; party leaders and big-money contributors to the party had an inordinate amount of influence on the outcome of the caucus elections and the convention results. But now most delegates to the national conventions are picked in state primaries—the wide-open primaries in which all party voters are welcome. The result is that the delegates—like the candidates—are reaching the national convention with less commitment to party bosses, less loyalty to party positions, and fewer obligations to party support. The "smoke-filled room" is a thing of the past.

Jeane Jordan Kirkpatrick, former Democratic and now Republican who was the ambassador to the UN under Reagan, appraises the significance of this trend:

> The capacity to appeal directly to voters makes it possible to bypass not only the party leadership, but the dominant political class, their standards and their preferences. The campaigns of George Wallace and Ronald Reagan could not have gotten off the ground without primaries. Nor could the campaign of George McGovern. Most observers believe that primaries give extremist candidates a better chance than they would otherwise have. . . .
>
> What caused the proliferation of primaries? Primaries are the institutional embodiment of the persistent American suspicion of organization. They reflect the conviction that in passing through the web of personal ambitions and structural complexities that compose a political party the voice of the people is distorted beyond recognition. In American tradition the populist instinct and the distrust of organization go hand in hand.

To repeat a crucial point made in the Congress chapter, a second reason for the decline of party influence is the creation of new money sources.

It used to be that the major political parties provided the *only* dependable machinery for collecting and distributing campaign funds. Party leaders squeezed money from rich businessmen, who in turn squeezed the politicians for favors. This kind of *quid pro quo,* afflicting every era but particularly virulent around the turn of the century, in what campaign financing expert George Thayer called "American's Golden Age of Boodle," was best seen in the careers of such men as Senator Boise Penrose of Pennsylvania.

One of the most powerful men in Congress, he had an appetite for corruption as hearty as his appetite for food (weighing 350 pounds, he could polish off four dozen oysters and a duck before tackling the main course). When labor leader Samuel Gompers appealed to him for help in passing anti-child–labor legislation in the U.S. Senate, Penrose protested, "But Sam, you know as damn well as I do that I can't stand for a bill like that. Why, those fellows this bill is aimed at—those mill owners—are good for $200,000 a year to the party. You can't afford to monkey with business that friendly."

So offensive had the purchasing power of big business become by 1907 that public opinion forced Congress to pass the Tillman Act, prohibiting direct corporate contributions to federal campaigns. But the law was not enforced. In 1925, Congress tried again by passing the Federal Corrupt Practices Act, which once more forbade corporate contributions to federal elections. It was moderately successful, but the smart fellows running big business still found numerous ways to get around the law. They gave themselves "raises" that were then paid over to their chosen candidates. Or they lent their candidates company planes and autos and office equipment; company employees were sometimes assigned full-time to the candidate's campaign—favors that were worth many thousands of dollars. And sometimes millions of dollars in corporate contributions were "laundered" through foreign banks in ways that made them very difficult to trace.

The crookedness of federal campaign financing reached a modern zenith in the Republican Party's reelection effort for President Nixon in 1972. The scheme, as Professor Larry Sabato reminds us,

> included practices bordering on extortion, in which corporations and their executives were, in essence, "shaken down" for cash donations. Up to $30 million was legally and illegally contributed by the business sector to Nixon in 1972, thanks to an ingenious "quota system" devised by the president's fundraisers. The system set as the expected "standard" contribution 1 percent of a wealthy individual's net worth or 1 percent of a company's gross annual sales, though this was

thoughtfully scaled down to a miserly $100,000 for large corporations. Eleven major American companies (including American Airlines, Goodyear, the 3M Company, and Gulf Oil*) and a number of excorporate executives were found guilty of illegal contributions.

The flagrant campaign corruption of the Nixon years once again created such public outrage that Congress had to pass reform legislation, the Federal Election Campaign Act of 1971 and a major amendment in 1974. As a result of two features of that amendment, parties lost their *primary* role as a collection agency for campaign funds.

On the one hand, the new law provided a way for federal funds to be substituted for private funds in presidential campaigns. In the presidential primaries, candidates would receive federal matching funds for all contributions of less than $250 from individuals. In the general election, government funds would pay *all* campaign expenses—so long as the nominees agreed not to accept any direct gifts from individuals. And of course, corporate donations were still banned, as they had been since 1907.

Greedier Congress

On the other hand, for Congress the 1974 law made changes that created even greater corruption than had existed before. It happened like this:

Congress refused to clean up its act with the kind of taxpayer-funded program that it set up for presidential races, which provides money for challengers as well as incumbents. Sitting members of Congress had no intention of helping those who wanted to take their seats from them. Furthermore, Congress wanted to encourage, not discourage, the flow of money. So it opened a rich source that had been

---

*Do not get the idea that Gulf was generous only with Richard Nixon. In the same presidential campaign, it had contributed to two other candidates, Wilbur Mills and Henry Jackson, both Democrats. Since those gifts were violations of the Corrupt Practices Act, Gulf lobbyist Claude Wild, Jr., was fined all of $1,000 and the corporation was fined $5,000. No wonder corporations were breaking the law without fear. Gulf had been doing so since the mid-1950s, distributing millions of dollars to presidents, members of Congress, and at least eighteen governors. Wild, who did most of the distributing, complained that it was "physically impossible for one man to handle that kind of money," so at various times he used seventeen couriers to deliver money to the hungry politicians. The Senate Ethics Committee voted five to one against taking action against any of the senators who accepted Gulf's illegal donations and the House Ethics Committee didn't even raise the question about members who benefitted from Wild's generosity. Gulf is cited here not as an exception but as a typical corporation on the make (Robert Sherrill, *The Oil Follies of 1970–1980* [New York: Anchor/Doubleday, 1983], p. 57).

outlawed for sixty-seven years: corporations. Members had always managed to get corporate money, of course, but they had to get it on the sly, under the table, and often with the help of party go-betweens. Now they gave themselves a way to go for it directly and legally—and without using the party as an undercover collection point. This was done, as mentioned in Chapter 4, by changing the law governing political action committees (PACs). Before the Federal Election Campaign Act and its amendments of the early 1970s, labor unions could contribute through PACs; corporations could not. Now they could.

What's more, while the act limited each individual to a maximum contribution of $1,000 per candidate per election, it permitted each PAC to give a candidate $10,000 per election (primary, runoff, and general). The new law says an individual can spend a total of $25,000 on *all* candidates in a year, but there is no ceiling on the total a PAC can spend—and in a typical election year there will be at least thirty PACs that each spend well over a million, and another thirty-five or forty PACs that spend over half a million. On top of this new freedom, the U.S. Supreme Court ruled in 1976 that any person or any PAC could spend as much money as it wanted to spend on behalf of candidates *if* it was done without the candidates' knowledge or cooperation. In other words, so long as the donors didn't ask permission of a candidate, they could go out and spend millions on billboards and television slots and so on to help him or her. At both the presidential and congressional levels, it was an open invitation for candidates and PACs to cheat by pretending they weren't working directly together.

With those changes in the election law, a new and perilous era began, for money makes the political world go round, and PACs—particularly business-sponsored PACs—have spun it dizzily.

Not long after the 1974 amendment passed, the U.S. Chamber of Commerce, the National Association of Manufacturers, and the Republican National Committee all began running seminars on PAC formation and to push corporate executives toward forming and financing PACs. In 1976, there were 1,242 PACs; in 1989 there were 4,828—and most of them were business PACs (including one for beer distributors, who named theirs—naturally—Six-PAC). They are gushing cash. And it has created two great dangers.

The first and most critical result is the money craze that has settled over Washington like a smog. One glum lobbyist put it this way:

> I'll tell you what's different about Washington now. Money. It's just more pervasive. This proliferation of PACs, these around-the-clock

fund-raisers—all for money. Everyone expects it. Unless you hit the drum, you're not in the game. Unless you give your 'max,' unless you lay out your $5,000 at a fund-raiser, you don't have access. And even five grand will only get you a return call these days.

Another lobbyist, who has been raising money for Democrats for years, complained, "Not so long ago, a senator or a fund-raiser would call and ask for $1,000 and you'd give them $500 and they'd be grateful. People now call and ask me to get my clients to give $100,000 or $200,000 or $250,000."

But if some of the donors are sick of the money rat-race, so are some of the receivers. John Glenn of Ohio, the former space hero, who was packing up to leave the Senate in 1998 after a twenty-four-year service, said, "I'd rather wrestle a gorilla than ask anybody for another 50 cents. Campaign financing, fund-raising, is the most stinking mess in government. To see an election coming up and not be raising money—that's a joy."

Splintered Interests

The second danger from PACs is that they have splintered politics into a thousand narrow issues, and have forced politicians to give up flexibility and the broad vision. To be sure, some of the richest and most potent—and sometimes meanest—PACs are built around a broad-based ideology: the National Conservative Political Action Committee, the National Congressional Club, and the Fund for a Conservative Majority on the right; the National Committee for an Effective Congress, the Fund for a Democratic Majority, and the Committee for the Future of America on the left. Although PACs such as these are not totally partisan, those with a liberal bias usually support Democrats and those with a conservative bias usually support Republicans, and in that respect they indirectly strengthen the two-party system.

But many PACs are fanatically concerned with a single passionate issue: abortion, prayer in the schools, support for Israel, gun control, and the like. These committees judge politicians not by their general voting record but by their votes on those particular issues. Most commonly, PACs are built around a single economic issue. To a degree, politicians who take money from PACs of this sort must shift their allegiance from parties to special-interest groups: medical interests, oil interests, labor union interests, auto industry interests, and so on. Selfish interests, as noted earlier, are a reasonable part of politics. But when they are coupled with so much money, they can have an unwholesome and disrupting influence.

A Surface Sameness

A third reason for the decline of party influence in politics has been the trend toward sameness. One of George Wallace's favorite explanations for running on a third-party ticket was that "there ain't a dime's worth of difference" between the two major parties. A great many Americans, including many who would disagree with everything else George Wallace ever said, have come to feel that the Democratic and Republican parties do overlap in policy at too many points.

Is this an accurate impression? The answer must be a waffling one: yes and no. There is no dramatic difference in the federal programs that operate during a Democratic administration from those that operate during a Republican administration. There is, however, a very noticeable difference in *emphasis.* Democrats are far more willing, and even eager, to spend money on social programs. The result was acknowledged by Robert Dole, the Republican candidate for president in 1996: "We do have this antipeople image that I think is unfair, but it is there."

Under the Reagan administration, the antipeople image grew much larger and became set in concrete. The atmosphere was so callous in this regard that even some of the most conservative—but politically sensitive—leaders of the party became uneasy. Senator Paul Laxalt of Nevada, one of Reagan's closest friends and advisers, was at the White House shortly before the president was to make his 1983 State of the Union address. Reagan and his aides were briefing Republican leaders on his plans for the year. After about an hour of this talk, Laxalt recalled later, he became alarmed because "I never heard the reality of unemployment raised except in passing." (At that time the unemployment rate was at a record high.) So Laxalt broke into the discussion and told his colleagues that he was "really bothered" by a recent incident in Minneapolis, where 12,000 unemployed workers applied for 200 jobs. The other Republican leaders dismissed the report, saying it had probably been orchestrated by local labor unions. "If that was orchestrated by the union," Laxalt replied, "then the people I saw interviewed on television were excellent actors. They had the ring of truth. This is middle-class America, people who want to work, and are out of work. Plain political and moral reality dictates that we address the problem."

Laxalt is an unusual Republican. For most leaders of that party, unemployment is usually rather far down on their list of problems to be faced. Republicans are much more concerned, as a group, with such things as a sound dollar and low inflation.

The apparent "sameness" of the parties is in effect a tribute to the success of the Democrats, going back to the 1930s when the character of the modern Democratic Party was developed under the presidency of Franklin Roosevelt. The 1930s were a time of critical economic depression. Under Roosevelt, the Democrats put together what is known today as the "welfare state." When private enterprise couldn't do the job, the government stepped in. Faltering businesses and failing banks received government financial assistance. Since one out of every five adults in the labor market was unemployed and the nearly bankrupt businesses of America weren't about to hire them, the government set up its own work programs—programs to build post offices and bridges, programs to build highways, programs to build dams and clear forests—and hired millions of the unemployed. The Social Security system was set up so that old folks who had saved nothing would have at least a small guaranteed income for their retirement. Government subsidies and loan guarantees were pumped into the housing market. And dozens of other programs were established to prop up the economy. In this effort to spend the country back to prosperity, the federal government had to go heavily into debt.

The Republican Party opposed all these steps. It advocated a balanced budget. It opposed government interference. It believed that a rigorous application of capitalism and free enterprise would rescue the faltering economy. It believed that if individuals couldn't take care of themselves, then they must depend on private charities.

That's how the Republicans felt in the 1930s. But as the years passed and it became evident that a great majority of the public, and of the business community as well, enjoyed the Big Brother role of the federal government in economics, the Republicans tacitly at first and then overtly adopted the Democratic programs. No longer did they oppose Social Security or federal work programs, and they certainly didn't oppose the bountiful subsidies that the federal government was handing out to Republican businessmen. By the 1960s, the once "radical" programs of Franklin Roosevelt were looked upon as standard pieces of the government furniture by both parties.

Reagan, an extreme conservative who was a hark-back to Republicanism of the 1920s, came into office vowing that he would reduce government spending so radically that the budget would be balanced within three years. At the end of three years, he was indulging in more deficit spending and rolling up a larger federal debt than any free-wheeling Democratic administration had ever dreamed of doing. Although, in comparison to the outlay during the last year of the Carter administration, Reagan sharply reduced environmental and consumer protection programs as well as social programs—food stamps, school aid programs, and the like—he still was spending more, much more, on these programs than had the last powerful Democratic president, Lyndon Johnson, father of the Great Society. It was the *manner* in which Reagan administered the government— tilting taxes in favor of the wealthy, adjusting regulations to help corporations and hurt consumers, showing an indifference to civil rights and civil liberties—not the total amount he spent doing it, that made the difference and let people know a conservative Republican was in office. And this manner of government continued to a somewhat lesser degree under George Bush when he moved into the White House in 1989.

Hardening Arteries

Meanwhile, the Democratic Party has become more conservative. It is no longer as flexible, as experimental, as progressive, as willing to take a chance as it was in the 1930s. The social programs are still around, but the party has lost some of its zest for them. It is no longer the party (as Vice President Alben Barkley described it) of the "poker-playing, whiskey-drinking, hiya-honey Democrats" who carried the banner of the underdog. After the 1970s, Democratic Party politics seemed almost as tuned to big business and the big banks as were those of the Republican Party.

Obviously, party labels, though still useful, are no longer so helpful as they once were. The voter cannot always be sure what the labels mean. Conservatives who voted for Nixon in 1968 could have sworn that he would never, never reopen diplomatic relations with Communist China or devalue the dollar or participate in deficit spending or agree to an arms deal with the Soviet Union. Those were things that a left-winger might do, but never a Republican. Right? Wrong. Nixon did them all. Liberals who voted for Jimmy Carter in 1976 hoped—on the basis of his campaign promises—that organized labor would have a louder voice in a Democratic White House, that the government would reform the tax laws to crack down on millionaires' loopholes, and that the giant corporations' power in government would be sharply restricted. None of these things happened.

Clinton won in 1992 by making the same promises, and, like Carter, he failed to carry them out.

Clinton further altered the traditional meaning of "Democrat" by being the leader of a cadre that called themselves "new Democrats," by which they meant their goal was to be fairly conservative in economic matters, but more or less traditional Democrats in social matters (equal rights, etc.). In many ways it was difficult to tell the "new Democrats" surrounding Clinton from just plain moderate Republicans, and in one moment of bitter self-analysis he said, "We're just a bunch of Eisenhower Republicans."

Indeed, he sometimes sounded like one. He proclaimed "the era of big government is past" (which of course it wasn't) and promised "the end of welfare as we know it"—slogans meant to convey the feeling that the liberalism bequeathed by Franklin D. Roosevelt's New Deal was dead in the Democratic Party.

From the beginning of his administration in 1993, Clinton's emphasis did not seem significantly different from that of the Republican he had just defeated. Clinton seemed more eager to promote a strong stock market and international trade than to promote programs that directly benefit the Democrats' traditional following: the unemployed, the lunchpail workers, the racial minorities, and the middle class.

This is not to say that he was indifferent to those groups; some of his programs helped them. And he might have taken a more traditionally Democratic approach if the House of Representatives had remained in the hands of a Democratic majority. But only two years into his presidency (as we mentioned in the chapter on Congress), there was a dramatic reversal of power under the Capitol dome. For the first time in forty years, the House was taken over by Republicans under the brilliant if eccentric leadership of Speaker Newt Gingrich of Georgia. The Senate was already in the hands of Republicans. To get his programs through this hostile environment, Clinton had to rely on threats of a veto and on compromise. For many Democrats, he compromised far too much.

Speaking for them was liberal pundit Jim Hightower: "Having Clinton as a Democratic president is like getting bitten by your pet dog—the bite will heal, but you never feel the same about that dog again."

Not the Same Old GOP

But if the tone and character of the Democratic Party leadership has undergone some startling changes in recent years, to some extent the same thing has happened to the Republican Party (of course, party character is a fluid thing and it can always change back). The Grand Old Party of today is not the GOP of your grandfather's day, and not even of your father's day. While major corporations and Wall Street fat cats are still—financially and in spirit—the main support of the

Republican Party, the rising influence of the religious right and the more demanding voice of small business has significantly diluted the party's old power source.

There are passionate differences developing between the conservative and the moderate wings of the Republican Party, and a further split between the economic conservatives and the social conservatives. For two decades, the social conservatives (many of whom make up what the press refers to as the "Christian right-wing") have complained that the GOP establishment has betrayed them by promising big things to get their votes and then giving little help on issues they consider paramount: abortion (they're against it), school prayer (they're for it), and homosexuality (against it), while concentrating mostly on tax, budget, and regulatory legislation.

That's only partly true. Actually, the Republican establishment has tried to please the Christian right by pushing antiabortion and pro-prayer legislation. And it treats gays as pariah. Senate Majority Leader Trent Lott told a television audience in 1998 that homosexuals are sick, "like kleptomaniacs and alcoholics." A spokesman for the Texas Republican Convention in Fort Worth that year likened a group of gay delegates to the Ku Klux Klan and child molesters.*

What the Republican mainstream establishment fears is that extremist interest groups will use their money (and they have many millions) to overwhelm political campaigns with their television advertisements in such a way that the more moderate message of the candidates themselves will be drowned out. Some, for instance, blame the huge volume of advertising by Christian conservatives for foisting an extremist image on Tom Bordenaro, the Republican candidate in a special California congressional election in 1998. He lost.

"Is this the future of campaigns?" asked Bordenaro. "Pretty soon, all we're going to have to do is file and sit back and let all these independent expenditures run the show. It's going to be rolling the dice whether you get into office or not."

Oddly, there are also grumbles from the big business wing of the party. Despite the fact that the Republican-controlled Congress has done many multibillion-dollar favors for corporations and rich individuals, some of the GOP's biggest contributors threaten to start

---

*By contrast, President Clinton in November 1997 became the first sitting president to address a gay and lesbian civil rights organization, although the White House made the breakthrough rather quietly. The party's support of homosexual rights doubtless hurts it politically on a national scale, but gay voters are important in some states and local races, and their campaign contributions run into the millions of dollars.

buying (so to speak) more Democrats if the Republican Congress doesn't become more profitable for them.

Getting squeezed in the middle are GOP politicians who are just plain pragmatists and don't want to chase off the independent voter by seeming to be either social extremists or corporate whores.

Ticket-Splitting

Losing faith in party labels, more and more voters are shunning them and calling themselves "independents." The rise of the independent voter has been the crucial development in American politics during the past forty years. Democratic membership has dropped, but Republican membership hasn't risen proportionately. The deserters have simply become "independent," and their influence on politics is seen in the decline of "straight-ticket" voting and the rise of "split-ticket" voting, something that the voting machines now make very easy to do (more than half the states don't even permit levers for straight-ticket voting). This is one reason for the chaos that grips Washington: There is no majority party in control of both the White House and Congress, with a cohesive program that most members of the party can agree on. Before 1956, no presidential election in the twentieth century—and only three in the nineteenth century—yielded a president of one party and a Congress of another. But it has happened in seven of the last ten elections.

Obviously, the electorate is somewhat schizophrenic; it has a split personality. Pollster Louis Harris asked the voters for a reason, and they told him 60 to 35 percent preferred a divided government because they want one party to check the other. "They just don't want one party of scoundrels in there," said Harris. "It's born of the cynicism toward politicians."

One should be highly skeptical of the voters' excuse. A much more probable reason for their ticket-splitting is that they sometimes prefer the Democrats' proven pork-barrel talents and sometimes the Republicans' old-fashioned notions. Another probability is that the nation has become "Southernized."

In the great period of Democratic unity and political power in Washington, during Roosevelt's New Deal, no region was more loyal to the party's economic policies than the South. Because it was the poorest region, it benefited the most from those policies. But when, in the 1960s, a Democratic president pushed through Congress (with strong resistance from southern members), a passel of civil-rights legislation, the old New Deal alliance began to break up. Party loyalty shifted sharply. In the 1950s, three-fourths of white southerners identified themselves as Democratic. By the 1980s, only a third called themselves Democratic. Meanwhile, in the North, many urban, ethnic, blue-collar Democrats, who had always voted Democratic because of labor alliances, became angry about the party's special efforts to bring blacks into the employment mainstream (threatening union seniority programs) and invading old ethnic neighborhoods with mostly black housing projects. Labor bosses still endorsed Democratic candidates for president, but it is estimated that 40 percent of the rank and file vote Republican.

In short, the economic self-interest that had been the glue holding the working-class and middle-class New Deal coalition together wasn't strong enough to withstand the acid of racism. Or perhaps it would be more accurate to say not racism but "antiminorityism," for the Democratic party also became the haven for those advocating women's rights and homosexual rights and many other minority rights—highly emotional symbols that prompted gut-wrenching reactions.

An Unfashionable Label

The fate of the party parallels the vicissitudes of the term "liberal," which is only natural because the Democratic Party is at bottom the liberal party. In the era of Franklin Roosevelt, "liberal" was a label that the party carried proudly.* Roosevelt himself called the Democratic Party "the bearer of liberalism and progress" and "the party of militant liberalism." After Roosevelt, the party avoided the label for strategic reasons, but many politicians still prized it, though it became less and less safe to do so as conservative Republicans in the 1950s equated liberals with "pinkos" and "parlor pinks." Arthur Schlesinger theorized that the popularity of liberalism comes in fifteen-year cycles. Perhaps so. After sinking in popularity in the late 1940s and throughout the 1950s, it revived in the 1960s and then sank again in the late 1970s.

---

*Everyone has his or her own definition of "liberal" and "conservative." One might say—with no guarantee of satisfaction—that a liberal is a person who believes government should boldly intervene in private affairs when necessary to promote social justice, and a conservative is a defender of the status quo who believes that, when change must come, it should come slowly and in moderation. But for the best, and probably the most accurate, definitions, one should turn (as in most of politics) to the humorists. Mort Sahl has ventured this definition: "Liberals feel unworthy of their possessions. Conservatives feel they deserve everything they've stolen." Perhaps the very best definition is by Ambrose Bierce: A Conservative "is enamored of existing evils, as distinguished from the Liberal, who wishes to replace them with others."

The label is still on the bottom of this cycle, as shown by the way Bush successfully thrashed his opponent with it in 1988. In describing Michael Dukakis, the one word Bush repeated most often, always in tones that implied it was a sexually transmitted disease, was "liberal." It was an effective bit of demagogy. Sometimes he slyly referred to it as "the abominable 'L' word." Not until the campaign was almost over did Dukakis, a lifeless and cautious candidate, come out of his shell, boast of being a liberal, and defend the noble traditions of liberalism in American politics. But his campaign had by then already died in the shroud of "liberalism" that Bush had wrapped around it.

Clinton did not have that trouble because, as Molly Ivins said, "only a fool or a Republican would mistake him for a liberal."

Power of Racism

The support of the South is still considered by many to be essential to winning the presidency, and Democratic candidates usually don't do very well in that region. Which isn't surprising. When President Johnson signed the Civil Rights Act of 1964—opening educational opportunities, jobs, and public accommodations to blacks—he turned to an aide and said, "I think we just delivered the South to the Republican Party for a long time to come."

By which he meant the white majority. And he was right. But why did he sound like that was such a change? In fact, his landslide victory in 1964 was the first time since 1948 that a Democrat had won a majority of white votes nationally, to say nothing of the South. Blacks give Democratic presidential candidates 80 to 90 percent of their support, but that usually isn't enough to make up for the whites who left the party.

In the two presidential elections following Johnson's signing of the Civil Rights Act of 1964, Democratic presidential candidates did not win a single southern state. However, though the situation was obviously precarious, it was not fatal, as Jimmy Carter showed when he carried every state of the Old Confederacy in 1976. His being a son (and former governor) of Georgia obviously made the difference by enabling him to win enough—though still not a majority of—white votes in that region. This spurt of loyalty from southern whites didn't last long. In his bid for reelection, he lost every state in the Old Confederacy. Twelve years later, the next Democratic winner was again a son of the Deep South, Bill Clinton of Arkansas, who won seven of the eleven Old Confederacy states—and nationally he became the first Democrat in three decades (since Lyndon Johnson in 1964) to win a plurality among whites. But in his successful bid for reelection in 1996, he won only four southern states, even though his Republican opponent was that bumbling old pol, Bob Dole.

Why the change in Carter's and Clinton's drop in popularity in Dixie between their election and reelection campaigns? Apparently both presidents had disappointed too many of their white southern brethren by appointing so many blacks to high federal offices and by pushing programs that would help blacks and Hispanics and other minorities.

The South is an extreme case. What about nationally?

In 1985, Democratic chairman Paul Kirk paid $200,000 for a study—5,000 interviews, an unusually large number for a survey—that concluded that if Democrats ever hoped to recover the white support needed to win the presidency, they must quit favoring programs to help the economic and social underclass. (Whites comprise more than 80 percent of the voting-age population, and CBS's 1988 exit poll showed 67 percent of the white voters had middle-class incomes.) The report noted that members of the white middle-class "have a whole set of middle-class economic problems today, and the Democratic party is not helping them. Instead, it is helping the blacks, Hispanics, and the poor. They feel betrayed." The report went on to say that middle-class whites

> view gays and feminists as outside the orbit of acceptable social life. These groups represent, in their view, a social underclass. . . . They feel threatened by an economic underclass that absorbs their taxes and even locks them out of jobs, in the case of affirmative action. They also fear a social underclass that threatens to violate or corrupt their children. It is these underclasses that signify their present image of the Democratic Party.

Party leaders felt the report was too hot to release, so they ordered all but a few copies destroyed. One of the copies leaked out four years later.

The kind of timidity expressed in that report has begun to change, however. Ethnic groups, feminists, and gays have begun to flex their muscles at the ballot box—and in campaign financing—as never before; and politicians welcome votes and dollars from almost any source (although Dole, with fanfare, did turn down contributions from a homosexual organization for his 1996 presidential campaign).

Making up 14 percent of the population, blacks are, as they have always been, the largest minority in the country, and while they overwhelmingly give support to Democratic candidates—if and when they vote—they have a low turnout (plus the fact that 14 percent of black men are currently or permanently barred from voting either because they are in prison or because they have been convicted of a felony).

Jesse Jackson, a Baptist minister and one of the national leaders of the civil rights movement, set out in the early 1980s to greatly increase black power at the polls. He was a veritable sorcerer in getting millions of blacks to register to vote and then turn out on election day. In 1984 he ran for the Democratic presidential nomination and although he made a couple of critical blunders (including alienating many Jews by calling New York "Hymietown"), he carried forty-one congressional districts and seven major cities, polling 3.5 million votes. Not bad for a beginner. In 1988, Jackson pulled off what must be considered one of the miracles of American politics. Out of an original field of six Democratic candidates, he finished second in the primaries with 7 million votes, or 29 percent of the total. More important, about 2 million of those votes came from whites—almost as many as had gone to establishment wheelhorses Albert Gore, Richard Gephardt, and Bruce Babbitt put together.

Jackson's successes had a trickle-down effect. David Dinkins, New York City's first black mayor, and Virginia's L. Douglas Wilder, the first elected black governor in the nation's history, were greatly helped by Jackson's own national campaigns and the vast black voter registrations he had galvanized. Equally important to the future of the Democratic Party, as journalist Marshall Frady has pointed out, was that "Where other civil rights leaders had mainly sought connections with the affluent white community, Jackson pioneered in seeking a link between blacks and the white working class."

Hispanic-Americans, many of whom are recent immigrants, are numerically and politically behind blacks on the national level—but they are gaining fast. From 1992 to 1996, the number of registered Hispanic voters rose by about 30 percent to 6.6 million, and Hispanic leaders hope to add another 2 million by the year 2000. These new voters are concentrated in populous states like New York, California, and Texas; and at least three out of four new Hispanic voters are registering as Democrats. But Democratic politicians know they had better not take them for granted because some Republican politicians—like Governor George W. Bush of Texas—are beginning to woo them eagerly. His brother Jeb Bush, whose wife is Hispanic, was recently elected governor of Florida with the help of Hispanic immigrants (primarily from Cuba) in south Florida.

Voter Disillusionment

Whatever their reason—whether because they feel that the major parties are no longer responsive to the ballot or because they feel there isn't "a dime's worth of difference between them"—more and more voters, or at least a higher percentage of the voters, are staying home on election day. Except for one paltry rise in 1984 and a hefty one in 1992, the turnout in presidential elections steadily declined for four decades: 62.8 percent of the voting-age population voted in 1960; 61.9 percent in 1964; 60.6 percent in 1968; 55.2 percent in 1972; 53.5 percent in 1976; 52.6 percent in 1980; 53.1 percent in 1984; 50.1 percent in 1988; 55.09 in 1992; 49.08 in 1996.

Let's take a look at some of those races.

In 1976, 70 million Americans stayed home rather than choose between Jerry Ford, who had proved his mediocrity through two years of a nonelected presidency, and Jimmy Carter, whose undistinguished term as governor of Georgia hardly indicated prime presidential qualities. Carter won with the votes of only about 27 percent of the eligible electorate.

Ronald Reagan's "victory" over Carter in 1980 was equally impressive for its negative quality. In Reagan, voters were offered a candidate who (according to his biographer, Lou Cannon) had said that the Watergate conspirators were "not criminals at heart," that trees caused more air pollution than autos did, that allowing abortions of malformed fetuses was "not different from what Hitler tried to do," that it was okay for U.S. corporations to bribe foreign governments, and that it might be a good thing if creationism was taught in schools instead of Darwinism. In Carter, the voters were offered a candidate, in political writer Theodore White's reasonably accurate description, "whose motives were pure but his thinking was muddled. He was for a government of charity and a government of austerity at the same time. His problem, in essence, was that he could not quite understand the world in which he lived. Nor his party, which he took over in shambles and left in shambles. Nor the Congress, whose partnership he sought yet disdained."

Given the choice between these two men, nearly half of the voting population stayed home. Many who did vote were motivated by disgust. Reagan won not because he was popular but because Carter had become so unpopular; polls taken by *The New York Times* and the television networks among voters just after they had cast their ballots showed that 38 percent of Reagan's supporters were actually voting *against* Carter while only 11 percent were attracted by Reagan's conservative agenda. "They voted for Reagan over Carter," political scientist Robert L. Peabody summarized, "as the lesser of two evils."

Much the same spirit determined the outcome of the 1988 race between George Bush and Michael Dukakis, a campaign that television commentator John Chancellor described as "insulting." Bush's part in the campaign was accurately defined by columnist Mary McGrory as "cheap and divisive, a cynical exercise in know-nothingism and intolerance," while Dukakis's appearances made him look and sound like (in the words of one of his aides) "a guy whose shoes are too tight." Political professionals in both parties agreed with Republican consultant Robert Goodman's assessment of the electorate's disillusionment and disgust with both candidates: "If the Constitution didn't require it, we wouldn't be having an election this year." No more than 90 million of the 182 million persons eligible to vote actually did so—about 50 percent or the lowest ratio since 1924.

But an even more depressing turnout would occur just two presidential elections down the pike. First, however, came a surprising upswing.

You will notice in our list of turnout percentages that the vote jumped 10 percent in 1992 over what it had been in 1988. Impressive! There were several reasons for the increase. For one thing, voters who had come to feel that presidential candidates were ignoring them were given, for the first time, a chance to confront the candidates in television town meetings. But perhaps the most potent force in shaking the public from its lethargy and apathy was the quirky little billionaire Ross Perot. In their book *Mad as Hell*, a history of the 1992 campaign, reporters Jack Germond and Jules Witcover correctly appraise Perot as "in a real sense the embodiment of the American voter who was fed up with politics as usual and who felt he did not have the luxury of keeping his mouth shut any longer."

Perot had no experience in politics (probably a plus with the public), was blunt and disparaging in his remarks about President Bush and the establishment, used statistics masterfully to show that ordinary taxpayers were being cheated, and generally left the impression that his one desire was to give the government "back to the people— 'the owners' of the country." Demagogue or true populist? It's hard to say, but his message so stirred the somnambulent electorate that, even though he made several crucial blunders (such as dropping out of the race and then coming back in again, and thereby seeming to be an irresolute wacko), he won a surprising 19 percent of the total vote and an even more significant 30 percent of the independent vote, only two percentage points below Bush.

But by the time the next presidential election rolled around in 1996, voters had slid back into apathy. In 1994, in a last spurt of rebellion, they had given majority power to Republicans in the House of Representatives for the first time in four decades. But that rebellion had backfired by causing gridlock in the power struggle between the White House and Congress. Washington seemed stuck in the mud. With another four-year dose of Clinton having an appeal only because the alternative was Republican Bob Dole—who carried all the bruises and plastic surgery of a politician who had been around Washington for thirty-five years—more than half the potential voters stayed home and Clinton was elected with only 49.24 percent of those who did turn out.

Disguised Apathy

The turnout and atmosphere for lesser political races can be just as bad, or worse. The typical legislator is sent to Washington with the active support of about 27 percent of the potential electorate in his or her political territory. In state and local elections, a candidate can usually win with the votes of less than 20 percent of the eligible electorate. In 1998, less than 17 percent of those old enough to vote turned out in statewide primaries. Ten states recorded their lowest turnout ever. It's part of a trend that has driven down participation by 25 percent in three decades.

On the surface, this is a puzzling situation. The slump in political participation has hit America at the same time that the government has taken great strides toward making the task easier. The Voting Rights Act effectively ended discrimination in the South toward black voters; residency requirements for federal elections have been eased for transients; more than half the population live in states where voters can register simply by returning a postcard. Until 1975 most American citizens who were not proficient in English could not vote with ease because the ballot was written only in English, but the Voting Rights Act has since required that bilingual ballots be provided in areas where the language minority population is greater than 5 percent. (In a place such as Los Angeles County, where Hispanics make up almost 30 percent of the population, this is obviously a significant lowering of barriers.) Still—the voters stay away. Why?

Ballots versus Bucks

The truth is, the experts don't know why. Some think that in good economic times—and the '90s were good—people lose interest in politics. Some theorize that many people have simply stopped having much faith in politics because they think their vote doesn't matter that much, in the scheme of things. This slice of the electorate has become disspirited at least partly because of what they hear—and see—of the influence of big-money lobbies and massive special-interest groups.

And who can blame them for feeling disspirited? Money talks, as never before in modern times. President Clinton kicked off an unusually gluttonous weekend of golf and fund-raising at a swanky Florida resort in November 1997 by telling the fifty loyal donors who were with him, "The party with the most money wins," and then extracting $50,000 from each of them. What did they get in return? Ultimately, who knows? But at the moment they got what they came for: the most important ear in politics. They told him their desires; he listened, and we may fairly assume he listened sympathetically.

Which doesn't mean they all got what they wanted from him, in terms of support for their corporate wish list. But they did get what most of the big contributors want first of all from the politicians they support: access. As Johnny Chung, the controversial fund-raiser for President Clinton, put it: "The White House is like a subway: You have to put in coins to open the gates."*

The great heaps of coins that were put into both Democratic and Republican gates of power created some of the most noxious headlines of the late 1990s. For $10,000 or more (usually much more), contributors might get to have coffee or dinner at the White House, or for really big bucks, get to spend the night in the Lincoln bedroom.† If the White House wasn't for sale, it at least seemed for rent.

Republican congressmen were quick to condemn the shamefulness of these shakedowns. But they were just as busy selling access. Millions of dollars were raised at dinners where trade associations and corporations were required to shell out from $10,000 to $100,000 a table and, in return, were promised a chance to snuggle up in "issue briefings" with the Republican Congressional leadership. The GOP method—plus the fact that it controlled Congress—raised twice as

---

*But direct contributions are not always necessary for access. Sometimes long-term chumminess will get you in, if you come from the right power circles. Vernon Jordan was a close pal, golfing partner, and confidant of President Clinton—at least until Jordan testified before the grand jury in the Lewinsky sex case—which surely was one reason dozens of major corporations like Philip Morris and American Airlines were pleased to make him a millionaire for representing them in Washington

†According to Russell Baker, a *New York Times* columnist of black humor, the biggest donors actually get to see the ghost of Abraham Lincoln: "Rumor has it that there is an ascending scale like this: For $2 million raised plus $300,000 cash, Lincoln walks silently through the bedroom. For $3 million raised and $400,000 cash, Lincoln pauses long enough to say, 'You can fool all the rich people some of the time.' For $5 million raised plus $500,000 cash, Lincoln stands at foot of bed and delivers the Gettysburg Address."

much as the Democrats managed to raise for the 1998 congressional elections.

Occasionally, the seedy atmosphere was brightened by an outlandishly candid participant. There was, for example, the wealthy oil entrepreneur Roger Tamraz, who wanted to talk to President Clinton about a scheme to build an Asian oil pipeline. Despite the National Security Council staff's warning that Tamraz had a "shady and untrustworthy reputation," he got into four White House events. Perhaps his donation of $300,000 to the Democrats explains Clinton's hospitality.

Testifying before a Senate committee, Tamraz was unusually blunt: "I'm saying that I did believe my contribution gave me access. It's the only reason, to get access." Referring to the fact that the $300,000 donation had not gotten the desired help, a Senator asked him, "Do you think that you got your money's worth?"

Tamraz responded, to peals of laughter from the Senators: "I think next time I will give $600,000."

In late 1997, Tilman Fertitta, a Houston multimillionaire, hosted a fund-raising dinner for President Clinton. Asked whether it was unfair for the wealthy to get such access to the president, he replied: "That's like saying someone who could afford front-row seats at a fight shouldn't go to it. That's the way the world works."

But what about those who can't afford even the cheapest seats in the peanut gallery? Politically speaking, that's most people. No wonder they're cynical, and they would be more so if they knew just how small, how elite, and how homogeneous the political donor class is. A study financed by the Joyce Foundation of Chicago found that the significant donors comprise just one-quarter of 1 percent of the population; 95 percent are white; 80 percent are men and over the age of forty-five, nearly half are over sixty; and 81 percent have annual family incomes higher than $100,000.

Populist columnist Bob Herbert, commenting on other findings in the survey, wrote:

> You want elite? Twenty percent of the donors had annual incomes higher than $500,000. . . .
>
> Most American families earn well under $50,000 a year and are struggling to make ends meet. They may be concerned about such matters as health coverage and financing their children's education, but it's the guy in the knickers strolling off the golf course who gets to go to the clubhouse and ring up his congressman.
>
> More than half of the campaign donors said they had talked with their member of Congress since the election. More than a third said they had been in touch with both of their senators.
>
> Have you talked with your senator or representative lately?

Birth of "People's Lobbies"

Voters are not apathetic because they don't care about how the nation is run. Their intense interest in that is shown by the fact that many have sought other routes for having an influence in government. In recent years, they have turned increasingly to citizen pressure groups— "public interest lobbies" or "people's lobbies," as they are often called. This is a dramatic new development that had its beginnings about the mid-1960s.

Two-thirds of the major public-interest groups came to life about that time and older groups have had their incredible growth since then. From 1970 to 1990, the Environmental Defense Fund grew 400 percent, the Sierra Club 700 percent, the National Audubon Society 800 percent, and so on.

Some of these "people's lobbies" have grown so large, in membership and wealth, as to take on the sheen of a business lobby. For example, the American Association of Retired Persons, which was founded in 1958 by a retired school principal, has around thirty-five million (middle-aged and older) members and assets of more than $355 million. It spends about $25 million a year to rent a ten-story building in Washington, complete with a marble lobby, and it pays its executive director about $350,000 a year. Its primary purpose (aside from making money, which has sometimes gotten it into trouble with the Internal Revenue Service) is to lobby Congress to protect Social Security and Medicare.

Organizing through Lobbying

Lobbies are as old as our government. Their freedom of operation is guaranteed by the Constitution. From the very beginning, special pleaders filled the rooms outside the House and Senate chambers—that is, they jammed the lobbies, for which they were named—as well as the taverns where congressmen might be found just as often. There, they seized the legislators' lapels and spilled out their needs (often accompanied by some money or a round of drinks). The lobbyists have almost always represented commercial, manufacturing, and banking interests. Profit, power, land acquisitions, franchises—in short, money—were usually behind their efforts, and they rarely were above passing around money to obtain their objective.

In some eras, the corruption of Congress by lobbyists became quite scandalous and open. In the early 1800s, one of the best-known lobbyists was a gent named Edward Pendleton, who operated a gambling house on Pennsylvania Avenue, within an easy hike of the Capitol, where congressmen were bribed in the form of fixed winnings. The relaxed morality imbuing Congress after the Civil War found many members, including House Speaker James G. Blaine, living like princes off bribes from industrial and business lobbyists. Special-interest legislation benefiting business profiteers shot through Congress without the slightest hitch.

When Woodrow Wilson moved into the White House in the early part of the twentieth century, he discovered the power of big money at work. He reported to the people, "Suppose you go to Washington and try to get at your government. You will always find that while you are politely listened to, the men really consulted are the men with the biggest stake—the big bankers, the big manufacturers, the big masters of commerce. . . . The government of the United States at present is the foster child of special interests."

Many would say that, though "people's lobbies" are now well represented, the rich interests denounced by President Wilson still have the most potent voice in Washington.

The two biggest waves of business lobbies into Washington came to oppose, reshape, or overturn the New Deal legislation of the 1930s and the Great Society legislation of the 1960s. There were 365 lobbyists registered in 1961; there were 23,011 (people's lobbyists as well as business lobbyists) in 1987—43 lobbyists for each member of Congress. They spend like drunken sailors. According to the Associated Press's first complete computerized study of lobby disclosures, done in 1998, businesses, interest groups of every sort, and labor unions spend $100 million a month in the direct lobbying of Congress and the executive branch. And that doesn't count the limited and part-time lobbying, the selling of "strategic advice" and public relations help, the lobbying of 600 professionals on behalf of foreign interests, and the entire field of "grass roots" lobbying, which has been estimated to generate $400 million or more a year. It also leaves out special-interest political contributions, which may not be exactly lobbying but the money sure opens the door for lobbyists. We're talking big bucks. The most extravagant lobbyist for 1997 was the American Medical Association, which spent $8.5 million in just the first six months. The highest-paid lobbyists—such as Jason Berman, head of the Recording Industry Association of America—can knock down $1 million a year. "Everybody in America," grumbled former House Speaker Tip O'Neill, "has a lobby."

The obvious reason for this, as one writer points out, is

> the ever increasing influence of federal law and regulation over the lives of all Americans, as well as over the businesses they operate and the groups they join. The federal government now has rules ranging from the establishment of whisky tax rates to the placement of toilets on construction sites, from the design of atomic power plants to the milk content of ice cream, from foreign arms sales to childproof tops on aspirin bottles. A single clause tucked away in the Federal Register of regulations can put a small-town manufacturer out of business or rejuvenate an industry that was on the brink of bankruptcy. The lobbyist who gets the clause removed, or puts it in, can be worth his salary for one hundred lifetimes. The very magnitude of federal spending [more than $1.6 trillion a year] reflects the stakes involved as competing groups try to get what they consider their fair share, or more.

Helpful Lobbyists

Before going further, let it be clearly understood that not all lobbying is bad. Some of it is very constructive, even essential. Many of the lobbyists who haunt the Capitol's hallways are walking encyclopedias in their specialty; they have scads of information at their fingertips—and information is vital to the successful functioning of Congress. Members cannot be expected to know everything they need to know to make intelligent judgments on such complex and diverse subjects as nuclear fission, natural-resource depletion allowances, offshore mineral exploration, union pension guarantees, and abortion. The experts they hire for their staffs can assist, but they are also unable to cope with all the issues that will confront a member in any given session. Information and guidance from outside experts—which is where lobbyists come in—can be extremely helpful.

As Terry Lierman, a health lobbyist and former staff aide for the Senate Appropriations Committee, told a reporter for *The New York Times:* "A good lobbyist is simply an extension of a congressional member's staff. If you're a good lobbyist and you're working something, all the members know where you're coming from. So if they want information and they trust you, they'll call *you* for information." But, of course, often the congressional members and staffs, rushed for time and crushed by ignorance, depend too heavily on lobbyists. Very often they even allow the lobbyists to write the legislation that affects the industries that hire them—the Cotton Council, for example, supplies the House cotton subcommittee with the bills that relate to the cotton industry. That's too cozy an arrangement.

Revolving Door

The dark, devious, and often harmful side of lobbying is that which makes its impact through money and cronyism. The most effective lobbyists are those who are both experts in their subject and pals with many important people in government. That's why most of the important lobbyists have themselves served at some time in government, making friends on the inside.

The revolving door between government and industry is oiled by money. Former high-level bureaucrats and politicians leave government to become well-paid lobbyists for big business—often the same big-business elements that they were allegedly regulating when they were in government. (Many were alumni of big business at the time they entered government; revolving doors, after all, do go in a circle.) A number of former top staff personnel for the Senate Banking Committee are now working as lobbyists for the American Bankers Association, which has 14,000 member banks and is one of the richest and most persuasive lobbying outfits around Washington. Joseph Califano, who was a former adviser to President Johnson and was Health, Education, and Welfare secretary under President Carter, is a lawyer-lobbyist whose clients, not surprisingly, include health-care organizations.

A perfect example of how the biggest names in corporate America succeed with the help of the right lobbyists can be seen in their 1998 campaign to protect a tax loophole that would be worth an estimated $1.8 billion.

Congress's Joint Committee on Taxation had slipped the loophole into the new tax code in 1996. What the loophole did was perform a magic trick: It allowed American multinational companies to escape U.S. taxation entirely on their overseas profits and at the same time reduce the taxes they must pay to the foreign countries in which they operate.

It took some slick bookkeeping to make it work, and the nation's biggest accounting firms were making lots of money teaching corporate giants like Philip Morris, General Motors, Microsoft, Exxon, and Hallmark Cards how to do the trick. The accountants didn't want the loophole removed from the law, and neither did the companies that were using it.

So when Treasury Secretary Robert E. Rubin tried to remove it, big business went all-out to stop him. It succeeded by hiring some of the best tax-lobbying talent in Washington, including many who had helped write the tax law in the first place. Notably, there was Kenneth Ties, who until the previous year had been the chief of staff on Congress's Joint Committee on Taxation, and Daniel Berman, who until the previous year had been the Treasury Department's top international tax lawyer.

There are around 1,000 former members of Congress still living; at least 185 of them stayed in Washington after they were retired or were defeated, and a good portion of them work as lobbyists. A shady past doesn't seem to hurt them. Bob Packwood, the Oregon Republican who was once the powerful chairman of the Senate Finance Committee, resigned after the Senate Ethics Committee voted to expel him for flagrant and repeated sexual misconduct. But he stayed in Washington and began knocking down $800,000 a year as a lobbyist (plus his full Senate pension). Dan Rostenkowski, Illinois Democrat and the even more powerful chairman of the House Ways and Means Committee, was sent to prison for fraud, but returned to Washington saying he expected to supplement his annual congressional pension of $104,000 with about $100,000 in lobbying fees.

Some do not register as lobbyists and do not like having the term applied to them; they prefer to be known as lawyers or consultants. Call them what you will, their business is selling influence—peddling their names and their renown.

Marlow Cook, who was a one-term senator from Kentucky, is candid about what he does. "It bothered me at first," he says, "lobbying, walking those same corridors with a briefcase that I'd walked before as a senator. But it's a beautiful, delightful, professional way to make a living. I hope I'm good at it. I had a dermatologist corner me at a cocktail party and ask me how a former senator could stoop to lobbying. I told him it beat the s—— out of squeezing pimples."

Wilbur Mills, once the conservative caesar of the House Ways and Means Committee, sold his wiles as a tax consultant and freely admitted, "I can't make this kind of money back in Arkansas." When the Ford Motor Company set out to fight the National Highway Safety Administration's efforts to get Ford to recall 20 million vehicles with transmissions that allegedly shifted from "park" to "reverse" by themselves, the car company hired William T. Coleman, Jr., former secretary of transportation. Peter Halle prosecuted antitrust cases when he was in the Department of Justice; now, as a member of the solid-gold law firm of Milbank, Tweed, Hadley and McCloy, he defends clients against antitrust charges. He thinks highly of the revolving door: "The government can attract better people if they know they can eventually leave; and a cadre of lawyers with government experience makes for more efficient and less costly private law." In short, he thinks government is a good training ground for anyone who wants to make bigger bucks as a lobbyist later on. You could fill a book with the names of people in Washington who, having passed through that revolving door, smile broadly on their way to the bank.

Foreign Invasion

According to a recent study by the nonpartisan Center for Responsive Politics, foreigners and their governments, businesses, and other organizations spend more than $500 million in open and legal attempts to affect the policy, the political climate, and the public opinion of the United States. It is illegal for foreign individuals, companies, and governments to give to U.S. politicians, but the U.S. subsidiaries of foreign corporations are free to do so. In the last presidential campaign, for example, the subsidiary of the giant Swiss drug company, Glaxo-Wellcome Incorporated, spent a whopping $6.5 million in lobbying and gave nearly $1 million in political contributions. Foreign tobacco, oil, and booze companies were almost as generous.

Of the 4,336 foreign agents registered with the Justice Department, about 200 read like they were lifted from a Who's Who of Washington; they are former top officials from the White House and elsewhere in the executive branch and former members of Congress. Some are hired to help foreign governments and foreign companies beat out American companies for a share of the American market.

After leaving Carter's White House staff, Stu Eizenstat worked for Hitachi and later went back through the revolving doors to join the Clinton administration. As Ken Silverstein points out in *Washington on $10 Million a Day: How Lobbyists Plunder the Nation,* the China lobby, with hundreds on its Washington payroll, has grown so swollen with ex-U.S. officials that it almost seems like a retirement home for them. There you will find such big guns as ex-Secretary of State Henry Kissinger, ex-Secretary of State Al Haig, ex-National Security Adviser Brent Scowcroft, and David Rothkopf and Lionel Olmer, both of whom had recently held international trade positions in the Commerce Department. Other Asian countries have recruited from the top of our government. Richard Allen, another former national security adviser, got rich representing the interests of Taiwan and South Korea. Former Democratic party chairman Charles Manatt has worked for Japanese electronics interests. When the Japanese company Toshiba was caught illegally selling sensitive technology to the Soviet Union, Congress was expected to impose serious sanctions against the company. But Toshiba spent $3 million to hire the right team of lobbyists—including former White House counsel Leonard Garment—and it got off with a scolding. In 1986, Stu Spencer, one of George Bush's top political advisers, received $25,000 a month from Panama for personally advising its strongman ruler, Manuel Noriega, who was indicted in this country two years later for selling drugs. Previously, Spencer worked for South Africa.

Often these lobbyists succeed in persuading our policy shapers to put cronyism and greed over national interest. Although even the Pentagon's arms experts warned that assisting China's missile program might result someday in their missiles landing on America, outfits like Boeing, which stood to reap huge profits, successfully lobbied President Clinton to relax restrictions on selling electronic and other equipment to China. Boeing's fortunes as an airplane manufacturer were closely tied to China, where in recent years it had sold about one in ten of its aircraft, so in 1997 it deployed twenty-five lobbyists, at a cost of $670,000, to convince Congress that despite China's unpredictable militarism, we needed closer commercial ties with that country.

No Washington official ever worked so enthusiastically in helping foreign lobbyists as the late Commerce Secretary Ron Brown, who, before joining Clinton's cabinet, was a lobbyist for an array of foreign business interests as well as for the regime of Haiti's Jean-Claude "Baby Doc" Duvalier, one of the Third World's cruelest and most corrupt dictators.

Among the most powerful foreign lobbies in Washington are those that fight for more military and economic aid. Foremost among these is the Israeli lobby. Working through Jews in the United States, who are big spenders in political campaigns, the Israeli lobby is so successful that in a typical year Israel gets about $4 billion in military assistance from the United States—about one-third of the assistance we set-aside for all our allies in the world, and half of it is in the form of an outright gift. Needless to say, the Israeli lobby is a key shaper of U.S. policy in the Middle East, by far more powerful than the Arab lobby, even though the latter has in recent years become much more sophisticated and generous in the money it spends in Washington.

"Lobbyist" and "lawyer" are often synonymous, so, of course, success often depends on hiring the right Washington law firm. None is "righter" when it comes to influence in high places than Akin, Gump, Strauss, Hauer and Feld, home of Clinton's golfing pal Vernon Jordan and, more importantly, home of the wily Robert Strauss, who has been a power broker in both parties for the past thirty years. Although it was Democratic President Lyndon Johnson who first brought fellow-Texan Strauss into Washington's inner circle, Strauss felt just as comfortable with Republicans. He served President Bush as ambassador to Russia in 1991 through 1992. Naturally, corporations that want to make deals in Russia line up to hire Akin, Gump. They also have an easy time getting loan guarantees for their Russian adventures from the U.S. government's Overseas Private Investment Corporation (OPIC), perhaps because OPIC is headed by Ruth Harkin, wife of Senator Tom Harkin. Prior to joining OPIC, she was a top corporate lawyer at Akin, Gump.

The Rise of People's Lobbies

For most of our nation's history, the public watched with seeming helplessness as this chummy relationship between business-industry lobbyists and government officials shaped our politics. Prior to the late 1960s, there were no powerful "public interest lobbies" or "people's lobbies." The nearest thing to one was the union organization, the American Federation of Labor and Congress of Industrial Organizations (AFL–CIO). However, the AFL–CIO had become fat, complacent, and narrow. It was interested in the routine labor issues, such as higher pay. But when it came to issues such as racism, pollution, consumerism, and militarism, big labor often found itself on the side of such powerful big-business lobbies as the National Association of Manufacturers and the U.S. Chamber of Commerce. Big labor opposed just about anything that might interfere with fatter profits and, therefore, fatter payrolls.

So, independent lobbies—people's lobbies—of all kinds began to spring up and thrive: Lobbies for women's liberation, for fair taxation, for more money for the cities, against pollution of all sorts, in defense of wild animals, for modernizing Congress, for auto safety, for legal abortion, for prison reforms—the list is a long one, and it continues to get longer as other problems arise. Some of the people's lobbies are big and well financed, while others can hardly afford a Xerox machine.

People's lobbies prove the old maxim: The squeaky wheel gets the most grease. Some people's lobbies really know how to yell, and lobbies that complain the loudest get the most help. Examples by the dozens could be given. One example is the difference in money spent to research cures for AIDS versus the money spent to research cures for hepatitis C.

Both diseases are potentially fatal. In the United States, hepatitis C affects four times more people than does HIV, the precursor to AIDS. Hepatitis C is already the leading cause for liver transplants, and each transplant can cost an average of $300,000. Each year there are an estimated 3,000 new infections and 10,000 deaths from hepatitis C in this country. There is no broadly effective treatment, and if none is developed over the next decade, the death rate from that disease could rise to 30,000 a year—a mortality rate roughly equal to that of AIDS in 1996.

Why is it that the National Institutes of Health spends only about $825 million on research for a cure for hepatitis C—which comes to about $6 per infected person—while spending more than $1.5 billion a year for research on HIV, or about $16 per infected person in this country?

One answer is that there is a huge and very vocal lobby pressing Congress to spend more money on AIDS. It is a sensitive "political" issue. But there is virtually no hepatitis C lobby, so Congress ignores the disease.

Enter: Ralph Nader

The big breakthrough year for people's lobbies was 1965, when Ralph Nader, the "father" of the consumer movement, burst upon the scene, although in those days he was so young as to hardly seem fatherly. The time was ripe for his appearance, and the cause of his appearance was very American indeed—the auto.

Between 1945 and 1960, traffic deaths had dropped in number almost every year. But after 1960, they began a strangely sharp increase. Senators Warren Magnuson, Robert Kennedy, and Abraham Ribicoff wanted to find out why. So they held hearings in 1965. Under congressional questioning, Frederick Donner, chairman of the board of General Motors, admitted that while GM had made a profit of about $1.7 billion the previous year, the corporation had spent only one-thousandth of that amount on research into auto safety. Such findings stirred public interest and anger.

A couple of months later, Ralph Nader published *Unsafe at Any Speed: The Designed-in Dangers of the American Automobile*. His premise was that the rising rate of traffic deaths was not caused primarily by motorist carelessness but by the poor and dangerous design of the automobiles. The book was favorably reviewed on the front page of *The New York Times*, and Nader was called to Washington to testify at Ribicoff's hearings; the book did not sell many copies and his testimony, while effective, was hardly enough to make him famous. But then he had a stroke of great luck. In March 1966, it was discovered that GM had hired a private detective to dig into Nader's political and sexual life to try to find something that would discredit the crusader.

That prompted Ribicoff to hold hearings to see if GM was trying to harass anti-auto–industry witnesses, and the private detective testified that GM had indeed hired him to "get something, somewhere, on this guy to get him out of their hair and to shut him up." GM's president, James Roche, publicly apologized.

That did it. Nader, a thirty-one-year-old lawyer who had been known only among the most limited circle of safety buffs in Washington, became nationally famous overnight and his book became a best seller. His continued crusading had a revolutionary impact. Largely because of it, the National Traffic and Motor Vehicle Safety Act of 1966 was passed, signalling, as University of California professor David Vogel has pointed out, the start of "a significant decline in business's influence over regulatory policy" in Washington that would continue strongly for the next ten years, and sporadically thereafter.

Before 1965, the auto industry was virtually free of federal regulation. Thanks to Nader and his supporters in and out of Congress, it is now tightly bound by regulations regarding safety equipment, gas mileage, and pollution emissions. The auto makers have been forced to recall many millions of cars to correct defective equipment.

On that success, Nader was able to develop a veritable empire of consumer organizations. He still wears rumpled suits and lives in a boardinghouse room and spends $20,000 a year on himself, but he raises several million dollars a year through lecturing and through contributions from about 100,000 persons to Public Citizen Incorporated, his fundraising agency that supports a cluster of lobbies that specialize in such issues as nuclear safety, tax reform, insurance fraud, hazardous drugs, and the environment.

Seldom has Washington seen such a dramatic demonstration of what one totally committed person can achieve, starting from scratch. Professor Vogel, who has written a history of the wars between consumer-environmentalists and big business, says that Nader

> more than any other single individual . . . effectively politicized the role of the consumer, articulating and giving political content to the frustration and anger of ordinary citizens. Most important, he became an inspiration to thousands of college graduates by providing them with a role model and an alternative vocation, namely, public-interest lawyer and advocate. The annual survey of American leaders conducted by *U.S. News & World Report* in 1974 found Nader to be the fourth most influential American, a ranking never before or since achieved by any business executive.

Vogel also gives Nader's organizations credit for "revitalizing two of the nation's oldest social regulatory agencies, the Federal Trade Commission and the Food and Drug Administration" and gives Nader personal credit as instrumental in the passage of a number of regulatory laws, including the Natural Gas Pipeline Safety Act (1968), the Radiation Control for Health and Safety Act (1967), the Wholesome Meat Act (1967), the Coal Mine Health and Safety Act (1969), the Comprehensive Occupational Safety and Health Act (1979), and the Clean Air Act Amendments of 1970. *One man!*

A Common Cause

But Nader was just part of the great people's lobbying movement that began to roll by the end of the 1960s. Common Cause, Friends of the Earth, the National Resources Defense Council, Environmental Action, the Center for Law and Social Policy, and the Consumer Federation of America were all established in either 1969 or 1970 to join forces with older groups, such as the Sierra Club and the Wilderness Society. The next decade opened with more than seventy consumer, environmental, and conservation organizations operating in Washington, lobbying for additional government restraints on the exploiters.

Probably next in importance to the Nader complex is Common Cause, with a membership of 250,000, it was founded in 1970 by John Gardner, former secretary of Health, Education and Welfare. Because of his weighty Establishment background and because Establishment money launched Common Cause (it got funds from Ford, Time, Allied Chemical, and so on), some expected Gardner to operate little more than just another civics club. But he was more militant than that, perhaps because he aimed Common Cause primarily at something even big business could support: more honesty and efficiency in government. "People," Gardner said,

> have a wholly unrealistic notion of the power of the president or of any elected official. If you replaced 10 percent of the officials with the best people in the country, which would change a lot of officeholders, and got the best possible president, it would still make very little difference toward fixing the things that are wrong. By the time they are elected, they've had to make their deals and the man is molded to the system. . . . To make the system work, you've got to be a little outside, on the sidelines.

The end of the 1960s was a perfect time for these lobbies to go to work because the public was with them; polls showed that between

1968 and 1973 the percentage of Americans agreeing with the statement "business tries to strike a fair balance between profits and interest of the public" fell from 70 to 18 percent. In the late 1960s and early 1970s, the public-interest lobbies won enactment of laws promoting drug safety, honest labeling, clean meat in the market, truth in lending, occupational safety, cleaner air, and cleaner water—and establishing agencies to enforce the new laws.

To the business community, that was a dark age, producing (as Professor Vogel puts it) "a series of political setbacks without parallel in the postwar period." Of course it was in fact an incredible renaissance of reform, comparable to the Progressive and New Deal periods.

The Cigarette Crusade

The impressive thing about the public-interest lobbying movement is that people of all ages and all shades of rebelliousness and ideology are part of it, and with a remarkable degree of unity.

It used to be that old folks—especially those who were no longer employed—acted as though they thought their role in life was to putter around at hobbies, keep quiet, and leave the fun of contention and social debate to younger people. No longer. Today, a significant portion of the old folks are militant and vocal. Politicians listen very respectfully to them because people at that age tend to vote more than do younger people. Moreover, they will become an increasingly potent political bloc. Now they make up 11 percent of the population, but within fifty years, as birth and death rates drop, that figure is expected to reach 20 percent.

John Banzhaf, a professor at the George Washington Law School in Washington, D.C., was among the young tigers. He teaches his students primarily through experience—urging them to find some governmental or corporate villain to sue.

Banzhaf himself, at the ripe old revolutionary age of twenty-seven, forced the television networks to surrender time worth millions of dollars to run antismoking ads. In fact, Banzhaf is the lawyer who forced cigarette ads off television and radio.

Weren't the cigarette companies urging Americans to participate in a debatable activity? And didn't the Federal Communications Commission, under its "fairness doctrine," require that the networks present both sides of controversial questions? Banzhaf sat down one night and addressed these questions to the FCC in a three-page letter. That was the simple way it began.

Eventually, the FCC agreed with him and issued orders to the networks to give up a "significant amount" of time for presenting antismoking ads. This ruling cost the networks about $75 million a year in broadcast time. And partly because the antismoking ads—prepared by the American Cancer Society and the American Heart Association—were so devastatingly effective, the cigarette companies were actually happy their commercials were banned from the air entirely as of January 1971.

By one measure, Banzhaf's victory was something of a miracle. After all, who would suppose that an unknown lawyer could dash off a letter to one of those impervious government agencies and wind up not only getting its cooperation but crushing a corner of Madison Avenue? But the moral of the story, or at least the moral that Banzhaf and other crusading attorneys would convey, is that the accomplishment should not be thought of as a miracle; it should be considered as an object lesson in the fact that average citizens have more power at their disposal than they imagine. Banzhaf says:

> We are having trouble with young people, because they are convinced that they can't beat the system. . . . I'm trying to show them that with many problems something can be done within the system. If I can win against the billion-dollar cigarette lobby, if Ralph Nader can take on the auto companies and win, if my students on a part-time basis can take on the ad agencies, the Federal Trade Commission, the Federal Communications Commission, the retail credit associations—it shows there are untapped resources within the system that the young can try.

Without instruction, the average citizen is not equipped to handle complex legal battles with government agencies or with large corporations. There is no handy-dandy kit to instruct an outraged citizen on how to sue Texaco Oil Company, say, for advertising clean restrooms and then not supplying them. But collectively, pooling their resources, any beleaguered group can afford a good lawyer and a court fight.

In short, the courts were rediscovered by the militant reformers. Changes that would take years to push through a reluctant Congress have sometimes been achieved in months through the courts. This recourse has given the people's lobbyists a bright new cockiness, the kind heard in a speech by Victor Yannacone at Michigan State University. Representing the environmental section of the American Trial Lawyers Association, Yannacone (who handled some of the landmark antipollution cases himself) reminded and urged the students:

This land does not belong to General Motors, Ford, or Chrysler; this land does not belong to Consolidated Edison, Commonwealth Edison, or any other private investor-owned utility company; this land does not belong to Penn-Central, B&O, C&O, Union Pacific, Southern Pacific, or any other railroad; this land does not belong to American Airlines, United Airlines, TWA, or any common carrier; this land does not belong to Minnesota Mining and Manufacturing Company, Minneapolis Honeywell, IBM, Xerox, Eastman Kodak, Polaroid, or any other company marketing technological marvels; this land does not belong to International Paper Company, Scott Paper, Boise Cascade, Weyerhaeuser, Crown Zellerbach, or any other paper products company; this land does not belong to United States Steel, Bethlehem Steel, Inland Steel, Crucible Steel, or any other steel company; this land does not belong to Anaconda, Kennecott, Alcoa, or any other nonferrous metal company; this land does not belong to any soulless corporation!

This land does not belong to the ICC, FPC, FCC, AEC, TVA, FDA, USDA, BLM, Forest Service, Fish and Wildlife Service, or any other federal or state alphabet agency!

This land does not belong to the president of the United States, the Congress of the United States, the governor of any state, or the legislatures of the fifty states. This land belongs to its people. This land belongs to you and this land belongs to me.

Don't just sit there like lambs waiting for the slaughter, or canaries waiting to see if the mine shaft is really safe. Don't just sit around talking about the environmental crisis, or worse yet, just listening to others talk about it.

Don't just sit there and bitch. Sue somebody!

All across the country the bright, militant propeople lawyers are doing just that. More important than whatever substantive successes these attorneys achieve is their demonstration that success does not always depend on being backed by a great deal of wealth or a powerful industry.

Big Business Fights Back

But whoa! Let's be realistic. Sure, success doesn't always depend on great wealth or a powerful industry. But the record shows that those forces usually do prevail. Plutocrats and corporations didn't get big and rich by being dumb. They catch on fast, and they are ruthless.

Since environmental and consumer and other pro-public lobbies have to do much of their fighting in court, do you think the corporations aren't going to make a very good effort to rig the judicial process?

Their most effective method is to pour campaign money into electing presidents who in turn will appoint pro-business judges to the federal bench. It sure worked out that way in the Reagan and Bush administrations.

But there are other ways corporations can shape judicial decisions. They don't exactly buy judges, but they do what they can to influence them. For example, in 1998 *The Washington Post* discovered that more than 100 of the 900 federal judges have attended expenses-paid, five-day seminars on property rights and the environment at resorts in Montana.

The seminars are paid for by foundations (supported by major corporations) that are also funding a wave of litigation against the government on environmental issues and property rights. Some of the cases will be decided by the judges who get these free "seminar" vacations—fishing, golfing, horseback riding—and five days of lectures on why environmentalists need to be held in check.

Though momentarily thrown off stride by the aggressiveness of the people's lobby movement, big business quickly adjusted, stepped up its lobbying efforts on all fronts, and even began to use some of the people's lobbies' own tactics. The success of the environmental and consumer activities spurred a corporate counterattack. The Business Roundtable was established in 1972 to promote the Fortune 500's view in Washington. Between 1974 and 1980, the U.S. Chamber of Commerce doubled its membership and trebled its annual budget to $68 million. In 1973, the National Association of Manufacturers, with 12,100 corporate members, moved its headquarters to Washington; by 1978, nearly 2,000 trade associations had headquarters there. By 1980 there were, in fact, more employees representing business— lawyers, lobbyists, trade-association personnel, public relations specialists, public-affairs consultants, and specialized journalists—in the Washington metropolitan area than there were federal government employees.

With a militarylike efficiency that business had not shown before in dealing with legislative issues, this army performed two functions: (1) It kept a close watch on all bills that might in any way affect business and quickly alerted businesspeople around the country to start phoning and writing their support or opposition to the bills, and (2) it cranked out smooth public-relations messages warning Congress and the public about what the business groups considered to be the adverse economic impact of consumer and environmental activism.

One result of this propaganda drive was to make many Americans start to think that regulation was a dirty word, that safety regulation and health regulation added unnecessarily to the cost of doing business.

By 1978 the business lobby's muscle had grown to the point that it could deal the consumer movement a stunning setback by defeating a bill that would have established a Consumer Protection Agency. At first, it seemed the bill couldn't possibly fail. All signs pointed in that direction. It had passed the House or the Senate five times in the previous seven years. Harris opinion polls showed that the public supported the idea of the agency by a margin of two to one. More than 150 consumer, labor, senior citizen, and similar organized groups endorsed the legislation. The White House had given the bill at least its official (if not enthusiastic) endorsement. And yet the bill was defeated in the House by a vote of 227 to 189.

How could it have happened?

It happened because an estimated 450 business organizations let Congress know how they felt.

House Speaker Tip O'Neill said that in his quarter century in Congress he had "never seen such extensive lobbying." To stir up grass-roots support for their opposition to the bill, business lobbies hired the North American Precis Syndicate (NAPC) to send out canned editorials and cartoons denouncing the consumer agency to 3,800 newspapers and weeklies. According to the NAPC, these propaganda articles appeared 2,000 times—never identified as having come from the business lobby—and stirred a letter-writing blizzard. As Speaker O'Neill put it, "Those who are for the legislation, don't write. Those who are against it do." So, despite all the polls and the endorsements favoring the bill, the letter-writing campaign gave congressmen an excuse to vote against it, and a majority did just that.

The success of the business lobbies in defeating that bill shows that they had learned the major lesson taught by the people's lobbies—that the potentially most powerful force in politics is at the grass roots.

It was during this period that the great growth in business political-action groups was seen in Washington. Between 1976 and 1980, the number of corporate PACs and the amount they gave to campaigns nearly tripled. They were giving so much to Democrats (who, after all, were then in control of Congress) that one conservative Republican was stung to say "corporate managers are whores. They don't care who's in office, what party or what they stand for. They're just out to buy you." But along with those Democratic purchases, business had also learned to use money more subtly, more intellectually, and to propagandize the public in the hope of reaching legislators indirectly. In a typical year, Mobil Oil, for example, spent $4 million in advocacy advertising. This included full-page newspaper ads carrying clip-out coupons for readers to send to members of Congress. Mobil didn't call this lobbying. It called it an "educational campaign." But it was really the most effective type of lobbying.

Many corporations have taken to sending letters to their shareholders, urging them to write members of Congress and ask that they vote in such a way as to further the interest of these corporations.

For example, some of the largest utility companies, determined not to pay for helping to clean up the atmosphere, united in an organization cleverly named Citizens for Sensible Control of Acid Rain and spent $4.6 million to hire a public-relations firm that generated "constituents" letters urging members of Congress to defeat bills on acid rain. More than a million of these letters, filled with exaggerated estimates of the cost of acid-rain control, were distributed to shareholders with an appeal to sign and mail in "the postage paid, pre-addressed envelope provided for your convenience." When Congress was considering an increase in the federal tax on beer, the Beer Institute sponsored newspaper and magazine ads "on behalf of 80 million American beer drinkers," inviting readers to call a toll-free number and dictate a message to the operator, who sped it to the proper lawmaker by Western Union. Within a few weeks, some 20,000 mailgrams had flowed like warm suds into Capitol Hill offices. Thus is *vox populi* created.

The practical objective of letter-writing campaigns is not actually to get a majority of the people behind a position and to express themselves on it—for it would be virtually impossible to whip up that much enthusiasm—but to get such a heavy, sudden outpouring of sentiment that lawmakers *feel* they are being besieged by a majority. The true situation may be quite the contrary.

Another Cigarette Story

For those who are still drunk on optimism about the chances of ordinary people—even if well organized—to compete with the biggest corporate lobbies, the best way for them to sober up is to review the success of the tobacco industry.

A moment ago we told about the David-and-Goliath victory of Banzhaf in chasing tobacco advertisements off television. But that was just one skirmish. In most other battles of the "cigarette war" (as Richard Kluger calls it in his prize-winning book *Ashes to Ashes*), the tobacco industry has until recently escaped almost unscratched.

Since 1957, when the federal government issued its first official warning that cigarettes can kill you, an estimated 15.6 million Americans have indeed died from diseases traced to smoking. On average, the experts say, each victim lost twelve years of life for the pleasure of inhaling a toxic gas. Let's put that in perspective. In the forty years or so since that first warning from Washington, the cigarette war caused a dozen times more deaths than resulted from all our other wars, from Revolutionary through Vietnam, put together.

And yet, even though they know the dangers, more than 40 million Americans are still puffing away. Polls show that most would like to quit. So why don't they? Are they addicted to nicotine in the same way people get hooked on heroin and cocaine, and is that what the tobacco companies have aimed to achieve? There is already ample evidence that the answer to both questions is decidedly "yes." There is, for example, the inter-office memo of a Brown and Williamson senior vice president, circa 1963: "We are, then, in the business of selling nicotine, an addictive drug."

While the industry denied under oath that it had ever targeted the youth market, internal documents show this was a lie. A memo circulated by R. J. Reynolds, creator of "Joe Camel," reads: "Realistically, if our company is to survive and prosper, over the long term, we must get our share of the youth market. In my opinion, this will require new brands tailored to the youth market."

Over the years, thousands of independent studies proved that smoking causes various cancers, heart disease, and other fatal illnesses. Meanwhile, the industry was pouring many millions of dollars into advertising that portrayed smoking as just a harmless little pastime that made the smoker seem glamorous and sophisticated. Not until 1990 did any tobacco company admit that smoking could be risky. This admission by the most successful of all the cigarette giants, Philip Morris, was tucked away in its annual report, and its candor was perhaps partly motivated by the fact that some of its top executives— all smokers, of course—had been stricken with heart and lung ailments. Furthermore, the admission did not come until evidence of the industry's brutal duplicity had been revealed through lawsuits and congressional hearings.

How did Big Tobacco get by with it for so long, without any real opposition from the government? The answer involves a number of pressure groups, including tobacco farmers (mostly in the South, which is the region where many of Congress's leaders hail from), truckers who haul those "coffin nails" to market, and the press and sporting events that hugely profited from tobacco advertising.

But the cigarette manufacturers' main line of defense was money—lots and lots of their own money—used like the Mafia would use it: to hire armies of lawyers and to pay off politicians. With an income of $55 billion a year, making the tobacco industry's profit margin double that of any other industry, they had plenty of it to spread around.

As the century wound to a close, many observers thought that at last public revulsion at the conduct of the industry would force Congress to act. The national mood seemed to be shifting in that direction. Several states forced multibillion dollar settlements from the cigarette companies as compensation for medical expenses, and dozens of other states were lined up to do the same. Then in the late 1990s, Congress began considering legislation that would make the companies pay a penalty of more than $368 billion (tax-deductible) over twenty-five years and would force them to stop tempting youth with their ads (it's estimated another 4,000 teens start getting hooked every day).

But the cigarette moguls knew how to handle the situation. In 1995 (the year Republicans took total control of Congress), the industry poured five times more into Republican Party treasuries than it did the year before, and *The New York Times* observed that it was obviously buying protection: "The surge in donations comes when the industry is facing the most serious threats from Washington in its history." The gusher continued. A coalition of the five biggest tobacco companies poured more than $72 million into lobbying and campaign contributions between 1996 and 1998, most of into Republican pockets, of course.

Result: In 1998, the congressional bill to regulate and punish the tobacco industry didn't even come to a vote.

The amazing thing is not that the big-business lobby often wins but that it sometimes loses. When environmentalists try to save the redwood trees, for example, or prevent the pollution of rivers by sawmill waste, or stop the overharvesting of timber from federal lands, they are going up against some of the most powerful industries in the country, such as the American Forest and Paper Association, a $60 million a year lobbying giant. All the environmentalist lobbies put together have only a trifling fraction of that kind of money to work with.

The Happy Payoff

And yet, even against such odds, the people's lobbies have won some stunning victories and the nation is better off as a result. It was the pounding from the environmentalists that made the government shape up on the enforcement of pollution laws. As a result, many rivers and the Great Lakes, once dying, are beginning to stir with new aquatic life, and some water supplies that once imperiled the health of whole cities are safe to drink again. Fish swim again in the Naugatuck River in western Connecticut, where no aquatic life could survive in the 1950s. The Detroit River, in which ducks died by the thousands after simply paddling about, and which was considered biologically dead in the 1950s and 1960s, now supports salmon, pike, brown trout, and walleye. In upstate New York, the Mohawk River, once a sewer for the raw wastes discharged by Utica and other municipalities, is now clean enough to permit the return of perch, bass, and other pollution-sensitive fish.

It was the constant critical attention of the public-interest lawyers that forced regulatory bodies such as the Federal Trade Commission and the Food and Drug Administration to show some enthusiasm for law enforcement in recent years. As a result, highly flammable materials that endangered children and some highly toxic pesticides that endangered farmers and food consumers have been taken off the market.

As with the PACs, the strength of the citizens' lobby movement is that it is built around issues, not parties. This issue orientation is the result of increased education. In 1950, only about 13 percent of adult Americans had some college education. Today, more than 25 percent have been to college. Researchers have found that issues are generally more important than party loyalty in determining votes. The trend has frightened many politicians who would prefer that voters troop blindly to the polls and pull the Democratic or the Republican lever without analyzing the politicians' records on such matters as strip-mining, taxation, the proliferation of nuclear power plants, industrial subsidies, and conflict of interest. The increased number and increased influence of groups that lobby for special causes are in fact changing the character of the American political process, weakening the two national parties and throwing the old-guard politicians into confusion. Whether this trend is mostly beneficial or mostly harmful has yet to be seen; it surely is some of both.

But the parties and the politicians have brought it on themselves, and they will simply have to adjust to this relatively new citizen response. Seeing that the normal electoral channels often do not get the job done, or at least that the normal channels need some reaming out, the people have learned to attack their problems in extra-electoral ways—by lawsuits, mass demonstrations, picketing, sit-downs, camp-ins, letter-writing blizzards, and threats and pressures and coaxings of all sorts.

Above all else, the people's lobbyists have become masters of publicity and counterpublicity.

As means for permanent reform, their techniques may leave something to be desired. But while the machinery of government is being repaired, the people will just have to go on innovating. Government is problem solving, and if the problems are not solved swiftly enough by officials chosen for the job, then the people—intemperate, illogical, impulsive, and flighty though their techniques may sometimes be—must do whatever is necessary to lead their leaders.

Vox Populi

And speaking of leading the leaders, we must not forget the most omnipresent technique, the opinion poll. It carries the weight of the largest pressure group of all, the general public. And it, too, is organized in a way—by the pollster and by the questions asked. The power of the opinion poll is awesome. Many politicians literally shape their votes and their careers around them. Bill Clinton rarely made a move without consulting his private polls. As we have seen, Ronald Reagan even waited for a pollster to tell him if Libya would be a "popular" country to bomb. When John W. Warner was first running for the Senate in Virginia, he was asked his position on a proposed constitutional amendment. Warner turned to his pollster, Arthur Finkelstein, and asked, "Art, where do we stand?"

Because the public's opinion is often emotionally volatile and based on only the shallowest knowledge of facts and history,* it

---

*Let's face it: A great many of our fellow citizens are dim bulbs in the marquee of democracy. Example number 1: At the very height of the scandal that would eventually force the resignation of House Speaker Jim Wright—a scandal that was on the front page of every newspaper and on every network evening news program for many weeks—polls showed that 60 percent of the electorate had no idea who Mr. Wright was. Example number 2: Although the Sandinistas and the contras had been fighting in Nicaragua for years, in a war that bitterly divided politicians in this country and that was the cause of the biggest scandal of the Reagan administration, a Gallup poll in 1988 showed that only half of U.S. adults knew the name of the country where the war was being waged. (Diane Ravitch, Historian of Education at Teachers College, Columbia University, for Washington Post Syndicate, October 28, 1988).

Example number 3: In July of 1989, the U.S. Supreme Court handed down the most important and most controversial judgment on abortion in sixteen years. A month later, a *New York Times*–CBS poll showed that 59 percent of those interviewed hadn't yet heard enough about the case to be able to comment on it (*The New York Times*, August 3, 1989).

Obviously, a great many people go through life in a haze and their opinions are worthless.

sometimes doesn't take much—perhaps nothing more than a television news bulletin—to move it sharply in one direction or the other. Nevertheless, politicians take opinion polls very seriously and can be persuaded by them unless the poll goes against (1) a powerful special-interest group or (2) a long-standing policy. For example, in recent years polls have consistently shown that the public would favor spending less on defense and more on domestic programs. This, however, goes against not only the specific pressures of the powerful military–industrial lobby but against long-standing defense policy built on an ever-increasing Pentagon budget. So the polls are ignored.

Nevertheless, where the public's opinion is steadfast and strong on a given subject, and it doesn't butt heads with either a politically dominant pressure group or with an entrenched government policy, it can—and has—shaped history via polls, probably much more than people realize. One can easily imagine Clinton's conviction and ouster in the Lewinsky scandal if the public's opinion had not been overwhelmingly in favor of his remaining in office. The Fourth of July myths are sometimes right: In this country, what the average person on the street thinks does count, and sometimes counts heavily. Although he is probably biased because of his profession, Barry Sussman, who was for years *The Washington Post*'s pollster, could be altogether correct when he sees that public opinion has shaped recent history in several crucial ways:

> It was the mounting of public opinion that forced an end to the war in Vietnam, overrunning one president, Lyndon Johnson, in its path. It was public opinion that finally made a reluctant Congress move toward the impeachment of Richard Nixon, forcing him to resign. In large part it has been public opinion that has brought the nuclear-power industry to its knees, leaving it gasping. . . .
>
> In early 1984, it was public opinion that made Reagan bring the U.S. Marines home from Lebanon only days after saying he would never 'cut and run.' Public opinion made Reagan stop crusading against the Social Security system. . . .
>
> I would go as far as to state that the nuclear-arms treaty between the United States and the Soviet Union, signed by Reagan and Gorbachev in a love feast in Washington in December 1987, was also in the main the result of pressure applied by the citizenry. . . .

If Sussman is right, it must make the late George Gallup very happy, on whatever cloud he now resides, for when he and a handful of other pollsters launched the profession of scientific opinion sampling half a century ago, it was for the purpose, Gallup once said, of giving the "citizen a way to make his wishes known to government" and thereby count almost as an equal with "the organized minorities in America, with their pressure organizations and their lobbyists in Washington."

CHAPTER 8

The Media and Government

Politics, Profits, and Propaganda

*Well, when you come down to it, I don't see that a
reporter could do much to a president, do you?*

DWIGHT EISENHOWER

JUDGING BY WHAT HAS USUALLY OCCURRED, EISENHOWER
was correct to think that a president need not worry about anything
a reporter, a mere mouse in the White House corner, could do to him.
But as President Nixon discovered, perhaps *two* reporters are a different matter. Two young reporters, Bob Woodward and Carl Bernstein of
The Washington Post, were largely responsible for uncovering the
Watergate scandal—an exposé that press scholar Ben H. Bagdikian
correctly appraised as "the greatest political news story of our time."

In its efforts to secure information that the government preferred it
not have, the press has won a number of flamboyant victories. For
example, it uncovered a number of secret military ventures. Top Air
Force officers were caught authorizing illegal bombing raids over
North Vietnam and making fake reports of their activities. A couple
of years after the press revealed the massacre by U.S. soldiers of 347
Vietnamese civilians at the hamlet called My Lai 40, the press found out
about another massacre of 155 Viet civilians by U.S. soldiers that the
Pentagon had tried to cover up.

And of course there was the revelation of the "Pentagon Papers,"
those documents leaked by Dr. Daniel Ellsberg that showed step-by-step

how the United States became enmeshed in a hopeless war in Southeast Asia. It was the most important leak of confidential government documents in our history.

However, most reporters who cover Washington would agree that such victories are unusual and that official secrecy usually carries the day.

Shortly after the Pentagon Papers came to light, CBS commentator Bernard Kalb asked Maxwell Taylor, "Well, what do you make, General, of the people's right to know when decisions of this dimension [getting into and escalating the Vietnam war] are taken?" Taylor replied:

> I don't believe in that as a general principle. You have to talk about cases. What is a citizen going to do after reading these documents [the Pentagon Papers] that he wouldn't have done otherwise? A citizen should know those things he needs to know to be a good citizen and discharge his functions—not to get in on the secrets which simply damage his government and indirectly damage the citizen himself.

Most officials, military and civilian, at the top of the federal hierarchy share the belief that the government should tell the people only enough to make them step along briskly and discharge their "functions" for the state.

When Lou Cannon of *The Washington Post* asked President Reagan why Secretary of State Alexander Haig had left the cabinet (Was he fired? If he quit, why did he quit?), President Reagan responded, "Lou, if I thought that there was something involved in this that the American people needed to know with regard to their own welfare, then I would be frank with the American people and tell them." And at an embassy cocktail party, when CBS correspondent Ike Pappas got into a heated discussion with CIA Director William J. Casey, a notorious liar, over the CIA's refusal to give the press reasonable access to agency information, Casey said, "Who elected you to tell the American people what they should know? When we think they should know something we will tell you about it."

By and large, those who hold to that grim Papa-knows-best doctrine are successful in forcing the press to operate within specific borders. The press and the government are not equal adversaries; the government frustrates the press at almost every turn. The moral of *The New York Times*' printing of the Pentagon Papers was only that the press is free to print what it can get by luck and stealth, not that it is free to get all that the public should know. The Pentagon Papers episode serves as a reminder to realists of just how little information the press normally gets from the government. "There are really two levels at which the press operates in Washington," said Richard Dudman, once chief of the *St. Louis Post-Dispatch's* Washington bureau. "Mostly we operate at the level at which the scenario is done by government P.R. flacks. When something like the Pentagon Papers comes along, you suddenly get a swift look at reality—at what's really going on in this town," most of which, tucked safely away in files all over town, neither the press nor the public will ever know about.

Data, Propaganda, and Power

Information is the oil that makes the wheels of government go round. It is the heart of democracy; as political scientist James David Barber points out, "Democracy is not only a structure of power, it is also a special kind of conversation: a deliberation meant to result in the consent of the governed—an informed consent, a persuaded consent."

The two million people in the federal bureaucracy spend most of their time collecting and dispensing information. Most of this information is highly practical and even, in our complex economy, downright necessary. From the weather reports to the monthly price index and from labor statistics to census data, federally collected information has an enormous impact on the way farmers and businessmen and housewives and all of us chart our future.

In addition, the government—or portions of the government—serves as its own muckraking reporter. Most of the news stories that reveal dirty work on the part of politicians and bureaucrats originate *not* with journalists but with investigators on the public payroll—at regulatory agencies and particularly on congressional committees. These investigators dig up the information and set down their findings in formal reports; then the press expands on the material and takes it to the public, getting undue praise for "exposures."

Perhaps the most important recent example of this was in the uncovering of multibillion-dollar corruption at the Department of Housing and Urban Development, which some have appraised as the worst scandal since Watergate. It was those excellent bureaucrats, the inspectors general at HUD, not the press, who sounded the alarm. In fact, they had an extremely difficult time getting anyone to listen. For nearly a decade, they sent to Congress detailed reports of fraud at HUD; these reports were available to the press, which ignored them, as Congress had, until 1989, when the scandal finally broke wide open.

Although the press must be given credit for relentlessly uncovering the Watergate scandals in its early stages and forcing Congress finally to enter the hunt for White House corruption, it should not be forgotten that the crucial evidence—the existence of the White House tapes—was revealed as the result of the work of Senate investigators. Without the damning evidence of the tapes, President Richard Nixon would probably have survived the scandal. Likewise, it was a Senate investigation that uncovered multimillion-dollar briberies involving U.S. corporations and foreign governments, plus illegal multimillion-dollar campaign contributions to U.S. politicians. It was the House Banking Committee and the Senate Committee on Government Operations that produced monumental studies illuminating the dangerous interlocking directorships and stock ownerships between banks and other industries. It was a Senate investigation that first revealed the scope of the Teamsters' corruption. It is investigators in both houses of Congress—not in the press—who regularly turn up the truly stunning examples of defense profiteering. Until the Reagan administration doused their fires, it was investigators in such regulatory agencies as the Federal Trade Commission and the Food and Drug Administration who published data on shoddy, dangerous products and on business swindles.

Without this assistance, the press would be lost, for it covers regulatory agencies and the Pentagon in an almost casual fashion. For example, only a couple of dozen newspapers ever send reporters to the Pentagon, and only two newspapers, *The New York Times* and *The Washington Post*, assign as many as two reporters to that department—although it eats up the lion's share of our budget. For guidance to the closets where the skeletons are, the press depends heavily on the many members of the bureaucracy and the federal legislature who are basically honest and who feel that the public deserves to be told even the bad news about its government.

Is It Legal?

However, not all the 20,000 public-information and public-affairs workers, moviemakers, broadcasters, writers, editors, and advertising specialists who work for the federal payroll are there to spread legitimate and useful information about government activities. Much of their work is also pure propaganda, aimed at misleading, overstating, understating, disguising, and inciting. Since 1913, federal law has prohibited the use of federal funds "to pay a publicity expert unless specifically appropriated for that purpose." Congress almost never "specifically" appropriates money for publicity, and yet, barely disguised among the bureaucracy's information specialists, are scores of the proscribed publicity experts—nobody knows for sure how many. They are almost never officially identified as such, but they are easy to spot because of their total commitment to making their bosses and their corners of government seem much more important than they are and glossing over defects. Their job is to puff, to aggrandize, and basically to con the public. (Congress doesn't complain about violations of the 1913 law, perhaps because its members are just as guilty of breaking it as is the White House.) No matter how small an agency may be, it invariably will have a public-relations staff. Some of the biggest publicity offices are truly awesome: The Defense Department's public-information and public-relations force costs $35 million a year.

To promote itself and propagandize its efforts, the government has become one of the top twenty advertisers in the country. Each year it spends more than $230 million through newspapers, magazines, and television to "sell" such things as the beauty of national parks, boat safety, train riding, and stamp collecting. The government spends enough money on moviemaking (roughly half a billion dollars a year) to rival the B-grade budgets of Hollywood, but the federal product is usually rather low in plot and drama. There are thousands of films on such subjects as how to brush your teeth and how to get a thrill out of hydrofoil racing. In a two-year period, the government's drug-abuse agency turned out fifty-two films on why one shouldn't use dope, and many of the scripts seemed to be the same. The government never believes in saying something just a dozen times when it has the money to repeat itself a hundred times.

In short, under the guise of supplying "information," government propagandists smother the press under an avalanche of obfuscating press releases.

The hope for digging beneath this surface of puffery and secrecy rests with the 15,000 or so reporters in Washington. But this is a very misleading roll call. Most of them are reporters for trade publications and newsletters, not reporters for what are called newspapers and magazines of "general circulation." To be sure, the army of general-circulation journalists is growing enormously. About 1,500 reporters were accredited to cover Congress in 1961; today, there are more than 5,000 carrying Congressional press cards. Over at the White House, when President Truman ordered the dropping of the atomic bomb on Japan in 1945, he broke the news to the entire press corps—twenty-five reporters. Today, nearly 2,000 reporters carry White House press passes. But again, numbers such as those are misleading. Very few of the people accredited to cover Congress actually do so in more than a perfunctory fashion, and most of the reporters in the White House press corps are mere hangers-on. In the entire 15,000 Washington journalist corps, no more than a few hundred have the ability, time, inclination, or support of their employers to cope with the federal politicians' and the bureaucrats' complex wiles. Although members of this elite group of journalists constitute what is undoubtedly the finest capital press corps in the world, they are too few and they work under too many handicaps (some created by themselves) to do the job that needs to be done.

The Handicaps from Within: Money

The almost hopeless odds against these reporters is to a great extent the fault of the media industrialists who hire them. Most of the Washington press corps represent newspaper and television companies that are corporately comfortable and defensive of the status quo. Press industrialists do not believe, ordinarily, in hiring tough reporters to make "their" government uncomfortable or to stir the rabble to suspicions that perhaps things should be put in different hands. The First Amendment has been good to the lords of the press; it has put great wealth next to their skins. Most of them are going to show their gratitude by employing reporters who are content to write about the positive side of government—about contracts for new dams and about auto safety awards.

The bigwigs of any administration and the press industrialists understand each other. The patriotism of press industrialists is no different from that of any other group of industrialists, which means that their idea of serving the country is to defend all aspects of private enterprise and all necessary commercial imperialism, including the politicians who serve these best.

To be sure, there are exceptional occasions when powerful politicians and publishers fall out and engage in a blood feud. Mrs. Katherine Graham, chairman of the board of the Washington Post Company, has often been tolerant of the stupidities of her favorite politicians, but in the Watergate investigation the Nixon crowd handled her wrong. They publicly insulted her newspaper, and they privately threatened and insulted her. In one telephone interview with Carl Bernstein early in the investigation, Attorney General John

Mitchell fumed: "Katie Graham's gonna get her tit caught in a big fat wringer if that's published!" Enough was enough, and she decided, she says, "Either I go to jail, or they go to jail." Seldom do reporters get to benefit from such a wholesale declaration of war by a publisher, but it is significant that apparently this publisher was stung to pursue the story not entirely for the public's welfare but also for personal revenge.*

Even though the Nixon administration and the press quarreled like old marrieds, behind the cash register they found true love. Although Nixon sent his vice president, Spiro Agnew, into the public arena to denounce the "concentration of power" that was developing in the newspaper field because of the increasing number of monopolies, he threw his weight (successfully) in support of legislation that allowed many newspapers to engage in monopolistic practices with total immunity from antitrust laws. And his administration pushed legislation to help television and radio stations fight off challenges to their licenses by "public interest" groups.

However beneficial their activities generally are, the press lords of the United States—the Hearsts, the Grahams, the Chandlers, the Sulzbergers, and their peers—have at least one eye on profits at all times. The barons of television have both eyes there. *The New York Times* television critic John J. O'Connor once said, "Everyone knows the networks operate from a base of undiluted greed." That may be an exaggeration, but the networks' priorities do raise serious questions. Their evening news programs usually contain twenty-three minutes of national news, of which no more than eight minutes originates in Washington. As one group of surveyors appraised the situation, "the typical thirty-minute network news show would take no more than one page of *The New York Times* if it were set into print." When a network devotes only eight minutes to the president, the Congress, the Supreme Court, and the bureaucracy, it obviously views news as just a minor pause between the quiz shows and the situation comedies.

Compared to television in terms of coverage, newspapers are well named. Still, no major newspaper gives more than 40 percent of its

---

*The Post, like other papers, usually is quite generous in showing courtesies to the people of the Establishment. When Chief Justice Warren Burger appeared at his front door with a gun (some say it was a pistol, some say a shotgun) to greet two of *The Washington Post* reporters, the newspaper's executive editor, Benjamin Bradlee, decided not to print a word about that startling apparition. Top People, after all, should hide each other's dirty linen so far as is possible. Thus, too, when the Supreme Court declined to take a case in which a woman was suing Arthur O. Sulzberger, publisher of *The New York Times,* in a paternity suit (he had already paid her $41,000 in settlement), neither *The Washington Post* nor *The New York Times* printed a word about it.

space to non-advertising material; and in this 40 percent, news must share space with comics, crossword puzzles, astrology charts, letters to the editor, editorials, columns, and "features." Some newspapers give no more than 20 percent of their "news" space to real news.

Press Not "Free"

The reason is very simple: The more space that is devoted to advertising, the more money the publishers make. A managing editor in Samuel I. Newhouse's vast newspaper chain once said of his boss, "Sam never pretended to be a public benefactor. He doesn't claim to be with the people. He's a capitalist." All publishers are capitalists. And most of them are very successful ones. The Times-Mirror Company (publishers of the *Los Angeles Times* and several other papers) consistently ranks among the top 200 corporations in America; the corporation has more than $3 billion in sales in a typical year.* The Chicago Tribune Company and Hearst earn more than a billion dollars a year; the New York Times Company and the Washington Post Company (which also owns *Newsweek* and several television stations) each have sales of well over two billion dollars a year.

With money of that sort involved, the phrase "free press" invites cynical jokes. A. J. Liebling wrote, "Freedom of the press is reserved for those who own one." Not many can afford the privilege. Not many can afford to compete with the big businesses (or even the medium-size businesses) of the press; competition among newspapers has disappeared in 97 percent of American cities. The First Amendment was aimed at fertilizing diversity of opinion, but the growing monopoly among newspapers squelches the very thing that the writers of the Constitution were trying to preserve. The monopolistic character of the newspaper industry is heightened further by the fact that three out of five of the nation's 1,600 daily newspapers are under chain ownership—and the trend is growing. Each paper in the Hearst, Gannett, Newhouse, Cox, Knight-Ridder or Times-Mirror chain is not automatically like every other, but there is not much editorial variety.

---

*If income alone is not enough to tell you how big these monstrous newspapers are, consider this: The *Los Angeles Times* consumes around 500,000 tons of newsprint (paper) every year, which makes it the ninth largest newsprint-consuming "nation" in the world. That is, the *Times* all by itself consumes more newsprint than any nation, except for China, Australia, France, West Germany, Britain, Japan, or the United States. And since the newspaper already consumes 90 percent of what China's entire population consumes, it probably will move into eighth place any day now. (Letter from James Tisdale, vice president of Smurfit Newsprint Corp. to *Los Angeles Times* former publisher, Tom Johnson.)

Homogenized opinion is the rule. Every member of the chain is only too sensitive to the thinking of the editorial flagship paper (where the publisher of the chain holds court), which is concentrated on making money and defending a system that allows the freedom of the press to be enormously profitable. Profits, after all, were the purpose behind the chain's expansion in the first place.

In 1980 (the last time such a poll was taken), members of the American Society of Newspaper Editors were asked if they felt free to publish news that might harm the corporate owners of their newspapers. One-third said they would be afraid to publish such news—and doubtless many more of the polled editors were simply too ashamed of their restrictions to answer honestly.

Not that high profits are necessarily a bad thing. Indeed, some of the best newspapers are the most profitable. Wealth insulates them from some of the petty and brutal pressures that force weaker papers to cover up the scandals of the business community (which is to say, their advertisers) or to print servile puffery. But it is also true that concern for profits in the boardroom rubbing against concern for news in the newsroom can result in a schizophrenic quality—a fitful inconsistency. Reporters must answer to editors, who must answer to publisher-owners, who ultimately set the tone and direction of the news-gathering organization. To be sure, some publishers—those who feel that selling news is a higher calling than, say, selling hot tubs—may encourage wide latitude and aggressiveness in reporting specific stories, even stories that embarrass their business friends, but few publishers are so open-minded as to permit their own newspapers to challenge the very system and social structure of which they are an important part.

One of the rare publishers was Ned Chilton, owner of the *Charleston Gazette* in West Virginia. It was a fairly normal day at the *Gazette* when, after editorially denouncing E. F. Hutton as a "scumbag company" and the Manville Corporation as "slimy," its editorial page declaimed, "If free enterprise is the wave of the future of the world, then the Lord help the world. What is increasingly becoming clear about this economic system is that it places greed above all other concerns."

Most other publishers considered Chilton rather bizarre for speaking out like that.

Conflicts of Interest

And why are they so reticent to follow his example? For a clue to the answer, drop by the boardroom at any big media enterprise and see who's there. Sitting around *The New York Times*'s boardroom table in a typical year, for example, were representatives of Merck, Morgan Guaranty Trust, Charter Oil, American Express, Bethlehem Steel, IBM, Scott Paper, Sun Oil, First Boston Corporation, Ford Motor Company, and Manville Corporation (a connection that may explain why *The Times* has gone rather lightly on Manville's poisoning of so many of its workers with asbestos dust).

And that is not an unusual lineup. Conflict-of-interest interlocking directorates are the rule. Every major media corporation in America has board members representing international banks, defense industries, top insurance companies, multinational oil companies, airlines, auto corporations, and so on. You will look long and hard before you find a media board of directors on which sits an official from a consumer organization.

When, in 1976, a serious effort was made in Congress to break up the major oil companies (big advertisers) into smaller units to promote competition, only three daily newspapers in the country—the *St. Louis Post-Dispatch*, the *Charleston Gazette*, and the *Arkansas Democrat Gazette*—came out editorially in favor of the idea. When oil and gas prices quadrupled in the early 1970s, only a few newspapers assigned investigative reporters to follow up rumors that the oil companies were creating phony shortages to gain higher profits. The banking, housing, agricultural, and other industries crucial to everyday life are covered only spasmodically by the press, and the stories usually land on the financial page—which is not exactly the page most people turn to first. The press didn't start giving front-page coverage to the vast scandals of the savings and loan industry in the late 1980s until the looters had carried off the store. "Why," asked Tom Wicker, a *New York Times* editor with an unusually sensitive conscience, "why has it been left mostly to people outside the press to raise the great issue of consumerism in America?" It's true; not until Ralph Nader and other consumer and environmental radicals raised Cain did the press begin to wake up to the cheating and abuses in the marketplace—unsafe autos, filthy rivers, cancer-causing food additives, dangerous pesticides.

Baffling and irritating is the tendency of even the best newspapers to ignore important news stories that are just handed to them, or are available at no cost at all. When the General Accounting Office (GAO), for example, found that the Internal Revenue Service had $5.5 billion worth of inaccurate accounts and that the Customs Service could not give an accurate accounting for tons of illegal drugs and millions of dollars of cash it had seized from smugglers, the GAO sent copies of both reports to all major news organizations. But *The New York Times*, *The Washington Post*, *The Wall Street Journal*, and *Los Angeles Times*—the newspapers with the most influence—printed not a word about these bureaucratic sins. That sort of thing happens all the time.

They Don't Invest in Reporters

What happened at the Times-Mirror Company in 1997 clearly illustrates the priorities of big newspaper corporations. The *Los Angeles Times* was making gobs of money but its owners wanted more, so they brought in Mark Willes to be publisher. Willes knew absolutely nothing about newspapers. Until recently, he had been a vice president of the cereal maker, General Mills. Drawing on that background, he announced that he wanted to market newspapers like they were cake mixes or Hamburger Helper. His first act—which, among reporters, earned him the nickname "The Cereal Killer"—was to cut 2,200 jobs, 10 percent of them in the newsroom.

Between trips to the bank, publishers love to give speeches lamenting the public's perception of them as money-grubbers. This is from a speech at Yale by Arthur Ochs Sulzberger, publisher of *The New York Times:* "We are often perceived as merely another form of big business—in business to make money just like everyone else—and our service to the community goes unperceived."

That lament was made in a year the Times corporation earned over a billion dollars for its "service."

The year before, Katherine Graham, whose family fortune is estimated at $250 million and whose media corporation, including *The Washington Post,* regularly knocks down two billion a year, complained in a speech at the University of Georgia, "What is not clearly perceived by the public—and even on occasion, by our own people—is this: Financial success is not a luxury in today's world, but a necessity. . . . It gives us the ability to pursue the news, no matter how unpopular, costly or even dangerous that might be."

Sure. But as Tom Goldstein, the dean of journalism at Columbia University, correctly responds, the Graham argument would be more convincing if so many publishers weren't "merely successful but fabulously wealthy" and if they were not so stingy about hiring more and better reporters to get the job done right. While *The Washington Post's* profits went up 815 percent in the 1980s, its number of employees increased only 21 percent.

Once in a while newspapers like *The Times* and *The Post* actually do something with their wealth that proves Graham's point: Only newspapers loaded with dough can handle the big investigations. No better example of that has been seen in recent years than *The New York*

Times's success in exposing the crookedness of Columbia/HCA Healthcare Corporation, the country's largest hospital chain. Early in 1997, *Fortune* magazine described Columbia as America's "most admired" health-care company. Wall Street analysts loved Columbia because of its profits. Many government leaders were convinced that Columbia set the ideal standards for the future of that industry. Little did they know. *The New York Times* was about to reveal the truth in a four-part, 16,878-word series, which showed Columbia had fleeced the government of millions of dollars. As a result of the series, some of Columbia's managers were indicted for fraud, others were fired, and the corporation itself was the target of an ongoing criminal investigation.

Digging into the hidden records of such a vast corporation could not have been done except by a newspaper of *The Times*'s wealth and equipment (30 million billing records were analyzed). *The Times* assigned four reporters to work on the story full-time for fourteen months, at a total cost, including salaries, of $625,000. The investment yielded one of the decade's best examples of public service journalism.

Although the nation's two most influential dailies are occasionally willing to splurge on that kind of heroic achievement, ordinarily they seem to think their shareholders would be unhappy if they hired more than four or five reporters each to cover the 535 members of Congress and their thousands of mischief-making employees on a regular basis, or more than two reporters each to cover the magicians at the Pentagon who make all those billions of dollars disappear.

Coverage of consumer and environmental issues in recent years has improved greatly. But even today these issues arouse only intermittent aggressiveness on the part of the press. No more than a dozen reporters check in regularly at the Federal Trade Commission and no more than two dozen routinely appear at the doors of the Department of Energy, the Occupational Safety and Health Administration, the Food and Drug Administration, and the Securities and Exchange Commission—agencies that are supposed to prevent our getting swindled, poisoned, and physically abused.

For that matter, the overwhelming majority of congressional committee sessions are held without the presence of a single member of the general-interest press or television. The reporters don't go because their editors don't insist that they go, and their editors don't insist they go because the publisher obviously isn't all that eager to have such coverage in his or her newspaper.

Beginning with the Reagan years and encouraged by that administration's unwillingness to enforce antitrust laws, big business has reveled in an orgy of corporate mergers. Some economists fear that the growing concentration of corporate wealth points to an ominous decline in free enterprise. That fear, however, is rarely conveyed in the nation's newspapers. Their silence isn't surprising. After all, no industry has had more mergers than the newspaper industry—big papers cannibalizing smaller ones, big chains buying up smaller ones. How could they convincingly preach against the evils of merging? And how could they unhypocritically crusade against antitrust violations, seeing as how the press long ago persuaded Congress to make newspapers virtually immune from antitrust laws?

How to Buy Support

Indeed, of all the many favors the media has obtained from federal politicians—cushy tax and tariff laws, exceptions from child-labor laws, and so on—none has been so rewarding as the nobly titled Newspaper Preservation Act, sometimes called the "failing newspaper act." The act exempted many newspapers from antitrust laws by allowing supposedly competing newspapers to share the same business offices and printing plant and to split the profits. The act was supposed to be used only to help a newspaper that, without antitrust immunity, would go out of business. And to some extent it was used for that purpose. But primarily it served as a license to operate gold mines. Daily newspapers earn an average of about 19 percent on sales, which is more than double the average for other manufacturing businesses, but the companies with joint operating agreements earn about *twice* what other papers earn.

After Congress passed the law, the question was: Would Nixon sign it? Earlier administrations had rejected the idea, but the Nixon gang, with an eye on the 1972 campaign, happily submitted to the entreaties of a lobby led by the Hearst, Scripps-Howard, and Cox media conglomerates.

The trade-off was embarrassingly obvious. Ben Bagdikian, tells it this way:

> In the previous three presidential elections . . . a third of all Hearst papers had endorsed the Democratic candidate, as had a third of the Cox papers and half of the Scripps-Howard papers. In 1972 . . . every Hearst paper, every Cox paper, and every Scripps-Howard paper endorsed Nixon. Scripps-Howard ordered a standard pro-Nixon editorial into all its dailies. Cox ordered all its editors to endorse Nixon (causing one editor to resign in protest).
>
> Without the chains whose local papers benefited from the White House reversal on the Newspaper Preservation Act, Richard Nixon

would have had, with the exception of Barry Goldwater in 1964, the lowest newspaper support of any candidate since World War II. Instead, he had the highest newspaper support of any candidate in U.S. history.

Obviously, portions of the press had happily engaged in a pyrotechnical sellout to a president who within two years would resign in disgrace.*

Another round of the "failing newspaper" charade came in the late 1980s, when the two richest chains, Knight-Ridder and Gannett, claimed that their Detroit newspapers, the *Free Press* and *The News*, were losing so much money that one of them would expire unless they were allowed to merge under the Newspaper Preservation Act. Many industry analysts were convinced that this claim was a hoax the chains were using to achieve a monopoly that would let them bilk their Detroit advertisers. Everyone agreed that if they *were* allowed to merge, the two papers could become incredibly profitable. The joint-operating agreement had to be approved by U.S. Attorney General Edwin Meese. At that time Meese was himself being investigated for conflicts of interest and other sleaze, and editorial cartoonists across the country were portraying him in various guises—pig and rat being the favorites. But not at the *Detroit Free Press* or at *The Miami Herald*, home base for the Knight-Ridder chain; at those two newspapers, the editorial cartoonists were under strict orders from management to draw nothing critical of Meese. This little editorial sellout was rewarded by Meese's approval of the merger.

Why Not Full Disclosure?

If publishers were compelled to disclose all their financial operations, the public would be better able to understand why publishers act the way they do and why they require no more from their reporters than they do. If it is desirable that the public be told that Representative Dan Burton, chairman of the committee investigating campaign finance abuses, received huge contributions from lobbyists and might be influenced by this, it would also be desirable for the

---

*In its eagerness to curry favor with the nation's top politicians, the Establishment press does not always ask for a *quid pro quo*. Often it offers the soothing favor of silence for free, playing the part of a wimp and expressing no editorial opinion at all in a political race, thereby guaranteeing that no candidate is offended.

readers of the *Los Angeles Times* and other newspapers owned by the Chandler family to know that the Chandlers also own oil wells, book-publishing companies, lumber companies, television stations, and enormous land and farming interests, and have been directors of the Santa Fe Railway, Kaiser Steel, Pan American World Airways, Safeway grocery stores, Security First National Bank, and Buffum's department stores. Isn't it conceivable that the Chandlers are influenced from time to time as a result of these holdings?

The Hearst empire includes not only a chain of newspapers and magazines both here and in Britain, and radio and television stations, but also water and power companies, paper-pulp companies, vast real estate in New York and San Francisco and elsewhere, book-publishing houses, movie companies, and wire syndicates.

When the Scripps-Howard newspaper chain stoutly opposed federal legislation that would have benefited trucking companies, its readers might have been better able to judge the quarrel if they had known of the many close ties between Scripps-Howard and the railroad industry.

The point to remember is that the press industry is just that—an industry. It is big business. Many of the most powerful newspapers have left their traditional ways and evolved, as former Chief Justice Warren Burger has pointed out, "into modern corporate conglomerates in which the daily dissemination of news . . . is no longer the major part of the whole enterprise."

That evolution is dangerous. The danger is evident if one remembers that the important role of journalism is setting the agenda for national attention. Only those problems that are deemed "newsworthy" have a chance of getting solved. Not until journalists decided to make racial discrimination the big news story of the early 1960s did major legislation to relieve the problem get passed in Congress. Not until filth and poisons in America's daily life became an "in" news topic did reform legislation emerge. Politicians, like the public in general, measure the boundaries of life to an unsettling degree by what they read in the newspaper and hear on the six o'clock news. Until a problem is emphasized in these formats, it often does not receive sufficient recognition to trigger the momentum of political reform. And when monopolistic, multibillion-dollar corporations control more and more of the press, it is only natural that the news agenda will be shaped by the outlook of big business. The latter is often characterized by caution, love of the status quo, intolerance of radical ideas, fear of risk, and fear of the restless underdog.

The New Media Empires

In the first edition of his classic *The Media Monopoly,* published in 1983, Ben Bagdikian wrote that fifty corporations "control what America sees, hears, and reads." By 1997, he had changed his count to ten corporations. Indeed, by then the merged conglomoration of the media world was awesome. Media empires—television, newspapers, book publishers, all under one dictatorship, so to speak—had been established.

Consider what happened in 1995 in two mergers. First came the purchase of Capital City/ABC Inc., the nation's top television network, by Disney Company, the world's largest entertainment factory. For $19 billion, Disney—which already was a strong contender in television and movies—got ABC's network of 225 affiliates, 10 television stations, 21 radio stations, radio networks serving more than 3,400 stations, controlling interest in ESPN and ESPN2, seven daily newspapers, scads of weeklies and shopping guides, and specialty books and magazines.

A few weeks later Time Warner paid $5 billion for the Turner Broadcasting System. The combined companies were a media colossus, pairing Turner's cable networks—CNN, TBS, TNT, and the Cartoon Network—with Time Warner's vast interests in publishing, music, cable systems, Home Box Office, and film production.*

Does the "bottom line" fanaticism of multibillion dollar conglomerates like these have a chilling effect on news and other serious television? The question is profoundly important because television is where most Americans get their news. The television moguls, as Kevin P. Phillips accurately puts it, "have this incredible power to beam into our living rooms the political agenda for the nation: They choose the people who say in the morning or in the evening who is good and who is bad, what happened in the world, what you are to think about. . . ."

Look what's happening: Yes, today there are more programs labeled "news" than even the most deeply addicted news junkie could ever watch. Counting cable, there are maybe 100 stations, some broadcasting around the clock, with the latest, up-to-the-minute, breathless reports on items like weather, crime, and liposuction. But this is stuff which, if news were considered a meal, would amount only to stale *hors d'oeuvres.* These are mere nibbles around the edge of the important things happening in the world.

---

*A partial listing of Time Warner's holdings include Time-Life books; Book-of-the-Month Club; Little, Brown publishers; Warner Brothers studio; and such magazines as *Fortune, Time, Life, Money,* and *Sports Illustrated.*

CBS's *60 Minutes* is one of the few hangovers from the vigorous, investigative era. International news, once the pride of network television, has been cut back one-third since the 1980s. Documentaries, once the crown jewels of the networks, are so rare that documentary-makers have become the starving artists of the television industry. Meanwhile, the networks are pouring money into tabloid television—syndicated talk shows that offer interviews with witches, bigamists, bigots, male strippers, child molesters—what critics call "the Freaks of the Week."

Right-wing conservatives with a pro-corporation slant dominate talk radio. Liberal commentators who step on the toes of the mighty rarely survive. Consider the fate of Jim Hightower, a Texas "populist" talk show host who had 2 million listeners on 150 ABC radio stations. His "Hog Report," introduced with much squealing and slurping, reported which corporations were giving how much in campaign contributions to which politicians, and how politicians were paying them back in tax giveaways. He talked about "corporate puppets in Congress." He didn't let his own employers off the hook. He accused ABC-TV of "kissing the toes" of the giant tobacco companies. After Disney bought ABC, he scolded his new employer for its cheapskate labor practices and complained, with a reference to Mickey Mouse, "Now I work for a rodent." He was fired.

With the boardroom paying close attention to what comes out of the newsroom, you shouldn't expect to hear much on CBS or NBC about the mismanagement of nuclear waste. After all, CBS is now owned by Westinghouse, one of the nation's largest suppliers of nuclear power, and NBC is owned by General Electric, another nuclear power supplier.

And don't expect to hear much, if anything, on NBC or on the public broadcasting system about the sleazy campaign-funding record of Archer Daniels Midland, the giant grain dealer. As journalist Frank Rich has pointed out, that corporation has made a long and successful "effort to minimize tough broadcast journalistic scrutiny of its political contributions and resulting corporate pork by sponsoring not just ABC's *This Week* but NBC's *Meet the Press*, PBS's *News-Hour* and NPR's *All Things Considered.*"

The influence of money on newscasting is enough to make a viewer cynical. When public television rejected several prize-winning documentaries about corporate corruption and waste, many critics reasonably believed it was because PBS did not want to offend corporate sponsors, who now provide nearly 30 percent of the "public" network's money.

America's newest media mogul, Rupert Murdoch, is both frightening and depressing—if he is a portent of the future. Australian-born, Murdoch is global. His News Corporation dominates the newspaper and television markets in Australia and Britain, and his satellite Star TV beams five channels into thirty-nine countries, from Israel to Indonesia.

He became a U.S. citizen in 1985 strictly for commercial reasons, as he admits. It was the only way the Federal Communications Commission would permit him to buy a network. In 1995, the FCC cleared his purchase of Fox TV, which is the biggest owner of television stations in terms of viewership, reaching 40 percent of the nation. His News Corporation also owns Twentieth Century Fox movie studios, *The New York Post, TV Guide,* HarperCollins book publishers, and dozens of other media enterprises here and abroad. They earn $9 billion a year, most of it in the United States, but because of an offshore tax ploy, he pays virtually no taxes to the U.S. government.

Murdoch-controlled media have prospered around the world by stressing what William Shawcross, Murdoch's biographer, accurately called "titillation, sensationalism and vulgarity." Fox TV has already shown ample signs of all three. His newspapers in England have specialized in printing hoaxes, fabricated news, racial scare stories, and propaganda to promote his own ultraconservative political agenda. Some of that last tendency has crept into *The New York Post*. People who have worked for him say he constantly meddles in editorial policy and directs the slanting of political reporting. Typically, because he wanted to increase his business with China, he ordered his book publishing company to reject a book critical of China's brutal dictators.

"News is a commodity that is of no more importance to Rupert Murdoch than a television sitcom," says press critic Alex S. Jones. "He crafts news for the audience, but in fact his sense of what the audience wants is skewed to sensation and a lowering, not an elevation, of standards."

Do Bank Robbers Hold Press Conferences?

The dangerous power of the television empires to manipulate news was dramatically illustrated in the way the major networks threw a cover of silence over the Telecommunications Act of 1996, which was the first big change in telecommunications law in sixty years.

The congressional debate over that legislation centered on the question: What should be done with the "digital spectrum" (an electronic spectrum which would allow television companies to own many new channels and give them marketing opportunities never before imagined)? Should it be auctioned to the television industry, which would bring an estimated $70 billion into the U.S. Treasury? Or should the digital spectrum be *given* to the industry?

If the questions had been carefully explained to the public, of course people would have overwhelmingly encouraged Congress to demand an auction. But it was never explained to the public. The print press gave it little attention. And the networks ignored it entirely. From the introduction of the legislation in May 1995 until its passage in February 1996, the evening news shows on the major networks—NBC, CBS and ABC—gave this monumentally important story a total of nineteen minutes—and in none of that brief time did they mention the possibility of an auction. The topic was simply blacked out for nine months. And during that long silence, the broadcasters poured millions of dollars into congressional campaigns to buy their votes. Result: The public was robbed of $70 billion.

Silence on the network news programs allowed the crime to take place. As Charles Lewis, head of the Center for Public Integrity put it, "The broadcasters didn't want to discuss it because that would have been like a bank robber stopping in the middle of a bank robbery and calling a press conference in front of the bank and saying, 'Look what we're doing here.' The last thing the broadcasters wanted to stir up was a public discussion."

Glitz Pays Off

It would be quite misleading to discuss how money shapes the news by talking only of the income of corporations and publishers. The color of green tints the news right down to the reportorial level on the major newspapers. It must be somewhat difficult for the highest-paid newspaper reporters in New York and Washington to identify with working stiffs when they are earning as much as members of Congress. Even so-so reporters on the big newspapers commonly earn more than twice the national average income. But the media stars on television are in a different galaxy altogether, with multimillion-dollar salaries commonplace. Television anchors get paid more in a year than most Americans earn in a lifetime. Do they sympathize with lower-income Americans? Diane Sawyer, who was being paid $7 million a year by ABC, crusaded against "welfare cheats," which is what she considered the single mother she interviewed on one program. This mother couldn't support herself and her four-year-old child on her monthly welfare check of $600, so she secretly (the welfare department would have considered it a fraud) worked two low-pay, part-time jobs that brought her total annual income up to $16,700. Sawyer, who earned much more in one day than that woman earned in a year, scolded: "You know people say you shouldn't have children if you can't support them."

Sam Donaldson of ABC contributed to a segment on *Prime Time Live* attacking federal farm subsidies. Donaldson, who earned an estimated $2 million from ABC, did not mention that he was collecting nearly $100,000 in federal subsidies for what he calls his "little ranching business" (totaling a mere 20,000 acres) in New Mexico.

Some old-timers like Walter Cronkite, CBS's revered anchor in the pre-Dan Rather days, deplore the drift toward elitism. In his recent memoir he writes,

> It does seem to me that these gigantic multimillion-dollar incomes must remove the anchorpeople from any pretense of association with or even understanding of the average person.

When he started out as a reporter, a long generation ago,

> nearly all of us newspeople, although perhaps white-collar by profession, earned blue-collar salaries, were part of the 'common people.' We drank in our corner bars with our friends, the cops and firemen, the political hacks from City Hall, the shoe salesmen and the ribbon clerks. . . . We could identify with the average man because we were him. That perhaps still exists at some levels of journalism and in some communities, but certainly in Washington and the major cities the press . . . incomes elevate them to the upper strata of political and business society, where their friends are among the rich and the powerful.

But for some of the media celebrities, the salary is just the beginning of what has sarcastically, and accurately, been called "buckraking." The lecture circuit for them is a gravy train. (But to their credit, the best known anchors, Tom Brokaw, Dan Rather, and Peter Jennings, don't indulge in this.) Just about anyone whose face is familiar on television can expect to knock down at least $15,000 for an hour of blather before some special-interest group. David Gergen, a columnist at *U.S. News & World Report* and a long-time commentator on public television, earned $466,625 in speaking fees in one recent year. Network news stars like Donaldson and Cokie Roberts can pocket $30,000 for a speech.

Some of the payoffs are unseemly, to say the least. At a time when tobacco companies were under fire from the press, Steve Roberts, then with *U.S. News & World Report*, accepted a reported $30,000 to speak at a Philip Morris conference. When Congress was in the midst of the health-care reform battle, Lesley Stahl of CBS was paid $20,000 to moderate a program for an insurance company that would be crucially affected by the outcome of the battle. Would that fee affect her reporting?

As mentioned previously, some of the biggest stars have turned their backs on the lecture circuit, or donate their fees to charity. "I call it white-collar crime," says Tom Brokaw of NBC. "That's just what I think it is." James Wooten, once a reporter for *The New York Times* and now a senior correspondent for ABC News, says, "The availability of money now, in the quantities journalists are earning from lectures, from TV, from columns—that availability may represent proper capitalism, but in its essence it is corrupting. It becomes the *raison d'etre* of one's life. Reporters should not do things mainly for money. And many of them do, as I sometimes have."

The Revolving Door

Putting aside the question of what big money does to news judgment, there is the serious question of what the revolving door does to it. Christopher Matthews used to be press agent and propagandist for Tip O'Neill when he was House speaker. Before that, Matthews was a speech writer for President Jimmy Carter. Now he is Washington bureau chief for the *San Francisco Examiner,* a syndicated columnist, and sometimes a commentator for CBS News. Ron Nessen, who was press secretary to former President Gerald Ford, became news director for the Mutual Radio Network. David Gergen, who was a White House spokesman under Reagan and Bush, moved over to become a columnist at *U.S. News & World Report* and then went back briefly to help Clinton. James Fallows, later an editor of *U.S. News,* was a speech writer for President Carter. Bill Moyers was press aide to President Johnson before moving into the high-salaried television fraternity. Tom Johnson, president of CNN, worked in the Johnson White House. Jack Rosenthal was press aide to Robert Kennedy; now he runs *The New York Times* Sunday magazine. David Burke was a principal assistant to Senator Edward Kennedy before winding up as president of CBS News. Diane Sawyer, a multimillion-dollar face on television news, was for years a hireling of Richard Nixon. Pat Buchanan, famous for frothing on television, held important press-office posts under both Nixon and Reagan. Dorrance Smith, once on President Ford's staff, became executive producer of ABC's weekend news. Leslie Gelb was a *New York Times* reporter at the State Department, quit to become assistant secretary of state during Carter's term, and then went back to *The Times* to become deputy editorial page editor.

That is only a fraction of the list that could be made up of the national journalists who have come through the revolving politics–press door. What happens to the press when it is so thickly populated at the top by what David Broder correctly describes as "a power-wielding clique of Insiders"? Having worked as propagandists and deal-makers for politicians, are they too sympathetic toward the old gang they used to be part of? Or are about to become part of? What is the public supposed to think of the press's vaunted reputation for objectivity when *Time* magazine's story on the Bush transition period was written by the man about to be employed as Vice President Dan Quayle's press secretary?

The Self-Censorship of Bias

Some self-censorship is motivated by one of the most natural of human passions: bias. Journalists simply like some politicians better than others, and it shows in their coverage (or lack of coverage).

During presidential campaigns, the press enjoys the role of impudent critic, and even enjoys seeing itself as a giant killer. Usually it fills these roles by constantly harping on one personal defect—or imagined defect—in a candidate. For example, in 1972, Senator Edmund Muskie, considered the front-runner for the Democratic nomination, was driven out of the race when some of the press reported (and mentioned again and again) seeing him cry because he was so angry at things the *Manchester, N. H. Union-Leader* had written about his wife; the crying was interpreted as weakness. (Some of the reporters admitted—years later—that maybe they had been mistaken about seeing him cry; maybe it was just snow melting on his cheeks.) In 1987, the press hounded Senator Gary Hart out of the almost certain Democratic nomination by alluding to him as a woman-chaser, and in 1988 Republican candidate Bob Dole was seriously hurt by the press's steady references to his bad temper. Dole's old age was the focus in 1996.

But perhaps it is because presidential candidates take their show on the road that the Washington press corps feels more enthusiastic about snapping at their heels. In the day-to-day coverage of the capital's political establishment, most Washington reporters place a very, very high premium on gentlemanly forbearance. Is a certain senator a heavy drinker? Is a ranking representative a "casual" cocaine snorter? Is a top bureaucrat a financial wheeler-dealer on the side? Does an agency official beat his wife, severely and often? Stuart Taylor, Jr., a reporter in *The New York Times'* Washington bureau, mentioned these activities in an article and went on to say, without seeming to blush, that journalists have "a strong feeling that officials as well as others should be able to live their private lives in peace," meaning no bad publicity, so long as it doesn't interfere with "an official's fitness to discharge a public trust." That sounds admirably broadminded, but in fact all that consideration for private lives is just a timorous excuse for not offending the people in power—or at least those in power that the press likes and admires.

Most members of the press like Bill Clinton, though the vigor with which they pursued evidence of his close friendship with Monica Lewinsky in 1998 might make one think otherwise. From his earliest career, reporters could have made much more out of Clinton's womanizing if they had wanted to. As David Maraniss points out in his Pulitzer Prize–winning biography, Clinton had for years had an incredible reputation for philandering, and it was fear of what that reputation would do to him that kept him from jumping into the presidential race in 1988 when his fellow philanderer, Gary Hart, was forced to quit. When Clinton ran for president in 1992 and his alleged affair with Gennifer Flowers, an ex-lounge singer, came up, the press gave heavy coverage to it, but only briefly; and some reporters even brought pressure on their colleagues—successfully—to put an end to questions on that subject. While the press truly exploded over the Lewinsky affair, eventually it acted almost ashamed of itself for having done so—a reversal that *The New York Times* sarcastically labeled "The Press's Mea Culpa Epidemic."

There was a time when the two most important money committees in Congress were chaired by falling-down drunks—Russell Long in the Senate and Wilbur Mills in the House—and many members of the press corps knew it. But Long was a good ol' boy from Louisiana who loved to tell jokes. Reporters liked him. Not a word was printed about his problem until he finally reformed and the press could write glowing stories praising him for his revival. As for Mills, an easy-going fellow from Arkansas who sometimes hosted members of the press at his favorite bar, the Silver Slipper, reporters might not have ever mentioned his problem if he hadn't gone swimming in the Tidal Basin with his girlfriend, a stripper called the "Argentine Bombshell." Neither the cops nor the press could ignore that.

When Congressman Wayne Hays of Ohio was caught putting his mistress on his staff at taxpayers' expense, newspapers kept it on the front page for days and the television networks gave the running account of Hays's sexual adventures top priority. One cannot suppose that the press was motivated strictly by outrage over an elected official's use of public money for private pleasures. If that were the case, reporters would not have ignored President Kennedy's alleged affairs with a Mafia moll, with several actresses, and with two White House secretaries who, according to *Time* magazine, "displayed few secretarial skills" and "usually were assigned quarters near the president and were assigned the code-names 'Fiddle' and 'Faddle' by the Secret Service." But *Time* didn't write that until twelve years after the fact. Indeed, the same periodicals that sounded so shocked by the Hays affair and kept the congressman in the headlines had known about the Kennedy escapades at the time they were happening, but covered them up and wrote not a line about them until years after Kennedy was dead.* Why the different treatment? One explanation is that until lately any president got comparatively kid-glove treatment from the press when it came to his private life. But another likely explanation is that Kennedy was highly popular with the press; he was considered a nice guy. Hays, on the other hand, was not only one of the most powerful people in Congress but also one of the most despised. Many of his colleagues and most members of the press considered him an obnoxious bully. They delighted in embarrassing him. For all its preachments about objectivity, the press is subject to the frailties of favoritism.

Nixon was justified in complaining that the press played favorites. Carl Albert, then Speaker of the House of Representatives, had a serious drinking problem. Sometimes he got drunk at the Zebra Lounge; sometimes, while drunk, he picked fights; now and then he would try to drive his car home, with loud, fender-bending results. Rarely did even a whiff of this get into the newspapers or on television, though dozens of reporters were aware that these things were happening. But Albert was a pleasant, innocuous little guy, and apparently the press felt protective of him. This greatly rankled President Nixon, who told his aide, John Ehrlichman, "If that were me, there outside the Zebra Lounge, drunk and running into things, the cops taking me home, my picture would be on every television station in the country. Isn't there some reporter with guts to run this story?" According to Ehrlichman, Nixon tried to plant a story about Albert's drunkenness with a friendly reporter, but failed.

In modern times, perhaps the greatest harm from the press' vulnerability to personal bias came with its coverage of Senator Joseph

---

*In his memoir of life as a White House correspondent, Robert Pierpoint tells of covering Kennedy when he attended a party at Palm Springs, and seeing Kennedy disappear into the back of a presidential limousine with a woman who was not Kennedy's wife. "As the light went on inside the car," writes Pierpoint, "we got a brief glimpse of his young friend just before she disappeared into the president's arms. Then the light went out again." Later he saw her "disengaging herself" from Kennedy and receiving a "brief farewell kiss." Pierpoint says he reported nothing of what he had seen "although I might report a similar incident were I to witness it today" (Robert Pierpoint, *At the White House* [New York: Putnam, 1981], pp. 193–194).

McCarthy of Wisconsin in the early 1950s. McCarthy created an anti-communist hysteria in government that led to widespread witch-hunting. Hundreds of officials were fired because they were suspected of being "procommunist." When McCarthy frowned, even the most patriotic Americans trembled. He was a thug, a liar, a con man; but he wielded tremendous power because he knew how to manipulate the press. From early 1954 until the end of 1956, he was rarely off the front page. How did he achieve this power? Because most reporters liked him personally; they appreciated his easy accessibility; and they loved to cover him because he was colorful and created wonderful—if false—stories for them. David M. Oshinsky, who has written the most complete biography of McCarthy, tells us that "before long a strange and mutually supportive bond had emerged between" the senator and the reporters covering him.

> With few exceptions . . . the press was quite fond of McCarthy. Its members knew he was a fountain of sordid misinformation. . . . But they loved to kibbitz with him, swap stories, have a few drinks, or play some cards. One of his sternest critics commented, "You knew very well that he was a bum—still, you liked this kind of bum." . . . At the same time, they viewed Joe as a "dream story," a guy who put those lucky enough to cover him on page one, where every reporter feels he belongs. The press flocked to McCarthy because he was bizarre, unpredictable, entertaining, and always newsworthy.
>
> Time after time, newspapers printed his distortions and falsehoods under banner headlines on the front page only to find, much later, that McCarthy had made a sucker of them. And yet, because he was privately amiable and publicly a good show, the press kept coming back for more—and thereby strengthened his savage crusade.

The Reagan Love Affair

If the press can unmake presidents, as Nixon discovered, it can also go a long way toward making a president. Ronald Reagan is the perfect example. Though it had treated him with some disdain as a candidate, as soon as he was sworn in, the press became overwhelmingly biased in his favor, particularly during his first two years in office. It was in that early period that his public-relations image was inflated to such a degree that Congress began looking upon him as the Man with the Magic Tongue, a kind of pied piper who could lead us back into a Hollywood wonderland where, if you simply ignore them, nasty things like the national debt and racism and poverty disappear somewhere over the rainbow.

To be sure, every president has a "honeymoon" period with the press at the start of his administration, and that's only proper, for a president should be allowed a few months to learn his way around the White House before he is subjected to sharp criticism. But Reagan got more than a honeymoon. He got an orgy.

The Washington press establishment had been bored by the up-tight and preachy President Carter. So Reagan, with his nice-guy personality, his aw-shucks grin, and his trunk full of vaudeville jokes (a personality practiced for many years in "best friend" roles in Hollywood's B-grade movies), was enthusiastically embraced by the press and other Washington insiders.

Although there had been no evidence of a socko personality in the 1980 campaign, which Reagan won by less than 51 percent of the popular vote, almost immediately after he moved into the White House, the press began discovering (for itself) qualities in Reagan that the public had obviously missed. It coined and endlessly repeated its cliché description of Reagan as "the great communicator." Press critic Mark Hertsgaard has correctly pointed out that Reagan's reputation as the great communicator was in fact amplified and sustained—until much of the nation began to believe it—by news coverage that was "little short of adulatory."

At the end of Reagan's first year in office, Haynes Johnson, a columnist for *The Washington Post* who usually repeated the Establishment line, said, "For the first time in years, Washington has a president that it really likes"—thereby indirectly confessing the press' loss of objectivity.

With *The Washington Post, The New York Times, Time* and *Newsweek* magazines, *The Wall Street Journal,* and other influential periodicals parroting praise of Reagan's "likeability" and "popularity," it was only natural that members of Congress got the idea that the press was talking about Reagan's popularity not only in Washington but in the nation at large. Intimidated (as they easily are), the federal legislators decided that they had better not oppose his programs lest they enrage their constituents. Consequently, in his first two years in office, Reagan won a number of crucial legislative victories—some of them highly damaging to the country—that he would never have won if the press had not softened Congress with its endless refrain of Reagan's "popularity."

Was he really as popular as the press made out? Not at all. Two scholars at the University of California, San Diego, have written:

> The record shows that in his first two years in office, precisely the
> period during which his reputation as a popular leader was firmly

established in the media and while opposing politicians ducked and covered to avoid his supposed juggernaut of popularity, Ronald Reagan regularly scored lower approval ratings than any other newly elected president since World War II.

Not only did Reagan average a significantly lower rating with the general public during his first two years for *job performance* than had Carter, Nixon, Johnson, Kennedy, or Eisenhower, he also scored significantly less than those presidents did in *personality approval*.

"So why," ask our two kibitzers, "should a sense of Reagan's enormous popularity have been firmly planted when the leading polls consistently contradicted it? Why did reporters apparently believe and write as if Reagan's popularity was inviolate and transcendent?" Why did *Newsweek* magazine, for example, claim that Reagan's popularity ratings were "the highest in polling history," when all evidence pointed to the exact opposite?

Their answer, an accurate one, is that the Washington reporters who covered Reagan were less interested in what the president's policies were doing to the rest of the country than they were in personally being entertained by him. They *liked* him, so they felt the people in Peoria must or should like him, too. In other words, Reagan's popularity was grotesquely inflated "thanks to a surprisingly insular Washington establishment that ignored the polls and confirmed its own face-to-face impressions by talking to itself."*

The Herd Instinct

Laziness, an unwillingness to offend friendly political sources, peevish envy of successful colleagues, devotion to journalistic "stylishness" (a cultural preference for the going thing), philosophical uncertainty and anxiety that induce the press to move with extreme

---

*The press's weird insistence on Reagan's popularity continued throughout his time in office and even after he left Washington. On April 20, 1989, while reporting George Bush's early popularity ratings, *The New York Times* referred to Reagan as "one of the most popular presidents in American history." To which Thomas Ferguson, political science professor at the University of Massachusetts, responded in *The Nation* that "this ever-popular and seemingly indestructible refrain monumentally distorts the truth." He pointed out that the Gallup Poll averages for Reagan's entire period in office showed his job approval rating at 52 percent, not impressively higher than Carter's 47 percent or Nixon's 48 percent and below Lyndon Johnson's 54 percent. Reagan wasn't in the same league with Kennedy, 70 percent, Eisenhower, 66 percent, or Roosevelt, 68 percent. Even the lowest scorers, Ford and Truman at 46 percent were closer to Reagan than Reagan was to Kennedy, Eisenhower, or FDR (*Nation*, April 22, 1989).

caution—what does all of that add up to? It often adds up to herd journalism: Editors and reporters trotting off in the same direction, grazing the same hillsides, going after the same stories, covering them the same way, interpreting the government's actions in the same light, swallowing the same excuses, believing the same rumors, and patting each other on the back for the mutual limitations of "responsible journalism"—by which most of them mean not taking risks, not going after the hard ones, not "embarrassing the profession" by upsetting the Establishment. There's a clubby, lazy, selfish reason why reporters covering the same beat are content to follow the pack: If one of them should break away and dig up a hard-hitting story on his or her own, others would be obliged to get out and do some extra work, too.

When the Watergate burglary took place, almost the entire national press corps dismissed it as an event of no consequence—or, worse, as a story that *The Washington Post* was blowing all out of proportion in order to hurt President Nixon unfairly in the approaching presidential campaign. In his history of the Watergate affair, J. Anthony Lukas notes:

> Most newspapers dismissed the Watergate burglary as a joke; their favorite word for it that fall was "caper." Ben Bagdikian, writing later in the *Columbia Journalism Review,* reported that of the 433 reporters in the sixteen largest newspaper bureaus in Washington, fewer than fifteen reporters were assigned full time to the Watergate story. The average Washington bureau had no one on the story full time. . . .
> And most newspapers, magazines, and television networks devoted relatively little attention to Watergate in the months before the election.

Big-name reporters were reluctant to offend the White House. Columnist Joseph Kraft, for example, wrote that "President Nixon and John Mitchell couldn't have been involved [in Watergate] because they are too honorable and high-minded, too sensitive to the requirements of decency, fair play, and law." But the two young metropolitan reporters—Bob Woodward and Carl Bernstein of *The Washington Post*—who had uncovered the scandal, went right on digging to the bottom of what was probably the biggest story of the century. Fortunately, they were unencumbered by social ties with the White House, the FBI, and the CIA—any of whom would have been happy to take them aside in a friendly way and try to convince them, over a bottle of beer, that there was nothing to the story.

But after the handful of real diggers had uncovered enough dirt to force Congress to set up a joint committee to investigate Watergate, the rest of the press rushed to cover the scandal. The herd that had been so hard to get excited when the job was difficult came stampeding in for the relatively easy task of covering the public hearings. Now just about everyone in the press began sounding tough. Jumping on the president became the new press fad.

But fads die out. And the hypercritical attitude that reached flood tide at the time of Nixon's resignation gradually slacked off during the Ford and Carter administrations. By the time Reagan arrived in Washington, the press had reverted to its customary attitude of caution and deference in dealing with the White House. The once-stampeding herd resumed munching grass. Aggressive journalism was no longer faddish, and those who practiced it began to feel self-conscious.

"The return to deference," *The Washington Post* executive editor Ben Bradlee explained, "was part of the subconscious feeling we had. . . . You know, initially, after Watergate the public was saying about the press, 'Okay, guys, now that's enough, that's enough.' . . . I think we were sensitive to that criticism much more than we should have been, and that we did ease off."*

The Press Conference Carnival

The herd instinct is institutionalized in the press conference, particularly the White House press conference. Here, everything is orchestrated. Indeed, the press corps assembles in front of the president like an orchestra, and when the president nods his head or points at a favored reporter, that person rises and plays his or her little tune of inquiry.

Actually, the modern press conference should more accurately be called the television conference. While the senior "print" reporter gets to open the conference with the first question and close it with a "Thank you, Mr. President"—a dubious honor bestowed in recent years on Helen Thomas, correspondent for United Press International wire service—the conference as a whole is structured on behalf of the

---

*Bradlee's excuse for going soft is quite misleading. The public didn't ask the press to back off. At the time of the Watergate investigation, a Gallup poll showed that only an insignificant portion of the public—15 percent—felt the Nixon administration was being treated unfairly by the press. And shortly after Reagan came to power, *The Washington Post's* own poll-taker, Barry Sussman, found in an extensive survey that most people felt "that reporting on public figures is too soft and that the media are in bed with the leadership in Washington. . . . The number thinking there is too little investigative reporting far exceeds those thinking there is too much" (Barry Sussman, *What Americans Really Think* [New York: Pantheon, 1988], pp. 121–122).

television networks, because, with at least 20 million Americans watching this little show, it's the networks that count.

If the press conference was structured to suit the print journalists, it would not be broadcast at all, and the reporters would be allowed to shoot endless follow-up questions at the president until they got to the heart of the issue, or until he refused to answer. And he would be allowed to go off the record, if necessary, to give enlightening details that would clarify the administration's position. But under the glare of television lights, and with the nation watching, a reporter is limited to only one follow-up question and the president can dodge and parry with a witticism or a rambling answer that leaves everything as muddled as before.

A clever president who is also a good actor can turn the press conference into a one-act play in which he stars, with a supporting cast of journalists desperate to get their faces on national television. As Hedrick Smith put it, Ronald Reagan made the press corps "characters in the presidential TV serial." Part of Reagan's act was to address the reporters in a friendly way, calling to them by their first names as he grinned and sometimes winked, making him seem "a patient father figure dealing with unruly children—a very subtle but effective put-down." What the national audience wasn't aware of, said Smith, was that Reagan actually knew very few of the reporters and relied on a seating chart to recognize them. If the seats got mixed up, Reagan called reporters by the wrong names—"still affecting familiarity." The show must go on.

Television reporters fight for a chance to participate in this charade. Nothing is so valued as an opportunity to sit on the first row. No matter how vacuous their questions might be, or how meaningless the response they evoke from the president, at least they are *seen* by their employers and by the public, bobbing up and down—and to be seen is everything.

Robert Pierpoint, for twenty years White House correspondent for CBS, says that "top network executives put heavy pressure on their correspondents to be recognized by the president. It is one of the criteria they use in judging how well their White House correspondents are doing. Their reasoning has more to do with show business than with news; it is an emphasis on visibility, not quality. But network news is always, to one degree or another, show business."

A White House press conference is anything but a spontaneous event. The president and his advisers even go through a dress rehearsal, in which he practices handling some of the more likely questions to come up at the real press conference. It's at the dress rehearsal that he is given the seating chart and photos of all the reporters who will be there. As crucial as knowing where the friendly reporters are sitting (sometimes with questions planted by his aides) is knowing where the tough reporters are he should avoid.

There have been great differences in the willingness of presidents to meet with the press. Clinton was an expert at dodging or disarming tough questions at these conferences; but there was a limit to his talents, so, for obvious reasons, he refused to have a single press conference for a ten-month stretch during the peak of his sex scandal. Franklin Roosevelt (though he really despised the press, he relished the opportunity to manipulate it) had seven informal sessions each *month*. Richard Nixon and Reagan had an average of only one press conference every two months, and sometimes Reagan had only four conferences in an entire year because he hated these events and distrusted the press; he was a good actor, but he was too lazy to do the studying necessary to prepare for the questions. Also, he was hard of hearing.

The dress rehearsals, of course, do not prevent blunders from occurring at the real press conference. This was particularly true under Reagan, who not only refused to take the rehearsals very seriously but often used them as an opportunity for a stand-up comic routine—and his staff got ulcers worrying about whether he intended to repeat his gags when he confronted the press. At least once he did just that, with a terrible P.R. backlash. It was in October 1983, when the Senate was debating whether to establish a national holiday for Martin Luther King, Jr.

Senator Jesse Helms of North Carolina opposed the holiday because he suspected King of harboring "a strong sympathy for the Communist Party and its goals." Helms demanded that the FBI open its "raw files" on King, but the bureau refused to do so, saying the files would remain sealed until the year 2027.

During the press conference rehearsal that October, one of Reagan's aides asked him, "Do you think Martin Luther King was a Communist?"

"Well," Reagan responded with a half-grin, "we'll know in thirty-five years, won't we?"

Everyone at the rehearsal laughed, nervously; they thought it was a good insider's gag, but surely he wouldn't repeat it when asked that question at the real press conference.

But he did. And before the public storm died down, Reagan was forced to apologize to King's wife.

So frequently did Reagan goof up that there was a period when his closest advisers urged him to stop holding press conferences altogether. Some outside political observers have urged that *all* presidents do away with the televised version because it seems like such a poor way for the press and the public to discover anything, except to see that the president is still healthy enough to stand on his feet and to hear that he is still mentally capable of putting together several sentences in sequence.

Pseudopatriotic Self-Censorship

One of the duties of the press is to never assume that the government's policymakers are correct, to be skeptical, and to seek out opinions contrary to the prevailing ones. The more important the issues, the more important this is. And yet, on the whole, the press fails to carry out this duty, and ironically its failure is keenest during periods of international crisis, when government leaders are most apt to go off half-cocked and a cool-headed press would be most useful.

This failure was most dramatically demonstrated in the press's willingness to withhold criticism of the policies leading us into the disastrous Vietnam War.* Tom Wicker has admitted the "failure of the American press" to "adequately question the assumptions, the intelligence, the whole idea of America in the world—indeed the whole idea of the world—which led this country into the Vietnam War in the 1960s. It is commonplace now, when the horse has already been stolen, to examine those assumptions. But where were we at the time we might have brought an enlightened public view to bear on that question?"

When Senator Ernest Gruening on March 10, 1964, delivered the first speech in the Senate advocating a pull-out of our troops in Southeast Asia, neither *The Washington Post* nor *The New York Times* printed a word of his message. Reviewing this remarkable failure in 1971, Jules Witcover of *The Los Angeles Times* observed:

> This single incident tells much about the performance of the Washington press corps in covering the Vietnam War. It represents not simply the misreading of the significance of a single event; more critically, it pinpoints the breakdown of a cardinal principle of newsgathering, especially early in the war: pursuit of all points of view.

---

*There were a few notable exceptions. The *Chicago Tribune* opposed the early commitments in Vietnam, and the *St. Louis Post-Dispatch* opposed the war all the way.

While the Washington press corps in those years diligently reported what the government said about Vietnam, and questioned the inconsistencies as they arose, too few sought out opposing viewpoints and expertise until very late, when events and the prominence of the Vietnam dissent no longer could be ignored. Gruening and other early dissenters from official policy in and out of the Senate attest that they found very few attentive ears among Washington reporters in the early 1960s.

Aside from being pro-war by neglect throughout all the years of the Vietnam build-up, the press was also pro-war in the contents of its stories and broadcasts.

When Seymour Hersh uncovered the story of the My Lai massacre, he had difficulty getting his stories published, despite the fact that it was probably the biggest news story of 1969. When the massacre series did catch fire in the public's imagination,

> Suddenly, nearly every war correspondent who had been in Vietnam had an atrocity story to tell. *Time*'s correspondent Frank McCullough had had nothing to say about atrocities when, in December 1967, he had written a farewell assessment of Vietnam after covering the war for four years. Now, McCulloch recalled having seen men pushed from aeroplanes, shot with their hands tied behind their backs, and drowned because they refused to answer questions.

Other reporters lined up to add their tales of past horrors.

Why did they wait for Hersh's example of truth-telling? Why had they not written about these things at the time they happened? Obviously, because they were censoring themselves or they were being censored by their editors and publishers.

In his 1995 autobiography, Ben Bradlee, the legendary editor of *The Washington Post*, admitted, "In my time as editor, I have kept many stories out of the paper because I felt—without any government pressure—that the national security would be harmed by their publications." What made him think his judgments in such matters were superior to government officials who, he went on to say, "more often than not, in my experience, use the claim of national security as a smoke screen to cover up their own embarrassment"?

Whatever his excuse for self-censorship, it met the standards of Katherine Graham, who, looking back on her long career as publisher of *The Post*, said, "There are some things the general public does not need to know and shouldn't. I believe democracy flourishes when the government can take legitimate steps to keep its secrets and when the press can decide whether to print what it knows."

Bay of Pigs

Next to the self-censorship of the Vietnam War, perhaps the most damaging was that which helped lead to the invasion of Cuba at the Bay of Pigs.

In November 1960, Carey McWilliams, editor of the *Nation,* learned that the next issue of *Hispanic American Report* was to contain an article by Ronald Hilton, then director of Stanford's Institute of Hispanic American and Luso-Brazilian Studies, in which he reported that the CIA was training Cuban exiles at a hidden base in Guatemala. The "secret" was well known to Guatemalans, according to Hilton, as was the purpose of the training.

McWilliams phoned Dr. Hilton for further details and wrote an editorial for the November 19 issue of the *Nation* in which he outlined the upcoming cloak-and-dagger adventure and urged that the rumor "be checked immediately by all U.S. news media with correspondents in Guatemala." The *Nation* sent seventy-five proofs of that editorial to the major news centers of New York, including the wire services and *The Times,* with no results. On April 7, nearly five months after the *Nation*'s editorial, *The Times* printed its own account of the pending military experiment, but by this time it was too late to reverse the disastrous chain of events leading to the Bay of Pigs. And even in its April 7 story, *The Times* withheld information it had on the involvement of the CIA and the nearness of the invasion date.

After the debacle, it was discovered that *The Miami Herald* had also withheld a story of the pending invasion—written and set aside at about the same time the *Nation* was trying to alert the press—and that the *New Republic* had written an exposé one month prior to the invasion that was killed by the publisher, Gilbert Harrison, at the request of the White House. *The Times, The Miami Herald,* and the *New Republic* obviously saw themselves as an adjunct of the government and as a supporter, through silence, of government propaganda, for the State Department was issuing lies on the hour in an effort to hide the gambit.

As it turned out, the press' patriotism was as stupid as the government's policy making. Even President Kennedy admitted it, telling Turner Catledge, then *The Times*' managing editor, "If you had printed more about the operation, you would have saved us from a colossal mistake."

Government officials have quite naturally come to think of publishers and editors and network officials as handmaidens of the government, and also see reporters in that way.* And indeed, many reporters have proved willing to be flunkies for the Establishment. In recent years, to the great embarrassment of the press, it has been revealed that more than 400 journalists have "cooperated" with the CIA in planting stories and acting as conduits for self-serving leaks and blatant propagandizing. Some have served as intelligence agents. Some of the reporters actually took money from the CIA for their work; some did it simply because they enjoyed being chums with spies or because they felt it was the patriotic thing to do. At one time, the CIA had as many as 800 "propaganda assets" (its phrase for recruited newsmen) at work secretly; most were foreign journalists but a large minority were U.S. journalists. Asked if the CIA ever told such agents what to write, William E. Colby, the former CIA director, replied, "Oh, sure, all the time." CIA memos uncovered by congressional investigators have told of successes in getting *The New York Times* and *The Washington Post* to use news stories in accordance with "our theme guidance."†

How to Keep a Reporter Down

When the Washington press corps isn't being sold out by management, and when it isn't being opiated by star-spangled orthodoxies, and when it isn't being cannibalized by envious peers, and when it isn't exhausting itself chasing politicians who are out of town on four-day weekends and bureaucrats who are out of the office on three-hour lunches, there are still other handicaps.

Many other handicaps. Why? Because, although they often work together with an openness and a constructiveness that is found in no other nation in the world, our government and our press are natural enemies. The reasons for this animosity are obvious. First of all, part of

---

*Irritated by surprisingly tough questions from one newsman, Secretary of State Rusk interrupted a news conference to ask angrily, "Whose side are you on, anyway?" Kennedy sometimes asked, without blushing, that reporters exercise self-censorship. Johnson frequently implied that reporters who veered from simply printing administration handouts on the war and on foreign policy were "aiding the enemy."
†Being an agency that depends so heavily on manipulating minds, and having almost unlimited funds at its disposal, the CIA also became notorious for indulging itself in buying pieces of the press. At various times it has owned or subsidized more than fifty newspapers, news services, or radio stations in this country and, mostly, overseas. It financed the writing and publishing of more than 250 English-language books, of which at least a score was published by reputable book houses in this country.

the business of the press is, to put it bluntly, to embarrass fools and catch rascals, and the government, in every era, is unfortunately infiltrated by a great many of both, who do all they can to frustrate their pursuers. Second, it is much more comfortable, even for honest and efficient members of government, to work without members of the press peering over their shoulders.

The government's antagonisms are usually revealed not in personal attacks on members of the press, but merely in attempts to frustrate and manipulate them. There are a number of very effective ways to achieve this.

Secrets and More Secrets

The most impressive device for keeping the public from finding out what's going on is simply the rubber stamp that transforms ordinary information into "Secret" or "Confidential" or "Eyes Only" or some other cloak-and-dagger pigeonhole. There are more than 120,000 officials in 100 government agencies with the authority to declare what information should be kept secret. The bureaucrats have gone crazy with their little rubber stamps.

It's a costly craziness. Congress estimates that the federal government—not counting the Central Intelligence Agency, which may spend as much on secrecy as the rest of the government combined—spends more than $5 billion a year keeping secret documents secret. The Pentagon's secrecy consumes 90 percent of the $5 billion. But some unlikely agencies—would you believe $1,153,000 for the Department of Agriculture?—also spend big money to keep classified documents from becoming public.

Probably more than 90 percent of the papers in the State Department are classified. The Pentagon uses 19,000 guidelines for deciding on the level of secrecy (each paragraph in a classified paper may get a different rating). Estimates of the Pentagon's inventory of classified documents range up to 200 million pages, with some of the documents going back to the Civil War. Documents marked "Secret" are the commonest thing in town. It has reached a point of total absurdity, as brief glimpses behind the curtain show. Press clippings have been stamped "Secret," as have appointment calendars. Looking over some documents at the Pentagon, *The New York Times* reporter Richard Halloran found this "secret" paragraph: "The Air Force must be able, in conjunction with other U.S. forces and our allies, to deter aggression and defeat it, should aggression occur." The United States Information Agency declassified seventy-seven "highly sensitive" studies that included such red-hot documents as "Opinions and Values of Egyptian Students in West Germany" and "Media Habits of Spanish Intellectuals."

But whether or not high-level government information bears a stamp, it is guarded jealously—sometimes almost psychopathically—and reporters who obtain it without going through routine channels are looked upon as virtually subversive. President Nixon commonly wiretapped the telephones of reporters and of his own officials who he thought might be supplying the reporters with unauthorized data. He set up a special investigating unit—called "the plumbers"—specifically to track down the sources who were talking to reporters and shut them up: that is, to plug the leaks. Reportedly, his "plumbers" at one point proposed setting fire to the Brookings Institution and then going in disguised as firemen to recover some government documents that had been taken there. On another occasion one of Nixon's aides proposed "getting rid" of columnist Jack Anderson, who was regularly publishing confidential data that embarrassed the Nixon administration.

President Carter came into office promising an "open" administration, but by 1978 he was bitterly complaining of an "epidemic" of unauthorized disclosures to the press. He moved vigorously to tighten control over the flow of information. At the Justice Department, some lawyers were required to sign affidavits about their contacts with reporters. As a result of this badgering by their superiors, they became unwilling to talk to reporters.

President Reagan used several methods for sharply reducing the flow of information. He issued an order requiring 250,000 present and former top-level employees of the State Department, the Defense Department, the White House, the National Security Council, the Justice Department, and several other agencies to get permission from a Publications Review Board (just as Central Intelligence Agency officials had been required to do for many years) before publishing anything—even fiction, even a letter to the editor. Also, Reagan ordered federal employees with access to classified information submit to lie detector tests if they were suspected of unauthorized talking to reporters. If they refused to take the test, they could be fired.

To complete the intimidation, Reagan's Justice Department, with the help of the U.S. Supreme Court in the case of *United States* v. *Samuel Loring Morison,* resharpened a very old law and held it at the heart of the press. Morison was a government official who also sometimes wrote articles and supplied information to the British magazine *Jane's Defence Weekly.* His work for the magazine was strictly legal, until one day he passed to it three photographs of Soviet military aircraft taken by a U.S. satellite. The photos were hardly a "secret" to the Soviets, since they were of their own equipment. So how did publication of the pictures hurt U.S. security? Probably it didn't. But the photos were nevertheless "classified" and it was against regulations for Morison to leak them. The Justice Department prosecuted him under the Espionage Act of 1917, which makes it a crime to disclose information "relating to national defense" to anyone not entitled to receive it. The law was aimed at real spies, not at reporters. Several presidents had asked Congress to expand the Espionage Act to stop even the passing or reporting of classified information by bureaucrats and the press, but Congress had always refused. Nevertheless, Reagan decided to use the law against Morison *as if* he were a real spy, and the Supreme Court in 1988 said Reagan had the right to do it. Morison went to prison for two years.

Jack Landau, executive director of the Reporters' Committee for Freedom of the Press, believes that Reagan's censorship efforts were the stiffest since the restrictions of the Second World War.

Under Presidents Bush and Clinton much of the paranoia of the Reagan years disappeared.

President Clinton ordered that most documents older than twenty-five years be declassified. There is a billion-page backlog of documents of that vintage that could be made public, but only 1 percent of the $5 billion budgeted for declassification is being spent, so it's unlikely that the job will ever be completed. Furthermore, there is stiff resistance from the military and intelligence agencies.

Nowhere is resistance stronger than at the CIA. In 1993 the CIA publicly pledged to release files on its most important covert actions of the Cold War—a stack of files reportedly taller than fifty Washington Monuments—and to complete the release within a matter of months.

The promise is still unfulfilled. In 1997 CIA officials claimed that files on one of the agency's most notorious escapades—the overthrow of the government of Iran in 1953—had been "lost" or destroyed years ago. Other important files were reportedly burned. A history professor who served for six years on the CIA's moribund declassification panel left in disgust, saying the CIA wasn't serious about opening its old files and had used the panel simply as a "brilliant public relations snow job."

Leaks

The best antidote to secrecy is "leaks"—the anonymous, unauthorized disclosure of information to the press. Leaks have been a part of American politics and government since the early days of the republic. They are absolutely essential. If leaks were stamped out, the public would learn only what the government wants it to know, which would seldom be enough for the intelligent conduct of a democracy.

A recent survey of current and former senior federal officials revealed that 42 percent of them had deliberately leaked information to the press. Howard Simons, former curator of the Nieman Foundation at Harvard University and a former managing editor of *The Washington Post,* considered it no big deal: "If you live and work as a journalist in Washington long enough, several things about national security and the press become self-evident. . . . The first thing that you learn is that it is impossible, not just improbable, but impossible to do your job without bumping into a secret."

It is no accident that *The Wall Street Journal* winds up with the best leaks on insider trading, or that *The Washington Post* and *The New York Times* get the most fulsome leaks regarding State Department and Pentagon policies. These things are the result of the basic law of leak physics: Secrets always seek the outlet of greatest impact.

Investigative reporters like Woodward and Bernstein have become folk heroes of a sort, and they deserve their adulation, no doubt. But the melancholy truth is that virtually all major stories are uncovered only because somebody in government *wants* them uncovered. And that's true of most middle-status stories as well. Most of the headlines begin with a leak. Sometimes the leaker is a federal employee who is tired of seeing the public pushed around or cheated by the government; sometimes the leaker is a federal employee who wants to get even with the boss or a colleague; sometimes it is an official who wants to put the reporter in his or her debt. But most often the leaker is an official within the administration who simply wants to use the press to influence a decision, to promote policy, to persuade Congress, or to give a signal to foreign governments.

Leaks are also one way the government communicates with itself. If a presidential aide is afraid to confront the president directly with bad news, he or she can get the message across via a leak to a favored reporter. If a cabinet officer is unable to get past the White House palace guard to present a case, he or she can leak a memo to the press. And, in a roundabout way, it will land on the president's desk with the delivery of the next morning's newspaper.

When President Bush tried to get John Tower confirmed as defense secretary by the Senate, Tower's background was given a rigorous check by the FBI and the details of the investigation were passed along to the White House and to Congress. It was supposed to be secret, and in fact the full report was never made public. But by the time Tower's nomination went down in flames, both sides had leaked so much of the report—Democrats leaking details of drinking and wenching, Republicans leaking testimony praising Tower—that the secrecy lay in shreds.

Although every president hates the unauthorized leakers within his administration, it is also true that every president (and every other top official in government) loves to use leaks for his own purposes. When the press was getting information out of the State Department that he didn't want it to get, Lyndon Johnson upbraided a group of startled officials in that agency by shouting, "You're just a bunch of goddamned puppy dogs, running from one fire hydrant to the next." But Johnson himself was constantly whispering self-serving tidbits into the ears of favored reporters. Columnist Carl T. Rowan recalls that when Johnson was vice president he arrived in Vietnam furious with officials there for passing secrets to reporters. And yet—"About an hour later I stumbled upon a cluster of U.S. newsmen in a frantic huddle on a Saigon sidewalk. I peeked inside and there was Lyndon Johnson, reading to them from a 'top secret' cable that he had just received from Kennedy."

Episodes like that are what prompted *Times* columnist James Reston to observe wryly that "government is the only known vessel that leaks from the top."

The Perils of Leaking

The leak system, obviously, is accompanied by dangers. The chief danger is that reporters, in their passion for "scoops," will rush to use leaks without checking them for accuracy or adequately weighing their potential for harm. A perfect example occurred in 1989 when Rita Braver of CBS News reported that Representative William H. Gray III, a Pennsylvania Democrat, was the focus of a criminal investigation by the Justice Department. The story broke during Gray's campaign to become the first African American to serve as House majority whip. Obviously Braver was using a leak from somebody who wanted to ruin Gray's effort. Several days after the story was broadcast, the Justice Department denied its accuracy. Although Gray did win the post of whip, the false leak did serious, if temporary, damage to his reputation. Why didn't the Justice Department punish the leaker? Because it is often impossible to find the offender. In this case, two senior attorneys from the criminal division and eleven FBI agents spent a year hunting the guilty party—taking 109 sworn statements, reviewing thousands of telephone records and phone message slips and appointment calendars, and giving a dozen polygraph tests to department employees—but all in vain.

The bigger the story, the more dangerous the leak system becomes because when the story is big enough to shock the nation, the resulting competition among reporters for leaks of increasing shock value can get out of control. One published leak often leads to a counter-leak—which in turn can develop into a daisy chain of leaks. In such an atmosphere, proper professional restraint may weaken. With the reporters wanting to look good in the eyes of their editors and their competitors, ambition and vanity often win out over caution and common sense. This makes the press extremely vulnerable to being used—"used" in the sense that it is manipulated by self-serving politicians and bureaucrats.

This kind of manipulation became dramatically evident when the Monica Lewinsky sex scandal swirled around President Clinton. Advocates for both sides—the White House and the prosecutor's office—leaked facts, guesses, rumors, and presumptions constantly, and the press used them with little restraint or effort to check their accuracy.

Many leaks came directly from prosecutor Kenneth Starr and his chief deputy, as Starr admitted in a long interview with Steven Brill, a legal expert. These leaks, which were in violation of the bar's ethical code, helped convict Clinton in the public's mind long before the grand jury completed its investigation. That isn't the way justice is supposed to be arrived at in this country.

But the press was also guilty. "What makes the media's performance a true scandal, a true example of an institution being corrupted to its core," says Brill, "is that the competition for scoops so bewitched almost everyone that they let the man in power [Starr] write the story."

An auxiliary corruption that comes from leaks, seldom noticed by the public but widely felt in the Washington press corps, is a corruption of the spirit of competition. The interplay of the top Eastern newspapers with the government discourages some of the excellent reporters whose only sin is in working for newspapers of the "wrong" geography. If reporters for the non-Eastern elite press are unable to open doors and get their share of leaks because of their lack of status, to that degree—and it is a serious degree—the size of the Washington press corps is effectively reduced, and its power is effectively cut. By favoring *The Washington Post* and *The New York Times,* as they do, federal officials have (although probably not by design) dealt a blow to the rest of the press corps.

Delays and More Delays

Although Washington is headquarters for the most centralized major government in the world, a reporter seeking data that could embarrass the bureaucracy may quickly discover that the government has become suspiciously decentralized. "Oh, *that* information," the reporter will be told, "isn't in this office. The only place you can get that is in our regional office in Atlanta," or Denver or Jacksonville or Chicago—anywhere away from Washington.

The regulatory agencies often tell reporters that they do not keep data on such things as travel expenses, costs of investigations, complaints from consumers, or the sales volume and profits of corporations accused of breaking the law. Even if it is evident that they are lying, what is a reporter going to do about it?

If convinced that the agency does in fact have the data being sought, reporters can sue under the Freedom of Information Act to have the information produced. But this technique is extremely time-consuming and uncertain, at best.

Whether bureaucratic officials block the flow of information to the press because they are malicious or because they are stupid, the results are the same: irritating delays. A *Baltimore Sun* reporter, trying to get information about coal-mining safety, ran into this maze:

> I called the Department of Labor and explained what I wanted to know. That, said the nice voice on the other end, was the kind of information we should be able to get from the Occupational Safety and Health Administration. But the nice voice at OSHA suggested we ask the Mining and Health Administration instead. The voice at the other end of *that* line said we had a good question, which might be answered by the Office of Statistical Operations of the Bureau of Labor Statistics. The voice at that end referred us to the Office of Information. The Information Office said we might call the Office of Industrial Relations or the Office of Inquiries and Correspondence. Industrial Relations was kind, but didn't have the information and didn't know who else might. Inquiries and Correspondence thought the best source was the Office of Occupational Safety and Health Statistics. And there, the nicest voice of all said we had a complicated question, but he was sure he would be able to find a meaningful answer. The next day he called back to say he had found it. He said he would mail it.

The consumption of time is (next to secrecy) a government's best way to keep the press at bay. Many topics are too timely to survive a long delay.

On the other hand, when investigative reporters are in a position to wait it out and defeat the government's delaying tactics, the payoff is sometimes very impressive. For example, *The Washington Post* and *The New York Times* asked the Energy Research and Development Administration and the Nuclear Regulatory Commission to supply their joint estimates of how much nuclear material had been lost or stolen from government-subsidized laboratories and factories during the past thirty years. When the agencies expressed reluctance to supply the information, the newspapers sued for it under the Freedom of Information Act. Then the journalists sat back and waited, and waited, and waited. At the end of two years, the government finally admitted the startling truth: It had lost—somehow, but it wasn't sure how—more than 8,000 pounds of nuclear material, enough to make five hundred Hiroshima-sized atomic bombs.

Sweet Talk and Threats

For reporters, sweet talk, little favors, pats on the head, or a social game of tennis are much more dangerous than threats. It is the problem of reporters who get caught up in the swirl of the officialdom they are supposed to be watching, the reporters who think they are important because they had lunch at a posh restaurant with a top-echelon politician, the reporters who get by with calling Senator Edward Kennedy "Teddy"—it's acknowledged to be one of the most crippling of professional diseases.

"When a reporter falls for the messiah complex," says Jerry Greene, once chief of the *New York Daily News* bureau, "and when his complex combines with that of a bureaucrat who thinks he is important, Christ, you need a shovel to clean the room. Send a young reporter to the White House and let him indulge in a presidential trip or two and he isn't worth a damn for six months. He gets on a first-name basis with these clowns, he gets to indulge in fancy drinks and big hotel rooms that he couldn't otherwise afford, and he's wiped out."

The old-timers are just as vulnerable to the chummy syndrome. Mingling with the mighty does something to them. They operate from the Olympian heights, and they perceive the rabble below through the heady fog that comes from being on a first-name basis with political big shots. They associate with the people who are making the news in a cordial backroom atmosphere, and amidst the laughter and clinking of glasses they begin to see things the way their sources see them.

Arthur M. Schlesinger, Jr., one of President Kennedy's advisers, has disclosed that Kennedy, in making his cabinet selections, asked for suggestions from Arthur Krock of *The New York Times,* Marguerite Higgins of the *New York Herald Tribune,* and other top reporters and columnists who secretly—or at least not publicly—served as his unofficial advisers. Having rubbed knees at the council table with the president himself and having been flattered with solicitations for guidance in such important matters, could these press people possibly have written objectively about the Kennedy administration? Were there not favors done for them that they could not forget—and which they would be expected to keep in mind when writing about Kennedy? Indeed, yes. Schlesinger quotes Robert Kennedy as saying that one reason President Kennedy selected Douglas Dillon to be secretary of the treasury was that columnist "Joe Alsop was a tremendous booster of Douglas Dillon. In view of all the favors that Alsop had done I don't think there's any question that this was a factor." The favor locked Alsop into the administration's loop forever, but that wasn't hard to do because Alsop was part of the Old Boy network that long ago lost track of the line between government and the press; he was one of the dozens of journalists who did spy work for the CIA on the side and later boasted of it.

When George Will privately coached Reagan in forensics and then went on television to praise the results—a most unprofessional conflict of interest—he was merely continuing a tradition of duplicity set years before by such chaps as the legendary Walter Lippmann, who gave Kennedy advice on what to say in his inauguration speech and then praised the speech in his column. Having learned from personal experience how unrewarding such toadyism is, Lippmann in his retirement warned younger reporters of "the most important forms of corruption in the modern journalist's world . . . the many guises and disguises of social climbing on the pyramids of power."*

A certain amount of probing and criticism is tolerated in this symbiotic arrangement. A top official will allow reporters who are close and friendly to disagree within accepted limits. Even to criticize him within accepted limits. That's part of the game. But the official sets the limits—and to this extent his reporter pals are corrupted.

The reporter who must cover one beat regularly or cover one congressional delegation is subjected to what are perhaps even more relentless demands to string along. Columnist Robert Walters elaborated:

---

*Of course, some journalists love to flaunt their social climbing. Columnist Will, who let everyone know that he was a frequent luncheon confidant of Mrs. Reagan, even turned off some of Reagan's closest associates. White House press secretary Larry Speakes called Will "the most pompous and arrogant among the whole legion of egotists, prima donnas, and problem children who report on the White House" (Larry Speakes, *Speaking Out: Inside the Reagan White House,* with Robert Pack [New York: Scribners, 1988], p. 219).

You get invited to the agency's parties. Not that the bureaucrats are consciously trying to co-opt you. They just want to get to know you better and make you feel more kindly toward them. But then if you get into a shoving match with them over some story, you get the stick instead of the carrot. You not only don't get invited to the parties, what's more important, you don't get invited to the background briefings. The same goes for reporters covering for Wyoming or Nebraska or Connecticut papers at the Capitol. It becomes a totally symbiotic relationship.

If you go to enough congressional parties and talk with enough drunk administration aides and legislative aides, you sure enough find out quick where a senator's faults are, which special interests he's responsive to, and how they repay him. But it's suicide to the hick reporters if they write it. Their congressional offices just cut them off with no more tips on what's going to happen. I don't know of any cases where that's actually happened, but I know that small newspaper reporters fear it, and they just won't write tough stories about the politicians they regularly cover for exactly that reason.

Reporters for big newspapers suffer from the same party-circuit complex. When Dr. Peter Bourne, President Carter's adviser on drug controls, was found to have signed a prescription for a much-abused drug made out to a fictitious person, the press had a field day. It was a front-page scandal immediately. Bourne resigned, but not before a second round of stories appeared, quoting unidentified sources who claimed to have seen Dr. Bourne smoking marijuana and snorting cocaine at a Washington party seven months earlier. One of the stories was broken by columnist Jack Anderson; the other by *The Washington Post*. But neither Anderson nor *The Post* told the whole story: The "unidentified sources" they were quoting were, in fact, their own reporters, who had been at the party where Bourne allegedly had taken the cocaine. The disturbing questions raised are these: Why didn't these reporters write about Bourne's activities at the party immediately afterward? Why did they wait seven months? Was it because they didn't feel it was "right" to reveal illegal activities of a fellow party-goer? Or did they just feel that it was safer to tell all when it appeared that Bourne was finished as a government official and therefore could do them no more good as a source?

Probably the latter, for it is a cruel fact of life in the Washington jungle that although the press will give special protection to good sources, it will also devour them if their usefulness seems about to end in scandal. House Speaker Jim Wright discovered this unhappy truth in 1989. As the third most powerful politician in Washington and therefore as the constant source of rich, off-the-record tidbits, he had been treated with deference by the press corps, which sometimes covered up for him. For example, in 1987 *The Washington Post, The New York Times* and *The Wall Street Journal* learned that Wright's assistant, John Paul Mack, had brutally attacked a young woman in 1973 and been sentenced to fifteen years in prison; after two and a half years, Wright got Mack (who was linked to Wright's family by marriage) out of jail and gave him a job on his staff, where he rose to the top. Here was a socko human-interest story, but neither *The Post* nor *The Times* nor *The Journal* wrote a word about it in 1987. Why not? Was it because they thought it unfair to dig up fourteen-year-old dirt on a man who had obviously rebuilt his life? Or was it because the papers didn't want to lose entree to the House Speaker? The answer came two years later when Wright, once considered almost invulnerable, seemed likely to be driven from office by a congressional investigation of his ethics. In the midst of that struggle, at a time when the disclosure was particularly damaging to Wright, *The Post* broke its silence and wrote up Mack's crime in all its bloody details. Other parts of the media, not wanting to be left behind, joined in. The symbiotic relationship between press and sources can be treacherous.

President Johnson thought he knew how to coddle and threaten the White House press corps. He gave 374 individual interviews in his first fifteen months of office (by comparison, Nixon gave none), and he thought surely the press must love him as a result; when he found out it didn't, he tried getting tough. On one occasion the White House press plane was mysteriously diverted to a field other than the one the president's plane had landed at, and the reporters were left to catch up with him any way they could. Some had to hitchhike aboard a garbage truck. A reporter who wrote about Johnson as a "people eater"—meaning one whose ego and demands devoured those around him—was told he would not get to speak to Johnson again until he had written a nice story to cancel out the other. Occasionally, a White House reporter who was dictating a story on the telephone would be startled by Johnson's breaking in on the line and criticizing something the reporter was telling his home office. He had been eavesdropping.

President Carter's relationship with the press quickly cooled once he was in office. Although reporters treated him, generally, to soft and friendly stories during his first three years, they went relentlessly after one of his oldest cronies, Thomas Bertram Lance, whom he had appointed director of the Office of Management and Budget. Reporters uncovered so many questionable activities in Lance's practices as a Georgia banker that he felt obliged to resign. Carter, furious, began to hold the press at a greater distance. Doors in the White House were closed. Reporters found it extremely difficult to get interviews with even the lowliest White House officials. When James Wooten, a reporter for *The New York Times,* described Carter in an article as a brooding and humorless taskmaster, tough on subordinates, who "seems to be retreating more and more into the sanctuary of his little study," Carter and his top aides reacted much in the same vengeful manner as Nixon would have. Jody Powell, Carter's press aide, tried to find out from which employees Wooten had gotten his information so that they could be fired. (He was unsuccessful.) And Wooten suddenly found himself running into such a wall of resistance from all important sources at the White House that *The Times* decided it might be expedient to shift him to a different beat.

Pique, even presidential pique, seldom has the frightening effect on the press that officialdom desires. Except, of course, with the television and radio networks. They are, of all the news media, the most easily frightened. Panic is a normal condition for them. They have their excuses, but they are only excuses. Bill Monroe, who used to be one of Washington's editors for NBC, argues that the networks' fears are justified because the Federal Communications Commission, which has life and death powers over all radio and television stations, "has a Democratic majority when a Democrat is in the White House and a Republican majority when a Republican is in the White House. So it is a board with a certain political tone to it that is guiding television editors on certain decisions in areas where no government body would dare tell newspaper editors what to do. Under these circumstances, is television a free element of a free press? No, it is not. Where it gets FCC guidance, it is a captive of seven men who owe their jobs to the White House."

If ever a fear was based on the flimsiest hypothesis, this one that hovers around television business offices certainly is. Not one of the hundreds of television stations—neither those owned by networks nor those owned by others—has ever lost its license because of its news coverage. But the very thought of risking one of those golden licenses for something as transient as a hard-hitting news story turns the corporate heart to Jell-O. And as long as this is true, the politicians of the day will take advantage of it.

Network officials sometimes admit they are willing to be spoon fed. ABC News vice president, Jeff Gralnick, put it this way: "It's my job to take the news as they choose to give it to us and then, in the amount of time that's available, put it into the context of the day or that particular story. . . . The evening newscast is not supposed to be the watchdog on the government." Indeed, the evening news is not only *not* a watchdog, it is not even a good bulletin board.

Not all fears of high-level revenge for aggressive reporting are unwarranted, however. The big boys in government have shown they are willing to play rough with the press. When several newspapers began printing the Pentagon Papers, the Nixon administration obtained a temporary injunction prohibiting the newspapers from continuing to publish these documents. For fifteen days that restraint was in effect before the Supreme Court lifted the ban. The press claimed a victory, but in fact it was a chilling defeat: For the first time in our nation's history, American newspapers had been restrained by a court order from printing the news.

Reagan played the roughest of all when he sent the military to invade the island of Grenada in 1983 without informing the press. It was the first war—if the conquest of such a tiny nation by such a powerful nation can be called a war—in U.S. history that the public was denied coverage by a free press. In the early, crucial days of the fighting, reporters were banned from the island; the only "news" releases and television films issued for public consumption were those concocted by the Pentagon's propaganda staff. Indeed, the fanatical secrecy of the Reagan administration was best symbolized by something that happened in that invasion. Vice Admiral Joseph Metcalf III, commander of the task force, ordered his ships to actually fire at any boats that attempted to take reporters to the island. They were willing to kill the press.

Usually, however, the military is content simply to hold the press hostage. Hundreds of reporters who flew down to cover the 1990 invasion of Panama were locked up in Army buildings as soon as they landed and were denied access even to a telephone.

In the Persian Gulf War, the press was reduced to being nothing but a mouthpiece for the military brass. Journalists were permitted to cover the war only in "pools" accompanied at all times by Pentagon "public affairs" escorts, and all their dispatches were reviewed in advance by military censors. A press photographer who tried to work outside the pool system was held for six hours by U.S. Marines who threatened to shoot him if he left his automobile. That was typical. Malcolm Brown, a reporter for *The New York Times*, wrote during that conflict: "Nearly all the reporters who have tried to reach American front-line units have been arrested at one time or another, and sometimes been held up to twelve hours in field jails."

Did accuracy suffer from the military's tight control? You bet. While the fighting was going on, military propagandists put out lots of television clips showing precision-guided bombs—the so-called "smart bombs"—going down chimneys or in the doors of Iraqi targets. Viewers would assume our bombers had incredible efficiency. What the military didn't tell the public until the war was long over was that "smart bombs" made up only 7 percent of all the U.S. explosives dropped on Iraq and that 70 percent of the 88,000 tons of bombs that were dropped in the forty-three days of war missed their targets.

The most disturbing part of this censorship was that very few publishers and editors strongly protested the way their reporters were treated or the way the news was manipulated, and polls showed that the American public by a wide margin approved of the military's suppression of information from the battlefront.

Lies and More Lies

Most officials tell the truth most of the time, but their record for veracity drops off dramatically when questions begin touching important nerve centers. Furthermore, it is an operational rule to expect all officials to lie or play ignorant when to do otherwise would be to inconvenience themselves or to disturb their work. Given the character and perspective of most politicians and public officials, it is probably natural that they act in this way. Their first objective is to survive in office, and they feel that the best way to survive is to duck criticism, to shift the blame to others, to sidestep hot issues, to always have a cartload of excuses and alibis ready in case of emergency. This is simply the protective coloration of the official animal—chartreuse, combining the natural hues of ambition and fear.

Presidents probably don't lie any more than other politicians, but because they hold center stage, presidential lies seem particularly dramatic and are indeed particularly damaging. In recent decades, fate and the ballot box have given America several presidents who reached historic heights of mendacity. Examples of presidential lying are so numerous, especially in foreign affairs, that reporters often despair of having it otherwise and ask only that the lies be flamboyant ones that make good copy. No modern president supplied more of that type than Lyndon Johnson did. To hide the horrible blunders of the Vietnam War, he would lie about how many American soldiers had been killed and instructed his secretary of defense, Robert McNamara, to report only half the costs of the war.

One of his most elaborate falsehoods was spun in an effort to win public support for his invasion of the Dominican Republic. On April 23, 1965, there was a revolt in that country. When President Johnson sent in the Marines, reporters intimately familiar with the workings of our State Department and with the situation in the Dominican Republic wrote that our fighters were sent to prevent a communist coup. The State Department denied this, and so did President Johnson, both insisting that the only reason Marine and Army personnel were being sent to the Caribbean nation was to protect American citizens living or visiting there. To make his point, President Johnson said in a news conference on May 5, that "there has been almost constant firing on our American Embassy. As we talked to Ambassador Bennett [on the phone], he said to apparently one of the girls who brought him a cable, he said, please get away from the window, that glass is going to cut your head, because the glass had been shattered, and we heard the bullets coming through the office where he was sitting while talking to us." By June 17, Johnson had really warmed up to the subject. He held another news conference in which he further explained his intervention:

> some 1,500 innocent people were murdered and shot, and their heads cut off, and as we talked to our ambassador to confirm the horror and tragedy and the unbelievable fact that they were firing on Americans and the American Embassy, he was talking to us from under a desk while bullets were going through his windows and he had a thousand American men, women, and children assembled in the hotel who were pleading with their president for help to preserve their lives.

None of this was true. William Tapley Bennett, Jr., who had been the ambassador under seige, later told reporters that no bullets came through his office, nor did he take cover under his desk, nor were there any beheadings, nor were any American citizens harmed or even threatened. In fact, the only two American citizens hurt during the revolt were two newsmen shot down without provocation by our own Marines.

For marathon lying, President Nixon probably holds the record. For a ten-month stretch after the Watergate burglary, Nixon either personally or through his aides denied that he or his White House staff were aware of, much less took part in preparations for, the whole complex of political skulduggery known collectively as Watergate. He also denied for ten months that the White House had participated in a cover-up of the scandal.

Finally, when the pretense obviously could be kept up no longer, Nixon's press aide announced that all previous denials were "inoperative"—as nice a word as was ever concocted to wipe out ten months of false information.

Nixon was also loose with the truth in foreign affairs. On his instructions, the Air Force indulged in 3,630 secret bombing sorties over Cambodia during a fourteen-month period in 1969 and 1970. After this took place, Nixon told Congress that "we have respected Cambodia's neutrality for the past five years." He sent a faked report to Congress to support this claim and to hide the bombing raids. Not until 1973 did the truth come out.

Realizing that the public was fed up with presidential lies, Jimmy Carter was astute enough to make "I'll never lie to you" one of his most frequently repeated promises during the 1976 campaign. After taking office he seemed committed to honoring the promise, though he was caught giving false and misleading information during a couple of highly controversial interludes (when his director of the OMB, Bert Lance, was being investigated, and when Carter was secretly arranging for the firing of a Republican district attorney in Philadelphia who was prosecuting Democratic politicians too ardently). But in general, Carter gave the electorate a welcome relief from the presidential forked tongue.

Political psychologists have yet to give a good explanation for the ironic fact that Carter, one of our most candid and truthful presidents, was not as admired as Ronald Reagan, who raised the scope of lying—if that is too harsh a word for you, then substitute "dissembling" or "disinformation"—to such gargantuan proportions that entire books were written about it. And, of course, it became a lush harvest for comics. Said satirist Mort Sahl, "George Washington couldn't tell a lie, Nixon couldn't tell the truth, and Ronald Reagan can't tell the difference." And in reference to Reagan's sloppy handling of facts, a performer playing the president in the off-broadway show *Rap Master Ronnie* said, "If you're right 90 percent of the time, why quibble over the remaining 3 percent?"

The satirist was making a point that White House reporters could appreciate: They could never be sure whether Reagan was deliberately lying or just incredibly misinformed. The effect was the same. Here is a sampling from his hundreds of false statements:

- Reagan, trying to show how oppressive the tax laws are, said, "If you took all the books of regulations and rules in the Income Tax

Code and put them all on a shelf, the shelf would be fifty-seven feet long to hold them all." He merely overstated by fifty-six-and-a-half feet.

- Arguing against abortion on the grounds that even very small fetuses are viable human beings, Reagan said, "I think the fact that children have been born prematurely even down to the three-month stage and have lived, the record shows, to grow up and be normal human beings, that ought to be enough for all of us." Pure science fiction. But even after the American College of Obstetrics and Gynecologists corrected the president, pointing out that at the end of three months, fetuses are only three-and-a-half inches long and none has ever been known to survive, Reagan kept repeating his claim.

- Twice Reagan told Jewish groups that he understood and sympathized with their cause, since he had himself seen the devastation of the Holocaust while filming the liberation of the concentration camps at the end of the Second World War. Not true. Reagan never left the United States during the war. His entire military service was in Hollywood, making Army training films at the old Hal Roach studios.

- Some of Reagan's most impressive lies followed the press's exposure of his secret sale of arms to Iran in an effort to win the release of a handful of U.S. hostages. When the scandal first broke, Reagan said, on November 13, 1986, "We did not—repeat, did not—trade weapons or anything else for hostages, nor will we." Nearly four months later, he revised his recollection in this foggy way: "A few months ago I told the American people I did not trade arms for hostages. My heart and my best intentions still tell me that's true, but the facts and evidence tell me it is not." And finally on March 26, 1987, he admitted that he had been lying all along, that his deals with Iran "settled down to just trading arms for hostages, and that's a little like paying ransom to a kidnapper"—which was exactly what he had promised never to do.

When the press gets hit with as many lies and inaccuracies as Reagan fired, they can't all be checked out in time, and many will be printed. And as Willie Brown, San Francisco's mayor, once said, "In this crazy political business, at least in our times, a lie unanswered becomes the truth within twenty-four hours."

Nevertheless, there is still the question of why the press—until the Iran-contra flood of falsehoods forced it to pay closer attention to

Reagan's dark side—was so tolerant of his lies. Mark Green offered as good an explanation as any: "Many in the media didn't pursue Reagan's misstatements because few of them wanted to believe that the leader of the free world was either a chronic liar or an amiable dunce."

Now and Then a Few Victories

One of the more candid fellows to pass through government was Arthur Sylvester, assistant secretary of defense for public affairs under Kennedy and Johnson. His two most famous declarations were (1) "The government has the right to lie," and (2) "Look, if you think any American official is going to tell you the truth, then you're stupid. Did you hear that?—*stupid.*"

Sylvester made the second statement after reporters had caught Defense Department officials lying again, and he was arguing that it was no big deal. Stinging him to this outburst of candor was one of the smaller victories achieved by the Washington press corps. Even the small ones are counted, however, because victories of any kind are scattered, spasmodic, often incomplete, always costly in time and sometimes in money. Although the capital's reporters are outwitted far more often than they outwit, they have done enough to make this the Era of the Press. Never before have journalists had such a profound impact on government. Far more than most Americans probably realize, the foreign policy and most certainly the economic and social-reform policies of the past twenty years have been shaped to some degree by names that many people in Peoria have likely never heard of: Morton Mintz, Brooks Jackson, Jeffrey Birnbaum, Gregory Vistica, William Greider, Ken Silverstein, Donald Barlett, James Steele, Jeff Gerth, to name a few of the reporters who, even on their off days, have been zealous enough to make politicians blush and bureaucrats sweat and all to promise that they will reform at least a little.

CHAPTER 9

The Economy

Manipulating That Mysterious Spigot

*Politics is business, that's what's the matter with it.
That's what's the matter with everything.*

LINCOLN STEFFENS

*Capitalism is the extraordinary belief that the
nastiest of men for the nastiest of motives will
somehow work for the benefit of us all.*

JOHN MAYNARD KEYNES

NEXT TO THEIR DEMOCRATIC, OR REPUBLICAN, FORM OF GOV-
ernment, Americans are proudest of what they consider to be their
free-enterprise, capitalist economy. Indeed, for most people, democracy
and capitalism are inseparable. On the eve of the nation's two hundredth birthday, President Gerald R. Ford proclaimed, "My resources
as president—and my resolve as president—are devoted to the free-
enterprise system. I do not intend to celebrate our Bicentennial by re-
versing the great principles on which the United States was founded."
That is part of our patriotic myth.

The year of the Declaration of Independence, 1776, was also the year
in which Adam Smith published his great work *The Wealth of Nations*.
In it, people could, for the first time, read a sensible formula for a free
economy—that is, an economy free from government interference
and regulation. In such an economy, everyone would work for profit,
and their efforts to compete for customers would produce goods in

quantities never before seen, at prices within reach of all. Smith believed that this unfettered and unregulated marketplace would result in a "universal opulence which extends itself to the lowest ranks of the people." In short, he preached an economic democracy (if not an economic anarchy). Government's role in this scheme was only to guarantee that the rules of competition would be allowed to prevail.

The Free Economy Isn't Free

Adam Smith's was an impossible ideal. Its weakness was that it depended on the willing participation of capitalists, and capitalists are willing to risk competition only up to a point—beyond which they prefer to surrender some of the "freedom" of their enterprise in exchange for the security of government assistance and protections. It has been that way for more than two hundred years.

The men who wrote the Constitution were men of wealth. They wanted a government that would leave them alone, but they also wanted a government that would enable them to acquire more. Thus, they wrote into their document stipulations that would protect private property, guarantee debts, sanctify contracts, and ensure the circulation of sound money. They set up the legal framework of a free-enterprise economy but made sure that the government would stand behind it. The result is that, from the beginning, government has interfered with and subsidized "free" enterprise in various ways. For example, shipbuilders, who made up one of the largest colonial industries, got an immediate bonus from independence: The second and third acts of the nation's first Congress imposed higher duties on goods moved in foreign ships.

When President Calvin Coolidge remarked, "The business of government is business," he was only enunciating a philosophy that had lived with vigor in one corner or another of the federal hierarchy since the nation's founding. James Madison, in *The Federalist* papers, sounds exactly like an early Coolidge in declaring that "the regulation of these various and interfering [economic] interests forms the principal task of modern legislation." In other words, the business of government was business then, too. Both Coolidge and Madison were thinking not merely of business, but of big business. Fat cats controlled the Constitutional Convention. As Charles Beard has pointed out, "Not one member represented in his immediate personal economic interests the small farming or mechanic classes."

In the nineteenth century, the state as well as the federal governments subsidized or built roads, canals, and railroads; many states actually entered into the manufacturing business. States also invented the corporate form of business organization, allowing individuals to hide behind a corporate body. High tariffs subsidized domestic industry by making foreign goods expensive by comparison. Finally, as small companies gave way to huge corporations, and competition to oligopoly or monopoly, the government had to step in and save us from free enterprise by establishing regulatory agencies such as the Interstate Commerce Commission and the Federal Trade Commission. So, while the myth of free enterprise still lingers in the backs of our minds, the fact of government's intrusion in the marketplace has long been accepted and even welcomed. Most Americans, while holding firmly to an ideology that condemns "big government" and "deficit spending" and favors "individual initiative," also strongly support government spending to reduce unemployment, control pollution, protect consumers, and provide aid to the impoverished and the sick. This dual viewpoint is a unique political contradiction that Americans have come to feel very comfortable with—a delusion that combines independence and dependence with breathtaking dexterity.

Many economists seriously doubt that any vestige of classic free-enterprise capitalism will survive in this country. Some contend that it has already been erased by big government, big unions, and big corporations, and that the United States is in fact well on the way to being a planned economy. But whatever its defects and however unfair, the combination of free enterprise and government interference made the United States the richest, most successful, and for a long while probably most efficient nation in history—and possibly the happiest, if happiness can be measured by the accumulation of material goods.

It is easy to look into our personal lives to see that the government is everywhere to some degree, shaping our economic lives down to the smallest detail through three forces: taxation, subsidization, and regulation.

If you were born in a hospital, it was probably a hospital built wholly or in part with federal funds. Poor or rich, as soon as you appeared in this world, the government permitted your parents to count you as a tax deduction.

When you went to school, your lunch was probably subsidized to some extent by the U.S. Department of Agriculture. Your school was built with tax dollars (if it was a public school), and your books were bought with tax dollars. You walked to school on sidewalks, or drove to school on streets, paid for with tax dollars.

The auto you drive was built according to certain government-prescribed safety and performance standards. The gasoline it burns has to meet certain government-prescribed standards.

All your life you have eaten food from cans or boxes or bottles that bore descriptive labels imposed by government decree. The meat you eat was first passed by government inspectors. The orange juice you drink came from oranges picked by workers who lived in camps that were supposed to meet government-set sanitation standards.

If you or your parents borrowed money from the bank to pay your way through college, the interest rate was influenced by the Federal Reserve System. When you deposit money in the bank, the Federal Deposit Insurance Corporation guarantees that your money (up to a certain amount) is safe, even if the bank goes out of business.

When you go to work, the government will require you to pay a certain amount each week into the Social Security Trust Fund. It will also require your employer to withhold income tax from your paycheck. As for your employer, there is a good chance that part of his or her income is from government contracts or government subsidies or government tax rebates (incentives).

If you fail to find employment—and if there are enough others who have your bad luck—the government will probably spend millions of dollars in make-work projects to give you employment. Or, if you lose your job, the government will pay unemployment compensation for a time.

When you retire, you can draw monthly checks from the Social Security system, and when you are sick, you can get help from the Medicare system. And when you die, the government will tax your estate. If you were a veteran, it will help pay for your burial.

From birth to death—and in far more varied and complicated ways than the above brief biography would indicate—the government molds your financial security (or lack of it), your material pleasures and pains, and the economic environment in which you exist. Is this true free-enterprise capitalism? Consider the standard working definition of capitalism as "an economic system in which the means of production—factories, farms, mines, and so forth—are owned by private individuals or firms rather than by the state, and in which the primary method of distributing incomes is the competitive marketplace." If that is an acceptable definition, then obviously we are not living in a system of free-enterprise capitalism. We are, instead, living in a system of state capitalism—meaning, a system where private ownership and income distribution are inextricably entwined with the government actions of taxation, subsidization, and regulation.

Some "Revolution"

For the Labor Day weekend in 1988, seven adult friends met at a rented vacation house on the Atlantic seashore. They were economically middle class, including a bookkeeper, a painting contractor, and a musician among their number. Five of the seven had master's degrees. One evening they took stock of their lives and found that none of them, despite their good educations and hard work, had prospered. Only one member of the group owned a home. Only one owned a new car. Two had some savings, but less than $5,000. Four were still trying to pay off their student loans. No one in the group could imagine ever putting together enough money to send his or her children to college.

In a letter to *The New York Times* telling about this meeting of friends, the painting contractor wrote:

> I recalled that when my father was my age, and also a painting
> contractor, he bought a house for one family in Westchester, a
> seven-room Colonial on three-quarters of an acre. He paid $19,000
> for it in 1963. (I wish we had kept it; it recently was resold for close
> to $200,000.) Twenty-five years later, at the same age and with the
> additional full-time income of a spouse, I can't afford to buy the house
> I grew up in. Most of the time, I have blamed myself for our plight, but
> the weekend gathering was reassuring, in a sad way, because it turned
> out that my contemporaries found themselves struggling, and feeling
> guilty, in similar ways. . . .
>
> I must wonder where are the prosperous times we're supposed to
> be in the midst of? Or are we in the midst of a cruel joke? It seems
> that the disparities are great today between rich and poor, and that
> somewhere buried under the avalanche of positive economic indicators
> is an overburdened, under-rewarded middle class.

That letter was written near the end of what its admirers called the "Reagan economic revolution," which was praised by President Bush and inherited by him. It was a revolution that greatly benefited Wall Street gamblers, merger maniacs, businesses that sought fewer regulations, and multinational corporations that wanted to strip their U.S. plants and set up operations in cheap labor markets overseas.

It was a revolution in which business ethics and productivity declined sharply, while profits rose just as sharply. The salaries of the top officials in the major corporations were commonly in the million-dollar-plus range. A dealer in "junk bonds" made $1 billion in one year, and although he was indicted for fraud, many on Wall Street looked upon him as a piratical hero.

But during the "Reagan economic revolution" the middle-income workers and the "working poor" and the outright poor had a different kind of luck. The top 20 percent of the population received 40 percent of the nation's total income in a typical year, and the bottom 20 percent earned only 5 percent of the total. And the gap between rich and poor continued to widen. The number of "working poor" between the ages of twenty-two and sixty-four increased by 60 percent in the decade.*

As for the just plain poor, when the Reagan revolution ended, the United States could claim that it had the highest rate of poverty in the industrial world.

The reason we go back to the Reagan administration and stress its revolution is that it set the pattern for what continued on through the Bush and Clinton administrations, to the very end of the century.

The Poor and the Very Poor

Since we have referred to the "poor" so often, and will again, it's time we said who they are. In 1965, the Social Security Administration developed definitions of poverty-level incomes that have ever since been the basis for the government's official definition of poverty. The formula was worked out by determining the cost of a "minimally adequate diet" and multiplying that by three (social workers figure most poor people spend one-third of their income on food). Since 1965, price increases have forced the poverty line upward. In 1966, the government—with an arbitrariness that is supposed to pass for omniscience—decided that $3,317 was the minimum that an urban family of four could earn before it sank into poverty. That was, of course, a ridiculously low estimate. It was meant to be a base subsistence figure: no movies, no newspapers, no medical or dental care, little meat, little clothing, and so on. By the mid-1990s, the government had raised its official poverty line to $16,000 a year for a family of four.

Even at that unrealistically low poverty ceiling, 14 percent of the population—one person in every seven—is caught below it. And these statistics hide the true condition of many of the poor; no distinction is made between the poor person earning $16,000 a year and the poor person earning $1,000 a year, or nothing. Congressional investigators

---

*And who are the "working poor"? Although most poor people of all levels work if they can, the clumsy expression "working poor" is used by economists to mean the one-fifth of our population who live above the poverty line and below the middle-income bracket. For a four-member household this means earning between $16,000 and $25,000—and in two-thirds of these households it takes two wage-earners to reach that range.

visiting communities in the hills of West Virginia found shacks that had no running water but did have electricity—though the people living in them could afford only one light bulb and moved that bulb from room to room. In a typical shack, the refrigerator contained only a small slab of roast—and ice. Nothing else. In another, the refrigerator held only several slices of bread, some peanut butter, some vinegar, and a tray with a scrap of meat—for a family of three. Three million Americans have no homes at all and can be found living in large cardboard boxes in the park or slumped in the corner of subway terminals.

Life at the Bottom

Through a crazy quilt of assistance programs, the problem of improving the lives of the dirt poor has been attacked with some success—up to a point—ever since the 1930s.

When the stock market fell apart in 1929 and the U.S. economy was ruined, one out of four workers in America was jobless. There had never before been an economic disaster of that scope in this country. Unlike today, there was nothing to fall back on—no unemployment compensation, no established welfare programs, no food stamps, no government-subsidized job retraining programs, no Social Security.

All those things came after Franklin Roosevelt became president in 1933 and established a new philosophy of government: "Modern society, acting through its government, owes the definite obligation to prevent the starvation or dire waste of any of its fellow men and women who try to maintain themselves but cannot."

In the succeeding decades, the idea took such deep root as to be almost accepted as a a truism. Many billions of dollars are pumped through the national budget to support what some have called "the guaranteed society"—much of it to help individuals who need a hand up (but bear in mind that corporations get much more "welfare" than individuals do). Three decades after the beginning of Roosevelt's New Deal, in the 1960s, Lyndon Johnson's "war on poverty" expanded the safety net for poor people.

These movements to help the needy, however, had their opponents. Indeed, even many people sympathetic to the poor came eventually to feel that welfare was a bog in which poor people—many of them smart and able-bodied—seemed to be imbedded permanently, living just from day-to-day, hopeless. In New York City in the 1980s there were 64,000 adult welfare recipients who had never had one day's work in their lives. Not one. There was a widespread feeling among Americans that something was dreadfully wrong with a system that supported two or three generations of the same family and made no real effort to help them get off the dole.

The public's impatience with those who seemed stuck forever on welfare was exploited by politicians, conservative Democrats as well as Republicans, who portrayed the needy as leeches. This exploitation reached a fresh intensity during the administration of Ronald Reagan, beginning in 1981. To hear Reagan scorn the welfare state, you would never have guessed that his own family was rescued from hunger by his father's job in one of Roosevelt's most famous antipoverty efforts: the Works Progress Administration (WPA). The WPA, supported entirely by federal funds, hired jobless men and women for make-work projects.

Reagan's administration slashed support for the poor. Food stamps, special nutrition for women and children, housing grants, medical help for children, job training—all were cut.

His propaganda campaign against welfare was viciously misleading. His most notorious distortion was summed up in "The Chicago Welfare Queen," which became a classic in the Republican repertoire and was repeated for years by the party faithful. Here is Reagan's phony anecdote: "There's a woman in Chicago. She has eighty names, thirty addresses, twelve Social Security cards, and is collecting veteran's benefits on four nonexisting deceased husbands. And she's collecting Social Security on her cards. She's got Medicaid, is getting food stamps, and she is collecting welfare under each of her names. Her tax-free cash income alone is over $150,000."

All of that was pure fantasy. The woman did not exist. But fantasies, repeated often enough, can have a powerful effect.

The Distortions Pay Off

By the 1990s, after twelve years of Presidents Reagan and Bush, the reputation of "welfare" had reached its lowest level in sixty years. The demonizing of the poor had become a favorite pastime for political conservatives and talkshow extremists. The public was badly confused. "To take the starkest example of this public confusion," writes William Greider, "the majority of the people who are officially poor— more than 60 percent of them—receive *no* cash assistance from the government whatever. Yet popular resentment assumes the opposite. Nearly 40 percent of the poor receive nothing at all from the government, neither cash nor other kinds of aid."

Those who get help from the government aren't exactly looting the treasury. The average welfare family receives less than $9,000 a year in benefits. And contrary to the complaints of right-wingers, most welfare recipients want to get off the dole. Seventy percent, on their own initiative, find work within two or three years. The other 30 percent includes a smattering of deadbeats, but it is made up mostly of people who have no marketable skills, or are physically or mentally disabled, or have to stay home to take care of someone in the family who is too young or too old or too sick to take care of him- or herself.*

By 1996 the momentum for changing welfare was so intense that President Clinton and the Republican Congress found it politically profitable to cooperate in radically thinning the welfare rolls so they could both claim credit in that election year. Having passed the new welfare-reduction legislation, both sides boasted that the changes in welfare would "save $58 billion over seven years." (In the same budget, according to the Center for the Study of Responsive Law, there was business welfare—tax breaks and subsidies—totaling $167.2 billion.)

The Toll Begins

The new legislation ruled that no one could be on welfare for more than five years in a lifetime. Some states followed up with legislation limiting lifetime welfare to two years. By 1998, there had been a cut of at least 20 percent in the welfare rolls nationally, and early evidence suggested that only about half of those who left the rolls had jobs. Some critics estimated a million more children had been pushed into deeper poverty by the legislation. Several of the important federal antipoverty programs were killed. Congress stopped allocating money for building low-income housing, even though fifteen million families qualified for such assistance.

Whites had a much easier time finding work, leaving the welfare rolls heavily populated by blacks and Hispanics, by a two-to-one margin. But whatever their color, most who moved into the workforce faced jobs paying $7 an hour, or less—in some places, a whole lot less: the Mississippi Delta, for instance—where 41 percent of the people live in poverty and a mother with two children on welfare gets $120 a month plus $315 in food stamps.

---

*Oregon, one of the most progressive states, has in recent years radically reduced its welfare rolls by helping recipients find jobs. It estimates that 75 percent of those remaining on welfare suffer from mental problems, 42 percent lack a high school education and 30 percent have criminal records. But it wasn't always easy finding work for people like the woman with a seventh-grade education, who weighed 325 pounds, and had serious body odor. A company finally hired her, but only after the state agreed to pay most of her salary for the first six months, and supplied her with lots of deodorant.

When a Delta mother is forced off welfare, where does she go to work? The unemployment rate hovers around 10 percent. Jobs, when they exist at all, are usually distant. Of the twenty-seven Greenville, Mississippi, women placed in jobs in one recent month, ten had to commute to a catfish plant in Eudora, Arkansas. To get there, the women were carried in a school bus on a trip that started at 6:30 in the morning and took an hour. Arriving at the plant, they put in earplugs and donned steel-lined safety gloves, for they would use saws to help gut the 100,000 catfish processed every day. The plant's comptroller says, "You work in the cold, you work in the wet—and of course you're around fish guts all the time."

For that, the women were paid $5.15 an hour.

The Difficulty of Distributing Wealth

Is wealth distributed unfairly? That question is at the center of all economic debates in this country. Some politicians have built highly successful careers espousing theories of distribution. Huey Long, for example, with his enormously popular Share the Wealth Plan, advocated that any fortunes above $8 million be taxed away and distributed to the population at large. Such visionaries are considered radicals and demagogues, but in fact the American economic system has for many years been shaped and reshaped (by Establishment economists, too) around the belief that some people have far too little—and something should be done to even things out a bit.

But how should the distribution be accomplished? That is the multibillion-dollar question, and it has never been answered satisfactorily. One obvious method is taxes. Reform politicians have been trying for many years to use taxes to significantly reduce the great fortunes. They have failed. In 1935, in the middle of this century's worst depression, President Roosevelt asked Congress to increase estate taxes because "inherited economic power is as inconsistent with the ideals of this generation as inherited political power was inconsistent with the ideals of the generation that established our government." Roosevelt got the taxes he asked for, and they are still on the books (although revised many times in the interim), but they mock his intent.

Just how big a mockery the inheritance tax is can be measured by the fortunes of the three wealthiest families in America in the 1930s: the Rockefellers, the DuPonts, and the Mellons. In 1937 they were together worth more than $1.2 billion. Today the three families' fortunes are together worth more than $15 billion.

The mockery of the inheritance tax continues today. Despite progressive taxation of large estates, the children of the rich start with enormous financial advantages; through the creation of elaborate trusts, these children are left with very large fortunes upon the death of their parents. Fifty percent of the Forbes 400 in 1996 had started their business lives with $50 million or more in family wealth or by inheriting a large company.

If one goes to the top of the pyramid, the contrast between rich and poor becomes awesome and, if one is trying to figure out some way to improve the distribution of wealth, even more troublesome. The top .5 percent of the population control more than 35 percent of the nation's wealth, according to the Joint Economic Committee of Congress, which points out that this tiny golden sliver of the population also controls most of the nation's business assets—58 percent of unincorporated business and 46.5 percent of corporate stock owned by individuals. They also hold 62 percent of state and local bonds.

Remember, that's just the top one-half of 1 percent of the nation's households.

The concentration of individual wealth among the rich and the super rich and the concentration of corporate wealth have resulted in

> a significant erosion of the [political] power of those on the bottom half of the economic spectrum, an erosion of the power not only of the poor but of those in the working and middle classes. At the same time, there has been a sharp increase in the power of economic elites, of those who fall in the top 15 percent of the income distribution.
>
> These distortions have created a system of political decision making in which fundamental issues—the distribution of the tax burden, the degree to which the government sanctions the accumulation of wealth, the role of federal regulation, the level of publicly tolerated poverty, and the relative strength of labor and management—are resolved by an increasingly unrepresentative economic elite.

Life at the Very Top

"Such is the decadence of the 1990s," writes Russell Baker, "that millionaires who fancy themselves rich now have multimillionaires rolling on the floor in laughter. A million is small change these days."

Indeed, becoming a millionaire is an increasingly easy goal to reach. If you measure a millionaire by what he's *worth*—by his savings and possessions—home, art, autos, and so forth—as well as his income, there are several million of them, but most are merely plump cats. On the other hand, if you count only the truly fat cats—those whose *income* each and every year is one million dollars or more—their ranks are much smaller, but growing. According to the Internal Revenue Service, their number increased from 13,505 in 1979 to 68,064 in 1994. Those are the latest official figures available, but it is safe to estimate that with the skyrocketing stock market of the late '90s, that number has jumped at least another 5,000.

Who are these moguls? They include entertainers, of course, like David Letterman, who collects about $14 million a year for cracking jokes on late-night television, and many top professional athletes, such as the 1998 world champion New York Yankees baseball team, whose average salary was $2,440,791.

Perhaps the best way to illustrate how fat some of the fattest cats are is to point out that when the stock market took a sharp dip in the second half of 1998, Sanford Weill, chief executive at Travelers Group, lost half the value of his stocks. Poor fellow! That left him having to survive on a mere $785 million. Charles Schwab, head of the discount brokerage that bears his name, lost $229 million. That left him holding stock worth only $1.8 billion. That's *billion.*

Some Americans are so wealthy that it's foolish to even talk of what they earn, since from interest alone they could be raking in millions every few days. The technology industry has eleven billionaires, led, of course, by Bill Gates, chairman of Microsoft, whom Forbes *ASAP* magazine estimates to be worth nearly $90 billion.

The late 1990s were considered good times for many people, but they were best at the top. An analysis by *The New York Times* of the compensation of chief executives at America's biggest companies found that the average salary plus bonuses for 1997 was $2.1 million—a 12.3 percent increase over 1996. (If the value of stock options was counted, the average total pay was $8.7 million, a 37.8 percent increase over 1996.) "By contrast," *The Times* notes, "wages for the average American worker increased 3.5 percent."

The wage gap between the top and bottom is widening. According to *Business Week,* CEOs now make 419 times the average factory worker's salary; that's up from 42 times as much in 1980.

Rewarding the "Killers"

There is a perverse irony among these riches. Some corporate executives have grown very rich simply by making many of their employees poorer—by firing them. When a corporation lays off thousands of its workers, Wall Street interprets that as a brilliant economic move (fewer workers handling the same workload equals "higher productivity"). So the downsized corporation's stock rises, sometimes sharply, and the chief executive of the corporation is rewarded. *Newsweek* magazine did a roundup story on what it called "Corporate Killers," which it illustrated with dozens of fellows like Robert Allen, chief executive at AT&T, who fired 40,000 workers and was rewarded with a salary of $3,362,000. American Express gave its chief executive, Harvey Golub, $33.2 million in 1997, a hefty 229 percent pay raise, as 3,300 workers were pushed out the door.

Another of the weird, perverse ironies in the corporate world is that top executives who fail at their job are nevertheless often lavishly rewarded. Boeing Company's chief executive, Phil Condit, was paid $5.6 million even though his company lost $178 million in 1997, and the same year Ray Irani, chief of Occidental Petroleum, took home $101.5 million while the company was losing $390 million.

Michael Kazin, professor of history at American University, says, "A century ago, many prosperous Americans at least felt a twinge of guilt about the gap between their swelling bank accounts and the single-digit daily wages paid to manual workers. Today, that twinge is gone. Few rich Americans seem troubled that their pile rests on the hard, anonymous labor of thousands of people, here and abroad, who often lack access to good health care and education for their children."

Life in the Middle Class

Americans may pity the poor and envy the rich, but they admire the middle class. That feeling may be a bit of smugness because the middle class is where most of us are, socially and economically. Smug or not, the preservation of that class is of paramount importance, because, as *Time* magazine once stated the obvious: "Any substantial decline in the middle class—even if it is partially psychological—would be ominous for the United States as a whole. It is the middle class whose values and ambitions set the tone of the country."

The middle class (along with the poor and working poor) entered the 1990s worse off than they were in the early 1970s. Figuring in inflation, their incomes had been stagnant. By the middle of the decade, things had improved somewhat for the average family, but it was still true, as one political anaylist lamented: "The median U.S. family income . . . no longer assured the middle-class status and lifestyle that median earnings had brought ordinary households twenty or thirty years earlier."

What was once the world's largest, expanding middle class now seems to be shrinking. In the twenty-six years from 1947 through 1973, the median income *doubled* even after adjusting for inflation. But in the next twenty-four years, it increased only 1.6 percent. In other words, the typical family in the middle of the income scale—seems to be on a slippery slope.

What is the middle class? The answer to that is rather vague. If "middle class" is measured by income, economists and politicians see it sprawling from $25,000 a year to $80,000 a year—depending on the size of the family and where they live. The median income for today's typical middle-class couple with two children is probably around $40,000 to $45,000, but it probably takes both parents working full-time to bring in that much.

Putting children through college on an income of that size, with tuitions rising two and a half times the rate of inflation in recent years, takes the talents of a magician. Putting together a down payment on a home isn't easy either. (It's getting tougher. In 1973, 43.6 percent of couples aged twenty-five to twenty-nine owned homes; by 1997, only 35 percent did. Among thirty to thirty-four year olds, the figure fell to 52.6 percent from 60.2 percent.)

Temps and Mergers

The last half of the 1990s found few in the middle class out of work. But more than ever before in recent decades, their jobs were risky. Partly, as we mention elsewhere in this chapter, the permanence of employment declined because many corporations "downsized" their U.S. workforces and shifted factories, at least in part, to foreign countries. But another reason was the trend toward hiring temporary workers to do the work that had previously been done by permanent employees. In 1975, companies hired an average of 250,000 temporary workers on a daily basis. In the late 1990s, they were hiring ten times that many "temps"—2.5 million—and the number was climbing.

The high-tech industries are particularly fond of temps. At Microsoft, for example, about one-fourth the 22,000 workers are rated "temporary," although in fact some have worked there for more than five years at high-prestige, high-technology jobs. They are well paid, but their health and vacation benefits are pale imitations of those enjoyed by regular Microsoft workers. By avoiding the cost of auxiliary work benefits like health care, corporations can save millions of dollars.

Many of the best middle-class jobs are in the largest industries, which were the industries that merged wildly in the 1980s and 1990s. Nine of the ten largest mergers in U.S. history were completed in 1998. Top executives often made fortunes in these mergers, but they were costly to middle-income workers because one of the main reasons companies combine is to save money by firing overlapping staffs and getting the same work done by fewer workers. It is estimated that 10 percent of the half-million jobs lost in 1998 was the result of mergers.

The Middle-Class Range

Bear in mind, the middle class covers a wide range of incomes because some workers are skilled and some are unskilled. Having a college degree is certainly not always a prerequisite for skills; but it often is, and in the mid-1990s only 24 percent of Americans aged twenty-five and older had bachelor degrees or higher. The college educated in this country are still a distinct minority.

The entry-level wages of college graduates rose modestly (economists differ on how much) between the early 1970s and the late 1990s, but entry-level wages for those with only a high school diploma fell by 24 percent. Even the most dangerous of low-skill work lost pay. In the 1980s, union laborers removing asbestos from old buildings in New York City were paid $31 an hour. Today union wages for that work is $19.90 an hour—and respirators are not always furnished.

Thirty years ago, presidential candidates, particularly the Democratic ones, stressed their eagerness to help the underdogs of society, the poor and the working poor. But beginning with Reagan and Bush, and continuing with Clinton, candidates have preferred to pose as the champions of the middle class. A typical remark from Clinton in 1992: "The rich get the gold mine and the middle class gets the shaft. It's wrong and it's going to ruin the country."

It may be callous for the politicians to have changed their pitch, but it is smart politics. The middle class is where most of the votes are. The lower their income, the less people vote. Populist radio commentator Jim Hightower notes that "the great number of electoral drop-outs are people making less than $25,000 a year. It doesn't take a degree in sociology to figure out that these people are telling us they don't see much improvement in their lives from the economic policies of either major party." Maybe so, but the sad truth is that by ignoring the ballot box, the have-nots simply throw away their best chance to make politicians help them climb to the next level, the middle class, which may not be paradise but it sure beats poverty.

The Social Security "Fix"

No government program is more beloved by middle-income and low-income Americans than the Social Security system. And for good reason.

Created in 1935, Social Security has been the government's most dependable and most efficient social help program. It's a pay-as-you-go arrangement, with deductions from the income of current workers going into a fund that helps support 44 million people: 31 million retirees, 7 million survivors (widows and children of workers who had paid into the system), and 6 million disabled people. For many retirees, it is their only income, and for 55 percent of the elderly, it supplies more than half their income. Social Security has cut elderly poverty from 35 percent in 1959 to just over 10 percent today.

It plays no favorites. It pays out to rich, middle class, and poor. Perhaps somewhat illogically, 3.2 percent of all benefits, about $8 billion, goes to those with incomes over $100,000, and in a typical recent year, 29,843 families with a household income of more than $500,000 also received Social Security benefits, averaging $16,426.

Despite Social Security's popularity and its success in providing a better life for millions of elderly and/or disabled Americans, the calls for the "reform" of Social Security are growing louder. Most, but not all, of the noise comes from economic conservatives who have never been supporters of government social programs. William Greider says, "Deep in the Republican soul lurks an abiding contempt for the Social Security system, a prejudice lingering from New Deal days when conservatives saw it as the vanguard of socialism." But that is mainly true of rich establishmentarians and their congressional allies, not ordinary-income Republicans who, polls regularly show, are just as much in favor of having this cushion for their retirement years as Democrats are.

The "reformists" argue that the population of elderly is growing so fast that by the year 2019 the Social Security Trust Fund will be paying out more in benefits than it takes in—and it will be on its way to bankruptcy. This is a Chicken Little argument. Actually, as Peter Coy, a *Time* magazine economics editor, and others have pointed out, there is no chance the trust fund will start sucking air for at least another thirty years, and to prevent it from happening then will require only a few minor adjustments. A very slight raise in payroll deductions, or adding on a year or two to the age at which retirees can tap into the system, would make Social Security sound far into the future. An even better way to add to the fund would be to deduct from salaries above $72,600—which is presently the cut-off point for deductions.

The law establishing the Social Security Trust Fund required that it be invested exclusively in government securities, which pay about 2.3 percent after inflation. The "reformers" want to change the law to let at least some of the trust fund be invested in the stock market. They point out that over its history, the market has averaged a return of 7 percent. The difference, compounded over decades, would be enormous.

Needless to say, the principal advocates of this kind of change are the money managers who would stand to profit from it. As *The New York Times* commented, "Wall Street is ecstatic at the idea that billions upon billions of dollars that today are invested only in government securities might suddenly fuel the stock market. Its enthusiasm is hardly without self-interest. If fund managers are permitted to skim just 1 percent in management fees, it would mean new Wall Street revenues of $10 billion to $40 billion a year by 2015, and far more in the next century."

Those who propose putting taxpayers' retirement funds into stocks tend to gloss over things like risk. The market has always been volatile, fickle, a gamble. Some say (with exaggeration) that the main difference between Wall Street and Las Vegas is that the former doesn't have floorshows. What would happen to the trust fund if the stock market took a prolonged and severe downturn, as it did in this country in the late 1920s and throughout the 1930s, or as the Japanese stock market did throughout the 1990s?

Just as risky are the questionable ethics of Wall Street. No less an expert than Arthur Levitt, Jr., chairman of the Securities and Exchange Commission (SEC), which polices the stock market, warned that "fraud and sales-practice abuses would empty the pockets of novice investors."

The market's history is full of examples to support his warning. Every year dozens of fund managers and brokers are suspended or barred from the securities business for what the National Association of Securities Dealers calls "failing to observe high standards of commercial honor." That's a nice way of saying that some were just plain crooks. Some worked for the most reputable brokerages, such as Merrill Lynch and Smith Barney. Does the Mafia have ties to Wall Street? In 1997, the chief regulator of the Nasdaq market admitted, "We believe the presence exists."

If Congress thinks governments would be safer than individuals from the predatory instincts of supposedly reputable brokerages, it should study what happened to Orange County, California, whose government lost $1.7 billion by gambling on bonds, on the advice of such reputable firms as Merrill Lynch. Because of those lost funds, the county had to severely slash its social service programs—programs to provide food and medical care and shelter for the poor. In other words, hurt the worst by Orange County's debacle were society's most vulnerable—the same kind of people, as SEC boss Levitt warned, who would be hardest hit if a comparable disaster happened to Social Security.

And even Wall Street's brightest money managers are not always clever enough to beat the stock market's odds. Consider the fate of the giant hedge fund, Long Term Capital Management, which was run by some of the most illustrious wizards of Wall Street, plus a former vice chairman of the Federal Reserve Board, plus two Nobel Prize economists, and a horde of PhDs. Dozens of brokerage firms, banks, and university endowments invested in Long Term's scheme to juggle bond prices. They made huge profits for a couple of years, but in 1998 the fund lost 90 percent of its assets—at least $4 billion. Fearing that a total wipe-out would do dire things to the stock market, the Federal Reserve rounded up fourteen Wall Street bankers to rescue the fund.

Does the government want "geniuses" like that gambling with our Social Security Trust Fund?

Taxation

The most distasteful—and yet perhaps the most necessary—part of participatory democracy is paying the bills. The government doesn't run on patriotism. It runs on money, and the only place to get the money is from the people and from business.

There are all sorts of ways to measure the burden of taxes. The Tax Foundation calculates that the average taxpayer has to work until May 4 of each year—or 124 days—just to pay federal, state, and local taxes. "Calculated another way," says the Foundation, "two hours and forty-three minutes of work out of an eight-hour day is needed to pay taxes to the three levels of government."

The main questions are: Do taxes come from the right people at the right rates? And do we get what we want from taxes?

Most of the federal government's operating expenses are supported by the income tax, personal and corporate. The income tax was sold to the general public early this century as a way to "soak the rich." Poor people were supposed to be left untouched, the middle class only brushed, and rich people hit relatively hard. Initially, the new tax followed that pattern, but even the rich were hardly "soaked," since the highest rate was only 6 percent and in its first year the tax fell on only one-half of 1 percent of the population. But beginning with the costly demands of World War II in the 1940s, the middle class began to be taxed a bit more heavily (but not painfully) and for the first time the rich were truly soaked.

That continued for a few years after the war. In 1955, while the effective federal tax rate for the average-income family was 9 percent, millionaires and others in the top 1 percent income bracket had an effective tax of 85.5 percent. But ever since the 1950s, Congress has been increasingly kind to the wealthy and increasingly tough on ordinary people. Down, down, down came the tax rate on the wealthiest—down to 70 percent in 1964, to 50 percent in 1981. Today the richest enjoy a rate of 39.6 percent—slightly less than half the 1955 rate. Meanwhile, the rate for the average family earning around $35,000 to $40,000 has risen to 28 percent. In other words, today the average family's tax rate is nearly three-fourths as high as a millionaire's.

No wonder Americans are cynical about taxes. When Washington politicians pass something they call "tax reform" legislation, which they do quite often, it only means corporations and the richest 10 percent of families are going to get much fatter. The resulting benefits of the so-called Tax Reform Act of 1986, for example, gave those with an income of $30,000 to $40,000 a tax savings of $467. But those with an income of $1 million and up saved $281,033.

"Reforms" launched by the Reagan administration were a bonanza for big business, cutting the tax load on corporations by nearly 40 percent. On the average, corporations were so unburdened of taxes that, as a Library of Congress study noted, "The present set of tax rules is not much different from the effects of having no corporate tax at all." That was no exaggeration. Investment tax credits given to General Electric in 1981, for example, were so generous that GE not only paid no federal taxes between 1981 and 1983—a period in which its net profit exceeded $5 billion—but it also received tax rebates of more than $300 million.

To stop that kind of nonsense, Congress passed another "reform" in 1986, the Corporate Minimum Tax, which supposedly would force big business to make at least token payments. And token they often are, with a giant like Chase Manhattan handing over only 1.7 percent of its income. Not content, big business persuaded the Clinton administration to quietly cut the Corporate Minimum Tax in half.

Backdoor Spending

There are special tax benefits—loopholes or preferences—for everyone: the rich, the poor, the middle class, businesses, farmers, preachers, soulless corporations. In fact, each year the federal government gives away about $200 billion by *not* collecting taxes that it would collect if certain exemptions had not been written into law. Some economists call this "backdoor spending."

One of the most prevalent, and most treasured, tax breaks is the deduction allowed for interest homeowners pay on their mortgage. Consider two families earning the same income and occupying homes of equal value. The family buying its home deducts mortgage interest and pays less income tax than the other family, which is renting. Is that fair? Homeowners sure think so. Renters don't.

The richer you are and the bigger home you can afford, the more deductions you get. A 1995 congressional study showed that the owner of a $1.25 million house with a $1 million mortgage would enjoy a tax deduction of about $380,000. Is it fair to ask taxpayers to subsidize the mortgage payments of those rich enough to buy homes in Aspen, Colorado, where the median price is $1.51 million? The question of fairness hovers over a great deal of the federal tax code.

According to Steve Brouwer, in *Sharing the Pie,* "In 1995 [a typical year] the federal government lost $51 billion in tax revenues because of mortgage deductions, nearly twice the amount, $26 billion, spent on all low-income housing programs and rental subsidies" for the poor. . . . "The richest 5 percent of Americans, those with incomes over $100,000 a year, collected 44 percent of the homeowner subsidy in 1995. . . ."

Because of sharply lower rates and a variety of tax concessions, corporations contribute a much smaller share of federal revenues today, by percentage, than they did four decades ago. In the 1950s, corporations paid 39 percent of all income-tax revenue, and individuals paid 61 percent. In the 1990s, the corporate share dropped to 19 percent; the individual share rose to 81 percent.

There's an endless variety of tax breaks corporations get. For example, in March 1989, an Exxon tanker spilled ten million gallons of oil after running aground in the harbor at Valdez, Alaska. It was the worst pollution of coastal waters in U.S. history. And who subsidized the cleanup? The U.S. taxpayer, that's who. The clean-up bill was expected to run around $500 million, of which Exxon, the nation's richest oil company, would pay only one-fifth. But not really even that much. Aside from raising the price of its gasoline to make customers pay for its part of the cleanup, Exxon would get a direct subsidy from the government by being allowed to deduct 34 percent of the expense from its taxable income as "a routine cost of doing business." U.S. taxpayers would have to make up this revenue loss to the U.S. treasury.

Uppercrust Cheaters

Public unhappiness with the tax system is to be expected. But why has it increased in recent years? No single answer is enough. Partly, it is because ordinary people, with good cause, suspect that Leona Helmsley, New York's notorious hotel queen, who evaded $4 million in taxes, was only telling it like it is when she said, "We don't pay taxes. Little people pay taxes."

The Internal Revenue Service discovered that between 1977 and 1993, the number of Americans who made $200,000 or more each year grew by more than fifteen-fold, but the number of people in that income group who paid *no* income taxes grew nearly twice as fast. How did they do it? Some hired lawyers and accountants who know how to use deductions, credits, and gimmicks to reduce tax payments far below the official rate—or wipe them out entirely.

But some who pay nothing simply cheat. An Internal Revenue Service audit of nearly 50,000 taxpayers found that the frequency of tax cheating is at least twice as high among the top 3 percent of taxpayers as among the bottom half. Because the IRS's enforcement staff is at an unprecedented low level, the cheaters—including the largest corporations that underreport $15 to $20 billion income each year—are usually not caught. What this means is that you and I, through the failure of IRS enforcement, are lending the tax evaders $100 billion, interest-free, each year, or an incredible $2 *trillion* in the last two decades.

The public's unhappiness also can be traced to the growing awareness of failed programs that gobble up the tax dollars, such as the military blunders (discussed in Chapter 3, on the Cold War) and the bungling of the federal red-tape artists (discussed in Chapter 6, on the bureaucracy).

For the most part, Americans have given with a good heart to build highways, to strengthen defense, and to upgrade social-aid programs such as health care, job training, and housing subsidies. But they have seen too much of their contributions siphoned off by fraud or by harebrained excesses, such as the Ronald Reagan Building and International Trade Center, the second-biggest government building ever constructed (the Pentagon is the biggest), at a cost of $816 million—a mere $448 million more than Congress had planned for. And was it really worth $40 million to investigate the marital infidelities of one president? Many opinion polls in 1997 and 1998 resoundingly said no!

Some cheats and crooks are very inventive—such as the government worker who defrauded $856,000 for a subway system that didn't exist, or the Puerto Rican barber's school that charged the government $5 million to train 1,000 veterans who were not enrolled, or the South Carolina doctor who charged the government for pulling healthy teeth from poor children, or the doctor who billed the government for seven tonsillectomies on the same patient.

Always remember: Abuses of the federal budget through mismanagement and fraud are not abstract, paper losses; they mean that the typical taxpayer is being robbed of hundreds of dollars every year—no different from being held up in a dark alley at gunpoint, except that this thief usually wears a tie.

Subsidization

For the first 140 years of our nation's life, federal spending never exceeded 3 percent of the gross national product except during wars and the immediate postwar periods. Of that 3 percent, two-thirds was devoted—even in peacetime—to paying the costs of past wars and the costs of supporting veterans and their widows. Civilian expenditures by the federal government rarely exceeded 1 percent of the gross national product. (The "gross national product" (GNP) means, in a loose way, the value of all the goods and services produced by everyone, privately, corporately, and governmentally. The GNP is, simply, the sum of a nation's production.)

But all that changed in the 1930s. As a result of the catastrophic depression that struck the nation in 1929 and continued until our entry into the Second World War in 1941, private industry was unable to heal itself. It had to have help merely to survive, and the only source of outside help was the federal government. It was during the 1930s that "pump-priming," as a political-economic phrase, came into common use. Pump-priming, as defined by the *Oxford English Dictionary,* means "to pour water down the tube with the view of saturating the sucker, so causing it to swell, and act effectually in bringing up water." In the 1930s, private industry's pump was sucking air, so President Franklin Roosevelt poured enough money into the nation's economic pump to make it start operating again, at least fitfully. He did it by putting millions of the unemployed on the federal payroll to build dams, post offices, roads, and other needed projects—or simply to lean on shovels. The objective was to put lots more money into circulation.

Economic pump-priming did not end with the depression of the 1930s; it has been going on ever since. Today federal spending amounts to more than 25 percent of the GNP, and if you add in state and local government spending, the total comes to about 37 percent of the GNP.

Big federal spending has become a permanent part of our economic machinery. Some farmers plan their harvests around the promise of government price support. Some railroads, rescued from bankruptcy by borrowing billions of dollars from the government (money that will never be repaid), continue to depend on annual multimillion-dollar subsidies. The aircraft industry depends on government contracts for much of its income. The perpetual building of federally subsidized highways supports thousands of contractors. Most of the so-called foreign-aid funds are not sent abroad but are spent right here at home: In a recent year, about three dollars out of four called "foreign" aid went to private U.S. companies, universities, and private volunteer groups that contracted to "aid" foreigners.

Most of the federal programs have created dependency, with the result that although every president comes into office with passionate promises to economize, to slash expenditures, to tighten the federal belt, each soon concludes that a major overall reduction in the budget is extremely difficult to achieve and perhaps even dangerous to attempt. The reason: Much of the nation's economy hangs by the federal budget. More than one of every twenty workers—soldiers, bureaucrats, politicians—are on Uncle Sam's payroll. Forty-four million people are on Social Security; 2.8 million are federal civilian retirees. In addition, millions of people get federal food stamps, receive Medicaid, and are on Medicare. About one-fifth of the federal budget goes for defense— meaning guns and planes, of course, but also pays for welders and electricians and scientists as well as dividends to the stockholders at all those defense factories.

Sometimes the government's budgetary involvement with the personal well-being of Americans takes on dramatic proportions, as when, in 1983, the Environmental Protection Agency offered to buy the entire town of Times Beach, Missouri—eight hundred homes and fifty businesses for $33 million—because the city had been inundated by waters contaminated with poisonous chemicals and the 2,500 people of Times Beach faced economic ruin.

Equally dramatic, and much more costly, is the government's frequent rescue of failing corporations. Because they are so necessary to the economic life of the nation, railroads have benefited especially from this largesse. When the Penn Central Transportation Company, the nation's largest railroad, went bankrupt, partly as a result of shabby service and sometimes lawless management, it did not die; it called for help and the federal government stepped in and rescued it with a variety of economic bandages (meanwhile permitting many of the Penn Central officials who had managed the company into disaster to stay on the job). Part of the rescue included blending Penn Central's passenger service with the defunct or near-defunct passenger service of a dozen other railroad companies and calling the new amalgam the National Passenger Railroad Corporation (or Amtrak).

In most countries of the world, natural monopolies, like railroads and utilities, are directly owned and run by the state—often with good results. But it is the American way to preserve at least the forms (and certainly the profits) of free enterprise. Sometimes we seem to be adept at getting the worst of both worlds, capitalist and socialist, when either free competition or public ownership would be better than an unholy mixture.

The sort of arrangement whereby the taxpayers subsidize the corporation and cushion its losses while its shareholders walk away with the profits (if there are any) may seem somewhat unfair to the taxpayers. But the fabric of the nation's economy is too interwoven to permit even the most foolishly managed companies, if they are large enough, to die. If Penn Central, for example, had collapsed, it would have probably carried down with it many of the nation's largest banks, which had loaned the corporation billions of dollars; and if these banks had collapsed, the repercussions throughout our business and industrial structure might have been truly disastrous. So bigness has helped to kill free enterprise.

Special Subsidies to Banks

No industry is so babied as are the banks and the savings and loan organizations. Although in recent years, these institutions have been caught laundering billions of dollars for drug syndicates and other organized criminals, although they have wasted great wealth by backing wild speculative ventures for their pals and by lending scads of money to people and nations who were terrible risks, although they have repeatedly shown little interest in playing by the rules laid down by their regulators,* almost never do their crooked officials actually go to jail and seldom do those officials convicted of reckless judgment even pay severe financial penalties. As usual, the taxpayer gets soaked.

And one of the biggest soakings comes as the result of the too-big-to-fail policy, which we just discussed in regard to Penn Central. Of the ten largest banks to fail in our entire history, six went out of business in the 1980s. One that should have died was Continental Illinois

---

*Banks are regulated by the Comptroller of the Currency, the Federal Reserve Board, the Federal Deposit Insurance Corporation (FDIC), and (for state-chartered banks) state banking supervisors. Savings and loan institutions were regulated by the Federal Home Loan Bank Board and the Federal Savings and Loan Insurance Corporation (FSLIC) until the industry's crisis of 1988–1989 revealed the total incompetence of the FSLIC. It was then put out of business and its duties turned over to the FDIC.

National Bank and Trust of Chicago, which the federal government saved from death only by a transfusion of several billion dollars. By rights, Continental was already a "failed bank" and thereby did not officially qualify for a loan from the FDIC, but the FDIC forked over the billions anyway. Why? Because the top 1 percent of commercial banks hold nearly 35 percent of all bank assets. If one of them went under, the banking system right down to Podunk's Main Street would be shaken (and so would Wall Street). So the powers that be in Washington felt that Continental—at that time one of the biggest—despite all its stupidity and criminalities, must be saved.

Imagine the seismic effects that may haunt the future, as our banks explode in size. After Congress legalized interstate banking, regional banks gobbled up statewide chains. Then regional banks expanded further into super-regional giants like Nationsbank. The next leap was to a national, coast-to-coast customer base, which BankAmerica and Nationsbank took in a 1998 merger. Half a dozen national bank chains will no doubt soon follow.

As Jeffrey E. Garten, dean of the Yale School of Management, put it so well:

> The most worrisome problem is that these new Goliaths will touch every American citizen and corporation and will be so intertwined with major financial firms around the world that they will never be allowed to fail.
>
> Knowing that they cannot go belly-up, these firms may take even more risks than they now do. Taxpayers may be called upon to shore them up when they get into big trouble.

S&L Crooks

As for the savings and loan institutions, at least 500 of them were considered insolvent by 1989. Could they be revived? Perhaps. But there was considerable debate over how much blood would have to be taken from the American taxpayer—probably $150 billion or more—and injected into these losers in order to revive them.

It all came about, as you have doubtless suspected, through greed. Oversimplified, it happened like this: During the second half of the 1970s and for the first couple of years of the 1980s, the worldwide oil boom resulted in the deposit of many, many billions of dollars in U.S. banks. The money lenders, infected with "oil fever" in the same way that California and Alaska were once infected with "gold fever," thought the boom would never end. They had so much money coming in, they didn't know how to lend it out fast enough. They practically begged nations with wobbly credit ratings (such as Brazil) to come in and take as much as they wanted—at exorbitant interest rates, of course. Mexico, an important oil-producing nation in its own right, went on a building spree that it couldn't pay for fast enough simply by selling its oil, so it turned to the giant Yankee banks and borrowed a mere $80 billion.

And in this country, the banks and savings and loan institutions, particularly in the oil-producing states of the southwest, began lending money at a mad pace, to fast-talking wildcatters and corporate con-men, to developers who changed the skyline of every town and city near an oil derrick. S&Ls, which were originally established to help ordinary Americans buy homes, became more interested in bankrolling resort condos and gambling casinos. It's estimated that at least 10 percent of the loans were fraudulent and many more were irrational. The banks and S&Ls were practically throwing money out their windows. Golly, it was fun!

But the fun and games ended in 1982 when the bottom fell out of the oil market. Insolvency strangled dozens of banks, large and small, that had gambled too much on a boom that was now kaput. The poor-credit nations that had borrowed billions got caught in the depression that followed and could barely pay the interest, much less the principal, on their multibillion-dollar loans.

As for the S&Ls that had footed the cost of building skyscrapers and shopping centers and apartment complexes and palaces across the oil states—they were suddenly left holding many fortunes of worthless promissory notes.

But that wasn't the end of it. When a bank or an S&L "fails," it doesn't just close its doors and disappear, leaving depositors empty-handed. That's what happened to banks that failed in the Great Depression of the 1930s. But since then the federal government has constructed "safety nets" that permit savings institutions to fail without carrying all their depositors down with them.

The best known of the safety nets is the Federal Deposit Insurance Corporation, which pays off depositors (up to $100,000 per depositor) when a bank gets in deep financial trouble. If the FDIC can't handle the problem alone, the Federal Reserve Board subsidizes the bank with huge loans. The S&Ls have a similar insurance program, but there was so much looting of the S&Ls that its insurance program went bankrupt and its role as a safety net was taken over by the FDIC and the government. This was one of the most shameful episodes in our economic history, and taxpayers were caught in the middle of it. The enormity of the bail-out can be seen in the comparison offered by columnist Neal

Peirce: "Just $10 billion to $20 billion of the $150 billion we're squandering on S&L misdeeds would modernize or renovate every sub-par unit of public housing in America. . . ."

Sweetheart Deals

One feature of these rescue missions is stunningly unfair to taxpayers. You might logically suppose that when a failing bank or S&L is saved with federal money, then the federal government would be the one to profit when the lending institution regains its feet. No, no, that's not how the system works.

Consider the American Savings and Loan Association of Stockton, California, once the nation's largest insolvent "thrift" institution. The Federal Home Loan Bank Board provided $2 billion to shore it up and then allowed a group headed by rich Texans to buy 70 percent of American Savings for a mere $550 million in cash and insured the new owners against loss. In other words, the new owners couldn't possibly lose, but they stood to gain billions of dollars.

Hundreds of ailing savings and loan institutions were disposed of in the same giveaway fashion. Big-time financiers and Wall Street deal-makers lined up by the score to get an S&L.

When it comes to subsidies and sweetheart deals, nobody gets better treatment from the federal government than the money lenders.

And no criminals enjoy such forgiveness. Because government overseers often do a sloppy job, very few of the insiders who loot billions from their own banks and thrifts get caught, and those that are caught get extremely light punishment. At the American Heritage Savings & Loan in Chicago, for example, executives made $15 million in fraudulent loans, causing the company to collapse and costing you and me $45 million to clean up. The longest sentence handed out: one year and a day. Complained Anthony Valukas, a U.S. attorney in Chicago: "If someone had walked in the door of the bank with a note saying this is a robbery and walked out with $1,500, I dare say he would have received five to ten years in prison."

Regulation

As we discussed in greater detail in Chapter 6 on the bureaucracy, the government regulates the marketplace through dozens of agencies and cabinet departments, which reach deep into our lives to fix the rules for everything from the label on a bottle of aspirin tablets to the color of the air that we breathe. To varying degrees, the government regulates what we see on television, how fast we drive, how high we fly, the prices of timber and oil, the size of our mortgage payments, what stocks we can buy, what and how many animals and fish we can kill, how much wheat or tobacco we can grow, whom we can hire, what minimum wages we must pay, the construction of our cars, what medicines we can buy, what hair dye we can use, and so on and so on and so on, in a thousand other ways.

The motivation behind some of these regulations is primarily safety and health, or honesty in marketing. But whatever the primary motivation, all these regulations affect the economy.

Some seemingly simple government regulations are complicated by conflicting humanitarian interests—the minimum wage, for example. About eight million Americans earn the federally mandated minimum wage; 85 percent are 18 and older, 60 percent are women, 86 percent work in service occupations, and 35 percent are in poor families. Through the 1980s the minimum stayed at $3.35 an hour, as food prices rose 27 percent and rents 49 percent. Many experts considered it totally unfair and unrealistically low. Congressional Democrats in 1989 offered legislation to raise it in three yearly hikes to a total of $4.55 an hour—which still would give a worker an income far below poverty wages for a family of four. That wasn't asking too much, was it?

Then why, when Congress passed the raise, did President Bush—at the urging of the U.S. Chamber of Commerce and many business organizations—veto it? The raise would have had a slight inflationary effect and cut into profits, of course.* But it was more complicated than that, and the reasons were not *all* based on hard-hearted greed. Some were based on the need to survive. Many businesses, already operating on a very tight profit margin, are at a severe disadvantage in competing with foreign countries where labor costs, compared to those in the United States, are minimal.

---

*Bush said his opposition to such a "large" increase was based on its inflationary effect, even though the first step of the increase was to be a mere 50 cents. At the same time, he proposed reducing the tax on capital gains, an action that would be truly inflationary. Capital gain is the difference between the purchase price of an asset and its higher resale price at some later date. Since wealthy people have most assets, a lower capital-gains tax would benefit them the most. The Senate majority leader, George J. Mitchell of Maine, seemed puzzled: "The president's own capital gains tax proposal would give the top 1.1 percent of all taxpayers, those with incomes in excess of $200,000, an average tax cut of almost $31,000 a year. How can anyone justify wanting to give a $30,000-a-year tax cut to the richest Americans and at the same time opposing 50 cents an hour more for the poorest Americans?" (*The New York Times*, April 12, 1989).

And some U.S. companies—particularly in the garment, restaurant, and meat-processing industries—that do pay at least the legal minimum wage are also faced with unfair competition in this country from "sweatshops" (officially defined as businesses that "regularly violate both wage or child labor and safety or health laws"). Once found mainly in New York City and Chicago, the sweatshops have spread from coast to coast, and hundreds of thousands of workers—many of them Hispanic and Asian immigrants, legal and illegal—are being exploited. Virtually all are paid less than the minimum wage.

Some businesses argued that if they had to raise their minimum wage, they would have to lay off workers—and isn't a $3.35 job better than no job at all? Those who stood to be fired would probably agree; those who kept their jobs at the higher rate wouldn't.

Pushed by Democrats at a time when they were still controlling Congress, the minimum wage was raised to $4.25 in 1991. There it was stuck for the next five years, finally bumping up to $4.75 in 1996 and then to $5.15 in 1997. But passing a minimum wage and enforcing it are two dramatically different things. Alan Krueger, a Princeton labor economist, estimates that 2 to 3 million workers are being illegally paid less than the minimum. Law-breakers are rarely caught and penalties are rare and light.

Violations occur most often in trucking and apparel work. A Cornell study of nonunion long-haul truck drivers found about half earned less than $4.25 an hour if their pay was divided by their actual hours worked. In a survey of seventy-six randomly selected southern California garment factories, the government found 43 percent had recently violated the minimum wage law. The worst offenders were diabolic, like the El Monte, California, operator of a garment sweatshop who kept eighty-one Thai immigrants imprisoned for years, forcing them to work long hours for $1 an hour. The government squeezed $1 million out of him for back pay, but that was only a fraction of what he really owed the workers.

Import Complexities

One of the government's major levers for controlling the economy—or trying to control it—is its imports policy. It seems sometimes more shaped by luck, good or bad, than by rational planning. Consider the "free trade" policies promoted by multinational corporations and their allies in both Republican and Democratic administrations for the past three decades. The theory was that by doing away with virtually all trade barriers in this country—and trying to persuade other countries to do likewise—we would be able to sell more of our products abroad, thereby increasing the number of attractive jobs in this country.

"Each additional billion dollars in exports creates nearly 20,000 jobs here in the United States," President Bush said in 1991. Two years later President Clinton said exactly the same thing. What neither mentioned was that trade goes in both directions, and that for each additional billion dollars in *imports*, many U.S. jobs would be lost.

And lose them we did. Under Washington's lopsided "free trade" policy, the United States in the last two decades has imported hundreds of billions of dollars more manufactured goods than it sold abroad. And because of all those imported products, an estimated 2.6 million manufacturing jobs as well as thousands of skilled computer-based jobs were wiped out in this country. That isn't to say unemployment went up. In fact, by the end of the '90s, the United States had its lowest unemployment rate in thirty years. But the *type* of employment changed. The number of high-paying, full-time manufacturing jobs dropped sharply. And workers who were bumped from those payrolls often wound up with part-time manufacturing jobs or in much lower-paying service jobs, which usually have no pension programs and rarely a medical program.

The "global economy" is here to stay, and it would be economically suicidal and irrational to try to shut it out with high tariffs. Indeed, there's no reason we can't participate in such a way as to benefit other nations while also benefiting our own. But at present there are many harmful defects. Consider:

- We have permitted some major trading partners, particularly in Asia, to take unfair advantage of our open-door policy. Japan is one of many examples. Rejecting the reciprocity of free trade, Japan blocked imports of U.S.–made television sets. At the same time, it licensed our technology and exported so many Japanese-made sets to this country at such low prices that they drove our television companies out of business. We once had half a dozen major television manufacturers—RCA, Zenith, and so forth. All are gone now, and with them went thousands of jobs.

  Japan has thought up some absurd reasons for barring our products. American skis, for example, were barred as "unsafe" because the Japanese customs inspectors insisted Japanese snow was different.

- General Electric was once the world's premier manufacturer of home appliances. It no longer manufactures any; it simply assembles them from parts made in other countries by cheap labor (but considering the price of these commodities, you'd never know the labor was cheap). Turning manufacturing plants into merely assembly plants is now commonplace in the United States.

- China refuses to buy from Boeing, the world's leading manufacturer of jet aircraft, unless Boeing lets Chinese factories make some of the crucial parts that go into the planes. Other foreign buyers make the same demand for other products.

  Today, 50 percent of the parts of a Boeing 777 are made outside the United States and shipped back here for assembly. Result: Boeing reduced its U.S. workforce by one-third and the company is in danger of losing control of its technology through Chinese duplications.

Our Companies Go Abroad

Many U.S. corporations decided the best way to compete in the global economy was to shut down factories in this country and open factories in lands where workers accept pitifully low wages. Corporations that paid $12 an hour for production-line workers in this country saw their profits soar when they moved their factories to countries where workers are paid $12 a week.

- For example, Nike Incorporated, the firm that produces athletic shoes for less than $6 a pair and sells them for up to $120, does not have a single factory in this country. Instead, it employs 450,000 people—many as young as fourteen—in Southeast Asia. An investigation of Nike plants in Vietnam found young women working 10 and one-half hours a day, six days a week (in violation of Vietnam law), in excessive heat and noise and in foul air, for slightly more than $10 a week. The workers may suffer, but Nike Incorporated doesn't. It earned $800 million in 1996 from sales of $9.2 billion.

- Texas Instruments is designing some of its more sophisticated computer chips in India, where computer scientists come cheap, by U.S. standards. As of 1995, 75,000 Indians were working on computer programs, mainly for the American market.

Next Stop, Mexico

The disparity in wages came closer to home, and made the use of cheap workers more convenient for our corporations, when Congress passed the North American Free Trade Agreement (NAFTA) in 1993. NAFTA opened the borders of both Canada and Mexico. In terms of trade, those countries and the United States virtually became one.

President Clinton pushed for passage of NAFTA by evoking all sorts of glorious visions of the future. By opening the Mexican border, he predicted, we could solve most of our immigration problems with Mexico. The economy of our southern neighbor would greatly expand, thousands of well-paying jobs would be created on that side of the border, and Mexicans would stay home and work rather than steal into this country. And with the Mexican economy booming, he said, that would become an enormously profitable market for U.S. goods.

None of this happened. What was supposed to be a rich market for us went flat; before NAFTA, the United States sold $5.4 billion more to Mexico than Mexico sold to us; two years after NAFTA, we were buying $15.4 billion more than we sold to them. The hordes of illegal immigrants poured over the border in ever-larger waves. Thousands of U.S. factory workers lost their jobs as their employers moved to Mexico.

The vast majority of the 2,700 factories—called maquiladoras—along the border on the Mexican side are owned by U.S. corporations. Desperate for work at any wage, Mexicans eagerly take jobs that pay as low as $3.40 a *day*, which was Mexico's minimum wage in 1998. More experienced workers may earn $1.50 an hour. Most of the workers live in filthy ghettoes surrounding the factories, in huts with dirt floors, no running water, no sanitation. By U.S. standards, the workers have few rights. For example, pregnant workers are usually harassed into quitting or are fired outright, so the company won't have to pay maternity benefits.

- General Motors has become Mexico's largest private employer, with 72,000 workers at fifty factories. GM pays Mexican workers $1 to $2 an hour to make auto parts and assemble vehicles that it once paid U.S. workers $22 an hour to produce in Michigan.

  GM's move to Mexico is just part of its global expansion. It is also building plants—$2.45 billion spent on them in 1997 alone—in Argentina, Brazil, Poland, Thailand, and China.
- The availability of cheap labor in Mexico has been used as a threat to depress wages in this country. In our low-wage

southern states, union organizers claim that since the passage of NAFTA, one in ten employers has threatened to move to Mexico if workers vote to unionize—and 12 percent of the companies actually did shut down to avoid a union contract.

It Isn't Hopeless

Since greed is at the bottom of all these problems, they may never be fully solved, but a number of reasonable reforms would help. Worth considering:

- We should stop being a pushover and force our foreign trading partners to accept the fact that "free trade" means "fair trade"—with them giving as much access to our products as we give to theirs.
- If one of our companies sets up shop in China, for example, their products, when shipped back to the U.S. market, should be hit with a tariff equal to the difference between Chinese and U.S. wages.
- Treaties should be worked out—and enforced—with other countries that would make U.S. companies operating abroad give environmental and workplace protections (safety and health) equal to those required in the United States. Supposedly that was part of the NAFTA agreement, but it has been ignored.

Trying to Regulate the Big Boys

Perhaps the most intelligent—and certainly the most ambitious—regulations we have are the Sherman Antitrust Act of 1890 and the Clayton Act of 1914. The first was inspired by the need to break up John D. Rockefeller's Standard Oil Trust, which, by gobbling up dozens of smaller companies, had come to control 95 percent of the oil refining industry in this country. The second was inspired by the need to break up the dangerous concentration of economic power held by what was then known as the Money Trust. A lot of people never heard of these laws, which is understandable, for they are the most *unused* major laws on our statute books. And that's too bad, because the Sherman and Clayton Acts contain the very heart and spirit of what we think of as the free-enterprise system. Their goal is to obtain the highest degree of fair pricing and business competition, or, to put it in the negative, to prevent unfair competition and the ripping-off of consumers—to prevent a bullying concentration of economic power. There are several very strict taboos: Companies are not supposed to get together to decide on a common price for their product (price-fixing).* They aren't supposed to price their products so low that potential competitors are discouraged from entering the market (predatory pricing). Mergers that might help one company dominate or control an industry—monopoly—is the biggest taboo of all.

Actually, very few major industries are in danger of being taken over by a true monopoly, although Microsoft's 90 percent control of the world's personal computer operating systems would probably qualify, and so would Boeing Aircraft Company, which, after it bought McDonnell-Douglas in 1996, became the only—yes, only—manufacturer of commercial jets in the United States.

But it is not uncommon for an industry to be dangerously dominated by something called an oligopoly, where a handful of large firms, rather than just one, pretty much run the show. For instance, it's hardly likely that real competition exists among the prime military contractors. A wave of mergers beginning in 1985 left only four: Lockheed-Martin, the number one military contractor; Boeing; Northup Gruman; and Raytheon Company. These four now represent about two-thirds of all military products' sales. Similar domination exists in the tobacco industry, where three companies, American Brands, Liggett and Meyers, and R. J. Reynolds, have more than 80 percent of sales sewed up.

The antitrust laws are supposed to prevent, or at least punish, unfair pricing and the unfair concentration of market power. And sometimes they do. Archer Daniels Midland (ADM), the planet's largest grain processor, was prosecuted in 1996 and fined $100 million for conspiring to fix prices. (The fine, by the way, was a pittance to ADM, which has annual revenues of over $13 billion.) The biggest merger ever challenged by the Justice Department was its lawsuit in 1998 to block Lockheed-Martin's acquisition of Northrup Grumman, for $8.3 billion. Lockheed, a veritable octopus, had already swallowed twenty-six other military contractors since 1990. The merger of Lockheed and Northup, the number one and number three military contractors, would have created a dangerous monopoly over many crucial items in the defense budget.

---

*One of the outstanding injustices of the antitrust system is that, because of the McCarran–Ferguson Act, the $400-billion insurance industry is exempt from it. (Americans spend more on insurance than on anything else except food and shelter.) Insurance companies could raise rates 1,000 percent or more, in concert, without fear of antitrust prosecution (*The Washington Post,* June 2, 1987).

Regrettably, the antitrust laws are regularly bent out of shape, if not broken, and the lawbreakers usually get by with it. The Federal Trade Commission and the Justice Department's antitrust division, the two parts of government that are supposed to police this conduct of corporations, have never had a record of much militancy, and during the Reagan and Bush administrations they were virtually starved to death for operating funds. There was a tidal wave of mergers and acquisitions, resulting of course in fewer and larger corporations. To its credit, the Clinton administration put more muscle into antitrust enforcement, examining large corporate mergers with more vigor than had been seen since the 1970s. But the twelve years of Reagan and Bush indifference had allowed a momentum to develop that couldn't be slowed down, and the merger mania that had begun in those years became even more maniacal in the Clinton era.

Mergers and acquisitions activity reached a record $347 billion in 1994, only to have the record smashed in every year thereafter, with 1998 topping $1.7 trillion. Would there ever be an end? Drug companies, banks, high-tech companies, railroads, paper and utility companies, corporations of every brand seemed eager to tie the knot. Nothing like it had been seen since the era between 1895 and 1904, when 1,800 U.S. companies combined into just 157 companies, including the oil, steel, and auto giants.

Why should consumers worry? What's the danger? The danger is that by reducing competition to fewer and fewer giants, the survivors more easily come to an "understanding" on prices and market shares. Since the really critical industries in this country are controlled by no more than eight corporations, it is relatively easy for them to reach such agreements.

When Competition Sours

It should be remembered, however, that in some industries rampant, wide-open competition does not—in the long run—serve the best interests of the consumer. Sometimes the most beneficial competition is that which is controlled by the federal government.

The airlines offer a good example. For many years, the government closely regulated airline rates and routes. The airlines could make changes, could offer a variety of fares, but they had to get permission from the Civil Aeronautics Board (CAB) before they did. The airlines could fight for customers, but the CAB was there, like a referee in a boxing match, to see that they only hit each other above the belt. The system worked fine.

But Congress, encouraged by the Carter administration, decided to change it, ending regulations in 1977 and throwing the referee out of the ring as a way, the politicians thought, to "encourage competition." And so it did—for a while. In the early days of deregulation, twenty-two new airlines entered the business, and the old airlines expanded. There was a wide variety of fares, many of them cheaper than in the pre-1977 regulated days.

But then things started going sour. The dog-eat-dog atmosphere caused some airlines to drop "unprofitable" routes, leaving many small cities without any air service. And then the airlines began gobbling each other up in a merger frenzy; the Justice Department approved twenty-one straight applications for mergers. As for the new, smaller airlines, some became casualties to fare wars, some were driven out of business because the big lines crowded them out at the airports and prevented their getting boarding gates. Of the twenty-two airlines that began interstate service after 1977, only five remained alive at the end of the first decade.

Now, only a handful of big airlines control all the major routes, and it is a much tighter and more profitable control than in the days when the industry was run by the CAB. The five biggest airlines carry nearly 70 percent of the traffic. *One* airline controls more than half of all flights at each of the eighteen "hub" airports across the country, and at some of these hub airports one airline controls 80 percent of the traffic. At airports dominated by one or two airlines, fares are 27 percent higher than the national average.

How did it happen? When enough of the competition had been eliminated, the remaining giants simply got together and divided up the country (an antitrust violation, by the way) and agreed among themselves which companies would dominate which markets. Acting in collusion (another antitrust violation) in the winter of 1988, the major airlines decided with one stroke to end many of the "bargain" fares that had been the selling point for deregulation in the first place. Alfred E. Kahn, who had been President Carter's chief architect of deregulation, had to admit that his bright idea hadn't turned out so brilliantly, after all: "Ten years after the airlines were deregulated, much of what we worked to achieve is threatened by the emergence of large areas of monopoly power."

And ten years after he said that, the same ruthless monopolies were still in power. In a significant and surprising departure from the government's twenty-year policy of support for airline deregulation, the Department of Transportation (DOT) in 1998 finally got around to challenging the abuses. DOT had the reputation of being a toothless tiger, for although it had had the authority to stop unfair practices in air transportation since 1979, it had never done so. But now Secretary of Transportation Rodney E. Slater said the government would levy fines to stop major airlines from driving out new competitors by unfair practices, such as flooding the market with cheap seats and then, when the competitor was gone, raising fares to three or four times their normal level.

Debt

It is not uncommon for the federal government to spend more than it takes in, although nine times in the last fifty or so years it has managed to balance its budget or come up with a small surplus. And ordinarily the federal debt has been nothing to worry about because (until recently) the growth of the debt has never been greater than the growth of the national economy. In other words, just as a person who has a good job and gets regular raises can handle a reasonable amount of debt, the federal government, with periodic and moderate adjustments upward of its income (taxes and fees), has been able to handle the normal debts that come with a flexible, aggressive attempt to spread the good things of life over a larger number of citizens.

Extreme conservatives, however, have always made "debt" the nastiest four-letter word in the language of government finance. (Or at least that was their line until their hero, Reagan, ran up the largest d*** in the nation's history.) For many years the holy grail that they sought was a balanced budget; nothing, to them, was so sacred as that.

So it was only natural that when Reagan ran for the presidency against the incumbent, Jimmy Carter, in 1980, he came down hard on the extra debt that had accumulated during the four Carter years.

Carter had had a little bad luck. Because oil-producing nations overseas had raised the price of oil an astounding 1,000 percent since 1973, and because energy prices influenced all other prices, there had been double-digit inflation toward the end of his term in 1980, and this inflation was written into the cost of doing the government's business, too. Thus, the annual deficits (the difference between income and expenditures) totaled $195 billion under Carter. The deficit for his last year alone was $59.5 billion.

To hear Reagan talk during the 1980 campaign, Carter had destroyed the government. It was, said Reagan, a "runaway deficit" that proved "the federal budget is out of control." He vowed that he would balance the budget within two years—"by 1983 if not earlier."

This was just one of the many promises that Reagan made no effort to keep. In fact, he went out of his way to break them. If Carter's last budget of $590 billion was "out of control," what did that make Reagan's last budget of well over $1 trillion? And did he improve upon Carter's "runaway" deficit of his last year, $59.5 billion? Not exactly. For the eight years of Reagan's administration, the annual deficits *averaged* $185 billion, or three times larger than Carter's *largest* annual deficit.

How and why did he do it? How could Reagan have made such a monstrous mistake? And why did he let the mistake continue for eight long years?

The answer to the "how" is that Reagan was fanatically determined to cut taxes. Next to "debt," "taxes" is the dirtiest word in the ultraconservative's vocabulary. So, in his very first year in office, he persuaded Congress to cut taxes, even though the nation was at that moment in a sharp recession—in fact it was experiencing the worst economic deterioration since the Great Depression of the 1930s.

In hard times, there is just naturally less money floating around for the government to tax. So, even if Reagan had *not* cut taxes, the government's income would have dropped and we would have gone further into debt. But when Reagan *did* cut taxes, on top of the natural slump, the debt became humongously large. And when he left office, the accumulated debt of the United States, which had been $914 billion in Carter's last year, was moving toward $3 trillion.

To visualize $3 trillion, let's quote from The Man himself. Deploring the nearly trillion-dollar debt he inherited from Carter, Reagan said: "If you had a stack of thousand-dollar bills in your hand only four inches high, you'd be a millionaire. A trillion dollars would be a stack of thousand-dollar bills sixty-seven miles high." When Reagan left office, to pay off the national debt you would have needed (using his figures) a stack of thousand-dollar bills 201 miles high.* He had managed in the eight years of his administration to increase the national debt by more than the sum of *all previous deficits* since the Republic was founded.

Why did Reagan do it (and why did his successor, President Bush, continue the Reagan economic policy)? That is a very dark question,

---

*We have gone along with Reagan's figures even though—as usual—his math is inaccurate. A trillion dollars would actually be a stack 63.13 miles high. But what's a few miles of thousand-dollar bills, one way or another, to a politician?

because, as Benjamin Friedman, Harvard economics professor, writes in *Day of Reckoning,* either the debt was the accidental result of well-intentioned stupidity or it was the result of an incredibly immoral and cunning scheme by conservatives to force people to give up programs they would otherwise have been able to afford. The debt is now so large that just its interest payment—$248 billion a year—is the second largest item in the budget, next to defense. This is money that otherwise could be spent on social programs to feed the hungry, house the homeless, help needy young people through college, train the unemployed for new jobs, and so forth. Because the interest on the debt must be paid, these programs will be cut back or cut out.

How does the government raise the money to pay the deficit, and the interest on it? First, it sells U.S. Treasury securities, which are snatched up by people wealthy enough to buy U.S. bonds in $5,000 and $10,000 minimums. (Ninety-three percent of all bonds are held by the richest 10 percent of the population.) That takes care of the deficit. Then the government uses taxes, mostly from working-class Americans, to pay off the bonds and the interest on them. This is a redistribution of wealth from bottom to top. Ronald Reagan was elected in 1980 by persuading most American voters to oppose the doctrine of "redistribution," by which he plainly meant to arouse their anger at the thought of taking tax dollars from hard-working, risk-taking Americans and transferring these same tax dollars to the Undeserving Poor, including welfare queens in designer jeans (as he described them). Ironically, during his eight years in office, the doctrine of redistribution continued—but in the opposite direction: toward those he considered the Deserving Rich.

Senator Daniel Moynihan of New York summed it up this way: "For the foreseeable future, it will require one-quarter of each citizen's personal income tax to pay the interest on money borrowed during the [Reagan] years. This is elementally a transfer of wealth from working parents in the Bronx to holders of long-term Treasury bonds living in Palm Beach."

Few ordinary taxpayers would disagree with Mark Shields when he says,

> Nobody really enjoys paying taxes. But American taxpayers have been able to take some comfort from the knowledge that their tax dollars did help sometimes to build a school and to improve the nation. However, there is no such consolation from income taxes used to pay off wealthy bondholders who are profiting at the nation's expense.

No Medicare prescription is filled; no math books purchased; no toxic waste dump is cleaned up by taxes that pay the interest bill on the national debt.

Managing the Money

Of the government's myriad regulatory functions that influence the economy, none is so important as its power to regulate the supply and flow of money.

Government officials and politicians can shape the economy through two routes—monetary policy (regulating the money supply) and fiscal policy (spending and taxation). Actually, they use a combination of the two.

Monetary policy is the effort to influence the level of prices by regulating the amount of money in circulation through the central bank, which is called the Federal Reserve System (or simply the "Fed"). Increasing the amount of money in the banking system increases the amount of credit that is available and lowers the interest rates. This stimulates borrowing. Businesses are encouraged to expand, and consumers are encouraged to buy. If business expansion and consumer purchases reach too fast a tempo, the economy heats up. Prices may soar. That is inflation. To control it, the Federal Reserve System restricts the flow of money and credit. When money becomes scarcer, its price (interest) goes up; neither business nor consumer can afford the higher interest rates, so they stop borrowing from banks and put away their credit cards. The economy grows chilly. Production is cut back. People are thrown out of work. And inflation is supposed to decline.

The monetary way of controlling the economy is somewhat crude. It depends on lower interest rates to stimulate the economy, and it depends on higher interest rates and consequent unemployment to depress the economy. The economy of a major industrial nation like the United States is much too complicated in scope, and too subtle in its parts, to be regulated in that way with any efficiency. If used alone, monetary policy can work, but only in a clumsy way, like swatting a fly with a two-pound hammer.

Nevertheless, the power to control the flow of money (and credit) lies at the very heart of the economic system. It is a power that can reach into every home. If used improperly, it can bring on heavy unemployment or runaway inflation. And because power over the money supply is so crucial to the health of the nation, the Constitution specifically put it into the hands of the people's representatives in Congress. Article I, Section 8, of the Constitution provides that Congress shall have the power "to coin Money [and] regulate the Value thereof."

Oddly enough, Congress permanently ducked this responsibility long ago, just as it has shed many of its other regulatory responsibilities. In 1913, worried by a series of financial crises that pointed to the need for closer supervision of the national banking system, Congress passed the Federal Reserve Act. This established the Federal Reserve System, whose main machinery is the Federal Reserve Board (in Washington, D.C.) and twelve district Federal Reserve Banks. The Fed supervises the operations of all national banks and many state banks. It controls the nation's money supply, decides on the interest rates to be charged by banks, and keeps an eye on bank management.*

The Fed is one of the most powerful, most secretive, and least understood parts of the bureaucracy. It is a little kingdom unto itself, with an independent budget of about $2 billion a year, a workforce of 25,000 employees, an air force of forty-seven Lear jets and small cargo planes, and a fleet of vehicles, including personal cars for fifty-nine Fed bank managers. It operates in monarchical style, like the $100 million district bank in Minneapolis, which sits on nine acres of prime riverfront, with a ten-story stone clock tower overlooking terraces and gardens. It offers robot-attended, automated vaults, plus an indoor pistol range, a fitness center, and subsidized dining. A full-time curator oversees the Fed's collection of paintings and sculptures.

But for all its grandeur, the Fed's huge empire is archaic and inefficient. Despite huge shifts in the nation's population and economy, the basic structure of the Federal Reserve System is virtually the same as it was when created in 1913. Back then, Fed banks were sited according to the politics and population of the day, and today these locations

---

*Briefly, this is the manner in which the Federal Reserve Board juggles the money and credit supply: Banks would either lend or invest every cent that came their way unless they were required to hold something in reserve. The Federal Reserve Board has the authority to say how much its members should hold in reserve. If, for example, the reserve requirement were $2 on hand for every $10 on deposit, and if the Fed decided it would like to put more money in circulation, it could drop the reserve requirement to say, $1 per $10. This action does not simply free the extra $1; it multiplies the $1 nearly tenfold through a complex ripple effect. (Banking is full of such hocus-pocus, which you have to take on faith.) Thus, when the Fed drops the reserve requirement, it literally gives the banks much more money to deal with and to profit from, and this plentiful supply effectively lowers interest rates on the borrowing of money. If the Fed, however, wants to tighten the economy, it can simply move in the reverse direction and increase the reserve requirements, also jacking up interest rates.

make little sense. Missouri, once an economic and political power because of its riverboat economy, has two Fed banks; booming Florida has none. California and its vast economy has only one Fed bank—which also serves eight other states and covers 20 percent of the U.S. population.

The Fed has some very undemocratic features and some dangerous built-in conflicts of interest. For one thing, the district Federal Reserve Banks that presumably supervise private banks are, in fact, owned by the private banks. Furthermore, private banks elect six of the nine directors of each district Federal Reserve Bank. The other three members are appointed by the Fed's Board of Governors in Washington. The seven members of the Board of Governors (appointed by the president to fourteen-year terms) usually have a banking background. Consumers, small businesses, and family farmers are almost never represented on the Board of Governors; it has rarely had a black or female member.

Thus, as Henry S. Reuss pointed out when he was chairman of the House Banking Committee, although the Fed is very independent of Congress, it is not at all independent of big-banking and big-business interest groups. "It is precisely these two groups which have an unhealthy dominance within the Fed's structure. The Federal Reserve System has a built-in conflict of interest by reason of the extremely narrow spectrum of America which is represented on the boards of directors of the twelve regional banks."

Dangerous Secrecy

The chief characteristic of the Fed is secrecy. It does not publicly discuss national monetary policy, interest rates, foreign bank matters, bank mergers, holding companies, or changes in stock-market margin requirements. In fact, the Fed keeps the public closed out of most of its discussions about everything. The most startling secrecy is that which surrounds the activities of the Fed's Open Market Committee (made up of the Board of Governors and five district bank presidents). On the third Tuesday of every month, these twelve men gather in a closely guarded conference room at the Fed's white marble palace in Washington and decide on the money supply. For forty-five days, the Open Market Committee keeps its decision a secret; it then makes a skimpy report to Congress. In other words, the policy it launches in secret will have been in operation long enough to affect the economy—for good or for ill—before the representatives of the people learn what happened.

Aside from the general accusation that it is operated primarily for big banks and big business, not for the people at large, critics of the Fed also charge that in its official role as watchdog of banking practices, it has too often proved toothless and sleepy. Investigations by journalists and members of Congress in recent years have found that the Fed covered up for dozens of the biggest banks, which, as a result of stupid and sometimes crooked conduct—as mentioned earlier in the section on bank subsidies—were in rickety condition. One reason they had performed in shaky and shady ways was that they had received virtually no supervision from the Fed.

Critics also argue that the basic undemocratic quality of the Fed is worsened by the fact that it is thoroughly dominated by one person, its chairman. Members of the congressional banking committees and other leaders of the nation's financial world frequently describe the Fed chairman in such terms as "the second most powerful man in America, just behind the president" and "the key man for what's going to happen to our economy and the world economy, for that matter."

No one person, nor any board, is smart enough to direct a monetary policy that has such global impact. Many observers believe that the Fed has guessed wrong more often than it has guessed right, and that it has been the cause of every major recession since the Second World War.

There is something to be said for that argument, as you will see in the careers of the last two chairmen of the Fed, Paul Volcker and Alan Greenspan, to whom we will shortly return.

Fiscal Control: Casting Bread upon the Waters

Monetarists, like the stuffy chaps who run the Fed, are usually relegated to the financial pages. The reason is obvious: They are considered rather dull. Their approach is essentially negative; their fundamental goal is to prevent the economy from running wild. Stability is the monetarist's ideal.

But economists who put their faith in the fiscal approach to shaping the national economy get the front pages. They believe that when we get into economic trouble we can rescue ourselves by juggling the rate of taxation and the rate of government spending. They do believe that thrift is sometimes called for, but they are best known as spenders. They believe that federal bread cast upon the waters at the right time always comes back well buttered. Simply stated, this is how the fiscal technique is supposed to work:

If there is inflation loose in the land, the government can take money away from the people by taxing them, and it can ease back on the amount of money it permits to seep into the economy through government spending programs. Theoretically, the combined effect will be that the people will have less money in hand; having less money, they will buy fewer things; when the demand for goods drops, prices will drop—and inflation will thereby be curbed.

To cure recessions and depressions, the fiscal policy works in the opposite way. Reducing taxes and increasing government expenditures to get more money in circulation increases the public's buying power; as people buy more, industry steps up its production and hires more people; as more people are hired, the market expands—and boom times are on the way.

Reliance on fiscal policy to pull the nation out of the economic dumps came into popularity in the 1930s. John Maynard Keynes, a British economist, was its most famous theoretician. President Franklin Roosevelt was its most famous practitioner. It was Keynes's belief (and some sarcastic critics would say that Roosevelt joined him in the belief) that it didn't matter in the slightest how government threw money around in times of depression—just so it threw plenty of it around. Keynes's most famous dictum was that if the government couldn't think of any other way to spend itself back to prosperity, it should bury gold and hire its citizens to dig for it. The spending policy worked (helped along by the unprecedented spending of the Second World War). FDR's New Deal and Keynes's theory just may have kept the United States from taking totalitarian remedies in the 1930s.

Until the 1930s, it was taken for granted that there would be sharp business cycles and that when the economy hit the bottom of one of those cycles, a lot of people would be out of work. Tough luck. But eventually the cycle would start moving up again, and presumably the unemployed would find work. It was a freewheeling, you're-on-your-own attitude; the government was not expected to step in and give the unemployed a helping hand. But the Great Depression of the 1930s brought a gloom to the country that it had never felt before. Toward the end of President Herbert Hoover's term (1929–1933), between 12.5 and 17 million people (at least one-third of the labor force) were jobless, and those lucky enough to remain on a payroll were earning from 40 to 60 percent less than three years earlier, before the stock market crash.

Such statistics do not even begin to convey the wretchedness of life then. In the fall of 1931, for example, more than 100,000 Americans applied for jobs in the Soviet Union in response to an ad asking for 6,000 skilled workers. Several hundred homeless women were forced to sleep in Chicago's parks; some of them were schoolteachers, who for eight of the thirteen months from April 1931 to May 1932 had received no pay from the city. Hunger riots swept through Oklahoma City, Minneapolis, and New York City.

If the situation was not hopeless, it certainly seemed as if it were. There was absolutely no sign that the economy would reverse itself in the normal cyclical way. The national feeling was not merely pity and self-pity, but fear and panic. Many people were convinced that capitalism had failed. Many believed that a democracy could not rescue itself from so great a slump. There were open and serious discussions about the possible need for changing our form of government; a shift to a benevolent dictator was not an uncommon suggestion—and, most significantly, some of these suggestions came from the wealthiest and most powerful people in the country, who were, of course, just the folks who might be able to bring about such a change.

The trauma of the 1930s was so severe that the relationship of the government to the economy changed completely. This change came about largely because Roosevelt established the notion that if a critical number of Americans could not find work anywhere else, the government must become the "employer of last resort." Previously, the operating philosophy in both the government and the private-business sector was that if a person really tried hard enough—showed pluck and initiative—a job somehow would become available. All one needed—so that good old American notion went—was enough "get up and go."

Of course, the truth has always been that people with the lowest incomes rarely get started toward upward economic mobility without a boost, and that boost will not likely come from any source but government. Roosevelt was the first president to act on that truism. He was willing to give direct relief where necessary, but he preferred to offer emergency government employment as a way of supplying income without destroying pride.

In 1935, he set up the Works Progress Administration (WPA), to create "socially useful" jobs. He asked Congress for $1.4 billion to start it off. Never before had a president sought so much money for a single purpose. The WPA, the largest public-service employment program in United States history at that time, built 110,000 public buildings, laid 16,117 miles of water mains and water distribution lines, built 651,087 miles of roads and highways and 48,680 miles of curbing, and constructed 77,965 bridges and viaducts and 600 airplane landing fields. There is scarcely a town in the United States today that does not have a school, post office, playground, or hospital built by WPA workers, who earned $50 a month.

The make-work programs of the 1930s were so successful that the creation of public jobs is now one of the first remedies that politicians consider when there is a sharp recession. Thus, even President Reagan, who did not believe in government handouts, signed a $4.3 billion Emergency Jobs Bill when unemployment approached 11 percent. Keeping a count of the unemployed to determine when artificial job-making may be necessary is considered a standard necessity of government (prior to the 1930s, no government agency seriously attempted to tally the unemployed on a regular basis). The reason is not only humanitarian, but practical—for government economists need to know the size of the leak in the fiscal bucket. Aside from the human costs of joblessness—destroyed hopes, increased tension, reduced standards of life, and more crime, drug abuse, and mental illness—government economists recognize that for every 1 percent increase in unemployment there is a loss to the nation of $50 billion in unproduced goods, at least $14 billion in uncollected taxes, and more than $2 billion in unemployment compensation.

Since 1934, the government—whether led by Democratic or Republican administrations—has been Keynesian in its commitment to intervention in the marketplace. The extent of that devotion is written into the federal budget. In the early 1930s, before we decided that spending would be our salvation, the annual budget averaged $5 billion. Today, the budget is $1.7 trillion—three hundred times larger, although the population is only slightly more than twice as large.

As mentioned in Chapter 3 on the Cold War, the most dramatic and controversial part of our fiscal policy is centered in the defense budget, which accounts for about one-fifth of the total federal budget.

Actually, nobody in government pretends that the defense budget is only for defense. A great deal of it—perhaps most of it—is used simply to keep Americans employed and corporate profits high. "Yes, there is a military–industrial complex," says Michigan Democratic Senator Carl Levin, voicing a typical politician's rationale, "but it's not necessarily sinister. It's people. It's jobs." The Pentagon, which represents the ultimate in Keynesian spending, is allowed to fill its stocking in a year-around Christmas without much protest from Congress because the military budget accounts for such a significant share of employment: one out of every ten jobs, directly or indirectly. And that's also why there is not even much protest over Pentagon waste. The brass aren't worried. They know that many Americans feel about military spending as did those workers in some West Coast defense plants during the Vietnam War, who sported lapel buttons that read, "Don't Bite the War That Feeds You."

Inflation: The Case of the Shrinking Dollar

Politicians who worry about the nation's economic health are generally concerned about two things: inflation and unemployment. Traditionally, Democrats have worried more about unemployment because it afflicts people and Republicans have worried more about inflation because that afflicts dollars. Like all [generalizations,] that generalization is accurate up to a point.

That old devil inflation is the loss of dollar power; that is, it now takes five dollars (or more) to buy what one dollar would have bought thirty years ago. Inflation is usually the result of what economists call *demand-pull*—"too many dollars chasing too few goods," is the way they put it. (Actually this is an inaccurate phrase. High demand rarely results in scarcity. When demand is high, sellers simply jack up prices with the assurance that a well-heeled public will pay what they ask. Automobiles, for example, don't become scarcer when demand is high.) Normal inflation for the first quarter-century after the Second World War ran from about 2 to 4 percent a year. Except for persons on very low fixed pensions, with no chance to supplement their income, that kind of inflation is not at all harmful and can be helpful, for inflation means there is an abundance of money in circulation, and where there is an abundance, there is a better chance for some of it to trickle down to the workers on the bottom. That's why, during normal times, most people don't mind moderate inflation.

The people who don't like inflation of *any* amount are big bankers and other big businesspeople—in short, the people who have most of the money. For them, the absence of inflation means a "sound dollar" and "wage stability." It means that high employment is not disturbing their great wealth. Therefore, it is customary for bankers and businesspeople to advocate a very tight fiscal policy as well as a very tight monetary policy. They do not approve of government spending on social-welfare programs (although they do approve of government spending on defense and on the subsidization of big business). They approve of high interest rates. They also approve of a "reasonably" high unemployment rate because, ordinarily, this will tend to keep inflation down.

When a president puts his economic policies together, he will hear advice from both sides: Those who think the government's primary objective should be prodollar (to fight inflation, to achieve a sound dollar, to achieve price stability) and those who think the government's primary objective should be propeople (to stimulate the economy and maintain a high employment rate). The character of a government's economic policy is shaped by the judgment of whether high unemployment is a greater evil than high inflation—and at what point one becomes a greater evil than the other.

And that brings us back to Paul Volcker.

Killing the Economy to Save the Dollar

When inflation reaches unusually high levels, the Federal Reserve Board will take radical actions to strengthen the dollar. Whether the president will encourage the Fed or will resist the Fed depends on whether his sympathies lie mainly with the financial world or with the people. During the last period of hyperinflation that forced the president to take sides—in the last years of the Carter administration and the first years of the Reagan administration—the people were deserted. The pattern for the fight against that hyperinflation was set by Carter when, in 1979, he appointed Paul Volcker to head the Federal Reserve Board. Volcker—who, as president of the New York Federal Reserve Bank, had become a darling of Wall Street, the big-business community, and the international financial bankers—set out with one goal: to help the money lenders.

Because of inflation, the value of the dollar on the international market had dropped. The international bankers were screaming because the loans they had made overseas were losing value. When dollars became cheaper, foreign borrowers could pay off their debts more easily.

What Volcker did was sharply reduce the supply of money. The effect was immediate and cruel. As the supply plummeted, its price (interest) soared. Debtors and would-be debtors everywhere, in this country and abroad, were crushed.

Nobody can say Volcker had done it in a sneaky fashion. Before his appointment, he had warned Carter that he would take drastic action and do what the banking world wanted him to do. He cut the guts out of the economy to boost the dollars.

By 1983 the battle against inflation appeared to be won. The dollar's shrinkage had been cut to 3.9 percent annually. But at what a price! The dollar had been rescued by crushing large groups of people. That had been Volcker's intention. When he took the job, he publicly warned, "The standard of living of the average American has to decline." And oh, how it did decline. The Fed tightened the money supply as never before in modern times; this allowed banks to raise interest rates so high that ordinary people and ordinary businesses couldn't afford to borrow. By the middle of 1982, personal and business bankruptcies were at a fifty-year high. Auto sales were the worst in twenty years, housing sales the worst in forty years. Net farm sales were the lowest in half a century. The Census Bureau said 34.4 million Americans, or 15 percent of the population, fell below the poverty level in 1982. At the end of the year, 6.27 million Americans were collecting jobless benefits, but millions of other jobless Americans weren't covered by unemployment insurance. An estimated 2 million homeless Americans were to be found all across the country living in church shelters, in abandoned buildings, and in broken-down cars with license plates from far away. The desperation of the unemployed could be seen dramatically in places like Milwaukee, where a factory announced it had 200 openings—and 20,000 hopefuls lined up in twenty-degree weather to apply for the jobs.

In July 1979, the month before Volcker became chairman, the unemployment rate was 5.7 percent. For nearly the first five years of his term, the jobless rate averaged 8.2 percent, and at its highest point was 11 percent, and that didn't count millions of others who had given up looking for work. Remember, each one of those percentage points meant another million Americans out of work. We should not think of them merely as statistics, however, but as Jeff Faux interpreted their misery:

> The human costs of Volcker's austerity have been enormous. Professor Harvey Brenner of Johns Hopkins estimates that a 1 percent increase in the unemployment rate sustained for six years will produce about 37,000 deaths from heart attacks, suicide, homicide, cirrhosis of the liver, and so forth. It will result in about 7,500 new admissions to state

prisons and mental hospitals. Add to this the destroyed marriages, battered wives, and abused children, the hunger and the drug addiction, and the very question of whether the Volcker program was "worth it" or merely obscene. Who has the scales to balance such costs against any economic benefits?

However, Faux gives Volcker credit for "faithfully" representing "his constituency of bankers and financiers—which is more than one can say for either of the political parties, whose constituency is supposed to be the country." Exactly. The Fed's chairman does not appear on the scene on the half shell, like Venus. He is appointed by politicians.

The Next Fed Czar

Volcker's successor, Alan Greenspan, had a spotty record as an economist. His fanatical allegiance to low inflation cost two presidents their jobs.

In 1974, as chairman of the Council of Economic Advisers, he was so eager to fight inflation (which wasn't really high) that he persuaded President Ford to reduce government spending right in the middle of a sharp recession, which just made the recession worse. The voters blamed Ford—voters always credit or blame the president for economic conditions—and dumped him in the 1976 election.

Temporarily out of government service, Greenspan hired out as a consultant for some reckless and unsavory savings and loan companies that wanted to persuade federal authorities to loosen regulations and let the S&Ls gamble more of their depositors' money on investments in junk bonds and speculative mortgages. Of the seventeen S&Ls Greenspan endorsed in a letter to the Federal Home Loan Bank Board as superbly run businesses, fifteen went broke within four years. The failure of one of these S&Ls cost taxpayers $3 billion.

Notwithstanding Greenspan's failures, President Reagan appointed him chairman of the Federal Reserve in 1987, and Bush inherited him two years later, to his sorrow. To keep a lid on inflation (which again wasn't high), Greenspan raised interest rates, creating a recession that lasted into the 1992 election, and voters took it out on Bush.

President Clinton reappointed Greenspan to the Fed, but he held him at arm's length. In Clinton's second term, the nation enjoyed exceptional prosperity, and the stock market—because of wild buying on the Internet and because of a heavy influx of foreign investors— reached its highest point in history. And yet inflation remained low.

Little of this could be credited to Greenspan or the Fed. Much more important was Treasury Secretary Robert Rubin, a very rich, former Wall Street whiz, who was much craftier about international finance, was savvy about domestic politics, and was modest enough to admit that in achieving success in money matters, it comes down to the question, as he put it: "Luck or skill? We'll never know."

But let's leave the esoterica of high finance behind and turn to something that's easy to grasp: health, the need to take care of it, and what it's doing to our pocketbooks.

Medical Muddle

Residents of the United States spend more than $1 trillion a year on health care. That averages to about $4,000 per person—almost twice as much per capita as any other developed country in the world. The yearly total is expected to rise to $2.1 trillion within eight years. Yes, our doctors and nurses are superbly trained and our hospitals are excellently equipped, but obviously the cost of it all is much too high—especially when you consider that forty-three million Americans have no health insurance of any kind and another forty million are underinsured. Neither group is receiving the kind of medical help they need. Often when these groups become seriously ill, they are forced to "crawl around like health-care beggars asking for some kindly doctor's or hospital's *noblesse oblige*," as Princeton economist Uwe E. Reinhardt puts it, or they accept the fact that they can't afford to go to the doctor and just stay home and rough it out; fourteen million seriously ill Americans did that in one recent year, according to a survey by the A. Robert Wood Foundation.

The most vulnerable citizens are often the least protected; eighteen million youngsters under age eighteen are not covered by any health plan. Thirty percent of the kids in America have never seen a dentist. Twenty-six percent of women of child-bearing age have no maternity coverage, with the result that the nation's infant mortality rate is among the developed world's highest. Why doesn't the government expand its coverage to help those left out? One reason is that under the present system, there is some doubt that the government could afford to take on more patients because physicians and hospitals are jacking up their prices so fast.*

*Don't get the idea that health care subsidies go mainly to the needy. Because of tax breaks for health insurance and medical payments, the government indirectly spends the same amount on health care for the well-to-do as it does for the poor (*The New York Times*, August 22, 1989).

Some countries, such as our neighbor, Canada, have health care for *all* their people, subsidized by the government. But that's a form of socialism, and because "socialism" is (for no logical reason) a dirty word in the United States, efforts to establish a similar kind of universal health care here have always failed. President Clinton made an effort in 1995—rather half-heartedly—to get Congress to accept a modified plan of that sort, but he failed miserably.

The nearest we come to universal health care are Medicare and Medicaid, created in 1965. Medicare is an insurance program funded by payroll taxes paid by workers and their employers, and it kicks in when one reaches sixty-five and starts getting Social Security. After that, participants continue to fund it by a monthly fee of $43 (as of 1998, but it will rise). Medicare pays 80 percent of doctors' charges, but beneficiaries must pay for most prescription drugs and also pay $760 at the start of a hospital stay.

Medicaid, which is free to participants, covers drugs as well as doctors and hospital fees. It is supposed to be for all people at the very bottom of the economy, but in fact it covers less than half the poverty population. That's because states, which pay up to half the cost of Medicaid, are allowed to set the standards of eligibility. This leaves the poor's fate in the hands of some very wacky and stingy legislators. Coverage varies wildly. For example, in North Carolina, to qualify for Medicaid, a person's earnings must be 26 percent below the poverty level (the federal poverty level as of 1998 was $8,052 for an individual and $10,860 for a couple). In Illinois, a person can earn no more than 46 percent of the poverty level.

How do those with little money and no coverage cope with illness? Consider Mr. Breedlove of Arkansas. A self-employed mechanic who must support a crippled wife and two children, he earns about $5,000 a year, but the Arkansas legislature rates him as too well off to be covered by Medicaid. So, like many in his situation, he doctors himself. On one occasion, he tried to anesthetize himself with alcohol and then used a pocketknife to try to dig out a rotten and aching tooth. Failing in that, he drove to the nearest free clinic, fifty miles away in Little Rock.

A Rough Beginning

Medicare and Medicaid were not easy to push through Congress in 1965. Even though studies showed that a great many older people couldn't get health insurance and couldn't afford to pay for medical care without it, the American Medical Association, speaking for the great majority of doctors—and its close ally, the American Hospital

Association—bitterly opposed any government health program because they feared it would result in a sharp reduction in their income. Many doctors publicly swore they would destroy the programs by not participating in them.

President Johnson knew that if this threat was carried out, Medicare would fail. To win the doctors over, he allowed them to set their own fees under Medicare, with only the vaguest guidelines—that is, the government promised to pay "reasonable charges" based on what doctors customarily charged and what the prevailing charges were in an area. But since the government did not determine what was a customary and prevailing rate, the doctors were in fact left free to charge just about anything they wanted. So they hiked their fees. In 1966, the first year of Medicare, the average physician's earnings rose 11 percent. And of course their earnings continued to climb. But eventually the doctors had abused the system so much that the goverment fixed limits on fees.

Medicare was also a great bonanza for the hospital industry because at first it was paid on a cost-plus basis. Thus for the first twenty years, whatever the private hospitals charged the government, however ridiculously bloated the charges might be, was paid without protest. But greed got out of control, and by the 1980s hospital costs were ballooning at a rate of 19 percent a year, threatening to drive Medicare into bankruptcy.

In an effort to control doctor and hospital charges, the government encouraged the growth of health maintenance organizations (HMOs), which are usually owned by insurance companies. They collect money from the insured and contract with doctors, hospitals, laboratories, and so forth, to provide services to their subscribers. HMOs are not in the business for humanitarian reasons. They are in it to make money, and they make a higher profit when patients are delivered less service. Today, managed care plans are entrenched in the economy, enrolling 61 percent of the population, including millions of people covered by Medicare and Medicaid. Industries have steered 85 percent of their employees into managed care.

More Unhappiness

But by the end of the '90s, the HMOs were getting very mixed reviews. On the whole, industrialists were happy with them because they were cutting what companies had to pay for their employees' health programs. This was done by making it much harder for patients to be treated by higher-priced specialists and harder for them to get high-priced drugs, even if both were needed. Many patients resented what they considered to be the HMOs stinginess—a stinginess that they felt sometimes put their lives at risk.

And doctors were particularly unhappy. Traditionally, doctors had ruled the medical roost by controlling the treatment of their patients. They decided which drugs patients should take and which patients should be hospitalized, for how long, and in which hospitals. But doctors who went to work for HMOs found that many of these decisions would be made by cost-cutting accountants and bookkeepers. A typical complaint came from Dr. Jane Jackman, president of the 18,000-member Illinois State Medical Society: "When I see a patient, she needs a quick diagnosis. But I have to get permission for any tests that costs more than $100 that I don't do in my own office. I have to call an 800 number to the managed care office for a decision of whether it can or cannot be done." Some HMOs allowed doctors to spend an average of only ten to twelve minutes with a patient, and if they habitually spent more time than an HMO manager felt was necessary, they risked being fired.

In short, many doctors came to feel they were being robbed of their traditional autonomy and closeness with patients, and many—especially doctors who were specialists—believed the HMOs were seriously restricting their income. While under normal circumstances it is probably hard for most Americans to work up much concern for members of a profession whose average annual income approaches $200,000, in fact many patients did sympathize with the doctors because the restrictions affected them, too.

And many government officials were outraged because the HMOs, which in the early 1990s had begged to service Medicare and Medicaid patients, had by the late 1990s started dropping hundreds of thousands of these patients because, they complained, the government wasn't paying enough.

If they were losing money, it was at least partly because of the profiteering of drug companies. Drug prices (and profits for U.S. drug makers) are rising by a staggering 16 percent a year. This drives HMOs and employers crazy. At Chrysler, the car company, spending for employees' prescription drugs rose 86 percent in five years, to more than $220 million. California's Medicaid program for the poor ran 10 percent over its $1.4 billion drugs budget for 1998 because drug prices had skyrocketed.

As for the elderly, prescription drugs are the single largest health-care expense (some pay as much as one-third of their income on drugs); about 19 million elderly people in the United States have little or no drug coverage at all. Nor do an estimated 43 million younger

Americans who overflow various categories—the unemployed, the working poor, immigrants, illegal aliens, single mothers in part-time jobs—who lack insurance of any kind.

Opportunities for Reform

From what we have said about the economic structure and the economic machinery of our nation, it is obvious that a number of reforms are desperately needed. Money and credit must not be looked upon as sacred in themselves but as the device by which greater happiness can be spread over a greater number of Americans. Those who control the economic machinery must be made responsive to the general welfare rather than to the prosperity of their own small group. How can we bring this about? It is never safe to make a flat assertion to an economic question, but perhaps some of the following ideas are worth considering.

First, we should make the Federal Reserve System a part of the democratic apparatus, not a club for bankers. Most important, the Fed itself should be restructured so that its governors are directly responsible to the people's elected representatives in Congress and the White House. That can hardly be considered a radical idea when even *Fortune* magazine, the capitalists' favorite light reading, says that "the concept of the Fed as an independent body, within but not of the government, clearly needs to be modified in a period when presidents are actively trying to guide the economy with closely coordinated fiscal and monetary policies." That's *Fortune*'s way of saying, and quite rightly, that considering the Fed's spotty record, there would be little to lose if it were stripped of its independence and transformed into a political instrument through which the people could make their own mistakes.

The tax system, obviously, should also be drastically overhauled so that the tax loopholes, tax shelters, and tax preferences for the moneyed class and corporations that cost the government an estimated $200 billion in revenue every year can be eradicated or modified to achieve greater equity between rich, middle class, and poor.

Reform of the economic structure so as to significantly improve the position of middle- and low-income families is the most difficult reform that the general voting public could attempt to achieve. The reason is simple. Those with the most to lose—that is, those with the greatest share of the wealth—have the most potent weapon in politics: big money. Money buys politicians to protect money, and big money buys more politicians to protect more money.

Reforms of any nature—whether they relate to the management of the public's money or to the management of the banking system—are not likely to get far. There is not only the power of the bank lobby to consider, but the pressure placed on Washington politicians by the sheer financial massiveness, the Great Presence, of the banking industry, which controls almost 60 percent of all the assets in all the financial institutions in the country.

It is almost unfair to single out the banks in this way, however, because the interrelationship of corporate wealth in this country includes much more than the banks. A study by the Senate Subcommittee on Reports, Accounting, and Management in 1978 analyzed the 130 largest companies in America. The thirteen largest companies were interlocked through board membership with an average of 70 percent of the 117 other companies in the study. The thirteen supergiants were American Telephone and Telegraph, BankAmerica, Chase Manhattan, Citicorp, Exxon, Ford, General Motors, Manufacturers Hanover, Metropolitan Life, Mobil, J. P. Morgan & Company, Prudential Insurance, and Texaco. *All* of the thirteen except BankAmerica were interlocked directly or indirectly with one another.

That kind of economic concentration, that kind of tight clubsmanship at the top, does not go unnoticed by our politicians. When the elite of the banking community make their wishes known to Washington, it is apparent to all within earshot that they speak not merely for bankers but for the most powerful level of *all* industry. It is this kind of concentration, greater today than ever before but even more frightening because it has been of such long duration, that gives the following warning a special piquancy:

> The great monopoly in this country is the money monopoly. So long as that exists, our old variety and freedom and individual energy of development are out of the question. A great industrial nation is controlled by its system of credit. Our system of credit is concentrated. The growth of the nation, therefore, and all our activities are in the hands of a few men who, even if their actions be honest and intended for the public interest, are necessarily concentrated upon the great undertakings in which their own money is involved and who, necessarily, by every reason of their own limitations, chill and check and destroy genuine economic freedom. . . .

That was Woodrow Wilson speaking as the twentieth century got under way—fourteen presidencies ago. Since much the same complaint could be made today, it's enough to generate considerable pessimism about the hope for change. But, in fact, despite the concentration of economic power at the top that the people still must compete against, much has been accomplished since Wilson's day. The twentieth century saw an impressive increase in economic and social fair play. The moneyed elite may have the biggest voice in the lobbies of Washington (and the state capitals), but the final voice has been heard at the ballot box, where ordinary citizens have exerted enough pressure to bring about a much more humane, healthier, and better-paid society than existed in Wilson's day.

The ten-hour workday is no more. The six-day work week is obsolete. It's no longer fashionable for corporate bosses to break up labor strikes by hiring thugs to beat and sometimes kill striking workers, as happened as late as the 1930s. Although many millions of Americans are still without medical coverage, other millions, as we have pointed out, are protected by government programs—something that was not even dreamed possible in the first half of the century. Though there is still a dangerous amount of gambling on Wall Street, federal oversight established in the 1930s has made the Street much less of an ethical swamp. And there are government regulators—far too few to do a really good job, it's true, but they didn't exist at all in Wilson's day—who try to protect us from unfair pricing, unfair labor practices, dangerous drugs, and impure foods.

Many improvements have been made in just the last three decades. In 1960, only 41 percent of all adults in America had finished high school and only 7.7 percent had finished college. A generation later, the percentage finishing high school had doubled (82 percent) and the percentage finishing college had tripled (23 percent). The terrors of old age still exist, as we have indicated in this chapter, but they have been pushed back on a wide scale. While only 14 million Americans were getting Social Security checks in 1960, today the checks are going to more than 44 million.

Our successes have resulted from our dissatisfaction with past ills, but enough ills remain to inspire plenty more dissatisfaction. Compared to a generation ago, a higher percentage of Americans live in poverty today; national saving and investment, measured against the size of the economy, are much lower; the gap between the well-off and the rest of society is considerably wider than it was three decades ago. And although many corporations are beginning to show that they understand it is profitable to have a social conscience, too many other corporations still don't realize that, as economist Robert Lekachman put it, "Greed is not enough."

CHAPTER 10

So You Want to Go into Politics

The first mistake in public business is going into it.
BENJAMIN FRANKLIN
Poor Richard's Almanac, *1758*

*Politics is such a torment that I would advise every one
I love not to mix with it.*
THOMAS JEFFERSON, 1800

OBVIOUSLY, THE JUDGMENT OF THE WISE MEN QUOTED ABOVE
(and many others as well) has been widely ignored. The temptation to
win and use political power, through appointment or through the ballot box, has overwhelmed the more spirited members of every generation. Some who read this book will be among those who can't resist
that temptation. And why should you? *Somebody* has to run things;
it might as well be you.

Do You Have What It Takes?

If you do turn your talents to politics, you might as well "think presidential." Don't be so modest as to suppose you are unfit to compete in
the same arena as the politicians who have been turning out for the big
race in recent years. Most of them have had only moderately impressive political records on the way up. Jesse Jackson, one of the most fascinating of the candidates, had no political experience at all before he
decided he wanted to be president. Gird up your confidence with the

assurance that, as Frank Moore Colby has written, "politics is a place of . . . strangely modest requirements, where all are good who are not criminal and all are wise who are not ridiculously otherwise."

And do not think, if you are a woman or belong to a minority group, that the presidency is off-limits to you. Perhaps at this moment, yes. But attitudes are changing radically. Only one woman has made it to the national ticket of a major party: Representative Geraldine Ferraro, the Democrats' vice-presidential candidate in 1984. But in 1999, Elizabeth Dole, wife of former presidential candidate Bob Dole, and herself a national leader of the Red Cross, was for a time rated as a serious candidate for the Republican presidential nomination. Women are no longer thought of as just vice-presidential material, although Christine Todd Whitman, the Republican governor of New Jersey is often mentioned as a perfect prospect for that position. What a change! Thirty years ago, people used to laugh when a woman said she was going to run for mayor. They don't laugh any more. Texas, for example, a state that considers itself *muy macho*, not long ago had women mayors in seventy-six communities, including six of its largest cities; and just to complete the picture, Texans elected one of their most colorful women, Ann Richards, to be governor. As for the U.S. Congress, women are so commonplace there that newspapers long ago stopped writing feature stories about them when they are elected. California, never bashful about taking the lead in such matters, elected women to both its Senate seats; then Maine did the same.

Racial minorities are also beginning to break through the political barriers. No black can be nominated for a spot on a national ticket? They're getting close. Jesse Jackson—by far the best debater of all the candidates in 1988—came in second in the presidential primaries that year, and for one golden moment it looked like he might actually win the nomination; what's more, he got almost as many white votes as Al Gore, Richard Gephardt, and Bruce Babbitt combined. And don't forget Gen. Colin Powell, mastermind of Desert Storm and former chairman of the Joint Chiefs of Staff; the Republicans made some sounds of wanting him on their national ticket in 1996.

Dropping down the political scale, blacks rarely win a U.S. Senate seat (the last was Carol Mosely-Braun, Illinois Democrat, whose one term ended in 1999), but they make up almost as high a percentage of the U.S. House of Representatives as they do in the general population. And Hispanics are moving up fast, with twenty-one in the House at last count. In recent years, blacks have been mayors of our largest cities—New York; Los Angeles; Chicago; Washington, D.C.; Detroit; Atlanta; Philadelphia. Perhaps their success in the last five of those cities can be accounted for by the black majorities, or near majorities, in their populations. As a rule, a black candidate can expect to get no more than 20 percent of the white vote (white candidates have the same expectation among black voters, when they run against a black).

But there are dramatic exceptions. In 1989, the nation got its first black governor when Virginia elected Democrat Douglas Wilder, grandson of slaves, to its highest office—and he got 40 percent of the white vote. And don't forget the support whites gave to Jesse Jackson (mentioned previously).*

So let our imagination leap forward two decades, to a time when sex and race are no longer handicaps. Let us further imagine you have used your political apprenticeship well in the intervening years. While developing a good reputation in business (or the arts, or law, or education) you served a dozen years in your state legislature, where you built a reputation as a persuasive orator. You chaired a committee that created legislation to make massive welfare reforms that will save your state billions of dollars (the conservatives love you for it) while concentrating the payments on the people who really need them (the liberals love you for it). It's such a model piece of legislation that other states are rushing to adopt it, too, and as the person who guided it into existence, you are developing something of a national reputation. You have helped your party raise a great deal of money, and the party leaders are solidly behind you and eager to try to nominate you for the governorship or the U.S. Senate.

And after that . . . the brass ring?

You have begun asking yourself if you should take their blandishments seriously. Should you, at least in the most private retreats of your heart, cultivate an ambition to run for the highest office in the land?

To answer that question, you must first answer several others:

- Are you willing to campaign at such a fever pitch that your mind becomes frazzled and your tongue begins to twist, as it did for Edward Kennedy when he spoke to the "fam farmlies of Iowa"?

---

*Jackson would have done much better still if he had not had the reputation—sadly ironic for a member of an abused minority—of mistreating his female campaign workers (see Elizabeth O. Colton's *The Jackson Phenomenon* [New York: Doubleday, 1989]) and of being intolerant of Jewish Americans. Although Jews are traditionally strong supporters of Democratic underdogs, Jackson never recovered from the 1984 campaign when he had called New York City "Hymietown." Jews gave Jackson only 3 percent of their votes in 1988.

- Are you willing to travel around the country at such a mad pace that you don't know where you are and, like Gerald Ford, tell the good people of Indiana how glad you are to be back in Illinois?
- Are you willing to put up with physical exhaustion, bad food, maddeningly repetitious welcoming committees, lack of sleep, and airplane rides that go up and down like an elevator and finally make you so groggy that you say to an aide, as Richard Nixon did, "Bob, from now on I don't want to land at any more airports?"
- Are you willing to make speech after speech after speech after speech until you become sick of the sound of your own voice and hypersensitive to the reaction of your audience and fall into a fit of anger when you don't think you have been appreciated enough, as John Kennedy did after speaking to a sullen group in rural South Dakota? "After the election," he swore as he entered his plane to take off for the next stop, "fuck the farmers."
- Are you willing to demean yourself by going hat-in-hand to moneyed people to beg for contributions? The first-tier candidates have fund-raisers who do the begging for them. But if you are a wild card in the pack, you must spend at least half your time personally on the phone, wheedling and cajoling people to help you keep going—sometimes begging for no more than a few thousand bucks, a thousand at least—and then beat your pride into unconsciousness and go back to them the next day to cadge a few thousand more. Do you have the guts to do that sort of thing month after month, before and during the primaries?
- Can you steel yourself to stay away from your family for days on end, never getting a home-cooked meal, sleeping night after night in those stale-aired, monotonously similar hotel rooms, giving up at least a couple years of normal life just to see if you *may* have a chance for the nomination?
- Are you willing to have the press pry into your private life? (Remember that fraternity or sorority party, when you got drunk and pushed the housemother into the swimming pool? It could come back to haunt you.) If, on your way to the presidential races, you served in a state legislature or in Congress, chances are there were a few occasions when you cut deals or cast votes you would just as soon forget. Do you think your opponents or the press will let you forget them now, as you get closer to the nomination? There's nothing unfair about such investigations, but they are uncomfortable—can you take it?

- When your consultants insist that your very best ideas to benefit your country—which you would like to take to the people in thoughtful, half-hour speeches over national television—be reduced to fifteen- or thirty-second sound bites, full of razzle-dazzle and glitz, will you swallow your pride and smother your good taste and let them do it?
- Do you have the strength to keep your desire and ambition sufficiently under control that they don't tempt you into doing things you would be ashamed of, even if you should win? When, near the end of a bitter and close contest, your consultants urge you to lie about your opponent and distort the record, will you do it? Adlai Stevenson once put it this way: "The hardest thing about any political campaign is how to win without proving that you are unworthy of winning."

The Springboards

So the party's leaders have come to you, stroked your ego, and assured you that you are the party's bright hope for winning the White House in a few years—*if* you are elected to the office that will be the best springboard to launch you toward the presidency.

What *is* the best springboard?

Don't underrate a governorship. Having served two terms as governor of California—a state which, if it were a nation, would have the sixth largest gross national product in the world—Ronald Reagan was sitting pretty. Jimmy Carter, as a one-term governor of a relatively insignificant state, Georgia, wasn't in such a good position but somehow, miraculously, he brought it off. Bill Clinton was from an equally insignificant state, Arkansas, but he had been elected governor five times and was nationally known as an up-and-comer. And if he hadn't run such an inept campaign, Michael Dukakis might have parlayed his Massachusetts governorship into the presidency.*

But your best route is probably by way of the U.S. Senate. The Senate is the surest springboard for getting into the vice presidency,

---

*As this book was being written, George W. Bush, governor of Texas, was seen as the almost certain Republican presidential candidate in 2000, with most pundits believing he would make it to the White House, either then or in a later election. His leap into the ranks of presidential contenders, however, had nothing to do with his having previously won renown as a politician; in fact, he had held no office until becoming governor and his governorship was quite ordinary. He was flying strictly on his name as the son of George Herbert Walker Bush, the last Republican president.

and you can't have a better springboard than the vice presidency from which to take that final plunge.

Since the 1940s, five of ten presidents first served as vice president, and three of the five vice presidents who won promotion to the White House had served in the Senate; the other two (Gerald Ford and George Bush) came out of the House.

The foremost preparation for election to the Senate is to achieve name recognition. This can be done either by holding other political jobs or by catching the public's attention in other professions. (Would New Jersey have elected Bill Bradley to the U.S. Senate if he hadn't been a famous basketball player? Would California have elected George Murphy if he hadn't first won hearts as a song and dance man in the movies? Would Ohio have elected John Glenn if he hadn't been the first U.S. astronaut to circle the globe?) Gimmicky campaigning may do the trick, too—the kind, for instance, Lawton Chiles success- fully used to win a Senate seat in 1970. "Walkin' Lawton," he billed himself, and walked from one end of Florida to the other (1,000 miles)—the first politician to campaign in that way.

If you wanted to win a Senate seat today, you would have to raise between $4 million and $10 million, depending on the size of the state you were running in. And, looking to the future, you would have to raise that amount, not once, but several times, because you aren't likely to be considered as a vice-presidential prospect until you have been reelected at least once. What's more, by the time you run for the Senate, fifteen or twenty years from now, the race will probably cost twice as much.

Why do senators have the inside track? One answer is that presi- dential nominees usually like to have a running mate who brings some glamour, and the Senate is considered a somewhat glamourous place. The press focuses more on Washington than on any state capi- tol, so senators with some seniority have a better chance to get their little acts on national television than even the most powerful gover- nors, and a better chance than most members of the House, with their limited fiefdoms.

Strange Balances

But glamour is only part of it. When a presidential candidate picks his running mate, he is even more interested in getting somebody who can supply him with (1) a tactical demographic leg up—that is, the ability to deliver Texas or California or Illinois, or young people, or women—and (2) a "balanced ticket," which usually means a running mate with a different ideology. Thus, liberal easterner Kennedy picked moderate-conservative southwesterner Johnson (who could help him get Texas). Moderate-conservative westerner Nixon picked eastern right-winger Agnew. Right-wing westerner Reagan picked moderate-conservative easterner Bush. Bush picked ultraconservative Dan Quayle of Indiana. But Clinton broke the pattern, and we'll get back to that in a moment.

Sometimes the balancing act was positively nutty. It made no sense at all for moderate-liberal New Englander Dukakis to pick the very conservative Texas Senator Lloyd Bentsen as his vice-presidential running mate. Bentsen, a straightforward tory on economics, was perhaps the most important congressional leader in pushing through Reagan's tax cuts for rich people; he was notoriously cozy with big business lobbyists; he was a steely hard-line militarist who supported U.S. intervention all over the globe; he belonged to segregated clubs.* Since Dukakis opposed *all* of those activities and attitudes, it was absurd for him to pick as a running mate a politician who, if Dukakis should die in office, would step in to give the country leadership *opposite* to what Dukakis was promising.

But at least Bentsen was acknowledged to be a very smart guy. Neither brilliance nor a deep commitment to public service, however, is a requirement for the vice president's job, as was dramatically demonstrated by Bush's selection of Senator Daniel Quayle for it.† Quayle, who had barely a C− grade average in college and was therefore ineligible for Indiana University Law School, used family connections (his uncle is the publisher of the *Indianapolis News*) to get in anyway and the same family connections to obtain his first job in the Indiana attorney general's office. An editor at the family newspaper, who also was a National Guard major general, helped young Dan get a coveted place in the guard, to avoid being sent overseas during the Vietnam War. Quayle spent the war writing press releases at home. His service in the U.S. Senate was inconspicuous, to say the least; he was best known for supporting whopping Pentagon budgets and favoring armed intervention in foreign countries—which, in light of his own country-club service in the National Guard, led some angry Vietnam vets to label him a hypocritical "chicken hawk."

---

*Bentsen resigned from the clubs for the duration of the campaign, and then rejoined them.

†Poor Quayle, he quickly became the butt of many jokes about his intellectual prowess. A typical joke: "Quayle thinks *Roe* v. *Wade* is two ways to get across the Potomac."

Why would Bush choose such a fellow for his vice president? Many Republicans were baffled. Apparently it was the old balancing act. Some of Bush's advisers told *Newsweek* that moderate-conservative Bush liked Quayle because he was "a young right-winger outspoken enough to please the conservatives but malleable enough not to over-shadow his boss," and besides he was young enough to appeal to the baby boomers.

As we said a moment ago, Clinton broke the pattern. In picking Al Gore to be his vice president, there was no geographical or intellectual "balancing." They were from neighboring southern states (Arkansas and Tennessee). They were about the same age and of about equal ambitions. They were both moderate-to-liberal. And they were probably about equally smart. What really made their relationship remarkable was its closeness. Gore sat in all major White House planning sessions, and he was not slow to give his opinions even if they sharply differed from Clinton's. And Clinton took his advice seriously. Gore had unprecedented authority for a vice president, and author Elizabeth Drew is probably correct to say that he was "the most influential vice president in history." Of course, there was one "balancing" matter: Gore had done military service and Clinton hadn't. Not exactly a big deal.

Another Bad Joke

Sometimes presidential nominees seem to pick their running mates as a kind of bad joke. Such was Richard Nixon's choice of Spiro Agnew, the former governor of Maryland. (Actually he was chosen because right-wing southerners liked him.) Agnew was a bumptious buffoon and a crook as well (he resigned halfway through his second term as vice president, having been charged with tax violations, bribery, extortion, and conspiracy). Perhaps Nixon didn't know Agnew's many defects when he picked him the first time; but he knew them full well by the time they ran for reelection, and held him in total contempt. Nixon's White House aide John Ehrlichman has written, "Nixon called Agnew his 'insurance policy' when someone raised the subject of the president's physical safety. 'No assassin in his right mind would kill me,' Nixon laughed. 'They know that if they did they would end up with Agnew!'"

The best known—and most repulsive—description of the vice presidency was given by one who held it, John Nance Garner: "It ain't worth a bucket of warm spit." But in one respect he was wrong, which is why politicians with ambitions to reach the White House yearn for the job. When John Kennedy offered Senator Lyndon Johnson the chance to be his running mate, he thought Johnson, then the most powerful member of Congress, would surely turn it down. But Johnson lunged at the opportunity.

After all, to a vice president, the Oval Office is "only a heartbeat away."

And because they can smell the power almost within their grasp, vice presidents have been willing to swallow their pride when the president's staff treats them like a servant (as Kennedy's staff often treated Johnson), or when the president makes them compromise their own beliefs (as Johnson often forced Humphrey to do).

The Hatchetmen

The worst abuse occurs when presidents use their running mates as the bad cop in a good-cop-bad-cop routine. While the president piously sticks to the high road, he lets his running mate get down in the gutter. While Eisenhower acted the role of the great statesman in the 1952 campaign, he sent forth vice-presidential candidate Nixon to do the snarling and gut-knifing. Because Democratic nominee Adlai Stevenson was a mild-mannered gentleman and an intellectual, Nixon made innuendoes that he was an effeminate Communist sympathizer by calling him "Side-saddle Adlai . . . clothed in State Department pinks." Ike would never have said such a thing, nor would he have said, as Nixon did, that Truman and Stevenson covered up a Communist conspiracy and were "traitors" to their party. With Nixon saying it, Ike didn't have to.

When Nixon became president, he used Agnew as he had been used himself, as a political hit man. Many of Agnew's speeches were written by Pat Buchanan, a particularly vicious ideologue. But Nixon would personally go over the speeches, inserting even more vicious language, before he sent Agnew out on the hustings to assassinate characters. After one such editing job, Nixon turned to Buchanan and laughed grimly, "This really flicks the scab off, doesn't it?"

Are You Squeaky Clean?

Since, hypothetically, we have placed you well into your young political career, we can only hope that you have behaved yourself up to now, because should you announce for the presidential race—or if you are chosen as a vice-presidential nominee—your past and present will be plowed and replowed by the press and by your opponents. If they turn up even one bone, they will never quit hunting for the rest of the skeleton, and they will rattle those bones for the rest of your political life.

Not even the minor candidates are safe from close inspection. *The Wall Street Journal* reported that Pat Robertson, a television evangelist running for president as a Republican in 1988, had married his wife—contrary to his claims—just a few weeks before their first child was born. Senator Joseph Biden, trying for the Democratic nomination in 1988, also ran into trouble when the press discovered that he had falsified his college records and was plagiarizing parts of his speeches. But because Robertson and Biden had no chance to win, those revelations were mere embarrassments, not history-shaping exposés.

Gary Hart's trial by publicity, on the other hand, clearly falls into the latter category. In May 1987, *The Miami Herald* revealed that Hart, then the prohibitive favorite to win the Democratic nomination, had been fooling around with Donna Rice, a Miami model. Hart, who was married but had a reputation as a womanizer, apparently spent the night with Rice in a Washington townhouse. There was also solid evidence that he had sailed with her to the Bahamas, for an overnight stay, aboard a boat appropriately named *Monkey Business*. The press hullabaloo that followed those revelations made campaigning so unpleasant for Hart that he dropped out. He reentered the race a few months later, only to find that the press was still relentless in pursuing him with questions about his private life. By that time, too, there were suspicions of irregularities in the way he had raised money.

He asked a group of students at the University of Iowa:

> Why are my personal life and campaign finances front-page, eight-column banner headline news and lead stories for nightly news when the real issues—hunger, homelessness and illiteracy—are routinely buried by those same media organizations?
>
> I've asked myself in all this, What's going on? I made a personal mistake and I've publicly apologized for it. But it seems to me that that has nothing to do with my ability to govern or lead this country.

Many Americans agreed with him. But many others believed that anybody stupid enough to offend the public by womanizing so openly was too stupid to be a serious presidential candidate. In any event, deplorable as it may be, the public is simply more interested in candidates' pratfalls and escapades than it is in how the candidates propose to cope with hunger, homelessness, and illiteracy. And the press, again perhaps deplorably, gives the public what it prefers.

Unpredictable Public

There is no ironclad rule about this. Sometimes the public is strangely forgiving of past sins, as it was of Clinton. Grover Cleveland had an illegitimate son, whom he acknowledged and supported. His political opponents tried to exploit it ("Ma, Ma, where's Pa? Gone to the White House, Ha, Ha, Ha!" went their campaign song), but he was elected anyway.

When Franklin Roosevelt was assistant secretary of the Navy, he had authorized recruiting forty-one enlisted men—ten of them between the ages of sixteen and nineteen—to take part in illegal sexual acts to trap homosexuals.

When the public learned that the Navy had used their boys as sexual decoys, all hell broke loose. A Navy court was quickly convened and Roosevelt was summoned to testify. He swore he had nothing to do with organizing the homosexual-hunting group. The court clearly did not believe him, but let him off with a mild reprimand. A Senate subcommittee then took up the investigation and concluded that Roosevelt had lied and had shown "an utter lack of moral perspective" and "an abuse of the authority of his high office" by encouraging the young men to take part in the "beastly acts that had been performed on them." He was described as the mastermind of one of the most shameful episodes in Navy history.

When that investigation was held in 1921, Roosevelt's very promising political career seemed to have been destroyed forever. And yet only eleven years later he would be elected president for the first of four times.

Usually though, the public never forgets or forgives. Compare the experiences of Cleveland and Roosevelt with what happened to Senator Edward Kennedy. On the night of July 18, 1969, he and friends and members of his staff had a party on Chappaquiddick Island, Massachusetts. During the evening, he went for a ride with one of the young women, Mary Jo Kopeckne. The car ran off a bridge. Miss Kopeckne drowned. Much mystery surrounded Kennedy's role. Why were the senator and the young woman alone in the car to begin with? Was he actually in the car, as he swore, when it went into the water? Why hadn't he reported the accident until the next morning?

Kennedy was never charged with a serious crime, but the stink of Chappaquiddick clung to him and permanently ended any chance that he would ultimately follow his brother into the White House, as most political observers had previously presumed was inevitable. Every time Kennedy is mentioned as a possible candidate, the old questions of Chappaquiddick are brought up again, and his balloon goes flat. Since the public's forgiveness can't be counted on, anyone with political ambitions had better keep his or her nose very clean.

Enslaved by Television

Do you think this fellow could be elected president?

> [He was] a stout, dumpy-looking man who wore a tight, side-curling wig on his balding head. His arms and legs looked too small for his body, his head seemed to come right out of his shoulders as if he had no neck, and his heavy-lidded eyes and small, prim mouth were flanked by large jowls. . . . But his personality also gave him problems. He was socially awkward, tactless, and often smug and haughty. He was uncomfortable with, and even distrustful of, most other people and once wrote his wife, Abigail, "There are very few people in this world, with whom I can bear to converse." At the same time he was fussy, sensitive to criticism, jealous, and highly irritable. When he was aroused he would throw his arms about and speak impulsively without restraint or caution, reaping criticism and mockery from his listeners.

That is a description of John Adams, one of our very best presidents. Fortunately for him, and for the country, he lived in an age when politicians were not sold like pizzas. Although he was a man of great principle, learning, integrity, and courage, it's doubtful that he would be seriously considered as a candidate for high office today. Brilliance and integrity no longer offset physical ugliness and severe social eccentricities in an age that demands reasonably good looks, a smooth style, and total obeisance to the great one-eyed god, television. At every step of your way up in politics, but particularly if you try for the presidency, you will be packaged almost solely for that medium; for anyone with pride, that can be a most unpleasant experience. You will not be allowed to be yourself; you will be revamped.

One of the services that party officials offer new candidates in major political races is a crash course at a "candidate school"—including, most importantly, training in how to act cool, natural, and in control on television even when, in fact, the candidate is extremely hot under the collar because of a barrage of hostile questions. Susan Peterson, one of Washington's "media trainers," explains, "Ultimately, if I have done my job right, they will look completely untrained." There in a nutshell is one of the accepted routes to success in television politics: Training to seem untrained—or, in short, to be what you aren't.

Nixon: Saved by Television

The watershed year for political television was 1952. In the previous presidential election, only 3 percent of the population owned television sets. Then the electronic monster swept the nation, and by 1952, 45 percent of the nation's households owned sets.

No politician benefited or suffered more from the coming of television than Richard Nixon. If he hadn't been saved by television, he would never have been vice president, much less president. And if it weren't for television, he wouldn't have had to wait an extra eight years before winning the presidency.

Here's how television saved Nixon: Less than two months before the end of the 1952 campaign, disgruntled Republicans leaked to the press that Nixon had a secret slush fund, set up by several rich backers. The slush fund amounted to $18,000; by today's standards, it is small potatoes, but in those days, when a Senator's salary was only $12,000, it was enough to make headlines. Republican presidential nominee Eisenhower was furious. After all, he had been telling the voters to throw the Democrats out of the White House because they were corrupt, and suddenly here was his running mate exposed for having taken questionable funds.

But while Eisenhower debated whether to force Nixon off the ticket, Nixon went on television to defend himself. The result was his legendary "Checkers speech," perhaps the most famous political pitch of modern times.

Nixon told the 58 million people who were gazing into their television screens that the slush fund was not secret. (That was false; it was secret.) He said he had done no favors for the contributors. (False; one of the contributors, for example, had gotten into trouble gambling in Cuba and Nixon had asked the State Department to help him.) Then he started passing the soap. He said he wasn't going to quit. "I am not a quitter. And Pat's not a quitter. [Pat was his wife.] After all, her name was Patricia Ryan, and she was born on St. Patrick's Day, and you know the Irish never quit." (Not true; although Pat was her nickname, she had been christened Thelma Catherine, and she was not born on St. Patrick's Day but on the day before.) Then he listed his debts, to show that he was just a po' boy, and went on: "And that's what we owe. It isn't very much. But Pat and I have the satisfaction that every dime that we've got is honestly ours. I should say this, that Pat doesn't have a mink coat. But she does have a respectable Republican cloth coat, and I always tell her that she would look good in anything."

And then came the three-handkerchief pitch. He said that he would be willing to give back most of the gifts he had received, but he would never, never give back a little black and white cocker spaniel named Checkers, given to him by a Texan. "And you know the kids, all the kids, loved the dog, and I just want to say this, right now, that regardless of what they say about it, we are going to keep it."

Americans had just witnessed their first political soap opera. And most had loved it. Occasionally, as Nixon had talked, tears had welled up in his eyes. (The drama professor who had taught Nixon how to cry in college, watching his old student weeping on television that night, had exclaimed, "Here goes my actor.") Many women who watched, including Eisenhower's wife, wept along with him. Nixon stayed on the ticket.

Television had demonstrated what Theodore White called "its primitive power . . . when, in one broadcast, it had transformed Nixon from a negative vice-presidential candidate, under attack, into a martyr and an asset to Dwight Eisenhower's presidential campaign."

Nixon: Victim of Television

Eight years later, Nixon would be involved in the next historic development in political television—the very first of the presidential debates that have since become standard fare—but this time the medium would betray him. Bear in mind, candidates John Kennedy and Nixon were entering uncharted waters. Not only was television a relatively new medium under any circumstances, but never before had presidential candidates submitted themselves to long television debates. *Four* debates in all. An average of 70 million Americans would watch each debate, an incredible audience, almost as big as the audience that had tuned in for the climactic White Sox–Dodgers meeting in the 1959 World Series. The stakes were enormous, and neither candidate was experienced at television performance. Stage presence, physical bearing, makeup, ability to stand up to the intense lights—what did they know about such things?

Kennedy had had a couple of extra days to rest and to practice with his aides in answering the kind of questions that would be asked by the debate panel. Nixon had had no time to rest or to practice; what's more, he was recovering from an illness and looked pale and haggard.

He had lost weight; his collar was loose around his neck. Under the best of circumstances, he had a five o'clock shadow; under the bright television lights, the shadow was so heavy it looked like he hadn't shaved for days. Kennedy, in contrast, looked cool, debonair, rested, and cocksure. Which he was.

Appearances made the difference. According to opinion polls, people who heard the debate on radio, where appearances were irrelevant, felt that Nixon had got the better of Kennedy. But every poll of television-watchers indicated that Kennedy had clobbered Nixon. That first debate in 1960 showed the permanent ascendancy in the television age of imagery over thought. What politicians *said* would never again amount to as much as the way they *looked* to viewers slumped on the living-room couch.

In the following debates, Nixon bounced back. He was better prepared for the questions, he looked more rested and in control—and he covered his five o'clock shadow with pancake makeup. But that first debate probably cost him the very slender margin by which he lost his bid that year for the presidency (Kennedy won the election by a trivial 112,000 votes). Polls showed that, of the 4 million who claimed to have made their choice of candidates based on the debates, 3 million voted for Kennedy. Speaking not only of the debates but of the entire campaign, Kennedy said after he won the presidency, "It was TV more than anything else that turned the tide."

One Big Theater

These days, it is taken for granted that all major political campaigns are primarily built on television. A candidate's grasp of issues is secondary to the way he or she looks on the screen. The situation has become so absurd that even serious reporters treat the candidates' battle of television images as real news. In the 1988 presidential race, *Newsweek* reported Bush as winning "the all-important battle of backdrops," and Jeff Greenfield, ABC News political reporter, thought it a significant contrast of televised images that "George Bush is almost always outdoors, coatless, sometimes with his sleeves rolled up, and looks ebullient and Happy Warrior-ish. Mike Dukakis is almost always indoors, with his jacket on, and almost always behind a lectern." Who cares?

It used to be that national political conventions were exciting television extravaganzas, much more exciting than Oscar night in Hollywood, but similarly drawing their excitement from the fact that the television audience still didn't know who would be the winners. Indeed, even into the '70s delegates to the conventions didn't know who would win because bartering for votes was still going on right there in the convention hall. But today, because of the primaries, everyone knows who will be the presidential nominee long before the convention opens. And even though convention managers spend around $50 million trying to make the setup entertaining with multilevel podiums, giant television screens, balloon drops, and other hoopla, the events are usually boring. The 1996 Republican convention in San Diego was so boring that Ted Koppel and his *Nightline* crew packed up in the middle of it and went home. Koppel said, "This convention is more of an infomercial than a news event. Nothing surprising has happened. Nothing surprising is anticipated."

If you are a rising politician who is asked to make a nominating speech at a convention, conduct yourself according to two rules: (1) Don't be dull; (2) don't be long-winded. Following the first rule, Ann Richards, at the 1988 Democratic convention, got delegates to whooping and laughing with her jibes at George Bush, delivered in a Texas drawl. True, it wasn't great humor, except by convention standards. Example: "Aw, don't blame George for what he says! He was born with a silver foot in his mouth!" (That moment of nationwide fame later helped elevate her into the governorship of Texas.) At the same convention, failing to follow either rule number one or rule number two, Bill Clinton made a nominating speech so long and so dull that finally the ABC network cut away and put on a movie. After thirty-two agonizing minutes, Clinton said, "In closing," and the delegates applauded wildly.

For excitement, television debates have stolen the show from the conventions. At these, Clinton excels, but not without a great deal of training beforehand, not only with his staff subjecting him to many hours of mock debates but—as we are told by James Carville, one of Clinton's "spin" experts—precise drilling on such important matters as "when to look at the other candidates on the stage, when to look at the press, when to look at the camera—the basic things you have to execute on television." You think the movement of the eyes aren't that important in a debate? Think again. During one of the Bush–Clinton debates, the camera caught Bush just as he glanced impatiently at his wristwatch while Clinton was speaking. For days thereafter, television commentators referred to that as a major blunder because it looked like Bush had lost interest in what was going on.

Transplants and Orange Dyes

The television age has turned politicians into primpers and preeners. Because camera crews favor close-ups, politicians turn to cosmetics. Not many go so far as Reagan did for a television appearance, with rouge and lipstick and eyeshadow. But hairpieces, hair transplants, permanents, dye jobs, eyebrow trimming, eyelash coloring, and facials are becoming routine. Politicians with bald heads, usually considered a cinematic negative, sometimes cleverly put them to use as a campaign device. Jim Jones, a very bald ex-congressman, sought to unseat Senator Don Nickles, who was blessed with a handsome head of golden, blow-dried hair. Jones made the best of the situation by running thirty-second television ads in which he held up a blow-dryer and boasted: "I will be able to spend more time on my constituents' business because I won't need one of these." (Clever, but Nickles still won.)

There are risks in phony hair colorings. When Senator Alan Cranston ran for president, a bad dye job turned his remaining hair a strange orange, drawing snide remarks in the press. Dyes tend, treacherously, toward that range of the spectrum. Reagan was once described as "prematurely orange," but then he hired a better beautician. Presidential candidate Bob Dole found a dye that gave his hair an authentic black, but it was so shiny it made him look like a hero of the silent movies, so he gave it up.

As the obsession with appearance and symbols and sloganeering has increased, the use of anything resembling a rational appeal to the electorate has declined sharply. Partly because ad time is so expensive, and partly because advertising experts who sell politicians have the same mentality as those who sell soda pop, political ads are getting shorter and shallower. The brevity of the time available often determines the kind of attack. Charles Guggenheim, one of the veterans in the business, says, "Create doubt. Build fear. Exploit anxiety. Hit and run. That's what can be done best in thirty seconds." And these days, thirty seconds is considered a generous allotment indeed.

The Stupidity of the Selective Process

Presidential campaigns have become incredibly drawn-out rituals. Candidates rev up two years before the first ballot is cast in the first caucus state (Iowa) or the first primary state (New Hampshire). Six months prior to the showdown in those states, the press begins to whoop it up, reporting the odds on this candidate or that. It's like a horse race—or the start of a series of horse races—with Iowa and New Hampshire the first heat.

What happens to candidates in those two states will help determine several key things. Those who win or place high will thereafter find rich people much more willing to bet on them. And they will also get the deluxe treatment from the press. Having helped create the artificial importance of Iowa and New Hampshire, the press tends to use those states to weed out what it hastens to assume (for its own convenience) are also-rans. David Broder, *The Washington Post*'s political guru, argues rather foolishly that the press does not have the personnel or space to fully cover all major candidates as long as they are in the running; therefore, after New Hampshire, "we have to reduce the number of candidates treated as serious contenders. Those news judgments will be arbitrary—but not subject to appeal. Those who finish first or second in Iowa and New Hampshire will get tickets from the mass media to play the next round. Those who don't, won't."

Old-Fashioned Iowa

Why should the voters of, say, California or Florida or Texas or New York—which have heavy ethnic populations and all the problems that go with teeming populations: traffic jams, heavy drug traffic, thousands of homeless, and environmental problems—pay more than passing notice to the way Iowa responds to presidential candidates? As *The Almanac of American Politics* accurately points out,

> To this day many aspects of Iowa life seem unaffected by the twentieth century. Most Iowans still live on farms or in small towns, not in large cities or surrounding suburbs. The state has no military installations and virtually no defense industry. Iowa politics, therefore, has not been afflicted with the ills which seem to result from rapid urbanization.

Furthermore, Iowa's population is almost solidly white Anglo-Saxon Protestant: Less than 2 percent of its population is black; less than 1 percent is Hispanic.

But candidates spend months in Iowa, attending county fairs, tea parties, church suppers, hog-judging contests, and quilting bees. They ride around the state on bicycles and hay wagons and horses, pretending to be "one of the folks." Why do they do it? Because the press, always willing to magnify the insignificant in politics, is watching closely and telling the world every detail. That *can* be of great importance to the dark horses in the race, as has been clear since 1976, when Jimmy Carter, virtually an unknown, won the Iowa Democratic caucuses (although he was an inept speaker to large audiences, he had magic in small gatherings, of the Iowa living-room sort) and immediately achieved a national identity that carried him to the White House. Ever since, candidates have gone to Iowa dreaming of being "Carterized." (Just as often, however, the results in Iowa are of no great benefit to the winners. In 1988, Richard Gephardt, who took the Democratic prize, and Bob Dole, who took the Republican, almost immediately thereafter lost momentum and never recovered it.)

New Hampshire: A Fraud?

But the importance of Iowa's caucuses is not nearly so grotesquely inflated by the press and a gullible public as is the importance of New Hampshire's primaries. It is a strange ritual, this thing that happens every four years, with dozens of candidates, hundreds of journalists, and sometimes thousands of campaign volunteers swarming over that small state, slogging their way through the snow and the mud. Rarely will they encounter anything but a white face (the population is less than .5 percent black; and about 1 percent Hispanic). The largest newspaper in the state, the *Manchester Union Leader,* has been one of the most irresponsible in the nation, regularly slandering candidates it does not like and spreading beneficial lies for its favorites, but its influence is waning. Traditionally a hidebound state, New Hampshire is loosening up a bit; it even elected a woman for governor. But it is still a long way from representing a cross-section of America.

New Hampshire is not all that its own publicists and a lazy national press have touted it to be. Writer Henry Allen offers a touch of the jaundiced truth:

> New Hampshire is a fraud. Which is to say that behind that idyll of white-steepled, sleigh-belled, town-meeting, republican-with-a-small-R America lurks a much realer and hidden New Hampshire—the souvenir hustlers, backwoods cranks, motorcycle racing fans, out-of-state writers, dour French Canadians and tax-dodging Massachusetts suburbanites who have conspired, as New Hampshire has conspired for two centuries, to create an illusion of noble, upright, granite-charactered sentinels of liberty out of little more than a self-conscious collection of bad (if beautiful) land, summer people, second-growth woods full of junked cars and decaying aristocracy, lakes howling with speedboats, state liquor stores that are open on Sundays and the most vicious state newspaper in America. . . .
>
> The question is not who they think they are, to be holding us hostage every four years with their presidential primary. Instead, who do we think they are, to let them get away with it, this white,

tight and right smidgen of a place, this myth-mongering bastion of
no-tax/no-spend conservatives with no minorities to speak of and
a total of .43 percent of the American people?

How did it happen? New Hampshire's emergence from a sleepy
no-place to a powerful omen-state occurred in 1956. Estes Kefauver
had just finished presiding over a series of televised U.S. Senate investigations into organized crime, and he wanted to parlay that national exposure into the Democratic presidential nomination. Few
experts took his candidacy seriously. More should have. Kefauver became "the first man to recognize how, in the dawning age of television and quickening social conscience, a 'down-home boy' could use
the primaries to appeal to ordinary people over the head of their
anonymous 'bosses.'" Kefauver—who pretended to be a rube from
Tennessee but who was in fact an extraordinarily sophisticated political manipulator—became "the first man to see the primaries as the
corridor to power."

The corridor began with the New Hampshire primary, which previous politicians had treated almost with contempt. After all, the state
had only eight votes of the total of 1,372 that would be counted at the
national convention. Why should front runners knock themselves out
to win the hearts of that backwater domain?

That's the way Adlai Stevenson felt. He had been the Democratic
presidential nominee in 1952 and was the front runner to repeat in that
role. He already had New Hampshire's Democratic party establishment in his pocket. Why court the mere handful (25,000) of Democratic
voters? So he didn't.

But Kefauver spent three months visiting every little town, talking
to storekeepers, buying a shirt or a toothbrush or a pair of galoshes to
show he was more than a transient. His pitch was simple, offered in his
Tennessee drawl: "I'm Estes Kefauver. I'm here to ask for yer he'p.
Don't let those Chicago gangsters take our party away from us." (That
last was in reference to Stevenson's being from Illinois.)

Not only did he win—this beginner in national politics won by *84*
percent. Immediately he had the glamour of the victorious underdog,
and using that, he blitzed to another victory in the next primary,
Minnesota, upsetting the most powerful state machine west of the
Mississippi. Again he was on the front page of every newspaper, and
suddenly, thanks to his exploitation of the two primaries through the
new-fangled television, he was no longer seen as the hopeless outsider
but as a strong contender, which he continued to be in one slam-bang
primary after another, from coast to coast—and that is what the pri-

mary season has remained, a coast-to-coast marathon. Since Kefauver lit the fire, it has never gone out.*

In one respect, the use of primaries—which have more than doubled in number since Kefauver found them so fruitful—has had a healthy populist influence on politics. But the exaggerated importance of the New Hampshire primary and the Iowa caucuses, simply because they are "firsts," seriously damaged any effort to operate the presidential campaigns in a sensible fashion.

Reform, or Is It?

The distortions of Iowa and New Hampshire influence could not be allowed to last forever. The pride of too many heavily populated states was being bruised. They felt they weren't getting the attention—and, in some instances, the electoral power—they deserved because their primaries came too late to matter as much as they should. So they began climbing up the calendar. First came the establishment of "Super Tuesday," when eleven states, including the electoral powerhouses of Florida, Texas, Ohio, Michigan, and Illinois, agreed to move their primaries up to the second Tuesday in March.

California, the nation's most populous state, hadn't helped choose a major party's nominee since 1972 because for decades its primary was in June. So in 1996 it moved the primary to late March. Still feeling left out, in 1998 it moved up again, this time to March 7, right on the heels of the Iowa caucuses and the New Hampshire primary. And California was joined in this powerhouse move by New York and at least four other eastern states, in what would amount to a giant national primary on a single day. Given all the above date changes, the nominating process has been reduced to about four weeks.

Until the new arrangement has been tried for a few elections, a final judgment can't be made. On the one hand, many political scientists argue that having diverse, populous states like California and New York vote early in the process will force candidates in both parties to appeal to broader, national concerns instead of narrower local issues or the extreme positions in each party. Others argue that the clustering of the big primaries at an early date will not give a dark-horse candidate who does well in Iowa and New Hampshire enough time to exploit his success by raising the money needed for a fair run in the later primaries. Those taking this side include some Republicans who complain that the trend toward earlier primaries left their party in 1996 with an

---

*Kefauver missed the presidential nomination, but got to be Stevenson's running mate.

establishment candidate, Bob Dole, while stacking the deck against fresher faces who might have run a stronger campaign against President Clinton.

Polls

Without the help of pollsters, many candidates feel as if they were blind, standing on a vast field in a starless night. On the other hand, some campaign professionals believe that polls are wildly overrated. Does a candidate really have to take a poll to find out what people want, what they hope for, what they fear? John White, former chairman of the Democratic National Committee, says, "Good politicians already know what people are worried about. If you've got a candidate who doesn't know, get yourself another candidate."

Do politicians need to take a poll to find out if they have a chance? Jimmy Carter would have been a fool to fashion his career by the polls. In October 1975, polls showed he had only 3 percent of the public's support. Thirteen months later he was the newly elected president. George Bush had a virtually nonexistent poll rating throughout most of 1979, yet kept plugging away and almost took the GOP nomination from Reagan in 1980. Many political scientists feel these early campaign polls—just "name recognition" tests—are worthless.

In a presidential race, polls can have a crucial impact. Six months before the 1968 election, both Gallup and Louis Harris showed Richard Nixon far ahead of Hubert Humphrey. As a way to predict the outcome of the race, the polls may have been worthless—but they served Nixon as a magnet for money. Contributors who wanted to own part of a winner came through with big bucks. "When the polls go good for me, the cash register really rings," said Nixon. For the reverse reason, the register wasn't ringing for Humphrey. Contributions began to dry up. Television stations and newspapers, leery of being left with big debts from a loser, forced Humphrey to pay cash for time and space, and although he was picking up strength toward the end, he just didn't have enough money to launch the kind of homestretch sprint he needed. He lost the race by less than 1 percent of the popular vote. If the polls hadn't cut off his contributions, he could have bought the ads and it is likely he would have pulled off the victory.

Frequently, major newspapers, in collusion with the networks, hire pollsters to go sample the electorates' feelings at a given moment in a campaign, and then they report those findings. But when they do, they are not merely reporting public opinion, they are helping to shape it. People may read the polls and say to themselves, "Aha, Candidate A has it wrapped up, so although I like Candidate B better, there's no reason to waste my time voting for him." Or, "Candidate X is five percentage points ahead, so there must be something wrong with Candidate Y." Marvin Kalb has pointed out that the height of irresponsible journalism of this sort was reached by ABC News when the network "devoted more than half of its evening newscast on October 12 [1988] to a state-by-state poll that declared Mr. Bush the winner a month before anyone voted."

Money, Money, Money

Money may be "the mother's milk of politics," as Jesse Unruh, once the Poo-Bah of California politics, used to say. Certainly there's no substitute for money when it comes to paying the bills for time on television, for newspaper ads, for the high-priced experts that swarm over every candidate's headquarters, for bumper stickers and campaign literature, and for all the etceteras that go into running for office.

But money is also the poison of politics. It can be poison whether it is your money or the money of others. The poison, or at least the souring, of a candidate's own money could be seen in the 1998 gubernatorial race in California, where Al Checchi, a half-billionaire businessman, spent $40 million of his own money—more than any other nonpresidential candidate in American history. One of the dangers of digging deep into your own pocket is that, if your pockets are deep enough, many people will interpret it as either trying to bully or to buy your way into office. Checchi lost. The politician who beat him, veteran state official Gray Davis, wasn't exactly a piker—his spending (of other people's money) in the primary beat the old California record of $9 million.

There are other examples to show that depleting your own wealth guarantees nothing, except that you will be poorer for it. A study by the Center for Responsive Politics in Washington found that of 149 candidates for the House and Senate in 1995–1996 who each put more than $100,000 of their own money into their campaigns, only nineteen won.

But the real poison is in being financed by others who expect something in return, as most big contributors do. The danger is most dramatically evident at the presidential level, of course, because no presidential candidate is taken seriously unless he or she can raise at least $20 million. Increasingly large amounts will be needed because, as we have pointed out, the primaries are being crowded together. The time between the first and last primaries is evaporating. Candidates won't have time to put in many personal appearance to shake hands or hold rallies. Even candidates for governor in California barely try to do it—the state is just too big. So the presidential primaries that really count will all come down to a humongously expensive bicoastal war of television advertising. And remember: That's just for the primaries.

Phony "Independent" Funds

The two main methods of raising money are through political action committees (PACs), discussed in chapters 4 and 7, and by leaning on people of wealth. Because PACs are primarily the conduits of money from corporate executives and other special interests, they lend themselves to great corruption. Reform laws passed in the 1970s strictly limit to modest amounts the money individuals, groups, or PACs can legally give directly to candidates; and, in the general presidential election, the two major-party candidates are supposed to use *only* federal subsidies. But these laws are broken so consistently that they might as well not exist. One way to get around the law is for PACs to spend money "independently" of the candidates, but on their behalf. That kind of money—completely phoney in its "independence"—isn't counted as a contribution, but it can have a tremendous impact on a campaign. For example, the costliest and most influential political ad of Bush's 1988 campaign—the "Willie Horton furlough" ad, which we will discuss later—was paid for by an outfit called the National Security Political Action Committee (NSPAC). Although NSPAC had long-standing ties with the Republican Party and the ad was filmed by a former employee of Bush's media manager, the organization claimed it was acting "independently" of Bush.

Another way of getting around the federal restrictions on the size of an individual gift to a presidential candidate (no more than $1,000 in the primaries and no donations in the general) is by giving money in the guise of contributions for "party building" and "get-out-the-vote" drives. These are favored outlets for rich contributors' "soft money"—or "sewer money," as it is more accurately called, to identify its suspicious odor. Of course the money is actually used as backdoor financing for the candidates.

Crooked, yes, but who's watching? Congress periodically holds hearings on the scandal, but does nothing. The Federal Election

Commission, the orphaned oversight agency of big-money politics, is so broke and so shorthanded that its top officials admit they will never get around to really investigating the 1996 election—the most expensive and probably the most corrupt presidential election ever held, with the two presidential campaigns spending $271.5 million in soft money, more than a tenfold increase over what was spent a decade earlier.

Crooked "Coffees" Pay Off

The 1996 campaign was full of such illegalities as money laundering, hidden foreign donations, and solicitations in the White House. Early in 1995, White House Counsel Abner Mikva had issued an official warning to everyone working on the premises: "Campaign activities of any kind are prohibited in or from government buildings. This means fund-raising events may not be held in the White House; also, no fund-raising phone calls or mail may emanate from the the White House." Mikva was citing a law that went back to 1883.

Other presidents and their staffs had broken that law. But none were such wild scofflaws as the Clinton crowd. Dozens of phone calls soliciting money were made from the White House, including calls from Clinton himself and from Vice President Gore. For a big enough contribution, fat cats were allowed to spend a night in the Lincoln bedroom. More than a hundred "coffees" were held at the White House to loosen the pocketbooks of big spenders, including a Chinese arms merchant and a convicted drug dealer. More than $25 million was received from about 1,500 people who attended coffees in 1995 and 1996.

And the Republicans, who always raise more corporate money than Democrats, were up to their own brand of shenanigans. And so were all members of Congress. A senator in a middling large state, for example, will have to raise about $6 million to finance his or her reelection campaign. That means having to solicit an average of $3,000 every day during their six years in office. Where will they get it, and what will their donors want in return? They will insist, "Oh, just good government." Uh huh, yeah—but what else?

Every step of your way up the political ladder, you will have to hold your nose as you see how other politicians go about financing campaigns, and see how you are expected to do the same. It's hard to get away from the smell of corruption. That's the bad news.

The good news is, the smell varies in intensity at different levels of politics—and once in awhile the air is almost clean.

Of the several standard ways candidates have of raising money, direct-mail solicitation is one of the most innocent because it depends on small contributions from many people. When a politician sends you a form letter asking for campaign support and you send back $5 or $25 or $50, it would be laughable to suggest that, for that kind of money, any *quid pro quo* arrangement had been worked out or that you had tried to buy influence with the candidate.

Direct-mail solicitation depends mainly on the emotionalism of the content of the letter, which is almost always negative. The standard theme is, "If you don't send money to elect me, those rotten liberals will seize the government and make slaves of us all," or, from the other side, "If you don't give until it hurts, the neofascists led by my opponent will destroy all our liberties."

Direct-mail specialists, however, don't rely on just one pitch. Walt Lukens, who headed Bob Dole's presidential mail solicitations, tried forty-two different ways of saying, "Send money quick."

Whose Words Will You Speak?

Assuming that your graduation from college will certify you as capable of sensibly marshalling your thoughts on paper, there is no reason why you, in your political career, can't actually write your own speeches. From time to time, politics has been blessed with practitioners who are that creative. And sometimes the results are truly remarkable. When one thinks of original rhetoric, one always recalls the story of Lincoln's writing the Gettysburg Address on the back of an envelope as he rode to the battlefield.

Unlike today, there also used to be many extemporaneous speakers—extemporaneous in the sense that they did not need notes and certainly nothing like a teleprompter for guidance—such as William Jennings Bryan, probably the most popular orator of an era that loved speechifying. With one speech (which included that immortal line, "You shall not press down upon the brow of labor this crown of thorns, you shall not crucify mankind on a cross of gold"), Bryan catapulted himself into the Democratic nomination in 1896.

But in fairness to contemporary candidates who hire stables of writers and who do need to refer to notes and teleprompters, it must be pointed out that in Bryan's day, before radio and television created national audiences, a politician didn't wear out a speech so fast. There was *time* in those days—time for a single speech to be edited and recrafted, and given again and again, all the nuances thoroughly practiced, until it seemed very "extemporaneous" indeed. Bryan's "Cross of Gold" speech, for example, was in fact a potpourri of parts of a number of speeches he had made, and repeated, on numerous occasions.

Politicians today usually hire others to put words in their mouths. And this has been true of presidents for at least the last fifty years. Consequently, some of the catchy phrases that have lived on and become an important part of history were in fact born in the minds of hirelings operating out of the public's sight.

For example, one of the most famous presidential expressions of the last fifty years came out of Eisenhower's farewell speech in which he warned the nation of the "military-industrial complex." The speech was written for him by Malcolm Moos, who would later be president of the University of Minnesota.

Some of the catchiest presidential phrases were uttered by Franklin D. Roosevelt, all of which were written by his rather extensive stable of writers. For example, one of his most famous statements, from a speech in his 1936 reelection campaign, was

> Never before in all our history have these forces [which he called "economic royalists"] been so united against one candidate as they stand today. They are unanimous in their hate of me—and I welcome their hatred. I should like to have it said of my first administration that in it the forces of selfishness and lust for power met their match. I should like to have it said of my second administration that in it these forces have met their master.

That portion of the speech had been written by Stanley High, the so-called punchline man, who, ironically, had been a speechwriter for those "economic royalist" Republicans in 1932 and would work for them again in 1940 and 1944. Speechwriters don't necessarily mean what they write; they merely write it well. They are mercenary soldiers.

Harry Truman fought from an underdog beginning to win the 1948 election with some very feisty speeches, from which he gained the nickname "Give 'Em Hell Harry." He toured the country giving hundreds of razzle-dazzle talks from the back of a train. Some of it was extemporaneous, of course, but some of it was written by Clark Clifford (who, over the next four decades, would become Washington's preeminent presidential adviser and fixer). It was Clifford who stuck "gluttons of privilege" (to describe Republicans) and "the Slave Labor Act" (to describe the Taft-Hartley Act) in Truman's mouth.

The Words Were Peggy's

One reason for Bush's victory in 1988 was that his chief speech-writer was Peggy Noonan, who had learned how to use shovel and spatula as one of Reagan's speechwriters. Left to his own devices, Bush's style ranges from inarticulate to cliché-ridden; he is noted for his "upbeat paroxysms of preppie polemic." Noonan transformed him, particularly in his acceptance speech at the Republican National Convention—a speech so intelligently crafted that it wowed the press and public and gave him momentum that he never lost. Some of the phrases of that speech were repeated so often by the candidate and the press during the campaign—"read my lips," "kinder, gentler nation," "a thousand points of light," and so on—that they too became clichés. From now on, books of aphorisms will list them under the name of Bush. But they were pure Noonan.

There is more than a touch of phoniness in all this. And one must wonder how Noonan, in her thirties, could have an accurate perspective for Reagan, in his seventies or Bush in his sixties. Or consider Richard N. Goodwin, who, just two years out of law school, was the number two speechwriter for John Kennedy (behind only Ted Sorensen). How could such a young fellow possibly grasp the variety of subject matter that a politician of presidential calibre must master? The answer is, he couldn't. He wasn't expected to. A speechwriter can get by on bluff and posturing and air-bag generalities. In his memoirs, Goodwin tells of writing a speech Kennedy was to give in the 1960 campaign to dairy farmers. He admits that he had never seen more than ten or twelve cows in his entire life:

> I was describing a problem that I—a child of city streets—knew nothing about. "I don't think people, even farmers, can follow all this stuff," I told Sorensen. "I can hardly understand it myself, and I wrote it." "That's not the point," Sorensen explained. "They don't follow it. But at least they know Kennedy's talking about something."

On another occasion, Goodwin was assigned to write a speech about arms control. "Of course I didn't know anything about arms control. But that didn't seem to matter. . . . My job was not to make policy, not to create, but to translate the ponderous melange of fact and opinion into a brief, readable piece suitable for a moderately ignorant public." That's how speechwriters and politicians get by with winging it: They know they are dealing with a public that is at least moderately ignorant about most issues.

Politics might be swept by a refreshing breeze if politicians wrote their own speeches again. No matter how clumsy the speeches might be (though many politicians are in fact capable of achieving eloquence without help), no matter how windy or misleading or devoid of substance, at least they would be authentic representations of the politician's mind, not merely a collection of rhetoric that he had given his stamp of approval to.

But, practically, it is probably wise that politicians turn the task over to others, for if they wrote their own speeches they might be tempted to speak from the heart, factually and with candor—and that can be politically dangerous.

When Adlai Stevenson accepted the Democratic presidential nomination in 1952, he said:

> The ordeal of the twentieth century—the bloodiest and most turbulent of the Christian age—is far from over. Sacrifice, patience, understanding and implacable purpose may be our lot for years to come. Let's face it—let's talk sense to the American people. Let's tell the truth, that there are no gains without pains. . . . Better we lose the election than mislead the people and better we lose the election than misgovern the people.

Some consider it the finest speech of the era. He wrote it. He went on writing all of his own speeches. Maybe he used them to tell too much of the truth. Anyway, he lost.

With Bill Clinton, the nation got another literate president (a former Rhodes scholar) who put his literacy to work. His staff included a team of speechwriters, of course, but Clinton would rewrite and rewrite their work so many times that the end product was mostly his own, at least in tone and spirit. His chief sin was that he enjoyed putting down his ideas so much that his speeches often ran on much too long. And what made them even longer was that he was a great ad libber, and when he made a point he saw his audience warming to, he would pause for a long ad-libbed aside. Some of his State of the Union speeches lasted nearly an hour and a half.

The Top Handlers

By the time you begin flying in the upper reaches of politics, you will have discovered that it is impossible to run all of your own campaign. Certainly, you can make the important judgment calls; you can decide if your campaign is going to be positive or negative; you can decide if you are going to build a campaign on the important issues, or go with the crowd and offer voters the quickie ads that are catchy but say little; you can decide if you are going to accept special-interest money or reject it. But you simply won't have time to lay out your campaign schedule, line up your speaking engagements, and make appointments with your backers; you can't personally supervise all the campaign workers to see that they aren't goofing up; you won't have the time or expertise to research the local issues that you must mention at various campaign stops, or to supervise the filming of your campaign ads, and so on and so on.

For all those things, you will recruit an army of mercenaries—call them consultants, advisers, handlers, or whatever. They will insist that you jump through hoops of their fashioning; they will want to drape you, like a mannequin, with their ideas. They will want to package you. You may resist, but for the most part you will probably give in.

The packaging of political candidates and political issues is certainly not a new phenomenon, but the modern expertise has turned candidates and issues into commodities—marketing them with the same kind of high-pressure advertising and public relations campaigns that are used to sell automobiles. Today, counting local advertising agencies, there are literally thousands of full-time professional consultants working the political fields. Even by the 1950s there were so many that the chairman of Michigan's Democratic Party predicted, "Elections will increasingly become contests not between candidates but between great advertising firms" and other consultants. He was too pessimistic. Politics has not yet become that perverted, and it is unlikely that the major candidates will ever become only puppets for their propagandist handlers.

But it is also true that sometimes, when candidates surround themselves with strong-willed, extremely competent and ruthless advisers, they almost *seem* to be puppets. Such was the case with George Bush in 1988. Having made the decision to wage the nastiest campaign necessary for victory (which we will discuss shortly), he put himself in the hands of gut-fighting experts and carried out their program to the last thrust and parry.

At the top of Bush's team was his rich friend, James Baker III, the charming svengali who, beneath his gentlemanly exterior, is hard as steel and believes in the take-no-prisoners kind of politics. He had been running campaigns since 1970, when Bush tried unsuccessfully to become a senator from Texas. When President Ford was ten points behind Jimmy Carter in the opinion polls in 1976, Baker took over Ford's campaign and brought him to within one percentage point of victory. And in 1980, Baker was the strategist who, after Bush's presidential campaign failed, manipulated Reagan into naming Bush as his running mate. This smoothie was the key strategist in Bush's 1988 effort.

The most fascinating rogue was his campaign manager, Lee Atwater. He had been a campaign consultant since 1974 and had developed a reputation for dirty tricks.

In 1980, a Democratic candidate for a congressional seat accused Atwater of planting questions with reporters about the fact that he had electric-shock therapy as a teenager. Asked about that, Atwater said he would not answer charges by someone who had been "hooked up to jumper cables."

Another notorious incident from Atwater's past was a South Carolina race in which he was accused of inducing a minor-party candidate to state publicly of the Democratic candidate—a man of Jewish faith—that he shouldn't win because he did not "believe that Jesus Christ has come yet." That charge is not to be laughed at in the Bible Belt of the Deep South. The Democrat lost.

(After Bush's election, Atwater was appointed head of the Republican National Committee, which soon started spewing the same kind of venom. For one thing, it issued a press release falsely implying that House Speaker Tom Foley was a homosexual.)

Another warrior in Bush's campaign was Roger Ailes, his media adviser. Ailes gained lasting notoriety in Joe McGinnis' book, *The Selling of the President 1968,* as the genius who remade Nixon into a visually marketable product. One of Ailes' memorable quotes from that book is, "You put him [Nixon] on television, you've got a problem right away. . . . He looks like somebody hung him in a closet overnight and he jumps out in the morning with his suit all bunched up and starts running around saying, 'I want to be president.' That's why these shows are important. To make them [the public] forget that." Ailes may not have been a clean fighter, but he was extremely effective in manipulating the press because (in his opinion) the press covers only three things, "visuals, attacks and mistakes. You try to avoid mistakes and give them as many attacks and visuals as you can."

Smears, Lies, and Other Nastiness

You can expect to get mud all over yourself, either from that which drips out of your hands as you fling it at your opponent or (if you don't play that way) from the mud hurled in your direction. Some of it flies through the air in almost every election; some elections are notoriously nasty, and that's been true from the beginning.

Campaign rumor-mongers called Andrew Jackson's mother a prostitute. They intimated that John Quincy Adams had once been a pimp. Labeling opponents as black or part-black used to be a common campaign trick; it happened not only to Jackson but to, among others, Abraham Lincoln and Warren Harding. Theodore Roosevelt was called a drunkard and drug addict. Rumors were spread that Woodrow Wilson's mind was afflicted by syphilis. Franklin Roosevelt was rumored to be a Jew (real name: Rosenfeldt) and probably mad, which was why there were bars on the White House windows—to keep him from hurling himself from the second floor. Martin van Buren was rumored to dress in women's corsets. Cleveland, when he wasn't fathering bastards, was rumored to spend his time abusing Mrs. Cleveland and making unnatural demands of her. So it went, all the way back to George Washington, who was rumored to have invited visitors to Mount Vernon to sleep with his pretty slave women.

For modern nastiness, let's start with the 1972 presidential campaign. Fearing that the unusually popular racist George Wallace might run as an independent and draw away too many supporters of President Nixon, the Nixon gang illegally used Internal Revenue Service records to smear the Alabama governor. That smear didn't work, but the Nixonites didn't have to think up another dirty trick because on May 15, 1972, at a campaign stop-over in Maryland, Wallace was shot and paralyzed. With him out of the race, Nixon's strategists turned their dirty tricks on the candidate who at the first of 1972 was believed most likely to wind up with the Democratic nomination: Edmund Muskie. As early as the summer of 1971, Patrick Buchanan (a hard right-winger in the administrations of both Nixon and Reagan) had said in a memo, "Senator Muskie is target A as of midsummer for our operation . . . to visit upon him some political wounds that would not only reduce his chances for nomination—but damage him as a candidate, should he be nominated."

The dirty tricks started in New Hampshire. Two weeks before the primary, a forged letter was planted with the *Manchester Union Leader,* saying that when Muskie campaigned in Florida he had made insulting remarks about Americans of French-Canadian origin (a group that carried some political clout in the New England states). Because of the letter and other sabotage, Muskie did much worse than expected, both in New Hampshire and in the primaries that followed. Along with planting stink bombs at Muskie rallies, stealing the keys from cars used in Muskie parades, scheduling fake meetings, and mailing out pamphlets lying about Muskie's record, Nixon operatives who had infiltrated the Muskie camp stole his campaign schedule and grievously disrupted it in a variety of ways; for a campaigner, nothing is more essential than keeping on schedule. Nixon spies also stole Muskie campaign stationery on which they forged letters that accused Senator Jackson of being a homosexual and Senator Humphrey of getting drunk and using call girls paid for by lobbyists.

By late April, Muskie had been harassed out of the race.

With similar tricks—forged letters, slander, forged advertisements—the Nixon gang helped destroy all the Democratic candidates except the one they wanted to run against, the weakest, George McGovern. As Pat Buchanan had written in a memo shortly after Muskie's withdrawal: "We must do as little as possible at this time to impede McGovern's rise."

Adlai Stevenson in 1954 came up with this Confucianist epigram: "He who slings mud generally loses ground." Unfortunately, he was wrong. The most expert mudslingers often win ground, and often enough ground to include the election. The latest proof came in 1988.

Bush's Motivation

But before we analyze the mudslinging technique of George Bush, let's pause to analyze his motivation. Most people who have known Bush intimately swear that he is genteel and fair-minded. Then what caused this genteel Dr. Jekyll to turn into a campaigning Mr. Hyde? Aside from a consuming ambition, the likeliest explanation is desperation.

He was desperate to overcome his own reputation. A few words of explanation:

Bush had, on the surface, a shining résumé. He had come out of the Second World War with Navy air medals on his chest, had served in Congress, then as Nixon's United Nations' ambassador, then as President Ford's ambassador to China, and then headed the CIA for a year. After running a strong race against Reagan for the GOP nomination in 1980, he had become Reagan's vice president for eight years. Unfortunately for Bush, his handling of those assignments had not left him with the reputation of a strong, decisive, deep-thinking person. On the contrary. The feeling around Washington was that—except for his election to Congress, where he left no mark—he had gotten each of those jobs primarily because he was something of a brown-noser who would follow orders quietly and not rock the boat. He had the reputation of delegating major issues to his aides and letting others conduct the debates.

The record shows that he attended many White House meetings at which details of the Iran-contra illegalities were discussed, but that he never opened his mouth while these discussions were going on. Later he would try to dodge his part in the scandal by claiming he didn't know what the discussions were all about. Such an excuse left people only to decide: Is he a liar or a dolt?

During the 1988 campaign, *The Washington Post* came out with several full-scale profiles of Bush. They were anything but flattering. One profile noted: "According to numerous associates, past and present, Bush has in common with his current boss, Ronald Reagan, a limited attention span. 'You have to stand between him and the window or he will spend his whole time looking out the window, daydreaming,' said one frustrated official after an economics briefing with Bush." Others who had known Bush for years, and liked him, conceded that he had compromised his principles so often in his political climb that it was hard to know what he stood for.

The Wimp Factor

Every time a reporter was within range, Democratic leaders would talk about Bush as a person of weak character. South Carolina's Democratic chairman Frank Holleman said, "Bush is a fundamentally weak personality and a weak candidate. That's why we have a chance" in the upcoming election. Senator John Breaux of Louisiana said his home folks, particularly the blue-collar workers, "liked Ronald Reagan for the same reason they liked John Wayne. He was a figure of strength. They don't see that with Bush." Robert Slagle, Democratic chairman of Bush's adopted home state of Texas, told reporters that "most Texas males don't really think Bush is very masculine. They don't identify with him." And Democratic National Chairman Paul G. Kirk called Bush the "quintessential establishment Republican country-clubber" who was known to "cringe with trepidation" at a phone call from his mother. And the cruelest cuts of all were delivered by former President Carter, who called Bush "silly" and "effeminate."

Bush was even getting some harsh criticism of the same sort from his own party; George Will, the influential right-wing columnist, had for some time been referring to Bush as a "lap dog."

The media constantly hazed Bush about his reputation. A year before the election, *Newsday* was out with a cover story, "Bush Battles the Wimp Factor," supporting the theme with a poll that showed 51 percent thought Bush's reputation as a wimp would hurt him.

This was the early aura surrounding George Bush that prompted Democrats, at their national convention in July 1988 to launch an unkind assault of giggling at Bush.

That strategy backfired.

The Wimp Strikes Back

Buried under all that quietude—under the Andover, Yale, old-school-tie, old-New-England-family exterior—was some grit, and the Democrats made a mistake by stirring it up. Aware that he was being dragged under by the wimp reputation, Bush struck back. If the Democrats thought he was a wimp, he was going to show them that he was the meanest wimp they had ever run into.

He and his campaign staff launched their attack with crafty care. They brought together in a secret meeting at Paramus, New Jersey, thirty voters—all of them moderate or conservative Democrats—and conducted a "market test" of propaganda they were thinking of using in the campaign. Hidden behind a two-way mirror, five of Bush's top aides—campaign manager Atwater, media consultant Ailes, pollster Robert Teeter, chief of staff Craig L. Fuller, and senior adviser Nicholas F. Brady—watched as another staff member talked to the thirty guinea pigs about some of the things Dukakis had done and some of the things he stood for; naturally, these things were laid out in an extremely biased fashion.

The effect was dramatic. At the beginning, all thirty had been for Dukakis. By the time the propaganda spiel was finished, only fifteen were for him. "I realized right there," Atwater would say later, "that we had the wherewithal to win . . . and that the sky was the limit on Dukakis's negatives."

Out of that laboratory experiment came the design for a campaign that was extraordinarily negative, extraordinarily unfair and distorted—but also extraordinarily effective. What it boiled down to, as Clark Clifford joked sourly, was that Bush "appealed to traditional American values—bigotry, envy, greed, chauvinism and fear." As a result of the testing of the thirty, the Bush campaign depended on distorting these issues:

- *Patriotism.* In 1977 the Massachusetts legislature passed a bill requiring public school teachers to open each day with a pledge of allegiance to the flag. Following an advisory ruling by the state's supreme court that such a law was unconstitutional, Governor Dukakis vetoed it. Legally, it was probably the right thing to do, because in 1943 the U.S. Supreme Court had ruled that a state could not require teachers or pupils to salute the flag. That ruling protects individuals, no matter how few in number, from being compelled by the government to profess beliefs they may not hold.

But Bush used Dukakis' veto to suggest that he was unpatriotic, implying that Dukakis did not want children to pledge allegiance. In fact, all he wanted was that they not *have* to. To keep the distortion rollicking along, Bush visited flag factories everywhere and when the cameras came zeroing in, he would mention the veto again. (Ironically, this Dauntless Defender of the Pledge sometimes misrecited it, as ". . . and to the liberty for which it stands.")

A spirited and sarcastic rebuttal from Dukakis about Bush's willingness to play politics with the Constitution might have shut him up. But Dukakis, being neither spirited nor sarcastic, resorted to legalistic explanations that bored the average voter. And when he tried to cancel Bush's ploy by holding his rallies in front of an enormous flag the size usually flown on top of a Cadillac agency, and asking crowds to join him in pledging allegiance, it only worsened the situation by giving television reporters an opening to mention again why he felt forced to do these things.*

- *The Environment.* As Reagan's vice president, Bush had personally taken an important role in weakening the enforcement of environmental laws and had defended the

---

*Bush's big to-do over the pledge of allegiance was a classic case of demagogy. In fact, there is nothing at all sacred about the pledge. It popped up first, with virtually no attention, in a magazine called *The Youth's Companion* in 1892 to mark the four hundredth anniversary of Christopher Columbus' arrival. For many years thereafter, it was recited only sporadically and with no pretense that it was an official pledge. After the First World War, some cities and states began making the pledge compulsory in school. A few religious groups, primarily the Jehovah's Witnesses, refused to salute the flag or promise their allegiance to it because they felt that would be worshipping a graven image, in violation of their beliefs. Frenzied patriots responded by burning some churches, breaking into Jehovah's Witnesses homes and wrecking them, and sometimes, after forcing the Witnesses to take castor oil, marching them out of town. The children in these families were bullied relentlessly at school. Finally, after too long a delay, the Supreme Court came to their rescue in 1943 in the case of *West Virginia State Board of Education* v. *Barnette*. But the best comments did not originate in that court but with Judge Irvin Lehman of the New York Court of Appeals in 1939: "The flag is dishonored by a salute by a child in reluctant and terrified obedience to a command of a secular authority which clashes with the dictates of conscience. The flag cherished by all our hearts should not be soiled by the tears of a little child" (*The New York Times,* September 2, 1988).

administration's 43 percent cut of the budget for water-pollution control. Since it was impossible to make his own record look good, Bush set out to divert the public's attention by attacking Dukakis' environmental record as governor of Massachusetts. A central part of the attack was a slick television ad showing a pool of yukky sludge near a sign reading "DANGER/RADIATION HAZARD/NO SWIMMING." The voice message that went with the visual, by condemning Dukakis for failing to clean up Boston harbor, clearly implied that the picture was of that harbor. It wasn't. The photo was taken at a Navy base where the sign had been erected to warn swabbies against swimming in waters where a nuclear submarine had recently been parked.

• *Law and Order No. 1.* Dukakis's philosophical position was that of a moderate with a patina of liberalism. Bush wanted to make him appear a soft-headed, left-wing kook. He decided to do it by using Dukakis' membership in the American Civil Liberties Union for his symbol.

The ACLU has been around for three generations. In that time it has often supported issues that—though they seemed radical at the time—proved to be what a majority of Americans would come to believe in. The ACLU has had clients and causes across the entire spectrum, from far left to far right, because it has no interest in ideology but only in pushing the Bill of Rights to the farthest possible limits to protect freedoms.

For example, the ACLU represented Japanese-Americans who fought internment in the Second World War; endorsed the integration of public schools and other civil rights for blacks during the 1960s; backed women's rights for abortion but at the same time supported the free-speech rights of antiabortion protestors; helped win the right to a lawyer for indigent criminal defendants; and supported Col. Oliver North's claim that when he was forced to testify before Congress, his rights against self-incrimination had been violated.

Unfortunately for Dukakis, the ACLU's more inflammatory efforts were what stuck in the public's mind and gave Bush his opening. It supported the right of Nazis to march in the heavily Jewish Chicago suburb of Skokie and the right of the Ku Klux Klan to hold a rally in Mississippi—both events being simply freedom-of-speech issues to the ACLU.

Its kookier clients had left the ACLU with a tainted reputation in the minds of many people, and it was this taint that Bush emphasized when he kept calling Dukakis a "card-carrying member" of the ACLU. That simple symbol registered quickly and effectively; Dukakis was left to defend himself with an involved explanation of the history of the ACLU and of the points he agreed and disagreed with it on—the kind of explanation that the network news shows found too boring to carry.

- *Law and Order No. 2 (Plus Racism).* The centerpiece of racism in the Bush television assault was the infamous Willie Horton commercial.

"Weekend Passes," the name of the thirty-second advertisement, opened with side-by-side photos of Bush and Dukakis. Then the announcer, alternating photos of the two candidates, explained that Bush believed in the death penalty and that Dukakis not only opposed the death penalty but "allowed first-degree murderers to have weekend passes from prison." Then, zap, the television audience was shown the mugshot of a very black man, glowering ominously. Announcer: "One was Willie Horton, who murdered a boy in a robbery, stabbing him nineteen times. Despite a life sentence, Horton received ten weekend passes from prison. Horton fled, kidnapped a young couple, stabbing the man and repeatedly raping his girlfriend."

As the announcer went through this litany, the words "KIDNAPPING" and "STABBING" and "RAPING" flashed on the screen.

The last photo was of Dukakis, with the announcer intoning "Weekend prison passes. Dukakis on crime."

Ugly stuff, but socko impact. No political ad of the campaign was so much talked about, or so persuasive. Campaign manager Atwater knew that in selecting a black rapist he would ring a psychic bell of alarm with most Americans, for that color coupled with that crime has always created a kind of social panic. From 1930 to the mid-1960s (when the Supreme Court ruled it was too heavy a punishment), 455 men were executed for rape; 90 percent of them were black. In June of 1988, Atwater told a Republican group, "If I can make Willie Horton a household name, we'll win the election." Horton did become a household word.

You may ask, "Well, if the Massachusetts prison furlough program released a murderer for weekend outings and he raped a woman and stabbed her companion on one of those weekends, then shouldn't Dukakis, as governor of the state, bear some of the blame for the program?"

If that was all that there was to say about it, the question would be a good one and the political advertisement could be defended, whatever the color of the skin of the chief participant. But in fact there's a lot more to say.

Massachusetts' furlough program was not established by Dukakis but by Dukakis' Republican predecessor as governor. Far from being a program singular to Massachusetts, virtually every state allowed furloughs from prison; so did the federal government. California had a prison furlough program as far back as when Ronald Reagan was its governor. And most of these programs included furloughs for murderers, drug dealers, and other serious felons—for a day, for the weekend (as with Willie Horton), or, as was true of the federal program, for as long as a month. Virtually all prison authorities have for years encouraged furloughs as a way to ease prisoners into the outside world, rather than dump them there suddenly. So for Bush's propagandists and Bush himself to pin the furlough idea on Dukakis was, to say the least, a hefty distortion.

Negative Impact

Why are smears, half truths, and distortions so effective? One theory comes from Mark Mellman, a Democratic pollster: "One of the fundamental facts of psychology is that negative information is processed more deeply than positive information. People say they hate the stuff, but that's not the point. The point is, they absorb the information."

What does that kind of campaign do to the nation? Clearly, such campaigns breed bitterness and cynicism among the voters and thereby destroy the electoral process. Exposed to more negative television advertising than had ever been seen before in a presidential contest, two out of three Americans in 1988 told pollsters they wished the country didn't have to put up with either candidate. If most saw Dukakis as a dud, many others saw Bush as what even the gentle Russell Baker called "a monster" of deceit. Exit polls showed that although 41 million people voted for Dukakis, about 20 million of them didn't really like him—they just detested Bush.

The Bush-type campaign, of course, was not new. After Richard Nixon won his first political campaign by smearing Congressman Jerry Voorhis as a Communist, for example, he said, "I knew Jerry Voorhis wasn't a Communist. . . . But it's a good political campaign fire to use. I had to win. That's the thing you don't understand. The important thing is to win."

We hear the same in the dramatic scenario described by journalist Jim Fain, who says that when Bush wanted to ease up on the mud-slinging and go back to the high road, his tough advisers like Lee Atwater would ask, "Do you want to win?" and Bush would continue to lay aside his conscience. "Bush," wrote Fain, "craved the presidency so desperately he was willing to sacrifice personal honor for the honor of office, to betray the code his parents had taught him, to barter his soul. It was classic Faust."

As for what that kind of campaign does to the people who run it, that of course can't be known. But surely it is reasonable to suppose that a heavy psychic and spiritual price is paid by a candidate who turns himself completely inside-out to win the prize.

Russell Baker observed that as soon as the last ballot was counted, "the monster of the campaign" disappeared and "there he was, old preppy Bush back again." But can character and integrity be restored so easily—if at all?

It is interesting to note that Bush did not throw mud in his reelection campaign in 1992—perhaps because his conscience won out, or perhaps because the genius of dirty tricks, Lee Atwater, had died, or perhaps because opinion polls were beginning to show that the public was fed up with negative campaigning. (Consultants who favor dirty tricks may say, "Yeah, and look what happened: He lost.")

At least for this historical moment, things seem to be getting better. The Clinton–Dole encounter in 1996 was notably free of gutter tactics.

But some kind of mud is always available, and perhaps by the time you run for high office, it will be in vogue again. In that case, you will have to decide if the winning-is-everything philosophy suits your style.

If it doesn't, maybe you should turn for advice to some of the great losers of the past. Like Barry Goldwater.

"In my life," wrote Goldwater,

> I've personally spoken to and shaken hands with about 20,000,000 Americans. The one question I've been asked more than any other is this: Should a young person go into politics? Unhesitatingly, I've always answered yes. But . . .
>
> You must have the courage to accept considerable criticism, much of it unjustified. You must feel it in your gut and have the courage to accept defeat and continue toward your goals. Finally, you must believe in yourself, in your principles and in people. Of all of those, I considered my belief in people to be my greatest strength. I genuinely liked people, and still do. If you don't love people, don't go into politics.

If you do, it will show in the way you campaign for their votes.

Index

AARP. See American Association of Retired Persons (AARP)
ABM system. *See* anti-ballistic-missile (ABM) system
ABM treaty (1972), 166
abortion rights
  Rehnquist Court and, 287–288
  Roe v. *Wade* and, 283–284
Abourezk, James, ix, 199, 200
"Abscam" (Arab scam), 222
abuse of power, by President, 22–24
accountability, of bureaucracy, 342–343
accused
  Burger Court and, 280–281
  rights of, 243, 274–275
Acheson, Dean, 122, 126
Achille Lauro (ship), 142–143
ACLU, 543–544
acquisitions, mergers and, 483
Adams, John, xi
  wars and, 79
adversary system of justice, 246–247
advertising, advocacy, 386–387
advice and consent, 82
advisers. *See also* staff
  congressional, 179–180, 181–182
  presidential domestic, 49–57
  presidential foreign policy, 85–91
advocacy advertising, by big business, 386–387
AEC. *See* Atomic Energy Commission (AEC)
affirmative action programs, 262
Afghanistan, 97, 159
  CIA and, 153–154
AFL-CIO. *See* American Federation of Labor and Congress of Industrial Organizations (AFL-CIO)
African Americans. *See* blacks
agencies
  losing touch with government, 318–324
  regulation and, 475
Agnew, Spiro, 401
  as Nixon's hatchetman, 515
  as running mate, 513, 514
Agriculture, Department of (USDA), 303, 318

diseases from outside the U.S. and, 313
aides
  congressional, 178–179, 181–182
  in Reagan White House, 30
AIDS lobby, 378–379
Ailes, Roger, 537, 541
Air Force One, 37–38
airlines
  oversight of, 309–310
  regulation of, 483–485
airplanes. *See also* military; weapons
  presidential, 37–38
air pollution, 314
Akin, Gump, Strauss, Hauer & Feld, 377, 378
Alabama, expenditures on defending poor in, 243–244
Alaska National Interest Lands Act (1980), 171
Albert, Carl, 177, 418
Albright, Madeleine K., 92
Alexander, Bill, 222
Allen, Henry, 525–526
Allen, James B., 180
Allen, Richard, 376
Allen, Robert, 461
Allende, Salvador, 153
Alliance for Progress, 148
allies, policy toward, 99
Alsop, Joe, 438
Alsop, Stewart, 170
Ambrose, Stephan E., 43
Amendments to Constitution. *See also* Bill of Rights; specific Amendments
  procedural rights and, 242–243
American Association of Retired Persons (AARP), 371
American Brands, 482
American Federation of Labor and Congress of Industrial Organizations (AFL-CIO), as public interest lobby, 378
American Heritage Savings & Loan, 241, 475
American Hospital Association, 501–502

American Independent Party, 350
American Medical Association, government health care and, 500–501
American Savings and Loan Association (Stockton, California), 475
American Society of Newspaper Editors, 403
Amtrak (National Passenger Railroad Corporation), 471
Anderson, Jack, 431, 439
Anderson, Martin, 54n
Andrews, T. Coleman, 138
anti-abortionists, 287–288, 344–345
anti-ballistic-missile (ABM) system, 166
anticommunism, 165. *See also* communism
    Central Intelligence Agency (CIA) and, 151–152
    communism and, 127
    of McCarthy, 418–419
    as policy-making tool, 135n
    Supreme Court and, 272
antipersonnel land mines, treaty abolishing, 84
antisegregation laws, congressional votes for, 233
anti-smoking ads, 382–383
antitrust laws, 481–483
    corporate mergers and, 406–407
appearance, on television, 522–523
appellate courts, 248
Arbatov, Georgi, 167
Arbenz, Jacobo, 152–153
Archer, Bill, 192
Archer Daniels Midland (ADM), 411, 482
Argesinger v. *Hamlin*, 243
armed forces. *See also* Military; Pentagon; war-making powers
    after Cold War, 117
    homosexuals in, 7
    in Russia, 114–115
    size of, 136
    standing military and, 134–136
Armed Services Committee, Thurmond and, 215
Armey, Richard, 203
arms and armaments
    as commodity for sale, 154–155
    costs of, 121
    manufacturers of, 117
Arms Control Export Act (1976), 104
Arms Export Control Act, 107
arms race, 129

Army Corps of Engineers, 190
    spending by, 300
Army National Guardsmen, 134n
Army Ordnance Association, 137
Article II (Constitution), on Chief Executive, 20–21
Ashes to Ashes (Kluger), 387
Asia, 82. *See also* specific countries, issues, and wars
    economic crisis in, 155
Aspin, Les, 164
assassinations
    attempts, 58, 191, 304
    gun control and, 190–191
    of Kennedy, 57–58
assault weapons, ban on, 60n
assertive presidents, power of, 29–30
assistant floor leaders, in House, 205–206
atomic bomb, at Hiroshima and Nagasaki, 159–160
Atomic Energy Commission (AEC), 161, 162, 293n, 309, 329
attorney, rights to, 243, 274–275
attorney general, FBI and, 321n, 322–323
Atwater, Lee, 537, 541
Auchter, Thorne, 338
audiotaping, in White House, 2, 250
audits, federal, 333–334
auto industry
    Nader and, 379–381
    regulation of, 380
Axis powers, 124

B-1 bomber, 140
B-2 Stealth bomber, 140–141
Babbitt, Bruce, 307, 365, 508
"backdoor spending," 467–468
Bagdikian, Ben H., 394, 407–408, 410, 422
Baker, Bobby, 50
Baker, Donald M., 180
Baker, Howard, Jr., 25n, 171–172, 178
Baker, James A., III, 41, 50–51, 91, 92, 536
Baker, Russell, 369n, 459, 545
Baker v. *Carr*, 273
Bakke, Allan P., 262
balance of power, among branches of government, 19
Ball, George, 166
Baltimore Sun, delays and, 436
BankAmerica, 473
bankruptcy, government subsidization and, 471

banks, subsidies to, 472–475
Banzhaf, John, 382–383
Barber, James David, 45, 397
Barkley, Alben, 358
Barlett, Donald, 447
"Battle of the Budget, The (1973)", 71
Bay of Pigs, 85, 95
   CIA and, 319
   press coverage of, 428–429
Beard, Charles, 450
Beech Aircraft Corp., 223
Beirut, 105
Bell, Griffin, 250
benefits, of government, 347–348
Bennett, Charles E., 139
Bennett, William Tapley, Jr., 444
Bentsen, Lloyd, 231, 513
Berle, Adolf, 339
Berlin blockade, 125
Berman, Daniel, 374–375
Berman, Jason, 372
Bernstein, Carl, 394, 400, 422
Best Congress Money Can Buy, The
   (Stern), 230
bias, self-censorship of, 416–419
Biden, Joseph, 516
Bierce, Ambrose, 362n
big business. *See also* business
   Bush and, 91–92
   Clinton and, 92–93
   fighting back by, 384–391
   regulation of, 481–485
big government, 451
Big Tobacco, 387–389
Billings, Leon G., 180
Bill of Rights. *See also* Constitution;
   specific Amendments
   electorate and, 266
   procedural rights and, 242
   and states, 274
   Warren Court on, 273–275
bills. *See* legislation; specific acts
bipartisanship. *See also* partisanship
   in Congress, 202, 204–205
Birnbaum, Jeffrey, 447
birth defects, from nuclear testing, 162
Black, Hugo, 243, 255, 256, 264n, 271
Blackmun, Harry A., 254, 255, 257,
   259, 280
   Roe v. Wade and, 283–284
blacks. *See also* civil rights; race and
   racism
   congressional hiring of, 182
   in elective offices, 508–509
   segregation of, 275–276

   voting by, 364–365
   welfare cutbacks and, 457–458
Blaine, James G., 372
Blasi, Vincent, 284
Bloomingdale, Alfred, 342
Board of Governors. *See* Federal Reserve
   System ("Fed")
Boeing Co., 146, 155, 166, 482
   China and, 479
Boeing-McDonnell, 146
Boesky, Ivan, 240
Bok, Derek, 240
Boland Amendment (1985), 107
Bolling, Richard, 171, 189, 190
Bolschwing, Otto von, 151
bomber gap, 118
bombers, 140–141
bonds, national debt and, 487
"boodle." *See* "pork barrel"
Boodman, Sandra G., 317
Bork, Robert H., 279
Bosnia, 159
Bourne, Peter, 439
Bowles, Chester, 51
Boyd, Margaret, 296
Boyers, Bill, 26
Bradlee, Benjamin, 401n, 423, 427
Bradley, Bill, 512
Bradley, Omar, 135n
Brady, Nicholas F., 541
Brandeis, Louis D., 257
Braver, Rita, 434
Brennan, William J., 254, 257n, 272, 285
Brethren, The: Inside the Supreme Court
   (Woodward and Armstrong), 257
Brewster, Daniel, 230
Breyer, Stephen, 289
bribery
   campaign contributions as, 229–231
   corporations, governments, and, 398
   FBI and, 323
   political contributions and, 227–229
Bribes (Noonan), 229
Bright, Stephen B., 244n
Brill, Steven, 435
Brock, David, 229n
Brock, William, III, 215
Brockway, David, 180
Broder, David, 171, 415
Brokaw, Tom, 414–415
Brouwer, Steve, 468
Brown, Edmund G. ("Pat"), 238
Brown, George, 193
Brown, Linda, 276
Brown, Malcolm, 442

Brown, Ron, 92, 377
Brown, Willie, 446
Brown & Williamson, 388
Brown v. Board of Education, 252, 262,
    275–276
Bryan, William Jennings, 532
Brzezinski, Zbigniew, 88
Buchanan, Patrick, 415, 538
    smearing by, 538, 539
budget. *See also* defense spending; econ-
    omy; national debt; spending
    Chief Executive and, 21
    of Defense Department, 134–135
    governmental spending and, 471
buildings
    congressional, 177–178
    government-owned, 301
Bumpers, Dale, 234
Bundy, McGeorge, 103n
Bunning, Jim, 165
bureaucracy, 290–294
    accountability of, 342–343
    agencies in, 293n
    Congress and, 325–327
    "contract bureaucrats" and, 294–295
    criticisms of, 298–299
    defined, 292n
    environmental revolution and,
        314–315
    "good guys" in, 315–318
    Housing and Urban Development
        under Reagan and, 336–337
    indifference of, 304–306
    "iron triangle" and, 326–327
    losing touch with government by,
        318–324
    new within old, 328
    payroll for, 294
    president and, 327–329
    under Reagan, 333–339
    reform of, 329–333, 340–343
    size of, 301–304
    spending by, 298–300
    treatment of underdogs by, 306–313
    workers allotment to agencies,
        310–311
    work production of, 296–297
Bureau of Land Management, corrup-
    tion and, 337–338
Bureau of National Affairs, 241
Burford, Anne Gorsuch, 338
Burger, Warren E., 245, 246, 251, 255,
    256, 257, 280, 401n, 409. *See also*
    Burger Court
Burger Court, 278–284

Bakke ruling by, 262
Roe v. Wade and, 283–284
Burger Court, The: The Counter-
    Revolution That Wasn't (Blasi), 284
Burke, David, 415
Burns, Arnold I., 335
Burns, Arthur, 109–110
Burton, Dan, 15, 408
    campaign contributions and, 229
Bush, George H.W., 4, 19n
    advisers of, 50–51
    big business and, 91–92
    challenges to, iv–v
    communism and, 129–130
    domestic policy of, 60–61
    economic luck of, 43
    foreign policy of, 91–92, 94
    Horton, Willie, and, 530, 544
    Iran-contra and, 90
    minimum wage and, 476
    mud-slinging against Dukakis by,
        539–545
    national debt and, 486
    negative campaigning by, 541–546
    Panama and, 84
    Persian Gulf War and, 158–159
    philosophy of, 60–61
    polls and, 528
    presidential treatment and, 42
    Reagan depression and, 25–26
    running mate of, 513–514
    speech writing for, 534
    spending under, 358
    Sununu and, 52
    Supreme Court appointments of,
        253, 254
    Tower nomination and, 433–434
    UN police action and, 150
    voter disillusionment and, 367
    welfare cutbacks and, 456–457
Bush, George W., 511n
    Hispanic-Americans and, 365
Bush, Jeb, Hispanic-Americans and, 365
business. *See also* big business; lobbying
    in arms and armaments, 154–155
    bureaucratic reform efforts and,
        332–333
    Burger Court and, 281
    CIA operations and, 152–154
    corporate executive wealth and,
        460–461
    court favoritism toward, 267–268
    media ownership by, 400–416
    Post Office reform and, 341–342
    regulation and, 268

Business Roundtable, 385
Butler, Smedley D., 79
Byrd, Robert, 181, 212–213

cabinet divisions, 329
Caddell, Patrick, 86
Califano, Joseph, 374
California
    expenditures on defending poor in,
        243–244
    primary election of, 527
Cambodia, 79, 104
    invasion of, 133
campaign funding, 369–370, 529–532.
    See also bribery; ethics; political ac-
    tion committees (PACs)
    contributions and, 369–370
    ethics and, 227–229
    by homosexuals, blacks, ethnic
        groups, feminists, and gays, 364
    by lobbyists, 372–373
    political party organizations and
        corruption in, 352–355
    polls and, 528
campaigning, 509–510
Camp David, Maryland, 37
Canada
    health care in, 500
    NAFTA and, 480
cancer, from nuclear testing, 162
candidates. *See* campaign funding; po-
    litical campaigns; politics; specific
    candidates
Cannon, James, 25n
Cannon, Joseph (Uncle Joe), 207
Cannon, Lou, 56, 366, 396
Capital City/ABC Inc., 410
capitalist economy, 448–450
Card, Andreas, 308
Caribbean region, 79
Carlucci, Frank, 331
Carroll, Eugene J., 84
Carswell, Harrold, 234
Carter, Jimmy, 3–4, 128–129, 511
    advisers to, 52, 96
    ambiguity of, 59–60
    bureaucracy and, 293, 329
    character of, 5, 27–29
    China and, 83
    Civil Service reform and, 331
    deal-making by, 68–69
    domestic politics and, 47
    economic luck of, 43
    Energy Department and, 329
    foreign policy advisers and, 86

foreign policy and, 76, 88, 100,
    104–105
human rights policy of, 100–101
image of, 63–64
Iran hostage crisis and, 59
judicial appointment by, 250
liberal pledges by, 358
lifestyle as president, 37
lying and, 445
national debt and, 485–486
political organizing and, 348
polls and, 528
press corps and, 440–441
secrecy under, 431
as southern Democratic, 363
Supreme Court and, 253
voter disillusionment and, 366–367
war and, 80
weapons malfunctions and, 142
Carter Library, 40
Carville, James, 522
Casey, William J., 89, 150–151, 396
Castro, Fidel, 95
casualties, in Vietnam War, 24
Catledge, Turner, 428
caucus, House Democratic, 216
caucus states, Iowa as, 523–525
censorship, by government, 442–443
Center for Defense Information, 117
Center for Public Integrity, 413
Center for Responsive Politics, 529
Central America, 99, 101
    CIA in, 97
    Reagan and, 122
Central Intelligence Agency (CIA), 87,
    97–98, 150–152, 319–324
    advice from, 95, 96
    Bay of Pigs and, 428–429
    Bush and, 91, 539
    disruptive tactics in U.S., 320
    media and, 396
    secrecy of, 430, 432
    spying by, 150–152
C-5A transport, 142
chairmanships. *See* committees (congres-
    sional); seniority system (Congress)
Chancellor, John, 367
Chandler family, 401, 409
Chappaquiddick, Kennedy, Edward,
    and, 517–518
character, of political leaders, 4–6
cheating, on taxes, 468–470
Checchi, Al, 529
"Checkers speech" (Nixon), 519–520
Chenoweth, Helen, 15

Chiang Kai-shek, 124
Chicago Tribune Company, 402
Chief Executive, 20–21. *See also* president(s); specific powers
  war-making powers of, 78
Chile, 153
Chiles, Lawton, 512
Chilton, Ned, 403
China
  Boeing and, 479
  Bush and, 94
  Carter and, 83–84
  communism in, 124–125
  human rights and, 101–102
  lobbying and, 377
  military in, 165
  Nixon and, 83–84, 131
Chou En-lai, 88
Christian Coalition, 16
Christian right-wing, 360
Christopher, Warren, 92
Chung, Johnny, 369
Church, Frank, 193
church and state, Rehnquist Court
  and, 286
Churchill, Winston, 130
CIA. *See* Central Intelligence
  Agency (CIA)
cigarettes
  crusade against, 382–383
  tobacco industry successes and,
    387–389
Cisneros, Henry, 49
Citadel Press, presidents ranked by, 4
Citizens for Reliable and Safe
  Highways (CRASH), 309
Citizens for Sensible Control of Acid
  Rain, 387
citizens' lobby movement. *See* "people's
  lobbies"
Civil Aeronautics Board (CAB), 293n
  regulation by, 483–484
civil liberties, Supreme Court and, 265
civil rights, 238
  in federal bureaucracy, 295
  Rehnquist Court retreat from,
    286–287
  Supreme Court and, 270
  Warren Court and, 275–277
Civil Rights Act (1957), Thurmond fili-
  buster against, 199
Civil Rights Act (1964), 68, 277,
  278, 363
  congressional ignoring of, 181
  Title VII of, 287

Civil Service. *See also* bureaucracy
  creation of, 329n
  production and income in, 296–297
  reform efforts, 331
Clark, Joseph, 170
classes. *See* middle class; poverty;
  wealth
classified documents, 430–431
Clay, Lucius D., 135n
Claybrook, John, 308
Clayton Act (1914), 481
Clean Air Act (1970), 170, 314
  Amendments, 381
Clean Water Act, 171, 314
clerks, Supreme Court, 259
Cleveland, Grover, 517
Clifford, Clark, 533, 541
Clinton, Bill, xii, 368, 417, 511. *See also*
  Lewinsky, Monica
  advisers of, 49
  behavior during and after impeach-
    ment, 16–17
  campaign funding for, 232, 369
  committee investigations of, 195
  Congress and, 7–8, 203–205
  declassification of documents
    under, 432
  defense industry and, 145
  economic luck of, 43
  federal judicial appointments by, 251
  foreign policy of, 76, 79, 92–93
  forgiveness of, 517
  funding solicitation by, 531
  homosexual rights and, 360n
  HUD and, 337
  human rights and, 101–102
  image of, 65–66
  impeachment of, 11, 14–16
  Jones, Paula, and, 11–12
  land mines agreement and, 84
  NAFTA and, 7–8
  "new Democrats" and, 358–359
  nominating speech by, 522
  Old Confederacy and, 363–364
  opinion polls and, 391
  personal touch and, 67–68
  power use by, 6–7
  presidential treatment and, 42
  press conferences of, 425
  ranking of, 3, 4
  reelection of, 9–10
  running mate of, 513, 514
  second administration of, 10–17
  Secret Service and, 38–39
  speech writing by, 535

travel style of, 39
unpopularity of, 8
welfare cutbacks under, 457–458
womanizing by, 2
Clinton, Hillary, 11
Coal Mine Health and Safety Act (1969), 182–183, 381
Cochran, Thad, 204
"cocoonizing" of president, 56
codes of ethical conduct, in Congress, 220–221
Coelho, Tony, 179
Colby, Frank Moore, 508
Colby, William E., 429
Cold War. *See also* specific presidents and issues
   defense spending during, 116
   end of Soviet Union and, 112–114
   ideological conflicts during, 126–130
   Kennedy and, 95
   lessons of, 162–163
   nuclear weapons and, 159–162
   Reagan and, 120–122
   U.S. after end of, 115–119
Coleman, William T., Jr., 375
Cole v. *Young*, 272
collective security, 78–79, 148
college, middle-class incomes and, 462
Colson, Charles, 69
Colton, Elizabeth O., 509n
Columbia/HCA Healthcare Corp., 406
Comeback Kid. *See* Clinton, Bill
Commager, Henry Steele, 111, 269
commerce, Congress and, 77
Committee for the Re-Election of the President (CREEP), 22, 280
committees (congressional), 192–197
   ethics and, 219–220
   guidance by, 196–197
   jurisdiction of, 194
   power and prestige of, 194–196
   select, 194–195
   Senate leadership of, 213
   seniority and, 214–217
   standing, 215
   and workload of Congress, 196–197
Common Cause, 229, 381–382
communism. *See also* anticommunism
   Central Intelligence Agency (CIA) and, 152–154
   in China, 124–125
   containment of, 125–126
   exaggerating threat of, 127
   fears of, 118, 123–124
   Reagan and, 120–122
   after World War II, 120
Communist party, 127–128
competition
   in defense industry, 145–146
   elimination of, 483–485
Comptroller of the Currency, 472n
Condit, Phil, 461
confidence, inspired by president, 59–61
confirmation
   of federal judges, 251
   of Thomas, Clarence, 252
conflicts of interest
   in Congress, 188–189
   of media, 403–405
   under Reagan, 336–337
Congo. *See* Zaire (Congo)
Congress, 168–169. *See also* ethics
   aides in, 178–179, 181–182
   alcoholics in, 417
   bureaucracy and, 325–327
   campaign finance corruption and, 353–355
   campaign financing for, 369–370
   changing mood in, 205
   Clinton and, 7–8, 14–15
   committees in, 192–197
   composition of, 177
   conflicts of interest in, 188–189
   costs of salaries and facilities, 177–178
   courage in, 233–235
   debate in, 198–201
   electorate and, 172–175
   ethical issues in, 219–226
   failures of, 171
   Fed and, 490
   floor business of, 197–198
   foreign policy and, 76–77, 102–106
   greed in, 227–233
   income of members, 175–176, 188n
   investigations by, 193–194
   leaders of, 201–211
   mail to, 186
   military purchases and, 141–142
   mistakes in legislation of, 191–192
   Nixon and, 47
   party animosities in, 203–211
   periods of dominance by, 170–171
   President and, 66–73
   presidential success with, 19
   press coverage of, 406
   publicity and, 399
   qualities of members, 174–175
   racial and ethnic breakdown of, 177

Congress—*cont'd*
  Reagan and, 31, 47–48
  as reflection of electorate, 174
  reform of, 217–219
  responsibilities of, 182–184
  self-exclusion from social and legal
      rules, 181–182
  seniority system in, 175, 213–217
  solution to workload of, 196–197
  Speaker of, 205–207
  staffs and advisers to, 178–182, 186
  term limitations for, vi
  time allotment by, 184–186
  treaty-making powers of, 82–85
  war-making powers and, 78–82
Congressional Record, 198
Conlon, Richard, 178
Connally, John, 139
Connerly, Ward, 67
conservatives and conservatism
  anti-abortion crusade and, 288
  Democratic Party and, 358
  presidents and, 282
  Reagan and, 253
  Rehnquist Court and, 284–288
  in Republican Party, 360
  of Supreme Court, 251–254, 264
  on talk radio, 411
Constitution. *See also* specific
    Amendments
  amendment of, 23n
  on Chief Executive, 20–21
  Congress' money responsibilities
      and, 489
  electorate and, 266
  government efficiency and, iv
  impeachment and, 15, 16, 107
  as law, 238
  on Speaker of the House, 206
  strict constructionists and, 264
  Supreme Court and, 263
  writers of, 450
constitutional law, 260
consultants, bureaucracy and, 294–295
consumer movement, Nader and,
    379–381
containment policy, 125–126
contamination, of imported foods, 313
Continental Illinois National Bank and
    Trust of Chicago, 472–473
contraband, 311
"contract bureaucrats," 294–295
contras. *See* Iran-contra scandal
controversy, congressional voting and,
    233–235

Cook, Marlow, 375
Coolidge, Calvin, 35, 69, 450
  domestic politics and, 45
Corcoran, Thomas G., 57
corporate crime, 241
corporate executives, wealth of,
    460–461
corporate mergers, 406–407
Corporate Minimum Tax, 467
corporation(s)
  analysis of largest, 504
  economic reform and, 504–505
  foreign manufacturing locations
      and, 479
  government rescue of, 471
corruption. *See also* bribery; campaign
    funding; ethics; lying; specific scan-
    dals and issues
  in bureaucracy under Reagan,
      334–335
  in campaign financing, 530–532
  during Cold War, 116–117
  in Congress, 221–222
  in EPA under Reagan, 338–339
  in HUD under Reagan, 336
  in Interior Department under
      Reagan, 337–338
  lobbying and, 371–372, 374–375
  in OSHA under Reagan, 338
  political parties and, 352–353
  presidential advisers and, 49–50
  of Teamsters, 398
Corrupt Practices Act. *See* Federal
    Corrupt Practices Act (1925)
Corwin, Edward S., 76
costs
  of corporate crime, 241
  of political campaigns, 231
  of presidential trips, 38
Council of Economic Advisers, 328
  Greenspan and, 498
counsel, rights to, 243, 274–275
court-packing program, of Roosevelt,
    Franklin D., 269–270
courts. *See also* Supreme Court
  case backlog in, 245–246
  inconsistencies in, 245–247
  judge's authority in, 247–248
  politics and, 248–250
  system of, 240–247
Cox, Harold, 68
Cox media conglomerate, 407
Crane, Daniel B., 222
Cranston, Alan, 23, 199, 223, 523
creationism, teaching of, 284

CREEP. *See* Committee for the Re-Election of the President (CREEP)
crime and criminals, 238–240. *See also* courts; Supreme Court
assault weapons and, 60n
Burger Court and, 282
corporate, 241
rights of accused and, 243, 274–275
sentencing by race, 239
crises, presidential responses to, 57–59
Crisis (Jordan), 52
Cronkite, Walter, 414
"Cross of Gold" speech (Bryan), 532–533
C-12 transport plane, 222
Cuba, 79, 95, 96, 97
Culvahouse, A. B., 25n
Cuomo, Andrew, 337
Customs Service
reporting about, 404–405
violations of regulations, 311
Czechoslovakia, 125

daily schedule, of senator, 187–188
D'Alemberte, Talbot, 245
Dallek, Robert, xii
D'Amato, Alfonse, 229, 336
Daniel, Dan, 222–223
Daniel, John E., 339
Darman, Richard, 49, 58
Day of Reckoning (Friedman), 487
deal-making. *See* Congress; leaders
deals, presidential, 68–69
Dean, Deborah Gore, 336
Dean, John, III, 55
death penalty, 286
Deaver, Michael, 62–63, 335
debate. *See also* presidential debates
in Congress, 198–201
debt. *See* national debt
decision-making, by presidents, 93–96
DeConcini, Dennis, 306
Defense, Department of, 131. *See also* Military entries
public-information and public-relations force of, 399
defense industry
corruption in, 116–117
lack of competition in, 145
size of, 117
defense issues, Reagan and, 120–122
defense spending
for Cold War, 116
current, 164–167
economic benefits of, 139–144

economy and, 138
Japan vs. U.S., 164
deficit
Reagan and, 485–487
spending, 451
De Gaulle, Charles, 84
deities
political, 2
president as, xii
Delay, Tom, 203, 224
demand-pull inflation, 495
democracy, and capitalism, 448
Democratic Party. *See also* Congress; specific issues
anticommunists and, 128
congressional voting and, 202
conservatism of, 358
"new" Democrats and, 358–359
racism in South and, 363–364
sameness of political parties and, 357
Southern congressional leaders and, 215–216
Supreme Court nominations and, 251–252
demonstrations, 282, 344–347
departments of government. *See* specific departments
Dershowitz, Alan, 244
desegregation. *See Brown* v. *Board of Education*
Detroit Free Press, 408
Detroit River, 390
"dial-a-porn," 285
Diggs, Charles, 221
Dillon, Douglas, 438
Dinkins, David, 365
direct-mail solicitation, of campaign money, 532
Dirksen, Everett McKinley, 68, 198
Dirty Little Secrets: The Persistence of Corruption in American Politics (Sabato and Simpson), 210
dirty tricks, in presidential campaigns, 537
discretionary powers, abuse of, 107
discrimination. *See also* race and racism
in congressional hiring, 181–182
reverse, 262
disease, importation of, 313
Disney Company, 410
Divad anti-aircraft gun, 141
diversity, in FBI, 323
dole. *See* welfare system
Dole, Elizabeth, 508

Dole, Robert, 9, 356, 368, 416, 508, 523, 528
  campaign contributions and, 228–229
  funding solicitation by, 532
dollar. *See* inflation
dollar diplomacy, Bush and, 91–93
Domestic Policy Staff, 328
domestic politics
  Congress and, 170–172
  crises in, 57–59
  presidential advisers and, 49–57
  presidential enthusiasm and, 43–49
  presidential success in, 42–66
Dominican Republic, 79
  invasion of, 444
domino theory, 122
Donaldson, Sam, 414
Donner, Frederick, 379
doomsday plane, 37
DOT. *See* Transportation, Department of (DOT)
Douglas, William O., 255, 256, 264n, 271
Downey, Thomas J., 140
draft, 135–136
Drew, Elizabeth, 65
drug prices, 502
Dudman, Richard, 397
due process clause, of Fourteenth Amendment, 268, 274
Dukakis, Michael, 350n, 511
  Bush mud-slinging against, 539–545
  liberalism and, 363
  running mate of, 513
  voter disillusionment and, 367
Dulles, Allen W., 95, 150
Dulles, John Foster, 87
Duvalier, Jean-Claude "Baby Doc," 377

Eagleburger, Lawrence S., 91
Eastland, James O., 68
eavesdropping, on presidents, 2
economic crises, presidential responses to, 57
economy, 448–450. *See also* wealth; welfare system
  bank subsidization and, 472–475
  benefits of defense spending in, 139–144
  debt and, 485–488
  defense budget and, 138–139
  distribution of wealth and, 458–459
  fiscal control and, 491–495
  free, 450–452
  government involvement in, 451–452

  health care and, 499–500
  imports policy and, 477–481
  inflation and, 495–496
  middle class and, 461–463
  monetary control and, 488–491
  pump-priming of, 143
  reform of, 503–505
  regulation and, 475–477
  Social Security system and, 463–466
  of Soviet Union, 163
  subsidization and, 470–472
  taxation and, 466–470
Education, Department of, 293, 329
Edwards, Don, 26, 193–194, 249n, 265
Ehrlichman, John, 36, 55, 69, 250, 418
Eichmann, Adolph, 151
Eighth Amendment, 242
Eisenberg, Howard B., 243
Eisenhower, Dwight D., 26, 394
  attitude of, 59
  on Cold War, 116
  domestic politics and, 45–46
  foreign policy and, 87, 99
  image of, 63
  Khrushchev and, 118n
  speech writing for, 533
  Supreme Court appointments by, 254, 271
Eizenstat, Stu, 376
elderly, legislation for, 171
elections
  of Clinton, 6–7
  of Congress, 173n
  financial contributions to, 227–229
  popular majority in, 62n
  voter interest in, 366–368
electoral college, 350n
electorate
  changing mood of, 205
  character of leaders and, 5
  congressional failures and, 172–175
  Constitution and, 266
elitism, in media, 414
Ellsberg, Daniel J., 108, 394–395
El Salvador, death squads, 101
Emergency Jobs Bill, 494
emergency war powers, of president, 103n
Emerson, Ralph Waldo, x
employment. *See also* unemployment
  losses from import policy, 478–479
  public jobs and, 493–494
  Supreme Court and rights of, 285
Endangered Species Act (1973), 170
enemies list, of Nixon, 22

Energy, Department of, 161, 162, 293, 294–295, 297, 329
  natural gas bill and, 183
enlistments. *See also* draft
  voluntary, 135n
entrapment, 285
environment
  bureaucracy and, 314–315
  lobbying successes for, 390
  radioactive wastes and, 101
environmentalists, NAFTA and, 8
environmental legislation, 170–171
Environmental Protection Agency (EPA), 314–315
  corruption in, 338–339
  spending and, 471
EPA. *See* Environmental Protection Agency (EPA)
equal opportunity, in federal bureaucracy, 295
Ervin, Sam, Jr., 234–235
Escobedo, Danny, 275
Escobedo v. *Illinois,* 274–275
Espionage Act (1917), 431
ESPN, ESPN2, 410
Espy, Mike, 49
ethics. *See also* corruption
  congressional committees for, 219–220
  congressional franking privileges and, 223–224
  congressional greed and, 227–233
  congressional philosophy of, 224–226
  in government, ii–iii
  of presidential advisers, 50
  of Reagan staff, 54–55
  reforms in Congress, 219–224
ethnic groups
  in Congress, 177
  voting by, 364
Etzioni, Amitai, 227, 228
Evans, Daniel, 172
evil empire. *See* communism; Soviet Union
evolution
  of Supreme Court, 267–271
  teaching of, 284
executive. *See also* Chief Executive; presidency; president(s)
  expansion under Roosevelt, Franklin D., 21
executive agreement, 83
Executive Office Building, 36
Executive Office of the President, 36, 328

Executive Order 8248, 328
executives (corporate), wealth of, 460–461
exports, arms, 154–155
Exxon tanker, oil spill clean-up costs, 468

factories. *See also* manufacturing
  maquiladoras, 480
"failed banks," 472–473
Fain, Jim, 546
Faircloth, Lauch, 12
fairness doctrine, of FCC, 382
Fallows, James, 415
Falwell, Jerry, 285
Family Assistance Plan, 46–47
family values, Reagan and, 31
Farewell Address (Washington), 119
farms and farming, USDA and, 303
Faux, Jeff, 497–498
FBI. *See* Federal Bureau of Investigation (FBI)
FCC. *See* Federal Communications Commission (FCC)
FDIC. *See* Federal Deposit Insurance Corporation (FDIC)
Federal Aviation Administration (FAA), 309–310
Federal Bureau of Investigation (FBI), 319–324
Federal Communications Commission (FCC), 304–305, 412
  fairness doctrine of, 382
  press coverage, politics, and, 441
Federal Corrupt Practices Act (1925), 352, 353n
federal courts. *See also* courts; Supreme Court
  appointments to, 251
Federal Deposit Insurance Corporation (FDIC), 472n, 473
  credit institution failures and, 474
Federal Election Act (1974), 227
Federal Election Campaign Act (1971), 353, 354
Federal Home Loan Bank Board, 472n, 498
Federal Housing Administration, audit of, 334
Federalist, The, 33–34, 450
  government efficiency and, iv
  Hamilton in, 77, 106
federal judges. *See also* judges
  appointment of, 249
  Reagan appointment of, 253
Federal Power Commission, 293n, 329

Federal Reserve Board, 293n, 472n
Federal Reserve System ("Fed"),
    488–490
  economic reform and, 503
  Greenspan and, 498–499
  secrecy of, 490–491
  Volcker and, 496–498
Federal Savings and Loan Insurance
    Corporation (FSLIC), 472n
  insolvency of, 318
Federal Trade Commission (FTC), 293n,
    390, 483
  economy and, 451
  Nader and, 381
Fed's Open Market Committee, 490
F-18 fighter, 143
Feingold, Russell D., 205
Felrice, Barry, 308
feminists, voting by, 364
Ferguson, Thomas, 421n
Ferraro, Geraldine, 508
Fifth Amendment, 242, 263
filibusters
  in Senate, 199–200
  Supreme Court and, 262
finances, of media chains, 408–409
financial contributions, to political
    campaigns, 227–229
Finch, Robert, 302
Finkelstein, Arthur, 391
fireside chats, 62
firing. *See also* corporate executives
  of staffs, 462–463
First Amendment, 263, 265
  Burger Court and, 282
  freedom of the press and,
    402–403
  Rehnquist Court and, 285
First World War. *See* World War I
fiscal policy, 488, 491–495
Fitzgerald, Ernest, 315
Fitzhugh, Gilbert W., 302
flag burning, 285
floor (Congress), work done on,
    197–198
floor leader (House), 205–206
Flowers, Gennifer, 417
Flynt, Larry, 16
Foley, Thomas, 303, 537
Folsom, Jim, viii
food, imported diseases and, 313
Food and Drug Administration (FDA),
    315, 316, 390
  Nader and, 381
food stamps. *See* welfare system

Ford, Gerald R., 3, 4, 21n, 27, 87, 304,
    448, 510, 512
  foreign policy and, 100
  negative actions of, 70
  Nixon pardon by, 24
  PAC contributions and, 228
  presidential treatment and, 42
  Supreme Court appointment by, 253
Foreign Affairs, 125
foreign agents, lobbying by, 376–378
"foreign" aid, 471
foreign policy. *See also* Central
    Intelligence Agency (CIA); war-
    making powers
  changing, 99–102
  congressional role in, 102–106
  funding of, 76
  military, 130–133
  presidential, 74–78
  presidential advisers and, 85–91
  presidential power and, 93–96
  spying and, 150–154
  in transition, 155–158
  treaty-making powers and, 82–85
  war-making powers and, 78–82
Foreman, Ed, viii
Forestry Service, bureaucracy and, 325
Forrestal, James, 137
Fortas, Abe, 86, 256
For the Record (Regan), 54
Fortune magazine, 503
Fourteenth Amendment, 268
  Bill of Rights and, 274
  Brown v. *Board of Education* and,
    275–276
  due process clause of, 274
  Plessy v. *Ferguson* and, 275
  state sovereignty and, 276–277
Fourth Amendment, 263
  Burger Court and, 281
Fowler, Wyche, 228
Fox TV, 412
Frady, Marshall, 365
Frank, Barney, 203–204, 233
Frank, Jerome N., 255
Frankel, Max, 166
Frankfurter, Felix, 247–248, 255, 277, 278
franking privileges, congressional,
    223–224
Franklin, Benjamin, 34n, 506
fraud
  corporate crime and, 241
  in government, ii
  in weapons production, 144–148,
    163–164

Freedom of Information Act, 295, 436, 437
freedoms
    in Bill of Rights, 273–274
    of press, 431–432
free enterprise, and defense industry, 145
free-enterprise economy, 448–450,
    450–452
Freeh, Louis, 324
free press, 272
free speech, 272
free trade, 477–478
Friedersdorf, Max, 54
Friedman, Allen, 335n
Friedman, Benjamin, 487
Fritchey, Clayton, 118n
Fulbright, William, 78, 133
Fuller, Craig L., 541
funding
    of foreign policy, 76, 103
    of military weapons, 141–142
furlough program, Bush, Horton, and,
    544–545

gag rule, in Congress, 198
Gallup, George, 392–393
Gallup poll, 348n, 528
Gannett media conglomerate, 408
GAO. *See* General Accounting Office
    (GAO)
Gardner, John, 348, 381
Garfield, James, 329n
Garmatz, Edward, 189
Garment, Leonard, 376
Garner, John Nance, 514–515
Garten, Jeffrey E., 473
Gates, Bill, 460
Gavin, James, 156
Gazprom, 92
Gelb, Leslie H., 17, 415
gender. *See also* sexual harassment;
    women
    in Congress, 177
    discrimination by, 287
    of justices, 249n
General Accounting Office (GAO),
    145, 300
    experts in, 317–318
General Assembly, 149
General Electric, 479
General Motors, Nader and, 379–380
General Services Administration (GSA),
    scandals in, 300
Gephardt, Richard, 365, 508
Gergen, David, 60, 414, 415
Germany, World War II and, 124

Germond, Jack, 367
Gerth, Jeff, 447
Gesell, Gerhard A., 241n, 247
Gideon, Clarence, 243
Gideon v. *Wainwright*, 243, 274
Gingrich, Newt, ii, 142, 203, 205,
    208–209, 232
    changing congressional mood
        and, 205
    ethical issues and, 226
    ethics of, 223
    GOPAC and, 232
    as Speaker, 209–211
Ginsburg, Ruth Bader, 251, 289
Glenn, John, 181, 355, 512
global communism, 120
global economy, imports policy and, 478
Goden, Clarence Earl, 274
Goldman, Eric, 27
Goldman, Sachs and Company, 92–93
Goldstein, Tom, 245, 405
Goldwater, Barry, viii, 23, 26, 67, 184,
    292, 546
    on PAC money, 231
Golub, Harvey, 461
Gompers, Samuel, 352
Gonzalez, Henry, viii, 214
Goodman, Ellen, 157
Goodwin, Richard N., 26, 67, 86, 534
GOP (Grand Old Party). *See* Republican
    Party
GOPAC, 232
    Gingrich and, 226
Gorbachev, Mikhail, 91, 112, 129, 165
Gore, Albert, 7, 92, 365, 508
    funding solicitation by, 531
    as running mate, 513–514
Gore, Albert (Sr.), 215, 233
government. *See also* bureaucracy;
    economy
    abuses in, vii
    economic role of, 455–458
    economy and, 451–452
    ethics in, ii–iii
    lying to reporters by, 443–447
    media and, 394–397
    natural monopolies and, 472
    public attitudes toward, ii
    workers on payroll of, 471
Government Accounting Office, on com-
    position of bureaucracy, 295
Government by Contract (Hanrahan), 294
government rights, Burger Court
    and, 281
graft, in Congress, 222–223

Graham, Katherine, 400–401, 405, 427
Gralnick, Jeff, 441–442
Gramm, Phil, Clinton and, 68
grand jury, Burger Court and, 281
Grand Old Party (GOP). *See* Republican
    Party
Grant, Ulysses, 44
grants, bureaucracy and, 298–299
Gravel, Mike, 281
Gray, Boyden, 50–51
Gray, William H., III, 434
Great Communicator. *See* Reagan,
    Ronald
Great Depression
    fiscal policy during, 492–494
    presidential response to, 57
Great Red Scare (1919-1920), 123
Greece, 125, 126, 127
greed, in Congress, 227–233
Green, Mark, 447
Greene, Jerry, 437
Greenfield, Jeff, 521
Greenhouse, Linda, 266n
Green Party, 349
Greenspan, Alan, 491, 498–499
Gregg v. *Georgia*, 239
Greider, William, 98, 447, 456
Grenada, 80, 105–106
gridlock, between President and
    Congress, 8
Griscom, Thomas, 25n, 178
Gruening, Ernest, 109, 233, 426
GSA. *See* General Services
    Administration (GSA)
Guatemala, 152–153
    Bay of Pigs and, 428
Guggenheim, Charles, 523
Gulf War. *See* Persian Gulf War
gunboat diplomacy, 106
gun controls, 190–191

Haig, Alexander M., 26, 89, 91,
    376, 396
Haiti, 79
    U. S. troops in, 159
Halberstam, David, 99
Haldeman, H. R., 55
    on Nixon, viii
Hall, James E., 310
Halle, Peter, 375
Halloran, Richard, 146–147, 430
Halperin, Morton, 238
Halverson, Richard C., 172
Hamilton, Alexander, 106
    on foreign affairs, 77

on presidency, 33–34
    on treaty-making powers, 82
Hand, Learned, 247
"handlers," in political campaigns,
    535–537
Hanrahan, John D., 294
Harding, Warren G., 4, 44
Harkin, Ruth, 378
Harkin, Tom, 378
Harris, Louis, 361
Harris, Richard, 227
Harrison, Gilbert, 428
Harris poll, 528
Hart, Gary, iii, 225, 416, 417
    trial by publicity, 516
Hart Building, 177
Hastert, J. Dennis, 211
Hastings, Alcee L., 249n
Hatch, Orrin G., 251
Hawaii, "defense" highway on, 142n
Haynsworth, Clement, 233
Hays, Brooks, 219
Hays, Wayne, 417, 418
hazardous-waste sites, 314
health
    bureaucratic indifference to, 307–308
    importation of disease and, 313
Health and Human Services,
    Department of, 302, 329
health care, 499–500
    HMOs and, 501–502
    Medicare, Medicaid, and, 500–501
Health, Education and Welfare,
    Department of, 302, 329
health insurance plan, 171
health maintenance organizations
    (HMOs), 501–503
Health Standards Programs, 338
Hearst media empire, 401, 402, 409
Heinz, John, 175
Helms, Jesse, 12, 199, 203, 213, 425
Helms, Richard, 238
Helmsley, Leona, 469
Henkel, William, 65
Henry, Patrick, 33
hepatitis C, funding for, 378–379
Herbert, Bob, 370
Hersh, Seymour, 427
Hertsgaard, Mark, 420
Higgins, Marguerite, 437
High, Stanley, 533
high crimes and misdemeanors, im-
    peachment and, 11
high-tech industries, temp help at, 462
Hightower, Jim, 359, 411, 463

highways, accidents and, 308–309
Hill, Joe, 347n
Hilton, Ronald, 428
Hiroshima, bombing of, 159
Hispanic American Report, 428
Hispanic-Americans
  in elective offices, 508–509
  political parties and, 365
HMOs. *See* health maintenance organizations (HMOs)
Holbrook, Hal, viii–ix
"hold," on legislation, 200
Holleman, Frank, 540
Hollings, Ernest, 180
Holtzman, Elizabeth, 253
homeless, protests for, 346
homosexuals and homosexuality
  in military, 7
  political contributions by, 364
  political parties and rights for, 360
  sexual harassment and, 287
Honduras, 79
Hooks, Benjamin L., 287
Hoover, Herbert, 492
  economy and, 44
  salary of, 35–36
Hoover, J. Edgar, 321–324
Horton, Willie, 530, 544
House, Karen Elliott, 296
House Commission on Administrative
  Review, 185n
House Democratic caucus, 216
House of Representatives. *See also* committees (congressional); Congress;
  ethics; Rules Committee (House)
  election of, 173n
  Ethics Committee in, 220–221,
    222–226
  expulsion from, 222
  floor leader and assistant floor
    leader in, 205–206
  Judiciary Committee in, 14
  PAC system and, 232
  Post Office of, 223–224
  seniority system in, 216–217
  Speaker of, 205–211
  Ways and Means Committee in,
    217–218
House Un-American Activities
  Committee, 272
Housing and Urban Development
  (HUD)
  Clinton's efforts to reform, 337n
  corruption in, 336–337
  scandals in, 397–398

Hubbell, Webb, 50
HUD. *See* Housing and Urban
  Development (HUD)
human rights issues, 267, 268
  Carter and, 100–101
  in foreign policy, 101–102
Humphrey, Gordon, 233
Humphrey, Hubert, vi, 127–128, 198,
  201, 290
  Johnson and, 515
  polls and, 528
  smearing of, 539
Hussein, Saddam, 158
Hustler magazine, 285
Hutton, E.F., Company, 403
Hyde, Henry, 14n, 181

ideology
  Cold War conflicts over, 126–130
  PACs and, 355
illegal immigrants, 312
image, presidential, 61–66
immigrants, sweatshop employment
  of, 477
Immigration and Naturalization Service
  (INS), 311–312
impeachment, 34n
  of Clinton, 11, 14–16
  as control of presidential foreign policy actions, 106–111
  of Johnson, Andrew, 11n
  of judges, 249n
  measuring conduct for, 15–16
imports policy, 477–481
  job losses from, 478–479
  NAFTA and, 480–481
income. *See also* minimum wage
  of over 1 million dollars, 460
  congressional, 175–177
  congressional disclosure of, 188
  of middle class, 461–462, 463
  military pension as, 188n
  Social Security and, 464
  of temp help, 462–463
income floor, 46–47
income tax, 466–467. *See also* taxation
Independent Party, 349, 350
individual rights, Warren Court and,
  281
Indonesia, 97
industry
  bureaucratic reform efforts and,
    332–333
  middle-class jobs in, 462–463
  regulation of, 268

inflation, 495–496
   fiscal control and, 492
   Greenspan and, 498
   minimum wage increase and, 476
influence peddling, under Reagan,
   336–337
information. *See also* leaks; propaganda;
   secret documents
   media, government, and, 397–400
   secret, 430–432
information-gathering, presidential information and, 93–96
inheritance tax, 458–459
Inouye, Daniel K., 142n, 184
INS. *See* Immigration and
   Naturalization Service (INS)
integration. *See Brown* v. *Board of
   Education*
integrity
   Cold War and, 116–117
   of political leaders, 4–6
intelligence operations, 150–152. *See also*
   Central Intelligence Agency (CIA);
   spying
intercontinental missiles, in Cuba, 96
Interior, Department of, 306–307
   and corruption under Reagan,
   337–338
interlocking directorships, 398
Internal Revenue Service (IRS), 305
   reporting about, 404–405
   tax cheats and, 469
Internal Security Subcommittee
   (Senate), 272
interpretation of Constitution, by
   Supreme Court, 263–267
Interstate Commerce Commission
   (ICC), 293n, 301–302
   economy and, 451
intervention. *See also* Central
   Intelligence Agency (CIA); foreign
   policy; specific countries and wars
   in Haiti, 159
   movement from isolation to, 119–120
invasions, 84. *See also* foreign policy
investigative reporting, 411
investment
   by S&Ls, 473–474
   of Social Security Trust Fund,
   464–466
investment tax credits, 467
Iowa, as caucus state, 523–525
Iowa Beef Processors, 307
Iran, 80
   Carter and, 100

Clinton and, 92
   Shah in, 96
Iran-contra scandal
   Bush and, 540
   North and, 90, 247
   presidential staff and, 54
   Reagan and, 17
   Reagan staff and, 55
Iran hostage crisis, 59
   weapons malfunctions during, 142
Iraq, 97
   Iran war with, 158
   Persian Gulf War and, 158–159
Irish Mafia, under Kennedy, 41
iron curtain, 124–125
"iron triangle," 326–327
IRS. *See* Internal Revenue Service (IRS)
IRS Reform Act (1998), 306
isolation, movement toward interven-
   tion, 119–120
Israeli lobby, 377
Ivins, Molly, 363

Jackman, Jane, 502
Jackson, Andrew, Supreme Court
   and, 277
Jackson, Brooks, 447
Jackson, Henry, 353n
Jackson, Jesse, 365, 506, 508, 509
Jackson, Robert, 255
Jacobson, Max, 25
Jagoda, Barry, 63
jail terms, 239
Jane's Defence Weekly, 431–432
Japan
   atomic bombings of, 159–160
   defense expenditures in, 164
   Pearl Harbor and, 119
   trade policies of, 478–479
Japanese-Americans, rights of, 270
Jaworski, Leon, 221
Jefferson, Thomas, 506
   children by slave, 2
   presidential pomp and, 35
   wars and, 79
Jenner, William, 272
Jennings, Peter, 414
Jews, Jackson, Jesse, and, 365, 509n
Jiang Zemin, 102
Jim Crow, Supreme Court and, 264
jobs. *See* employment
"Joe Camel" advertising campaign, 388
John Paul II (Pope), 91
Johnson, Andrew, 11n
   impeachment of, 107

Johnson, Gregory Lee, 285
Johnson, Haynes, 420
Johnson, Lyndon B., xii, 74, 85. *See also*
   Vietnam War
   advisers of, 94–95
   attitude of, 59
   character of, 5
   on Civil Rights Act, 363
   Congress and, 67
   deal-making by, 68
   domestic politics and, 44–45, 46
   foreign policy and, 99–100
   on Goldwater, viii
   image of, 63
   after Kennedy assassination, 58
   leaks by, 434
   lying by, 443–444
   Medicare and, 501
   mental incapacity of, 26–27
   pension for, 35
   personal touch and, 67
   political organizing and, 348
   presidential treatment and, 41
   press corps and, 440
   propaganda and, 72
   ranking of, 3, 4
   as running mate, 513, 515
   spending under, 358
   travel style of, 39
   Vietnam and, 122
   war and, 79, 81
   "war on poverty," 455
Johnson, Tom, 415
Joint Chiefs of Staff, 131
Joint Committee on Taxation, loophole
   for lobbyists and, 374
joint resolution, foreign policy
   and, 82–83
Jones, Alex S., 412
Jones, David C., 131
Jones, Jim, 523
Jones, Norvill, 180
Jones, Paula, 11–12, 13
Jordan, Hamilton, 52, 86
Jordan, Vernon, 369n, 377
journalism. *See also* media
   "stylishness" in, 421–422
judges. *See also* courts; federal courts;
   Supreme Court
   authority of, 247–248
   jury selection and, 247
   as millionaires, 241n
   politics and, 248–250
   sentencing inconsistencies
      among, 245

   Supreme Court, 258–260
judicial review, 265
Judiciary Committee (House), Clinton
   impeachment and, 14
junk bonds, 453
"junkets" (trips abroad), 195, 222n
juries
   competence of, 246
   selection of, 247
justice. *See also* courts
   adversary system of, 246–247
   in U.S., 238–239
Justice, William Wayne, 249–250
Justice Department, antitrust division, 483

Kahn, Alfred E., 484
Kalb, Bernard, 396
Kalb, Marvin, 529
Kappel, Frederick R., 341
Katzenbach, Nicholas, 81
Kazin, Michael, 461
Kearns, Doris, 85
Keating, David, 176
Keenan, Patrick J., 244n
Kefauver, Estes, 526
Kelly, Brian, 52
Kelsey, Frances, 316
Kennan, George F., 125
Kennedy, Anthony M., 253, 254, 284, 288
Kennedy, Edward ("Teddy"), 233,
   437, 509
   Chappaquiddick and, 517–518
Kennedy, John F., 24
   advisers of, 51, 95
   bureaucracy and, 330
   cabinet selection, media, and, 437–438
   campaigning by, 510
   on congressional committees, 192
   coverage of affair, 417
   crisis after assassination, 57–58
   deal-making by, 68
   domestic advisers of, 51
   domestic politics and, 45
   Hoover and, 321n
   image and, 63
   Irish Mafia and, 41–42
   Khrushchev and, 85
   love affairs of, 2
   on Nixon, viii
   ranking of, 3, 4
   running mate of, 513, 515
   salary of, 35
   speech writing for, 534
   war and, 79

Kennedy, Patrick J., 198
Kennedy, Robert, 68, 321n, 379, 438
Kerry, John, 175
Keynes, John Maynard, 448, 492, 494
Khomeini, Ayatollah, 18
Khrushchev, Nikita, 118n, 149
  presidential incapacity and, 25
kickbacks
  in Congress, 221
  FBI and, 323
Kirk, Paul G., 364, 540
Kirkpatrick, Jeane Jordan, 351
Kissinger, Henry, 88, 91, 131, 376
Kluger, Richard, 387
Knight-Ridder media conglome-
  rate, 408
Knowland, William F., 271
Koop, C. Everett, 316–317
Kopeckne, Mary Jo, 517–518
Koppel, Ted, 522
Korea, 79, 97
  Carter and, 100
"Koreagate" scandal, 221
Korean War, 79, 150, 155–156
Kotz, Nick, 309
Kraft, Joseph, 422
Kristol, Irving, i
Krock, Arthur, 437
Kurtz, Howard, 173
Kuwait, 158

labels
  "liberal" as, 362–363
  for political parties, 358–359
labor. *See also* American Federation of
  Labor and Congress of Industrial
  Organizations (AFL-CIO)
  cheap, 479, 480–481
  civil federal force, 332
  communism and, 125
  NAFTA and, 8
  violation of regulations, 311
Labor Department, 311
LaFollette, Robert M., 350
laissez faire capitalism, 268
lame duck president, 32–33
Lance, Bert, 440–441, 445
Landau, Jack, 432
Landslide, The Unmaking of the President,
  1984-1988 (Mayer and McManus), 25n
Laos, 79
LaRocque, Gene, 117
Larson, Arthur, 46
Lavelle, John D., 133n
Lavelle, Rita M., 339

law(s). *See also* courts
  congressional self-exclusion from,
    181–182
  constitutional, 260
  defined, 236
  enforcement of Supreme Court rul-
    ings and, 277–278
  origins of, 238
  statutory, 260
  Supreme Court and, 267
law-and-order posture, of Burger Court,
  280–281
lawyers
  as lobbyists, 377–378
  right to, 243, 274–275
Laxalt, Paul, 356
Lazarus, Edward, 159
leaders. *See also* president(s)
  character and integrity of, 4–6
  congressional, 201–211
  of House, 205–211
  qualities of, v–x
  of Senate, 212–213
League of Nations, 119, 148
Leahy, Patrick J., 298
leaks
  of information, 432–435
  perils of, 434–435
  punishment for, 434–435
Lebanon, 79, 80, 105
  hostages in, 85
  Reagan and, 122
lectures, by media stars, 414
left wing. *See* liberal(s)
legal process
  adversary system in, 246–247
  speed of, 245–246
legislation
  Clinton and, 7–8
  committees and, 196–197
  congressional committees and,
    192–197
  environmental, 170–171
  under Johnson, Lyndon, 44–45
  "pork barrel," 189–192
  quality of, 182–184
  slowing passage of, 198–201
  social, 170–171
  vetoes of, 70
Lehman, William, 191
Lekachman, Robert, 505
Lemov, Michael R., 180
Leno, Jay, 98–99
Lens, Sidney, 112
Letterman, David, 460

Levin, Carl, 494–495
Levitt, Arthur, Jr., 465
Lewinsky, Monica, 10n, 12–14, 392, 417, 435
Lewis, Charles, 413
liberal(s)
    attitude toward federal government, 290–291
    as label, 362–363
    Rehnquist Court and, 282, 284
    Warren Court and, 272–277
libraries, presidential, 39–40
Libya, 85
Lieb, Julian, 27n
Liebling, A. J., 402
Lierman, Terry, 373
lies. *See* lying
life appointment, of federal judges, 250
lifestyle, of presidents, 36–40
Liggett and Meyer, 482
Light, Paul, 294
Lincoln, Abraham, ranking of, 3
Lippmann, Walter, 438
Littleton, Colorado, 191
Livingston, Robert, 14n, 211
lobbies. *See also* political action committees (PACs)
    congressional committee system and, 197
    political contributions and, 228
lobbying, 371. *See also* campaign funding
    by big business, 384–391
    by foreign agents, 376–378
    government-industry revolving door and, 374–376
    helpful, 373
    organizing through, 371–378
    "people's lobbies" and, 378–384
Lockheed, 139, 146
Lockheed-Martin, 482
Long, Huey, xi, 458
Long, Russell, xi, 417
Los Angeles Times, 402n, 405
Lott, Trent, 213, 360
    campaign contributions and, 229, 233
loyalty oath, 123–124, 271
Lucas Industries, 143
luck of President, in domestic politics, 43
Lukas, J. Anthony, 422
lying. *See also* corruption
    by government, 443–447
    by Johnson, 443–444
    by Nixon, 444–445
    in political campaigns, 537–546
    about welfare, 456–457

MacArthur, Douglas, 41, 112, 128
    Korean War and, 156
Machiavelli, Niccolo, 49
Mack, John Paul, 440
Mad as Hell (Germond and Witcover), 367
Maddox (ship), 108
Madison, James, 77, 450
    on foreign relations, 77
Mafia, 321, 323
    CIA and, 320
Magnuson, Warren, 193, 379
mail, to Congress, 186
majority leader, of Senate, 212
majority party (House), floor leader of, 205–206
majority whip, in Senate, 212
Manatt, Charles, 376
Manchester Union Leader, 416, 525, 538
Mansfield, Mike, 104
manufacturing
    foreign locations for, 479
    maquiladoras and, 480
Mao Tse-tung, 88
maquiladoras, 480
Maraniss, David, 9, 417
Marcantonio, Vito, 123
Marines, 105
Marshall, George, 127
Marshall, John, 277
Marshall, Thurgood, 68, 252, 255
Marshall Plan, 155, 226
Martin Marietta, 146
Matlock, Jack F., Jr., 114
Matthews, Christopher, 415
Mayer, Jane, 25n
McCain, John, 68, 205
McCarren-Ferguson Act, 482n
McCarthy, Eugene, i
McCarthy, Joseph, 95, 127, 272, 418–419
McCloskey, Robert G., 271
McClure, James A., 68–69
McCorvey, Norma, 283
McCullough, Frank, 427
McDade, Joe, 190
McDonnell-Douglas, 146, 482
McFarlane, Robert, 89, 90
McGee, David, 324
McGinnis, Joe, 537
McGovern, George, 22, 82, 137
McGrory, Mary, 23, 367
McIver, Stuart B., 4n
McKellar, Kenneth B., viii
McKinley, William, treaties and, 83
McLarty, Thomas F., III, 42
McLean, Kenneth A., 180

McManus, Doyle, 25n
McNamara, Robert, 94–95, 130, 443
McVeigh, Timothy, FBI and, 324
McWilliams, Carey, 428
media. *See also* Pentagon Papers;
    Watergate scandal; specific issues
    conflicts of interest of, 403–405
    control of, 402–403
    corruption uncovered by, 397–400
    empires of, 410–412
    full disclosure of financial opera-
        tions by, 408–409
    glitz in, 413–415
    government and, 394–397
    Newspaper Preservation Act and,
        407–408
    ownership by industrialists, 400–416
    polls and, 528–529
Media Monopoly, The (Bagdikian), 410
media stars, 413–415
Medicaid, 45n, 500–501
Medicare, 45n, 500–501
Meeds, Lloyd, 174
Meehan, Martin T., 205
Meese, Edwin, III, 107, 335, 408
Mellman, Mark, 545
Memoirs (Nixon), 131–132
mental incapacity, of President, 18–19,
    25, 26–27
Mercer, Lucy, 2
mergers and acquisitions, 406–407, 483
    in airlines industry, 484–485
    of media companies, 410
    middle-class jobs and, 462–463
Merit Systems Board. *See* U.S. Merit
    Systems Protection Board
Metcalf, Joseph, III, 442
Metzenbaum, Howard A., 191, 199,
    200, 233
Mexico, 76, 79
    NAFTA and, 480–481
Miami Herald, 408
    Bay of Pigs and, 428
Microsoft, 482
    temp help at, 462
middle class, 461–463
    incomes of, 461–462
    range of incomes in, 463
    under Reagan, 453–454
    taxation of, 466–467
    temp help and, 462–463
Middle East
    foreign policy and, 158
    Iran-Iraq war in, 158
Mikva, Abner, 531

military
    in China and United States, 165
    civilian alumni of, 136, 137
    in civilian policy positions, 130–131
    after Cold War, 117
    fraud and waste in, 144–148,
        163–164
    Reagan expenditures on, 121
    standing, 134–136
    in Vietnam War, 157
military bases, tax savings for closing,
    137–138
military foreign policy, 130–133
military-industrial complex, 109–110, 117
    creation of term, 533
military-industrial-political complex,
    136–138
military pension, 188n
millionaires, 459–460
Mills, C. Wright, 241
Mills, Wilbur, ix, 217–218, 353n, 375, 417
minimum wage, 476–477
Mining Law (1872), 325–326
minorities
    in elective offices, 508–509
    in federal bureaucracy, 295
Mintz, Morton, 447
Miranda v. *Arizona*, 275
missile gap, 118
missiles, in China, 165
Mississippi Delta, poverty in, 457–458
Mitchell, George, 2, 213
Mitchell, John N., 23, 55, 400–401
    corruption by, 337
Mobil Oil, advocacy advertising by, 387
Mobutu Sese Seko, 102, 151
moderates, in Republican party, 360
Mohawk River, 390
monarchy, presidency and, 33
Mondale, Walter, 155
monetary policy, 488–491
monetary restrictions, 76
money
    buying media support, 407–408
    managing economy and, 488–491
    media empires and, 410–412
money sources. *See also* campaign fund-
    ing; lobbying
    political party influence decline and,
        351–352
money supply, 488
Money Trust, 481
monopolies
    of money, 504
    natural, 472

Monroe, Bill, 441
Monroe Doctrine, 82
Moos, Malcolm, 533
morality
    in Congress, 219
    House censures and, 222
Morris, Anthony, 315
Morris, Dick, 9n
Morse, Wayne, 109, 199, 233
Moseley-Braun, Carol, 177, 508
Moss, John, 52, 194
Mossadegh, Mohammed, 152
Moyers, Bill, 415
Moynihan, Daniel Patrick, 97, 172, 487
"Mr. Chairman," 217
muckraking, 397
mud-slinging, in political campaigns,
    537–546
multinationals, Bush and, 91–92
Mundt, Karl, 272
Murdoch, Rupert, 226, 412
Murphy, George, 512
Murtha, John, 190
Muskie, Edmund, 416
    smearing of, 538–539
Myers, Michael J., 222
My Lai massacre, 110, 394, 427

Nader, Ralph, 308, 344
    lobbying by, 379–381
Nagasaki, bombing of, 159–160
Nation, the, Bay of Pigs and, 428
National Aeronautics and Space
    Administration, 293n
National Association of Manufacturers,
    354, 385
National Cancer Institute, federal bu-
    reaucracy and, 297
national debt, 485–488
    Reagan and, 485–487
National Emergency Airborne
    Command Post, 37
National Foundations for the Arts and
    Humanities, 45n
National Guard, 134n
National Highway Traffic Safety
    Administration (NHTSA), 308
National Institute of Mental Health, 299
National Institutes of Health, AIDS
    lobby and, 379
National Labor Relations Board, 293n
National Organization of Women, 346
National Progressives, 350
National Rifle Association, Second
    Amendment and, 248

National Science Foundation (NSF), 299
national security, waste and, 164
National Security Act (1947), 97, 131, 150
National Security Council (NSC), 89, 90,
    91, 126n, 328
National Security Industrial
    Association, 137
national security policy, president and,
    77–78
National Taxpayers Union, 176
National Traffic and Motor Vehicle
    Safety Act (1966), 380
National Transportation Safety Board,
    309, 310
Nationsbank, 473
Native Americans, bureaucratic treat-
    ment of, 306–307
NATO. *See* North Atlantic Treaty
    Organization (NATO)
natural gas bill, 183
Natural Gas Pipeline Safety Act
    (1968), 381
natural monopolies, 472
negative actions, legislation and, 70
negative campaigning, 537–546
negative powers, in Congress, 206
Nelson, Gaylord, 170
Nessen, Ron, 415
neutrality theory, 78
New Deal, 455
    Congress and, 204
    Keynes and, 492
    Roosevelt court-packing and,
        269–270
"new" Democrats, 358–359
New Hampshire, primary in, 523,
    525–527
Newhouse, Samuel I., 402
New Republic, 428
news, manipulation of, 412–413
News Corporation (Murdoch), 412
Newspaper Preservation Act, 407–408
newspapers, 401–402. *See also* media
New York, primary election in, 527
New York Herald Tribune, cabinet selec-
    tions and, 437
New York Times, 403–404, 405–406
    Bay of Pigs and, 428
    cabinet selections and, 437
    delays and, 437
    leaks to, 433, 435
    Pentagon Papers and, 108, 110
    protection of Speaker by, 440
NHTSA. *See* National Highway Traffic
    Safety Administration (NHTSA)

Nicaragua, 76, 79, 107, 157
  Iran-contra scandal and, 18
  Reagan and, 76
Nickles, Don, 523
Nike Inc., 479
Nixon, Richard, 272
  anticommunism of, 127–128
  audiotaping by, 2–3
  behavior of, viii
  China and, 131
  Congress and, 83, 170–171
  domestic politics and, 46
  as Eisenhower's hatchetman, 515
  environment and, 314
  foreign policy funding and, 104
  foreign policy of, 88
  image and, 63
  judicial appointments by, 250
  lifestyle in White House, 36
  lying by, 444–445
  media and, 401
  mental incapacity of, 26
  on negative campaigning, 545
  Newspaper Preservation Act and,
    407–408
  "plumbers" unit of, 431
  polls and, 528
  presidential treatment and, 41
  press conferences of, 425
  propaganda and, 71, 72
  public approval of, 62
  ranking as President, 4
  Rehnquist appointment and, 253n
  Republican reelection effort for,
    352–353
  running mate of, 513, 514
  smearing by, 538–539
  staff of, 55–56
  State Department and, 87
  Supreme Court and, 264
  Supreme Court appointments by,
    252–253, 279–280
  television and, 519–521
  threats by, 69
  values of, 59
  vetoes by, 70
  Vietnam War and, 110
  war and, 79
  Watergate and, 22–24, 394
  wiretapping by, 431
Nixon, Walter, impeachment of, 249n
Nofziger, Lynn, 335
Noise Control Act (1972), 170
Noonan, John T., Jr., 229
Noonan, Peggy, 534

Noriega, Manuel, 84, 151, 377
North, Oliver L., 89–90, 240–241, 247
North American Free Trade Agreement
  (NAFTA), 7–8, 480–481
North American Precis Syndicate
  (NAPC), 386
North Atlantic Treaty Organization
  (NATO), 79, 126, 148, 155
Northerners, congressional leadership
  and, 216
North Korea. *See* Korean War
Northrup Grumman, 141, 482
North Vietnam. *See* Vietnam War
NSC. *See* National Security Council
  (NSC)
nuclear arms, 126n
  Reagan and, 121–122
Nuclear Nonproliferation Treaty, 104
nuclear warheads, 165–166
nuclear weapons
  atmospheric testing of, 162
  Cold War and, 159–162

obscenity, Supreme Court on, 280
Occupational Safety and Health
  Administration (OSHA), 170,
  307–308
  corruption in, 338
O'Connor, John J., 401
O'Connor, Sandra Day, 249n, 253, 254,
  284
O'Donnell, Kenneth, 107
Office of Government Ethics, 50
Office of Management and Budget
  (OMB), 328
Office of the Independent Counsel, 11.
  See also Starr, Kenneth
Offices of Inspectors General, criminal
  investigations by, 318
oil and gas legislation, 199, 200
oil companies
  foreign policy and, 158–159
  media coverage of, 404
oil investments, S&L crash failures and,
  473–474
oil spill, clean-up costs for, 468
Oklahoma City bombing, 324
Old Boy network, 438
Old Confederacy, 363
Old Executive Office Building, 36
O'Leary, Hazel, 162
oligopoly, 482
Olmer, Lionel, 376
OMB. *See* Office of Management and
  Budget (OMB)

O'Neill, Tip, 27, 52, 91n, 106, 178, 415
  on business lobbying, 386
  ethical issues and, 225
  on lobbyists, 372
  Reagan and, 66
  as Speaker, 208
"one-man, one-vote" principle, 273
Open Door policy, 83
Operation Rolling Thunder, 94
opinion, of Supreme Court, 261
opinion polls, 391–393
Opinion Research Company, 348n
oral arguments, before Supreme Court,
  260–261
Orange County, government financial
  loss in, 465
oratory, in Congress, 198
Organization of American States, 148
Charter of, 84
organized prayer, 277–278
organizing
  through lobbying, 371–378
  through political parties, 348–351
  pressure through, 347–348
Osborne, John, 63
OSHA. *See* Occupational Safety and
  Health Administration (OSHA)
Oshinsky, David M, .419
Ottinger, Richard L., 196
Overseas Private Investment
  Corporation, 378
overthrow of government, Supreme
  Court on, 272

Packard, David, 139, 146
Packwood, Bob, 180, 375
PACs. *See* political action committees
  (PACs)
Padover, Saul K., 80
Palmer, A. Mitchell, 123
Panama, 84, 97
Panama Canal, 82
  Treaty, 198
Pan Am flight 103, 143n
Pappas, Ike, 396
Pardue, Michael Rene, 239–240
partisanship. *See also* bipartisanship
  in Congress, 203–211
Patman, Wright, 216
payroll, of bureaucracy, 301
PBS, money control and, 411
peacekeeping operations, 149
  in Balkans, 159
Pearl Harbor attack, 119
Pearson, James B., 185

Pecora, Ferdinand, 334
Pendleton, Edward, 372
Penn Central Transportation Company,
  471–472
Pennsylvania v. *Nelson,* 272
Penrose, Boise, 352
Penry, John Paul, 244
pensions
  Civil Service, 296
  congressional, 176, 177
  for ex-presidents, 36n
  military, 134
  presidential, 35
Pentagon, 117, 302. *See also* armed
  forces; defense spending; military
  growth of, 132–133
  loss of enemies and, 167
  manpower spending by, 133–136
  Reagan and, 121–122
  secret documents of, 430–431
  spending by, 300
Pentagon Papers, 108, 394–397
  Nixon revenge for, 442
"people's lobbies," 371, 372
  cigarette crusade and, 382–384
  Common Cause and, 381–382
  Nader and, 379–381
  rise of, 378–379
  successes by, 389–391
Pepper, Claude, 215
Percy, Charles, 22, 69, 215
perks. *See* Congress; income
Perot, Ross, 6, 349, 350
  voter response to, 367
Perry, Robert, 339
Persian Gulf War, 150, 158–159
  military inadequacy in, 147–148
  press in, 442–443
personality
  of McCarthy, 418–419
  of Reagan, 419–421
personal touch, presidential use of,
  66–68
pesticides
  regulation of, 170
  water pollution and, 314
Pettigrew, F. R., ix
pharmaceutical companies, 316
Philip Morris, 388
Phillips, Kevin P., 410
photo opportunities, presidential, 65
Pierce, Franklin, 35
Pierce, Samuel, 336
Pierpoint, Robert, 67, 424
Pizza Connection, 323

Planned Parenthood v. *Casey*, 254, 288
pledge of allegiance, Bush and, 541–542
Plessy, Homer, 275
"plumbers" unit, of Nixon, 431
Poindexter, John, 89
police, sentences for crimes, 239
police actions, of UN, 150
political action committees (PACs), 175,
     354–355. *See also* bribery
  campaign costs and, 231–233
  campaign funding and, 227–229,
     530–531
  Gingrich and, 226
political campaigns. *See also* political
     funding
  of Bush, George H.W., 541–544
  costs of, 231
  "handler" in, 535–537
  polls and, 528–529
  process of, 523–528
  reform of, 527–528
  smears, lying, and, 537–546
  television's role in, 521–522
political funding. *See* campaign funding
political parties. *See also* specific parties
  congressional animosities between,
     203–211
  congressional disloyalty to, 202
  congressional voting and, 201–203
  decline of influence of, 351–355
  inadequacy of labeling, 358–359
  organizing through, 348–351
  and pressure groups, 344–348
  racism and, 363–365
  sameness of, 356
  third parties and, 349
  ticket-splitting and, 361–362
  two-party system and, 349–351
political representation, equalization of,
     272–273
politics. *See also* voter disillusionment
  campaign funding and, 529–532
  courts and, 248–250
  handlers for campaign, 535–537
  involvement in, 506–511
  PACs and, 355
  polls and, 528–529
  presidential success in domestic,
     42–66
  profession and process of, i–xi
  reputation, behavior, and, 515–518
  sameness in, 356
  selective process for, 523–528
  smears, lies, and, 537–546
  speech writing and, 532–535

  springboards to, 511–515
  Supreme Court and, 251–252, 256
  television and, 518–523
Politics (Emerson), x
polls
  by Clinton, 9
  opinion polls and, 391–393
  in political campaigns, 528–529
  of presidential ranking, 4
pollution, 314–315
popularity, of Reagan, 419–421
population, immigration and, 311–312
Populists, 350
"pork barrel," Congress and, 189–192
pornography, Rehnquist Court and, 285
Posner, Victor, 240
Postal Service, congressional franking
     privileges and, 223–224
Post Office Department, reform of,
     341–342
Potsdam agreement, 83
poverty
  accused's rights and, 282
  legal help and, 243–244
  poor and very poor, 454–458
  under Reagan, 454
  right to counsel and, 243, 274
  welfare family and, 456–457
Powell, Adam Clayton, Jr., 219n
Powell, Colin, 508
Powell, Jody, 64, 441
Powell, Lewis F., Jr., 261–262, 280, 284
power(s). *See also* Congress; president(s)
  Clinton and, 6–7
  corruption and, 50
  electorate and, 5
  negative congressional, 206
  of presidency, 32
  of President, 29–30
  presidential foreign policy decision-
     making and, 93–96
  presidential image and, 62
  of Reagan, 30
  treaty-making, 82–85
  war-making, 78–82
"Power Game, The," 5–6
power-sharing, 77
prayer, organized, 277–278
precedents, Supreme Court and, 260
pre-emptive action, 126n
presidency, mystique of, 31–42
president(s). *See also* impeachment;
     presidency; press conferences; spe-
     cific presidents
  abuses of powers by, 22–24

advisers of, 49–57, 85–91
assertive, 29–30
backgrounds of, 511–512
and bureaucracy, 327–329
bureaucratic reform by, 331–333
confidence inspired by, 59–61
Congress and, 66–73
controls on foreign policies of,
    102–106
as deity, xii
demythologizing, xii
domestic politics success by,
    42–66
electronic eavesdropping on, 2–3
flattery of, 40–42
foreign policy and, 74–78, 99–102
image of, 61–66
impeachment as restraint on foreign
    policy power of, 106–111
imperial status of, 27–29
influence over bureaucracy, 333–335
judicial appointments by, 249, 250
lifestyles of, 36–40
limits on, 21n
lying by, 443–447
mental incapacity of, 18–19, 25
omniscience of, 93–96
pension for, 35, 36n
press coverage by, 40
ranking of, 3–4
running mates of, 512–514
salary of, 35
second terms of, 32–33
staffs of, 53–57
stress and incapacity of, 25–27
terms of, v, 32–33
travel styles of, 37–39
war-making powers and, 78–82
presidential campaigns. *See* political
    campaigns
presidential debates
    Bush-Clinton, 522
    between Nixon and Kennedy,
        520–521
presidential papers, 39–40
press. *See also* media; newspapers; press
    self-censorship; television
    control of, 402–403
    freedom of, 431–432
    government-media connections and,
        415–416
    herd instinct among, 421–423
    news manipulation and, 412–413
    ownership of, 400–416
    presidential coverage by, 40

presidential manipulation of, 71–72
    Reagan and, 419–421
press conferences, 423–426
press corps, presidential candidate be-
    havior and, 416–417
press secretary, media connections of,
    415–416
press self-censorship
    of Bay of Pigs, 428–429
    of bias, 416–419
    pseudopatriotic, 427–429
    of Vietnam War, 426–427
pressure groups, political parties and,
    344–348
primary elections
    dates of, 527–528
    Jackson, Jesse, and, 365
    New Hampshire and, 523, 525–527
priorities, of government, vi–vii
privacy rights, Burger court and, 281
private lives, of candidates, 416–417
pro-abortionists, 287, 344–345
pro bono legal work, 244
procedural rights, 242–243
pro-choice movement, 287
pro-life movement, 287–288
propaganda, 398–400
    anticommunist, 127–128
    presidential, 70–73
    against regulation, 385–386
property rights, 267, 268
protests. *See* demonstrations
Proxmire, William, 28n, 139, 142, 193,
    315, 332–333
Pryor, David, 172, 234
public. *See* electorate
Publications Review Board, 431
Public Citizen Inc., 380
public information, propaganda and,
    398–400
public interest lobbies, 378
publicity, Congress and, 399
public opinion, 346
    measuring of, 391–393
    research on, 348n
public service journalism, 405–407
pump-priming, 143, 470
punishment. *See also* sentences (court)
    of wealthy, 241n

Qaddafi, Muammar, 85, 89, 143
Quayle, Dan, as running mate,
    513–514
quorum, congressional floor work and,
    197–198

race and racism. *See also Brown* v. *Board of Education;* discrimination
  in Congress, 177
  and elective offices, 508–509
  political parties and, 363–365
  sentencing differences by, 239
radio. *See* media; talk radio
radioactive waste disposal, 161
Rafshoon, Gerald, 64, 86
Rand Corporation, 238–239
ranking of presidents, 3–4
Rap Master Ronnie (show), 445
Rather, Dan, 62, 414
Rayburn, Sam, 207
Raymond, Jack, 110
Raytheon Company, 166, 482
REA. *See* Rural Electrification Administration (REA)
Reagan, Nancy, 17, 54
Reagan, Ronald, iv, 4, 17–20, 511
  Achille Lauro hijacking and, 142–143
  as activist president, 30–31
  advisers of, 50
  appearance of, 523
  assassination attempt on, 58, 304
  bureaucracy and, 293, 294, 333–339
  Cold War and, 120–122
  communism and, 129
  Congress and, 66, 171
  congressional voting and, 202
  conservatism of, 357–358
  corruption under, 334–335
  in Costa Rica, 38
  cutbacks in poverty spending by, 456
  domestic legislation and, 47–49
  economic luck of, 43
  economy under, 453–454
  foreign policy and, 76, 85–86, 88–89, 105, 107
  human rights and, 101
  image of, 64–65
  imperial pomp and, 28
  incapacity of, 18–19, 25
  Iran-contra and, 17, 90
  lifestyle as president, 37
  lying by, 445–446
  military waste and, 163–164
  national debt and, 485–487
  Nicaragua and, 157
  opinion polls and, 391, 528
  power of, 30
  presidential treatment and, 42
  press and, 419–421
  press conferences of, 424, 425–426
  propaganda by, 71–72

  public jobs and, 494
  Qaddafi and, 143
  "reforms" of, 467
  Republicans and, 204
  secrecy under, 431–432
  staff of, 53–55, 56–57
  Supreme Court appointments by, 253, 254
  voter disillusionment and, 366–367
  war and, 80
  welfare cutbacks under, 456
redistricting, political boundaries and, 273
"Red Menace," 122
Red Scare
  of 1919-1920, 123
  in 1940s and 1950s, 123–124, 271
Reedy, George, 40, 94
reform
  of bureaucracy, 340–343
  of Congress, 217–219
  economic, 503–505
  ethics, 219–224
  Federal Election Act and, 227
  of presidential campaigns, 527–528
  resistance to bureaucratic, 329–333
  of Social Security system, 463–466
  of taxes, 467
Regan, Donald, 53–54
Regents of the University of California v. *Bakke,* 262
regulation, 475–477
  of auto industry, 380
  of banks, 472n
  of business and industry, 268
  business propaganda against, 385–386
  competition and, 483–485
  courts and, 247
  economy and, 451
  environmental controls and, 390
  inadequacy of, 307–308
  of large corporations, 481–485
  of savings and loans, 472n
regulatory agencies, corruption in, 398
Rehnquist, William H., 201, 250, 253n, 280. *See also* Rehnquist Court
Rehnquist Court, 284–288
Reich, Robert, 152
Reinhardt, Uwe E., 499
religion, Supreme Court and, 286
Remembering America (Goodwin), 26
rent control, 285
Reorganization Act (1949), 329
reporters. *See also* media; press

delays and, 436–437
governmental coverage by, 399–400
government lying to, 443–447
handicapping, 429–447
lack of investment in, 405–407
leaks and, 432–437
lying to, 443–447
media ownership and controls over,
  400–416
presidential coverage by, 40
revenge against, 442
secret information and, 430–432
sweet talk, threats, and, 437–443
television, 411
wiretapping of, 431
Reporters' Committee for Freedom of
  the Press, 432
representation, equalization of, 272–273
Republican National Committee, 354
Republican Party. *See also* Congress
antipeople image of, 356
changes in, 359–361
changing attitudes toward, 348n
after Clinton impeachment, 16
congressional voting and, 202–203
conservatives vs. moderates in, 360
Democratic programs adopted
  by, 357
Nixon reelection campaign and,
  352–353
racism in South and, 363–364
as third party, 350
Reston, James, 85, 434
Reuss, Henry S., 174, 490
reverse discrimination, 262
Reynolds, R.J., 482
Ribicoff, Abraham, 379, 380
Rice, Donna, 516
Rich, Frank, 411
Richards, Ann, 508, 522
Richardson, Elliot, 279n
Ridgeway, Matthew B., 156
Ridings, William J., Jr., 4n
rights. *See also* Bill of Rights;
  Constitution; procedural rights
in Bill of Rights, 273–274
human and property, 267
Rehnquist Court on, 285–286
right to counsel, poverty and, 243–244,
  274–275
right wing, 360. *See also* conservatives
Starr investigation of Clinton and,
  11–12
Rio Pact, 148
Roberts, Cokie, 414

Roberts, Steve, 414
Robertson, Pat, 516
Roche, James, 380
Rockefeller, John D., 481
Roe v. Wade, 254, 283–284, 287, 346
Rogers, Will, 58
Rogers, William P., 88
Rollins, Ed, 8–9, 52
Ronald Reagan Building and
  International Trade Center, 469
Roosevelt, Franklin D.
bank crisis and, 58
bureaucracy and, 330
Democratic Party and, 357
economy and, 44, 455
executive expansion under, 21
Executive Office and, 328
fireside chats of, 62
Great Depression and, 57, 492–494
Keynes and, 492
lame duck presidents and, 33n
liberalism and, 362
Mercer, Lucy, and, 2
past behavior of, 517
press conferences of, 425
pump-priming by, 470
ranking of, 3
Securities and Exchange Act and, 334
speech writing for, 533
Supreme Court and, 265, 269
taxation under, 458
Roosevelt, Kermit, 152
Roosevelt, Theodore, 30, 350
on courts, 268
Open Door policy and, 82
Rose, Sanford, 138
Rosenthal, Jack, 415
Rostenkowski, Dan, 224, 375
Rothkopf, David, 376
rotten apple theory, 122
Rowan, Carl T., 23, 434
Rowland, Robert A., 338
Rubin, Robert E., 93, 307, 374, 499
Ruby Ridge, 324
Ruckleshaus, William, 279n
Rudman, Warren B., 197
daily schedule of, 187–188
Rules Committee (House), 207, 215
rumors, in political campaigns, 537–539
running mates, 512–514, 515
Runyon, Marvin, 342
Rural Electrification Administration
  (REA), 301
Rusk, Dean, 78, 87, 429n
Russia, 76, 112–114

Sabato, Larry J., 210, 352–353
Sadat, Anwar, 89
safety, bureaucratic indifference to, 307–308
Safire, William, 10
Sagan, Carl, 116n
Sahl, Mort, 362n, 445
salaries
  congressional, 175–177
  presidential, 35
Sandinistas, 157
S&Ls. *See* savings and loans
Santa Clara County v. *Southern Pacific Railroad*, 268
Saudi Arabia, 158
savings and loans
  corruption in, 473–475
  FSLIC insolvency and, 318
  Greenspan and, 498
  regulation of, 472n
Sawyer, Diane, 413, 415
Saxbe, William B., 322
Scaife, Richard, 11–12
Scalia, Antonin, 253, 254, 256, 284
scandals. *See* specific scandals
Scarborough, Joe, 205
Schlesinger, Arthur M., Jr., 3, 48, 70, 93, 132, 330, 437–438
  liberalism and, 362
Schlesinger, James, 26, 320
Schwab, Charles, 460
Scowcroft, Brent, 91
Scripps-Howard media conglomerate, 407, 409
Seaborg, Glenn T., 161–162
SEATO, 148
Second Amendment, 248
Second World War. *See* World War II
secrecy, of Fed, 490–491
secret documents, reporters and, 430–432
Secret Service, 34n, 304
  Clinton and, 38–39
  protection for ex-presidents, 36n
securities. *See* Treasury securities
Securities and Exchange Act, Roosevelt, Franklin D., and, 334
Securities and Exchange Commission, 293n
security
  military-industrial complex and, 117, 118
  for presidents, 38
Security Council, 149
security risks, 272

sedition, 272
segregation. *See also Brown* v. *Board of Education;* race and racism
  congressional votes against, 233
  Plessy v. *Ferguson* and, 275
  Supreme Court and, 264
select committees, in Congress, 194–195
self-censorship. *See* press self-censorship
self-incrimination, 275
Selling of the President, 1968, The (McGinnis), 537
Semple, Robert, 59
Senate. *See also* committees (congressional); Congress; ethics
  Clinton impeachment and, 14–15
  filibusters in, 199–200
  graft in, 223
  leaders of, 206, 212–213
  as route to presidency, 511–512
  seniority system in, 216
  treaty-making powers and, 82
  war-making powers and, 77
Senate Foreign Relations Committee, 213
seniority system (Congress), 175, 213–217
sentences (court), inconsistencies among, 245
separate but equal treatment, 275–276
Serbia, 159
Sessions, William S., 323
Seven Days in May, 132
Seventh Amendment, 242
sex and sexuality. *See also* gender
  obscenity and, 280
sexual escapades, in Congress, 222
sexual harassment, 287
  in federal bureaucracy, 295
"shadow" workers, 294
Shah of Iran, 96, 152
Shapiro, Bernard, 180
Share the Wealth Plan, 458
Sharing the Pie (Brouwer), 468
Shawcross, William, 412
Shays, Christopher, 205
Sherman Antitrust Act (1890), 481
Shields, Mark, 487–488
Shivers, Allan, 277
Shoup, David, 125
Shultz, George, 88, 89, 90, 91
Shuster, Bud, 190
Sidey, Hugh, 72
Sierra Club, 381
Sikes, Robert L., 221

Sikorski, Gerry, 181
Silverstein, Ken, 376, 447
Simons, Howard, 433
Simpson, Alan, 204
Simpson, Glenn R., 210
Sinai, 80
Six-PAC, 354
Sixth Amendment, 242, 243
  Burger Court and, 282
  on speedy trial, 263
"60 Minutes," 411
slavery. *See also* race and racism
  Fourteenth Amendment and, 268
slush funds, 229
Small Business Administration, 318
smears, in political campaigns, 537–546
Smith, Adam, 448–450
Smith, Denny, 147
Smith, Dorrance, 415
Smith, Hedrick, 5, 30, 32, 424
Smith, Sharon, 296
Smith Act (1940), 272
Smithsonian Agreement, 71
smoking
  anti-cigarette crusade and, 382–383
  tobacco industry successes and,
    387–389
smuggling, 311
Social Security Administration
  (SSA), 306
Social Security system, 357
  health care and, 500
  number receiving, 505
  reform of, 463–466
Social Security Trust Fund, 464
social welfare programs. *See also* Social
  Security system; welfare system
  Congress and, 204–205
  government bureaucracy and, 392
society, bureaucratic indifference to
  needs of, 306–313
"soft" money, political contributions
  and, 228
Solomon, B. H, 198
Sorensen, Ted, 534
Souter, David, 254
South
  organized prayer in, 277–278
  political party alliances and,
    361–362
  racism and, 363
  racism and voting in, 363–365
South America, 79, 99
Southeast Asia, 148. *See also* specific
  countries and wars

Southerners, congressional leadership
  and, 215–216
South Korea. *See* Korean War
South Vietnam. *See* Vietnam War
Soviet Union. *See also* Cold War;
  Russia
  CIA and, 98
  end of, 112–114
  as enemy, 125–126
  nuclear weapons and, 160–162
  Reagan and, 129
  rivalry with, 120
  as World War II ally, 124–125
  World War II costs to, 163
Spanish-American War, 83
Spanish-speaking immigrants, 312
Speaker of the House, 205–209
  ethical issues regarding, 225–226
  Gingrich as, 209–211
Speakes, Larry, 105, 438n
special-interest groups, bureaucracy
  and, 339–340
Specter, Arlen, 15, 230
speech writing, for candidates, 532–535
Speiser, Lawrence, 266
Spencer, Stu, 376–377
spending. *See also* defense spending;
  taxation
  on Cold War, 116–117
  federal, 298–300, 470–471
  on political campaigns, 529–532
  by Reagan, 357–358
  on secrecy, 430
split-ticket voting, 361–362
spying, 93. *See also* Central Intelligence
  Agency (CIA); Federal Bureau of
  Investigation (FBI)
  CIA and, 97–98, 150–154
staff. *See also* advisers; specific
  presidents
  congressional, 178–182, 186
  presidential, 53–57
  of Supreme Court justices, 259
Stahl, Lesley, 414
Stalin, Joseph, 125
Standard Oil Trust, 481
standing committees, in Congress, 215
standing military, 134–136
stare decisis, 260
Stark, Fortney, 193, 218, 219
Starr, Kenneth, 11–12, 435
  investigation of Clinton by, 11–16
  Lewinsky and, 12–17
stars, media, 413–415
"Star Wars," revival of, 166

State Department, 87, 95. *See also* foreign policy; Military entries; specific individuals
state judges, selection of, 249–250
states
Bill of Rights and, 274
expenditures on defending poor in, 243–244
statutes. *See* law(s); Supreme Court
statutory law, 260
Stealth bomber, 140–141
Steed, Diane, 308
Steel, Ronald, 115, 119–120
Steele, James, 447
Steffens, Lincoln, 448
Stein, Herbert, 16
Stern, Phil, 230
Stevens, John Paul, 11, 254
Stevenson, Adlai, 127, 526
mud-slingers and, 539
Nixon and, 515
speech writing by, 535
Stewart, Potter, 284
Stockdale, James B., 108–109
stock market, Social Security Trust Fund and, 464–466
straight-ticket voting, 361
Strauss, Robert, 377
stress, presidential, 25–27
strict constructionists, on Supreme Court, 264, 280
Stubbs, Gerry E., 222
Students for a Democratic Society, 282
subcommittees (congressional), 192–197
subsidies, 139, 451–452, 470–472
subsidization, of banks, 472–475
Subversive Activities Control Board, 272
Sullivan, Richard J., 180
Sulzberger, Arthur O., 401, 405
Sununu, John, 52
super power, U.S. as remaining, 115–116
Supreme Court, 236–240, 248. *See also* courts; Roosevelt, Franklin D.
Burger Court and, 278–284
conservative revolution in, 251–254
enforcement of edicts, 277–278
evolving nature of, 267–271
future of, 289
influences on, 260–261
judicial review by, 265
mystique of, 255–258
operation of, 258–262
political struggle over, 251–252
Rehnquist Court and, 284–288
role of, 263–267

Roosevelt, Franklin D. and, 21
secrecy on, 257–258
tenure of justices on, 256
unanimous decisions of, 261–262
Warren Court and, 251, 272–277
Sussman, Barry, 392, 423n
Swanner, John, 224
sweatshops, 477
Swomley, John M., Jr., 135n
Sylvester, Arthur, 447

Taft, William Howard, 123, 351
talk radio, conservatives on, 411
Talmadge, Herman, 221
Tamraz, Roger, 370
tapes. *See* Audiotaping
tariffs, 77
economy and, 451
taxation, 466–470
benefits ("backdoor spending") and, 467–468
for congressional salaries and facilities, 177–179
mistaken provisions and, 191–192
Reagan, national debt, and, 486–487
reform of, 467
under Roosevelt, Franklin D., 458
savings from closing military bases, 137–138
uppercrust cheaters and, 468–470
tax reform, Carter and, 47
Tax Reform Act (1986), 467
tax reform bill, quality of, 183
Taylor, Maxwell, 396
Taylor, Stuart, Jr., 416
Taylor, Telford, 256
Teamsters, corruption of, 398
Teeter, Robert, 348n, 541
Teflon President, Reagan as, 65
Telecommunications Act (1996), 412–413
television, 401. *See also* media; reporters
cosmetics and, 522–523
impact of money on, 411
presidential elections and, 518–523
presidential image and, 63–64, 65–66
reporting on, 411
role in political campaigns, 521–522
temp help, 462–463
term limitations
for Congress, vi
for President, v
Texas, *pro bono* legal work in, 244
Texas Instruments, 479
thalidomide, 316
Thayer, George, 352

third parties, 349–350
Third World, 99
Thomas, Clarence, 251, 252, 254
Thomas, Helen, 423
Thompson, Frank, 41
threats, presidential, 69
thrifts. *See* savings and loans
Thurmond, Strom, 199, 214–215
ticket-splitting, 361–362
Ties, Kenneth, 374
time allotment, by Congress, 184–186
Time Inc., Nixon and, 72
Times-Mirror Company, 405
Time Warner, 410
Tisdale, James, 402n
Title VII, of Civil Rights Act (1964), 287
tobacco industry, successes by, 387–389
Tolchin, Martin, 40
Tonkin Gulf, 81, 108–109
Tonkin Gulf Resolution, 81n, 109
too-big-to-fail policy, 472–473
Topeka, Kansas. *See Brown* v. *Board of Education*
Tower, John, 225, 433–434
toxic wastes, 314–315
trade, imports policy and, 477–481
trade associations, 385
Transportation, Department of (DOT), 484–485
travel, by presidents, 37–39
Treasury securities, national debt and, 487
treaties, 148–149. *See also* United Nations
Senate and, 77
treaty-making powers, 82–85
trials. *See also* courts; judges; juries; Supreme Court
timely manner of, 263
Trident nuclear submarines, 147
Tripp, Linda, 13
truck accidents, 308–309
Truman, Bess, 35
Truman, Harry S, 30, 35
Cold War and, 126–127
communism and, 125
foreign policy and, 99
Korean War and, 79, 156
speech writing for, 533
Supreme Court appointments by, 271
UN police action and, 150
Truman Doctrine, 82, 127
trusts, inheritance tax and, 459
truth, press and, 447

Turkey, 126, 127
Turner Broadcasting System, 410
Twenty-fifth Amendment, 24
Twenty-second Amendment, 32
Twining, Nathan F., 126n
two-party system, 349–351
Tydings, Joseph, 69

underclass, Democratic party and, 364
unemployment
Fed and, 497–498
in Great Depression, 492–494
Harding and, 44
inflation and, 495–496
welfare system and, 458
"unholy trinity," 326
Union of Soviet Socialist Republics (USSR). *See* Soviet Union
United Fruit Company, 152
United Government Organization Manual, 301
United Nations, 148–149
United States
defense expenditures in, 164
intervention in world affairs by, 148–150
small country challenges to, 155–159
U.S. Chamber of Commerce, 354, 385
United States Information Agency, 430–431
U.S. Merit Systems Protection Board, 295
United States Postal Service, reform of, 341–342
United States v. *Samuel Loring Morison,* 431–432
universal health care, 500
Unruh, Jesse, 529
Unsafe at Any Speed: . . . (Nader), 379

vacations, of presidents, 37
Valuejet DC-9 crash, 310
Valukas, Anthony, 241, 475
Vance, Cyrus, 88
Vance, Leonard, 338
Vandenberg, Arthur, 126
vehicle designs, injuries and, 308
Veil (Woodward), 150–151
Veterans Affairs, Department of, 294
vetoes, 70
Vietnam War, 79, 81, 94–95, 110, 156
Congress and, 103–104
Ellsberg and, 108
Johnson and, 86
Kennedy and, 107–108

Vietnam War—*cont'd*
  presidential power and, 24
  press and, 426–427
  votes against, 233
Vincennes (ship), 143
Vinson, Frederick, 271
violence, by presidents, viii
Vistiga, Gregory, 447
Vogel, David, 380, 381, 382
Volcker, Paul A., 214, 491, 496, 498
Vonnegut, Kurt, iii
"voodoo economics," 71
Voorhis, Jerry, 545
voter disillusionment, apathy and, 368
voters. *See also* elections
  Clinton election and, 6–7
  use of power and, 5
voting
  blacks and, 365
  congressional party membership
    and, 201–203
  ethnic groups and, 364
  by feminists, 364
  Hispanic-Americans and, 365
  homosexuals and, 364
  lobbying and, 371
  voter disillusionment and,
    366–368
Voting Rights Act (1965), 45n, 278

Waco, 324
wage gap, 460
Waggoner, Joe, 218
Wainwright, Louis, 274
Wald, George, 117
Wallace, George C., 277, 304, 350, 356
  Nixon smearing of, 538
Wall Street. *See* stock market
Wall Street Journal
  leaks to, 433
  protection of Speaker by, 440
Walters, Robert, 438–439
war economy, permanent, 137
war-making powers, 78–82
Warner, John W., 391
"war on poverty," 455
War Powers Resolution, 103, 105
Warren, Earl, 255, 262, 271. *See also*
    Warren Court
  Eisenhower on, 254
Warren Court, 251
  application of Bill of Rights to states
    and, 274
  civil rights and, 275–277
  machinery of justice and, 273–275

political representation and, 272–273
  "revolutionary" nature of, 272–277
wars and warfare. *See* specific wars
Washington, George
  Farewell Address of, 119
  ranking of, 3
*Washington on $10 Million a Day: How
    Lobbyists Plunder the Nation*
    (Silverstein), 376
Washington Post, 400–401, 405, 429. *See
    also* Watergate scandal
  delays and, 437
  on Johnson's mental incapacity, 27
  leaks to, 435
  protection of Speaker by, 440
  Watergate and, 422
waste disposal, 314–315
Watergate scandal, 398
  abuse of presidential power and,
    22–24
  media and, 394
  Nixon's lying during, 444–445
  Nixon staff and, 55–56
  press response to, 422
water pollution, 314
  cleanup of, 390
Watkins, David, 49–50
Watt, James, corruption by, 336–337,
    337–338
Waxman, Henry A., 193, 195
Wayne, John, i
Ways and Means Committee (House),
    217–218
wealth. *See also* middle class
  concentration of, 459
  of corporate executives, 460–461
  distribution of, 458–459
  of founders of U.S., 450
  of newspaper publishers, 405
  under Reagan, 453–454
  value of, 459–460
Wealth of Nations, The (Smith), 448–450
wealthy
  judges as, 241n
  punishment of, 241n
weapons. *See also* arms race
  defective, 140–144
  economic benefits of, 139–144
  fraud and waste in, 144–148
  military foreign policy and, 130
  nuclear, 159–162
Weaver, James Baird, 350
Webster, William H., 323
*Webster v. Reproductive Health Ser-
    vices*, 288

Wedtech, Inc., 318
Weill, Sanford, 460
Weiss, Stephen Airel, 178
Weld, William F., 213, 335
welfare system, 454–458. *See also* Social
  Security system; social welfare
  programs
  Bush and, 456
  Carter and, 47
  Clinton and, 456–458
  Nixon and, 46–47
  Reagan and, 456
Westerners, congressional leadership
  and, 216
West Virginia State Board of Education v.
  Barnette, 542n
"whip," in House, 206
"whistle-blowers," 315–316
White, Byron R., 253–254, 256, 258, 284
White, E. B., 236
White, John, 528
White, Theodore H., 46, 520
white-collar crime. *See* corporate
  crime
White House
  defense of, 34n
  operating costs of, 36
  press conferences, 423–426
  staff, 328
"White House enemies," 22
whites
  political parties, racism, and,
    363–364
  welfare cutbacks and, 457
Whitman, Christine Todd, 508
Whitten, Jamie L., 190
Wholesome Meat Act (1967), 381
Wicker, Tom, 404, 426
Wild, Claude, Jr., 353n
Wilder, L. Douglas, 365, 509
Wilderness Society, 381
Will, George, 438, 540
Willes, Mark, 405
Williams, Jody, 84
Wilson, Charles E., 137, 221

Wilson, Meredith, 48
Wilson, Woodrow, 119, 372
  economic reform and, 504–505
  war and, 79
wimp factor, Bush and, 540–545
Wise, David, 97, 154
Witcover, Jules, 367, 426–427
Witness to Power (Ehrlichman), 36
Wofford, Harris, 51
womanizing, by politicians, viii
women. *See also* sexual harassment
  in high elective offices, 508
women's rights. *See also* gender
  Burger Court and, 283–284
  Roe v. *Wade* and, 283–284
Woodward, Bob, 150, 394, 422
Woodward, William, 43
Wooten, James, 415, 441
Works Progress Administration (WPA),
  456, 492–493
world affairs, U.S. intervention in,
  148–150
World Trade Center, bombing,
  153–154
World War I, 79, 119
World War II, 79, 119–120
  Soviet Union as ally in, 124–125
  Supreme Court and, 270–271
WPA. *See* Works Progress
  Administration (WPA)
Wright, Charles Alan, 258
Wright, Jim, ii, 168, 178, 208, 391n,
  439–440
  ethical issue and, 225–226

Yalta agreement, 83
Yannacone, Victor, 383–384
Yarborough, Ralph, 233
Yard, Molly, 346
Yates v. *United States*, 272
Yost, Charles, 127
Yugoslavia, 79, 98
  CIA and, 154

Zaire (Congo), 151

NOTES